everyWORD

SCRIPTURE | OUTLINE | COMMENTARY

THE GOSPEL ACCORDING TO LUKE

Volume 1
Chapters 1 – 13:21

NEW TESTAMENT | ENGLISH STANDARD VERSION

LMW

LEADERSHIP MINISTRIES WORLDWIDE
CHATTANOOGA, TN

every**WORD**™—LUKE (Volume 1)
Chapters 1 – 13:21

ENGLISH STANDARD VERSION

Copyright © 2020 by LEADERSHIP MINISTRIES WORLDWIDE.

All other Bible study aids, references, indexes, reference materials
Copyright © 1991 by Alpha-Omega Ministries, Inc.

Previous Editions of **The Preacher's Outline & Sermon Bible**,
New International Version NT Copyright © 1998
King James Version NT Copyright © 1991, 1996, 2000
by Alpha-Omega Ministries, Inc.

Please address all requests for information or permission to:
Leadership Ministries Worldwide
1928 Central Avenue
Chattanooga, TN 37408
Ph.# (423) 855-2181 FAX (423) 855-8616 E-Mail info@lmw.org
http://www.lmw.org

ISBN Softbound Edition: 978-1-57407-452-9
ISBN Casebound Edition: 978-1-57407-455-0

LEADERSHIP MINISTRIES WORLDWIDE
CHATTANOOGA, TN

Printed in the United States of America

DEDICATED

To all the men and women of the world who preach and teach the Gospel of our Lord Jesus Christ and to the Mercy and Grace of God

&

- Demonstrated to us in Christ Jesus our Lord.

  "In him we have redemption through his blood, the forgiveness of our trespasses, according to the riches of his grace." (Ep.1:7)

- Out of the mercy and grace of God, His Word has flowed. Let every person know that God will have mercy upon him, forgiving and using him to fulfill His glorious plan of salvation.

  "For God so loved the world, that he gave his only Son, that whoever believes in him should not perish but have eternal life. For God did not send his Son into the world to condemn the world, but in order that the world might be saved through him." (Jn.3:16-17)

  "This is good, and it is pleasing in the sight of God our Savior; who desires all men to be saved and to come unto the knowledge of the truth." (1 Ti.2:3-4)

everyWORD™

is written for God's servants to use in their study, teaching, and preaching of God's Holy Word . . .

- to share the Word of God with the world.
- to help believers, both ministers and laypersons, in their understanding, preaching, and teaching of God's Word.
- to do everything we possibly can to lead men, women, boys, and girls to give their hearts and lives to Jesus Christ and to secure the eternal life that He offers.
- to do all we can to minister to the needy of the world.
- to give Jesus Christ His proper place, the place the Word gives Him. Therefore, no work of Leadership Ministries Worldwide—no Outline Bible Resources—will ever be personalized.

CONTENTS

ACKNOWLEDGMENTS AND BIBLIOGRAPHY

Every child of God is precious to the Lord and deeply loved. And every child as a servant of the Lord touches the lives of those who come in contact with him or his ministry. The writing ministries of the following servants have touched this work, and we are grateful that God brought their writings our way. We hereby acknowledge their ministry to us, being fully aware that there are so many others down through the years whose writings have touched our lives and who deserve mention, but whose names have faded from our memory. May our wonderful Lord continue to bless the ministries of these dear servants—and the ministries of us all—as we diligently labor to reach the world for Christ and to meet the desperate needs of those who suffer so much.

THE GREEK SOURCES

Balz, Horst and Schneider, Gerhard M. *Exegetical Dictionary of the New Testament.* Grand Rapids: Wm. B. Eerdmans Publishing Co., 2003. Via Wordsearch digital edition.

Black, David Alan. *Linguistics for Students of New Testament Greek.* Grand Rapids, MI: Baker Publishing Group, 1988.

Burton, Ernest De Witt. *Syntax of the Moods and Tenses in New Testament Greek.* Grand Rapids: Kregel Publications, 1976. Via Wordsearch digital edition.

Cotterell, Peter and Turner, Max. *Linguistics and Biblical Interpretation.* Downers Grove, IL: InterVarsity Press, 1989.

Davis, William Hersey. *Beginner's Grammar of the Greek New Testament.* New York: Harper & Row, 1923.

Expositor's Greek Testament, Edited by W. Robertson Nicoll. Grand Rapids: Wm. B. Eerdmans Publishing Co., 1970.

Gilbrant, Thoralf and Harris, Ralph W. *The Complete Biblical Library Greek-English Dictionary.* Springfield, MO: World Library Press, Inc., 1989. Via Wordsearch digital edition.

Guthrie, George H. and Duval, J. Scott. *Biblical Greek Exegesis: A Graded Approach to Learning Intermediate and Advanced Greek.* Grand Rapids, MI: Zondervan, 1998.

Harris, Murray J. *Exegetical Guide to the Greek New Testament: John.* Nashville: B & H Academic, 2015.

Kittel, Gerhard and Friedrich, Gerhard. *Theological Dictionary of the New Testament.* Grand Rapids: Wm. B. Eerdmans Publishing Co., 1977.

Kostenberger, Andreas J., Merkle, Benjamin L., and Plummer, Robert L. *Going Deeper with New Testament Greek: An Intermediate Study of the Grammar and Syntax of the New Testament.* Nashville: B & H Academic, 2016.

Kubo, Sakae. *A Reader's Greek-English Lexicon of the New Testament and a Beginner's Guide for the Translation of New Testament Greek.* Grand Rapids, MI: Zondervan, 1975.

Moulton, Harold K., ed. *The Analytical Greek Lexicon Revised.* Grand Rapids, MI: Zondervan, 1977.

Practical Word Studies in the New Testament. Chattanooga, TN: Leadership Ministries Worldwide, 1998. Via Wordsearch digital edition.

Robertson, A.T. *A Grammar of the Greek New Testament in the Light of Historical Research.* New York: George H. Doran Company, 1915.

_____. A.T. *A Short Grammar of the Greek New Testament.* New York: A.C. Armstrong & Son, 1909.

_____. A.T. *Word Pictures in the New Testament.* Nashville, TN: Broadman Press, 1930.

Staats, Gary. *Christological Greek Grammar.* Austin, TX: Wordsearch Bible Software, 2001.

Strong, James. *Strong's Greek and Hebrew Dictionary of the Bible.* Public Domain. Via Wordsearch digital edition.

Thayer, Joseph Henry. *Greek-English Lexicon of the New Testament.* New York: American Book Co, n.d.

Vincent, Marvin R. *Word Studies in the New Testament.* Grand Rapids: Wm. B. Eerdmans Publishing Co., 1969.

Vine, W.E. *Expository Dictionary of New Testament Words.* Old Tappan, NJ: Fleming H. Revell Co., n.d.

Wallace, Daniel B. *Greek Grammar Beyond the Basics: An Exegetical Syntax of New Testament with Scripture, Subject, and Greek Word Indexes.* Grand Rapids, MI: Zondervan. 1997. Via Wordsearch digital edition.

Wuest, Kenneth S. *Word Studies in the Greek New Testament*. Grand Rapids: Wm. B. Eerdmans Publishing Co., 1966.

Young, Richard A. *Intermediate New Testament Greek: A Linguistic and Exegetical Approach*. Nashville: Broadman & Holman, 1994.

Zodhiates, Spiros. *The Complete Word Study Dictionary: New Testament*. Chattanooga, TN: AMG Publishers, 1992. Via Wordsearch digital edition.

THE REFERENCE WORKS

Berkhof, Louis. *Principles of Biblical Interpretation*. Grand Rapids, MI: Baker Book House, 1950.

Blomberg, Craig. *The Historical Reliability of the Gospels*. Downers Grove, IL: InterVarsity, 1987.

Bruce, F. F. *New Testament History*. New York: Doubleday, 1983. Via Wordsearch digital edition.

Bryant, T. Alton, ed. *The New Compact Bible Dictionary*. Grand Rapids: Zondervan Publishing House, 1967.

Butler, Trent C., ed. *Holman Bible Dictionary*. Nashville: Holman Bible Pub., 1991.

Carson, D. A. and Moo, Douglas. *An Introduction to the New Testament*. 2nd ed. Grand Rapids, MI: Zondervan, 2005.

Cruden's Complete Concordance of the Old & New Testament. Philadelphia: The John C. Winston Co., 1930.

Easton, Matthew G. *Illustrated Bible Dictionary*. Public Domain. Via Wordsearch digital edition.

Edersheim, Alfred. *The Life and Times of Jesus the Messiah*. Peabody, MA: *Hendrickson Publishers*. 1993. Via Wordsearch digital edition.

Evans, Craig A. and Porter, Stanley E. *Dictionary of New Testament Background*. Downers Grove, IL: InterVarsity Press, 2000. Via Wordsearch digital edition.

Gromacki, Robert. *New Testament Survey*. Grand Rapids, MI: Baker Book House, 1974.

Gundry, Robert. *Survey of the New Testament*. 4th ed. Grand Rapids, MI: Zondervan, 2003.

Guthrie, Donald. *New Testament Introduction*. rev. ed. Downers Grove, IL: InterVarsity, 1981, 1064 pp.

Habermas, Gary R. *The Historical Jesus: Ancient Evidence for the Life of Christ*. Joplin, MO: College Press, 1996. Via Wordsearch digital edition.

Hiebert, D. Edmond. *An Introduction to the New Testament*. 3 vols. Chicago: Moody Press, 1975-77.

Jensen, Irving L. *Jensen's Survey of the New Testament*. Chicago: Moody Press, 1981.

Josephus' Complete Works. Grand Rapids: Kregel Publications, 1981.

Kaiser, Walter, Jr., and Silva, Moises. *An Introduction to Biblical Hermeneutics: The Search for Meaning*. Grand Rapids, MI: Zondervan, 1994.

Klein, William W., Blomberg, Craig L., and Hubbard, Robert, Jr. *Introduction to Biblical Interpretation*. Nashville: W Publishing Group, 1993.

Larkin, Clarence. *Rightly Dividing the Word*. Philadelphia, PA: The Rev. Clarence Larkin Est., 1921.

Lockyer, Herbert. Series of books, including his books on *All the Men, Women, Miracles, and Parables of the Bible*. Grand Rapids, MI: Zondervan Publishing House, 1958-1967.

Marshall, I. Howard. ed. *New Testament Interpretation*. Grand Rapids, MI: Wm. B. Eerdmans Publishing Co., 1977, 406 pp.

Martin, Ralph. *New Testament Foundations*. 2 vols. Grand Rapids, MI: Wm. B. Eerdmans Publishing Co., 1975-78.

McGarvey, John William. *Lands of the Bible: A Geographical and Topographical Description of Palestine*. Public Domain. Via Wordsearch digital edition.

Morris, Leon. *New Testament Theology*. Grand Rapids, MI: Zondervan, 1996.

Nave's Topical Bible. Nashville, TN: The Southwestern Co., n.d.

Orr, James. *The International Standard Bible Encyclopedia*. Grand Rapids, MI: Wm. B. Eerdmans Publishing Co., 1939. Via Wordsearch digital edition.

Ramm, Bernard. *Protestant Biblical Interpretation: A Textbook of Hermeneutics*. Grand Rapids, MI: Baker Book House, 1970.

Ryrie, Charles. *Biblical Theology of the New Testament*. Chicago: Moody, 1959, 304 pp.

Scroggie, William G. *Guide to the Gospels*. London: Pickering and Inglis, 1948, rpt., 664 pp.

Tenney, Merrill C. *Genius of the Gospels*. Grand Rapids, MI: Wm. B. Eerdmans Publishing Co., 1951, 124 pp.

_____. *New Testament Survey*. Grand Rapids, MI: Wm. B. Eerdmans Publishing Co., 1961.

The Amplified New Testament. (Scripture Quotations are from the Amplified New Testament, Copyright 1954, 1958, 1987 by the Lockman Foundation. Used by permission.)

The Four Translation New Testament. (Including King James, New American Standard, Williams—New Testament in the Language of the People, Beck—New Testament in the Language of Today.) Minneapolis, MN: World Wide Publications.

The New Thompson Chain Reference Bible. Indianapolis: B.B. Kirkbride Bible Co., 1964,

Unger, Merrill F., Harrison R. K., (ed.). *The New Unger's Bible Dictionary.* Chicago: Moody Publishers, 2006. Via Wordsearch digital edition.

Water, Mark, *AMG's Encyclopedia of Jesus' Life & Time.* Chattanooga, TN: AMG Publishers, 2006. Via Wordsearch digital edition.

Willmington, Harold L. *Willmington's Bible Handbook.* Wheaton, IL: Tyndale House, 1997.

_____. *Willmington's Guide to the Bible.* Wheaton, IL: Tyndale House, 1981.

THE COMMENTARIES

Anyabwile, Thabiti. *Christ-Centered Exposition Commentary, Exalting Jesus in Luke.* Nashville: B&H Publishing Group, 2018.

Barclay, William. *Daily Study Bible Series.* Philadelphia, PA: Westminster Press, Began in 1953.

Barnes, Albert. *Barnes' Notes on the New Testament.* Grand Rapids, MI: Kregel Classics, 1962. Via Wordsearch digital edition.

Barton, Bruce, ed. *Life Application Bible Commentary.* Carol Stream, IL: Tyndale House Publishers, Inc., various dates. Via Wordsearch digital edition.

Baxter, J. Sidlow. *Explore the Book.* Grand Rapids, MI: Zondervan, 1960.

Bock, Darrell L. *Baker Exegetical Commentary on the New Testament, Luke 1:1-9:50.* Grand Rapids, MI: Baker Books, 1994.

_____. *Baker Exegetical Commentary on the New Testament, Luke 9:51-24:53.* Grand Rapids, MI: Baker Books, 1996.

_____. *The NIV Application Commentary: Luke.* Grand Rapids: Zondervan, 1996.

Boice, James Montgomery. *Expositional Commentary* (27 volumes). Grand Rapids, MI: Baker Publishing Group, various dates. Via Wordsearch digital edition.

Calvin, John. *Calvin's Commentaries.* Public Domain. Via Wordsearch digital edition.

Elwell, Walter A. *Baker Commentary on the Bible.* Grand Rapids: Baker Academic, 2001. Via Wordsearch digital edition.

Evans, Craig A. *The Holman Apologetics Commentary on the Bible: The Gospels and Acts.* Nashville: Broadman and Holman, 2013.

_____. *Understanding the Bible Commentary Series: Luke.* Grand Rapids, MI: Baker Books, 1990.

Exell, Joseph S. *The Biblical Illustrator, Mark.* Grand Rapids, MI: Baker Book House, 1953.

France, R.T. *Teach the Text Commentary Series: Luke.* Grand Rapids, MI: Baker Books, 2013.

Garland, David E. and Longman III, Tremper, ed. *The Expositor's Bible Commentary, Revised Edition, Volume 9: Luke and Acts.* Grand Rapids, MI: Zondervan, 2010.

Geldenhuys, Norval. *The New International Commentary on the New Testament, The Gospel of Luke.* Grand Rapids, MI: Kregel Publications, 1971.

Gilbrant, Thoralf and Harris, Ralph W. *The Complete Biblical Library New Testament Commentary.* Springfield, MO: World Library Press. 1992. Via Wordsearch digital edition.

Grogan, Geoffrey. *Focus on the Bible Commentary: Good News from Jerusalem.* Fearn, Ross-Shire, Scotland: Christian Focus Publications, 2003.

Hendriksen, William. *Luke.* Grand Rapids, MI: Baker Books, 1978.

Henry, Matthew. *Commentary on the Whole Bible.* Old Tappan, NJ: Fleming H. Revell Co.

Holman Bible editorial staff. *Holman New Testament Commentary.* Nashville, TN: Holman Reference, 2001. Via Wordsearch digital edition.

Hughes, R. Kent. *Luke: That You May Know the Truth* (Preaching the Word commentary series). Wheaton, IL: Crossway Books, 2014.

Ironside, H.A. *Address on the Gospel of Mark.* New York: Loizeaux Brothers, 1947.

Jamieson, Robert; Fausset, A. R.; and Brown, David. *Jamieson, Fausset & Brown's Commentary on the Whole Bible.* Public Domain. Via Wordsearch digital edition.

Larson, Bruce. *Luke: The Preacher's Commentary, Vol.26*. Nashville, TN: Thomas Nelson, 1983.

Lenski, R.C.H. *Commentary on the New Testament: Luke*. Peabody, MA: Hendrickson Publishers, 2001.

Luck, G. Coleman. *Luke: The Gospel of the Son of Man*. Chicago: Moody Press, 1960.

MacArthur, John. *The MacArthur New Testament Commentary* (34 volumes). Chicago: Moody Publishers, 2015.

MacDonald, William. *Believer's Bible Commentary*. Edited by Art Farstad. Nashville, TN: Thomas Nelson, 1995.

MacLaren, Alexander. *Expositions of the Holy Scriptures* (17 volumes). Grand Rapids, MI: Baker Publishing Group, 1988.

Marshall, I. Howard. *The New International Greek Testament Commentary, The Gospel of Luke*. Grand Rapids, MI: Wm. B. Eerdman's Publishing Co., 1978.

McGee, J. Vernon. *Through the Bible* (5 volumes). Nashville, TN: Thomas Nelson, 1990. Via Wordsearch digital edition.

Morris, Leon. *The Gospel According to Luke: An Introduction and Commentary* (Tyndale New Testament Commentaries). Grand Rapids, MI: Wm. B. Eerdman's Publishing Co., 1988.

Nolland, John. *Word Biblical Commentary, Luke 1:1–9:20*. Nashville, TN: Thomas Nelson, 1989.

Nolland, John. *Word Biblical Commentary, Luke 9:21–18:34*. Nashville, TN: Thomas Nelson, 1993.

Pate, C. Marvin. *Moody Gospel Commentary: Luke*. Chicago: Moody Press, 1995.

Pfeiffer, Charles F and Harrison, Everett F., eds. *The New Testament & Wycliffe Bible Commentary*. New York: The Iverson Associates, 1971. Produced for *Moody Monthly*. Chicago: Moody Press, 1962.

Phillips, John. *Phillips Commentary Series*. Grand Rapids, MI: Kregel, 2006.

Poole, Matthew. *Matthew Poole's Commentary on the Holy Bible*. Peabody, MA: Hendrickson Publishers, 1985.

Rice, John R. *The Son of Man: A Verse-by-Verse Commentary on the Gospel According to Luke*. Murfreesboro, TN: Sword of the Lord Publishers, 1971.

Sorenson, *Reformation Heritage Bible Commentary: Luke*. St. Louis, MO: Concordia Publishing House, 2014.

Swindoll, Charles R. *Swindoll's New Testament Insights: Insights on Luke*. Wheaton, IL: Tyndale House, 2016.

Tasker, RVG. *The Gospel According to St. John* (Tyndale New Testament Commentaries). Grand Rapids, MI: Wm. B. Eerdmans Publishing Co., 1960.

The Pulpit Commentary, Edited by H.D.M. Spence & Joseph S. Exell. Grand Rapids, MI: Wm. B. Eerdmans Publishing Co., 1950.

Thomas, W.H. Griffith. *Outline Studies in the Gospel of Luke*. Grand Rapids, MI: Wm. B. Eerdman's Publishing Co., 1950.

Tittle, Ernest F. *The Gospel According to Luke: Exposition and Application*. New York: Harper and Brothers, 1951.

Tyndale New Testament Commentaries. Grand Rapids, MI: Wm. B. Eerdmans Publishing Co., Began in 1958.

Various authors. *The IVP New Testament Commentary Series (20 volumes)*. Downers Grove, IL: InterVarsity Press, 1991-2009. Via Wordsearch digital edition.

Various authors. *The New American Commentary* (43 volumes). Nashville, TN: Broadman & Holman, various dates. Via Wordsearch digital edition.

Walvoord, John. *The Bible Knowledge Commentary New Testament: An Exposition of the Scriptures by Dallas Seminary Faculty*. Wheaton, IL: Victor Books. Via Wordsearch digital edition.

Wiersbe, Warren W. *The Bible Exposition Commentary*. Colorado Springs, CO: David C. Cook, 2004. Via Wordsearch digital edition.

ABBREVIATIONS

&	=	and	O.T.	=	Old Testament
bc.	=	because	p./pp.	=	page/pages
concl.	=	conclusion	pt.	=	point
cp.	=	compare	quest.	=	question
ct.	=	contrast	rel.	=	religion
e.g.	=	for example	rgt.	=	righteousness
f.	=	following	thru	=	through
illust.	=	illustration	v./vv.	=	verse/verses
N.T.	=	New Testament	vs.	=	versus

THE BOOKS OF THE OLD TESTAMENT

Book	Abbreviation	Chapters	Book	Abbreviation	Chapters
GENESIS	Gen. or Ge.	50	Ecclesiastes	Eccl. or Ec.	12
Exodus	Ex.	40	The Song of	S. of Sol. or Song	8
Leviticus	Lev. or Le.	27	Solomon		
Numbers	Num. or Nu.	36	Isaiah	Is.	66
Deuteronomy	Dt. or De.	34	Jeremiah	Jer. or Je.	52
Joshua	Josh. or Jos.	24	Lamentations	Lam.	5
Judges	Judg. or Jud.	21	Ezekiel	Ezk. or Eze.	48
Ruth	Ruth or Ru.	4	Daniel	Dan. or Da.	12
1 Samuel	1 Sam. or 1 S.	31	Hosea	Hos. or Ho.	14
2 Samuel	2 Sam. or 2 S.	24	Joel	Joel	3
1 Kings	1 Ki. or 1 K.	22	Amos	Amos or Am.	9
2 Kings	2 Ki. or 2 K.	25	Obadiah	Obad. or Ob.	1
1 Chronicles	1 Chron. or 1 Chr.	29	Jonah	Jon. or Jona.	4
2 Chronicles	2 Chron. or 2 Chr.	36	Micah	Mic. or Mi.	7
Ezra	Ezra or Ezr.	10	Nahum	Nah. or Na.	3
Nehemiah	Neh. or Ne.	13	Habakkuk	Hab.	3
Esther	Est.	10	Zephaniah	Zeph. or Zep.	3
Job	Job or Jb.	42	Haggai	Hag.	2
Psalms	Ps.	150	Zechariah	Zech. or Zec.	14
Proverbs	Pr.	31	Malachi	Mal.	4

THE BOOKS OF THE NEW TESTAMENT

Book	Abbreviation	Chapters	Book	Abbreviation	Chapters
MATTHEW	Mt.	28	1 Timothy	1 Tim. or 1 Ti.	6
Mark	Mk.	16	2 Timothy	2 Tim. or 2 Ti.	4
Luke	Lk. or Lu.	24	Titus	Tit.	3
John	Jn.	21	Philemon	Phile. or Phm.	1
Acts	Acts or Ac.	28	Hebrews	Heb. or He.	13
Romans	Ro.	16	James	Jas. or Js.	5
1 Corinthians	1 Cor. or 1 Co.	16	1 Peter	1 Pt. or 1 Pe.	5
2 Corinthians	2 Cor. or 2 Co.	13	2 Peter	2 Pt. or 2 Pe.	3
Galatians	Gal. or Ga.	6	1 John	1 Jn.	5
Ephesians	Eph. or Ep.	6	2 John	2 Jn.	1
Philippians	Ph.	4	3 John	3 Jn.	1
Colossians	Col.	4	Jude	Jude	1
1 Thessalonians	1 Th.	5	Revelation	Rev. or Re.	22
2 Thessalonians	2 Th.	3			

HOW TO USE
everyWORD™

❶ SUBJECT HEADING - ▶ John

B. Jesus the Light of the World:
The Special Witness of John the Baptist, 1:6–8

❷ MAJOR POINTS - ▶

1. John was a man sent from God[DS1]

2. John was a man sent on a very special
   mission

❸ SUBPOINTS & SCRIPTURE - - - - - - - - - - - - - - - ▶
   a. To bear witness of the Light
   b. That people might believe
3. John was a great man, but he was not
   the Light

⁶ There was a man sent from God,
whose name was John.
⁷ He came as a witness, to bear witness about the light, that all might
believe through him.

⁸ He was not the light, but came to
bear witness about the light.

Division I

The Witnesses to the Revelation of Jesus Christ, 1:1–51

B. Jesus the Light of the World: The Special Witness of John the Baptist, 1:6–8

1:6–8
Introduction

❹ COMMENTARY - ▶

Of all the people who bore witness of Jesus, one individual stands out as unique. John the Baptist was a very special witness of Christ. In fact, John's sole purpose on earth was to witness and
to bear testimony of the Light of the world. His purpose stands as a dynamic example for us.
As believers, our purpose is to bear the same witness as John: Jesus Christ is the Light of the
world. This is, *Jesus the Light of the World: The Special Witness of John the Baptist, 1:6-8*.
  1. John was a man sent from God (v.6).
  2. John was a man sent on a very special mission (v.7).
  3. John was a great man, but he was not the Light (v.8).

❶ Glance at the **Subject Heading**.
Think about it for a moment.

❷ Glance at the **Subject Heading** again, and then the **Major
Points** (1, 2, 3, etc.). Do this
several times, reviewing them
together while quickly grasping
the overall subject.

❸ Glance at **both** the **Major
Points** and **Subpoints** together
while reading the **Scripture**. Do
this slower than Step 2. Note
how these points sit directly
beside the related verse and
simply restate what the Scripture
is saying—in Outline form.

❹ Next read the **Commentary.
Note** that the *Major Point Numbers* in the Outline match those
in the Commentary. When applicable, a small raised number
(**DS1, DS2, etc.**) at the end of a
Subject Heading or Outline Point
directs you to a related Deeper
Study (shown on opposite page)
in the Commentary.

❺ and **❻** Finally, read the
Thoughts and **Support Scriptures** (shown on opposite page).

1:6

⁶ There was a man sent from God, whose
name was John.

1 John was a man sent from God.
Scripture makes a strong contrast between what had been
said about Christ and what is now being said about John.
Christ "was in the beginning"; He was "with God," and He
"was God" (vv.1-2). On the other hand, John was "a man"
who had come into existence at birth, just like every other
human who has ever lived. John had a biological mother and
father, whereas Jesus Christ had no human father; He was the only begotten Son of God (v.14;
Jn.3:16). John was not a divine being, not even an angel. He was a mere man.
  This man, however, was *sent from God*; and he was sent on a very special mission. Two facts
show this:
  ➤ The meaning of the word *sent* (see Deeper Study # 1).
  ➤ The phrase *from God* (Gk. para Theou), which literally means "from beside God." John was
    not only sent by God, he was sent from the very side and heart of God. John was only a
    man, but a man of high calling and mission, of enormous responsibility and accountabil-
    ity. He was a man sent uniquely by God, not by some other person.

  Luke recorded a fascinating fact about this unusual man: his name was not chosen by his parents, but by God Himself. The angel whom God sent to Zacharias, instructed him to name his son

8

**The everyWORD™ series and study system contains everything
you need for sermon preparation and Bible study:**

1. The **Subject Heading** describes the overall theme of the passage and is located directly above the Outline and Scripture
   (keyed *alphabetically*).
2. **Major Points** are keyed with an outline *number* guiding you to
   related commentary.
3. **Subpoints** explain and clarify the Scripture as needed.
4. **Commentary** is fully researched and developed for every point.

John (Lk.1:13). The name *John* means *gracious*. John was a man sent forth with a name to match his message: *God's grace* is now to enter upon the scene of world history.

> John answered, "A person cannot receive even one thing unless it is given him from heaven." (Jn.3:27)

> What is man, that you make so much of him, and that you set your heart on him? (Jb.7:17)

> What is man that you are mindful of him, and the son of man that you care for him? (Ps.8:4)

> Do you not know? Do you not hear? Has it not been told you from the beginning? Have you not understood from the foundations of the earth? It is he [God] who sits above the circle of the earth, and its inhabitants are like grasshoppers; who stretches out the heavens like a curtain, and spreads them like a tent to dwell in. (Is.40:21-22)

THOUGHT 1. Like John, we too, as believers, are sent by God to bear witness of Jesus Christ. Note three significant points about the servants and messengers of God:

➤ First, the servants and messengers of God are not sent forth by another person, but by God. We are sent forth as the ambassadors of God.

➤ Second, God's messengers are sent forth *from* God, from the very side and heart of God.

➤ Third, as God's messengers, we have received the highest of all callings and missions, the calling of telling the world about Christ and the mission of bringing others into a saving relationship with Christ. This is an enormous responsibility, and we must never lose sight of the sobering fact that we are accountable to God Himself for our faithfulness to this holy task.

> "You did not choose me, but I chose you and appointed you that you should go and bear fruit and that your fruit should abide, so that whatever you ask the Father in my name, he may give it to you." (Jn.15:16)

> Not that we are sufficient in ourselves to claim anything as coming from us, but our sufficiency is from God, who has made us sufficient to be ministers of a new covenant, not of the letter but of the Spirit. For the letter kills, but the Spirit gives life. (2 Co.3:5-6)

> All this is from God, who through Christ reconciled us to himself and gave us the ministry of reconciliation; that is, in Christ God was reconciling the world to himself, not counting their trespasses against them, and entrusting to us the message of reconciliation. Therefore, we are ambassadors for Christ, God making his appeal through us. We implore you on behalf of Christ, be reconciled to God. (2 Co.5:18-20)

> Of this gospel I was made a minister according to the gift of God's grace, which was given me by the working of his power. (Ep.3:7)

> I thank him who has given me strength, Christ Jesus our Lord, because he judged me faithful, appointing me to his service. (1 Ti.1:12)

DEEPER STUDY # 1

(1:6) **Sent—Apostle—Commission:** *Sent* (apestalmenos) means to send out; to commission as a representative, an ambassador, an envoy. Three things are true of the person sent from God.

1. He belongs to God, who has sent him out.
2. He is commissioned to be sent out.
3. He possesses all the authority and power of God, who has sent him out.

2 John was a man sent on a very special mission.

1:7

Two Old Testament prophets foretold John's special mission and purpose. Both Isaiah and Malachi prophesied that John would prepare the way of the Lord, who is the embodiment

⁷ He came as a witness, to bear witness about the light, that all might believe through him.

9

---

5. **Thoughts** help apply the Scripture to daily life.
6. **Support Scripture** provides one or more Bible verses that correspond to the Major Points and Subpoints.
7. **Deeper Studies** provide in-depth discussions of key words or phrases.
8. **Scripture Callouts** repeat segments of Scripture used in the Scripture and Outline sections below the Subject Headings.

➎ THOUGHTS

➏ SUPPORT SCRIPTURE

➐ DEEPER STUDY

➑ SCRIPTURE CALLOUTS

"Woe to me, if I do not preach the gospel!"
(1 Co.9:16)

THE GOSPEL ACCORDING TO LUKE

INTRODUCTION

AUTHOR: Luke (1:3). Luke is also the author of Acts.

The early church fathers held Luke to be the author of both the Gospel of Luke and Acts: Irenaeus (about A.D. 130-200); Clement of Alexandria (about A.D. 150-215); Origen (about A.D. 185-254); and Tertullian (about A.D. 160-200). (See *The Pulpit Commentary*, Vol.16. Grand Rapids, MI: Wm. B. Eerdmans Publishing Co., 1950, p.1f, for an excellent discussion on the introductory material on Luke.)

A study of both books bears evidence that Luke is the author. The writer was evidently a physician, as Greek medical terms are used. An analysis of the Gospel and Acts together shows the same style and language. There is also a clear understanding of the Roman and Greek world of the first century. The content of the two books shows a strong unity, with emphasis on the resurrection, the Holy Spirit, the person of Christ, and the ministry to the Gentiles.

There is also enormous evidence that the writer of Acts was an acquaintance of Paul. This is clearly seen in the "we" section of Acts. In three sections of Acts, there is a remarkable switch from "they" and "he" to "we." The "we" sections give a first-hand account (Ac.16:10-17; 20:5-21:18; 27:1-28:16).

1. Luke is first seen with Paul at Troas. He switches from using "he" and "they" to "we." Luke joined Paul on his journey to Philippi and evidently remained in Philippi until Paul returned from Jerusalem (Ac.16:10).

2. Luke later went to Jerusalem with Paul when Paul was arrested (Ac.20:5-21:15).

3. Luke is seen with Paul again while Paul was a prisoner in Caesarea. He also accompanied Paul the prisoner to Rome (Ac.27:1-28:15).

4. Paul calls Luke "the beloved physician" (Col.4:14; Phile.24).

5. Luke is the last one to remain with Paul in his imprisonment (2 Ti.2:11).

DATE: uncertain. Probably A.D. 58-62.

The author ends Acts abruptly with Paul's two-year imprisonment at Rome, so the writing would have been done a number of years after Jesus' ascension, just prior to the end of Acts. Another factor is that Luke says nothing about the Fall of Jerusalem. The fall of the city was prophesied by Jesus, and it actually took place in A.D. 70; therefore, the writing took place before A.D. 70. Considering these two factors, Luke must have written the Gospel sometime between A.D. 58-62.

TO WHOM WRITTEN: to "the most excellent Theophilus," a Gentile convert (Lu.1:3; Ac.1:1). The words "most excellent" indicate that he was a high official in the Roman government. The book of Acts is also personally addressed to Theophilus (see note, *Theophilus*-Ac.1:1 for more discussion).

PURPOSE: to set forth an eyewitness account of Jesus, the Son of Man, the Savior of the world.

Luke wished Theophilus to know the certainty of those things which he had believed. Thus, Luke sets out to write an orderly and accurate account of the whole life of Jesus (Lu.1:1-4).

SPECIAL FEATURES:

1. *Luke* is "The Gospel for Man" or "The Gospel for Gentiles." Luke shows that God is interested in all men everywhere, not just in the Jews (Lu.2:14, 32; 3:38; 4:25-27; 7:2-10; 9:51-54; 10:30-37; 13:29; 17:16; 24:47).

2. *Luke* is "The Gospel of Individuals." Luke shows that Jesus was deeply interested in individuals. He tells of Zechariah and Elizabeth, the parents of John the Baptist (Lu.1:5-25, 39-45; 67-79); of Mary and Martha (Lu.10:38-42); of Zacchaeus (Lu.19:2-10); of Cleopas and his companion (Lu.24:18); and of the

woman who anointed Jesus' feet in the home of Simon the Pharisee (Lu.7:36f). The parables in Luke also tend to stress individuals, whereas in Matthew they stress the Kingdom.

3. *Luke* is "The Gospel of Salvation." Luke uses the words "salvation" and "Savior" or their various forms many more times than any of the other Gospel writers.

4. *Luke* is "The Gospel of Outcasts and Sinners." Luke tells of the feast Matthew held for tax collectors and sinners (Lu.5:30); of the woman anointing Jesus' feet with her tears and wiping them with her hair (Lu.7:36–50); of tax collectors and sinners drawing near to hear Jesus teach (Lu.15:1). He alone tells of the Prodigal Son (Lu.15:11–32); of the Pharisee and tax collector (Lu.18:9–14); of Zacchaeus, the tax collecting "sinner" (Lu.19:1–10). Many of his parables center around outcasts (Lu.7:41f; 12:13–21; 16:1–12, 19–31; 18:1–8, 9–14).

5. *Luke* is "The Gospel of the Poor." Luke tells of the shepherds who were poor (Lu.2:8f); of Mary, who made the purification offering of the poor (Lu.2:24; cp. Le.12:8). He says that Jesus came to preach the Gospel to the poor (Lu.4:18–6:20), and the poor have the Gospel preached to them (Lu.7:22).

6. *Luke* is "The Gospel of Women." Luke's world was a world that treated women only as things, as little more than chattel property, knowing nothing of women's rights. But Luke gives them a special place. He shows how God honored Elizabeth, Mary, and Anna (Lu.1:5f; 2:25f). He tells about the widow of Nain (Lu.7:11–18); the sinful woman who anointed Jesus' feet (Lu.7:36–50); and three women who were healed of evil spirits: Mary Magdalene, Joanna, and Susanna (Lu.8:2–3). He writes about the sisters Mary and Martha (Lu.10:38–42); the bent-over lady (Lu.13:11–13); the widow who gave all to God (Lu.21:1–4); and the women who lined the road and wept as Jesus sagged under the weight and burden of the cross (Lu.23:27–31). He also includes women in some of his parables (Lu.15:8–10; 18:1–8).

7. *Luke* is "The Gospel of Children." The birth of Jesus and John the Baptist are given in detail (Lu.1–2). Luke's point is to show that God was at work even in the infant stages of the Savior. Luke alone gives the story of Jesus' boyhood (Lu.2:41–52). He alone emphasizes Jesus' ministry to the "only son" and "only daughter" of a desperate parent (Lu.7:12; 8:42; 9:38).

8. *Luke* is "The Gospel of Prayer" or "The Gospel of Devotion." Prayer is often emphasized.
   a. There are the prayers of Jesus: at His baptism (Lu.3:21); in the wilderness (Lu.5:16); before choosing the disciples (Lu.6:12); immediately prior to predicting His death (Lu.9:18); at the transfiguration (Lu.9:28f); when the seventy returned (Lu.10:17–24, esp. 21–22); before giving the Lord's Prayer (Lu.11:1); for Peter (Lu.22:32); in the Garden of Gethsemane (Lu.22:39–46); for His enemies (Lu.23:34); and on the cross (Lu.23:46). Most of these are recorded by Luke alone. They show Jesus facing every crisis of life with prayer.
   b. There are the parables of Jesus that deal with prayer: the friend at midnight (Lu.11:5–8); the unjust judge (Lu.18:1–8); the Pharisee and Publican (Lu.18:9–14).
   c. There are the exhortations and warnings about prayer (Lu.6:28; 11:2; 10:47; 22:40, 46).

9. *Luke* is "The Gospel of Praise." He uses the phrase "praising God" more than all the rest of the New Testament combined.
   a. Some of the great Christian hymns are taken from Luke. The "Ava Maria" from the words of the angel to Mary (Lu.1:28–33); "The Magnificat" from Mary's song (Lu.1:46–55); "The Benedictus" from Zacharias (Lu.1:68–79); the "Gloria in Excelsis" from the song of the heavenly angels (Lu.2:13–14); and "The Nunc Dimittis" from the rejoicing of Simeon (Lu.2:29–32).
   b. People are seen praising God when helped (Lu.2:20; 5:25–26; 7:16; 13:13; 17:15; 18:43).
   c. The words "joy" and "rejoicing" are used time and time again (for example Lu.1:14, 44, 47; 10:21).
   d. There are references to laughter (Lu.6:21) and merriment (Lu.15:23, 32) and to joy (Lu.15:6, 9; 19:6).
   e. The Gospel ends with joy (Lu.24:52) even as it began with joy (Lu.1:14).

10. *Luke* is "The Gospel of Christ's Passion." This is seen in three significant emphases.
   a. There are the many references to His death. Moses and Elijah discuss Jesus' death at His transfiguration (Lu.9:31). Luke says the time for Jesus to be received up has arrived (Lu.9:51); therefore, Jesus sets His face to go up to Jerusalem (Lu.9:51). Jesus refers to His death as a baptism and stresses a constraint to accomplish it (Lu.12:50). Jesus sends a message to Herod that after His ministry He will finish His course on the third day (Lu.13:32). He then continues to speak of perishing in Jerusalem (Lu.13:33–35). And Jesus foretells His passion in a statement that is unique to Luke (Lu.17:25).

b. There is lengthy space devoted to the passion narrative.

c. There are the times that Scripture is said to be fulfilled by Jesus' death (Lu.9:22; 13:33; 17:25; 18:31; 20:17; 22:37; 24:7, 26f, 44, 46).

11. *Luke* is "The Gospel of the Holy Spirit."

a. The persons involved in the preparation for the Savior's coming are said to be Spirit-filled and Spirit-led: John the Baptist (Lu.1:15), Elizabeth and Zechariah (Lu.1:41, 67), and Simeon (Lu.2:25–27).

b. The Holy Spirit is said to be active in the life and ministry of Jesus. Mary was told that the Holy Spirit would come upon her (Lu.1:35). John the Baptist predicted Jesus would be baptized with the Holy Spirit and fire (Lu.3:16). The Holy Spirit came upon Jesus after His baptism "in a bodily shape, like a dove" (Lu.3:22). The Holy Spirit filled and led Him into the wilderness to be tempted by the devil (Lu.4:1). Jesus returned from His temptations to begin His ministry in Galilee "in the power of the Spirit" (Lu.4:14). While preaching, He claimed "the Spirit of the Lord is upon me" (Lu.4:18). He rejoiced in the Spirit when the seventy returned and gave a good report (Lu.10:21); He told His disciples that the Father would give the Spirit to those who asked (Lu.11:13). He said that blasphemy against the Holy Spirit is an unforgivable sin (Lu.12:10). He told His disciples that the Holy Spirit would tell them what to say in emergencies (Lu.12:12). He closed His ministry by assuring His disciples, "Behold, I send the promise of my Father upon you. . . ." (Lu.24:49).

OUTLINE OF LUKE 1–13:21

everyWORD™ is *unique*. It differs from all other study Bibles and sermon resource materials in that every passage and subject is outlined right beside the Scripture. When you choose any subject below and turn to the reference, you have not only the Scripture, but also an outline of the Scripture and subject *already prepared for you—verse by verse.*

For a quick example, choose one of the subjects below and turn over to the Scripture. You should find this system to be a marvelous help for more organized and streamlined study.

In addition, every point of the Scripture and Outline is *fully developed in a* Commentary section with supporting Scripture at the end of each point. Again, this arrangement makes sermon or lesson preparation much simpler and more efficient.

Note something else: The subjects of *Luke* have titles that are both *biblical* and *practical.* The practical titles are often more appealing to people. This benefit is clearly seen for use on billboards, bulletins, church newsletters, and so forth.

A suggestion: For the *quickest* overview of *Luke*, first read all the Division titles (I, II, III, etc.), then come back and read all the individual outline titles.

OUTLINE OF LUKE

I. **THE ANNOUNCEMENT OF THE COMING OF JESUS, THE SON OF MAN, 1:1–2:52**
    A. Luke's Gospel Account: The Truth of the Word, 1:1-4
    B. Zachariah and Elizabeth, the Parents of John the Baptist: Godly Parents, 1:5-25
    C. Mary, the Mother of Jesus: Submission to God's Will, 1:26-38
    D. Elizabeth's Divine Revelation: A Very Unusual Testimony, 1:39-45
    E. Mary's Magnificent Song About God: God's Glorious Mercy and Deliverance, 1:46-56
    F. John's Birth and Naming: An Event for All Generations, 1:57-66
    G. Zachariah' Inspired Prophecy: God's Savior and His Forerunner, 1:67-80
    H. Jesus' Birth: Its Unusual Events, 2:1-24
    I. Simeon's Prophecy: Jesus' Life and Fate Foretold, 2:25-35
    J. Anna's Praise: The Child Jesus Is Praised by a Prophetess, 2:36-38
    K. Jesus' Growth as a Child, 2:39-40
    L. Jesus as a Young Boy in the Temple: His First Recognition of Messiahship, 2:41-52

II. **THE SON OF MAN'S COMING, 3:1–4:15**
    A. The Forerunner, John the Baptist: Launched the Pivotal Point in History, 3:1-6
    B. The Plain Message of John the Baptist: A Message for All Ages, 3:7-20
    C. The Baptism of Jesus: Obedience and God's Approval, 3:21-22
    D. The Genealogy of Jesus: The Roots of the Messiah, 3:23-38
    E. The Temptation of Jesus: Victory over Temptation, 4:1-15

III. **THE SON OF MAN'S ANNOUNCED MISSION AND PUBLIC MINISTRY, 4:16–9:17**
    A. Jesus Announces His Mission: A Graphic Picture of Rejection, 4:16-30
    B. Jesus Ministers and Makes an Amazing Impact: A Day in the Life of Jesus, 4:31-44
    C. Jesus Calls His First Disciples: Steps to Calling People, 5:1-11
    D. Jesus Cleanses the Untouchable, 5:12-16
    E. Jesus Proves His Amazing Power to Forgive Sins, 5:17-26
    F. Jesus Reveals His Great Mission: The Greatest Mission of All, 5:27-39
    G. Jesus Teaches That Need Supersedes Religion, 6:1-11
    H. Jesus Chooses His Men: Whom He Chose and Why, 6:12-19
    I. Jesus Teaches the Perils of the Material World, 6:20-26
    J. Jesus Teaches the New Principles of Life, 6:27-38
    K. Jesus Teaches His Rules for Discipleship: The Need to Watch, 6:39-45
    L. Jesus Teaches Two Foundations of Life: Genuine vs. Counterfeit Discipleship, 6:46-49
    M. Jesus Finds Great Faith in a Soldier: Great Faith, What Great Faith Involves, 7:1-10

CHAPTER 1

I. THE ANNOUNCEMENT OF THE COMING OF JESUS, THE SON OF MAN, 1:1–2:52

A. Luke's Gospel Account: The Truth of the Word, 1:1–4

Inasmuch as many have undertaken to compile a narrative of the things that have been accomplished among us,

² just as those who from the beginning were eyewitnesses and ministers of the word have delivered them to us,

³ it seemed good to me also, having followed all things closely for some time past, to write an orderly account for you, most excellent Theophilus,

⁴ that you may have certainty concerning the things you have been taught.

1. Luke's Gospel is a record of historical events

2. Luke's Gospel is a record of eyewitnesses and servants of the Word

3. Luke's Gospel is the record of a man who was led to write

4. Luke's Gospel is a record to establish the truth

Division I

The Announcement of the Coming of Jesus, the Son of Man, 1:1–2:52

A. Luke's Gospel Account: The Truth of the Word, 1:1–4

1:1–4
Introduction

The eternal destiny of every soul hangs on believing in Jesus Christ. But before people can believe in Christ, they must know the truth about Him. Luke begins his Gospel with a series of statements emphasizing that what he has to say is the truth about Jesus Christ. From the outset, Luke declares the glorious news that the Son of Man, God's Son, has come to earth to seek and to save all who are lost. Luke's Gospel is an accurate, orderly account of the truth about Jesus.

Luke intentionally crafts his introduction in the very form used by the historians of his day. His use of this form points strongly to the fact that he intended it to be circulated among churches and believers. This is, *Luke's Gospel Account: The Truth of the Word*, 1:1–4.

1. Luke's Gospel is a record of historical events (v.1).
2. Luke's Gospel is a record of eyewitnesses and servants of the Word (v.2).
3. Luke's Gospel is the record of a man who was led to write (v.3).
4. Luke's Gospel is a record to establish the truth (v.4).

1 Luke's Gospel is a record of historical events.

1:1

Luke's opening statement establishes that his Gospel is a record of historical events. He acknowledges the fact that *many* had written about the life and work of Christ. However, their accounts were neither as *complete* nor as *orderly* as Luke wished to record (see v.3). A quick comparison of the first two chapters of Luke with Mark and Matthew will

Inasmuch as many have undertaken to compile a narrative of the things that have been accomplished among us,

show this. Luke includes many more events than the other two Synoptic Gospels, and the Gospel of John had not yet been written at the time Luke completed his Gospel. The fact that *many* had written a record on the life of Christ is strong evidence that the events are true.

The events or *things* of Christ's life were *accomplished* or *fulfilled* (Gk. peplerophoremenon, pronounced *pep-lay-rah-phor-ay-men'-own*). This means that the *things* he was writing about, the events of Christ's life, were accomplished or fulfilled among the believers of that day. These *things* (events, matters) of Christ actually took place; they were purposeful; they were destined to be accomplished and fulfilled. Furthermore, Christ did not do these *things* secretly. He accomplished His earthly purpose—did the works God sent Him to do—in the presence of people who could testify to their truth.

Luke's point is, the *things* of Christ are a record of historical events that actually happened and that actually fulfilled the purpose of God. Indeed, the whole Bible, New Testament and Old Testament, is a record of these *things*. In the Old Testament, they are seen in prophecies and types. In the New Testament, they are seen as they were actually accomplished. The entire Bible tells the story of Jesus.

> For the Son of Man came to seek and to save the lost. (Lu.19:10)

> For God so loved the world, that he gave his only Son, that whoever believes in him should not perish but have eternal life. (Jn.3:16)

> Who, though he was in the form of God, did not count equality with God a thing to be grasped, but emptied himself, by taking the form of a servant, being born in the likeness of men. And being found in human form, he humbled himself by becoming obedient to the point of death, even death on a cross. Therefore God has highly exalted him and bestowed on him the name that is above every name, so that at the name of Jesus every knee should bow, in heaven and on earth and under the earth, and every tongue confess that Jesus Christ is Lord, to the glory of God the Father. (Ph.2:6–11)

> He has delivered us from the domain of darkness and transferred us to the kingdom of his beloved Son, in whom we have redemption, the forgiveness of sins. He is the image of the invisible God, the firstborn of all creation. For by him all things were created, in heaven and on earth, visible and invisible, whether thrones or dominions or rulers or authorities—all things were created through him and for him. And he is before all things, and in him all things hold together. And he is the head of the body, the church. He is the beginning, the firstborn from the dead, that in everything he might be preeminent. For in him all the fullness of God was pleased to dwell, and through him to reconcile to himself all things, whether on earth or in heaven, making peace by the blood of his cross. (Col.1:13–20)

> He himself bore our sins in his body on the tree, that we might die to sin and live to righteousness. By his wounds you have been healed. (1 Pe.2:24)

> I will put enmity between you and the woman, and between your offspring and her offspring; he shall bruise your head, and you shall bruise his heel. (Ge.3:15)

> I am poured out like water, and all my bones are out of joint; my heart is like wax; it is melted within my breast; my strength is dried up like a potsherd, and my tongue sticks to my jaws; you lay me in the dust of death. For dogs encompass me; a company of evildoers encircles me; they have pierced my hands and feet; I can count all my bones—they stare and gloat over me; they divide my garments among them, and for my clothing they cast lots. (Ps.22:14–18)

> What more was there to do for my vineyard, that I have not done in it? When I looked for it to yield grapes, why did it yield wild grapes? And now I will tell you what I will do to my vineyard. I will remove its hedge, and it shall be devoured; I will break down its wall, and it shall be trampled down. (Is.5:4–5)

> For to us a child is born, to us a son is given; and the government shall be upon his shoulder, and his name shall be called Wonderful Counselor, Mighty God, Everlasting Father, Prince of Peace. (Is.9:6)

THOUGHT 1. The early believers had no difficulty whatsoever believing the *things* of Christ. They actually saw these things accomplished, and "many" were writing an account of the events.

The "many" who wrote about the life of Jesus are not known by name. They are the silent and humble heroes of God, never known by the world, but well-known by God. Some of their writings served as a *source* for Luke (v.3). Note two observations.

1) Their ministry of writing was used greatly by God. Some of what they wrote was either included in the inspired *Gospel of Luke* or at least stirred thoughts in Luke's mind to record an event.

2) God's silent, quiet, and humble servants are always used by Him just as much as the ones out in the forefront. Their ministry is just as important, if not more so. Some who are last will most definitely be first.

> **And behold, some are last who will be first, and some are first who will be last. (Lu.13:30; see Mt.19:30; 20:16; Mk.10:31)**

2 Luke's Gospel is a record of eyewitnesses and servants of the Word.

Luke's Gospel is both a record of *eyewitnesses* and a record of *ministers* or *servants of the Word*. Luke himself was not an eyewitness of the day-to-day life of Christ. If he ever saw Christ personally, there is no mention of it. However, Luke was a constant and very dear companion of Paul (see Introduction—Luke; note—Ac.16:10). He also had contact with other apostles. What Luke says is that the sources of his writing were eyewitnesses of Christ and ministers of the Word of Christ. The apostles, of course, would be his primary sources. In addition, his information came from other disciples who followed Jesus either continuously or occasionally. Note these simple facts:

> *² just as those who from the beginning were eyewitnesses and ministers of the word have delivered them to us,*

➤ The ministers of the Word were eyewitnesses of both *The Word* (Christ Himself) and of the Word of Christ (His teaching, doctrine, and instructions).

➤ The ministers of the Word were eyewitnesses "from the beginning," eyewitnesses of every event and word of Christ, eyewitnesses of His life day by day.

➤ The ministers of the Word heard as well as saw Christ; some heard and saw Him day by day. Therefore, Luke's Gospel is a true record of both the acts and words of Christ.

➤ The ministers of the Word set out immediately to *minister* the Word to others. The word was of critical importance to them. They gave their lives to the ministry of the Word.

➤ The ministers of the Word did not create the Word (message) themselves. They were not ministering their own ideas and thoughts; they were ministering *the Word of God*.

➤ The ministers of the Word—through Luke—have given us a written Gospel that is an eyewitness account. It agrees exactly with what was seen, heard, and proclaimed by Christ and preached to the people of His day and to the world since then.

> **That which was from the beginning, which we have heard, which we have seen with our eyes, which we looked upon and have touched with our hands, concerning the word of life—the life was made manifest, and we have seen it, and testify to it and proclaim to you the eternal life, which was with the Father and was made manifest to us—that which we have seen and heard we proclaim also to you, so that you too may have fellowship with us; and indeed our fellowship is with the Father and with his Son Jesus Christ. And we are writing these things so that our joy may be complete. (1 Jn.1:1-4)**

3 Luke's Gospel is the record of a man who was led to write.

Luke states that it "seemed good to [him]" to write an account of Christ's life and works. God's Spirit led Luke to write his Gospel. The Holy Spirit stirred his spirit to produce an orderly account of Christ's life. Four facts point out just how strongly Luke felt led to record the life of Christ.

> *³ it seemed good to me also, having followed all things closely for some time past, to write an orderly account for you, most excellent Theophilus,*

First, Luke had thoroughly investigated the life of Christ. *Having followed, having had perfect understanding,* or *have investigated* (parekolouthekoti, *par-ay-kol-oo-they-kah'-tee*) means to study, to follow up, to search out diligently, to trace accurately, to become thoroughly acquainted with. Luke says that having been acquainted with and having investigated *all things* concerning Christ, he was determined to record the facts himself.

Second, Luke says he had investigated all things *for some time past, from the very first,* or *from the beginning* (anothen, *ahn'-oh-then*). This Greek word can and often does mean *from above*. Some scholars understand Luke to be saying that he had investigated the things *from above* (see Deeper Study # 1).

Third, Luke says he is writing *an orderly account* or *sequence* (kathexes, *kah-thex-ace'*). Luke is the only writer in the New Testament to use this word. He uses it in his Gospel only once and in *Acts* twice (Ac.11:4; 18:23). The question is, what does Luke mean by *orderly?* Consecutive or chronological arrangement? Logical arrangement? Subject arrangement? Inspired or Spirit-led arrangement? The meaning is not clear. Perhaps he is saying that he is writing a full account of the life of Christ and that his account is a *better arrangement,* that is, it has more order and is better arranged than those in existence.

Fourth, Luke is writing to a man named "Theophilus." Who was he? We are not told.

Luke calls him the "most excellent Theophilus." *Most excellent* (kratiste, *kra'-tis'-teh*) is a title of rank and honor. The same title is used of Felix and Festus (Ac.23:26; 24:3; 26:25). Whoever Theophilus was, he was a person who desired or needed to know about Jesus Christ. He was probably a convert for whom Luke deeply cared. Some feel he was a man investigating the validity of Christianity. Theophilus is the immediate reason Luke *felt led* to write. (see note, *Theophilus*—Ac.1:1 for more discussion).

THOUGHT 1. We need to be *prepared* to serve Christ. Like Luke, we should study, investigate, search out, become acquainted with the truth of Christ in order that we will be ready to serve Him, prepared to do whatever He calls us to do. In addition, we should follow the Lord's leading to serve Him, no matter the task. We should be both sensitive and obedient to the Spirit of Christ's leading in our lives.

> You did not choose me, but I chose you and appointed you that you should go and bear fruit and that your fruit should abide, so that whatever you ask the Father in my name, he may give it to you. (Jn.15:16)

> For all who are led by the Spirit of God are sons of God. (Ro.8:14)

> Do your best to present yourself to God as one approved, a worker who has no need to be ashamed, rightly handling the word of truth. (2 Ti.2:15)

THOUGHT 2. We can have great confidence in the truth and accuracy of the written record of Christ.

> All Scripture is breathed out by God and profitable for teaching, for reproof, for correction, and for training in righteousness. (2 Ti.3:16)

> And we have the prophetic word more fully confirmed, to which you will do well to pay attention as to a lamp shining in a dark place, until the day dawns and the morning star rises in your hearts, knowing this first of all, that no prophecy of Scripture comes from someone's own interpretation. For no prophecy was ever produced by the will of man, but men spoke from God as they were carried along by the Holy Spirit. (2 Pe.1:19–21)

THOUGHT 3. Note a tremendous challenge to us. Luke cared so much for one man that he dedicated himself to writing not just a long letter, but a whole book in order to instruct the man. Imagine the dedication and the days and months required! All for one person (initially)!

> What man of you, having a hundred sheep, if he has lost one of them, does not leave the ninety-nine in the open country, and go after the one that is lost, until he finds it? (Lu.15:4)

DEEPER STUDY # 1

(1:3) **Anothen:** Some scholars feel this Greek word should be translated here as *from above.* Several insights point to this translation.

1. If Luke meant *from some time past,* or *from the first or beginning,* why did he not use the same Greek word (arches, *ar-case'*) which he used in verse 2? It seems to be much more

accurate to say he chooses a different word (anothen) because he is saying something different, *from above*.

2. The prophets are said to have proclaimed things *from above*. Note what Scripture says about the proclamations of the prophets:

> **Concerning this salvation, the prophets who prophesied about the grace that was to be yours searched and inquired carefully, inquiring what person or time the Spirit of Christ in them was indicating when he predicted the sufferings of Christ and the subsequent glories. It was revealed to them that they were serving not themselves but you, in the things that have now been announced to you through those who preached the good news to you by the Holy Spirit sent from heaven, things into which angels long to look. (1 Pe.1:10–12)**

Scripture also says:

> **For no prophecy was ever produced by the will of man, but men spoke from God as they were carried along by the Holy Spirit. (2 Pe.1:21)**

3. Luke is certainly recording *all things from above,* investigating and searching diligently to write what "the Spirit of Christ in [him] was indicating" (1 Pe.1:11). He is certainly speaking as a holy man of God "carried along by the Holy Spirit" (2 Pe.1:21). He is certainly proclaiming the gospel of the Lord Jesus Christ, the good news of Him who came from above.

4 Luke's Gospel is a record to establish the truth.

Luke stated clearly his purpose for writing: he wanted Theophilus to be certain of the things he had been taught. Theophilus *had already heard* about Christ. But he *needed to know* the absolute truth of those things, to be firmly convinced of them and secure in them. Luke wrote to establish the truth of Jesus Christ in Theophilus' heart and mind.

⁴ that you may have certainty concerning the things you have been taught.

THOUGHT 1. Luke's account of Christ is the absolute truth. We can be absolutely certain, fully convinced, or secure in the truth of the things he wrote.

THOUGHT 2. Hearing the things of Christ, even being instructed in them, is not enough. We are to study and learn, to know the absolute certainty of them.

> **Now these Jews were more noble than those in Thessalonica; they received the word with all eagerness, examining the Scriptures daily to see if these things were so. (Ac.17:11)**

B. Zechariah and Elizabeth, the Parents of John the Baptist:
Godly Parents, 1:5–25

1. **They were parents with an interesting background**
   a. They lived in the time of Herod
   b. The father was a priest, and the mother was from a priestly family
2. **They were parents who lived righteously**

3. **They were parents with human problems**
   a. They had no child
   b. They were elderly
4. **They were parents who worshiped**

5. **They were parents who prayed and led others to pray**

6. **They were parents greatly favored by God**
   a. Their worship and prayers were favored by a visit from an angel

   b. Their prayers were answered: They received the promise of a son

   c. Their son was to be great
   d. Their son was to be a prophet

   e. Their son was to be the forerunner of the Messiah

⁵ In the days of Herod, king of Judea, there was a priest named Zechariah, of the division of Abijah. And he had a wife from the daughters of Aaron, and her name was Elizabeth.

⁶ And they were both righteous before God, walking blamelessly in all the commandments and statutes of the Lord.

⁷ But they had no child, because Elizabeth was barren, and both were advanced in years.

⁸ Now while he was serving as priest before God when his division was on duty,

⁹ according to the custom of the priesthood, he was chosen by lot to enter the temple of the Lord and burn incense.

¹⁰ And the whole multitude of the people were praying outside at the hour of incense.

¹¹ And there appeared to him an angel of the Lord standing on the right side of the altar of incense.

¹² And Zechariah was troubled when he saw him, and fear fell upon him.

¹³ But the angel said to him, "Do not be afraid, Zechariah, for your prayer has been heard, and your wife Elizabeth will bear you a son, and you shall call his name John.

¹⁴ And you will have joy and gladness, and many will rejoice at his birth,

¹⁵ for he will be great before the Lord. And he must not drink wine or strong drink, and he will be filled with the Holy Spirit, even from his mother's womb.

¹⁶ And he will turn many of the children of Israel to the Lord their God,

¹⁷ and he will go before him in the spirit and power of Elijah, to turn the hearts of the fathers to the children, and the disobedient to the wisdom of the just, to make ready for the Lord a people prepared."

¹⁸ And Zechariah said to the angel, "How shall I know this? For I am an old man, and my wife is advanced in years."

¹⁹ And the angel answered him, "I am Gabriel. I stand in the presence of God, and I was sent to speak to you and to bring you this good news.

²⁰ And behold, you will be silent and unable to speak until the day that these things take place, because you did not believe my words, which will be fulfilled in their time."

²¹ And the people were waiting for Zechariah, and they were wondering at his delay in the temple.

²² And when he came out, he was unable to speak to them, and they realized that he had seen a vision in the temple. And he kept making signs to them and remained mute.

²³ And when his time of service was ended, he went to his home.

²⁴ After these days his wife Elizabeth conceived, and for five months she kept herself hidden, saying,

²⁵ "Thus the Lord has done for me in the days when he looked on me, to take away my reproach among people."

7. **They were parents who found it difficult to believe the humanly impossible**[DS1]

8. **They were parents who had to be disciplined by God**

9. **They were parents who saw God fulfill His promise**

Division I

The Announcement of the Coming of Jesus, the Son of Man, 1:1–2:52

B. Zechariah and Elizabeth, the Parents of John the Baptist: Godly Parents, 1:5–25

1:5-25
Introduction

Every generation needs the example of godly parents. The parents of John the Baptist were godly, dynamic examples of what all parents should be. They were human, showing some weaknesses, but they were striking examples for all. In this passage, Luke tells us about them and about what God did for them and through them. This is, *Zechariah and Elizabeth, the Parents of John the Baptist: Godly Parents, 1:5–25.*

1. They were parents with an interesting background (v.5).
2. They were parents who lived righteously (v.6).
3. They were parents with human problems (v.7).
4. They were parents who worshiped (vv.8–9).
5. They were parents who prayed and led others to pray (v.10).
6. They were parents greatly favored by God (vv.11–17).
7. They were parents who found it difficult to believe the humanly impossible (vv.18–19).

8. They were parents who had to be disciplined by God (vv.20-22).

9. They were parents who saw God fulfill His promise (vv.23-25).

1:5

⁵ In the days of Herod, king of Judea, there was a priest named Zechariah, of the division of Abijah. And he had a wife from the daughters of Aaron, and her name was Elizabeth.

1 They were parents with an interesting background.

Luke introduces us to a godly couple who were privileged to play a key role in the coming of the Messiah. Zechariah and Elizabeth were blessed to be the vessels through whom the forerunner of Christ would be sent to the world.

a. They lived in the time of Herod.

The baby John was promised to his parents during the reign of Herod the Great. Herod's reign was a long and bloody one (37 B.C.-A.D.4). John was born right at the end of his reign (see DEEPER STUDY # 3—Mt.2:3-4).

b. The father was a priest, and the mother was from a priestly family.

John's father was Zechariah, which means *remembered of Jehovah*. He was a priest from the division of Abijah. Remember that all the male descendants of Aaron were priests. There were over twenty thousand at this time and only one temple, so they had to be divided into groups (1 Chr.24:1-6). Zechariah served in the eighth group or division (1 Chr.24:10). There were twenty-four groups, and each group served in the temple for one week, twice a year.

John's mother was named Elizabeth, which means *one whose oath is to God*. The daughter of a priest, she was a pure and virtuous woman. We know this because a priest was required to marry a virgin (Le.21:14).

1:6

⁶ And they were both righteous before God, walking blamelessly in all the commandments and statutes of the Lord.

2 They were parents who lived righteously.

Zechariah and Elizabeth were godly people. Scripture states specifically that they "were *both* righteous." They were joined together and committed to each other, and they lived for God and for each other as husband and wife.

Scripture also states that they were "righteous *before God*." Their godliness was not merely external. They were exactly what they appeared to be, what *God* knew them to be. Together they came "before God" seeking Him, that is, seeking to please Him and to live as He said. Accordingly, they walked "in *all* the commandments and statutes [ordinances, requirements] of the Lord." They controlled their thoughts, minds, tongues, and behavior, diligently seeking to please the Lord in all they did. And they did so *blamelessly*. This, of course, does not mean they were perfect. It means they were faithful, living in such a way that no one could charge them with open sin. They were a stumbling block to no one; they lived honestly before both God and other people.

1:7

⁷ But they had no child, because Elizabeth was barren, and both were advanced in years.

3 They were parents with human problems.

Living righteously did not free Zechariah and Elizabeth from problems. They had to face the problems of this world just as all persons do. But there was a difference: they were righteous before God. Therefore, they had the presence of God to help them through the problems. Two serious problems burdened this godly couple's hearts.

a. They had no child.

Zechariah and Elizabeth were childless. This was a terrible calamity to the people of that day. Children were considered a blessing from God, a great heritage of the Lord. In fact, a Jew whose wife could not bear children was thought to be cut off from God. The husband was expected to divorce his wife, remarry, and bear children. Therefore, being childless was a critical problem to Zechariah and Elizabeth, a problem that weighed ever so heavily upon their hearts and never left their minds. They felt disfavored and displeasing to God.

b. They were elderly.

All the problems that come with age stood as a threat before Zechariah and Elizabeth. On top of all the burdens old age brings (Ec.12:1-7), their advanced years sealed their excruciating fate. They would *never* have a child. They would never know the joys of parenting. They would die without a descendant, without an heir, for Elizabeth was now too old to conceive.

> **So that you may be sons of your Father who is in heaven. For he makes his sun rise on the evil and on the good, and sends rain on the just and on the unjust. (Mt.5:45)**

> **Reproaches have broken my heart, so that I am in despair. I looked for pity, but there was none, and for comforters, but I found none. (Ps.69:20)**

4 They were parents who worshiped.

1:8-9

Zechariah and Elizabeth worshiped and served God faithfully. Zechariah had been chosen and ordained by God to be a priest, and he was faithful to that call. He was steadfast in his duties despite the lack of blessings from God, that is, being childless (v.8). Remember that bearing a son in that day and time was considered one of the greatest blessings and signs of God's approval. Not having a son was thought to be an indication of God's disapproval.

> [8] Now while he was serving as priest before God when his division was on duty,
> [9] according to the custom of the priesthood, he was chosen by lot to enter the temple of the Lord and burn incense.

Zechariah was given the holy privilege of burning incense in the temple (v.9). In the temple's daily worship, incense was burned upon the altar by a priest before the morning sacrifice and after the evening sacrifice. The offering of incense symbolized that the sacrifices were being offered up to God in the sweetest and most prayerful of spirits. The aroma of the incense was just like prayer; it enveloped the sacrifice and carried it before the very throne of God.

The priests considered the burning of incense to be the highest privilege of the priestly functions. However, because of the large number of priests, some never had the opportunity to offer it up to God. Just who received this privilege was determined by drawing lots. On this particular day, Zechariah experienced one of the greatest days of his life. The lot fell upon him. He was the priest chosen to offer the incense.

The point is, Zechariah was faithful to God's call. He had been chosen and ordained by God to be a priest, and he had accepted and given his life to that call. He was faithful in his worship despite his *problems and lack of blessings* from God (being childless).

> **Blessed is the man who remains steadfast under trial, for when he has stood the test he will receive the crown of life, which God has promised to those who love him. (Jas.1:12)**

> **Behold, we consider those blessed who remained steadfast. You have heard of the steadfastness of Job, and you have seen the purpose of the Lord, how the Lord is compassionate and merciful. (Jas.5:11)**

5 They were parents who prayed and led others to pray.

1:10

Zechariah was praying while he offered the incense up to God, and he had led the people to pray while he sought the Lord in their behalf. He had led them to be a praying people. They were as involved in the prayer and worship as he was. (What a lesson for congregations!)

> [10] And the whole multitude of the people were praying outside at the hour of incense.

> **Again I say to you, if two of you agree on earth about anything they ask, it will be done for them by my Father in heaven. (Mt.18:19)**

> **Seek the LORD and his strength; seek his presence continually! (1 Chr.16:11)**

> **When he calls to me, I will answer him; I will be with him in trouble; I will rescue him and honor him. (Ps.91:15)**

6 They were parents greatly favored by God.

God is bound to bless and highly favor any parent who is righteous, who worships, who prays, and who leads others to worship and pray. Zechariah and Elizabeth were faithful to the Lord in

1:11-17

all these areas, in spite of the fact that God had not seen fit to bless them with children. Consequently, Zechariah and Elizabeth were greatly favored by God. The Lord showed His favor on this godly couple in five unusual ways.

¹¹ And there appeared to him an angel of the Lord standing on the right side of the altar of incense.
¹² And Zechariah was troubled when he saw him, and fear fell upon him.
¹³ But the angel said to him, "Do not be afraid, Zechariah, for your prayer has been heard, and your wife Elizabeth will bear you a son, and you shall call his name John.
¹⁴ And you will have joy and gladness, and many will rejoice at his birth,
¹⁵ for he will be great before the Lord. And he must not drink wine or strong drink, and he will be filled with the Holy Spirit, even from his mother's womb.
¹⁶ And he will turn many of the children of Israel to the Lord their God,
¹⁷ and he will go before him in the spirit and power of Elijah, to turn the hearts of the fathers to the children, and the disobedient to the wisdom of the just, to make ready for the Lord a people prepared."

a. Their worship and prayers were favored by a visit from an angel (vv.11–12).

This couple's need was met by God in a very personal way: God sent an angel to Zechariah. Note the angel appeared on the right side of the altar of incense, the very place of prayer (v.11). It was while he was praying, in the act of obedience, that God met his need in this special way.

When the angel appeared to Zechariah, the righteous man was gripped in the soul-strangling clutch of fear (v.12). But the angel had come with good news for this faithful priest and his barren wife.

b. Their prayers were answered: They received the promise of a son (vv.13–14).

The angel informed Zechariah that God had heard his prayer. The angel's announcement reveals what this righteous man had been praying about: he had been pouring his heart out to God about being childless, despite his age (v.13).

Although Scripture does not say so, it is safe to assume that, as a faithful Jew, Zechariah had also been praying for the redemption of Israel, for the coming of the Messiah? *Both* prayers were now being answered. Elizabeth was to bear a son, and the Messiah was to be born.

Their son was to be named John, which means *the grace of Jehovah*. Not only would his birth bring joy to his parents, but to *many* (v.14). He would cause his parents to rejoice because of his life. He was to be everything that parents could want in a child. He would not shame them, but he would bring joy to their hearts. He would cause many to rejoice because of his contribution to society. He would bring joy to all their friends, and he would bring joy to the nation as a whole. Many would rejoice in such a commitment and contribution as his.

c. Their son was to be great (v.15a).

The angel announced that John would be great, not just in people's eyes, but in the sight of the Lord. He would be great in the sight of God Himself because of his *faithfulness* (obedience). He would live a *disciplined* and *controlled* life, abstaining from wine and strong drink and from the very appearance of evil.

THOUGHT 1. Note the traits that made John great. How desperately believers need the same traits in our own lives!

I appeal to you therefore, brothers, by the mercies of God, to present your bodies as a living sacrifice, holy and acceptable to God, which is your spiritual worship. Do not be conformed to this world, but be transformed by the renewal of your mind, that by testing you may discern what is the will of God, what is good and acceptable and perfect. (Ro.12:1-2)

I thank him who has given me strength, Christ Jesus our Lord, because he judged me faithful, appointing me to his service. (1 Ti.1:12)

THOUGHT 2. The point to see about Zechariah and Elizabeth is that God did hear their prayer and bless them richly. He favored them because they were faithful to Him.

> If you abide in me, and my words abide in you, ask whatever you wish, and it will be done for you. (Jn.15:7)

> And whatever we ask we receive from him, because we keep his commandments and do what pleases him. (1 Jn.3:22)

d. Their son was to be a prophet (vv.15b–16).

John was ordained by God to be a prophet. Like Jeremiah, God chose John for this special office before he was conceived (Je.1:5). He would be filled with the *Holy Spirit* from the very first, while he was yet in his mother's womb. He would be a vessel chosen by God for a very special service, *fitted* in a very special way (v.15b). Like that of the prophets of old, John's ministry would result in many of God's people turning back to Him (v.16).

e. Their son was to be the forerunner of the Messiah (v.17).

The angel saved the most glorious news about John until last: Zechariah and Elizabeth's son would be the forerunner of the promised Messiah. Note what the angel said: "He will go before Him . . . to make ready for the Lord a people prepared" (Mal.3:1). John's ministry was to be like that of Elijah, the greatest of the prophets (Mal.4:5-6; see Mt.11:10; 17:10). The same *spirit* and *power* that marked Elijah's ministry would mark his ministry as well.

7 They were parents who found it difficult to believe the humanly impossible.

Zechariah just could not believe the message and the promise of God. He had been praying, but apparently, he had not thought God would answer, certainly not by doing the impossible—by overruling the laws of nature. Note that Zechariah's question was the question of unbelief. He asked the very same question asked by Abraham (Ge.15:8), but Zechariah asked the question in a spirit of unbelief. He informed the angel that he and Elizabeth were too old to have children (v.18).

The very Word and promise of God should have been enough to convince Zechariah, but he was weak in faith. He had to ask for additional assurance. He asked for a sign—a sign other than *God's Word and promise* as sent through the angel, who identified himself as Gabriel (v.19; see Deeper Study # 1).

[18] And Zechariah said to the angel, "How shall I know this? For I am an old man, and my wife is advanced in years."
[19] And the angel answered him, "I am Gabriel. I stand in the presence of God, and I was sent to speak to you and to bring you this good news."

DEEPER STUDY # 1

(1:19) **Gabriel:** means the *man of God* or the *hero of God* or the *mighty one of God*. Note that Gabriel said two things about himself . . .
  1. He is the one who actually stands in the presence of God.
  2. He is the one who brings good news to people.
      ➤ He shared the restoration of Israel with Daniel (Da.8:16; 9:21f).
      ➤ He shared the birth of the forerunner with Zechariah (Lu.1:13f).
      ➤ He shared the birth of the Messiah with Mary (Lu.1:26f).

8 They were parents who had to be disciplined by God.

Zechariah had failed to believe God; therefore, he had to be disciplined and taught to grow in trust more and more. Zechariah had asked for a sign. He had let his tongue speak instead of his heart.

1:20-22

²⁰ "And behold, you will be silent and unable to speak until the day that these things take place, because you did not believe my words, which will be fulfilled in their time."
²¹ And the people were waiting for Zechariah, and they were wondering at his delay in the temple.
²² And when he came out, he was unable to speak to them, and they realized that he had seen a vision in the temple. And he kept making signs to them and remained mute.

Therefore, God gave him a sign—the sign of stopping his tongue during the nine months before John was born (v.20).

Zechariah had failed to receive the Word of God. Consequently, God took away his ability to share the Word with other people. He had spoken words of distrust and unbelief; therefore, God saved him from speaking any more words of distrust and unbelief.

Note that Zechariah tarried in the temple much longer than usual (v.21). The people became restless, wondering what had happened. When he came out, he was supposed to lead the people in a benediction, but he was unable to speak. All he could do was motion with his hand (v.22). Even though Zechariah could not speak, the people could tell that he had been in the presence of God. They thought he had seen a vision. Despite Zechariah's unbelief, he had still lived a faithful life before God; therefore, God still met him and gave His promise to him and his wife. What hope for us all, even when our faith is weak!

THOUGHT 1. Every true child of God knows the discipline of God's loving hand. His discipline differs with each of us, but each of us can recognize His discipline nevertheless (see outline and notes—He.12:5–13).

> And have you forgotten the exhortation that addresses you as sons? "My son, do not regard lightly the discipline of the Lord, nor be weary when reproved by him. For the Lord disciplines the one he loves, and chastises every son whom he receives." (He.12:5–6)
>
> Those whom I love, I reprove and discipline, so be zealous and repent. (Re.3:19)
>
> Know then in your heart that, as a man disciplines his son, the LORD your God disciplines you. (De.8:5)
>
> Blessed is the man whom you discipline, O LORD, and whom you teach out of your law. (Ps.94:12)
>
> My son, do not despise the LORD's discipline or be weary of his reproof, for the LORD reproves him whom he loves, as a father the son in whom he delights. (Pr.3:11–12)
>
> Correct me, O LORD, but in justice; not in your anger, lest you bring me to nothing. (Je.10:24)

THOUGHT 2. God will not allow people to disbelieve and distrust forever. The day is coming when he will stop all disbelief and distrust just as He did with Zechariah.

1:23-25

²³ "And when his time of service was ended, he went to his home.
²⁴ After these days his wife Elizabeth conceived, and for five months she kept herself hidden, saying,
²⁵ "Thus the Lord has done for me in the days when he looked on me, to take away my reproach among people."

9 They were parents who saw God fulfill His promise.

In spite of Zechariah's lapse in faith, God fulfilled his promise to him and Elizabeth. Elizabeth conceived the promised child (v.24). God proved Himself faithful to this couple who were faithful to Him. These verses reveal two glimpses into this godly couple's faithfulness to the Lord.

First, they were responsible (v.23). Zechariah had lost his voice completely. Yet he fulfilled his duties, despite being disciplined with the infirmity. He did what he could, responsibly and faithfully. What an example!

Second, they withdrew into the presence of God (vv.24–25). After Zechariah completed his duties, he returned home. Most likely, Zechariah stayed close to home, walking in meditation and prayer because of his experience and being unable to talk with others. But note especially

Elizabeth's behavior. She hid herself for five months. Why? For the same reason any of us would withdraw after being visited by such an angelic being with so great a message. She needed time alone with God to absorb all that was happening and to prepare herself for the rearing of one who was destined to be so greatly used by God.

Note how the thought that she was hiding her pregnancy from the public is inaccurate. She hid herself only for the first five months of her pregnancy. Her pregnancy became public after the five months (see vv.39–40, 57).

THOUGHT 1. Note a crucial point. The call to special service necessitates a period of preparation, especially the preparation of oneself in the presence of God. Time alone with God for meditation and prayer over God's call is essential.

> Let us draw near with a true heart in full assurance of faith, with our hearts sprinkled clean from an evil conscience and our bodies washed with pure water. (He.10:22)

> Draw near to God, and he will draw near to you. Cleanse your hands, you sinners, and purify your hearts, you double-minded. (Jas.4:8)

> Is anyone among you suffering? Let him pray. Is anyone cheerful? Let him sing praise. (Jas.5:13)

> The LORD is near to the brokenhearted and saves the crushed in spirit. (Ps.34:18)

> Be merciful to me, O God, be merciful to me, for in you my soul takes refuge; in the shadow of your wings I will take refuge, till the storms of destruction pass by. (Ps.57:1)

C. Mary, the Mother of Jesus: Submission to God's Will, 1:26–38

(Mt.1:18–25)

1. The angel Gabriel was sent by God to Nazareth

2. Mary was pure, a virgin[DS1]

3. Mary was highly favored by God

4. Mary was very human
   a. Greatly troubled

   b. Fearful

5. Mary was told she was to bear the Messiah
   a. His name: Jesus[DS2]
   b. His great person
      1) Son of the Most High
      2) Son of David[DS3]

   c. His eternal kingdom

6. Mary was expected to believe the miraculous
   a. Her perplexity
   b. Her conception: By the Holy Spirit and the power of God
   c. Her child: The Son of God

7. Mary was encouraged to believe that nothing is impossible with God
   a. God's other miracle

   b. God's great power

8. Mary was submissive

26 In the sixth month the angel Gabriel was sent from God to a city of Galilee named Nazareth,

27 to a virgin betrothed to a man whose name was Joseph, of the house of David. And the virgin's name was Mary.

28 And he came to her and said, "Greetings, O favored one, the Lord is with you!"

29 But she was greatly troubled at the saying, and tried to discern what sort of greeting this might be.

30 And the angel said to her, "Do not be afraid, Mary, for you have found favor with God.

31 And behold, you will conceive in your womb and bear a son, and you shall call his name Jesus.

32 He will be great and will be called the Son of the Most High. And the Lord God will give to him the throne of his father David,

33 and he will reign over the house of Jacob forever, and of his kingdom there will be no end."

34 And Mary said to the angel, "How will this be, since I am a virgin?"

35 And the angel answered her, "The Holy Spirit will come upon you, and the power of the Most High will overshadow you; therefore the child to be born will be called holy—the Son of God."

36 "And behold, your relative Elizabeth in her old age has also conceived a son, and this is the sixth month with her who was called barren.

37 For nothing will be impossible with God."

38 And Mary said, "Behold, I am the servant of the Lord; let it be to me according to your word." And the angel departed from her.

Division I

The Announcement of the Coming of Jesus, the Son of Man, 1:1–2:52

C. Mary, the Mother of Jesus: Submission to God's Will, 1:26–38

(Mt.1:18–25)

1:26–38
Introduction

It is fascinating that so little information is given about Mary in the Bible. Many would consider her to be the most significant woman in world history. Yet, we know so little about her. However, what is said is striking and sets before us a tremendous example of *submissiveness to God's will*. Submissiveness to God is an absolute essential for every believer, and it is the trait for which the mother of our Lord is remembered. This is, *Mary, the Mother of Jesus: Submission to God's Will,* 1:26–38.

1. The angel Gabriel was sent by God to Nazareth (v.26).
2. Mary was pure, a virgin (v.27).
3. Mary was highly favored by God (v.28).
4. Mary was very human (vv.29–30).
5. Mary was told she was to bear the Messiah (vv.31–33).
6. Mary was expected to believe the miraculous (vv.34–35).
7. Mary was encouraged to believe that nothing is impossible with God (vv.36–37).
8. Mary was submissive (v.38).

1 The angel Gabriel was sent by God to Nazareth.

1:26

After sending the angel Gabriel to announce the birth of John, God sent His special messenger on a second mission involving the birth of Jesus (see DEEPER STUDY # 1—Lu.1:19). The time of this mission is given: it was six months after Elizabeth's conception that God sent Gabriel to an obscure

> 26 In the sixth month the angel Gabriel was sent from God to a city of Galilee named Nazareth,

village, Nazareth of Galilee. Galilee bordered Gentile or heathen nations; therefore, it was sometimes called Galilee of the Gentiles. Nazareth was a despised city, considered inferior by the rest of Israel. The Nazarenes were a conquered people especially despised by the Romans. The city and its citizens were the object of deep prejudice by Jews and Romans alike (see Jn.1:46; see DEEPER STUDY # 4—Mt.2:23; 13:53–58.)

THOUGHT 1. God is no respecter of persons or places. He sends a message to Nazareth as readily as He does to Jerusalem (see Lu.1:5–25), to a believer in Nazareth (Mary) as quickly as he does to a believer in Jerusalem (Zechariah).

THOUGHT 2. A place, whether city or nation, is not judged by its institutions and advantages, but by the righteous people within its borders (see Ge.18:23f).

2 Mary was pure, a virgin.

1:27

The very first piece of information given about Mary is that she was a virgin when Gabriel appeared to her and when she subsequently conceived Christ. She had never been touched by a man, not immorally. This is unmistakably and clearly stated. She confirmed the fact herself (see v.34). This fact is significant because, over seven hundred years prior, God had

> 27 to a virgin betrothed to a man whose name was Joseph, of the house of David. And the virgin's name was Mary.

revealed through the prophet Isaiah that the Messiah would be born of a *virgin* (Hb. alma; Is.7:14; see DEEPER STUDY # 1).

Unsurprisingly, skeptics and infidels have attacked Christ's virgin birth for centuries, and they continue to do so today. One of their most common arguments is that the Hebrew word *alma* can mean a young woman with a questionable character, that it does not necessarily refer to a virgin. However, this argument is weak. When a Hebrew spoke of a young woman (alma) he meant virgin. This is clear when the word *alma* is studied. The word is used six times in the Old Testament, always referring to a young woman with pure character.

➢ Rebekah, the young woman, was certainly a virgin (Ge.24:43). The whole context verifies the point.

➢ Miriam, the young sister of Moses, was also pointed to as a virgin by the context (Ex.2:8).

➢ Young women of pure character were those who were worthy to participate in the worship of God (Ps.68:25).

➢ The young women who were worthy of Solomon's love were not of impure character (Song 1:3).

➢ There were young women who were contrasted with queens and concubines—women who were not virgins (Song 6:8).

➢ The maiden (young woman) of *Proverbs* was contrasted with the adulterous woman (Pr.30:19–20).

In view of the heavy weight of this argument, the logical translation of *alma* is virgin. Of course, the virgin birth does not rest on this argument alone. However, we need to realize that unbelief snatches at every little gnat, trying its best to add everything it can to disprove the deity of Christ.

THOUGHT 1. Humanity desperately needs to turn from its unbelief and to trust Christ wholeheartedly. He is the only hope for the human race.

> For God so loved the world, that he gave his only Son, that whoever believes in him should not perish but have eternal life. (Jn.3:16)

> And just as it is appointed for man to die once, and after that comes judgment. (He.9:27)

The second piece of information given about Mary is that she was betrothed (espoused, engaged) to Joseph. Being betrothed was something like a modern-day engagement, except it was more binding, both legally and practically. During this one-year period, sexual contact with another person was considered to be adultery, just as it was in marriage, and resulted in stoning. The betrothal was so binding that if it were broken, a divorce had to be secured.

Mary and Joseph were both godly, so godly that God could choose them to be the parents of His Son. It was impossible that God would have chosen an immoral man and woman to bear and rear His Son, not when He had the power to control the events.

THOUGHT 2. Mary's purity teaches two striking lessons.

1) God expects both women and men to be sexually pure, abstaining from sexual relations with a man or woman until they are married.

2) God is looking for pure women and men to use in the ministry of the gospel and in meeting the desperate needs of the world.

> You have heard that it was said, "You shall not commit adultery." But I say to you that everyone who looks at a woman with lustful intent has already committed adultery with her in his heart. (Mt.5:27–28)

> But sexual immorality and all impurity or covetousness must not even be named among you, as is proper among saints. (Ep.5:3)

> For this is the will of God, your sanctification: that you abstain from sexual immorality; that each one of you know how to control his own body in holiness and honor, For God has not called us for impurity, but in holiness. (1 Th.4:3–4, 7)

> Older women likewise are to be reverent in behavior, not slanderers or slaves to much wine. They are to teach what is good, and so train the young women to love their husbands and children, to be self-controlled, pure, working at home, kind, and submissive to their own husbands, that the word of God may not be reviled. (Tit.2:3–5)

It is these who have not defiled themselves with women, for they are virgins. It is these who follow the Lamb wherever he goes. These have been redeemed from mankind as firstfruits for God and the Lamb. (Re.14:4)

Who shall ascend the hill of the LORD? And who shall stand in his holy place? He who has clean hands and a pure heart, who does not lift up his soul to what is false and does not swear deceitfully. (Ps.24:3-4)

DEEPER STUDY # 1

(1:27) **Jesus Christ, Virgin Birth:** in looking at the virgin birth of Christ, people need to think deeply and honestly. Both are necessary: people must be honest, and they must engage in concentrated thought. One question needs to be asked: Why would God's Son have to enter the world through a virgin? Or more simply put, why was Christ born of a virgin? Why was a virgin birth necessary? (Note: Mary confirmed that she was a virgin, v.34.)

1. The birth of God's Son required a miracle. He could not be born through the natural process as other humans are. If He had been born as other people, His very birth would indicate that He was no more than mere man. Very simply, any person who enters the world through a man and a woman is a mere man or a mere woman. He or she can be nothing more. But this is not so with Christ. Christ already existed. Therefore, if God wanted to send His Son into the world, He would have to choose another way. All Christ needed was a body. As He Himself said to God the Father: "A body have you prepared for me" (He.10:5).

2. The birth of God's Son required a combined act on God's part and on a woman's part. If God's Son were to become a human and identify with human beings, He had to come through the process of conception through a woman. Why? Because human beings can only come through the woman. Therefore, if God wanted to send His Son into the world, He would have to perform a miracle, causing Mary to conceive by an act of His divine power.

3. The birth of God's Son required a miraculous nature—both a divine nature and a human nature.
   ➤ He had to be born of a woman to partake of human nature (see He.2:14-18).
   ➤ He had to be born through a miraculous act of God so as not to partake of humanity's corruption. This was critical if we are to escape corruption and live forever. Think about it. Our faith must be in an incorruptible Savior if we are to be covered by His incorruption. God had to identify with us by becoming one with us and by conquering our depraved and doomed nature (see DEEPER STUDY # 3—Mt.1:16 for more discussion).

4. The birth of God's Son required the birth of a perfect nature. Why? Because a perfect life needed to be lived. Righteousness, that is, perfection, needed to be secured. An Ideal Life (that is, a perfect, righteous life) had to be lived so that it could stand for and cover all people in perfection and in righteousness. Honest thought confesses that no human being has been or is perfect. Every human falls short (Ro.3:23). Our *falling short* of God's glory is tragically pictured in the ultimate fate of life: death.

   But God acted. God did everything to secure righteousness and perfection for humanity. He took every step and performed every act necessary to *save His people* from their sins and from death. He did it from beginning to end, from birth to exaltation. God sent His Son into the world, not through a *man* and a woman but through a miraculous act of His own upon the virgin Mary. Jesus Christ was thereby the God-Man. This says at least four things (see notes—Ro.5:1; DEEPER STUDY # 2—8:3 for more discussion).

   a. As God-Man, Christ was able to consummate both the human and divine. He had the capacity and innate power not to sin (see DEEPER STUDY # 3—Mt.1:16). Therefore, His Godly nature empowered Him to live righteously, never doing wrong and always choosing and doing right (He.5:8; 2 Co.5:21). By living a sinless life, Christ was able to secure righteousness, the Ideal Righteousness, that will cover and stand for all people.

b. As God-Man, Christ was also able to bear the sins and the judgment of sin for all people. When He died, He died as the Perfect and Ideal Man. Therefore, His death is able to cover and stand for all.

c. As God-Man, Christ was able to arise from the dead. Note the phenomenal words: ". . . His [God's] Son, who was descended from David according to the flesh [that is, made a man]; and was declared to be the Son of God in power, according to *the Spirit of holiness* by his resurrection from the dead" (Ro.1:3-4). He lived a perfect and holy life by which He became the Perfect and Ideal Man; therefore, His resurrection covers and stands for every person.

d. As God-Man, Christ was exalted to sit at the right hand of the Father—to live eternally in the heavenly dimension of being, in God's very own presence. As the Perfect and Ideal Man, His exaltation into the heavenly or spiritual dimension is able to blaze the path into heaven for every person. He is the forerunner into heaven for every individual (He.6:20). His exaltation as the Ideal Man covers and stands for the exaltation of everyone.

5. The birth of God's Son required the creative Word of God. God created the world by simply speaking the Word. God always creates by the power of His Word and the power of His Word alone. Therefore, when God chose . . .

   • to create a body for His Son, He created that body by simply speaking the Word (He.10:5)
   • to send His Son into the world, He sent His Son by simply speaking the Word

It is the same with the new birth or the re-creation of a person's spirit. It is by the Word of God, God's simply speaking the Word, that we are born again. The act of the spiritual birth, of the re-creation, is not seen, felt, or touched. Nothing physical happens, but the re-creation does occur. *It occurs by the Word of God* (see 1 Pe.1:23).

6. The birth of God's Son required the virgin birth because Christ is the *only begotten* Son of God. He is God's only Son, who possesses all the nature and fullness of God Himself (Ph.2:6-7; Col.2:9). Therefore, His birth had to be different. He had to enter the world differently from others, for He is different by the very nature of His being. He had to enter the world in such a way as to proclaim His divine nature, yet in such a way that would allow Him to partake of human nature. This is critically important. His birth had to involve both the act of mankind and of God Himself. Why? Because the Son of God had to be proclaimed to be the Son of God.

   ➤ There is no salvation apart from His *being* the Son of God.
   ➤ There is no salvation apart from His being *proclaimed* to be the Son of God.

We can be saved only if the Son of God *is*, only if He exists, and only if He is *proclaimed*. The Son of God must *exist*, and we must *hear* of Him if we are to be saved. He and His message are both essential. His virgin birth proclaims Him to be the *only begotten* Son of God, the only Son sent into the world by the direct and miraculous intervention of God.

7. The birth of God's Son satisfied the requirement of a second Adam, a second man . . .

   • born just like the first Adam, by the Word of God using natural substance
   • born to become what the first Adam failed to become: the Representative Man, the Ideal Man, the Pattern, the Perfect One in whom all people could find their Representative, their Ideal, their Pattern, their Perfection
   • born to be what Adam failed to be: the Man who always chose to love and obey God in all things, thereby passing on the nature of the ideal righteousness and perfection that can stand for and cover all
   • born to provide what the first Adam failed to pass on to humanity: the Way to God, the Truth of God, and the Life of God which all can trust and follow (Jn.14:6).

- born to offer what the first Adam failed to pass on to humanity: the nature of righteousness and life, both life abundant and life eternal (see Ro.5:15-19; Jn.10:10)

8. The birth of God's Son required an espousal or betrothal state of Mary and Joseph, and not a single or married state. Why?
   ➢ Because a single woman would cause far more questioning and heap far more contempt upon Christ and His followers.
   ➢ Because a married woman would not be a virgin and God's Son had to be born of a virgin as indicated by the points above.

   The betrothal state provided the ideal marital relationship for God to use in sending His Son into the world (see note 2—v.27). The fact that Jewish society used the betrothal relationship as a preparation for marriage shows how God was preparing the world for the coming of His Son (see DEEPER STUDY # 1—Ga.4:4.)

   But when the fullness of time had come, God sent forth his Son, born of woman, born under the law. (Ga.4:4)

THOUGHT 1. A question needs to be asked. Why is it so hard to believe that God can cause Mary to miraculously conceive? Why is it so hard to believe that God exists and that "God so loved the world, that he gave his only Son, that whoever believes in him should not perish but have eternal life" (Jn.3:16)?

THOUGHT 2. Just imagine what science can do in the fertilization of female eggs today. Is God not able to do so much more? How foolish our unbelief causes us to act. The problem is not God, but our faith: "For nothing will be impossible with God" (Lu.1:37; 18:27; see He.11:6, which is a warning to all).

3 Mary was highly favored by God.

Imagine how Mary must have felt when an angel suddenly appeared to her! In greeting Mary, Gabriel said three simple, yet meaningful, things to her.

> [28] And he came to her and said, "Greetings, O favored one, the Lord is with you!"

First, the angel said that she was highly favored by God. Note the angel did not immediately tell Mary *how* she was to be favored by God, that she was God's choice to bear and to be the mother of the Messiah. That came later in the conversation. The angel had to give her time to adjust to the shock of his spectacular appearance. For right now, he simply announced that she was favored by God—*a unique privilege.*

THOUGHT 1. Just think! God does *favor* us: He saves us, gifts us, uses us. We are favored by the God of the universe—a phenomenal privilege and an awesome responsibility to make ourselves available to receive His favor.

Second, the Lord was with Mary. She did not walk through life alone. Mary's life had pleased God to the point that He could favor her and be with her. She allowed God to walk with her and look after her life, so God was able to be with her. This means that God . . .
- *had been* with her (past)
- *was* with her (present)
- *would be* with her (future)

No matter where Mary had to walk or what she had to do, God promised to be with her. What God had chosen Mary to do would not be easy, but she would not go through it alone; He would be with her.

Third, among all women, Mary was the most blessed. It should be noted that this clause is not in the oldest and most reliable manuscripts. Nevertheless, the point is made later in this passage:

Mary was to be blessed and to be called blessed by people of all generations (v.48; see Jud.5:24 for a similar declaration by Deborah concerning Jael).

1:29–30

²⁹ But she was greatly troubled at the saying, and tried to discern what sort of greeting this might be.

³⁰ And the angel said to her, "Do not be afraid, Mary, for you have found favor with God."

4 Mary was very human.

Mary's response to the angel's appearance and words reveals that she was very human—a normal human being no different from anybody else. She was both troubled and stricken with fear.

a. Greatly troubled (v.29).

Mary was deeply troubled by what the angel told her. It was the message that caused her to be troubled, the fact that . . .
- she was highly favored
- the Lord was with her
- she was blessed among women

Mary was troubled because she did not understand how God could so greatly favor a person like herself. She never expected to be greatly favored by Him. This fact reveals her deep humility. Mary was not a proud, self-centered, flighty, or frivolous young lady who was conscious of herself or felt that she merited and deserved the attention of others. She was a young lady who loved God and had determined to live a pure and responsible life. Apparently, from her response throughout this passage, she had a sweet spirit that was full of softness, warmth, and tenderness. She was responsive and willing, subjective and giving, thoughtful and kind. However, Mary never dreamed she was anyone special. Therefore, when she heard that God was to favor her and use her in a very special way, she became troubled. How could she, so ordinary and humble, do anything special for God? What a striking example Mary is!

b. Fearful (v.30).

Mary's fear is understandable, for an angelic being from God stood before her. He stood in all the dazzling splendor that is necessary to reveal that he was truly from God. In addition, she feared the message that the angel had been sent to deliver to her. For this reason, Gabriel immediately assured her that he had been sent with good news from God.

> But he gives more grace. Therefore it says, "God opposes the proud but gives grace to the humble." (Jas.4:6)

> For though the Lord is high, he regards the lowly, but the haughty he knows from afar. (Ps.138:6)

> "All these things my hand has made, and so all these things came to be," declares the Lord. "But this is the one to whom I will look: he who is humble and contrite in spirit and trembles at my word." (Is.66:2)

1:31–33

³¹ "And behold, you will conceive in your womb and bear a son, and you shall call his name Jesus.

³² He will be great and will be called the Son of the Most High. And the Lord God will give to him the throne of his father David,

³³ and he will reign over the house of Jacob forever, and of his kingdom there will be no end."

5 Mary was told she was to bear the Messiah.

Mary was told by the angel just *how* God has favored her, what this meant to her life. She was to bear and be the mother of the Messiah. Gabriel proceeded to reveal three startling and profound truths about Mary's Son.

a. His name: Jesus (v.31).

Mary was actually told what she was to name the Messiah: *Jesus* (see DEEPER STUDY # 2). Christ's Father chose His name to express the purpose for which He was sending His only Son.

b. His great person (v.32).

Mary's Son would be called the *Son of the Most High* or *Highest*. The Highest, of course, is God. Therefore, Jesus is the Son of God, that is, of the very nature of God. He is "God over all, blessed forever. Amen" (Ro.9:5).

Mary's Son was to be the Son of David and was to receive the throne of David. The fact that David is referred to as His father means that He was of the line of David. Mary was a descendant of David; therefore, Christ Himself would be a descendant of David (see DEEPER STUDY # 3).

c. His eternal kingdom (v.33).

Mary's Son would be Israel's king, and He would reign over an eternal kingdom. For this reason, Jesus would teach that His kingdom would not be of this earth, for nothing on this earth lasts forever (Jn.19:36). Therefore, the kingdom was to be spiritual, by which it would be eternal (see DEEPER STUDY # 3—Mt.19:23-24).

DEEPER STUDY # 2

(1:31) **Jesus** (Gk. iesous, pronounced *ee-yay'-soos*): Savior; "He will save." The Hebrew form is *Joshua* (yasha), meaning "Jehovah is salvation" or "He is the Savior." The idea is that of deliverance, of being saved from some terrible disaster that leads to perishing (see Jn.3:16; see also Lu.9:23; Ro.8:3; Ga.1:4; He.2:14-18; 7:25).

DEEPER STUDY # 3

(1:32-33) **Jesus Christ, Son of David:** Christ is the Son of David, a descendant of David. Note two truths.

1. Christ is to reign upon the throne of David. But it will not be the people who will give Him the throne. They will not allow Him to rule over them. The throne will be given to Him by God. God will be the One to place Him upon the throne and give Him the rule over the people (see note—Mt.1:1).

2. The promise of ruling over the house of Jacob and of possessing a kingdom forever apparently has both a literal and a spiritual meaning, both a temporal and eternal meaning (see DEEPER STUDY # 3—Mt.19:23-24; note—Lu.3:24-31; DEEPER STUDY # 3—Jn.1:45; DEEPER STUDY # 4—1:49; note—Ro.11:1-36, esp. 11:25-36).

---

6 Mary was expected to believe the miraculous.

Mary was expected to believe the miraculous, but she was puzzled. She was not doubting or distrusting the message. She was not asking for some sign or proof like Zechariah (v.18). She was simply asking for more information for the sake of understanding, not confirmation of the Lord's word.

34 And Mary said to the angel, "How will this be, since I am a virgin?"

35 And the angel answered her, "The Holy Spirit will come upon you, and the power of the Most High will overshadow you; therefore the child to be born will be called holy—the Son of God."

a. Her perplexity (v.34).

Mary's question was logical and appropriate. She was single and had never been with a man sexually. How could she—a virgin—possibly bear a child?

b. Her conception: By the Holy Spirit and the power of God (v.35a).

The angel explained how Mary would conceive: "The Holy Spirit will *come upon you*." Mary would not conceive after the manner of men—naturally, but *after the manner* of God's

Spirit—supernaturally and miraculously. What is the manner or operation of God's Spirit? How does the Spirit work? God's Spirit sets apart and activates, creates and re-creates by *the Word of God*. God's Spirit simply speaks, and it is done (see Deeper Study # 1, pt.5—v.27). Some skeptics have suggested that the Holy Spirit came upon Mary sexually. This concept is blasphemy! There is no such idea as a *crude mating* between the Holy Spirit and Mary. God's Spirit simply speaks and it is done, no matter what is to be done.

The angel went on to say that God's power would *overshadow* (episkiasei, *eh-pis-kih-ah'-say*) Mary. God Himself was going to look after the whole matter. The child's conception and growth during pregnancy and His birth and life were under the shadow and wing of Almighty God. Greek scholar A. T. Robertson remarks that the Greek word translated *overshadow* is the same word . . .

> "used of the shining bright cloud at the Transfiguration of Jesus (Mt.11:27; Lu.10:21; Jn.5:19f.). Here it is like the Shekinah glory which suggests it (Ex.40:38) where the cloud of glory represents the presence and power of God."[1]

It was God's power that saw to the whole operation, not the presence or power of an angel or of a man or of any other creature.

c. Her child: The Son of God (v.35b).

The angel told Mary that her child would *be holy*, "the Son of God." Note the most critical point: who "the Son of God" is:

➤ He is "the holy One" born by the power and the Word and the will of God through the virgin Mary.

➤ He is "the holy One" whom "God sent forth . . . born of a woman" by His power, Word, and will (Ga.4:4).

THOUGHT 1. Like Mary, we are to believe the miraculous. We serve a God who can and does operate outside the boundaries of the natural. The difference in Mary and Zechariah is that Mary asked in faith, while Zechariah asked in doubt (Jas.1:5–6). Mary asked for information; Zechariah asked for confirmation. We should believe God, believe the miraculous, never doubting His Word or His power.

He said to them, "Because of your little faith. For truly, I say to you, if you have faith like a grain of mustard seed, you will say to this mountain, 'Move from here to there,' and it will move, and nothing will be impossible for you." (Mt.17:20)

And Jesus said to him, " 'If you can'! All things are possible for one who believes." (Mk.9:23)

Commit your way to the LORD; trust in him, and he will act. (Ps.37:5)

Trust in the LORD with all your heart, and do not lean on your own understanding. (Pr.3:5)

1:36–37

³⁶ "And behold, your relative Elizabeth in her old age has also conceived a son, and this is the sixth month with her who was called barren. ³⁷ For nothing will be impossible with God."

7 Mary was encouraged to believe that nothing is impossible with God.

The angel sought to assure Mary of the miracle God would perform within her and to strengthen her faith in God's power. Pointing to two facts, he challenged her to believe that God can do the impossible.

a. God's other miracle (v.36).

The angel informed Mary of another miracle: her cousin Elizabeth, who was beyond childbearing age, had conceived a son in her old age and was now six months pregnant. The fact that God could cause her cousin to conceive in her old age demonstrated God's power. Visiting Elizabeth would encourage Mary.

---

1 A. T. Robertson, James Swanson, ed., *Word Pictures in the New Testament* (Nashville: Holman Reference, 1958). Via Wordsearch digital edition.

b. God's great power (v.37).

With people, much is impossible. But to say that all things are possible with humans is far from the truth. When Mary heard and meditated on the simple statement, "For nothing will be impossible with God," she was bound to be encouraged. The statement was simple and striking. It could be easily remembered and understood.

THOUGHT 1. God expects us to believe Him and His power, regardless of circumstances and our feelings of insignificance.

> But Jesus looked at them and said, "With man this is impossible, but with God all things are possible." (Mt.19:26)

> I know that you can do all things, and that no purpose of yours can be thwarted. (Jb.42:2)

> Our God is in the heavens; he does all that he pleases. (Ps.115:3)

8 Mary was submissive.

Mary submitted to God's will and plan for her. Her response was immediate and brief, only one short sentence, yet it was striking, meaningful, and beautiful.

> ³⁸ And Mary said, "Behold, I am the servant of the Lord; let it be to me according to your word." And the angel departed from her.

Mary said that she was the Lord's *servant* (doule), which literally means slave-girl. Mary was saying that she was a bond-slave, willing to sell herself out completely to God. She would possess herself no longer but would give herself completely to God.

God's will became her will. She surrendered totally to obey God. She would serve as He willed, being completely obedient and fulfilling His purpose entirely. She would act "according to [the] *word*" the angel had spoken to her from God.

Imagine what Mary was thinking, the enormous depth of her trust and dedication to God. Her submission to God's will brought a great deal of uncertainty, potential shame, and even the possibility of death. Consider what Mary had to face:

➤ *The idea of being an unwed mother* (Lu.1:26f; Mt.1:18)—who of that day would ever believe Mary's story? Required was a willingness to be available to God regardless of the price.

➤ *Joseph's discovery of her pregnancy* (Mt.1:19)—the shock of broken trust and of personal embarrassment were more than a person could be expected to bear (Mt.1:20). Required was a willingness on Joseph's part to forget self completely.

➤ *The threat of being condemned to death because of adultery* (De.22:23f)—she had to face the possibility of being stoned because she would appear to be immoral (see Jn.8:5). Required was a total disregard for her own life (Ac.20:24).

THOUGHT 1. Surrender to God is an absolute essential both for salvation and service.

> For whoever does the will of my Father in heaven is my brother and sister and mother. (Mt.12:50)

> So therefore, any one of you who does not renounce all that he has cannot be my disciple. (Lu.14:33)

> And the world is passing away along with its desires, but whoever does the will of God abides forever. (1 Jn.2:17)

> I delight to do your will, O my God; your law is within my heart. (Ps.40:8)

> Teach me to do your will, for you are my God! Let your good Spirit lead me on level ground! (Ps.143:10)

D. Elizabeth's Divine Revelation: A Very Unusual Testimony, 1:39–45

1. **Mary visited Elizabeth**
   a. She hurriedly traveled to a town in Judah
   b. She entered Elizabeth's home and greeted her
   c. Elizabeth welcomed Mary with a divine revelation
      1) Heard Mary's greeting
      2) Felt her baby leap within
      3) Was filled with the Spirit
      4) Spoke loudly, exuberantly
2. **Elizabeth proclaimed the uniqueness of Mary and her child**
3. **Elizabeth proclaimed that Mary's child was her Lord**
   a. The great confession
   b. The clear sign

4. **Elizabeth proclaimed that Mary would receive the promise because of her faith**

³⁹ In those days Mary arose and went with haste into the hill country, to a town in Judah,
⁴⁰ and she entered the house of Zechariah and greeted Elizabeth.
⁴¹ And when Elizabeth heard the greeting of Mary, the baby leaped in her womb. And Elizabeth was filled with the Holy Spirit,
⁴² and she exclaimed with a loud cry, "Blessed are you among women, and blessed is the fruit of your womb!
⁴³ And why is this granted to me that the mother of my Lord should come to me?
⁴⁴ For behold, when the sound of your greeting came to my ears, the baby in my womb leaped for joy.
⁴⁵ And blessed is she who believed that there would be a fulfillment of what was spoken to her from the Lord."

Division I

The Announcement of the Coming of Jesus, the Son of Man, 1:1–2:52

D. Elizabeth's Divine Revelation: A Very Unusual Testimony, 1:39–45

1:39–45
Introduction

Through the angel Gabriel, the Lord sent word to Mary that she had been selected to bear God's Son. The Lord confirmed the message by revealing this truth to Mary's cousin Elizabeth by the Holy Spirit. Elizabeth proclaimed the word about Mary's baby that had been revealed to her supernaturally. Her confession is crucial and needs to be studied in depth. Why is Elizabeth's confession about the baby conceived in Mary of critical importance? Because the baby was . . .

- Jesus (v.31)
- The Son of the Highest (v.32)
- The Son of David (v.32)
- The Ruler over the house of Jacob forever (v.33)
- The Ruler whose kingdom has no end (v.33)
- The One born of the Holy Spirit (v.35)
- The Son of God Himself (v.35)

Spoken by Elizabeth, Mary's cousin and John the Baptist's mother, this is the very first testimony ever given by human lips about Jesus. This is, *Elizabeth's Divine Revelation: A Very Unusual Testimony, 1:39–45.*

1. Mary visited Elizabeth (vv.39–42).
2. Elizabeth proclaimed the uniqueness of Mary and her child (v.42).
3. Elizabeth proclaimed that Mary's child was her Lord (vv.43–44).
4. Elizabeth proclaimed that Mary would receive the promise because of her faith (v.45).

1 Mary visited Elizabeth.

After Mary's encounter with the angel, she went to see her cousin, Elizabeth. It would a memorable visit that the Lord would use in a special way in both ladies' hearts.

a. She hurriedly traveled to a town in Judah (v.39).

Mary went with *haste* (Gk. spoudes, pronounced *spoo-dace'*) to see her cousin Elizabeth. The Greek word means speed, diligence, care, earnestness, zeal. The idea is that Mary went with purpose and earnestness. She was not going on a casual, friendly visit. She had a very specific reason for going, a meaningful purpose. She was going so that she and Elizabeth could encourage and share with each other. They both had similar situations. God had performed a miracle for both, moving supernaturally upon their bodies. He gave life to Elizabeth's barren womb for the son of Zechariah to be conceived, and He created

39 In those days Mary arose and went with haste into the hill country, to a town in Judah,
40 and she entered the house of Zechariah and greeted Elizabeth.
41 And when Elizabeth heard the greeting of Mary, the baby leaped in her womb. And Elizabeth was filled with the Holy Spirit,
42 and she exclaimed with a loud cry, "Blessed are you among women, and blessed is the fruit of your womb!"

a child in the virgin Mary's womb. Mary in particular could be encouraged, for Elizabeth was already six months pregnant. The six months' pregnancy was visible evidence that God had already acted upon her miraculously. It should be noted that Mary knew about Elizabeth's miraculous conception, but Elizabeth did not know about Mary's conception.

Zechariah and Elizabeth lived in a town in Judah. The town is unknown today, but most commentators think it was the same as Hebron. Hebron is said to be in the hill country of Judah and to belong to the priests (Jos.21:10-11).

b. She entered Elizabeth's home and greeted her (v.40).

When Mary arrived at Zechariah and Elizabeth's home, she entered the house and greeted her cousin. Neither of the happy ladies anticipated what would happen next.

c. Elizabeth welcomed Mary with a divine revelation (vv.41-42a).

At the *very* moment Elizabeth heard Mary's greeting, Elizabeth felt her baby leap in her womb (v.41a). The baby had leapt or kicked before, but this leap was different from all the others. It was a sign to Elizabeth that the baby within Mary was someone very, very special, someone who was about to be revealed by the Holy Spirit.

Instantly, the Holy Spirit filled Elizabeth and gave her a very special spirit of prophecy (v.41b-42a). The Holy Spirit seized her and led her to greet Mary as the mother of the Messiah, the coming Lord. Note: Elizabeth was living an obedient life before God. This was the reason God was able to use her and the Holy Spirit was able to speak through her.

Elizabeth spoke loudly and exuberantly. She was full of joy and exaltation for the Messiah, full of unusual emotions. Under the influence and impulse of the Spirit of God, she was being guided to proclaim that Mary's Baby was "the Lord" (vv.43, 45).

2 Elizabeth proclaimed the uniqueness of Mary and her child.

The Holy Spirit led Elizabeth to proclaim that Mary and her child were unique from every other mother and baby. Elizabeth responded with a proclamation of praise. She was the *first* person to know about the birth of Christ other than Mary, and God saw to it that her first act was to honor His

42 and she exclaimed with a loud cry, "Blessed are you among women, and blessed is the fruit of your womb!"

Son. The very first earthly act toward Christ was a *proclamation of praise*. God would have His Son to be honored on earth even as He is honored in heaven.

> Through him then let us continually offer up a sacrifice of praise to God, that is, the fruit of lips that acknowledge his name. (He.13:15)

> But you are a chosen race, a royal priesthood, a holy nation, a people for his own possession, that you may proclaim the excellencies of him who called you out of darkness into his marvelous light. (1 Pe.2:9)

Elizabeth declared that, of all the women of the earth, Mary was uniquely blessed because of the child she was carrying. The "fruit of her womb" was blessed. Her next Spirit-stirred statement would proclaim why Mary's baby was so special (v.43).

THOUGHT 1. Elizabeth demonstrated a very sweet and humble spirit, a spirit of meekness and love. She was older, and by being the wife of a priest, she was recognized by the world as being of a higher social class and more honorable. Yet Mary, poor and unrecognized by the world, had been chosen by God to serve in a more special way. As great as Elizabeth's child would be, Mary's would be exceedingly greater. Elizabeth showed no envy or jealousy, no hurt or withdrawal. Contrariwise, she rejoiced over Mary's call. We need to demonstrate the same spirit Elizabeth demonstrated, and when we are filled with the Holy Spirit, we will.

> But the fruit of the Spirit is love, joy, peace, patience, kindness, goodness, faithfulness, gentleness, self-control; against such things there is no law. . . . Let us not become conceited, provoking one another, envying one another. (Ga.5:22–23, 26)

> Do nothing from selfish ambition or conceit, but in humility count others more significant than yourselves. Let each of you look not only to his own interests, but also to the interests of others. (Ph.2:3–4)

> Put on then, as God's chosen ones, holy and beloved, compassionate hearts, kindness, humility, meekness, and patience. (Col.3:12)

1:43–44

43 "And why is this granted to me that the mother of my Lord should come to me?
44 For behold, when the sound of your greeting came to my ears, the baby in my womb leaped for joy."

3 Elizabeth proclaimed that Mary's child was her Lord.

Elizabeth made a remarkable proclamation about Mary's baby, a truth she could only have known by divine revelation. She was under the power of the Holy Spirit; therefore, she was confessing this truth under the influence of God. This truth was that the coming child of Mary was the Messiah, the Son of the living God.

a. The great confession (v.43).
Elizabeth called Mary's Baby "my Lord." In a moment of inspiring power, the Holy Spirit revealed that the Babe was not only the promised Messiah, but He was the Son of the Highest, of God Himself (Lu.1:32, 35). There was no question that Elizabeth was using the term "Lord" in its highest sense. She was also contrasting her son with the Son of Mary. Her own son was to be great, but the Son of Mary was greater. He was *her Lord*, the Lord God Himself, the Son of the Highest.

b. The clear sign (v.44).
The sign of this revelation from the Spirit was unmistakable. Upon hearing the greeting of Mary as she entered the door, Elizabeth's heart leaped for joy and the baby in her womb leaped much more than usual. In Elizabeth's words, "The baby leaped in my womb *for joy* [exultation]." God caused the baby to *leap* (skirtao, *skeer-tah'-oh;* the word is strong, indicating a struggling leap) as a sign of great joy in the presence of One so great that Elizabeth would call Him "my Lord."

THOUGHT 1. Elizabeth's confession of her Lord was a very personal thing. She apparently never shared it with John. John did not know Jesus was the Messiah until Jesus' baptism (Jn.1:31–34). John had to discover and confess Christ for himself. So do we all. It is a *personal* decision.

> So everyone who acknowledges me before men, I also will acknowledge before my Father who is in heaven. (Mt.10:32)

He said to them, "But who do you say that I am?" Simon Peter replied, "You are the Christ, the Son of the living God." And Jesus answered him, "Blessed are you, Simon Bar-Jonah! For flesh and blood has not revealed this to you, but my Father who is in heaven." (Mt.16:15–17)

Whoever confesses that Jesus is the Son of God, God abides in him, and he in God. (1 Jn.4:15)

THOUGHT 2. One reason, perhaps the main reason, God's Spirit gave Elizabeth this revelation was to encourage Mary. *God sees to it that we are encouraged* when we need encouragement. Mary needed assurance, so God led her to where she could be assured. But note: she obeyed God. She went where God led her. It was while she was obeying that God was able to encourage her.

But even the hairs of your head are all numbered. Fear not, therefore; you are of more value than many sparrows. (Mt.10:30–31)

For I, the LORD your God, hold your right hand; it is I who say to you, "Fear not, I am the one who helps you." (Is.41:13)

But now thus says the LORD, he who created you, O Jacob, he who formed you, O Israel: "Fear not, for I have redeemed you; I have called you by name, you are mine." (Is.43:1)

4 Elizabeth proclaimed that Mary would receive the promise because of her faith.

Elizabeth proclaimed that God would reward Mary's faith. She would be *blessed* (makaria, *mah-kah'-ree-ah*)—favored and given great happiness—by the Lord. Because she had believed that God would do what He had promised her, she would see the performance of God's promises, the things told her from the Lord.

45 "And blessed is she who believed that there would be a fulfillment of what was spoken to her from the Lord."

By which he has granted to us his precious and very great promises, so that through them you may become partakers of the divine nature, having escaped from the corruption that is in the world because of sinful desire. (2 Pe.1:4)

Know therefore that the LORD your God is God, the faithful God who keeps covenant and steadfast love with those who love him and keep his commandments, to a thousand generations. (De.7:9)

He remembers his covenant forever, the word that he commanded, for a thousand generations. (Ps.105:8)

THOUGHT 1. God blessed Mary for two reasons:
1) Mary believed the Word of God sent to her (Lu.1:38). Contrast her belief with Zechariah's unbelief (Lu.1:20).
2) Mary was related to Christ in a very, very special way.

The same two facts are essential for us if we wish to be blessed by God.
1) We must believe the Word of God sent to us.

But he said, "Blessed rather are those who hear the word of God and keep it!" (Lu.11:28)

If you abide in me, and my words abide in you, ask whatever you wish, and it will be done for you. (Jn.15:7)

And we also thank God constantly for this, that when you received the word of God, which you heard from us, you accepted it not as the word of men but as what it really is, the word of God, which is at work in you believers. (1 Th.2:13)

2) We must become related to Christ by being born again and adopted into God's family.

But when the fullness of time had come, God sent forth his Son, born of woman, born under the law, to redeem those who were under the law, so that we might receive adoption as sons. And because you are sons, God has sent the Spirit of his Son into our hearts, crying, "Abba! Father!" (Ga.4:4–6)

E. Mary's Magnificent Song About God:
God's Glorious Mercy and Deliverance, 1:46–56

1. **God was the subject of her song**

2. **God was her Savior**

   a. Had considered her humble state
   b. Has caused her to be remembered

3. **God was to be exalted**
   a. His power
   b. His holiness
   c. His mercy

4. **God had reversed the order of things on earth**
   a. Had scattered the proud
   b. Had dethroned the mighty and exalted the humble

   c. Had filled the hungry and emptied the rich

5. **God had helped His people**
   a. Remembered His mercy
   b. Remembered His promise to send the Messiah
6. **Conclusion: Mary visited Elizabeth for about three months**

⁴⁶ And Mary said, "My soul magnifies the Lord,
⁴⁷ and my spirit rejoices in God my Savior,
⁴⁸ for he has looked on the humble estate of his servant. For behold, from now on all generations will call me blessed;
⁴⁹ for he who is mighty has done great things for me, and holy is his name.

⁵⁰ And his mercy is for those who fear him from generation to generation.
⁵¹ He has shown strength with his arm; he has scattered the proud in the thoughts of their hearts;
⁵² he has brought down the mighty from their thrones and exalted those of humble estate;
⁵³ he has filled the hungry with good things, and the rich he has sent away empty.
⁵⁴ He has helped his servant Israel, in remembrance of his mercy,
⁵⁵ as he spoke to our fathers, to Abraham and to his offspring forever."
⁵⁶ And Mary remained with her about three months and returned to her home.

Division I

The Announcement of the Coming of Jesus, the Son of Man, 1:1–2:52

E. Mary's Magnificent Song About God: God's Glorious
   Mercy and Deliverance, 1:46–56

1:46–56

Introduction

After Mary received confirmation of Gabriel's message to her through the revelation the Spirit gave to Elizabeth, she sang a beautiful song of praise to the Lord. Mary's song is known as the *Magnificat*. In some ways, it is similar to the Song of Hannah (1 Sa.2:1-10). However, there is a striking difference between the two songs. Hannah proclaimed a triumph over her enemies; Mary proclaimed God and His glorious mercy to the human race. Mary was proclaiming the salvation of God, a salvation brought about through the promised Messiah, her Savior. She prophesied that the Savior would be welcomed by those who reverenced Him (v.50); but He would be rejected by the proud, the powerful, and the rich (vv.51-53). This is, *Mary's Magnificent Song About God: God's Glorious Mercy and Deliverance,* 1:46-56.

1. God was the subject of her song (v.46).
2. God was her Savior (vv.47-48).
3. God was to be exalted (vv.49-50).
4. God had reversed the order of things on earth (vv.51-53).
5. God had helped His people (vv.54-55).
6. Conclusion: Mary visited Elizabeth for about three months (v.56).

1 God was the subject of her song.

⁴⁶ And Mary said, "My soul magnifies the Lord,"

Mary was not singing about herself; she was not praising herself. She was not thinking about things which she might accomplish. She said very definitively, "My soul magnifies *the Lord.*" The Lord was the subject of her song, the subject of her praise and rejoicing.

Mary was surely exhausted. She had just arrived from a long, strenuous trip and had not even had time to sit down. As soon as she walked in the door, Elizabeth began her Holy Spirit-inspired proclamation of praise. Mary's song followed right on the heels of Elizabeth's song. Mary forgot her fatigue, for her faith was being confirmed. She now knew that the angel who had come to her was not a figment of her imagination, not an illusion, not a false vision, not some dreamy state of mind (v.28). He was real; and his message that she, as a virgin, would bear the Son of God was true. Her faith was reassured and confirmed.

The word, *magnify,* as it is used in verse 46, means to declare the greatness of. The Greek word translated *magnify* (Gk. megalunei, *meh-ga-loo'-nay*) speaks of a continued, habitual action; that is, it became the habit of Mary's soul to magnify the Lord for using her to bear His Son, the Messiah and Savior. She kept on magnifying Him from that point forward.

THOUGHT 1. God assures and confirms the faith of us all. We believe and trust, and as the need arises, God steps in to confirm the reality of what we believe.

> Now faith is the assurance of things hoped for, the conviction of things not seen. (He.11:1)

> Know therefore that the LORD your God is God, the faithful God who keeps covenant and steadfast love with those who love him and keep his commandments, to a thousand generations. (De.7:9)

THOUGHT 2. The one thing that can overcome tiredness and exhaustion is an experience with God. More than anything else, the experience of *genuine* prayer and seeking God will cause a person to forget tiredness of body. How desperately we need to seek God!

> Come to me, all who labor and are heavy laden, and I will give you rest. (Mt.11:28)

THOUGHT 3. Mary was greatly blessed by God, yet she did not slip into the sin of pride, nor did she think that she was a favorite of God. The more we are blessed by God, the more dangerous the sin of pride becomes. We must learn to live praising God more and more. The more He blesses us, the more we must learn to praise Him.

> But you are a chosen race, a royal priesthood, a holy nation, a people for his own possession, that you may proclaim the excellencies of him who called you out of darkness into his marvelous light. (1 Pe.2:9)

> Sing praises to the LORD, who sits enthroned in Zion! Tell among the peoples his deeds! (Ps.9:11)

> Enter his gates with thanksgiving, and his courts with praise! Give thanks to him; bless his name! (Ps.100:4)

2 God was her Savior.

Mary declared that God was her Savior (v.47). This statement reveals the depth of her spiritual understanding: in the excitement and rejoicing of the moment, she grasped God's purpose for the miracle He would perform in her. At the same time, Mary recognized her need, that she was a sinner and needed a Savior just like everyone else. And, more importantly, she made a *personal confession*: "God [is] *my* Savior."

1:47–48

⁴⁷ "and my spirit rejoices in God my Savior,
⁴⁸ for he has looked on the humble estate of his servant. For behold, from now on all generations will call me blessed;"

a. Had considered her humble state (v.48a).

God saw Mary's humble (lowly) estate (state or condition). Mary recognized where she had come from, just how lowly a person she was. In the eyes of the world, she was a *nobody: poor, obscure, unknown, insignificant,* of *little purpose* and *meaning* in life. The very expression "looked on the humble estate of his servant" suggests that Mary was even considered the least within her own household.

THOUGHT 1. God usually chooses the least person to more clearly demonstrate His mercy and power.

> For consider your calling, brothers: not many of you were wise according to worldly standards, not many were powerful, not many were of noble birth. But God chose what is foolish in the world to shame the wise; God chose what is weak in the world to shame the strong; God chose what is low and despised in the world, even things that are not, to bring to nothing things that are, so that no human being might boast in the presence of God. (1 Co.1:26–29)

> And he said to him, "Please, Lord, how can I save Israel? Behold, my clan is the weakest in Manasseh, and I am the least in my father's house." (Jud.6:15)

THOUGHT 2. We must all know where we have come from, just how low we were when God saved us (Ro.3:23).

> But God shows his love for us in that while we were still sinners, Christ died for us. (Ro.5:8)

> The saying is trustworthy and deserving of full acceptance, that Christ Jesus came into the world to save sinners, of whom I am the foremost. (1 Ti.1:15)

THOUGHT 3. No matter how *low*, how *nothing* we may be, God cares and will reach down and out to us. He will take us by the hand, lift us up, and give us purpose, meaning, and significance. God will make us somebody and use us, giving us a full and meaningful life (Jn.10:10).

> Humble yourselves before the Lord, and he will exalt you. (Jas.4:10)

> For thus says the One who is high and lifted up, who inhabits eternity, whose name is Holy: "I dwell in the high and holy place, and also with him who is of a contrite and lowly spirit, to revive the spirit of the lowly, and to revive the heart of the contrite." (Is.57:15)

b. Has caused her to be remembered (v.48b).

Mary realized that all future generations of believers would celebrate what God had chosen to do *through her*. God would cause her to be remembered. All future believers would highly esteem her and her great dedication to God. At the same time, it is important to note what Christ said:

> As he said these things, a woman in the crowd raised her voice and said to him, "Blessed is the womb that bore you, and the breasts at which you nursed!" But he said, "Blessed rather are those who hear the word of God and keep it!" (Lu.11:27–28)

1:49–50

⁴⁹ "for he who is mighty has done great things for me, and holy is his name.
⁵⁰ And his mercy is for those who fear him from generation to generation."

3 God was to be exalted.

It is critical to understand that Mary was not boasting or relishing in the fact that she would be famous. To the contrary, she was humbly praising God for choosing her, a lowly, obscure young woman, to be a part of the greatest thing God has done for the human race. She was magnifying God for the great work He would do through her. In her song, Mary proclaimed three of God's glorious attributes.

a. His power (v.49a).

First, Mary proclaimed God's power. Two marvelous thoughts were in her mind:

➤ The promised Messiah was *now* to be born. The hope of the world was now to be fulfilled after so many generations of waiting. God's power was now to be demonstrated in a way never before witnessed.

➤ The promised Messiah was to be born *of a virgin!* It was to be an event and a method never before witnessed. A miracle was to be performed! The enormous power of God was to be demonstrated *even in the manner of the birth of the Messiah!* As Mary testified, "He who is mighty has done great things *for me.*"

> As he was drawing near—already on the way down the Mount of Olives—the whole multitude of his disciples began to rejoice and praise God with a loud voice for all the mighty works that they had seen. (Lu.19:37)

> O Lord, open my lips, and my mouth will declare your praise. (Ps.51:15)

> And let them offer sacrifices of thanksgiving, and tell of his deeds in songs of joy! (Ps.107:22)

b. His holiness (v.49b).

Second, Mary proclaimed God's holiness: "Holy is His name"; that is, God is to be set apart as different from and above all others (see note and DEEPER STUDY # 1—1 Pe.1:15-16). His very nature, His very being is different. God is both a *pure being* and *pure in being,* both a *perfect being* and *perfect in being.* God is *holy in name* and *holy in being,* set apart and different from all others.

> Who is like you, O LORD, among the gods? Who is like you, majestic in holiness, awesome in glorious deeds, doing wonders? (Ex.15:11)

> Exalt the LORD our God, and worship at his holy mountain; for the LORD our God is holy! (Ps.99:9)

c. His mercy (v.50).

Third, Mary proclaimed God's mercy. Mary was surely thinking of God's glorious mercy to her. He had proven to be her *personal* Savior (see note—vv.47-48).

> The steadfast love of the LORD never ceases; his mercies never come to an end; they are new every morning; great is your faithfulness. (Lam.3:22-23)

> Who is a God like you, pardoning iniquity and passing over transgression for the remnant of his inheritance? He does not retain his anger forever, because he delights in steadfast love. (Mi.7:18)

In addition, Mary praised God for His glorious mercy in finally sending the Messiah (Savior) to those who fear (reverence) Him. Note that Mary saw God's mercy passing down from generation to generation.

> Giving thanks to the Father, who has qualified you to share in the inheritance of the saints in light. He has delivered us from the domain of darkness and transferred us to the kingdom of his beloved Son. (Col.1:12-13)

> Through him then let us continually offer up a sacrifice of praise to God, that is, the fruit of lips that acknowledge his name. (He.13:15)

> But the steadfast love of the LORD is from everlasting to everlasting on those who fear him, and his righteousness to children's children. (Ps.103:17)

4 God had reversed the order of things on earth.

Mary proclaimed what the results of the Messiah's coming were to be for those of all nations and generations who trust in God. There were to be three results, and all three are given in the Greek aorist tense; that is, they are proclaimed as having already happened. Mary saw into the future, and standing there in the future, she proclaimed what the Messiah's coming had already done.

1:51–53

[51] "He has shown strength with his arm; he has scattered the proud in the thoughts of their hearts;

[52] he has brought down the mighty from their thrones and exalted those of humble estate;

[53] he has filled the hungry with good things, and the rich he has sent away empty."

What Mary saw was that the Lord had reversed the order of things on earth; He was "turning everything upside down."[1] And note: He had done it with "the strength of His arm," that is, not by love but by power.

a. Had scattered the proud (v.51).

The sending of the Messiah had scattered the proud. The proud are prideful in the "thoughts" or "imagination of their hearts." They think themselves better because of . . .

- looks
- person
- position
- wealth

- ability
- heritage
- achievement
- possessions

Mary predicted that at the end of time, the Lord will have scattered all such pride. By sending the Messiah, God had already decreed it as done; in effect, it was already done.

b. Had dethroned the mighty and exalted the humble (v.52).

By sending the Messiah, the Lord had dethroned the mighty and exalted the humble. The mighty are those who sit in positions of power, authority, and influence over others. The picture concerns those who use their power to . . .

- seek their own ends
- fail to serve
- deprive others
- push others down

- abuse others
- enslave others
- bypass others
- misuse others

Mary predicted that at the end of time, the Lord will have dethroned the mighty and exalted them of low degree (see notes—Mt.19:28). Again, in heaven, it is already done.

c. Had filled the hungry and emptied the rich (v.53).

The Lord had filled the hungry and emptied the rich by sending His Son. Those who were rich only in this world's goods are seen stripped of all their earthly goods and sent away empty. And those who had nothing of this world, but who put their trust in God, are seen as having received all good things (see note—Ep.1:3 for discussion).

1:54–55

[54] "He has helped his servant Israel, in remembrance of his mercy,

[55] as he spoke to our fathers, to Abraham and to his offspring forever."

5 God had helped His people.

Mary transitioned her song to what the sending of God's Son meant to Israel. She sang about two ways God had helped His covenant people by sending the Messiah.

a. Remembered His mercy (v.54).

In the Septuagint (the ancient Greek translation of the Hebrew Old Testament), *mercy* (eleos, *el'-eh'os*) is most commonly the equivalent of the Hebrew word *chesed*,

---

1 Warren W. Wiersbe, *Bible Exposition Commentary (Matthew-Colossians)* (Colorado Springs, CO: David C. Cook, 2008). Via Wordsearch digital edition.

which speaks of Jehovah's steadfast, faithful love for His people.[2] The people (Israel) desperately needed God's mercy and God's deliverance. They were enslaved by the Romans; therefore, they were frantic in their search for deliverance, so frantic that many were turning to false messiahs and other answers to escape their plight. Some were even finding their security in the Roman state and in humanistic answers instead of God. If a people ever needed God to remember His mercy, it was then. Mary proclaimed that the Lord had remembered His mercy.

b. Remembered His promise to send the Messiah (v.55).
God had promised the Messiah to the fathers of Israel, to Abraham and to Abraham's descendants. As the centuries had rolled on, many had no doubt questioned whether God would keep His word. But, at last, "the fullness of the time had come" (Ga.4:4), and God did exactly what He had promised Abraham approximately two thousand years before. God sent the Messiah, the Savior of the world (see DEEPER STUDY # 1—Jn.4:22; DEEPER STUDY # 1—Ro.4:1-25 for more discussion).

> **Jesus said to them, "If God were your Father, you would love me, for I came from God and I am here. I came not of my own accord, but he sent me." (Jn.8:42)**

> **So the Jews gathered around him and said to him, "How long will you keep us in suspense? If you are the Christ, tell us plainly." Jesus answered them, "I told you, and you do not believe. The works that I do in my Father's name bear witness about me, but you do not believe because you are not among my sheep. My sheep hear my voice, and I know them, and they follow me. I give them eternal life, and they will never perish, and no one will snatch them out of my hand. My Father, who has given them to me, is greater than all, and no one is able to snatch them out of the Father's hand." (Jn.10:24–29)**

> **Now the promises were made to Abraham and to his offspring. It does not say, "And to offsprings," referring to many, but referring to one, "And to your offspring," who is Christ. (Ga.3:16)**

> **I will bless those who bless you, and him who dishonors you I will curse, and in you all the families of the earth shall be blessed. (Ge.12:3)**

6 Conclusion: Mary visited Elizabeth for about three months.

1:56

Mary stayed with Elizabeth for about three months, the exact time that was needed for her and others to notice signs confirming pregnancy. She needed her cousin's encouragement until her pregnancy was rather obvious. Note the simple childlikeness of Mary, her need for the support and encouragement of her older cousin, who was probably more spiritually mature.

[56] And Mary remained with her about three months and returned to her home.

> **We who are strong have an obligation to bear with the failings of the weak, and not to please ourselves. (Ro.15:1)**

> **Bear one another's burdens, and so fulfill the law of Christ. (Ga.6:2)**

---

2   Thoralf Gilbrant, Ralph W. Harris, eds., *The Complete Biblical Library Greek-English Dictionary* (Springfield, MO: World Library Press, 1992). Via Wordsearch digital edition.

1. **The child's birth**
   a. Validated God's power, v.18
   b. Validated God's mercy
   c. Caused all to rejoice

2. **The child's name validated a prophetic witness**
   a. The child was circumcised: Given up to God
   b. The child's name was disputed

   c. The father confirmed the name John

3. **The child's birth caused several important results**
   a. The father was miraculously healed, and he praised God
   b. The people were awestruck
   c. The events were spread abroad

   d. The sense of destiny surrounded the child

⁵⁷ Now the time came for Elizabeth to give birth, and she bore a son.
⁵⁸ And her neighbors and relatives heard that the Lord had shown great mercy to her, and they rejoiced with her.
⁵⁹ And on the eighth day they came to circumcise the child. And they would have called him Zechariah after his father,
⁶⁰ but his mother answered, "No; he shall be called John."
⁶¹ And they said to her, "None of your relatives is called by this name."
⁶² And they made signs to his father, inquiring what he wanted him to be called.
⁶³ And he asked for a writing tablet and wrote, "His name is John." And they all wondered.
⁶⁴ And immediately his mouth was opened and his tongue loosed, and he spoke, blessing God.

⁶⁵ And fear came on all their neighbors. And all these things were talked about through all the hill country of Judea,
⁶⁶ and all who heard them laid them up in their hearts, saying, "What then will this child be?" For the hand of the Lord was with him.

Division I

The Announcement of the Coming of Jesus, the Son of Man, 1:1–2:52

F. John's Birth and Naming: An Event for All Generations, 1:57–66

1:57–66
Introduction

The birth of a child is exciting and holds a sense of anticipation—anticipation of what this new life will become. For every parent, the birth of a child is one of the most significant events of their lives. The birth of John held a special sense of excitement and anticipation. His birth was one of the most significant in human history, not just for his parents, but for the world. John's birth was a sign that the greatest event of world history—the coming of our Savior—was near. This is, *John's Birth and Naming: An Event for All Generations*, 1:57–66.

1. The child's birth (vv.57–58).
2. The child's name validated a prophetic witness (vv.59–63).
3. The child's birth caused several important results (vv.64–66).

1 The child's birth.

The birth of Elizabeth's child proclaimed a great message to the world. It trumpeted God's wonder-working power and His marvelous mercy. But it also announced even more glorious news: The Savior would soon be coming.

a. Validated God's power (v.57).

The child's birth confirmed God's unlimited power. As revealed earlier in the chapter, the birth of John involved a supernatural act of God. Elizabeth had conceived when she was old, beyond child-bearing years (vv.18, 36). An angel had visited her husband, Zechariah, to deliver the news that she would have a son (vv.11f.)

> 57 Now the time came for Elizabeth to give birth, and she bore a son.
> 58 And her neighbors and relatives heard that the Lord had shown great mercy to her, and they rejoiced with her.

The fact that the child was born just as God had said is evidence of His glorious power. God was able to control natural events and to send out the forerunner of the Messiah *exactly* as He had promised.

> But Jesus looked at them and said, "With man this is impossible, but with God all things are possible." (Mt.19:26)
>
> For nothing will be impossible with God. (Lu.1:37)
>
> I know that you can do all things, and that no purpose of yours can be thwarted. (Jb.2:2)
>
> Our God is in the heavens; he does all that he pleases. (Ps.115:3)

b. Validated God's mercy (v.58a).

The child's birth also confirmed God's mercy. The fact that John was born as a *baby of promise* demonstrated that God has mercy on people, even on an insignificant woman with a desperate need (see note—v.7).

> The LORD is merciful and gracious, slow to anger and abounding in steadfast love. (Ps.103:8; see vv.1–8 for a description of God's mercy)
>
> But the steadfast love of the LORD is from everlasting to everlasting on those who fear him, and his righteousness to children's children. (Ps.103:17)
>
> Praise the LORD! Oh give thanks to the LORD, for he is good, for his steadfast love endures forever! (Ps.106:1)

In addition, the fact that God would use John in His plan of salvation demonstrates God's mercy. The Lord gave John the unparalleled privilege of being greatly involved with the Messiah. Such a high privilege and call clearly demonstrated God's glorious mercy.

THOUGHT 1. The very same privilege is given to us. God wants to use every one of us in His plan of salvation, both to be saved and to bear witness of His salvation.

> This is good, and it is pleasing in the sight of God our Savior, who desires all people to be saved and to come to the knowledge of the truth. For there is one God, and there is one mediator between God and men, the man Christ Jesus. (1 Ti.2:3–5)

c. Caused all to rejoice (v.58b).

Elizabeth's neighbors and relatives rejoiced with her, and all believers since rejoice as well. By giving Elizabeth a son, God showed her great mercy. But the son He gave her was a merciful gift to the entire world. God has had mercy on the world, and John's birth was one of the significant proofs of His mercy. God sent the forerunner to proclaim the coming of the promised Messiah, just as had been prophesied in Scripture (Mal.31). The fact that the forerunner had been sent indicated that the Savior would soon be sent.

2 The child's name validated a prophetic witness.

The naming of Elizabeth's child created an interesting scene. But the name of this particular child was unusually significant. A prophecy was involved, and the child's name had to validate the prophetic witness.

1:59–63

⁵⁹ And on the eighth day they came to circumcise the child. And they would have called him Zechariah after his father,

⁶⁰ but his mother answered, "No; he shall be called John."

⁶¹ And they said to her, "None of your relatives is called by this name."

⁶² And they made signs to his father, inquiring what he wanted him to be called.

⁶³ And he asked for a writing tablet and wrote, "His name is John." And they all wondered.

a. The child was circumcised: Given up to God (v.59a).

All Jewish males were circumcised on the eighth day after birth (see DEEPER STUDY # 1—Ph.3:3; see Ge.17:12; Le.12:3). Circumcision was the Jewish ceremony where the child was offered up or dedicated to God. It was the rite or sign that the child was to be a follower of God, a true Jew. The day of circumcision was also the day on which the child was officially named.

b. The child's name was disputed (vv.59b–62).

In keeping with the custom of naming a child after a family member, some of the relatives naturally wanted the child to be named after his father, Zechariah. However, knowing that the angel had told Zechariah to name the child John, Elizabeth objected. The relatives took the matter to Zechariah, asking him to write the child's name out for all to see. They, of course, were expecting Zechariah to be pleased with their suggestion that the child be named after him.

c. The father confirmed the name John (v.63).

But Zechariah shocked them. He confirmed that the child was to be named John. He dared not doubt and disobey God again. He was already under the discipline of God for having disobeyed Him before.

The point is that the name John sealed the prophetic witness. The angel had told Zechariah what to name the child. His name was to be John, and Zechariah had borne witness to the angel's visit and promise, even to the angel revealing that the child was to be named John. John was the *prophetic name* given by God's messenger. Zechariah obeyed God and bore testimony to the prophecy; therefore, Zechariah sealed the prophetic witness by confirming the name John.

THOUGHT 1. The very fact that the child was named John adds proof to the whole event's being true, as having really happened.

THOUGHT 2. The prophetic witness is true. Zechariah confirmed it by naming the child John.

> But these are written so that you may believe that Jesus is the Christ, the Son of God, and that by believing you may have life in his name. (Jn.20:31)

1:64–66

⁶⁴ And immediately his mouth was opened and his tongue loosed, and he spoke, blessing God.

⁶⁵ And fear came on all their neighbors. And all these things were talked about through all the hill country of Judea,

⁶⁶ and all who heard them laid them up in their hearts, saying, "What then will this child be?" For the hand of the Lord was with him.

3 The child's birth caused several important results.

Some wonderful things occurred at and following John's circumcision and naming. His birth brought about several important results.

a. The father was miraculously healed, and he praised God (v.64).

As soon as Zechariah decreed that the baby would be named John, he was miraculously healed and began to praise God. Unable to speak, this good man who had doubted God's word had been shut up with his own thoughts *for nine months!* His *last* spoken words had been words of questioning, distrust, and unbelief (Lu.1:18). But when the Lord healed him—opened his ears and loosed his tongue—his *first* words were ones of praise to God.

b. The people were awestruck (v.65a).
When Zechariah was healed, a sense of fear swept over the neighbors and relatives. In this context, *fear* (Gk. phobos, *phoh'-bos*) does not mean terror and fright, but reverence. It means a reverential awe, a reverential fear of God. The people stood in reverence before the events, awe-struck over what was happening and wondering what else was going to happen. God was working. His mighty hand was evident.

c. The events were spread abroad (v.65b).
The news of John's birth and Zechariah's miraculous healing spread throughout Judea. God's hand upon the child was the subject of the countryside. (It *should* have been the subject of all. God's movement should always be at the very center of people's conversations.)

d. The sense of destiny surrounded the child (v.66).
The people of the community kept these things "in their hearts." They did not forget what they had heard. There was something unusual about the message surrounding the child; a sense of destiny hovered over him. As he matured, the people looked on, eager to see what he would become. Expectations were running high, and many were holding the things in their memory, waiting for the child to grow up and waiting to see what would happen.

THOUGHT 1. All four results we have just seen in subpoints a through d should be taking place in our lives. We should be praising God; we should be awe-stricken at the events; we should spread the events abroad; we should see the fulfillment of God's plan. We have the privilege of knowing just who John was, the forerunner of the Messiah Himself.

> And if you call on him as Father who judges impartially according to each one's deeds, conduct yourselves with fear throughout the time of your exile, knowing that you were ransomed from the futile ways inherited from your forefathers, not with perishable things such as silver or gold, but with the precious blood of Christ, like that of a lamb without blemish or spot. He was foreknown before the foundation of the world but was made manifest in the last times for the sake of you (1 Pe.1:17–20)

> A God greatly to be feared in the council of the holy ones, and awesome above all who are around him? (Ps.89:7)

> He sent redemption to his people; he has commanded his covenant forever. Holy and awesome is his name! The fear of the LORD is the beginning of wisdom; all those who practice it have a good understanding. His praise endures forever! (Ps.111:9–10)

THOUGHT 2. Note that Zechariah's obedience removed the discipline of God for his sin. Zechariah named the child John despite all the pressure from friends and the practice of the day to name the first son after the father. God had *told* Zechariah what to do in naming the child, and when he obeyed, the discipline of God was removed from his life. In our lives as well, God's discipline is not punitive, but corrective. When we turn from our sin to obeying the Lord, He will lift his discipline.

> For they disciplined us for a short time as it seemed best to them, but he disciplines us for our good, that we may share his holiness. For the moment all discipline seems painful rather than pleasant, but later it yields the peaceful fruit of righteousness to those who have been trained by it. Therefore lift your drooping hands and strengthen your weak knees, and make straight paths for your feet, so that what is lame may not be put out of joint but rather be healed. (He.12:10–13)

> If any of you lacks wisdom, let him ask God, who gives generously to all without reproach, and it will be given him. (Jas.1:5)

> And if you call on him as Father who judges impartially according to each one's deeds, conduct yourselves with fear throughout the time of your exile, knowing that you were ransomed from the futile ways inherited from your forefathers, not with perishable things such as silver or gold, but with the precious blood of Christ, like that of a lamb without blemish or spot. He was foreknown before the foundation of the world but was made manifest in the last times for the sake of you (1 Pe.1:17–20)

1. **Zechariah was filled with the Holy Spirit**

2. **Part 1: God's Savior**
   a. He is the one through whom God visited and redeemed His people[DS1]
   b. He is the mighty Savior of David's house

   c. He is the one prophesied from ancient times: He will save us from our enemies

   d. He is the one who fulfilled the promised mercy and covenant, the oath made to Abraham

      1) He enables us to serve God without fear

      2) He enables us to live righteously and to serve God forever

3. **Part 2: God's forerunner, John the Baptist**
   a. To be called the prophet of the Most High
   b. To prepare the Lord's way
   c. To proclaim salvation: Forgiveness of sins

   d. To proclaim the rise of the heavenly Son
      1) The Son was to come because of God's mercy
      2) The Son was to give light

4. **Conclusion: John's childhood fulfills the prophecy**

⁶⁷ And his father Zechariah was filled with the Holy Spirit and prophesied, saying,

⁶⁸ "Blessed be the Lord God of Israel, for he has visited and redeemed his people

⁶⁹ and has raised up a horn of salvation for us in the house of his servant David,

⁷⁰ as he spoke by the mouth of his holy prophets from of old,

⁷¹ that we should be saved from our enemies and from the hand of all who hate us;

⁷² to show the mercy promised to our fathers and to remember his holy covenant,

⁷³ the oath that he swore to our father Abraham, to grant us

⁷⁴ that we, being delivered from the hand of our enemies, might serve him without fear,

⁷⁵ in holiness and righteousness before him all our days.

⁷⁶ And you, child, will be called the prophet of the Most High; for you will go before the Lord to prepare his ways,

⁷⁷ to give knowledge of salvation to his people in the forgiveness of their sins,

⁷⁸ because of the tender mercy of our God, whereby the sunrise shall visit us from on high

⁷⁹ to give light to those who sit in darkness and in the shadow of death, to guide our feet into the way of peace."

⁸⁰ And the child grew and became strong in spirit, and he was in the wilderness until the day of his public appearance to Israel.

Division I

The Announcement of the Coming of Jesus, the Son of Man, 1:1–2:52

G. Zechariah's Inspired Prophecy: God's Savior and His Forerunner, 1:67–80

1:67–80
Introduction

As soon as Zechariah was healed of his muteness, he first praised the Lord and then prophesied. In the Latin translation, the opening word of his prophecy is *benedictus*. Consequently, Zechariah's prophecy is known as the *Benedictus* and is sometimes recited in worship services. Note that it is a prophecy about the coming Messiah (vv.68-75) and His forerunner, John the Baptist (vv.76-80). The person and ministry of both are predicted and proclaimed. This is, *Zechariah's Inspired Prophecy: God's Savior and His Forerunner, 1:67-80.*

1. Zechariah was filled with the Holy Spirit (v.67).
2. Part 1: God's Savior (vv.68-75).
3. Part 2: God's forerunner, John the Baptist (vv.76-79).
4. Conclusion: John's childhood fulfills the prophecy (v.80).

1 Zechariah was filled with the Holy Spirit.

1:67

Once Zechariah obeyed God, God removed His discipline and healed him of his deafness and dumbness (vv.62, 64). Immediately thereafter, God filled Zechariah with the Holy Spirit.

> [67] And his father Zechariah was filled with the Holy Spirit and prophesied, saying,

The infilling of the Holy Spirit indicated that Zechariah was forgiven his sin of unbelief. It was his questioning of God, his distrust and unbelief, that had caused him to be muted (vv.20-22). As soon as Zechariah demonstrated faith in God's promise, he was healed and was forgiven his sin (see vv.64-66).

Zechariah's being filled with the Holy Spirit is a picture of what happens to us. We believe and obey God, then God immediately forgives our sins and gives us His Spirit.

> **And Peter said to them, "Repent and be baptized every one of you in the name of Jesus Christ for the forgiveness of your sins, and you will receive the gift of the Holy Spirit." (Ac.2:38)**

2 Part 1: God's Savior.

1:68-75

The first part of Zechariah's prophetic song concerned God's Savior, the Messiah. He prophesied four truths about God's Son. Notice the verbs are in past tense as Zechariah is positioning himself in the future and looking back—proclaiming what the Messiah *had done.*

> [68] "Blessed be the Lord God of Israel, for he has visited and redeemed his people
> [69] and has raised up a horn of salvation for us in the house of his servant David,
> [70] as he spoke by the mouth of his holy prophets from of old,
> [71] that we should be saved from our enemies and from the hand of all who hate us;
> [72] to show the mercy promised to our fathers and to remember his holy covenant,
> [73] the oath that he swore to our father Abraham, to grant us
> [74] that we, being delivered from the hand of our enemies, might serve him without fear,
> [75] in holiness and righteousness before him all our days."

a. He is the one through whom God visited and redeemed His people (v.68).

Zechariah prophesied that the Messiah was the one through whom the Lord God of Israel visited and redeemed His people (see DEEPER STUDY # 1). It was God Himself who visited the earth in the Person of the Messiah. He had not neglected nor left the world alone. In the past, God had been actively involved in the world's affairs. He had sent His Word and His messengers to the world, but now God was becoming *personally* involved in the world. He was visiting the world Himself.

45

The purpose for God's visit was special and unusually significant. He came to redeem His people, to save and rescue them from sin and death and separation from God. The visit carried a tremendous, unparalleled cost; He had to pay the enormous price of redemption—a life for a life (see note, *Redemption*—Ep.1:7).

b. He is the mighty Savior of David's house (v.69).

The Messiah was the mighty Savior of David's house. The phrase *horn of salvation* is a reference to Christ. Throughout the Old Testament, the word *horn* was a symbol of strength, power, and might. The Messiah is called the *horn* or the *mighty One of salvation* because He alone possesses the might, the strength, and the power to save.

But note where the horn or the Messiah was raised up: "in the house of His servant David." King David was raised up by God to deliver and to rule over His people Israel for a period of time. But Christ was raised up to deliver and to rule over *all* of God's people, and His deliverance and rule were to be forever. The Messiah was the horn promised to David, the One who fulfilled the prophecies made concerning David (see note—Mt.1:1).

> There I will make a horn to sprout for David; I have prepared a lamp for my anointed. (Ps.132:17. See Ps.89:24, 29.)

c. He is the one prophesied from ancient times: He will save us from our enemies (vv.70–71).

Zechariah declared that the Messiah was the one prophesied throughout the ages. The idea is that God was working out His plan for the world. He was on the throne bringing to pass all that He had promised.

The Messiah had been foretold since the beginning of the world. When Satan first reared his poisonous head in the Garden of Eden, the Messiah was *the Seed of the woman* who was to break the serpent's head (Ge.3:15). When God first acted to form a people for Himself, He was the Seed promised to Abraham and his heirs (Ge.12:1-4; see DEEPER STUDY # 1—Ro.4:1-25).

The prophecies of the Messiah dealt with salvation. The Messiah was to save believers from their enemies and from all who hated them. Carnal people (the Jews, the fleshly, the worldly-minded) think of salvation as material and physical deliverance; but God never meant salvation to last only for a few short years, the years of a person's life. He cares much more for us than that. When God speaks of *salvation,* He means spiritual and eternal salvation, a deliverance and life that will never end. He is interested in saving us from the enemies that wage endless war against the spirit and enslave us both now and eternally: the enemies of sin, death, and condemnation.

d. He is the one who fulfilled the promised mercy and covenant, the oath made to Abraham (vv.72–75).

In addition, Zechariah prophesied that the Messiah was the one who fulfilled the promised mercy and covenant, the oath God made to Abraham. God promised Abraham that if he would leave his old country to follow Him, then Abraham would receive both the mercy of God and the covenant of faith. The covenant was based on "the promised Seed," Christ Himself. Thus Zechariah, under the inspiration of the Holy Spirit, was proclaiming the Messiah to be the fulfillment of the promised mercy and covenant to Abraham (vv.72-73). The Messiah was *the promised mercy and Seed to Abraham* (see DEEPER STUDY # 1—Ro.4:1-25 for detailed discussion; see De.6:9, 12-13; 1 Ki.8:23; Ne.1:5; 9:32).

➢ The Messiah brings God's mercy to mankind (the mercy promised to Abraham and his seed): the Messiah delivers us out of the hands of our enemies (vv.71, 74).

➢ The Messiah establishes the covenant of faith with mankind (the covenant promised to Abraham and his seed): the Messiah saves all who believe the promises of God just as Abraham believed (see Ro.4:1-25).

> No unbelief made him waver concerning the promise of God, but he grew strong in his faith as he gave glory to God, fully convinced that God was able to do what he had promised. That is why his faith was "counted to him as righteousness." But the words "it was counted to him" were not

written for his sake alone, but for ours also. It will be counted to us who believe in him who raised from the dead Jesus our Lord, who was delivered up for our trespasses and raised for our justification. (Ro.4:20–25)

When we believe, God's mercy delivers us for two very specific purposes. The first purpose is that we might serve Him without fear (v.74). God does not want us living in fear, fearing the future and the *evil powers* of this world. He does not want us fearing the pain of death and the coming judgment of hell. God wants us to have peace of mind and heart, to feel secure and to know meaning and purpose throughout all of life.

Since therefore the children share in flesh and blood, he himself likewise partook of the same things, that through death he might destroy the one who has the power of death, that is, the devil, and deliver all those who through fear of death were subject to lifelong slavery. (He.2:14–15)

Behold, God is my salvation; I will trust, and will not be afraid; for the LORD GOD is my strength and my song, and he has become my salvation. (Is.12:2)

The second purpose for God's deliverance is that we might live righteously and serve God "all our days"—both in this life and *forever* (v.75). God's deliverance changes us. It purifies us and transforms us that we might be holy as He is holy and righteous as He is righteous. His deliverance—His salvation—is the *only* answer for our depraved, sinful human nature.

For our sake he made him to be sin who knew no sin, so that in him we might become the righteousness of God. (2 Co.5:21)

And to put on the new self, created after the likeness of God in true righteousness and holiness. (Ep.4:24)

Filled with the fruit of righteousness that comes through Jesus Christ, to the glory and praise of God. (Ph.1:11)

For the grace of God has appeared, bringing salvation for all people, training us to renounce ungodliness and worldly passions, and to live self-controlled, upright, and godly lives in the present age, waiting for our blessed hope, the appearing of the glory of our great God and Savior Jesus Christ, who gave himself for us to redeem us from all lawlessness and to purify for himself a people for his own possession who are zealous for good works. (Tit.2:11–14)

But when the goodness and loving kindness of God our Savior appeared, he saved us, not because of works done by us in righteousness, but according to his own mercy, by the washing of regeneration and renewal of the Holy Spirit, whom he poured out on us richly through Jesus Christ our Savior, so that being justified by his grace we might become heirs according to the hope of eternal life. (Tit.3:4–7)

Sow for yourselves righteousness; reap steadfast love; break up your fallow ground, for it is the time to seek the LORD, that he may come and rain righteousness upon you. (Ho.10:12)

DEEPER STUDY # 1

(1:68) **Israel:** Zechariah addressed God as "the Lord God of Israel." Why did he limit God to being God of Israel? Why did he not address God as *the Lord God of the earth*? There are several reasons (see DEEPER STUDY # 1—Jn.4:22).

1. Israel was the chosen people of God, the people chosen to love, obey, and worship Him supremely.

2. As the *chosen* people of God, Israel had been given (entrusted with) both the Word and promises of God to a lost and dying world.

3. As the *recipient* of God's Word and promises, Israel was to be given the Messiah, His salvation and redemption.

4. As the *people* of salvation and redemption, Israel was given the task to make God known, to be the missionary force to reach a lost and dying world.

Zechariah was thinking of God's promise to Israel, of the glorious fact that the promise of the Messiah was now being fulfilled. He knew nothing of Israel's rejection of the Messiah, of God's turning to the Gentiles, of the birth of a new people (the church). Therefore, he did the natural thing: he praised the Lord God of Israel.

3 Part 2: God's forerunner, John the Baptist.

The second part of Zechariah's prophecy concerned John the Baptist. In the Spirit, the godly priest also declared four truths about *his* son.

1:76-79

⁷⁶ "And you, child, will be called the prophet of the Most High; for you will go before the Lord to prepare his ways,

⁷⁷ to give knowledge of salvation to his people in the forgiveness of their sins,

⁷⁸ because of the tender mercy of our God, whereby the sunrise shall visit us from on high

⁷⁹ to give light to those who sit in darkness and in the shadow of death, to guide our feet into the way of peace."

a. To be called the prophet of the Most High (v.76a).

John was to be the prophet of the Highest. Israel had had no prophet for some four hundred years. John was to be the first prophet since Malachi.

John would be a prophet of the Most High or Highest, of Christ, or of God Himself. *Most High* is a title for God. Here, it refers specifically to Christ. Thus, the deity, the very Incarnation of God in Christ, is being proclaimed. He is "God blessed forever" (Ro.9:5).

b. To prepare the Lord's way (v.76b).

John's mission was to prepare the Lord's way. He was to be the forerunner of the Messiah, the one who was to prepare the people for the coming of the Lord (see Lu.3:3-6).

c. To proclaim salvation: Forgiveness of sins (v.77).

John's message was the message of salvation, the forgiveness or remission of their sins. Note that salvation comes by the forgiveness of sin. Salvation is conditional. Our sins must be forgiven before we can be saved (Ep.1:7). John's purpose was to call people to repentance, to be forgiven of their sins.

d. To proclaim the rise of the heavenly Son (vv.78-79).

Through Zechariah's prophecy, the Holy Spirit portrayed the descent of Christ from heaven to earth as the rising of the sun in the morning. As Isaiah described it, "The people who walked in darkness have seen a great light" (Is.9:2). Note that Christ, the Messiah, is called "the Son of righteousness" (Mal.4:2; 2 Pe.1:19; Re.22:16). He is the "Dayspring from on High," the morning light, the rising sun who has "visited us." John was to proclaim the rise of the Messiah, and in particular two things about His rise:

First, the Messiah was being sent through the tender mercy of God.

> For God so loved the world, that he gave his only Son, that whoever believes in him should not perish but have eternal life. For God did not send his Son into the world to condemn the world, but in order that the world might be saved through him. (Jn.3:16-17)

> But God, being rich in mercy, because of the great love with which he loved us, even when we were dead in our trespasses, made us alive together with Christ—by grace you have been saved. (Ep.2:4-5)

Second, the Messiah was being sent to give light . . .

• to those who sit in darkness

> A light for revelation to the Gentiles, and for glory to your people Israel. (Lu.2:32)

> In him was life, and the life was the light of men. . . . The true light, which gives light to everyone, was coming into the world. (Jn.1:4, 9)

> And this is the judgment: the light has come into the world, and people loved the darkness rather than the light because their works were evil. For everyone who does wicked things hates the light and does not come to the light, lest his works should be exposed. But whoever does what is true comes to the light, so that it may be clearly seen that his works have been carried out in God. (Jn.3:19-21)

> Again Jesus spoke to them, saying, "I am the light of the world. Whoever follows me will not walk in darkness, but will have the light of life." (Jn.8:12)

> I have come into the world as light, so that whoever believes in me may not remain in darkness. (Jn.12:46)

- to those who are in the shadow of death

> Truly, truly, I say to you, whoever hears my word and believes him who sent me has eternal life. He does not come into judgment, but has passed from death to life. (Jn.5:24)

> Since therefore the children share in flesh and blood, he himself likewise partook of the same things, that through death he might destroy the one who has the power of death, that is, the devil, and deliver all those who through fear of death were subject to lifelong slavery. (He.2:14–15)

- to guide our feet into the way of peace

> Jesus said to him, "I am the way, and the truth, and the life. No one comes to the Father except through me." (Jn.14:6)

> Peace I leave with you; my peace I give to you. Not as the world gives do I give to you. Let not your hearts be troubled, neither let them be afraid. (Jn.14:27)

> I have said these things to you, that in me you may have peace. In the world you will have tribulation. But take heart; I have overcome the world. (Jn.16:33)

4 Conclusion: John's childhood fulfills the prophecy.

1:80

What we know about John's childhood is preserved only in this single verse. He grew as a normal boy physically, but he was different from the other children in three different ways.

> [80] And the child grew and became strong in spirit, and he was in the wilderness until the day of his public appearance to Israel.

First, John advanced far beyond other children spiritually. He grew "strong in spirit." He was a boy of strong heart and commitment, of strong will and decisiveness, of strong conscience and conviction, of strong drive and initiative. He was God's servant, a young man who was committed to follow, obey, and serve God.

Second, John lived in a different environment than most others—in the desert. The text seems to indicate that John's parents reared him in the wilderness. The wilderness or desert was an obscure place, a place of quietness, far from the worldliness of the cities and masses of people. The desert was made for meditation and thought, for seeking God.

Third, John stayed at his desert home until God called him to launch his ministry to Israel. This points to a life of obedience both to parents and to God.

THOUGHT 1. The crying need of the hour is for believers to grow in the Lord Jesus Christ—to grow strong in the spirit.

> And now I commend you to God and to the word of his grace, which is able to build you up and to give you the inheritance among all those who are sanctified. (Ac.20:32)

> So that we may no longer be children, tossed to and fro by the waves and carried about by every wind of doctrine, by human cunning, by craftiness in deceitful schemes. Rather, speaking the truth in love, we are to grow up in every way into him who is the head, into Christ. (Ep.4:14–15)

> But grow in the grace and knowledge of our Lord and Savior Jesus Christ. To him be the glory both now and to the day of eternity. Amen. (2 Pe.3:18)

CHAPTER 2

H. Jesus' Birth: Its Unusual Events, 2:1–24

(Mt.1:18–25; 2:1; Jn.1:14)

1. The miraculous taxation
  a. A world event used by God to fulfill His plan

  b. An event that forced Joseph to Bethlehem
    1) From Galilee
    2) Out of Nazareth
    3) Into Judea
    4) To the city of David, Bethlehem

  c. An event that led to the fulfillment of Scripture despite the world's plans

2. The shocking place of birth

3. The extraordinary appearance of an angel to common shepherds

  a. His appearance: Radiated the glory of the Lord all around them

  b. His message: Reassured the shepherds and brought good news

    1) A proclamation: The Messiah's birth[DS1, 2]

    2) A charge: Visit the child
    3) A sign: The location and setting

4. The spectacular appearance of a vast number of angels, the heavenly host

5. The excited shepherds' search for evidence
  a. They immediately decided to go to the scene

In those days a decree went out from Caesar Augustus that all the world should be registered.

2 This was the first registration when Quirinius was governor of Syria.

3 And all went to be registered, each to his own town.

4 And Joseph also went up from Galilee, from the town of Nazareth, to Judea, to the city of David, which is called Bethlehem, because he was of the house and lineage of David,

5 to be registered with Mary, his betrothed, who was with child.

6 And while they were there, the time came for her to give birth.

7 And she gave birth to her firstborn son and wrapped him in swaddling cloths and laid him in a manger, because there was no place for them in the inn.

8 And in the same region there were shepherds out in the field, keeping watch over their flock by night.

9 And an angel of the Lord appeared to them, and the glory of the Lord shone around them, and they were filled with great fear.

10 And the angel said to them, "Fear not, for behold, I bring you good news of great joy that will be for all the people.

11 For unto you is born this day in the city of David a Savior, who is Christ the Lord.

12 And this will be a sign for you: you will find a baby wrapped in swaddling cloths and lying in a manger."

13 And suddenly there was with the angel a multitude of the heavenly host praising God and saying,

14 "Glory to God in the highest, and on earth peace among those with whom he is pleased!"

15 When the angels went away from them into heaven, the shepherds said to one another, "Let us go over to Bethlehem and see this thing that has

happened, which the Lord has made known to us."

¹⁶ And they went with haste and found Mary and Joseph, and the baby lying in a manger.

¹⁷ And when they saw it, they made known the saying that had been told them concerning this child.

¹⁸ And all who heard it wondered at what the shepherds told them.

¹⁹ But Mary treasured up all these things, pondering them in her heart.

²⁰ And the shepherds returned, glorifying and praising God for all they had heard and seen, as it had been told them.

²¹ And at the end of eight days, when he was circumcised, he was called Jesus, the name given by the angel before he was conceived in the womb.

²² And when the time came for their purification according to the Law of Moses, they brought him up to Jerusalem to present him to the Lord

²³ (as it is written in the Law of the Lord, "Every male who first opens the womb shall be called holy to the Lord")

²⁴ and to offer a sacrifice according to what is said in the Law of the Lord, "a pair of turtledoves, or two young pigeons."

b. They rushed to see the baby for themselves

c. They excitedly shared the message wherever they went

d. They caused a stir among the people

6. **The humble, trusting mother**

7. **The heartened shepherds' worship of God**

8. **The unusual naming of the child by God Himself**
9. **The traditional observance of the legal ceremonies**
   a. Circumcision,[DS3] Ge.17:10–12
   b. Purification after childbirth, Le.12:6
   c. Dedication to the Lord, Ex.13:2, 12; Nu.18:6; Is.1:2

10. **The deliberate choice by God to have a poor family bear His Son**

Division I

The Announcement of the Coming of Jesus, the Son of Man, 1:1–2:52

H. Jesus' Birth: Its Unusual Events, 2:1–24

(Mt.1:18–25; 2:1; Jn.1:14)

2:1-24
Introduction

From the time that sin entered the world and separated mankind from God, God promised salvation to the human race. This salvation would come through a Savior who would defeat Satan:

> **I will put enmity between you and the woman, and between your offspring and her offspring; he shall bruise your head, and you shall bruise his heel. (Lu.21:34)**

This prophecy is referred to as the *Protoevangelium,* a compound Greek word which means "first gospel." Indeed, it is the first mention of the gospel—the good news of salvation—in God's

Holy Word. The very first mention of a Savior reveals that He would be virgin-born. The promised Savior would be the *offspring* or *seed* of the *woman*—not the offspring of a man *and* a woman.

Throughout the Old Testament, more and more about this Savior, the Messiah, is prophetically revealed. As the centuries rolled by, the promise remained unfulfilled. At long last, "when the fullness of time had come, God sent forth His Son, born of a woman . . ." (Ga.4:4). An unusual series of events surrounding the birth of God's Son fulfilled every single prophecy of Scripture. Through Luke, the Holy Spirit related and preserved the beautiful details of the Savior's birth. This is, *Jesus' Birth: Its Unusual Events,* 2:1-24.

1. The miraculous taxation (vv.1-6).
2. The shocking place of birth (v.7).
3. The extraordinary appearance of an angel to common shepherds (vv.8-12).
4. The spectacular appearance of a vast number of angels, the heavenly host (vv.13-14).
5. The excited shepherds' search for evidence (vv.15-18).
6. The humble, trusting mother (v.19).
7. The heartened shepherds' worship of God (v.20).
8. The unusual naming of the child by God Himself (v.21).
9. The traditional observance of the legal ceremonies (vv.21-23).
10. The deliberate choice by God to have a poor family bear His Son (v.24).

2:1-6

In those days a decree went out from Caesar Augustus that all the world should be registered.
² This was the first registration when Quirinius was governor of Syria.
³ And all went to be registered, each to his own town.
⁴ And Joseph also went up from Galilee, from the town of Nazareth, to Judea, to the city of David, which is called Bethlehem, because he was of the house and lineage of David,
⁵ to be registered with Mary, his betrothed, who was with child.
⁶ And while they were there, the time came for her to give birth.

1 The miraculous taxation.

The first event surrounding Christ's birth demonstrates how God carries out His purposes in and through world affairs (Pr.21:1). Caesar Augustus, the ruler of the Roman Empire, ordered all people to return to the place of their birth to be registered for the purpose of taxation. Unquestionably, the pagan emperor was stirred miraculously by God to issue *this* decree at *this* specific time.

a. **A world event used by God to fulfill His plan (vv.1-2).**
God used this taxation to fulfill His plan for the birth of the Messiah. It had been prophesied that the Messiah was to be born in Bethlehem, and Scripture had to be fulfilled. Joseph and Mary lived in Galilee, and Mary was now nearing the delivery of her child. How was God going to make sure that the child was born in Bethlehem? The taxation happened just at the right time and in the right way; that is, everyone had to return to the city of their birth to pay their taxes. God was miraculously controlling the events of the world, working all things out for good so that He might fulfill His promise to send the Savior into the world.

b. **An event that forced Joseph to Bethlehem (vv.3-4).**
The taxation forced Joseph to Bethlehem, the city of his birth. Note the great detail given in describing the journey to Bethlehem. Joseph went from the region of Galilee, out of the city of Nazareth, to the region of Judea, to the city of Bethlehem (v.4). The point is that Bethlehem was the prophesied city of the Messiah's birth (Mi.5:2). The Scribes understood it (Mt.2:5-6) and so did the common people (Jn.7:42). The taxation was certainly an event planned by God to fulfill Scripture.

c. **An event that led to the fulfillment of Scripture despite the world's plans (vv.5-6).**
The taxation led to the fulfillment of Scripture, despite human plans. Mary was about to deliver, and it seems that the child would be delivered in Nazareth. But God overruled. He either caused or used the taxation and saw to it that Joseph and Mary went to Bethlehem.
In summary, why was all this necessary? Why was it so critical that Jesus be born in Bethlehem?

➤ The Messiah was the prophesied Son of David (see notes—Lu.3:24-31; Mt.1:1; Deeper Study # 3—Jn.1:45; Deeper Study # 4—1:49 for discussion).

➤ David had been born in Bethlehem; therefore, it was necessary for the Son of David to be born there.

➤ Scripture foretold that the Messiah would be born in Bethlehem (Mi.5:2).

2 The shocking place of birth.

2:7

God's Son was not born in comfortable surroundings. Shockingly, He was born in a stable and laid in a manger or feeding trough. Jesus' birth is covered in one simple verse, yet much can be gleaned from it.

First, Jesus was born in a smelly stable. He was neglected and turned away by people from the very beginning. There was no room in the inn, and Mary was about to deliver. If someone had cared, room could have been made for her.

Second, Jesus was born in obscurity and loneliness. The birth took place away from people, all alone. Note that Mary herself wrapped the child in swaddling clothes and laid Him in a manger.

Third, Jesus was born in humiliation. He did not enter the world . . .

- in a hospital
- in a comfortable home
- in the home of a friend or relative
- under a doctor's care
- under the stars of heaven, nor even out in the open

> [7] And she gave birth to her firstborn son and wrapped him in swaddling cloths and laid him in a manger, because there was no place for them in the inn.

Instead, He came into the world via a smelly stable, the lowest imaginable place for a birth.

Fourth, Jesus was born into a corruptible world full of sin and selfishness, greed and unkindness. This is seen in that the world (represented in the innkeeper) was so wrapped up in its affairs that it could not help a woman bearing a child. No one would make room for Mary in the inn. Money and personal comfort were more important to all who had become aware of the situation.

THOUGHT 1. Note how so many missed the first coming of Christ. How many will be woefully unprepared for the second coming of Christ?

But watch yourselves lest your hearts be weighed down with dissipation and drunkenness and cares of this life, and that day come upon you suddenly like a trap. (Lu.21:34)

Training us to renounce ungodliness and worldly passions, and to live self-controlled, upright, and godly lives in the present age, waiting for our blessed hope, the appearing of the glory of our great God and Savior Jesus Christ. (Tit.2:12-13)

3 The extraordinary appearance of an angel to common shepherds.

2:8-12

Jesus' birth was accompanied by the appearance of an angel to a most unlikely group of men—shepherds. In the eyes of many, an angel would never appear to a shepherd. Shepherds were looked upon as anything but worshipers. Their reputation was lowly at best, and religious people snubbed and ignored them. They were despised because they were unable to attend services and to keep the ceremonial laws of washing and cleansing. Their flocks just kept them too busy, and the nature of their work hindered them from keeping the ceremonial requirements. What a beautiful foretaste of the salvation to come: God gave the first message of His Son to common shepherds, those looked upon as unfit to worship Him.

> [8] And in the same region there were shepherds out in the field, keeping watch over their flock by night.
> [9] And an angel of the Lord appeared to them, and the glory of the Lord shone around them, and they were filled with great fear.
> [10] And the angel said to them, "Fear not, for behold, I bring you good news of great joy that will be for all the people.
> [11] For unto you is born this day in the city of David a Savior, who is Christ the Lord.
> [12] And this will be a sign for you: you will find a baby wrapped in swaddling cloths and lying in a manger."

a. **His appearance: Radiated the glory of the Lord all around them (v.9).**

The angel's appearance was full of splendor and glory. The glory that surrounded him was *the glory of the Lord*—the shekinah glory (see note—Mt.17:5-8).

b. **His message: Reassured the shepherds and brought good news (vv.10-12).**

The angel immediately reassured the frightened shepherds that he had come with good news. In fact, it was the best news ever delivered from heaven to earth. He proclaimed the Savior's birth and charged the shepherds to visit the child. He then gave them a sign by which they would recognize the Messiah: they would find the baby lying in a manger (see DEEPER STUDIES 1, 2).

THOUGHT 1. The Savior was coming to call sinners to repentance; therefore, the first announcement of His coming was given to those viewed as sinners.

> And Jesus answered them, "Those who are well have no need of a physician, but those who are sick. I have not come to call the righteous but sinners to repentance." (Lu.5:31-32)

> For consider your calling, brothers: not many of you were wise according to worldly standards, not many were powerful, not many were of noble birth. But God chose what is foolish in the world to shame the wise; God chose what is weak in the world to shame the strong; God chose what is low and despised in the world, even things that are not, to bring to nothing things that are, so that no human being might boast in the presence of God. (1 Co.1:26-29)

DEEPER STUDY # 1

(2:11) **Jesus—Savior:** see DEEPER STUDY # 2—Lu.1:31; note—2:21.

DEEPER STUDY # 2

(2:11) **Christ—Messiah:** see DEEPER STUDY # 2—Mt.1:18; note—Lu.2:21.

2:13-14

13 And suddenly there was with the angel a multitude of the heavenly host praising God and saying,

14 "Glory to God in the highest, and on earth peace among those with whom he is pleased!"

4 The spectacular appearance of a vast number of angels, the heavenly host.

Suddenly, a multitude of the heavenly host appeared spectacularly to the lowly shepherds (v.13). The word "host" describes a huge army of angels, "ten thousand times ten thousand" (Da.7:10; see Ps.68:17). God either gave the shepherds a special sight into the spiritual world and dimension or caused the spiritual dimension to appear in the earth's physical dimension.

The angel choir called for glory to be lifted up to God "in the highest" (v.14a). This term means that God . . .

- is the highest possible being
- dwells in the highest realm possible, in heaven itself

In addition, the angels proclaimed peace, God's favor and good will toward humanity (v.14b). By *peace* is meant the peace of reconciliation. The alienation and separation, struggle and divisiveness, restlessness and fear caused by sin needed to be solved. The heavenly host was praising God that the alienation and separation were now being solved in the birth of the "Savior, who is Christ the Lord" (v.11).

> And through him to reconcile to himself all things, whether on earth or in heaven, making peace by the blood of his cross. (Col.1:20)

5 The excited shepherds' search for evidence.

Think of how you would feel if an angel visibly appeared to you and audibly delivered a message from God, and if a multitude of angels subsequently appeared to confirm that message! Unsurprisingly, the shepherds were overwhelmed with excitement at what they had seen and heard. However, they did not stand around and bask in the glorious experience. To the contrary, they sprang into action, searching for evidence of the Savior's birth.

> ¹⁵ When the angels went away from them into heaven, the shepherds said to one another, "Let us go over to Bethlehem and see this thing that has happened, which the Lord has made known to us."
> ¹⁶ And they went with haste and found Mary and Joseph, and the baby lying in a manger.
> ¹⁷ And when they saw it, they made known the saying that had been told them concerning this child.
> ¹⁸ And all who heard it wondered at what the shepherds told them.

a. They immediately decided to go to the scene (v.15).

The shepherds recognized that the Lord had spoken to them through the angelic messenger and had confirmed the message by the appearance of the heavenly host. They immediately decided to follow the angel's urging to go to the scene where the Messiah had been born.

b. They rushed to see the baby for themselves (v.16).

Luke reports that the shepherds went to the scene "with haste." These words convey a sense of extreme urgency. They did not hesitate or delay; they rushed or hurried. They felt an urgency to act and to act now. They wasted no time. When they arrived, they found the baby, just as the angel had said.

c. They excitedly shared the message wherever they went (v.17).

After first seeing the child themselves, the shepherds shared their experience wherever they went. They were the first to bear witness to the Savior of the world.

d. They caused a stir among the people (v.18).

The shepherds' testimony created a stir among the people. Note that nothing is said about these hearers' seeking out the child. They only wondered about what they heard; they never responded and never moved to find Him for themselves.

THOUGHT 1. Like the shepherds, we who have experienced Christ ought to share Him with others. How can we not? How can we be silent if we have truly come to know Him?

> But you will receive power when the Holy Spirit has come upon you, and you will be my witnesses in Jerusalem and in all Judea and Samaria, and to the end of the earth. (Ac.1:8)

> For we cannot but speak of what we have seen and heard. (Ac.4:20)

> To this day I have had the help that comes from God, and so I stand here testifying both to small and great, saying nothing but what the prophets and Moses said would come to pass: that the Christ must suffer and that, by being the first to rise from the dead, he would proclaim light both to our people and to the Gentiles. (Ac.26:22-23)

THOUGHT 2. Tragically, many people are like those to whom the shepherds witnessed. They hear about Christ, but they never respond to the message and find Him for themselves. They choose not to believe, to remain unchanged by the truth that the Savior has come.

> He was in the world, and the world was made through him, yet the world did not know him. He came to his own, and his own people did not receive him. But to all who did receive him, who believed in his name, he gave the right to become children of God. (Jn.1:10-12)

> Whoever believes in him is not condemned, but whoever does not believe is condemned already, because he has not believed in the name of the only Son of God. (Jn.3:18)

> For good news came to us just as to them, but the message they heard did not benefit them, because they were not united by faith with those who listened. (He.4:2)

6 The humble, trusting mother.

Luke paints a beautiful picture of Mary's humble, trusting heart. Mary had been told that her child was of God, truly of God. Above all others she knew that the Messiah, the very Son of God, had now come. She had been through so much: pregnant, yet unmarried; the possibility of being found out and of rumors heaped upon rumors; the discussions with Joseph and with her parents; the long trip from Nazareth; the exhaustion of giving birth without help in a smelly stable; the visit of some rough-hewn shepherds with an amazing story of the heavenly host's proclaiming the praises of God.

Mary was as weary and exhausted as a person could be. So much had happened, and she was at the very center of it all. No one could even begin to know the thoughts that had filled her mind for nine months, nor could anyone know the feelings and emotions of the experience. The wonder, the amazement, the astounding reality was too much to talk about. All she could do was continue in the humble sweetness that had so characterized her over the past months. She merely bowed once again in *humble adoration* to God and *quietly entrusted* all these things into God's keeping. Like priceless treasures, Mary stored all the details in the vault of her heart, where she would meditate on them and ponder the miraculous thing God had done through her.

2:19

¹⁹ But Mary treasured up all these things, pondering them in her heart.

2:20

²⁰ And the shepherds returned, glorifying and praising God for all they had heard and seen, as it had been told them.

7 The heartened shepherds' worship of God.

Shepherds were not usually religious people. Yet it was to a group of shepherds the angel had delivered the message of the Messiah's birth. It was shepherds who visited the newborn holy baby. And it was shepherds who are seen glorifying and praising God for His birth.

The shepherds were praising God for what they had *heard* and *seen*. God had spoken to them, and they had received the message. They obeyed God's instructions to seek out the Messiah; therefore, they had been privileged to see Him, and now they had reason to praise God. (How many hear and see, yet never respond and never praise God?)

> For I know the plans I have for you, declares the Lord, plans for welfare and not for evil, to give you a future and a hope. Then you will call upon me and come and pray to me, and I will hear you. You will seek me and find me, when you seek me with all your heart. (Je.29:11–13)

2:21

²¹ And at the end of eight days, when he was circumcised, he was called Jesus, the name given by the angel before he was conceived in the womb.

8 The unusual naming of the child by God Himself.

This child was named by His Father—by God Himself. Before He was ever conceived in Mary's womb, God had directed that He was to be named Jesus (Lu.1:31). The name *Jesus* (Iesous, *ee-yay'-soos*) means Savior or He will save. The Hebrew form of the name is Joshua which means *Jehovah is salvation*.

> This is good, and it is pleasing in the sight of God our Savior, who desires all people to be saved and to come to the knowledge of the truth. For there is one God, and there is one mediator between God and men, the man Christ Jesus, who gave himself as a ransom for all, which is the testimony given at the proper time. (1 Ti.2:3–6)

> But when the goodness and loving kindness of God our Savior appeared, he saved us, not because of works done by us in righteousness, but according to his own mercy, by the washing of regeneration and renewal of the Holy Spirit, whom he poured out on us richly through Jesus Christ our Savior, so that being justified by his grace we might become heirs according to the hope of eternal life. (Tit.3:4–7)

9 The traditional observance of the legal ceremonies.

In every aspect of His life, Jesus fulfilled the law of Moses (Mt.5:17). His parents were careful to observe every requirement of the law pertaining to His birth.

a. Circumcision (v.21).

The law called for every Jewish baby boy to be circumcised on the eighth day after his birth (Le.12:3; see DEEPER STUDY # 3). Joseph and Mary fulfilled this requirement for the Son of God.

> 22 And when the time came for their purification according to the Law of Moses, they brought him up to Jerusalem to present him to the Lord
> 23 (as it is written in the Law of the Lord, "Every male who first opens the womb shall be called holy to the Lord")

b. Purification after childbirth (v.22a).

After the birth of a boy, a woman was considered unclean for forty days (eighty for a girl). She could work around the home and engage in normal activities, but she could not take part in religious ceremonies. She was considered to be religiously, that is, ceremonially, unclean. After a woman's forty or eighty days were up, she was to make an offering in the temple (Le.12:1-8). Mary observed this ceremony of purification.

c. Dedication to the Lord (vv.22b-23).

God's law required that firstborn male children be consecrated to Him (see Ex.13:2, 12, 15; 22:9; Le.27:6; Nu.8:17; 18:15-16). A male child was presented (dedicated) in the temple when the family lived close to Jerusalem. Accordingly, Joseph and Mary dedicated baby Jesus to the Lord.

Why would Jesus, the Son of God, be subjected to the legal observances of the law? He was not a stranger to the covenants of God (circumcision). He had created the covenants Himself. He was not lacking in commitment (the Dedication Ceremony). He was God Himself, the One to whom all babies were dedicated, yet He was subjected to all the legal requirements. Why? Scripture answers the question:

> Do not think that I have come to abolish the Law or the Prophets; I have not come to abolish them but to fulfill them. (Mt.5:17; see note—Mt.5:17-18)

> But when the fullness of time had come, God sent forth his Son, born of woman, born under the law, to redeem those who were under the law, so that we might receive adoption as sons. (Ga.4:4-5)

> Therefore he had to be made like his brothers in every respect, so that he might become a merciful and faithful high priest in the service of God, to make propitiation for the sins of the people. For because he himself has suffered when tempted, he is able to help those who are being tempted. (He.2:17-18)

DEEPER STUDY # 3

(2:21) **Circumcision:** see DEEPER STUDY # 1—Ph.3:3.

10 The deliberate choice by God to have a poor family bear His Son.

Luke reports a significant detail: Mary offered two pigeons to the Lord as the sacrifice for her purification. This was the offering of the poor. Rich people were required to offer a lamb and a pigeon. Those who did not have the means to

> 24 and to offer a sacrifice according to what is said in the Law of the Lord, "a pair of turtle-doves, or two young pigeons."

offer a lamb could bring two turtledoves or pigeons (Le.12:6-8). This detail reveals the fact that God deliberately chose a poor family to rear His only Son in an ordinary home without luxuries.

THOUGHT 1. No matter what we have to bear in life, Christ has already borne it—even poverty (see note 3—Lu.2:40 for discussion). He knows the suffering we undergo; therefore, He is able to strengthen and carry us through the suffering.

> For we do not have a high priest who is unable to sympathize with our weaknesses, but one who in every respect has been tempted as we are, yet without sin. Let us then with confidence draw near to the throne of grace, that we may receive mercy and find grace to help in time of need. (He.4:15–16)

25 Now there was a man in Jerusalem, whose name was Simeon, and this man was righteous and devout, waiting for the consolation of Israel, and the Holy Spirit was upon him.

26 And it had been revealed to him by the Holy Spirit that he would not see death before he had seen the Lord's Christ.

27 And he came in the Spirit into the temple, and when the parents brought in the child Jesus, to do for him according to the custom of the Law,

28 he took him up in his arms and blessed God and said,

29 "Lord, now you are letting your servant depart in peace, according to your word;

30 for my eyes have seen your salvation

31 that you have prepared in the presence of all peoples,

32 a light for revelation to the Gentiles, and for glory to your people Israel."

33 And his father and his mother marveled at what was said about him.

34 And Simeon blessed them and said to Mary his mother, "Behold, this child is appointed for the fall and rising of many in Israel, and for a sign that is opposed

35 (and a sword will pierce through your own soul also), so that thoughts from many hearts may be revealed."

1. **Simeon, a man who walked closely with God**
   a. A man who was righteous and devout

   b. A man who looked for the Messiah
   c. A man who was led by the Holy Spirit
   d. A man who was given an unusual promise

   e. A man who was led by God's Spirit to go and prophesy over the child

2. **The child was God's salvation**

   a. The source of peace

   b. The one appointed to be God's salvation
   c. The one prepared for all people

   d. The light to unbelievers
   e. The glory to the believers of Israel
   f. The parents' amazement at the predictions
3. **The child was to cause the rise and fall of many**
4. **The child's fate was sealed**
   a. His fate: To be opposed and put to death
   b. His purpose: To reveal the inner thoughts of people's hearts

Division I

The Announcement of the Coming of Jesus, the Son of Man, 1:1–2:52

I. Simeon's Prophecy: Jesus' Life and Fate Foretold, 2:25–35

2:25–35
Introduction

When Joseph and Mary took the baby Jesus to the temple to be dedicated, they met two faithful, faith-filled servants of God. The first was a man named Simeon. Exactly who Simeon was is not known. Some think he was a priest, but Scripture does not say. All we know is what is recorded here. He was a man who had great faith in God and His Word, faith so strong that God was able to use him in a most magnificent way. He used Simeon to proclaim one of the greatest messages of all time: the events and fate of the child Messiah's life. This is, *Simeon's Prophecy: Jesus' Life and Fate Foretold*, 2:25-35.

1. Simeon, a man who walked closely with God (vv.25-27).
2. The child was God's salvation (vv.28-33).
3. The child was to cause the rise and fall of many (v.34).
4. The child's fate was sealed (vv.34-35).

2:25-27

25 Now there was a man in Jerusalem, whose name was Simeon, and this man was righteous and devout, waiting for the consolation of Israel, and the Holy Spirit was upon him.
26 And it had been revealed to him by the Holy Spirit that he would not see death before he had seen the Lord's Christ.
27 And he came in the Spirit into the temple, and when the parents brought in the child Jesus, to do for him according to the custom of the Law,

1 Simeon, a man who walked closely with God.

Simeon was a man who walked closely with God. He walked so closely that God was able to use him in a most magnificent way to encourage Joseph and Mary. Five things are said about him personally.

a. A man who was righteous and devout (v.25a).

Simeon was a righteous and devout man. *Righteous* or *just* (Gk. dikaios, *dik'-eye-os*) describes a person who is "upright, fair, honest, innocent, proper, above board in . . . behavior and dealings both with God and man."[1] It speaks of a person who fulfills obligations to the law and to others. Simeon was a man who treated other people as he should: justly.

Devout (eulabes, *yoo-lob-ace'*) means cautious and careful in relation to God. It speaks of having reverence for God and being very attentive to spiritual matters. Simeon was exceptionally careful in his relationship with God.

b. A man who looked for the Messiah (v.25b).

Simeon was a man who looked for the coming of the Messiah (see Deeper Study # 2—Mt.1:18). This is what is meant by "the consolation of Israel." Faithful believers among the Jews felt that Israel could find consolation only in the Messiah. They longed and yearned with all hope and patience for His coming. Joseph of Arimathaea was another example of one who "was looking [waiting] for the kingdom of God" to come through the Messiah (Mk.15:43).

Thought 1. The world can find consolation only in the coming of Christ. Indeed, Christ came and ministered here on earth, suffered and died on our behalf, was resurrected, and will one day return. Believers should long for Jesus to come again; they should anticipate Christ's return with all hope and patience (see 2 Pe.3:3-18).

> And to wait for his Son from heaven, whom he raised from the dead, Jesus who delivers us from the wrath to come. (1 Th.1:10)

> Henceforth there is laid up for me the crown of righteousness, which the Lord, the righteous judge, will award to me on that day, and not only to me but also to all who have loved his appearing. (2 Ti.4:8)

> Waiting for our blessed hope, the appearing of the glory of our great God and Savior Jesus Christ, who gave himself for us to redeem us from all lawlessness and to purify for himself a people for his own possession who are zealous for good works. (Tit.2:13-14)

> Beloved, we are God's children now, and what we will be has not yet appeared; but we know that when he appears we shall be like him, because we shall see him as he is. And everyone who thus hopes in him purifies himself as he is pure. (1 Jn.3:2-3)

---

1 *Practical Word Studies in the New Testament*, (Chattanooga, TN: Leadership Ministries Worldwide, 1998). Via Wordsearch digital edition.

c. A man who was led by the Holy Spirit (v.26a, 27).

Simeon was a man filled with the Holy Spirit. The idea seems to be that the Spirit was upon him continually. In most instances throughout the Old Testament, the Spirit only came upon people temporarily for special service. It is not said that the Spirit abode upon them continually; however, the Spirit does seem to have rested upon Simeon continually. This shows just how closely Simeon was living with God. He must have been a very, very special man, a man who held God ever so dear to his heart and whom God held ever so close to His heart.

d. A man who was given an unusual promise (v.26b).

The Holy Spirit had given Simeon an unusual promise. Apparently, Simeon was constantly studying the Scriptures, in particular searching the prophecies concerning the coming of the Messiah (1 Pe.1:10). At some point, the Holy Spirit revealed to him that he would not die until he had seen the Messiah, that the Messiah would come in his lifetime. What a thrilling promise! Just think how closely Simeon must have lived to God! He was unquestionably a very special person to God.

e. A man who was led by God's Spirit to go and prophesy over the child (v.27).

On the very day that Joseph and Mary were bringing the baby Jesus to the temple to be dedicated, Simeon was again led by the Spirit; he was led to go to the temple. This was the day which he had long anticipated, the day he was to see and embrace the Messiah. When the parents entered the temple with God's Son, Simeon immediately saw that this child was different from all the others; he recognized the baby as the Christ-child. He took the holy child up in his arms and proclaimed Him to be the long-awaited Messiah.

THOUGHT 1. The most important quality to notice about Simeon is his closeness with God. He is a man who stands as a dynamic example of *strong dedication*. Because of his *strong dedication*, God was able to bless Simeon beyond imagination.

> Though you have not seen him, you love him. Though you do not now see him, you believe in him and rejoice with joy that is inexpressible and filled with glory. (1 Pe.1:8)

> Keep yourselves in the love of God, waiting for the mercy of our Lord Jesus Christ that leads to eternal life. (Jude 21)

> I know your works, your love and faith and service and patient endurance, and that your latter works exceed the first. (Re.2:19)

> Love the LORD, all you his saints! The LORD preserves the faithful but abundantly repays the one who acts in pride. (Ps.31:23)

2 The child was God's salvation.

Once Simeon had embraced the Messiah, he broke out in song, proclaiming that the child he held in his arms was God's salvation. His song is called the *Nunc Dimittis*, its opening words in the Latin language.

a. The source of peace (v.29).

Simeon had seen and embraced the Messiah, God's salvation (v.30). Therefore, he was now ready to die in peace. Note that He believed and trusted God—all of God's promises. He praised God for fulfilling His Word. It was because of God's faithfulness that he was ready to die. The source of peace had come into the world and had given him peace, and now he was ready to depart from this earthly life (see note—Jn.14:27).

> Peace I leave with you; my peace I give to you. Not as the world gives do I give to you. Let not your hearts be troubled, neither let them be afraid. (Jn.14:27)

²⁸ he took him up in his arms and blessed God and said,

²⁹ "Lord, now you are letting your servant depart in peace, according to your word;

³⁰ for my eyes have seen your salvation

³¹ that you have prepared in the presence of all peoples,

³² a light for revelation to the Gentiles, and for glory to your people Israel."

³³ And his father and his mother marveled at what was said about him.

I have said these things to you, that in me you may have peace. In the world you will have tribulation. But take heart; I have overcome the world. (Jn.16:33)

b. The one appointed to be God's salvation (v.30).

The baby Simeon held in his arms was the one appointed to be God's salvation. He was appointed and prepared in "the definite plan and foreknowledge of God" (Ac.2:23). This statement is the confession of Simeon. He confessed that the child was God's salvation.

THOUGHT 1. Everyone needs to confess that Jesus is God's salvation, through whom God saves the world. There is no salvation apart from Him. We must make this message known throughout the world.

> So everyone who acknowledges me before men, I also will acknowledge before my Father who is in heaven. (Mt.10:32)

> And there is salvation in no one else, for there is no other name under heaven given among men by which we must be saved. (Ac.4:12)

> Whoever confesses that Jesus is the Son of God, God abides in him, and he in God. (1 Jn.4:15)

c. The one prepared for all people (v.31).

Simeon saw that God's salvation was not for any one people or nation or group. The Messiah had come to save all people. Anyone could now be saved, no matter who they were or what they had done. Prejudice and favoritism are unknown to God. He is not willing that any should perish.

> For I am not ashamed of the gospel, for it is the power of God for salvation to everyone who believes, to the Jew first and also to the Greek. (Ro.1:16)

> The Lord is not slow to fulfill his promise as some count slowness, but is patient toward you, not wishing that any should perish, but that all should reach repentance. (2 Pe.3:9)

d. The light to unbelievers (v.32a).

The child, God's salvation, came to be the Light of the world. Specifically, Simeon prophesied that He was to be a light for "revelation to the Gentiles," to the unbelievers of all nations, not just the Jewish nation. This simply means that He came to be the Revelation of God, to reveal the way, the truth, and the life to all people (see note, pt.4—Lu.1:76-79).

> Again Jesus spoke to them, saying, "I am the light of the world. Whoever follows me will not walk in darkness, but will have the light of life." (Jn.8:12)

> Jesus said to him, "I am the way, and the truth, and the life. No one comes to the Father except through me." (Jn.14:6)

e. The glory to the believers of Israel (v.32b).

The child, God's salvation, was also to be the glory of Israel. The fact that God sent His Son, the Savior through the Jews would be the greatest glory the nation had ever known. Tragically, His own people did not receive Him as their Messiah and Savior (Jn.1:11). In reality, the Messiah would only be the glory of all Israelites (Jews) who truly believed. Likewise, He was to be the glory of all who believe, no matter what nationality. While many of His own people would reject Him, many of the Gentiles would receive Him as their Savior. Isaiah prophesied of the salvation the Messiah would bring to Israel (and to all people):

➤ The believers would be justified.

> In the LORD all the offspring of Israel shall be justified and shall glory. (Is.45:25)

➤ The believers would be saved to live with God eternally.

> Whereas you have been forsaken and hated, with no one passing through, I will make you majestic forever, a joy from age to age. . . . Violence shall no more be heard in your land, devastation or destruction within your borders; you shall call your walls Salvation, and your gates Praise. The sun shall be no more your light by day, nor for brightness shall the moon give you light; but the LORD will be your everlasting light, and your God will be your glory. (Is.60:15, 18–19)

f. **The parents' amazement at the predictions (v.33).**

Jesus' parents marveled at Simeon's prophecies. His predictions would amaze anyone, but they were given for an additional reason. Joseph and Mary needed to be assured and encouraged. Their need was only natural. Imagine what they had been through and were yet to go through because of the child (see note—Lu.2:7; 2:40; DEEPER STUDY # 1—Mt.1:18-25). God saw to it that they were strengthened through this experience.

3 The child was to cause the rise and fall of many.

Simeon went on to prophesy that Mary's child was to cause the rise and fall of many. The child was to be what the Scripture calls the *stone of stumbling* and the *chief cornerstone.*

Many would stumble and fall over Him. They would not notice, look, choose, believe, or trust Him and the salvation He was bringing. They would simply choose another way other than God. Therefore, they would stumble and fall over Him just as they would stumble over a stone lying in their path.

At the same time, many would rise because of Him. That is, they would take notice, choose, and believe Him and the salvation He was bringing. Therefore, He would become their foundation, their cornerstone, and they would rise—be built—on Him.

> 34 And Simeon blessed them and said to Mary his mother, "Behold, this child is appointed for the fall and rising of many in Israel, and for a sign that is opposed"

THOUGHT 1. Decisively, Jesus Christ causes every person to make a choice. A person either rejects the Messiah, God's salvation, and falls (eternally); or accepts Him and rises (eternally) (see DEEPER STUDY # 7—Mt.21:42; DEEPER STUDY # 9—21:44 for more discussion).

> So the honor is for you who believe, but for those who do not believe, "The stone that the builders rejected has become the cornerstone," and "A stone of stumbling, and a rock of offense." They stumble because they disobey the word, as they were destined to do. (1 Pe.2:7-8)

> But the LORD of hosts, him you shall honor as holy. Let him be your fear, and let him be your dread. And he will become a sanctuary and a stone of offense and a rock of stumbling to both houses of Israel, a trap and a snare to the inhabitants of Jerusalem. And many shall stumble on it. They shall fall and be broken; they shall be snared and taken. (Is.8:13-15)

4 The child's fate was sealed.

Finally, Simeon prophesied the fate of the baby he held in his arms. At the same time the birth of Christ was being celebrated, His death was foretold. The salvation He was bringing could only come through His death. Truly, Christ was born to die.

> 34 And Simeon blessed them and said to Mary his mother, "Behold, this child is appointed for the fall and rising of many in Israel, and for a sign that is opposed
> 35 "(and a sword will pierce through your own soul also), so that thoughts from many hearts may be revealed."

a. **His fate: To be opposed and put to death (v.34b).**

Although God's Spirit moved Simeon to proclaim this prophecy, imagine how painful it was for Simeon to do this. This child was the "sign" that would be "opposed" or "spoken against." This statement speaks of Christ's death. He was to be opposed and eventually killed.

Simeon warned Mary of the intense grief she would feel seeing her Son, the only begotten Son of God, rejected and killed by unbelieving people. The sorrow she was to experience at the cross would be unbearably sharp and excruciating, like a sword piercing her soul (see Jn.19:25-27).

THOUGHT 1. Christ was a "sign" of both God's love and judgment. It is this truth that causes people to react. People want a god who brings only enough law and morality to give order to society. They want a god that allows them to live as they desire, not a God who demands total self-denial and obedience (see note and DEEPER STUDY # 1—Lu.9:23). They want a god of indulging love, not of sacrificial love; a god of license, not of demanding love. Therefore, when Christ is set before people as the Messiah of self-denying love and obedience, they react. Why? Because if they disobey Him and fail to live sacrificial lives, they bring judgment upon themselves.

THOUGHT 2. Within every society, Christ and His genuine followers are *spoken against* with varying degrees of reaction and persecution. The *speaking against* ranges all the way from simply ignoring believers to killing them (martyrdom). There is . . .

- ignoring
- ridiculing
- abusing
- hating
- imprisoning
- murdering
- persecuting
- slandering

> Remember the word that I said to you: "A servant is not greater than his master." If they persecuted me, they will also persecute you. If they kept my word, they will also keep yours. (Jn.15:20)

> Indeed, all who desire to live a godly life in Christ Jesus will be persecuted. (2 Ti.3:12)

> Do not fear what you are about to suffer. Behold, the devil is about to throw some of you into prison, that you may be tested, and for ten days you will have tribulation. Be faithful unto death, and I will give you the crown of life. (Re.2:10)

b. His purpose: To reveal the inner thoughts of people's hearts (v.35b).

The painful death of Mary's child—God's Son and the Savior—would serve a penetrating purpose. It would reveal the inner thoughts of people's hearts. "When people encounter Christ, their inner thoughts . . . are seen for what they are."[2] Those who are proud, rebellious, and hard-hearted reject Jesus. But those who are humble and aware of their sinful condition and need of salvation fall to their faces before Him in repentance, gratitude, and faith.

THOUGHT 1. Every individual either sees the love of God and surrenders to the saving grace of God, or else looks upon the cross as a repulsive sight and rejects the saving grace of God. They either see Christ's dying for their sins and receive the forgiveness of God offered by the cross, or else they recoil from the thought of sin within themselves and turn from the forgiveness of the cross (see note, pts. 2–4—Mt.16:21–23).

> Or do you presume on the riches of his kindness and forbearance and patience, not knowing that God's kindness is meant to lead you to repentance? (Ro.2:4)

> For the word of the cross is folly to those who are perishing, but to us who are being saved it is the power of God. (1 Co.1:18)

> To whom shall I speak and give warning, that they may hear? Behold, their ears are uncircumcised, they cannot listen; behold, the word of the LORD is to them an object of scorn; they take no pleasure in it. (Je.6:10)

> The wise men shall be put to shame; they shall be dismayed and taken; behold, they have rejected the word of the LORD, so what wisdom is in them? (Je.8:9)

> They made their hearts diamond-hard lest they should hear the law and the words that the LORD of hosts had sent by his Spirit through the former prophets. Therefore great anger came from the LORD of hosts. (Zec.7:12)

---

2   Various authors, R. Kent Hughes, ed. *Preaching the Word Commentary: Luke,* (Wheaton, IL: Crossway, 2015).

³⁶ And there was a prophetess, Anna, the daughter of Phanuel, of the tribe of Asher. She was advanced in years, having lived with her husband seven years from when she was a virgin,

³⁷ and then as a widow until she was eighty-four. She did not depart from the temple, worshiping with fasting and prayer night and day.

³⁸ And coming up at that very hour she began to give thanks to God and to speak of him to all who were waiting for the redemption of Jerusalem.

1. **Anna was a prophetess**
2. **Anna never lost hope over many, many years**
3. **Anna never grew bitter in the face of sorrow**
4. **Anna never ceased to worship—night and day**
5. **Anna knew the child instantly and gave thanks**
6. **Anna shared the message with all believers: He was the promised redemption (salvation)**

Division I

The Announcement of the Coming of Jesus, the Son of Man, 1:1–2:52

J. Anna's Praise: The Child Jesus Is Praised by a Prophetess, 2:36–38

2:36–38
Introduction

When Joseph and Mary took the baby Jesus to the temple to dedicate Him, they also encountered a godly woman named Anna. Nothing is known about Anna except what is given here by Luke. She was the daughter of Phanuel and was a descendant of the tribe of Asher. Apparently, her father's name had originated from the name of the place (Penuel) where Jacob wrestled with God face to face (Ge.32:24–30).

Anna's name means *gracious*. She seems to have been a person of enormous devotion, one who lived as though face to face with God, ever basking in His grace and sharing His grace with others.

A man, Simeon, had just borne witness that the child Jesus was the *Salvation of God*. Now a woman, Anna, bore the very same witness. Both a man and a woman acknowledged the child to be the Messiah, the Salvation of God. Both men and women of every generation are urged to hope in Him for salvation. Jesus is our hope, our only hope. This is, *Anna's Praise: The Child Jesus Is Praised by a Prophetess, 2:36–38*.

1. Anna was a prophetess (v.36).
2. Anna never lost hope over many, many years (v.36).
3. Anna never grew bitter in the face of sorrow (v.36).
4. Anna never ceased to worship—night and day (v.37).
5. Anna knew the child instantly and gave thanks (v.38).
6. Anna shared the message with all believers: He was the promised redemption (salvation) (v.38).

1 Anna was a prophetess.

There had not been a prophet in Israel for some three hundred years, yet God raised up a prophet, and a woman at that. This was quite unusual, for female leaders were very rare in that day. Like Simeon, apparently Anna also was a very special person, one who loved God and hoped in God with all her being (see v.37). She was evidently on a spiritual par with other saintly women used by God throughout Scripture such as Miriam, Hannah, and Deborah. As a prophetess, she was constantly studying the Word of God that she might be approved of God and proclaim the unsearchable riches of His grace (see 2 Ti.2:15; 4:2). Because Anna's hope was in God, God blessed her greatly. God will always bless the person who hopes in Him.

2:36

36 And there was a prophetess, Anna, the daughter of Phanuel, of the tribe of Asher. She was advanced in years, having lived with her husband seven years from when she was a virgin,

> Be strong, and let your heart take courage, all you who wait for the LORD! (Ps.31:24)

> Behold, the eye of the LORD is on those who fear him, on those who hope in his steadfast love. (Ps.33:18)

> And now, O Lord, for what do I wait? My hope is in you. (Ps.39:7)

> Why are you cast down, O my soul, and why are you in turmoil within me? Hope in God; for I shall again praise him, my salvation and my God. (Ps.42:11)

> For you, O Lord, are my hope, my trust, O LORD, from my youth. (Ps.71:5)

> Blessed is the man who trusts in the LORD, whose trust is the LORD. (Je.17:7)

2 Anna never lost hope over many, many years.

Anna had lived a long life and had not seen God's promise of Messiah fulfilled. Nevertheless, she still believed and still looked for the Messiah. She still looked for the salvation that God was to send to the world. She never lost hope and forsook her belief, but held fast, expecting God to keep His Word.

> As the Father has loved me, so have I loved you. Abide in my love. (Jn.15:9)

> And let us not grow weary of doing good, for in due season we will reap, if we do not give up. (Ga.6:9)

> Behold, we consider those blessed who remained steadfast. You have heard of the steadfastness of Job, and you have seen the purpose of the Lord, how the Lord is compassionate and merciful. (Jas.5:11)

> I am coming soon. Hold fast what you have, so that no one may seize your crown. (Re.3:11)

3 Anna never grew bitter in the face of sorrow.

Anna became widowed at a very young age. She had been married at an early age and had lived with her husband only seven years when he died. She remained a widow throughout the years, but not out of bitterness or disappointment. Apparently, she never remarried out of conviction—the conviction that her life belonged to God. Before her husband died, she had been committed to her husband; when her husband died, she apparently chose to commit her life totally to God. Therefore, she dedicated herself to serving Him and Him alone for the remainder of her life, placing her hope in God and in God alone. Anna never grew bitter in the face of deep sorrow, the sorrow of losing her husband while a young woman.

> To the unmarried and the widows I say that it is good for them to remain single, as I am. (1 Co.7:8)

> This is what I mean, brothers: the appointed time has grown very short. From now on, let those who have wives live as though they had none, and those who mourn as though they were not mourning, and those who rejoice as though they were not rejoicing, and those who buy as though they had no goods, and those who deal with the world as though they had no dealings with it. For the present form of this world is passing away. I want you to be free from anxieties. The unmarried man is anxious about the things of the Lord, how to please the Lord. But the married man is anxious about worldly things, how to please his wife, and his interests are divided. And the unmarried or betrothed woman is anxious about the things of the Lord, how to be holy in body and spirit.

But the married woman is anxious about worldly things, how to please her husband. I say this for your own benefit, not to lay any restraint upon you, but to promote good order and to secure your undivided devotion to the Lord. (1 Co.7:29-35)

2:36-38

4 Anna never ceased to worship—night and day.

Luke makes a phenomenal statement about this godly woman: she never left the temple, but worshiped God night and day. This statement either means that she had been given some kind of *room* at the temple or else she was at worship every day never missing a service (see Lu.24:53).

> [37] and then as a widow until she was eighty-four. She did not depart from the temple, worshiping with fasting and prayer night and day.

To Anna, the Lord was everything. She was totally devoted to God, sold out to Him completely, hoping in Him and in Him alone.

Anna's regular fasting and prayer indicate that she was extremely disciplined, possessing the consistency in devotions that so many lack. She fasted and prayed night and day despite being elderly, eighty-four years old. She did not give herself to the flesh as she grew old. She did not retire from nor cut back on her service to the Lord. Instead, she continued to devote herself to serving and hoping in God, praying and bearing witness as His servant.

> And he told them a parable to the effect that they ought always to pray and not lose heart. (Lu.18:1; see Ep.6:18; 1 Th.5:17)

> Therefore, my beloved brothers, be steadfast, immovable, always abounding in the work of the Lord, knowing that in the Lord your labor is not in vain. (1 Co.15:58)

> Seek the Lord and his strength; seek his presence continually! (1 Chr.16:11)

5 Anna knew the child instantly and gave thanks.

When Joseph and Mary brought their baby to the temple, Anna knew the child instantly and gave thanks to God for the Messiah. She was the Lord's servant, so the Lord guided her life step by step, taking care of her and looking after her welfare. Anna was so committed to God that God could guide her every step. He saw to it that her path crossed the

> [38] And coming up at that very hour she began to give thanks to God and to speak of him to all who were waiting for the redemption of Jerusalem.

path of the child Messiah. He fulfilled her hope. Note she came in at the very moment that Jesus was in the temple, and she immediately began giving thanks to God for the Christ-child. What is the message of her thanksgiving? *Redemption*. She praised God for His redemption. The child was the Messiah who was to redeem all people (see note, pts. 1, 2, 3—Lu.2:28-33; see note—Ep.1:7). She prophesied and proclaimed the same message as Simeon: the child Jesus is the glorious hope of humanity's redemption.

> And because of him you are in Christ Jesus, who became to us wisdom from God, righteousness and sanctification and redemption. (1 Co.1:30)

> Christ redeemed us from the curse of the law by becoming a curse for us—for it is written, "Cursed is everyone who is hanged on a tree." (Ga.3:13)

> In him we have redemption through his blood, the forgiveness of our trespasses, according to the riches of his grace. (Ep.1:7; see Col.1:14)

> He entered once for all into the holy places, not by means of the blood of goats and calves but by means of his own blood, thus securing an eternal redemption. (He.9:12)

> He sent redemption to his people; he has commanded his covenant forever. Holy and awesome is his name! (Ps.111:9)

> O Israel, hope in the Lord! For with the Lord there is steadfast love, and with him is plentiful redemption. (Ps.130:7)

6 Anna shared the message with all believers: He was the promised redemption (salvation).

Anna knew of others who were looking for the Messiah's coming, so she shared the glorious news with them (see Deeper Study # 2—Mt.1:18). She had seen the child-Messiah, the salvation of God, the glorious hope of all people. She wanted all who were eagerly anticipating the Savior's coming to know that He had come. The promised Redeemer had at last been sent by God. Salvation was here!

2:38b

[38] And coming up at that very hour she began to give thanks to God and to speak of him to all who were waiting for the redemption of Jerusalem.

Go therefore and make disciples of all nations, baptizing them in the name of the Father and of the Son and of the Holy Spirit, teaching them to observe all that I have commanded you. And behold, I am with you always, to the end of the age. (Mt.28:19–20)

And what you have heard from me in the presence of many witnesses entrust to faithful men, who will be able to teach others also. (2 Ti.2:2)

Let the redeemed of the LORD say so, whom he has redeemed from trouble (Ps.107:2)

³⁹ And when they had performed everything according to the Law of the Lord, they returned into Galilee, to their own town of Nazareth.

⁴⁰ And the child grew and became strong, filled with wisdom. And the favor of God was upon him.

1. Jesus was led by His parents to fulfill all the law
2. Jesus was reared in Nazareth

3. Jesus grew as a child: Physically, spiritually, and mentally
4. Jesus possessed God's grace

Division I

The Announcement of the Coming of Jesus, the Son of Man, 1:1–2:52

K. Jesus' Growth as a Child, 2:39–40

2:39–40
Introduction

God's Spirit chose to reveal very little in Scripture about our Savior's formative years. Virtually all we know about Jesus' childhood is contained in these two verses and the passage that follows (vv.41–52). The brevity of this information makes it all the more critical that we understand it. It is applicable to every parent who earnestly desires to bring their children up in the "disciple and instruction [training and admonition] of the Lord" (Ep.6:4), as well as to every young person who longs to be like Jesus. This is, *Jesus' Growth as a Child, 2:39-40.*

1. Jesus was led by His parents to fulfill all the law (v.39).
2. Jesus was reared in Nazareth (v.39).
3. Jesus grew as a child: Physically, spiritually, and mentally (v.40).
4. Jesus possessed God's grace (v.40).

1 Jesus was led by His parents to fulfill all the law.

2:39a

God's Spirit led Luke to highlight the fact that Jesus' parents fulfilled every detail required by the law concerning their Son—God's Son. Their faithfulness was critical to God's purpose for Jesus. God had sent His Son into the world to fulfill the law, not to destroy it. By keeping all the law, Jesus would

³⁹ And when they had performed everything according to the Law of the Lord, they returned into Galilee, to their own town of Nazareth.

be perfectly righteous and become the *Ideal Man*, the Man who would be the pattern for all people to follow.

Another way to say the same thing is that God has given us a perfect life to follow, not just written letters and words. By fulfilling the law and never failing in a single point, Jesus became the Perfect Man, the Ideal Life which we are to imitate. We are now to look to Jesus and follow Him instead of following the law. Jesus has fulfilled the law; therefore, He embraces and includes all the law *and more* in His life (see notes—Mt.5:17-18; DEEPER STUDY # 2—Ro.8:3).

In order to fulfill the law, Jesus had to keep the law and every observance of it. He had to "fulfill all righteousness" (Mt.3:15). Now note: by keeping all of the law, Jesus was symbolically predicting what He was to do for sinful human beings. He was going to secure righteousness and perfection by fulfilling the law, and thereby He was to become the Ideal Man. As the Ideal Man, whatever He did would cover any person who follows Him. The individual who follows Jesus is covered by His righteousness (perfection), His death, His resurrection, and His ascension. All who genuinely trust Jesus Christ to cover them with His righteousness are truly covered.

For these reasons God led Mary and Joseph to fulfill all the law for the child Messiah (also see notes—Lu.2:22–23; DEEPER STUDY # 3—Mt.8:20 for more discussion).

> But Jesus answered him, "Let it be so now, for thus it is fitting for us to fulfill all righteousness." Then he consented. (Mt.3:15)

> Do not think that I have come to abolish the Law or the Prophets; I have not come to abolish them but to fulfill them. (Mt.5:17)

> For God has done what the law, weakened by the flesh, could not do. By sending his own Son in the likeness of sinful flesh and for sin, he condemned sin in the flesh. (Ro.8:3)

> For as by a man came death, by a man has come also the resurrection of the dead. (1 Co.15:21)

2:39b

³⁹ And when they had performed everything according to the Law of the Lord, they returned into Galilee, to their own town of Nazareth.

2 Jesus was reared in Nazareth.

Luke reports the simple detail that after Jesus' dedication in the temple, His parents returned to Nazareth. He does not mention the details in Matthew's account . . .

- of their return to Bethlehem where the wise men visited them (Mt.2:1–12)
- of their flight into Egypt (Mt.2:13–15)
- of Herod's slaughter of the children (Mt.2:16–18)
- of the threat of Archelaus (Mt.2:19–22)

Nazareth was an ideal place for the child Messiah to be brought up (see DEEPER STUDY # 1). However, Nazareth was an obscure town, despised and reproached by other people (see Jn.1:46). Therefore, as with Jesus' birth in a stable, which was the lowest of places, He continued to identify with people in the most severe circumstances. He, too, knew what it was to be born and brought up in a despised place. From the very first, He *"made Himself of no reputation"* (Ph.2:7, KJV, NKJV).

> For Christ did not please himself, but as it is written, "The reproaches of those who reproached you fell on me." (Ro.15:3)

> For you know the grace of our Lord Jesus Christ, that though he was rich, yet for your sake he became poor, so that you by his poverty might become rich. (2 Co.8:9)

> But emptied himself, by taking the form of a servant, being born in the likeness of men. (Ph.2:7)

DEEPER STUDY # 1

(2:39) **Nazareth:** the hometown of Joseph and Mary and of Jesus Himself during His childhood and early manhood. There were at least two advantages to Jesus' being brought up in Nazareth.

1. It was a quiet town, small and obscure, ready-made for a close community and for neighborliness and quiet contemplation.

2. It was a town in touch with the modern life and world events of that day. Two of the major roads in the ancient world passed within eyesight of the hills surrounding the city: the road stretching between the great cities of the North and South (from Rome to Africa), and the road stretching between the great cities of the East and West. Jesus can be imagined sitting and standing on the hills observing (perhaps even meeting) some of the travelers and caravans using the major routes as they crisscrossed the world. He had opportunity to observe and study the nature and dealings of all kinds of people and nationalities as they used the major routes. How often His heart must have ached and wept as a child over a world lost and needing to be found.

3 Jesus grew as a child: Physically, spiritually, and mentally.

Luke's account emphasizes the fact that Jesus grew as a normal child. But note the added words: *became strong* (Gk. ekrataiouto, *eh-krat-ah-ee'-oo-tah*). This verb speaks of continuous vigorous growth. Scripture specifically states that the child Jesus did not just grow in wisdom, He was *"filled* with wisdom" (pleroumenon sophias, *play-roo'-men-on sof-ee'-ahs*). Simply stated, Jesus grew perfectly at every stage of life.

⁴⁰ And the child grew and became strong, filled with wisdom. And the favor of God was upon him.

> ➤ He grew physically as well as the human body could grow (perfectly well and healthy).
> ➤ He "became strong," as strong as a child could grow.
> ➤ He was "filled with wisdom," as much as a child could be filled.

No other child had ever been or ever will be perfect in growth at the various stages of childhood, but the Christ-child was. He grew as well as a child can grow: *filled* perfectly with all the qualities that can potentially fill a child.

Why did Christ come into the world as a child and not as a full-grown man? The first man, Adam, stood at the head of the human race as the natural representative of man, and he had been created as a full-grown man. Why not Jesus Christ, the second Adam? He, too, was sent into the world to stand at the head of the human race as the spiritual representative of humanity. Going through the stages of growth as a baby, then as a child, and then as a teenager is a humbling experience. Why did God subject His Son to such humiliation? There are at least three reasons.

First, Christ needed to set a striking example for every person, no matter the age, even for children. He stooped to fully experience what it is to be a helpless baby, then a dependent child, then a maturing teenager, and then an independent and responsible man. The very fact that the Son of God stooped so low is shocking to any thoughtful person. It sets a striking example of *humility and lowliness of mind* for every individual.

> **Do nothing from selfish ambition or conceit, but in humility count others more significant than yourselves. Let each of you look not only to his own interests, but also to the interests of others. Have this mind among yourselves, which is yours in Christ Jesus, who, though he was in the form of God, did not count equality with God a thing to be grasped, but emptied himself, by taking the form of a servant, being born in the likeness of men. And being found in human form, he humbled himself by becoming obedient to the point of death, even death on a cross. (Ph.2:3–8)**

Second, Christ needed to demonstrate a striking truth to all people: no person can enter heaven unless they first become as a little child. There was no better way to demonstrate this lesson than for the Son of God Himself to go through the humbling experience of becoming a child before becoming a man.

> **And said, "Truly, I say to you, unless you turn and become like children, you will never enter the kingdom of heaven. Whoever humbles himself like this child is the greatest in the kingdom of heaven." (Mt.18:3–4)**

Third, Christ needed to experience every human situation, condition, and trial in order to become the perfect sympathizer *or Savior.* For this reason, He experienced the most humiliating experiences possible. He experienced . . .

- being born to an unwed mother (Mt.1:18–19)
- being born in a stable, the worst of conditions (Lu.2:7)
- being born to poor parents (Lu.2:24)
- having his life threatened as a baby (Mt.2:13f)
- being the cause of unimaginable sorrow (Mt.2:16f)
- having to be moved and shifted as a baby (Mt.2:13f)
- being reared in a despised place, Nazareth (Lu.2:39)
- having His father die during His youth (see note, pt.3—Mt.13:53–58)
- having to support His mother and brothers and sisters (see note, pt.3—Mt.13:53–58)
- having no home, not even a place to lay His head (Mt.8:20; Lu.9:58)
- being hated and opposed by religious leaders (Mk.14:1–2)
- being charged with insanity (Mk.3:21)

- being charged with demon possession (Mk.3:22)
- being opposed by His own family (Mk.3:31-32)
- being rejected, hated, and opposed by listeners (Mt.13:53-58; Lu.4:28-29)
- being betrayed by a close friend (Mk.14:10-11, 18)
- being left alone, rejected, and forsaken by all of His friends (Mk.14:50)
- being tried before the high court of the land on the charge of treason (Jn.18:33)
- being executed by crucifixion, the worst possible death (Jn.19:16f)

Note that each of these experiences reaches the depth of humiliation. Christ stooped to the lowest point of human experience in every condition in order to become the perfect sympathizer (Savior). He can now identify with and feel sympathy for every circumstance we face.

> For surely it is not angels that he helps, but he helps the offspring of Abraham. Therefore he had to be made like his brothers in every respect, so that he might become a merciful and faithful high priest in the service of God, to make propitiation for the sins of the people. For because he himself has suffered when tempted, he is able to help those who are being tempted. (He.2:16-18)

> For we do not have a high priest who is unable to sympathize with our weaknesses, but one who in every respect has been tempted as we are, yet without sin. Let us then with confidence draw near to the throne of grace, that we may receive mercy and find grace to help in time of need. (He.4:15-16)

2:40b

⁴⁰ And the child grew and became strong, filled with wisdom. And the favor of God was upon him.

4 Jesus possessed God's grace.

Jesus possessed *God's favor* or *grace*. The idea is that God's grace rested on Jesus in its *full measure*, without any lack or shortcoming whatsoever.

Jesus was choosing to grow perfectly, coming short in nothing. Therefore, God showered Him with His grace, His favor. God favored Him by looking after and taking care of Him perfectly.

> For he whom God has sent utters the words of God, for he gives the Spirit without measure. (Jn.3:34)

> And because of him you are in Christ Jesus, who became to us wisdom from God, righteousness and sanctification and redemption. (1 Co.1:30)

⁴¹ Now his parents went to Jerusalem every year at the Feast of the Passover.

⁴² And when he was twelve years old, they went up according to custom.

⁴³ And when the feast was ended, as they were returning, the boy Jesus stayed behind in Jerusalem. His parents did not know it,

⁴⁴ but supposing him to be in the group they went a day's journey, but then they began to search for him among their relatives and acquaintances,

⁴⁵ and when they did not find him, they returned to Jerusalem, searching for him.

⁴⁶ After three days they found him in the temple, sitting among the teachers, listening to them and asking them questions.

⁴⁷ And all who heard him were amazed at his understanding and his answers.

⁴⁸ And when his parents saw him, they were astonished. And his mother said to him, "Son, why have you treated us so? Behold, your father and I have been searching for you in great distress."

⁴⁹ And he said to them, "Why were you looking for me? Did you not know that I must be in my Father's house?"

⁵⁰ And they did not understand the saying that he spoke to them.

⁵¹ And he went down with them and came to Nazareth and was submissive to them. And his mother treasured up all these things in her heart.

⁵² And Jesus increased in wisdom and in stature and in favor with God and man.

1. **Jesus' faithfulness in worship was noteworthy**
   a. His Parents were faithful
   b. His parents taught Him
   c. His special year: Became a man at age twelve
2. **Jesus' social development was normal**
   a. His parents left to return home
   b. He was missing from the caravan

   c. His parents thought He was with others, playing and socializing

   d. His parents returned to find Him

3. **Jesus' knowledge was surprising**
   a. He was found in the temple among the teachers, learning and asking questions
   b. He amazed everyone with the depth of His understanding and knowledge
4. **Jesus' mission was misunderstood by His parents**

5. **Jesus' first known recognition of Messiahship was at an early age**

6. **Jesus' obedience to His parents was absolute**

7. **Jesus' upbringing was normal and He grew in favor with both God and people**

Division I

The Announcement of the Coming of Jesus, the Son of Man, 1:1–2:52

L. Jesus As a Young Boy in the Temple: His First
   Recognition of Messiahship, 2:41–52

2:41–52
Introduction

As stated previously, this passage (along with the two preceding verses) is the only passage in Scripture that covers Jesus' childhood. It is important because it tells us about our Savior's formative years. In addition, its lessons for parents and young people are inexhaustible. But this section of Scripture is critical for another reason: it gives us the first *known* time that Jesus claimed to be the Messiah. As a young boy, Jesus knew who He was, and He knew His purpose for coming to earth. This is, *Jesus as a Young Boy in the Temple: His First Recognition of Messiahship*, 2:41-52.

1. Jesus' faithfulness in worship was noteworthy (vv.41–42).
2. Jesus' social development was normal (vv.43–45).
3. Jesus' knowledge was surprising (vv.46–47).
4. Jesus' mission was misunderstood by His parents (v.48).
5. Jesus' first known recognition of Messiahship was at an early age (vv.49–50).
6. Jesus' obedience to His parents was absolute (v.51).
7. Jesus' upbringing was normal and He grew in favor with both God and people (v.52).

2:41–42

[41] Now his parents went to Jerusalem every year at the Feast of the Passover.
[42] And when he was twelve years old, they went up according to custom.

1 Jesus' faithfulness in worship was noteworthy.

From the time Jesus was a young boy, He was faithfully involved in worship and instruction in the faith. Faithful worship and service to God were the habit of His parents, and they made sure it became their Son's—God's Son's—habit as well.

a. His parents were faithful (v.41).

Scripture carefully notes that Jesus' parents were faithful in their worship. It was their *custom* to keep the feast of the Passover every year. All male Jews who lived within twenty miles of Jerusalem were required by law to participate in temple worship three times a year: at Passover, Pentecost, and the Feast of Tabernacles (Ex.23:14-17). Women were exempt from the law, but they could attend if they wished. Note what Mary chose to do: both "parents went to Jerusalem every year." They were both faithful in their worship by choice, not by restraint.

b. His parents taught Him (vv.41–42).

Jesus' parents led and taught Him to be faithful in worship. It is not specifically said that Jesus went to Jerusalem with His parents every year, but it is implied that He did. Note the words "Now His parents went . . . every year at the . . . Passover." It was the custom for "all who could understand what they heard" to be present if at all possible (Ne.8:2).

Jesus' knowledge and ability to discuss issues with religious authorities (vv.46-47) indicates that His parents continually taught Him, seeing to it that He was in the synagogue worshiping and learning at every opportunity. (Of course, His amazing wisdom and understanding of spiritual matters was primarily due to the fact that He was God). God had placed the child Jesus into their hands as a *bundle of trust*. The child belonged to God. He had only entrusted the child's keeping into their hands to see that He was looked after and taught. It was Joseph's and Mary's responsibility to see that Jesus grew physically, mentally, and spiritually and to see that He became all He could become. The parents were faithful to their duty.

THOUGHT 1. What an example for all parents. Children are but a *bundle of trust* placed into our hands by God. They belong to God, not us. Therefore, we are to train up our children in the way they should go (Pr.22:6). Note two critical points.

1) Every child should be taught from the very first about God and worship, about the world and a person's responsibility in it.
2) Every child, when he or she comes of age, should be charged with becoming a "son (or daughter) of the law," a mature individual *before God*, being responsible and making their contribution to the world—*all in the name of the Lord*.

> **Fathers, do not provoke your children to anger, but bring them up in the discipline and instruction of the Lord. (Ep.6:4)**

> **You shall teach them diligently to your children, and shall talk of them when you sit in your house, and when you walk by the way, and when you lie down, and when you rise. (De.6:7)**

> **Assemble the people, men, women, and little ones, and the sojourner within your towns, that they may hear and learn to fear the Lord your God, and be careful to do all the words of this law. (De.31:12)**

> **Come, O children, listen to me; I will teach you the fear of the Lord. (Ps.34:11)**

> **Train up a child in the way he should go; even when he is old he will not depart from it. (Pr.22:6)**

c. **His special year: Became a man at age twelve (v.42).**
As it was for every Jewish boy, the age of twelve was a very special year for Jesus. When a Jewish boy reached thirteen years of age, he became a *son of the law* which meant that he was now considered a man and was expected to keep all the law. It was suggested that a boy be brought to the Passover Feast a year or two early so that he might become familiar with the Temple and the Feasts. When the eleven- and twelve-year old initiates arrived, they were naturally given a great deal of attention and special instruction (vv.46-47).

2 Jesus' social development was normal.

a. **His parents left to return home (v.43a).**

b. **He was missing from the caravan (v.43b).**

c. **His parents thought He was with others, playing and socializing (v.44).**

d. **His parents returned to find Him (v.45).**
From what happened in these verses, we learn that Jesus' social development was normal. His parents had finished their worship obligations and were returning home to Nazareth. Jesus had remained behind, but they did not know it. They thought He was off playing and socializing with some of the other families and children in the caravan. The caravans were large, and the roads were packed with thousands of pilgrims leaving the Feast. We can glean from this that Jesus was sociable and fit right in with people. The very fact that His parents would think He was off socializing with others points to a normal social development. In fact, they were so sure that He was socializing that they did not bother to look for Him until nightfall (v.44). When they did not find Him among their relatives and friends, they returned to Jerusalem to search for Him.

43 And when the feast was ended, as they were returning, the boy Jesus stayed behind in Jerusalem. His parents did not know it,
44 but supposing him to be in the group they went a day's journey, but then they began to search for him among their relatives and acquaintances,
45 and when they did not find him, they returned to Jerusalem, searching for him.

THOUGHT 1. A child's social development is important. Children are to be helped and encouraged, led and directed to play with others. However, they must also be taught how be . . .

- patient
- giving
- joyful
- loving

- kind
- helpful
- peaceful

- loyal
- caring
- disciplined

In addition, they need to be taught to avoid . . .

- bragging
- being revengeful
- being arrogant

- being jealous
- being selfish
- being easily provoked.

Let all bitterness and wrath and anger and clamor and slander be put away from you, along with all malice. Be kind to one another, tenderhearted, forgiving one another, as God in Christ forgave you. (Ep.4:31–32)

But now you must put them all away: anger, wrath, malice, slander, and obscene talk from your mouth. . . . Put on then, as God's chosen ones, holy and beloved, compassionate hearts, kindness, humility, meekness, and patience, bearing with one another and, if one has a complaint against another, forgiving each other; as the Lord has forgiven you, so you also must forgive. And above all these put on love, which binds everything together in perfect harmony. (Col.3:8, 12–14)

2:46–47

⁴⁶ After three days they found him in the temple, sitting among the teachers, listening to them and asking them questions.
⁴⁷ And all who heard him were amazed at his understanding and his answers.

3 Jesus' knowledge was surprising.

It took Jesus' parents three days to find Him. Imagine their sense of panic and worry! When they at last found Him, Jesus was in the very place where classes and discussion took place among the doctors of theology and religion. It was a prominent place, and it was a custom to hold open classes and discussions so that the public could listen and learn. At this point, Luke stresses the surprising knowledge of Jesus.

Of all the places a twelve-year-old boy could be, Jesus chose to go to the place where God's Word was discussed and taught—a remarkable fact!

a. **He was found in the temple among the teachers, learning and asking questions (v.46).**
Joseph and Mary found Jesus in the temple, sitting among the teachers of God's law. There were some very prominent Jewish scholars in that day, men who were very capable theologically. Among them were . . .

- Gamaliel, the great teacher of Saul (later called Paul) of Tarsus
- Hillel, one of the most revered liberal teachers with a large school of followers (see DEEPER STUDY # 1—Mt.19:1–12)
- Shammai, one of the most revered conservative teachers who also had a school of followers (see DEEPER STUDY # 1—Mt.19:1–12)
- Jonathan, who paraphrased the sacred books
- Simeon, who was to later succeed Hillel
- Nicodemus, who was so revered by his peers that he was sent to interview Jesus alone

Some of these scholars were probably engaged in the discussion with Jesus, for news of the young boy and his unparalleled understanding must have swept through the halls of the temple, stirring the curiosity of the most brilliant teachers. Remember, Jesus had been in the temple for at least three days. The point to note is how Jesus was making use of the opportunity He had. He was in Jerusalem exposed to these eminent scholars for only a few days, so He grasped the opportunity to learn—and perhaps teach—all He could.

Jesus had an unusual thirst for spiritual knowledge and understanding. Scripture expressly says that He was *listening* (Gk. akouonta, *ah-koo-on'-tah*) to what the teachers said. He listened closely, attentively, with rapt attention. He was "quick to hear" (Jas.1:19).

Scripture also reports that Jesus was *asking them questions* (eperotonta autous, *eh-per-oh-tone'-tah au-toos'*). He wanted answers, more understanding. He thirsted for truth and sought it.

b. He amazed everyone with the depth of His understanding and knowledge (v.47).

Perhaps most remarkable, Jesus *answered* their questions. Consider how unusual and amazing this fact was—and would be today: a twelve-year-old boy answering the questions of the greatest theologians of the day! His knowledge and understanding were so extraordinary that everyone was astonished, even the doctors—the master teachers. *Amazed* or *astonished* (existanto, *ex-is-tahn'-tow*) means that all were overwhelmed, bewildered, and perplexed at His understanding. Literally, it means they were beside themselves (2 Co.5:13), out of their minds with amazement.

> And coming to his hometown he taught them in their synagogue, so that they were astonished, and said, "Where did this man get this wisdom and these mighty works?" (Mt.13:54)

> The Jews therefore marveled, saying, "How is it that this man has learning, when he has never studied?" (Jn.7:15)

> In whom are hidden all the treasures of wisdom and knowledge. (Col.2:3)

> I have more understanding than all my teachers, for your testimonies are my meditation. I understand more than the aged, for I keep your precepts. (Ps.119:99–100)

> For to us a child is born, to us a son is given; and the government shall be upon his shoulder, and his name shall be called Wonderful Counselor, Mighty God, Everlasting Father, Prince of Peace. (Is.9:6)

> And the Spirit of the Lord shall rest upon him, the Spirit of wisdom and understanding, the Spirit of counsel and might, the Spirit of knowledge and the fear of the Lord. (Is.11:2)

THOUGHT 1. Jesus' thirst for God's Word teaches a striking lesson for both children and adults. We should *thirst* for knowledge and understanding, grasping every opportunity to learn the truth.

> So Jesus said to the Jews who had believed him, "If you abide in my word, you are truly my disciples, and you will know the truth, and the truth will set you free." (Jn.8:31–32)

> For this very reason, make every effort to supplement your faith with virtue, and virtue with knowledge. (2 Pe.1:5)

> Blessed is the one who finds wisdom, and the one who gets understanding. (Pr.3:13)

> Get wisdom; get insight; do not forget, and do not turn away from the words of my mouth. (Pr.4:5)

> The heart of him who has understanding seeks knowledge, but the mouths of fools feed on folly. (Pr.15:14)

> Buy truth, and do not sell it; buy wisdom, instruction, and understanding. (Pr.23:23)

4 Jesus' mission was misunderstood by His parents.

2:48

Mary's words to Jesus reveal that His parents did not fully understand His mission. After three days of sheer distress, she rebuked Jesus rather sternly. However, she forgot who her son was. It is not that she was not to teach and discipline or direct Him; she was. But He was now a young man by law, and He was where He should be, going about His Father's business.

> [48] And when his parents saw him, they were astonished. And his mother said to him, "Son, why have you treated us so? Behold, your father and I have been searching for you in great distress."

THOUGHT 1. Too often distress and sorrow cause us to *forget who Jesus is*. We allow circumstances to cloud our minds, to disturb us and bring sorrow into our lives. Consequently, we soon *forget Jesus*, His understanding of the situation and His business of ministering to our needs.

> Only take care, and keep your soul diligently, lest you forget the things that your eyes have seen, and lest they depart from your heart all the days of your life. Make them known to your children and your children's children. (De.4:9)

5 Jesus' first known recognition of Messiahship was at an early age.

In response to Mary's rebuke, Jesus reminded Mary of who He was. His statement is extremely significant, for it is the first time recorded in Scripture of Jesus claiming to be the Son of God. This fact is seen even more clearly when Jesus' answer is studied.

2:49-50

⁴⁹ And he said to them, "Why were you looking for me? Did you not know that I must be in my Father's house?"
⁵⁰ And they did not understand the saying that he spoke to them.

First, Jesus called God His Father. Joseph was standing there, so Jesus was no doubt gentle in the way He worded His statement. Still, He was clear and definite in referring to God as His Father. Exactly *when* Jesus grasped that He was the Messiah, the Son of God, is not known; and frankly, all suggestions are pure speculation. But this fact is known: at age twelve, He was conscious of a *unique relationship with God*, a relationship unlike other children. God was His Father, and He was the Son of God, the *unique Son* in the sense that He alone had been begotten of the Father.

Second, Jesus was saying to His mother that His Father (God) had been looking after Him. He had been in His Father's house, about His Father's business, doing what His Father wanted Him to do. Therefore, He was under His Father's care and watchful eye. Mary had no need to worry; His Father was taking care of Him.

Third, Jesus was saying that He had work to do for His Father (God) even if that work was not understood. He could not go home with Joseph and Mary until He had finished His Father's work. He first had to do what His Father willed.

> But Jesus answered them, "My Father is working until now, and I am working." (Jn.5:17)
>
> We must work the works of him who sent me while it is day; night is coming, when no one can work. (Jn.9:4)
>
> Jesus answered them, "I told you, and you do not believe. The works that I do in my Father's name bear witness about me." (Jn.10:25)
>
> I glorified you on earth, having accomplished the work that you gave me to do. (Jn.17:4)

THOUGHT 1. We need to *place ourselves under* God's care and watchful eye. A decision to follow Christ as Lord causes God to adopt us as His child and places us under the Father's care.

> Therefore do not be anxious, saying, "What shall we eat?" or "What shall we drink?" or "What shall we wear?" For the Gentiles seek after all these things, and your heavenly Father knows that you need them all. But seek first the kingdom of God and his righteousness, and all these things will be added to you. Therefore do not be anxious about tomorrow, for tomorrow will be anxious for itself. Sufficient for the day is its own trouble. (Mt.6:31-34)
>
> So we can confidently say, "The Lord is my helper; I will not fear; what can man do to me?" (He.13:6)

THOUGHT 2. Every person is to serve God first, even if their work is not understood. And it is often not understood. Sometimes, even our families may not understand or oppose our decision to serve God. We must be faithful to God and His call even if we are misunderstood and opposed.

> Remember also your Creator in the days of your youth, before the evil days come and the years draw near of which you will say, "I have no pleasure in them." (Ec.12:1)

2:51

⁵¹ And he went down with them and came to Nazareth and was submissive to them. And his mother treasured up all these things in her heart.

6 Jesus' obedience to His parents was absolute.

What Jesus did next is both beautiful and striking. Jesus was *submissive* or *subject* to His parents; He obeyed them. As the Son of God, He set the perfect example of what a child should be to His parents. He obeyed His parents despite the fact . . .

- that Joseph was not His true father
- that He was stronger in spirit than His parents

- that He was filled with wisdom
- that God was His Father

> **Children, obey your parents in the Lord, for this is right. Honor your father and mother (this is the first commandment with a promise), that it may go well with you and that you may live long in the land. (Ep.6:1–3; see Col.3:20)**

> **But if a widow has children or grandchildren, let them first learn to show godliness to their own household and to make some return to their parents, for this is pleasing in the sight of God. (1 Ti.5:4)**

> **Even a child makes himself known by his acts, by whether his conduct is pure and upright. (Pr.20:11)**

> **Listen to your father who gave you life, and do not despise your mother when she is old. (Pr.23:22)**

Note that Mary again kept all these things in her heart. In humble faith she said nothing; neither did she discuss the matter with relatives or neighbors, nor did she boast in her Son and His uniqueness. She became quiet, humbly waiting on God to use Jesus as He so willed. In due time, she knew that God would reveal Him and His salvation to the world.

7 Jesus' upbringing was normal, and He grew in favor with both God and people.

The brief, simple statement of Scripture suggests that Jesus' upbringing and development were normal: He *increased* (see Deeper Study # 1). As ones who love Jesus, believers would relish in our Savior's experiences of His childhood and teen years. However, all that God's Spirit wants us to know is contained in this single verse.

> 52 And Jesus increased in wisdom and in stature and in favor with God and man.

- ➤ Mentally, Jesus increased or grew in wisdom. He learned from teachers and from personal study and thought just as all children learned. Yet He differed from other children in that He learned perfectly, coming short in nothing.
- ➤ Physically, Jesus grew normally just as all other children grow.
- ➤ Spiritually, Jesus increased in favor with God. He looked to God in perfect obedience, and God nurtured Him in His perfect favor.
- ➤ Socially, Jesus grew in favor with other people. He was friendly, loving, caring, helpful, unselfish, pure, honest, and humble. He was welcomed and embraced by other families in His community.

THOUGHT 1. Parents have a responsibility to see to it that their children develop and grow normally in the four areas of life mentioned in this verse. If parents do not oversee and direct their children's development, they will not become what they need to be and what God wants them to be.

1) Children need to be encouraged to seek learning. If not, most will take what is assigned and do the minimum that is required. They need encouragement from parents, teachers, pastors, and others to pursue excellence.
2) Some children do not develop physically, not like they should. Some are incapable due to deformity or abnormality. However, other children fail to develop as they should because they do not get the physical exercise necessary to develop. They sit around, watching television and playing with electronic devices instead of being outside playing and working. Sadly, many parents fail to set an example for their children in this area. And, because of their own inactivity, they fail to see to it that their children get the exercise they need.
3) Children's hearts are tender and open to following the Lord. Their innocent minds are receptive to God's truth. Parents must introduce their children to Jesus and teach them His Word. They must set an example of obedience to and dependence on Christ. They must see to their children's spiritual development just as they provide for their education and physical needs.

4) Some children do not follow Jesus' example in developing socially. Some children are not welcomed by other families. Again, parents are usually to blame. Parents must both teach and model God's principles for human relationships and social behavior.

DEEPER STUDY # 1

(2:52) **Increased** (proekopten, *pro-ehk'-op-ten*): means to grow steadily, to keep advancing. The picture is that of Jesus' cutting His way through the advancing years just as a pioneer cuts through the wilderness to reach his destination.

CHAPTER 3

II. THE SON OF MAN'S COMING, 3:1–4:15

A. The Forerunner, John the Baptist: Launched the Pivotal Point in History, 3:1–6

(Mt.3:1–6; Mk.1:2–6; Jn.1:19–28)

In the fifteenth year of the reign of Tiberius Caesar, Pontius Pilate being governor of Judea, and Herod being tetrarch of Galilee, and his brother Philip tetrarch of the region of Ituraea and Trachonitis, and Lysanias tetrarch of Abilene,

1. John launched the most pivotal point in history

² during the high priesthood of Annas and Caiaphas, the word of God came to John the son of Zechariah in the wilderness.

2. John was called out of the wilderness

³ And he went into all the region around the Jordan, proclaiming a baptism of repentance for the forgiveness of sins.

3. John preached repentance and forgiveness of sin

⁴ As it is written in the book of the words of Isaiah the prophet, "The voice of one crying in the wilderness: 'Prepare the way of the Lord, make his paths straight.

4. John cried out prophetically (warning the world): Prepare, make the Lord's paths straight

⁵ Every valley shall be filled, and every mountain and hill shall be made low, and the crooked shall become straight, and the rough places shall become level ways,

  a. The humble will be exalted
  b. The proud will be made low
  c. The crooked and rough paths will be made straight and smooth

⁶ and all flesh shall see the salvation of God.'"

  d. The world will see God's salvation

Division II

The Son of Man's Coming, 3:1–4:15

A. The Forerunner, John the Baptist: Launched the Pivotal Point in History, 3:1–6

(Mt.3:1–6; Mk.1:2–6; Jn.1:19–28)

3:1–6
Introduction

The coming of Jesus Christ was the pivotal point of human history. When He came to earth, the world saw the Son of God Himself (1 Jn.1:1-3). Christ's impact upon the world can never be overstated. He changed the world so much that earth's years are numbered from the point of His coming.

Scripture declares that Jesus is coming to earth again. When He came the first time, He came as a Savior. However, He will not return as a Savior, but as a Judge—*the* Judge who will prove that He is the King of kings and Lord of lords, the God Incarnate, the Messiah. He is going to prove that He is the Salvation of God Almighty.

A Person of such magnitude, the Person whose coming was to be the pivotal point of history, needed a forerunner. He needed someone who could run ahead of Him and stir people to prepare for His coming. That forerunner was John the Baptist, a man who is an example to us all. This is, *The Forerunner, John the Baptist: Launched the Pivotal Point in History,* 3:1-6.

1. John launched the most pivotal point in history (v.1).
2. John was called out of the wilderness (v.2).
3. John preached repentance and forgiveness of sin (v.3).
4. John cried out prophetically (warning the world): Prepare, make the Lord's paths straight (vv.4-6).

3:1-2a

In the fifteenth year of the reign of Tiberius Caesar, Pontius Pilate being governor of Judea, and Herod being tetrarch of Galilee, and his brother Philip tetrarch of the region of Ituraea and Trachonitis, and Lysanias tetrarch of Abilene,
² during the high priesthood of Annas and Caiaphas, the word of God came to John the son of Zechariah in the wilderness.

1 John launched the most pivotal point in history.

Many dispute that the coming of Christ is the most significant event in history, but Scripture proclaims that God will someday reveal this fact to all. Luke dates the public presentation of Christ by marking significant events and historical rulers. The very first event was God's call of John, the Lord's forerunner (v.2). His ministry launched the most pivotal point in history.

Tiberius, the second Roman Emperor, began his reign in A.D. 14. By the time God called John, Tiberius was in the fifteenth year of his reign (v.1a). Accordingly, John's ministry began between A.D. 28-29.

Shortly before Christ's coming, the situation had grown so bad in Judea that Rome had to remove Archelaus from civil control and move in a military commander. Pontius Pilate was appointed as both the civil ruler of the region and a military commander (v.1b). Therefore, a Roman authority ruled directly over Judea by this time. Pilate held office from A.D. 26-36.

Herod Antipas was tetrarch of Galilee (v.1c). Tetrarch simply means a ruler over a fourth part. The son of Herod the Great, Herod Antipas inherited his territory at his father's death and ruled from 4 B.C. to A.D. 39. Note that he was the ruler over Galilee, the area where Jesus spent most of His time ministering (see DEEPER STUDIES 1, 2—Mt.14:1-14 for more discussion).

Philip was tetrarch of Ituraea and Trachonitis (v.1d). He was a reputable leader and was regarded as fair and just. Caesarea Philippi, where Peter made his great confession, was built and named after him (Mt.16:13-20). Nothing of importance is known about Lysanias, tetrarch of Abilene (v.1e).

Annas and Caiaphas were the High Priests at the time (v.2a). This statement throws a revealing light upon the high priesthood of Jesus' day. It shows just how political and corrupt the high priesthood had become. There was never to be more than one priest at any given time, for the priesthood was supposed to be for life and was supposed to be hereditary. But with the coming of Roman rule, the position of High Priest became a political power base. Rome used the position to secure power over Jewish life. They offered and gave the position to men who were cooperative and willing to let the people follow Roman rule. Between 37 B.C. and A.D. 26, twenty-eight different men were installed and removed as High Priests.

The point Luke is making is just this: the High Priest's office had become corrupted, and religious positions had become politically motivated. Annas, who had served as High Priest between A.D. 7-14, was still the power behind the throne. Caiaphas was officially the High Priest in Rome's eyes, but Annas was still the one to whom most Jewish leaders looked. This is actually seen during the trials of Jesus. Jesus was taken first to Annas, despite the fact that he was not the official High Priest (Jn.18:13).

These details set the stage for the presentation of Jesus Christ to earth. It was a critical time in Jewish and world history, the time God had appointed to send the human race a Savior.

> And saying, "The time is fulfilled, and the kingdom of God is at hand; repent and believe in the gospel." (Mk.1:15)

> Who gave himself for our sins to deliver us from the present evil age, according to the will of our God and Father. (Gal.1:4)

2 John was called out of the wilderness.

The place where John was reared was so slightly populated that it was known as a wilderness. The area consisted of only six small towns or villages scattered far apart. This remote spot was where God's call came to John; God found him in the most obscure place.

² during the high priesthood of Annas and Caiaphas, the word of God came to John the son of Zechariah in the wilderness.

God's call to John was a very personal matter. In fact, he never revealed how God spoke to him. Did God call him through a vision, through the appearance of an angel, through an audible voice, or through an inner sense? We do not know. John kept the matter in his heart; it was just too intimate, too meaningful an experience. And his heart was genuine and pure. He was not willing to lower his intimacy with God by talking about it and boasting in it, that is, by acting super-spiritual.

God's call was for John to serve Him rather than to serve institutional religion. John's father, Zechariah, was a priest, and the priesthood was by descent. When God called John, he was approaching thirty years of age, the age when he was to become a full-fledged priest by descent. He was supposed to have been in training for some five years, and when he reached the age of thirty he was to begin serving in the temple. But God's call to John was to a different ministry, a ministry that fitted into God's plans much more than institutional religion.

THOUGHT 1. The place where a person is does not matter; a person's heart is what matters. If our hearts are right toward God, God will call us no matter where we are. No one is hidden from God, no matter how obscure his or her residence is. God knows where we are, and His Word is not limited; it reaches even to the wilderness.

THOUGHT 2. Our first loyalty should always be to God, not to institutional religion—not to a denomination, a spiritual leader, or a church. God moves *outside* institutional religion as well as *within* institutional religion. This truth is seen in the coming of Christ. God worked both through John, who operated outside of the temple, and also through Simeon, probably a priest, and Anna, a prophetess within the temple (2:25–38). Note two facts.

1) *Institutional religionists* often frown and oppose those ministering *outside* their institution. They feel threatened, as though the *outside minister* is against them. Sometimes they are right; the outsider is sometimes against them. But if the outside minister is truly ministering for the Lord, there should be support and encouragement. However, too often cooperation is not given, for fear of the loss of authority, position, and security; therefore, they oppose *outside ministers*. Such motives are corrupt and need to be corrected. Ministers, both within and without institutional religion, need to be about God's call and business. They should not be wasting time struggling against each other. Time is too short, and God's call comes to people both within and without institutional religion. Each needs to support the other in God's calling.

2) We must serve God as He calls and wills. While God sometimes guides us through the counsel of others, we need to ultimately listen to what He says to *us*—what He communicates to our spirit through His Spirit. We need to always serve Him in the way *He* calls us to serve.

> You did not choose me, but I chose you and appointed you that you should go and bear fruit and that your fruit should abide, so that whatever you ask the Father in my name, he may give it to you. (Jn.15:16)

All this is from God, who through Christ reconciled us to himself and gave us the ministry of reconciliation; . . . Therefore, we are ambassadors for Christ, God making his appeal through us. We implore you on behalf of Christ, be reconciled to God. (2 Co.5:18, 20)

Of this gospel I was made a minister according to the gift of God's grace, which was given me by the working of his power. (Ep.3:7)

I thank him who has given me strength, Christ Jesus our Lord, because he judged me faithful, appointing me to his service. (1 Ti.1:12)

3:3

³ And he went into all the region around the Jordan, proclaiming a baptism of repentance for the forgiveness of sins.

3 John preached repentance and forgiveness of sin.

John preached "a baptism of repentance for the forgiveness of sins." His message to those who wanted to be forgiven of their sins was that they needed to repent and proclaim their repentance publicly through baptism. Baptism was the sign to their neighbors and the world that that they were repenting because they wanted God to forgive their sins. The order is as follows:

➢ A person wanted God's forgiveness of their sins.
➢ The person therefore made a decision to repent, to turn from sinful ways, and to change their lifestyle (see note and Deeper Study # 1—Ac.17:29-30).
➢ The person was immediately baptized.

John's message emphasized two simple truths. First, forgiveness of sins is conditional. People must repent to receive God's forgiveness.

Second, if a person's repentance is genuine, they will be baptized. Baptism follows repentance. Baptism is the immediate witness and sign that a person is repenting and changing their life. If a person is truly sincere in seeking God's forgiveness, truly sincere in turning away from sin and turning to God, they will be baptized. The Lord commands believers to be baptized. To refuse to be baptized is a sin of disobedience against God, a sin that reveals that a person is not genuinely repentant (see Deeper Study # 2—Mt.3:11; notes—Mk.1:3-5; Jn.1:24-26 for more detailed discussion on John's baptism).

And Peter said to them, "Repent and be baptized every one of you in the name of Jesus Christ for the forgiveness of your sins, and you will receive the gift of the Holy Spirit." (Ac.2:38)

I baptize you with water for repentance, but he who is coming after me is mightier than I, whose sandals I am not worthy to carry. He will baptize you with the Holy Spirit and fire. (Mt.3:11)

No, I tell you; but unless you repent, you will all likewise perish. (Lu.13:3)

Repent therefore, and turn back, that your sins may be blotted out. (Ac.3:19)

Cast away from you all the transgressions that you have committed, and make yourselves a new heart and a new spirit! Why will you die, O house of Israel? (Ezk.18:31)

"Yet even now," declares the LORD, "return to me with all your heart, with fasting, with weeping, and with mourning." (Joel 2:12)

3:4-6

⁴ As it is written in the book of the words of Isaiah the prophet, "The voice of one crying in the wilderness: 'Prepare the way of the Lord, make his paths straight.
⁵ Every valley shall be filled, and every mountain and hill shall be made low, and the crooked shall become straight, and the rough places shall become level ways,
⁶ and all flesh shall see the salvation of God.'"

4 John cried out prophetically (warning the world): Prepare, make the Lord's paths straight.

John warned the people that the Lord was coming. He called them to prepare the way for Him, to clear His path (see Deeper Study # 3—Mk.1:3). The Messiah's path was being made straight or smooth by John's preparing the people to receive Him (1:17). John called the people to prepare the way of the Lord into their individual hearts by repenting of their sins and seeking God's forgiveness. By turning from their sin, they would be ready to turn to Christ in faith, to believe in Him and receive the salvation He was bringing.

John quotes Isaiah 40:3-5 as his authority, identifying himself as the voice in the wilderness. As he proclaimed the points Isaiah had made, he was calling the people to prepare to meet the Lord. While these statements further develop the thought of the path of the Lord being made straight or smooth, they also teach spiritual lessons about the coming of Christ to the world.

a. The humble will be exalted (v.5a).

John declared that the Lord would fill every valley. *Every valley* refers to the humble believers of the earth. *Filled* means that they would be received, enriched, raised up, and exalted by repenting and believing in Christ.

b. The proud will be made low (v.5b).

The mountains and hills represent the self-sufficient and the self-confident, the prideful and the boastful, the conceited and the arrogant. They too must prepare to meet the Lord. If they are too proud to repent, they will lose everything they have and be brought low. They will be leveled, made as the dust of the earth.

c. The crooked and rough paths will be made straight and smooth (v.5c).

Every human being is a crooked sinner who has been bent out of shape by our sinful nature. We can only be made straight by repenting of our sins and believing in the Lord. He alone can change our corrupted hearts. He alone can straighten us out.

The rough places or ways can symbolize the ways of hopelessness, helplessness, loneliness, emptiness, insecurity, guilt, shame, sin, death, false religion, and empty worship. The Lord can make all of these smooth. He can level the paths of our lives and make a way of joy and peace.

d. The world will see God's salvation (v.6).

God's salvation would be seen by all flesh. Not only the Jews, but all people would see the Messiah, God's salvation to the world. When the way was prepared, the Savior would appear. God's salvation would be made available to all the people of the world.

John's preaching stirred thousands to prepare and to look for the Messiah. Apparently, it was the multitude who listened to John who eventually became followers of Christ. It was also the same multitude who created the excitement needed to spread the news of the Messiah's coming.

THOUGHT 1. Just as John did, we need to call people today to prepare the way of the Lord. Jesus is coming again. Every human being must stand before Him in judgment; we must all face Him. The salvation of God is available to all people. Our call is the same as John's: to call people to repentance and to receive Christ.

> Therefore you also must be ready, for the Son of Man is coming at an hour you do not expect. (Mt.24:44)

> Therefore stay awake—for you do not know when the master of the house will come, in the evening, or at midnight, or when the rooster crows, or in the morning. (Mk.13:35)

> Sow for yourselves righteousness; reap steadfast love; break up your fallow ground, for it is the time to seek the LORD, that he may come and rain righteousness upon you. (Ho.10:12)

> Therefore thus I will do to you, O Israel; because I will do this to you, prepare to meet your God, O Israel! (Am.4:12)

1. John preached condemnation

⁷ He said therefore to the crowds that came out to be baptized by him, "You brood of vipers! Who warned you to flee from the wrath to come?

2. John preached repentance
3. John preached against pride

⁸ Bear fruits in keeping with repentance. And do not begin to say to yourselves, 'We have Abraham as our father.' For I tell you, God is able from these stones to raise up children for Abraham.

4. John preached judgment

⁹ Even now the axe is laid to the root of the trees. Every tree therefore that does not bear good fruit is cut down and thrown into the fire."

5. John preached love and care for others

¹⁰ And the crowds asked him, "What then shall we do?"

a. The people: Were to love and care enough to share their material possessions

¹¹ And he answered them, "Whoever has two tunics is to share with him who has none, and whoever has food is to do likewise."

b. The tax collectors: Were to love and care enough to stop exerting their authority and cheating people

¹² Tax collectors also came to be baptized and said to him, "Teacher, what shall we do?"

¹³ And he said to them, "Collect no more than you are authorized to do."

c. The soldiers: Were to love and care enough to provide security and service to the nation

¹⁴ Soldiers also asked him, "And we, what shall we do?" And he said to them,

Division II

The Son of Man's Appearance, 3:1–4:15

B. The Plain Message of John the Baptist: A Message for All Ages, 3:7–20

(see Mt.3:7–12; Mk.1:7–8)

3:7–20
Introduction

Preparation is a key to success in any endeavor. When God sent His Son into the world, He sent a special messenger, John, to prepare the way for Him. An intriguing character, John accomplished his mission. When Jesus at last emerged on the world stage, a host of people were watching and waiting for Him. Most likely, these people were the first Christ-followers. They were prepared to receive Christ because they had obeyed John's plain and powerful message. What John had commanded them to do is what we all must do before we can receive Christ and the forgiveness He has provided: we must repent. This is, *The Plain Message of John the Baptist: A Message for All Ages,* 3:7–20.

1. John preached condemnation (v.7).
2. John preached repentance (v.8).

"Do not extort money from anyone by threats or by false accusation, and be content with your wages."

¹⁵ As the people were in expectation, and all were questioning in their hearts concerning John, whether he might be the Christ,

¹⁶ John answered them all, saying, "I baptize you with water, but he who is mightier than I is coming, the strap of whose sandals I am not worthy to untie. He will baptize you with the Holy Spirit and fire.

¹⁷ His winnowing fork is in his hand, to clear his threshing floor and to gather the wheat into his barn, but the chaff he will burn with unquenchable fire."

¹⁸ So with many other exhortations he preached good news to the people.

¹⁹ But Herod the tetrarch, who had been reproved by him for Herodias, his brother's wife, and for all the evil things that Herod had done,

²⁰ added this to them all, that he locked up John in prison.

6. John preached the Messiah's coming

    a. The Messiah's person
    b. The Messiah's baptism*DS1*

    c. The Messiah's judgment*DS2*

7. John preached many other truths

8. John preached against sin in high places
    a. He preached against the ruler's sin

    b. The result: Herod had John arrested

3. John preached against pride (v.8).
4. John preached judgment (v.9).
5. John preached love and care for others (vv.10–14).
6. John preached the Messiah's coming (vv.15–17).
7. John preached many other truths (v.18).
8. John preached against sin in high places (vv.19–20).

1 John preached condemnation.

John boldly preached the truth about people, telling them what they *were* and what they *had become.* They were "vipers," poisonous. They had allowed themselves to be poisoned and were now poisoning others. They were sick and doomed, and they were biting others, injecting their poisonous beliefs into them. God knew exactly what they were, and His wrath was coming upon them (see vv.8, 17). John

⁷ He said therefore to the crowds that came out to be baptized by him, "You brood of vipers! Who warned you to flee from the wrath to come?"

warned them that they needed to flee from the condemnation they were facing.

Matthew clarifies that John was speaking specifically to Israel's religious leaders, the Pharisees and the Sadducees (Mt.3:7). Jesus would later refer to them exactly as John did, as a "brood of vipers" (Mt.12:34; 23:33). John "saw straight through those [religious leaders] wanting to be baptized. They wanted one more credential behind their name, one more religious act they could tell everyone about."[1] As the teachers and leaders of the people, their judgment would be stricter than that of the people; they faced a "greater condemnation" (Jas.3:1, KJV).

> Whoever believes in the Son has eternal life; whoever does not obey the Son shall not see life, but the wrath of God remains on him. (Jn.3:36)

> For you may be sure of this, that everyone who is sexually immoral or impure, or who is covetous (that is, an idolater), has no inheritance in the kingdom of Christ and God. Let no one deceive you with empty words, for because of these things the wrath of God comes upon the sons of disobedience. (Ep.5:5–6)

> Kiss the Son, lest he be angry, and you perish in the way, for his wrath is quickly kindled. Blessed are all who take refuge in him. (Ps.2:12)

3:8a

[8] "Bear fruits in keeping with repentance. And do not begin to say to yourselves, 'We have Abraham as our father.' For I tell you, God is able from these stones to raise up children for Abraham."

2 John preached repentance.

John preached that people—including the religious leaders—needed to repent, and they should live in a way that demonstrates that they have genuinely repented; they should "bear fruits." Note that a person must first repent, then bear fruit. And the fruit must be consistent with repentance—fruit that shows a changed heart and a turning away from sin (see notes—Lu.3:3; note and Deeper Study # 1—Ac.17:29-30).

Thought 1. Genuine repentance bears fruit—the fruit of a changed life. There is no salvation without repentance, and there is no repentance without a changed life. We need to examine our lives for the fruits of repentance, examine ourselves to be sure we are truly "in the faith" (2 Co.13:5).

> No, I tell you; but unless you repent, you will all likewise perish. (Lu.13:3)

> So as to walk in a manner worthy of the Lord, fully pleasing to him: bearing fruit in every good work and increasing in the knowledge of God. (Col.1:10)

> Cast away from you all the transgressions that you have committed, and make yourselves a new heart and a new spirit! Why will you die, O house of Israel? (Ezk.18:31)

3:8b

[8] "Bear fruits in keeping with repentance. And do not begin to say to yourselves, 'We have Abraham as our father.' For I tell you, God is able from these stones to raise up children for Abraham."

3 John preached against pride.

John confronted the people's pride as Jews (see note—Ro.12:16; see 1 Co.4:10; 5:6). Many of the people—especially the religious leaders—believed they were acceptable to God simply because they were Jews, that is, because they were children of Abraham and of godly forefathers. They felt the righteousness of their fathers had saved them, and how they lived mattered little. They believed they were saved because they were *special*—special enough to be acceptable to God (see Deeper Study # 1—Ro.4:1-25). They thought that "they were guaranteed God's blessings and that the promise given to the patriarchs was guaranteed to all their descendants, no matter how they acted or what they believed."[1]

Many felt acceptable to God because they had undergone a religious ritual, that of circumcision. Consequently, they viewed the baptism John was mandating as simply a new ritual they needed to undergo.

John straightly informed these people that God could fulfill His covenant with Abraham apart from them. If the Lord so chose, He could take the stones of the wilderness and raise up spiritual descendants of Abraham (Ga.3:7-11).

---

1 Phillip W. Comfort and Grant R. Osborne, eds., *Life Application Bible Commentary*, (Carol Stream, IL: Tyndale House Publishers, 1996). Via Wordsearch digital edition

THOUGHT 1. Many people are prideful. They feel they are special enough to be acceptable to God, that God would never reject them. They feel acceptable because they . . .

- have godly parents
- have been baptized
- are not too bad
- are good enough

- are blessed with so much
- are somewhat religious
- are members of a church
- are regular worshipers

However, we can only be acceptable to God if we repent and believe in Jesus Christ.

Salvation is not inherited or hereditary. God has no grandchildren. Neither is salvation attained through submitting to some ritual or performing good works. The only way of salvation is through repentance and faith.

> He also told this parable to some who trusted in themselves that they were righteous, and treated others with contempt. (Lu.18:9)

> Know then that it is those of faith who are the sons of Abraham. And the Scripture, foreseeing that God would justify the Gentiles by faith, preached the gospel beforehand to Abraham, saying, "In you shall all the nations be blessed." So then, those who are of faith are blessed along with Abraham, the man of faith. For all who rely on works of the law are under a curse; for it is written, "Cursed be everyone who does not abide by all things written in the Book of the Law, and do them." Now it is evident that no one is justified before God by the law, for "The righteous shall live by faith." (Ga.3:7-11)

> For by grace you have been saved through faith. And this is not your own doing; it is the gift of God, not a result of works, so that no one may boast. (Ep.2:8-9)

> There are those who are clean in their own eyes but are not washed of their filth. (Pr.30:12)

4 John preached judgment.

John warned the people—especially the religious leaders—that they must all face God's judgment. He illustrated the coming judgment with the image of a woodman cutting down unfruitful trees:

> [9] "Even now the axe is laid to the root of the trees. Every tree therefore that does not bear good fruit is cut down and thrown into the fire."

- ➢ God is the Divine Woodman who cuts down the trees.
- ➢ The axe is already lying at the roots of the trees.
- ➢ The trees are *not yet* cut down, but all people are warned.
- ➢ There are many trees: some lofty (the proud), some stately (leaders), some diseased, some bearing good fruit, some bearing bad fruit, and some bearing no fruit at all.
- ➢ All trees that do not bear good fruit will be cut down and cast into the fire (see DEEPER STUDY # 4—Lu.16:24; DEEPER STUDY # 2—Mt.5:22).

> If anyone does not abide in me he is thrown away like a branch and withers; and the branches are gathered, thrown into the fire, and burned. (Jn.15:6)

> But now the righteousness of God has been manifested apart from the law, although the Law and the Prophets bear witness to it— the righteousness of God through faith in Jesus Christ for all who believe. For there is no distinction: for all have sinned and fall short of the glory of God. (Ro.3:21-23)

> But if it bears thorns and thistles, it is worthless and near to being cursed, and its end is to be burned. (He.6:8)

> For it is time for judgment to begin at the household of God; and if it begins with us, what will be the outcome for those who do not obey the gospel of God? And "If the righteous is scarcely saved, what will become of the ungodly and the sinner?" (1 Pe.4:17-18)

> Awake, you drunkards, and weep, and wail, all you drinkers of wine, because of the sweet wine, for it is cut off from your mouth. (Joel 1:5)

> For behold, the day is coming, burning like an oven, when all the arrogant and all evildoers will be stubble. The day that is coming shall set them ablaze, says the Lord of hosts, so that it will leave them neither root nor branch. (Mal.4:1)

5 John preached love and care for others.

John's blunt, fiery preaching stirred the people. Three different groups of people asked John how repentance would affect their lives, just what a changed life would mean. What kind of fruit should they bear? John answered in the most practical terms, explaining that genuine repentance would reveal itself primarily in the way they treated others.

3:10-14

¹⁰ And the crowds asked him, "What then shall we do?"

¹¹ And he answered them, "Whoever has two tunics is to share with him who has none, and whoever has food is to do likewise."

¹² Tax collectors also came to be baptized and said to him, "Teacher, what shall we do?"

¹³ And he said to them, "Collect no more than you are authorized to do."

¹⁴ Soldiers also asked him, "And we, what shall we do?" And he said to them, "Do not extort money from anyone by threats or by false accusation, and be content with your wages."

a. **The people: Were to love and care enough to share their material possessions (v.11).**

The first group was the crowds—the common, ordinary people. If they truly repented, they would love and care enough to share their material goods with those who were in need. John mentioned clothing and food, the basic necessities of life. Those who had *two tunics*—more than they needed—would share with those who had none. Likewise, they would share their food with the needy. Genuine repentance would transform them from being selfish to being gripped with mercy and unselfishness. They would give what they had. Such fruit would be evidence of repentance, of a life truly changed.

b. **The tax collectors: Were to love and care enough to stop exerting their authority and cheating people (vv.12-13).**

The tax collectors who wanted to be baptized asked the same question. If they truly repented, John replied, these despised government agents would love and care enough about others to stop exerting their authority and cheating people. Tax collectors in Jesus' day were so despised because they represented the Roman government and levied more taxes than necessary, pocketing the excess. A tax collector who genuinely repented would become a man of justice and fairness. He would love and care for others enough to treat them fairly and respectfully, to not take advantage of them just because he could.

c. **The soldiers: Were to love and care enough to provide security and service to the nation (v.14).**

The soldiers who came to John were probably Jews who had joined the Roman army or who had been drafted into service by the Roman government. Many soldiers abused their authority by extorting money, food, or other possessions from the common people or by forcing them to serve them (Mt.5:41). John said that soldiers who had genuinely repented would no longer abuse the people. Instead, they would be respectful and loving, truthful and honest, contented and responsible. He made this clear to the soldiers by specifying three ways they commonly abused people.

First, they would not extort money through intimidation. The Greek word for *extort money* or *intimidate* (diaseisete, *dee-as-ay-say'-teh*) means to shake violently, agitate, terrify. The idea is that some extorted money by terrifying people. Roman soldiers were, of course, posted to protect the interests of Rome. It was common for soldiers to allow illegal things to go on for a bribe.

Second, they would not accuse anybody falsely. If people did not pay a bribe or otherwise do what a soldier demanded, they were often falsely accused by the soldier.

Third, they would be content with their wages. Dissatisfaction and grumbling over wages was a common complaint of soldiers, and it often was the root of their extorting from common people. True repentance would make them content with what the Roman government paid them.

What then were the fruits that demonstrated a person was truly repenting? Very practically, *"the fruits of righteousness"* (Ph.1:11; see v.8). Genuine repentance is demonstrated by a changed life, especially in the way we treat others.

But the fruit of the Spirit is love, joy, peace, patience, kindness, goodness, faithfulness, gentleness, self-control; against such things there is no law. (Ga.5:22–23)

. . . (for the fruit of light is found in all that is good and right and true). (Ep.5:9)

And it is my prayer that your love may abound more and more, with knowledge and all discernment, so that you may approve what is excellent, and so be pure and blameless for the day of Christ, filled with the fruit of righteousness that comes through Jesus Christ, to the glory and praise of God. (Ph.1:9–11)

But the wisdom from above is first pure, then peaceable, gentle, open to reason, full of mercy and good fruits, impartial and sincere. (Jas.3:17)

6 John preached the Messiah's coming.

3:15–17

John's preaching was so powerful that the people questioned in their hearts if *he* were the Messiah (v.15). Sensing their thoughts, John cleared the air. He stated in no uncertain terms that he was not the one for whom the people were looking. He stressed three ways in which the Messiah would be greater than he.

a. The Messiah's person (v.16a).

The Messiah would be mightier and more worthy than John, both in person and work (baptism and judgment, vv.16–17). John made this unquestionably clear, stating that he was not worth the rank of a slave before Christ. Slaves were the ones who loosed the sandals and washed the feet of guests. He was as *nothing* before the Lord. What an attitude of humility!

15 As the people were in expectation, and all were questioning in their hearts concerning John, whether he might be the Christ, 16 John answered them all, saying, "I baptize you with water, but he who is mightier than I is coming, the strap of whose sandals I am not worthy to untie. He will baptize you with the Holy Spirit and fire. 17 His winnowing fork is in his hand, to clear his threshing floor and to gather the wheat into his barn, but the chaff he will burn with unquenchable fire."

b. The Messiah's baptism (v.16b).

The people were lined up before John to be baptized, but John made it clear that his baptism was far inferior to the baptism the Messiah would bring. The Messiah would not baptize people with water, but with the Holy Spirit and fire (see DEEPER STUDY # 1).

c. The Messiah's judgment (v.17).

The Messiah would be able to judge who was genuinely repentant and who was not. John could only take people at their word, but the Messiah would see their hearts. In the same way a farmer separated the wheat from the chaff, the Messiah would separate genuine believers from false believers. Note the meaning of the terms John uses in this illustration:

➢ The *winnowing fork* or *fan* (Gk. ptuon, *ptoo'-on*) is a symbol of the Messiah's power to pick out both the wheat and the chaff.
➢ The *threshing floor* is the earth which will be purged or cleansed of all chaff.
➢ The *wheat* represents believers who truly repent and bring forth fruit. They will be gathered into His barn (His kingdom or the new heavens and earth).
➢ The *chaff* represents those who only profess, who are counterfeit wheat. They lie on the floor (the earth) with the wheat, but they are not wheat. They will "[be burned] with unquenchable fire" (see DEEPER STUDY # 2).

DEEPER STUDY # 1

(3:16) **Baptism:** the word *baptize* (baptizo, *bap-tee'-zo*) means to dip, to immerse, to submerge, to place into. John's baptism was with water, but Jesus' baptism was *"with"* or *"in* (Greek, en) the Spirit and fire."

1. John's baptism was both a preparation and a symbol of the spiritual baptism that Jesus was to bring. John's water baptism meant two things.

First, it symbolized cleansing from all sin. The person was being prepared for the cleansing that Christ would provide.

Second, it symbolized separation or dedication. The person was setting their life apart to God in a renewed spirit of dedication. They were committing themselves to the Christ about whom John was preaching.

2. Jesus' spiritual baptism is a double baptism. The Greek preposition translated here as "with" is usually translated as "in" throughout the New Testament. Hence, it is accurate to say that the Messiah would baptize "in the Spirit and fire."

First, Jesus baptizes the person *in the Spirit*. He dips, immerses, and places the person in the Spirit. A person may be carnal and materialistic, but once they have been baptized into the Spirit by Christ, they become spiritually minded (Ro.8:5-7). The Jews had longed and looked for the day when the Spirit would come. The prophets had predicted His coming time and again; therefore, the people knew exactly what John was prophesying (see Ezk.36:26-27; 37:14; 39:29; Is.44:3; Joel 2:28). Note: John's baptism was called "the baptism of repentance"; that is, the person who repented was baptized. There could be no question; it was understood. If one repented and actually turned to the Lord, they were baptized.

Second, Jesus baptized the person *in fire*. Fire has several functions that graphically symbolize the work of Christ. It illuminates, warms, melts, burns, and utterly destroys. The difference between baptism with water and fire is the difference between an outward work and an inward work. Water only cleanses the outside; fire purifies within, that is, the heart.

Jesus Christ separates a person from their former life and purifies them within by the fire of His Holy Spirit. It should be noted that in John's mind the "baptism of fire" meant that the Messiah was to destroy the enemies of Israel. It was "the messianic fire of judgment" that was to come from the throne of David (see DEEPER STUDY # 2—Mt.1:18; notes—11:1-6; 11:2-3; DEEPER STUDY # 1—11:5; DEEPER STUDY # 2—11:6; note—Lu.7:21-23).

DEEPER STUDY # 2

(3:17) **Unquenchable Fire** (puri asbesto): this literally reads "with fire unquenchable." It is fire that cannot be quenched, snuffed out, extinguished. The idea is that the fire is everlasting, burning on and on and never ending (see DEEPER STUDY # 3—Mt.25:41).

3:18

[18] So with many other exhortations he preached good news to the people.

7 John preached many other truths.

In addition to repentance and baptism, John preached many other truths. Note the word *exhortations* (Gk. parakalon, *par-ahk-ah-lone'*). It is actually a verb which means to admonish, urge, beseech, entreat. John pierced the ears and the hearts of the people; he pressed and pressed upon the people their need to prepare for the coming of the Lord.

Now in a great house there are not only vessels of gold and silver but also of wood and clay, some for honorable use, some for dishonorable. Therefore, if anyone cleanses himself from what is dishonorable, he will be a vessel for honorable use, set apart as holy, useful to the master of the house, ready for every good work. (2 Ti.2:20-21)

"Yet even now," declares the LORD, "return to me with all your heart, with fasting, with weeping, and with mourning; and rend your hearts and not your garments." Return to the LORD your God, for he is gracious and merciful, slow to anger, and abounding in steadfast love; and he relents over disaster. (Joel 2:12-13)

8 John preached against sin in high place.

a. He preached against the ruler's sin (v.19).

b. The result: Herod had John arrested (v.20).

John was a bold preacher who neither feared nor sought the favor of any person. He even rebuked the ruler Herod for his evil life and carnal excess, for his terrible sin of adultery. John's faithfulness to proclaim the truth—even to those in high places—cost him his freedom, as Herod put him in prison. Ultimately, it cost him his life (see Deeper Study # 1—Mt.14:1-14).

> **19** But Herod the tetrarch, who had been reproved by him for Herodias, his brother's wife, and for all the evil things that Herod had done,
>
> **20** added this to them all, that he locked up John in prison.

> Now the works of the flesh are evident: sexual immorality, impurity, sensuality, idolatry, sorcery, enmity, strife, jealousy, fits of anger, rivalries, dissensions, divisions, envy, drunkenness, orgies, and things like these. I warn you, as I warned you before, that those who do such things will not inherit the kingdom of God. (Ga.5:19-21)

> It was also about these that Enoch, the seventh from Adam, prophesied, saying, "Behold, the Lord comes with ten thousands of his holy ones, to execute judgment on all and to convict all the ungodly of all their deeds of ungodliness that they have committed in such an ungodly way, and of all the harsh things that ungodly sinners have spoken against him." (Jude 14-15)

> Then the Spirit of God clothed Zechariah the son of Jehoiada the priest, and he stood above the people, and said to them, "Thus says God, 'Why do you break the commandments of the Lord, so that you cannot prosper? Because you have forsaken the Lord, he has forsaken you.'" (2 Chr.24:20)

C. The Baptism of Jesus: Obedience and God's Approval, 3:21–22

(Mt.3:13–17; Mk.1:9–11; Jn.1:29–34)

1. Jesus' obedience
   a. He was obedient along with the people
   b. He was obedient in prayer
2. God's signs of approval
   a. The heavens were opened, v.21
   b. The Spirit descended
   c. The voice of God spoke

²¹ Now when all the people were baptized, and when Jesus also had been baptized and was praying, the heavens were opened,

²² and the Holy Spirit descended on him in bodily form, like a dove; and a voice came from heaven, "You are my beloved Son; with you I am well pleased."

Division II

The Son of Man's Appearance, 3:1–4:15

C. The Baptism of Jesus: Obedience and God's Approval, 3:21–22

(Mt.3:13–17; Mk.1:9–11; Jn.1:29–34)

3:21–22
Introduction

Baptism is an outward picture of what takes places within us when we repent and believe in Jesus Christ unto salvation. This truth raises a question: why, then, was Jesus baptized? He was not a sinner. He was absolutely holy within and without. He had no need of salvation, no sins to be cleansed of. To the contrary, He was the ideal and perfect man, the only one who could provide salvation to the sinful human race.

While salvation is an outward picture of our salvation, it is something more. It is a step of obedience to God. This is one of the reasons Jesus was baptized, and it is one of the reasons we are to be baptized. This is, *The Baptism of Jesus: Obedience and God's Approval, 3:21–22.*

1. Jesus' obedience (v.21).
2. God's signs of approval (v.22).

3:21

²¹ Now when all the people were baptized, and when Jesus also had been baptized and was praying, the heavens were opened,

1 Jesus' obedience.

Baptism is an act of obedience to God. Jesus was baptized out of obedience to God. His obedience to His heavenly Father is seen in two acts.

a. He was obedient along with the people.

Jesus obeyed God by being baptized with the people. Note the words, "When all the people were baptized." Some scholars say Jesus was baptized *after* all the people were baptized; others *while* they were being baptized. It does not matter which is actually the case. The point is, Jesus was in the midst of the people, *obeying* God with them. He was doing exactly what God wanted, identifying with the people.

One thing sets these people apart from the rest of the public. They heard John's message and responded, doing exactly what God required. They were obeying God's call, doing what was right, obeying righteousness. Again, note that Jesus was baptized "when all the people were baptized," right along with them. He was doing at least two things (see outline and notes—Mt.3:13; 3:15; Mk.1:9-11 for more discussion).

First, Jesus was demonstrating that He, the Son of God, was *fulfilling all righteousness* (see note—Mt.5:17-18). He, too, was being obedient to God, *fulfilling every requirement* of God for humanity.

Second, Jesus was demonstrating His humiliation, that He was man, fully man. As man He was required to live obediently to God just as other people were. There was one difference, however; Jesus lived a sinless life, and by such He became the perfect and ideal man, the pattern for all people (see DEEPER STUDY # 3—Mt.8:20).

THOUGHT 1. Every individual should respond to the gospel of God; that is, they should seek God's forgiveness for their sins, repent, and be baptized. This is God's will for every human being. Every person should obey God and fulfill all righteousness. Baptism is an act of obedience; it is obeying God right along with other believers.

> **Then Jesus came from Galilee to the Jordan to John, to be baptized by him. John would have prevented him, saying, "I need to be baptized by you, and do you come to me?" But Jesus answered him, "Let it be so now, for thus it is fitting for us to fulfill all righteousness." Then he consented. (Mt.3:13-15)**

> **Whoever believes and is baptized will be saved, but whoever does not believe will be condemned. (Mk.16:16)**

> **Baptism, which corresponds to this, now saves you, not as a removal of dirt from the body but as an appeal to God for a good conscience, through the resurrection of Jesus Christ. (1 Pe.3:21)**

THOUGHT 2. By being baptized, Jesus showed His identification with the human race. No person is above any other person, not in the eyes of God. God's own Son had to obey Him; He had to be baptized as a *sign of obedience* to God. We, too, are to be baptized if we are truly repenting and seeking God to forgive our sins. We are not above God's will and His instruction to "repent and be baptized" (Ac.2:38).

> **Go therefore and make disciples of all nations, baptizing them in the name of the Father and of the Son and of the Holy Spirit, teaching them to observe all that I have commanded you. And behold, I am with you always, to the end of the age. (Mt.28:19-20)**

> **And Peter said to them, "Repent and be baptized every one of you in the name of Jesus Christ for the forgiveness of your sins, and you will receive the gift of the Holy Spirit." (Ac.2:38)**

> **And now why do you wait? Rise and be baptized and wash away your sins, calling on his name. (Ac.22:16)**

b. **He was obedient in prayer.**

While Jesus was being baptized, He was praying. His mind and thoughts were on God. He was in fellowship and communion with God. This is as it should be. Why would any person's mind be elsewhere while they are being baptized if they are sincere?

➤ Baptism is an *outward* sign of God's working *within* our hearts. The *inward working* and *inward grace of God is sought by prayer*. Thus, *true* baptism is the first act whereby we show that we are in communion with God.

➤ Baptism, the first significant act of discipleship, will be followed by a changed life. A changed life demonstrates that we have genuinely repented and sought God to forgive our sins. Therefore, even while we are being baptized, we should be in a spirit of prayer seeking God's grace and strength as we walk out into a wicked world.

➤ Baptism launches the new life of the believer. Baptism is to be our first act as a repenting believer, the first confession to the public that we want to change our lives and live for God (see DEEPER STUDY # 1—Ac.2:38 for more discussion). *Baptism is the first public confession of our inward prayer of confession to God.* Thus baptism, the outward public confession to other people, should follow right on the heels of our inward private confession to God. The spirit of prayer that started it all should be the same spirit of prayer that finishes it all. The prayer that confessed to God privately should continue right on through to the prayer that confesses to the public at large. In fact, from the very moment of the inward prayer of our confession to God, our hearts should continue in a spirit of prayer right on through life. Our very spirit should be a spirit of continued prayer. Such was Jesus' obedience in prayer. Such is to be our obedience in prayer. An unbroken communion with God in prayer is the longing of God for each of us.

THOUGHT 1. Throughout His earthly life, Jesus taught us the critical importance of prayer, both by precept and by His example. God wants us to live in fellowship with and in total dependence on Him. God promises to supply us with everything we need. His divine provision—whether for strength, wisdom, courage, forgiveness, material needs, power, or anything else—is received through prayer. We fail to receive because we fail to pray (Jas.4:2). Of all the elements of the Christian life, prayer is surely the most vital.

> And he told them a parable to the effect that they ought always to pray and not lose heart. (Lu.18:1)

> Rejoice in hope, be patient in tribulation, be constant in prayer. (Ro.12:12)

> Praying at all times in the Spirit, with all prayer and supplication. To that end, keep alert with all perseverance, making supplication for all the saints. (Ep.6:18)

> Continue steadfastly in prayer, being watchful in it with thanksgiving. (Col.4:2)

> Pray without ceasing. (1 Th.5:17)

> Evening and morning and at noon I utter my complaint and moan, and he hears my voice. (Ps.55:17)

3:22

²² and the Holy Spirit descended on him in bodily form, like a dove; and a voice came from heaven, "You are my beloved Son; with you I am well pleased."

2 God's signs of approval.

When Jesus was baptized, God was very pleased. Likewise, when we are baptized, God is very pleased, for we are *obeying* and *following* in the steps of Jesus. God showed His approval of His Son's baptism in three ways.

a. The heavens were opened (v.21).

When Jesus was baptized, the heavenly Father did an unusual thing: He opened the heavens. What was His purpose for this supernatural act?

First, God opened the heavens to give Jesus a very special sight and sense of God's glory and presence. The Lord's baptism was the launch of His ministry to the people of the world. He needed a special glimpse of His Father's glory along with the stamp of God's approval and power (see Ac.7:56; Ezk.1:1).

Second, God opened the heavens that day to reveal to John and perhaps to the others standing there (if the opening of heaven were visible to all) that Jesus was truly the Lamb of God who takes away the sin of the world (Jn.1:29). The classic commentator Matthew Henry remarks, "He that by his power parted the waters, to make a way through them to Canaan, now by his power parted the air, another fluid element, to open a correspondence with the heavenly Canaan. Thus was there opened to Christ, and by him to us, a new and living way into the holiest; sin had shut up heaven, but Christ's prayer opened it again."[1]

b. The Spirit descended.

The Holy Spirit descended on Jesus in "bodily form like a dove." The dove was a sacred bird to the Jews. It was a symbol of peace and gentleness, of purity and innocence. But even more significant, it was often identified with the Spirit of God. When the dove descended upon Jesus, it was the Spirit of God Himself coming upon Jesus. He was descending upon Jesus to identify Jesus as the Messiah and to endow Jesus with the power of God (see outline and notes—Mk.1:9-10). John went out of his way to stress that the Spirit's descent upon Jesus was unique: He descended, and He remained upon Jesus (Jn.1:32-33). The Holy Spirit entered the life of Jesus once for all, permanently and powerfully, in His full manifestation and unlimited power.

---

1 *Matthew Henry's Commentary on the Whole Bible,* (p.d.). Via Wordsearch edition.

c. The voice of God spoke.

God speaks to people in a number of ways, but He spoke to the world in an unusual—out of the ordinary—way when His Son was baptized: God spoke audibly. His actual voice was heard (2 Pe.1:17; see note—Mt.3:16-17). The God of heaven and earth *personally* testified that Jesus was His Son. The Father's audible pronouncement from heaven fulfilled two Messianic prophecies:[2]

➤ "You are My beloved Son" fulfilled Psalm 2:7:

> I will tell of the decree: The Lord said to me, "You are my Son; today I have begotten you."

➤ "With you I am well pleased" fulfilled Isaiah 42:1:

> Behold my servant, whom I uphold, my chosen, in whom my soul delights; I have put my Spirit upon him; he will bring forth justice to the nations.

THOUGHT 1. When we genuinely obey God and are baptized, God is pleased. He shows His approval in the same three ways.

1) God opens heaven up to us and gives us a very special sense of His presence, a sense of His approval, a sense that we are pleasing Him immensely.

> Blessed be the God and Father of our Lord Jesus Christ, who has blessed us in Christ with every spiritual blessing in the heavenly places. (Ep.1:3)

> But God, being rich in mercy, because of the great love with which he loved us, even when we were dead in our trespasses, made us alive together with Christ—by grace you have been saved— and raised us up with him and seated us with him in the heavenly places in Christ Jesus. (Ep.2:4-6)

2) God manifests and reveals His Spirit to us in a very special sense. We are obeying Him, and significant moments of obedience bring special manifestations of the Spirit (see note—Jn.14:21).

> Whoever has my commandments and keeps them, he it is who loves me. And he who loves me will be loved by my Father, and I will love him and manifest myself to him. (Jn.14:21)

> But, as it is written, "What no eye has seen, nor ear heard, nor the heart of man imagined, what God has prepared for those who love him"— these things God has revealed to us through the Spirit. For the Spirit searches everything, even the depths of God. (1 Co.2:9-10)

> In him we have redemption through his blood, the forgiveness of our trespasses, according to the riches of his grace, which he lavished upon us, in all wisdom and insight making known to us the mystery of his will, according to his purpose, which he set forth in Christ as a plan for the fullness of time, to unite all things in him, things in heaven and things on earth. (Ep.1:7-10)

> The mystery hidden for ages and generations but now revealed to his saints. To them God chose to make known how great among the Gentiles are the riches of the glory of this mystery, which is Christ in you, the hope of glory. (Col.1:26-27)

3) God's Word is heard. The fact that we are baptized is a sign that we have heard His command to be baptized, and because we are obeying Him, He continues to speak to us day by day as we seek His will in the Bible and prayer.

> That which we have seen and heard we proclaim also to you, so that you too may have fellowship with us; and indeed our fellowship is with the Father and with his Son Jesus Christ. (1 Jn.1:3)

> Behold, I stand at the door and knock. If anyone hears my voice and opens the door, I will come in to him and eat with him, and he with me. (Rev.3:20)

---

2 Douglas Sean O'Donnell. R. Kent Hughes, ed., *Matthew: All Authority in Heaven and on Earth* (Preaching the Word Commentary series), (Wheaton, IL: Crossway, 2013). Via Wordsearch digital edition.

D. The Genealogy of Jesus: The Roots of the Messiah,[DS1] 3:23–38

(Mt.1:1-17)

1. **Jesus was about thirty years of age when He began His ministry**

2. **Jesus is the Davidic heir: To be the Messianic King (see vv. 24–31, esp. v. 31, the son of David)**

3. **Jesus is the Adamic heir: To be the Messianic High Priest (see vv. 32–38, esp. v. 38, the son of Adam)**

4. **Jesus is the Godly heir: To be the Son of God, the Messianic Prophet of God**

[23] Jesus, when he began his ministry, was about thirty years of age, being the son (as was supposed) of Joseph, the son of Heli,

[24] the son of Matthat, the son of Levi, the son of Melchi, the son of Jannai, the son of Joseph,

[25] the son of Mattathias, the son of Amos, the son of Nahum, the son of Esli, the son of Naggai,

[26] the son of Maath, the son of Mattathias, the son of Semein, the son of Josech, the son of Joda,

[27] the son of Joanan, the son of Rhesa, the son of Zerubbabel, the son of Shealtiel, the son of Neri,

[28] the son of Melchi, the son of Addi, the son of Cosam, the son of Elmadam, the son of Er,

[29] the son of Joshua, the son of Eliezer, the son of Jorim, the son of Matthat, the son of Levi,

[30] the son of Simeon, the son of Judah, the son of Joseph, the son of Jonam, the son of Eliakim,

[31] the son of Melea, the son of Menna, the son of Mattatha, the son of Nathan, the son of David,

[32] the son of Jesse, the son of Obed, the son of Boaz, the son of Sala, the son of Nahshon,

[33] the son of Amminadab, the son of Admin, the son of Arni, the son of Hezron, the son of Perez, the son of Judah,

[34] the son of Jacob, the son of Isaac, the son of Abraham, the son of Terah, the son of Nahor,

[35] the son of Serug, the son of Reu, the son of Peleg, the son of Eber, the son of Shelah,

[36] the son of Cainan, the son of Arphaxad, the son of Shem, the son of Noah, the son of Lamech,

[37] the son of Methuselah, the son of Enoch, the son of Jared, the son of Mahalaleel, the son of Cainan,

[38] the son of Enos, the son of Seth, the son of Adam, the son of God.

Division II

The Son of Man's Appearance, 3:1–4:15

D. The Genealogy of Jesus: The Roots of the Messiah, 3:23–38

(Mt.1:1–17)

What proof is there that Jesus was the Messiah, the Son of God? Perhaps the most powerful evidence is that, when Jesus was baptized, God the Father spoke audibly from heaven, declaring that Jesus is His Son (v.22; Mt.3:17; Mk.1:11). Along with Matthew and Mark, Luke reports this extraordinary fact. In this passage, Luke offers another proof, a phenomenal point. He says that even the roots of Jesus, His genealogy, prove He is the Messiah (see DEEPER STUDY # 1). His roots give Him the right to claim Messiahship, to claim that He is the Savior, the Son of God. This is, *The Genealogy of Jesus: The Roots of the Messiah, 3:23–38.*

1. Jesus was about thirty years of age when He began His ministry (v.23).
2. Jesus is the Davidic heir: To be the Messianic King (see 24–31, esp. 31, the son of David) (vv.24–31).
3. Jesus is the Adamic heir: To be the Messianic High Priest (see 32–38, esp. 38, the son of Adam) (vv.32–38).
4. Jesus is the Godly heir: To be the Son of God, the Messianic Prophet of God (v.38).

DEEPER STUDY # 1

(3:23-38) **Jesus, Genealogy:** two significant facts are presented here. First, Luke follows Mary's line (genealogy), the line of Jesus' mother. Second, he traces Mary's line all the way back to Adam. By doing so, he shows that God's Son actually became a man. Jesus was the promised Messiah. Luke is writing to Gentiles who placed great emphasis on a transcendental God, a God way out in space someplace who was thought to be far removed from the day-to-day affairs of humans. Luke had to show that Jesus was a man, fully human. He was a man born of a woman, full of emotions and feelings and personal day-to-day experiences just like all other human beings.

Matthew's genealogy is different (Mt.1:1). Matthew was writing primarily to Jews who placed great emphasis on pure lineage. An impure lineage deprived a Jew of their nationality, of their right to be called a Jew; and tragically, this meant that they lost their right to be called a child of God. To combat this problem, Matthew traces Joseph's line all the way back through King David and Abraham, the founding father of Israel. He does this to show that Jesus had the legal right to the throne of David and to the promises made to Abraham. This is not to say that Jesus was the actual physical son of Joseph, but rather as the Son of God, Jesus was sent into the family of Joseph. By such He became the legal heir of Joseph (see DEEPER STUDY # 3—Mt.1:16; DEEPER STUDY # 2—Jn.8:23). This meant two things. First, Jesus was legally of the pure line of the Jewish nation. He fulfilled the Old Testament prophecies that said the Messiah would be born of the Jewish nation. Second, as a Jew and as the Son of God, Jesus had the legal right to claim Messiahship. He had the legal right to the throne of David and to the promises made to Abraham (see DEEPER STUDY # 1—Jn.4:22; DEEPER STUDY # 1—Ro.4:1-25; see Ge.12:1-3).

1 Jesus was about thirty years of age when He began His ministry.

Jesus did not launch His ministry until He was about thirty years of age. Why did He wait until He was this age? Some might reason that He could have helped so many more people if He had started ministering at a younger age. However, Jesus waited until He was thirty for some significant reasons, reasons that were important to validating and fulfilling His earthly ministry. Thirty was the age when the Levites began their work (Nu.4:47), and it was also the age when a Scribe was allowed to begin his teaching ministry. In addition, a man was thought to reach full development and maturity at the age of thirty.

3:23

23 Jesus, when he began his ministry, was about thirty years of age, being the son (as was supposed) of Joseph, the son of Heli,

Now, note a crucial point. Jesus needed to live thirty years as other people lived, learning and maturing in the day-to-day routine of life and responsibility (see He.5:8). Why? There are four primary reasons:

First, Jesus needed to prove faithful, to secure righteousness right down where people live, right in the day-to-day duties . . .

- of work (carpenter by trade)
- of family (became head of the house when Joseph died)
- of physical growth (grew and matured as all people do, day by day)
- of mental growth (studied and learned as all people do)
- of spiritual growth (sought God as all people should)

Second, Jesus needed to show (demonstrate, paint the picture of) how people should live in the routine of day-to-day living.

Third, Jesus needed to learn from the day-to-day experiences of life (as Man)—learn so that He could teach others from experience exactly how they should live.

Fourth, Jesus needed to learn from day-to-day experiences so He could better help people throughout their lives. By persevering through the experiences of life, He could better help people press on through their day-to-day experiences (see note—Lu.2:40 for detailed discussion).

> Therefore he had to be made like his brothers in every respect, so that he might become a merciful and faithful high priest in the service of God, to make propitiation for the sins of the people. For because he himself has suffered when tempted, he is able to help those who are being tempted. (He.2:17–18)

> Since then we have a great high priest who has passed through the heavens, Jesus, the Son of God, let us hold fast our confession. For we do not have a high priest who is unable to sympathize with our weaknesses, but one who in every respect has been tempted as we are, yet without sin. (He.4:14–15)

> Although he was a son, he learned obedience through what he suffered. (He.5:8)

3:24–31

24 the son of Matthat, the son of Levi, the son of Melchi, the son of Jannai, the son of Joseph,
25 the son of Mattathias, the son of Amos, the son of Nahum, the son of Esli, the son of Naggai,
26 the son of Maath, the son of Mattathias, the son of Semein, the son of Josech, the son of Joda,
27 the son of Joanan, the son of Rhesa, the son of Zerubbabel, the son of Shealtiel, the son of Neri,
28 the son of Melchi, the son of Addi, the son of Cosam, the son of Elmadam, the son of Er,
29 the son of Joshua, the son of Eliezer, the son of Jorim, the son of Matthat, the son of Levi,
30 the son of Simeon, the son of Judah, the son of Joseph, the son of Jonam, the son of Eliakim,
31 the son of Melea, the son of Menna, the son of Mattatha, the son of Nathan, the son of David,

2 Jesus is the Davidic heir: To be the Messianic King.

Luke traces the genealogy of Christ back to David, showing that Jesus was qualified to be the Messianic King because He was the Davidic heir (v.31). God had given to David and His seed (the Messiah) the promise of eternal government (2 Sa.7:12; Ps.39:3f; 132:11). The Jews believed these promises of God. Therefore Jesus, "who is called Christ" (Mt.1:16), was indeed the promised Son of Abraham, the promised Son of David (Mt.1:1).

Note how often Jesus was called the son of David (see Mt.12:23; 15:22; 20:30-31; 21:9, 15; Ac.2:29-36; Ro.1:3; 2 Ti.2:8; Re.22:16). It was the common title and popular concept of the Messiah. Generation after generation of Jews looked for the promised deliverer of Israel. The people expected Him to be a valiant, mighty general who would deliver and restore the nation to its greatness. In fact, they expected Him to make the nation the center of universal rule. He would, under God's authority, conquer the world and center the glory and majesty of God Himself in Jerusalem. And from His throne, the throne of David, He would execute "the Messianic fire of judgment" upon the nations and peoples of the world. (See DEEPER STUDY # 2—Mt.1:18; DEEPER STUDY # 3—3:11; notes—11:1-6; 11:2-3; DEEPER STUDY # 1—11:5; DEEPER STUDY # 2—11:6; Lu.7:21-23. Referring to these notes will show what the Jewish concept of the Messiah was.) Luke gave this detailed genealogy of Christ for a clear purpose: if he can prove that Jesus' roots (genealogy) go all the way back to David and Adam, then he will have shown how seriously one must take the claims of Jesus to be the Messiah (see DEEPER STUDY # 2—Mt.1:18).

The Messianic King was prophesied again and again in Scripture:

He shall build a house for my name, and I will establish the throne of his kingdom forever. (2 Sa.7:13)

You delivered me from strife with the people; you made me the head of the nations; people whom I had not known served me. (Ps.18:43)

May he have dominion from sea to sea, and from the River to the ends of the earth! . . . May all kings fall down before him, all nations serve him! (Ps.72:8, 11)

You have said, "I have made a covenant with my chosen one; I have sworn to David my servant: 'I will establish your offspring forever, and build your throne for all generations.' " Selah. (Ps.89:3-4)

Of old you spoke in a vision to your godly one, and said: "I have granted help to one who is mighty; I have exalted one chosen from the people. I have found David, my servant; with my holy oil I have anointed him, so that my hand shall be established with him; my arm also shall strengthen him. I will crush his foes before him and strike down those who hate him." (Ps.89:19-21, 23)

And I will make him the firstborn, the highest of the kings of the earth. . . . I will establish his offspring forever and his throne as the days of the heavens. His offspring shall endure forever, his throne as long as the sun before me. Like the moon it shall be established forever, a faithful witness in the skies. Selah. (Ps.89:27, 29, 36-37)

The LORD says to my Lord: "Sit at my right hand, until I make your enemies your footstool." The LORD sends forth from Zion your mighty scepter. Rule in the midst of your enemies! (Ps.110:1-2)

The LORD swore to David a sure oath from which he will not turn back: "One of the sons of your body I will set on your throne. . . . There I will make a horn to sprout for David; I have prepared a lamp for my anointed. His enemies I will clothe with shame, but on him his crown will shine." (Ps.132:11, 17-18)

He shall judge between the nations, and shall decide disputes for many peoples; and they shall beat their swords into plowshares, and their spears into pruning hooks; nation shall not lift up sword against nation, neither shall they learn war anymore. (Is.2:4)

In the year that King Uzziah died I saw the Lord sitting upon a throne, high and lifted up; and the train of his robe filled the temple. (Is.6:1)

For to us a child is born, to us a son is given; and the government shall be upon his shoulder, and his name shall be called Wonderful Counselor, Mighty God, Everlasting Father, Prince of Peace. Of the increase of his government and of peace there will be no end, on the throne of David and over his kingdom, to establish it and to uphold it with justice and with righteousness from this time forth and forevermore. The zeal of the LORD of hosts will do this. (Is.9:6-7)

There shall come forth a shoot from the stump of Jesse, and a branch from his roots shall bear fruit. . . . In that day the root of Jesse, who shall stand as a signal for the peoples—of him shall the nations inquire, and his resting place shall be glorious. (Is.11:1, 10)

Behold, a king will reign in righteousness, and princes will rule in justice. (Is.32:1)

Your eyes will behold the king in his beauty; they will see a land that stretches afar. (Is.33:17)

Behold, the Lord GOD comes with might, and his arm rules for him; behold, his reward is with him, and his recompense before him. (Is.40:10)

How beautiful upon the mountains are the feet of him who brings good news, who publishes peace, who brings good news of happiness, who publishes salvation, who says to Zion, "Your God reigns." (Is.52:7)

Behold, my servant shall act wisely; he shall be high and lifted up, and shall be exalted. (Is.52:13)

Behold, the days are coming, declares the LORD, when I will raise up for David a righteous Branch, and he shall reign as king and deal wisely, and shall execute justice and righteousness in the land. In his days Judah will be saved, and Israel will dwell securely. And this is the name by which he will be called: "The LORD is our righteousness." (Je.23:5-6)

But they shall serve the Lord their God and David their king, whom I will raise up for them. (Je.30:9)

For thus says the Lord: David shall never lack a man to sit on the throne of the house of Israel. (Je.33:17)

Thus says the Lord God: Remove the turban and take off the crown. Things shall not remain as they are. Exalt that which is low, and bring low that which is exalted. A ruin, ruin, ruin I will make it. This also shall not be, until he comes, the one to whom judgment belongs, and I will give it to him. (Ezk.21:26–27)

My servant David shall be king over them, and they shall all have one shepherd. They shall walk in my rules and be careful to obey my statutes. They shall dwell in the land that I gave to my servant Jacob, where your fathers lived. They and their children and their children's children shall dwell there forever, and David my servant shall be their prince forever. (Ezk.37:24–25)

Then the iron, the clay, the bronze, the silver, and the gold, all together were broken in pieces, and became like the chaff of the summer threshing floors; and the wind carried them away, so that not a trace of them could be found. But the stone that struck the image became a great mountain and filled the whole earth. (Da.2:35)

And in the days of those kings the God of heaven will set up a kingdom that shall never be destroyed, nor shall the kingdom be left to another people. It shall break in pieces all these kingdoms and bring them to an end, and it shall stand forever. (Da.2:44)

I saw in the night visions, and behold, with the clouds of heaven there came one like a son of man, and he came to the Ancient of Days and was presented before him. And to him was given dominion and glory and a kingdom, that all peoples, nations, and languages should serve him; his dominion is an everlasting dominion, which shall not pass away, and his kingdom one that shall not be destroyed. (Da.7:13–14)

Know therefore and understand that from the going out of the word to restore and build Jerusalem to the coming of an anointed one, a prince, there shall be seven weeks. Then for sixty-two weeks it shall be built again with squares and moat, but in a troubled time. (Da.9:25)

Afterward the children of Israel shall return and seek the Lord their God, and David their king, and they shall come in fear to the Lord and to his goodness in the latter days. (Ho.3:5)

The Lord roars from Zion, and utters his voice from Jerusalem, and the heavens and the earth quake. But the Lord is a refuge to his people, a stronghold to the people of Israel. "So you shall know that I am the Lord your God, who dwells in Zion, my holy mountain. And Jerusalem shall be holy, and strangers shall never again pass through it." (Joel 3:16–17)

In that day I will raise up the booth of David that is fallen and repair its breaches, and raise up its ruins and rebuild it as in the days of old. (Am.9:11)

He shall judge between many peoples, and shall decide disputes for strong nations far away; and they shall beat their swords into plowshares, and their spears into pruning hooks; nation shall not lift up sword against nation, neither shall they learn war anymore. (Mi.4:3)

But you, O Bethlehem Ephrathah, who are too little to be among the clans of Judah, from you shall come forth for me one who is to be ruler in Israel, whose coming forth is from of old, from ancient days. . . . And he shall stand and shepherd his flock in the strength of the Lord, in the majesty of the name of the Lord his God. And they shall dwell secure, for now he shall be great to the ends of the earth. (Mi.5:2, 4)

The Lord has taken away the judgments against you; he has cleared away your enemies. The King of Israel, the Lord, is in your midst; you shall never again fear evil. (Zep.3:15)

And say to him, "Thus says the Lord of hosts, 'Behold, the man whose name is the Branch: for he shall branch out from his place, and he shall build the temple of the Lord. It is he who shall build the temple of the Lord and shall bear royal honor, and shall sit and rule on his throne. And there shall be a priest on his throne, and the counsel of peace shall be between them both.' " (Zec.6:12–13)

Rejoice greatly, O daughter of Zion! Shout aloud, O daughter of Jerusalem! Behold, your king is coming to you; righteous and having salvation is he, humble and mounted on a donkey, on a colt, the foal of a donkey. I will cut off the chariot from Ephraim and the war horse from Jerusalem; and the battle bow shall be cut off, and he shall speak peace to the nations; his rule shall be from sea to sea, and from the River to the ends of the earth. (Zec.9:9–10)

The New Testament clearly establishes that Jesus Christ is the Messianic King:

Saying, "Where is he who has been born king of the Jews? For we saw his star when it rose and have come to worship him." . . . " 'And you, O Bethlehem, in the land of Judah, are by no means least among the rulers of Judah; for from you shall come a ruler who will shepherd my people Israel.' " (Mt.2:2, 6)

The Son of Man will send his angels, and they will gather out of his kingdom all causes of sin and all law-breakers. (Mt.13:41)

When the Son of Man comes in his glory, and all the angels with him, then he will sit on his glorious throne. (Mt.25:31)

Now Jesus stood before the governor, and the governor asked him, "Are you the King of the Jews?" Jesus said, "You have said so." (Mt.27:11)

And Jesus came and said to them, "All authority in heaven and on earth has been given to me." (Mt.28:18)

He will be great and will be called the Son of the Most High. And the Lord God will give to him the throne of his father David, and he will reign over the house of Jacob forever, and of his kingdom there will be no end. (Lu.1:32-33)

Nathanael answered him, "Rabbi, you are the Son of God! You are the King of Israel!" (Jn.1:49)

Jesus answered, "My kingdom is not of this world. If my kingdom were of this world, my servants would have been fighting, that I might not be delivered over to the Jews. But my kingdom is not from the world." Then Pilate said to him, "So you are a king?" Jesus answered, "You say that I am a king. For this purpose I was born and for this purpose I have come into the world—to bear witness to the truth. Everyone who is of the truth listens to my voice." (Jn.18:36-37)

Pilate also wrote an inscription and put it on the cross. It read, "Jesus of Nazareth, the King of the Jews." (Jn.19:19)

God exalted him at his right hand as Leader and Savior, to give repentance to Israel and forgiveness of sins. (Ac.5:31)

For to this end Christ died and lived again, that he might be Lord both of the dead and of the living. (Ro.14:9)

But each in his own order: Christ the firstfruits, then at his coming those who belong to Christ. Then comes the end, when he delivers the kingdom to God the Father after destroying every rule and every authority and power. For he must reign until he has put all his enemies under his feet. The last enemy to be destroyed is death. (1 Co.15:23-26)

That he worked in Christ when he raised him from the dead and seated him at his right hand in the heavenly places, far above all rule and authority and power and dominion, and above every name that is named, not only in this age but also in the one to come. And he put all things under his feet and gave him as head over all things to the church. (Ep.1:20-22)

Therefore God has highly exalted him and bestowed on him the name that is above every name, so that at the name of Jesus every knee should bow, in heaven and on earth and under the earth, and every tongue confess that Jesus Christ is Lord, to the glory of God the Father. (Ph.2:9-11)

Which he will display at the proper time—he who is the blessed and only Sovereign, the King of kings and Lord of lords, who alone has immortality, who dwells in unapproachable light, whom no one has ever seen or can see. To him be honor and eternal dominion. Amen. (1 Ti.6:15-16)

But when Christ had offered for all time a single sacrifice for sins, he sat down at the right hand of God, waiting from that time until his enemies should be made a footstool for his feet. (He.10:12-13)

Who has gone into heaven and is at the right hand of God, with angels, authorities, and powers having been subjected to him. (1 Pe.3:22)

And from Jesus Christ the faithful witness, the firstborn of the dead, and the ruler of kings on earth. To him who loves us and has freed us from our sins by his blood and made us a kingdom, priests to his God and Father, to him be glory and dominion forever and ever. Amen. Behold, he is coming with the clouds, and every eye will see him, even those who pierced him, and all tribes of the earth will wail on account of him. Even so. Amen. (Re.1:5-7)

And to the angel of the church in Philadelphia write: "The words of the holy one, the true one, who has the key of David, who opens and no one will shut, who shuts and no one opens." (Re.3:7)

The one who conquers, I will grant him to sit with me on my throne, as I also conquered and sat down with my Father on his throne. (Re.3:21)

And I looked, and behold, a white horse! And its rider had a bow, and a crown was given to him, and he came out conquering, and to conquer. (Re.6:2)

Then the kings of the earth and the great ones and the generals and the rich and the powerful, and everyone, slave and free, hid themselves in the caves and among the rocks of the mountains, calling to the mountains and rocks, "Fall on us and hide us from the face of him who is seated on the throne, and from the wrath of the Lamb, for the great day of their wrath has come, and who can stand?" (Re.6:15-17)

Then the seventh angel blew his trumpet, and there were loud voices in heaven, saying, "The kingdom of the world has become the kingdom of our Lord and of his Christ, and he shall reign forever and ever." (Re.11:15)

And I heard a loud voice in heaven, saying, "Now the salvation and the power and the kingdom of our God and the authority of his Christ have come, for the accuser of our brothers has been thrown down, who accuses them day and night before our God." (Re.12:10)

Then I looked, and behold, a white cloud, and seated on the cloud one like a son of man, with a golden crown on his head, and a sharp sickle in his hand. (Re.14:14)

They will make war on the Lamb, and the Lamb will conquer them, for he is Lord of lords and King of kings, and those with him are called and chosen and faithful. (Re.17:14)

Then I saw heaven opened, and behold, a white horse! The one sitting on it is called Faithful and True, and in righteousness he judges and makes war. His eyes are like a flame of fire, and on his head are many diadems, and he has a name written that no one knows but himself. . . . From his mouth comes a sharp sword with which to strike down the nations, and he will rule them with a rod of iron. He will tread the winepress of the fury of the wrath of God the Almighty. On his robe and on his thigh he has a name written, King of kings and Lord of lords. (Re.19:11–12, 15–16)

Blessed and holy is the one who shares in the first resurrection! Over such the second death has no power, but they will be priests of God and of Christ, and they will reign with him for a thousand years. (Re.20:6)

(Also see topical Bibles or reference works: God and Jesus Christ, Kingdom of.)

3:32–38

³² the son of Jesse, the son of Obed, the son of Boaz, the son of Sala, the son of Nahshon,
³³ the son of Amminadab, the son of Admin, the son of Arni, the son of Hezron, the son of Perez, the son of Judah,
³⁴ the son of Jacob, the son of Isaac, the son of Abraham, the son of Terah, the son of Nahor,
³⁵ the son of Serug, the son of Reu, the son of Peleg, the son of Eber, the son of Shelah,
³⁶ the son of Cainan, the son of Arphaxad, the son of Shem, the son of Noah, the son of Lamech,
³⁷ the son of Methuselah, the son of Enoch, the son of Jared, the son of Mahalaleel, the son of Cainan,
³⁸ the son of Enos, the son of Seth, the son of Adam, the son of God.

3 Jesus is the Adamic heir: To be the Messianic High Priest.

Luke proceeds to trace the genealogy of Christ all the way back to Adam to demonstrate that Jesus was the Adamic heir (v.38)—He was qualified to be the Messianic High Priest, the Perfect High Priest who represents humanity before God and God before humanity. This was the very *function* of the High Priest: to represent humanity before God and God before humanity. The High Priest bore the name of God before the people, and He carried the names of the people before God (Ro.8:33–34; Heb.2:17; 9:24; 1 Jn.2:1–2; see Is.49:16). In relation to the Messiah, this meant two things.

First, the Messiah must *know humans perfectly*, and He must *know God perfectly*. He must be the perfect God-Man in person, in being, in essence. He had to be a man, yes, but He also had to be God Incarnate in human flesh. He had to be born of Adam, that is, of Adam's seed, of human flesh; but He also had to possess the very nature of God. This was the only way humanity could ever have a perfect High Priest. It was absolutely necessary—because of the very nature of a depraved world—that a perfect High Priest be *perfect God-perfect man*.

Second, the Messiah must also *be able to represent God before humanity*, represent God perfectly; and He must *be able to represent humanity before God*, represent man perfectly. As Scripture says "[Messiah must] be faithful to Him who appointed Him" (He.3:2).

The Messiah had to live as perfect God in order to represent God to the human race. The Messiah also had to live as perfect Man (never sinning) in order to represent the human race before God (if man was to be represented as perfect before God). Scripture declares that Jesus did live a perfect life, that He never sinned (2 Co.5:21; He.4:15; 9:28; 3:5).

The Messianic High Priest was typified by two men or priests in the Old Testament:

➤ By Melchizedek.

And Melchizedek king of Salem brought out bread and wine. (He was priest of God Most High.) And he blessed him and said, "Blessed be Abram by God Most High, Possessor of heaven and earth; and blessed be God Most High, who has delivered your enemies into your hand!" And Abram gave him a tenth of everything. (Ge.14:18–20)

The LORD has sworn and will not change his mind, "You are a priest forever after the order of Melchizedek." (Ps.110:4)

➤ By Aaron.

Then you shall bring Aaron and his sons to the entrance of the tent of meeting and shall wash them with water and put on Aaron the holy garments. And you shall anoint him and consecrate him, that he may serve me as priest. You shall bring his sons also and put coats on them, and anoint them, as you anointed their father, that they may serve me as priests. And their anointing shall admit them to a perpetual priesthood throughout their generations. (Ex.40:12-15)

The Messianic High Priest was prophesied in Scripture:

Their prince shall be one of themselves; their ruler shall come out from their midst; I will make him draw near, and he shall approach me, for who would dare of himself to approach me? declares the LORD. And you shall be my people, and I will be your God. (Je.30:21-22. Note how the governor draws near in High Priestly fashion.)

And say to him, "Thus says the LORD of hosts, 'Behold, the man whose name is the Branch: for he shall branch out from his place, and he shall build the temple of the LORD. It is he who shall build the temple of the LORD and shall bear royal honor, and shall sit and rule on his throne. And there shall be a priest on his throne, and the counsel of peace shall be between them both.' " (Zec.6:12-13)

The New Testament clearly establishes that Jesus Christ is the Messianic High Priest:

Therefore, holy brothers, you who share in a heavenly calling, consider Jesus, the apostle and high priest of our confession, who was faithful to him who appointed him, just as Moses also was faithful in all God's house. (He.3:1-2)

Since then we have a great high priest who has passed through the heavens, Jesus, the Son of God, let us hold fast our confession. For we do not have a high priest who is unable to sympathize with our weaknesses, but one who in every respect has been tempted as we are, yet without sin. Let us then with confidence draw near to the throne of grace, that we may receive mercy and find grace to help in time of need. (He.4:14-16)

And no one takes this honor for himself, but only when called by God, just as Aaron was. So also Christ did not exalt himself to be made a high priest, but was appointed by him who said to him, "You are my Son, today I have begotten you"; Although he was a son, he learned obedience through what he suffered. And being made perfect, he became the source of eternal salvation to all who obey him. (He.5:4-5, 8-9). (See outline—He.4:14-5:10 for overview. See outlines—He.4:14-7:28 for full picture.)

4 Jesus is the Godly heir: To be the Son of God, the Messianic Prophet of God.

Jesus is the Godly heir, the Son of God, the One qualified to be the Messianic Prophet of God Himself. God acted directly in sending the world Jesus, the Second Adam, just as He acted directly in creating the first Adam. Jesus was sent directly by God to be the Messianic Prophet of God. Jesus Christ Himself proclaimed what the Messianic Prophet of God was to do:

[38] the son of Enos, the son of Seth, the son of Adam, the son of God.

And he came to Nazareth, where he had been brought up. And as was his custom, he went to the synagogue on the Sabbath day, and he stood up to read. And the scroll of the prophet Isaiah was given to him. He unrolled the scroll and found the place where it was written, "The Spirit of the Lord is upon me, because he has anointed me to proclaim good news to the poor. He has sent me to proclaim liberty to the captives and recovering of sight to the blind, to set at liberty those who are oppressed, to proclaim the year of the Lord's favor." And he rolled up the scroll and gave it back to the attendant and sat down. And the eyes of all in the synagogue were fixed on him. And he began to say to them, "Today this Scripture has been fulfilled in your hearing." (Lu.4:16-21)

The Messianic Prophet of God was prophesied in Scripture:

The LORD your God will raise up for you a prophet like me from among you, from your brothers—it is to him you shall listen. (De.18:15)

The people who walked in darkness have seen a great light; those who dwelt in a land of deep darkness, on them has light shone. (Is.9:2)

There shall come forth a shoot from the stump of Jesse, and a branch from his roots shall bear fruit. And the Spirit of the LORD shall rest upon him, the Spirit of wisdom and understanding, the

Spirit of counsel and might, the Spirit of knowledge and the fear of the LORD. And his delight shall be in the fear of the LORD. He shall not judge by what his eyes see, or decide disputes by what his ears hear, but with righteousness he shall judge the poor, and decide with equity for the meek of the earth; and he shall strike the earth with the rod of his mouth, and with the breath of his lips he shall kill the wicked. (Is.11:1–4)

Behold my servant, whom I uphold, my chosen, in whom my soul delights; I have put my Spirit upon him; he will bring forth justice to the nations. He will not cry aloud or lift up his voice, or make it heard in the street; a bruised reed he will not break, and a faintly burning wick he will not quench; he will faithfully bring forth justice. He will not grow faint or be discouraged till he has established justice in the earth; and the coastlands wait for his law. (Is.42:1–4)

How beautiful upon the mountains are the feet of him who brings good news, who publishes peace, who brings good news of happiness, who publishes salvation, who says to Zion, "Your God reigns." (Is.52:7)

Behold, upon the mountains, the feet of him who brings good news, who publishes peace! Keep your feasts, O Judah; fulfill your vows, for never again shall the worthless pass through you; he is utterly cut off. (Na.1:15)

The New Testament clearly establishes that Jesus Christ is the Messianic Prophet of God (see above statement of Christ, Lu.4:16–21):

And the crowds said, "This is the prophet Jesus, from Nazareth of Galilee." (Mt.21:11)

Fear seized them all, and they glorified God, saying, "A great prophet has arisen among us!" and "God has visited his people!" (Lu.7:16)

Nevertheless, I must go on my way today and tomorrow and the day following, for it cannot be that a prophet should perish away from Jerusalem. (Lu.13:33)

For he whom God has sent utters the words of God, for he gives the Spirit without measure. (Jn.3:34)

When the people saw the sign that he had done, they said, "This is indeed the Prophet who is to come into the world!" (Jn.6:14)

When they heard these words, some of the people said, "This really is the Prophet." (Jn.7:40)

"I have much to say about you and much to judge, but he who sent me is true, and I declare to the world what I have heard from him." . . . So Jesus said to them, "When you have lifted up the Son of Man, then you will know that I am he, and that I do nothing on my own authority, but speak just as the Father taught me." (Jn.8:26, 28)

So they said again to the blind man, "What do you say about him, since he has opened your eyes?" He said, "He is a prophet." (Jn.9:17)

For I have not spoken on my own authority, but the Father who sent me has himself given me a commandment—what to say and what to speak. And I know that his commandment is eternal life. What I say, therefore, I say as the Father has told me. (Jn.12:49–50)

Do you not believe that I am in the Father and the Father is in me? The words that I say to you I do not speak on my own authority, but the Father who dwells in me does his works. . . . Whoever does not love me does not keep my words. And the word that you hear is not mine but the Father's who sent me. (Jn.14:10, 24)

No longer do I call you servants, for the servant does not know what his master is doing; but I have called you friends, for all that I have heard from my Father I have made known to you. (Jn.15:15)

For I have given them the words that you gave me, and they have received them and have come to know in truth that I came from you; and they have believed that you sent me. . . . I made known to them your name, and I will continue to make it known, that the love with which you have loved me may be in them, and I in them. (Jn.17:8, 26)

CHAPTER 4

E. The Temptation of Jesus: Victory over Temptation, 4:1–15

(Mt.4:1–17; Mk.1:12–15)

And Jesus, full of the Holy Spirit, returned from the Jordan and was led by the Spirit in the wilderness

² for forty days, being tempted by the devil. And he ate nothing during those days. And when they were ended, he was hungry.
³ The devil said to him, "If you are the Son of God, command this stone to become bread."

⁴ And Jesus answered him, "It is written, 'Man shall not live by bread alone.'"

⁵ And the devil took him up and showed him all the kingdoms of the world in a moment of time,

⁶ and said to him, "To you I will give all this authority and their glory, for it has been delivered to me, and I give it to whom I will.
⁷ If you, then, will worship me, it will all be yours."
⁸ And Jesus answered him, "It is written, 'You shall worship the Lord your God, and him only shall you serve.'"
⁹ And he took him to Jerusalem and set him on the pinnacle of the temple and said to him, "If you are the Son of God, throw yourself down from here,
¹⁰ for it is written, 'He will command his angels concerning you, to guard you,'
¹¹ and 'On their hands they will bear you up, lest you strike your foot against a stone.'"
¹² And Jesus answered him, "It is said, 'You shall not put the Lord your God to the test.'"
¹³ And when the devil had ended every temptation, he departed from him until an opportune time.

1. **Jesus' preparation to serve God**[DS1]
   a. He was filled with the Spirit and led by Him
   b. He spent time alone with God
   c. He was tried and tested—tempted by the devil
   d. He fasted and prayed

2. **Jesus' first temptation: To meet His needs by His own power**
   a. Satan's appeal: For Jesus to misuse His power
   b. Jesus' answer: People need more than bread—they need God's life or spiritual food

3. **Jesus' second temptation: To fulfill God's purpose through compromise**
   a. Satan's enticement: He shows the world's possessions and glory
   b. Satan's claim: He controls the world and its glory
   c. Satan's offer: He will give the world to anyone he wills
   d. Satan's appeal: For Jesus to worship and follow him
   e. Jesus' answer: He must worship and follow God alone

4. **Jesus' third temptation: To prove Himself through sensationalism**
   a. Satan's appeal
      1) For Jesus to choose another way
      2) For Jesus to misuse and twist the Scripture to suit His own ends
      3) For Jesus to give people heightened sensations—a religion of feelings and emotions
   b. Jesus' answer: God is not to be tempted— God's way alone is to be followed

5. **Jesus' victory: Satan left Him for a while**

a. Jesus' great power
b. Jesus' great fame

c. Jesus' great ministry

14 And Jesus returned in the power of the Spirit to Galilee, and a report about him went out through all the surrounding country.

15 And he taught in their synagogues, being glorified by all.

Division II

The Son of Man's Appearance, 3:1–4:15

E. The Temptation of Jesus: Victory over Temptation, 4:1–15

(Mt.4:1–17; Mk.1:12–15)

4:1–15
Introduction

In every area of life, Jesus has led us to victory over Satan. This includes the area of temptation. Victory over temptation is essential before we can fully enjoy the abundant life Christ came to give us (Jn.10:10). In addition, it is essential to serving God effectively. God's Word promises that He will always provide a way for us to escape temptation (1 Co.10:13). In this passage, Jesus showed us that way. No temptation has ever confronted us that Jesus Christ has not confronted. In His confrontation, Jesus reveals what lies behind each temptation and how to conquer it. Once it has been conquered, we can then live a victorious life and serve God effectively. This is, *The Temptation of Jesus: Victory over Temptation*, 4:1–15.

1. Jesus' preparation to serve God (vv.1–2).
2. Jesus' first temptation: To meet His needs by His own power (vv.3–4).
3. Jesus' second temptation: To fulfill God's purpose through compromise (vv.5–8).
4. Jesus' third temptation: To prove Himself through sensationalism (vv.9–12).
5. Jesus' victory: Satan left Him for a while (vv.13–15).

4:1–2

And Jesus, full of the Holy Spirit, returned from the Jordan and was led by the Spirit in the wilderness
2 for forty days, being tempted by the devil. And he ate nothing during those days. And when they were ended, he was hungry.

1 Jesus' preparation to serve God.

Jesus was about to launch the most important work ever performed by any person. His work would determine the eternal fate of the world and of every individual in the world. To accomplish His critical work, Jesus had to be strengthened and prepared perfectly, without flaw. Two things were involved in His preparation.

First, Jesus' preparation involved God's plan. Our Lord had to be totally committed to carry out God's plan no matter what happened. God's plan was the cross, the way of sacrifice and suffering in order to help others. Jesus would always be tempted to choose the easier course of self, power, and glory. He needed to gain the victory over these temptations *once and for all*. This does not mean that He would not be tempted again; He would. But He needed a strong moment of victory to show that He could conquer the temptation (see DEEPER STUDY # 1).

Second, Jesus' preparation involved a personal need for strength and assurance. The only way Jesus could be strengthened and gain assurance was to be tempted. He had to struggle against temptation to become tough and strong as a human being, and to be assured that He could conquer and be victorious over the trials of life.

If Jesus had to be prepared to serve God, how much more do we! These verses give four essentials that were a part of our Lord's preparation, and they are necessary for our preparation to serve God as well.

a. He was filled with the Spirit and led by Him (v.1a).

Jesus was *full of the Holy Spirit*. Note the emphasis on the Holy Spirit. He is mentioned twice in this verse.

Jesus had a dramatic experience with the Spirit at His baptism. The Holy Spirit came upon Him visibly in the form of a dove (3:21–22). Now, as the Savior prepared to launch His ministry, Jesus was *led by the Spirit* (egeto en to pneumati, *ay'-get-oh in tow new'-mah-tee*) in the wilderness. Note the Greek word "*en*." It means *in*, which means that Jesus was led not only *by the Spirit* but also *in the Spirit*, step by step and day by day. We must be *in the Spirit* to be led *by the Spirit*.

b. He spent time alone with God (v.1b).

Time alone with God is necessary for preparation to serve Him. Therefore, the Holy Spirit led Jesus to the wilderness to spend time alone with God.

c. He was tried and tested—tempted by the devil (v.2a).

Jesus was led to be tried and tested. Trials toughen us, make us stronger, and give us greater assurance so that we can face whatever lies ahead.

d. He fasted and prayed (v.2b).

Jesus was led to fast and pray, two absolute essentials in one's preparation to do a great work for God.

THOUGHT 1. Jesus' preparation is applicable to His servants today. What Jesus needed to serve God effectively is what we need as well.

1) We need to be filled with the Spirit and to learn to recognize the Spirit's leading in our lives (Ro.8:14; Ga.5:16; Ep.5:18).
2) We need to step away from the world and its distractions and get alone with God on a regular basis, even if only for a few minutes or an hour. From time to time we also need an extended retreat, a day or several days when we focus only on God and communing with Him (Mt.14:13; Mk.5:31; Mk.9:2).
3) We need to accept trials and tests as a part of God's work in our lives to strengthen and mature us (Jas.1:2–4, 12; Ps.66:10).
4) As the Lord leads, we need to incorporate the spiritual discipline of fasting into our prayer lives. Resisting our physical appetites in order to focus on spiritual things brings unusual spiritual clarity to our minds and hearts, and it produces spiritual power (Mt.17:21; Ac.14:23; Da.9:3).

> **And after he had dismissed the crowds, he went up on the mountain by himself to pray. When evening came, he was there alone. (Mt.14:23)**
>
> **However, this kind does not go out except by prayer and fasting. (Mt.17:21 NKJV)**
>
> **And do not get drunk with wine, for that is debauchery, but be filled with the Spirit. (Ep.5:18)**
>
> **Count it all joy, my brothers, when you meet trials of various kinds, for you know that the testing of your faith produces steadfastness. And let steadfastness have its full effect, that you may be perfect and complete, lacking in nothing. (Jas.1:2–4)**
>
> **For you, O God, have tested us; you have tried us as silver is tried. (Ps.66:10)**

DEEPER STUDY # 1

(4:1-2) **Tempt** (Gk. peirazo, *pay-rah'-zo*): peirazo is used here in Scripture with both good and bad associations. In the good sense it means to test, to try, to prove. Its purpose is not to defeat or to destroy. The idea is not that one is tempted, seduced, enticed, and pulled into sin by the Holy Spirit (see Jas.1:13), but that one is tested, proved, strengthened, reinforced, and purified through the trials of temptation.

The bad sense of course involves tempting, seducing, enticing, and pulling someone away from God into the way of sin, of self, and of Satan (Mt.4:1; 1 Co.7:5; 1 Th.3:5; Gal.6:1; Jas.1:13-14). Scripture states that this is what Satan is doing here.

Yet at the same time, the text says Jesus was led into the wilderness by the Spirit. Matthew's account says He was "led up by the Spirit into the wilderness *to be tempted*" (Mt.4:1, emphasis ours). The Spirit did not seduce or entice Jesus to do evil, but He led Jesus into circumstances whereby He could learn obedience and discipline. Satan's motivations were evil—as they always are—but the Spirit used the temptation to strengthen Jesus. Through such trials, Jesus was to be perfected and enabled to help all those who suffer trials (He.4:15-16; 5:8; see notes—Mt.4:2-4; 4:5-7; 4:8-10).

Six things need to be said about overcoming temptation.

1. Temptation to sin has its bottom root in passion and appetite (Mk.7:20-23; Jas.1:14). It comes directly from within, from the heart, not from without. And it does not come from God. Scripture clearly states that God does not tempt any person with evil (Jas.1:13). God does not tempt anyone in a bad sense. What He does is look upon His people as we endure temptation, and He strengthens us to bear the temptation. In this way He teaches us discipline and obedience for a greater work (Ro.8:28; 2 Co.1:3-4; He.5:8; 1 Pe.1:6-7).

2. No person faces any temptation that is not common to all people (1 Co.10:13).

3. God does not allow the believer to be tempted beyond what we are able to bear. God always provides a way to overcome temptation (1 Co.10:13).

4. Jesus Christ understands temptation. He was tempted in every way that we are tempted, yet He never sinned (He.2:18; 4:15).

5. Jesus Christ is a sympathetic High Priest in helping us through temptation (He.2:17-18; 4:15).

6. Temptation is overcome (a) by submitting to God and resisting the devil (Jas.4:7-8; 1 Pe.5:8-9), and (b) by using and obeying Scripture to combat temptation (Lu.4:4; see De.4:8; 4:12; 6:13, 16; 8:3; 10:20).

4:3-4

[3] The devil said to him, "If you are the Son of God, command this stone to become bread."

[4] And Jesus answered him, "It is written, 'Man shall not live by bread alone.'"

2 Jesus' first temptation: To meet His needs by His own power.

Satan tempted Jesus in three ways. The first way was enticing Jesus to meet the necessities of life by His own power.

a. Satan's appeal: For Jesus to misuse His power (v.3).

Satan's temptation was for Jesus to misuse His supernatural power as God (see note—Mt.4:2-4). Jesus was very hungry. He had the power to create food and to meet His need, and the tempter tempted Him to use His power to benefit Himself. But note the wrong in this temptation. Jesus would have been misusing His power by using it in an improper way. His power had not been given to use on Himself, but to demonstrate His deity by showing people that He was the Son of God. Never once did He use His power on Himself or for His own ends—not even when He was hanging on the cross (see Mt.26:42; Lu.23:35). He always used His power to help others, thereby demonstrating and giving evidence that what He was claiming was true: He is the Son of God sent to save the world.

The point is, Satan wanted Jesus to prove His Messiahship by *centering* His attention and power on Himself. If Jesus had used His power on Himself...

- He would be trusting Himself and not the Father, acting completely independent of the Father and the Father's will

- He would be saying that people could use their abilities solely to benefit themselves instead of helping a world lost in need
- He would be teaching that people could use their abilities to build themselves up (pride) instead of honoring God and His will

b. Jesus' answer: People need more than bread—they need God's life or spiritual food (v.4).
Jesus fired back at Satan with Scripture (De.8:3), answering that life is about more than satisfying our physical appetites. We need something more than physical food to live. We need to be fed spiritually. We need our spiritual needs met. The point is that Jesus alone can meet people's spiritual needs; therefore He, the Son of God, must use His power only as God wills (see note—Mt.4:2-4 for detailed discussion).

THOUGHT 1. We all have needs, the very necessities of life . . .

- food
- clothing
- shelter
- friends
- acceptance
- recognition
- self-esteem
- work
- rest and recreation

These needs are legitimate. However, the problem arises when we are tempted . . .

- to use our ability independent of God, forgetting His will and doing our own thing
- to focus our ability on ourselves, getting and banking more and more instead of meeting the needs of a desperate world
- to use our abilities to build ourselves up instead of acknowledging God as the Source of our abilities. Too many seek fame, honor, and praise for selfish ends. Too many want to be recognized as superior and better, as having more position, authority, clothes, houses, cars, lands, and looks

The great wrong with this is twofold.

1) We misuse our ability. Forgetting God and His will, we focus on self.
2) We live for the physical and not for the spiritual, for receiving and not for giving. There is a spiritual hunger that is not met by bread, that is, the physical and material (see note—Ep.1:3 for detailed discussion).

> Jesus said to them, "I am the bread of life; whoever comes to me shall not hunger, and whoever believes in me shall never thirst." (Jn.6:35)

> This is the bread that comes down from heaven, so that one may eat of it and not die. I am the living bread that came down from heaven. If anyone eats of this bread, he will live forever. And the bread that I will give for the life of the world is my flesh. (Jn.6:50-51)

> Like newborn infants, long for the pure spiritual milk, that by it you may grow up into salvation. (1 Pe.2:2)

> How sweet are your words to my taste, sweeter than honey to my mouth! (Ps.119:103)

> Come, everyone who thirsts, come to the waters; and he who has no money, come, buy and eat! Come, buy wine and milk without money and without price. Why do you spend your money for that which is not bread, and your labor for that which does not satisfy? Listen diligently to me, and eat what is good, and delight yourselves in rich food. Incline your ear, and come to me; hear, that your soul may live; and I will make with you an everlasting covenant, my steadfast, sure love for David. (Is.55:1-3)

> Your words were found, and I ate them, and your words became to me a joy and the delight of my heart, for I am called by your name, O Lord, God of hosts. (Je.15:16)

3 Jesus' second temptation: To fulfill God's purpose through compromise.

The second way Satan tempted Jesus was to entice Him to seek His ambition (God's kingdom) through compromise (see note—Mt.4:8-10). Jesus had come to earth to seek and to save people *eternally*, to secure their loyalty for God, and to set up the kingdom of God forever (see DEEPER STUDY # 3—Mt.19:23-24). This was Jesus' ambition. The only way to fulfill this ambition was by the cross (freeing people from sin, death, and judgment). "The Father had already promised to give the Son all the kingdoms of the world (Ps.2:7-8), but first the Son had to suffer and die (Jn.12:23-33; Re.5:8-10)."[1] Note what happened in this temptation: Satan offered Jesus a way to bypass the cross and still receive these kingdoms.

4:5-8

> [5] And the devil took him up and showed him all the kingdoms of the world in a moment of time,
> [6] and said to him, "To you I will give all this authority and their glory, for it has been delivered to me, and I give it to whom I will.
> [7] If you, then, will worship me, it will all be yours."
> [8] And Jesus answered him, "It is written, 'You shall worship the Lord your God, and him only shall you serve.'"

a. **Satan's enticement: He shows the world's possessions and glory (v.5).**

Satan took Jesus to a high peak and showed Him all the kingdoms of the world. The vision occurred "in a moment of time"—in an instant. What Luke describes is "a physical impossibility, and most likely is meant to indicate some sort of diabolic [rapid sequence of images, as in a dream], flashed before Christ's consciousness, while His eyes were fixed on the silent, sandy waste."[2] Apparently, Satan supernaturally *flashed* across Jesus' mind all the kingdoms of the world in their enormous glory.

b. **Satan's claim: He controls the world and its glory (v.6a).**

Satan claimed that he controls the possessions and glory of the world. Sometime later, Jesus substantiated Satan's claim, saying that Satan is "the ruler of this world" (Jn.12:31; 14:30). Other Scriptures say that he is "the prince of the power of the air" (Ep.2:2) and the "god of this world" (2 Co.4:4).

c. **Satan's offer: He will give the world to anyone he wills (v.6b).**

Satan offered Jesus all the possessions and glory of the world. The world was under His dominion and control; therefore, he could give it to whomever he wished.

d. **Satan's appeal: For Jesus to worship and follow him (v.7).**

Satan, however, had one condition. Jesus had to worship Satan, that is, follow and obey the way of Satan's world. Jesus had to compromise Himself . . .
- by compromising His standards and behavior
- by compromising His loyalty and faithfulness to God
- by compromising His ministry and mission

e. **Jesus' answer: He must worship and follow God alone (v.8).**

Note Jesus' answer: He was quick and decisive, totally dependent on Scripture to conquer the temptation (De.6:13). He must worship, follow, and serve God alone, not the way and standards and evil of the world. He would follow God even if it meant not realizing His ambition. There is a right way and a wrong way to achieve one's end and purpose; and He, the Son of God, would choose the right way.

---

1 Warren W. Wiersbe, *The Bible Exposition Commentary*, (Colorado Springs, CO: David C. Cook, 2002). Via Wordsearch digital edition.
2 Alexander Maclaren, *Expositions of Holy Scripture,* (p.d.). Via Wordsearch digital edition.

THOUGHT 1. The *power* and the *glory* of the world come from many things. *Worldly power and glory* come from . . .

- houses
- lands
- wealth
- authority
- influence
- success

- cars
- possessions
- stimulation
- excitement
- fame
- position

Figuratively speaking, Satan takes us up to a mountain and shows us what the world has to offer. To receive it, we must do but one thing: worship Satan, that is, follow the path of *worldliness*. Many people choose to accept Satan's offer, feeling that if they compromise and go along with the world (everyone else), they will get what they want and move ahead much faster.

There is nothing wrong with ambition and desiring to fulfill our calling in life. There is nothing wrong with experiencing the power and the glory—the earthly benefits and rewards—of whatever our calling is. The wrong is found in following Satan (evil) when tempted to satisfy our desires and ambitions instead of following God.

> For what will it profit a man if he gains the whole world and forfeits his soul? Or what shall a man give in return for his soul? (Mt.16:26)

> Do not be conformed to this world, but be transformed by the renewal of your mind, that by testing you may discern what is the will of God, what is good and acceptable and perfect. (Ro.12:2)

> For the grace of God has appeared, bringing salvation for all people, training us to renounce ungodliness and worldly passions, and to live self-controlled, upright, and godly lives in the present age. (Tit.2:11-12)

> Do not love the world or the things in the world. If anyone loves the world, the love of the Father is not in him. For all that is in the world—the desires of the flesh and the desires of the eyes and pride of life—is not from the Father but is from the world. (1 Jn2:15-16)

4 Jesus' third temptation: To prove Himself through sensationalism.

4:9-12

Satan's third temptation was for Jesus to be sensational. Challenging Jesus' deity, he dared God's Son to jump off the pinnacle of the temple. This time, the deceiver threw Scripture at the Savior. Twisting God's Word, Satan said that God would cause angels to catch Him. God would never let Him be dashed to bits (Ps.91:11-12). Therefore, when the people saw the angels float Him to the ground, they would be stunned into belief and become His followers immediately. (Remember Jesus had not yet performed a miracle. Satan had no idea of the miracles to come, nor that people would be slow to believe even with all the evidence of signs and wonders.)

⁹ And he took him to Jerusalem and set him on the pinnacle of the temple and said to him, "If you are the Son of God, throw yourself down from here,

¹⁰ for it is written, 'He will command his angels concerning you, to guard you,'

¹¹ and 'On their hands they will bear you up, lest you strike your foot against a stone.'"

¹² And Jesus answered him, "It is said, 'You shall not put the Lord your God to the test.'"

a. Satan's appeal (vv.9-11).

Satan's temptation was subtle and strategic. His carefully-crafted appeal actually presented three enticements.

First, Satan tempted Jesus to choose some way other than God's way (see note and DEEPER STUDY # 1—Lu.9:23). God's way was the way of the cross and of identifying with the human race in His trials and sufferings. (See He.4:15-16. Then see He.2:14-18 with Jn.3:16; see also He.5:7-9.)

Second, Satan tempted Jesus to misuse Scripture by twisting it to suit His purposes. Scripture did say that God would take care of His Son no matter what. The heavenly angels were given charge to help Him in everything.

Third, Satan tempted Jesus to give people sensations, a religion of feelings. People do not want a life of self-denial and sacrifice, of too much discipline and control. They want the spectacular, something that will be a quick fix, something . . .

- to stir their emotions and flesh
- to stimulate their feelings and give gratification
- to meet their needs with less and less effort
- to feed their body and soul without cost

b. Jesus' answer: God is not to be tempted—God's way alone is to be followed (v.12).

As in the previous temptations, Jesus responded to the enemy's attempt to bring Him down with Scripture. Jesus' answer was straightforward and decisive: "You shall not put the Lord your God to the test" (De.6:16). There is no way other than God's way; God's way alone is to be pursued and followed. And God's Word is not to be stretched or twisted (presumed upon) trying to make another way. People must be taught the truth. The way to God is the way of the cross.

THOUGHT 1. At some point, all people are tempted to bypass God, to choose another way. The way of the cross is hard and difficult, yet it is the only way to God (see note and DEEPER STUDY # 1—Lu.9:23). Trying to devise another way to God only spells doom (see Jn.14:6; 1 Ti.1:15; 2:5–6; Tit.3:4–7).

> Since, therefore, we have now been justified by his blood, much more shall we be saved by him from the wrath of God. (Ro.5:9)

> For the word of the cross is folly to those who are perishing, but to us who are being saved it is the power of God. For it is written, "I will destroy the wisdom of the wise, and the discernment of the discerning I will thwart." (1 Co.1:18–19)

> But far be it from me to boast except in the cross of our Lord Jesus Christ, by which the world has been crucified to me, and I to the world. (Ga.6:14)

> And through him to reconcile to himself all things, whether on earth or in heaven, making peace by the blood of his cross. (Col.1:20)

THOUGHT 2. Some try to twist or stretch Scripture . . .
1) To allow them to do what they want (sin).
2) To devise some way to God other than the cross.

> But we have renounced disgraceful, underhanded ways. We refuse to practice cunning or to tamper with God's word, but by the open statement of the truth we would commend ourselves to everyone's conscience in the sight of God. (2 Co.4:2)

> Do your best to present yourself to God as one approved, a worker who has no need to be ashamed, rightly handling the word of truth. (2 Ti.2:15)

> And count the patience of our Lord as salvation, just as our beloved brother Paul also wrote to you according to the wisdom given him, as he does in all his letters when he speaks in them of these matters. There are some things in them that are hard to understand, which the ignorant and unstable twist to their own destruction, as they do the other Scriptures. (2 Pe.3:15–16)

> You shall not add to the word that I command you, nor take from it, that you may keep the commandments of the Lord your God that I command you. (De.4:2)

4:13–15

[13] And when the devil had ended every temptation, he departed from him until an opportune time.
[14] And Jesus returned in the power of the Spirit to Galilee, and a report about him went out through all the surrounding country.
[15] And he taught in their synagogues, being glorified by all.

5 Jesus' victory: Satan left Him for a while.

a. Jesus' great power (v.14a).

b. Jesus' great fame (v.14b).

c. Jesus' great ministry (v.15).

Jesus' period of fierce temptation concluded in a compelling and encouraging way: Satan *departed from Him*. The enemy left Jesus alone, but only for a while. The victory was won;

the temptation was conquered, and Satan was routed for a while. When another opportune time arose, the deceiver would be back; but for now, Jesus had peace and freedom to carry on His ministry.

Immediately after this victory, Jesus' ministry began to flourish. His great power—the power of the Holy Spirit—was evident as He taught and ministered to people. News of His marvelous ministry spread like wildfire, and His fame was reported abroad. As He ministered in the synagogue, the admiring crowds recognized that there was something different about Him.

THOUGHT 1. Victory over temptation does not mean a person is freed forever from temptation. In this life temptation will always return. It did for Jesus; it will for us (see note and DEEPER STUDIES 1, 3—Mt.4:1–11).

> And he said to his disciples, "Temptations to sin are sure to come, but woe to the one through whom they come!" (Lu.17:1)

> Simon, Simon, behold, Satan demanded to have you, that he might sift you like wheat. (Lu.22:31)

> Be sober-minded; be watchful. Your adversary the devil prowls around like a roaring lion, seeking someone to devour. (1 Pe.5:8)

THOUGHT 2. Victory over temptation will lead to great results in our lives. It will give us more power, a greater testimony, and a greater ministry.

> Blessed is the man who remains steadfast under trial, for when he has stood the test he will receive the crown of life, which God has promised to those who love him. (Jas.1:12)

> The one who conquers, I will grant him to sit with me on my throne, as I also conquered and sat down with my Father on his throne. (Re.3:21)

III. THE SON OF MAN'S ANNOUNCED MISSION AND PUBLIC MINISTRY, 4:16–9:17

A. Jesus Announces His Mission: A Graphic Picture of Rejection, 4:16–30

(Mt.13:53–58; Mk.6:1–6)

1. **Scene 1: Jesus visited His hometown and entered the synagogue on the Sabbath (His weekly custom)**

2. **Scene 2: Jesus' dramatic reading from the prophet Isaiah—concerned the Messiah**

   a. The Messiah was to be anointed by the Spirit
   b. The Messiah was to preach the gospel (good news)
   c. The Messiah was to minister

   d. The Messiah was to preach the era of salvation

3. **Scene 3: Jesus' phenomenal claim**
   a. The people paid rapt attention

   b. Jesus claimed to be the Messiah

4. **Scene 4: The people's skeptical response**
   a. First: They were impressed
   b. Second: They questioned
   c. Third: They demanded proof—insisted He heal (prove) Himself, that is, work miracles

5. **Scene 5: The people's painful rejection**

   a. Illustration 1: Only one needy widow had her needs met in Elijah's day—because only one widow accepted Elijah

---

¹⁶ And he came to Nazareth, where he had been brought up. And as was his custom, he went to the synagogue on the Sabbath day, and he stood up to read.

¹⁷ And the scroll of the prophet Isaiah was given to him. He unrolled the scroll and found the place where it was written,

¹⁸ "The Spirit of the Lord is upon me, because he has anointed me to proclaim good news to the poor. He has sent me to proclaim liberty to the captives and recovering of sight to the blind, to set at liberty those who are oppressed,

¹⁹ to proclaim the year of the Lord's favor."

²⁰ And he rolled up the scroll and gave it back to the attendant and sat down. And the eyes of all in the synagogue were fixed on him.

²¹ And he began to say to them, "Today this Scripture has been fulfilled in your hearing."

²² And all spoke well of him and marveled at the gracious words that were coming from his mouth. And they said, "Is not this Joseph's son?"

²³ And he said to them, "Doubtless you will quote to me this proverb, '"Physician, heal yourself." What we have heard you did at Capernaum, do here in your hometown as well.'"

²⁴ And he said, "Truly, I say to you, no prophet is acceptable in his hometown.

²⁵ But in truth, I tell you, there were many widows in Israel in the days of Elijah, when the heavens were shut up three years and six months, and a great famine came over all the land,

²⁶ and Elijah was sent to none of them but only to Zarephath, in the land of Sidon, to a woman who was a widow.

²⁷ And there were many lepers in Israel in the time of the prophet Elisha, and none of them was cleansed, but only Naaman the Syrian."

²⁸ When they heard these things, all in the synagogue were filled with wrath.

²⁹ And they rose up and drove him out of the town and brought him to the brow of the hill on which their town was built, so that they could throw him down the cliff.

³⁰ But passing through their midst, he went away.

b. Illustration 2: Only one needy leper was cleansed in Elisha's day—because only one leper accepted Elisha

6. Scene 6: The people's true spirit
   a. An insane wrath and closed-mindedness
   b. An insane assault: To silence Jesus

   c. The insane behavior of the people failed

Division III

The Son of Man's Announced Mission and Public Ministry, 4:16–9:17

A. Jesus Announces His Mission: A Graphic Picture of Rejection, 4:16–30

(Mt.13:53–58; Mk.6:1–6)

4:16–30
Introduction

From the outset of His public ministry, Jesus did not hesitate to let people know who He was. He revealed that He was the Messiah, and His claim was rejected by the people of His day. Tragically, it is still rejected by people today. This is, *Jesus Announces His Mission: A Graphic Picture of Rejection*, 4:16–30.
   1. Scene 1: Jesus visited His hometown and entered the synagogue on the Sabbath (His weekly custom) (v.16).
   2. Scene 2: Jesus' dramatic reading from the prophet Isaiah—concerned the Messiah (vv.17–19).
   3. Scene 3: Jesus' phenomenal claim (vv.20–21).
   4. Scene 4: The people's skeptical response (vv.22–23).
   5. Scene 5: The people's painful rejection (vv.24–27).
   6. Scene 6: The people's true spirit (vv.28–30).

1 Scene 1: Jesus visited His hometown and entered the synagogue on the Sabbath (His weekly custom).

4:16

¹⁶ And he came to Nazareth, where he had been brought up. And as was his custom, he went to the synagogue on the Sabbath day, and he stood up to read.

Jesus returned to His hometown of Nazareth where He had been reared (see DEEPER STUDY # 4—Mt.2:23). As was His custom, He entered the synagogue for worship on the Sabbath. He was faithful in His worship of God and faithful to the assembling of God's people. This synagogue was the one Jesus had attended as a child. It was a small community synagogue where everyone would know everyone else. Jesus and the congregation were neighbors; some were close to His family.

The synagogue had no preachers or ministers as most churches today do (see DEEPER STUDY # 2—Mt.4:23). The leaders would simply invite a person to read and preach. They had been hearing a good deal about their neighbor Jesus, so they invited Him to read and preach this Sabbath.

2 Scene 2: Jesus' dramatic reading from the prophet Isaiah—concerned the Messiah.

Out of reverence for God's Holy Word, Jesus stood to read the Scripture (v.16). The synagogue's leaders handed Jesus the book of Isaiah from which to read (v.17). He unrolled the holy scroll to a passage which declared five specific prophecies about the Messiah (see Is.61:1-2).

4:17-19

¹⁷ And the scroll of the prophet Isaiah was given to him. He unrolled the scroll and found the place where it was written,
¹⁸ "The Spirit of the Lord is upon me, because he has anointed me to proclaim good news to the poor. He has sent me to proclaim liberty to the captives and recovering of sight to the blind, to set at liberty those who are oppressed,
¹⁹ to proclaim the year of the Lord's favor."

THOUGHT 1. We should always have reverence for the Scripture, both in hearing and in reading it.

> And Ezra opened the book in the sight of all the people, for he was above all the people, and as he opened it all the people stood. (Ne.8:5)

> Though the cords of the wicked ensnare me, I do not forget your law. (Ps.119:61)

a. **The Messiah was to be anointed by the Spirit (v.18a).** Isaiah had prophesied that the Messiah would be anointed by the Spirit. He would be both *called* and *equipped* by the Spirit (see Lu.3:21-22).

THOUGHT 1. When God calls, He anoints; He equips the messenger with His Spirit, who goes with the messenger wherever God sends him or her.

> And it is God who establishes us with you in Christ, and has anointed us. (2 Co.1:21)

> But you have been anointed by the Holy One, and you all have knowledge. (1 Jn.2:20)

b. **The Messiah was to preach the gospel (good news) (v.18b).**
The Messiah would *preach the gospel* or *proclaim good news* (euangelisasthai, *yoo-ang-ghel-is-sas'-thigh*). It is from this Greek word that we get our word "evangelize." The Messiah would preach to two classes of people.

First, He would preach to the poor. The *poor* means not only poor in material possessions but also *poor in spirit* (see DEEPER STUDY # 2—Mt.5:3).

Second, He would preach liberty or deliverance to the *captives* (aichmalōtois, *aheekh-mall'-oh-tois*). This Greek compound word literally means to be captured at spear point and speaks of prisoners of war. Here, it refers to those in spiritual captivity, "those who have become captives of the devil" (see note, *Redemption—Ep.1:7*).[1]

c. **The Messiah was to minister (v.18c).**
Isaiah prophesied that the Messiah would have a threefold ministry. He would heal the *brokenhearted* (KJV, NKJV).[2] Note that He was not only to help the brokenhearted, He was to *heal* the brokenhearted, those who were . . .

- crushed by grief
- shattered
- opposed
- cut off
- blemished by sin
- violated by sin

- infected
- diseased
- weakened
- subdued
- injured
- bankrupt

In addition, the Messiah would give sight to the *blind*, not only to those who were spiritually blind, but to those who were blind physically. And He would set at liberty those who were

---

1   Spiros Zodhiates, *The Complete Word Study Dictionary: New Testament*, (Chattanooga, TN: AMG Publishers, 1992). Via Wordsearch digital edition.

2   The Greek texts from which the ESV and most other modern versions are translated do not include this statement, which is a part of Isaiah 61:1.

oppressed. He would set free those who had been battered, bruised, and broken into pieces physically, mentally, emotionally, psychologically, and spiritually.

d. The Messiah was to preach the era of salvation (v.19).

The Messiah was to preach the era of salvation. The term *year of the Lord's favor* or *acceptable year* means the era, the age or day of salvation (see 2 Co.6:2). It means that the age of the Messiah had come. The time had come when God had chosen to provide His salvation to the human race.

Note a significant point. Jesus was reading from Isaiah 61:1-2, but He abruptly stopped in the middle of verse 2. Why? Because the last part of the verse had to do with judgment and Jesus' present ministry was salvation, not judgment. His future ministry will be to judge the world (Is.61:2b; see Is.58:6).

3 Scene 3: Jesus' phenomenal claim. 4:20-21

After reading Isaiah's prophecy of the Messiah, Jesus rolled up the scroll, handed it back to the synagogue attendant, and sat down. Sitting was the posture for preaching in the synagogue. The people present eagerly anticipated what Jesus would say about the Scripture He had just read.

> [20] And he rolled up the scroll and gave it back to the attendant and sat down. And the eyes of all in the synagogue were fixed on him. [21] And he began to say to them, "Today this Scripture has been fulfilled in your hearing."

a. The people paid rapt attention (v.20).

All eyes *were fixed on Him* (Gk. esan atenizontes autō, *ay-sahn' ah-ten-id-zon'-tes aw'-tow*), a descriptive phrase meaning focused, gazing, spellbound. They stared at Jesus in rapt attention; their eyes were locked on Him, eagerly waiting to see what He had to say.

b. Jesus claimed to be the Messiah (v.21).

The voice of God's Son pierced the air, announcing that Isaiah's prophecy was being fulfilled that very day, in their presence—a phenomenal claim! The words *this day* or *today* are important. The people thought of the Messiah's coming and the Messianic age in terms of the future. Jesus proclaimed that He was the Messiah—that the Messianic Age was then and now—that all the Scripture of Isaiah was *fulfilled* in Him. He proclaimed . . .

- that He was the one upon whom the Spirit dwelled
- that He was the one anointed to preach the gospel to the poor and captives
- that He was the one who would heal the brokenhearted
- that He was the one who would give sight to the blind
- that He was the one who would free the oppressed
- that He was the one who was preaching the acceptable year of the Lord, the age of salvation

> **He said to them, "But who do you say that I am?" Simon Peter replied, "You are the Christ, the Son of the living God." And Jesus answered him, "Blessed are you, Simon Bar-Jonah! For flesh and blood has not revealed this to you, but my Father who is in heaven." (Mt.16:15-17)**

> **But Jesus remained silent. And the high priest said to him, "I adjure you by the living God, tell us if you are the Christ, the Son of God." Jesus said to him, "You have said so. But I tell you, from now on you will see the Son of Man seated at the right hand of Power and coming on the clouds of heaven." (Mt.26:63-64)**

> **And he said to them, "O foolish ones, and slow of heart to believe all that the prophets have spoken! Was it not necessary that the Christ should suffer these things and enter into his glory?" (Lu.24:25-26)**

> **The woman said to him, "I know that Messiah is coming (he who is called Christ). When he comes, he will tell us all things." Jesus said to her, "I who speak to you am he." (Jn.4:25-26)**

> **Jesus said to her, "I am the resurrection and the life. Whoever believes in me, though he die, yet shall he live, and everyone who lives and believes in me shall never die. Do you believe this?" She said to him, "Yes, Lord; I believe that you are the Christ, the Son of God, who is coming into the world." (Jn.11:25-27)**

4 Scene 4: The people's skeptical response.

When Jesus claimed to be the Messiah, the people responded favorably to Him at first. But their attitude toward Him changed suddenly and drastically. The people's response to Jesus' claim deteriorated from being *impressed* to being *offended* to *demanding proof.*

4:22–23

²² And all spoke well of him and marveled at the gracious words that were coming from his mouth. And they said, "Is not this Joseph's son?"
²³ And he said to them, "Doubtless you will quote to me this proverb, '"Physician, heal yourself." What we have heard you did at Capernaum, do here in your hometown as well.'"

a. **First: They were impressed (v.22a).**

The people in the synagogue were impressed with Jesus' eloquence, His charm and winning words, and the power of His message. Note the word *marveled* (ethaumazon, *eh-thaw'-mah-zon*). It means they were amazed and astonished at the gracious words flowing from His mouth. They were taking *pride* in one of their own neighbor's being so capable.

b. **Second: They questioned (v.22b).**

As the realization that Jesus was one of their own set in, the people's attitude toward Him changed. They began to question if He was who He claimed to be, the Messiah. This was a quick reversal in their thought processes. Sitting there listening, questions began to arise in their thoughts, such as: "Is not this Joseph's son?" Matthew is even more descriptive. The people were sitting there glancing around, asking in their minds, "Is not this . . . His mother . . . His brothers . . . His sisters. Are they not all with us? . . . And they took offense at Him" (Mt.13:55–57). *Took offense* means they stumbled over Him. They could not accept that someone from their own town—someone whom they had known since a child—could be the Messiah, the Son of God.

c. **Third: They demanded proof—insisted He heal (prove) Himself, that is, work miracles (v.23).**

Before the people dared speak it, Jesus told them what they were thinking. In their minds they were demanding proof, insisting in their thoughts that He had to prove Himself by working miracles in their midst, just as He had been reported to do in other places. It appears they were still processing things in their minds. They were sitting there listening to Him, but their thoughts were *stumbling* over His claim to be the Messiah. As God, Jesus knew their thoughts, so He stopped His message and directed a statement to them: "You are thinking, saying to me, Physician, heal, prove yourself. Prove yourself by doing the miracles you did in Capernaum."

As a side note, the fact that Jesus knew what the people were thinking should have served as a proof of His claim. It should have made the people realize that He was more than an ordinary man.

THOUGHT 1. Many are impressed with Jesus Christ at first, but when they are presented with His claims and the cross, they become offended and demand proof. His claim to be the Incarnate God in human flesh—to be the virgin-born Son of God—who must die for humanity's sin by being crucified upon a vulgar cross, is offensive to some. Many refuse to accept such phenomenal claims and vulgar scenes. They want a religion of grand images, beautiful pictures, and soft words.

> So Jesus said to him, "Unless you see signs and wonders you will not believe." (Jn.4:48)

> For Jews demand signs and Greeks seek wisdom, but we preach Christ crucified, a stumbling block to Jews and folly to Gentiles. (1 Co.1:22–23)

5 Scene 5: The people's painful rejection.

Jesus continued to speak, directing His remarks to His hometown audience. He knew they had already rejected Him in their hearts and minds. Therefore, He would not gratify their curiosity and demand for signs, nor would He continue to preach to them. Instead, He would give a twofold warning.

First, He stated bluntly that no prophet is *accepted* in His hometown (v.24). Jesus' neighbors had rejected Him, and He knew it. They could not hide the fact. They had (as is so often the case) . . .

- allowed familiarity to breed contempt
- thought it farfetched that the claims of a hometown boy could be true
- given in to envy among neighbors

Note the words "His hometown" or "His own country." Jesus was likely thinking of all Israel as well as Nazareth. The Jewish nation as a whole would eventually reject Him, the true Messiah.

Second, Jesus warned the crowd that God would reject those who reject His prophet, the Messiah. He warned the people by recalling two well-known stories in the history of Israel. The audience could not miss the point. In the past, God had not shown mercy to people who just *thought* they were "God's people" (the Jews), but He had shown mercy to those who had accepted Him—those whose hearts were turned toward Him.

> 24 And he said, "Truly, I say to you, no prophet is acceptable in his hometown.
> 25 But in truth, I tell you, there were many widows in Israel in the days of Elijah, when the heavens were shut up three years and six months, and a great famine came over all the land,
> 26 and Elijah was sent to none of them but only to Zarephath, in the land of Sidon, to a woman who was a widow.
> 27 And there were many lepers in Israel in the time of the prophet Elisha, and none of them was cleansed, but only Naaman the Syrian."

a. Illustration 1: Only one needy widow had her needs met in Elijah's day—because only one widow accepted Elijah (vv.25–26).

Jesus illustrated His point first by referring to the needy widow in Elijah's day. As far as is known, she was the only widow who had her needs met by God in the time of severe famine. Many were without food, destitute and starving; yet God sent His prophet to help only this one person—and she was a despised Gentile. Why? When there were so many others who *professed to be God's chosen people*, why would God help only this one poor widow? Why would God turn away from the Jews to another person? The point is clear. She was the only one whose heart was turned toward God and who accepted Him.

b. Illustration 2: Only one needy leper was cleansed in Elisha's day—because only one leper accepted Elisha (v.27).

Jesus went on to point out the one leper who had his leprosy cleansed by Elisha. When God sent Elisha to heal Naaman, Elisha passed by many Jewish lepers, many who thought they were the chosen people of God. But the prophet stopped to help none of these. He was sent to heal the Syrian Gentile, the one person whose heart accepted God.

THOUGHT 1. Salvation requires more than mere profession, more than just thinking one is chosen of God and that one will never be rejected by God. A person's heart must be turned toward God (repentance) and must accept God (belief) in order to be saved.

> Whoever believes in him is not condemned, but whoever does not believe is condemned already, because he has not believed in the name of the only Son of God. . . . Whoever believes in the Son has eternal life; whoever does not obey the Son shall not see life, but the wrath of God remains on him. (Jn.3:18, 36)

> I told you that you would die in your sins, for unless you believe that I am he you will die in your sins. (Jn.8:24)

> Take care, brothers, lest there be in any of you an evil, unbelieving heart, leading you to fall away from the living God. (He.3:12)

6 Scene 6: The people's true spirit.

Jesus had declared that God would turn and give His mercy to others if His chosen people rejected Him. God would turn to those who were responsive to Him. He would not continue to appeal to those who were always rejecting and hardening their hearts (vv.25–27). These words of warning were more than the skeptical Nazarenes could bear. They suddenly grew hostile and violent and "rose up" against Jesus.

4:28–30

28 When they heard these things, all in the synagogue were filled with wrath.
29 And they rose up and drove him out of the town and brought him to the brow of the hill on which their town was built, so that they could throw him down the cliff.
30 But passing through their midst, he went away.

a. An insane wrath and closed-mindedness (v.29a).

The people got the point Jesus was making and were "filled with wrath." *Filled* (eplēsthēsan, *eh-place-thay'-sahn*) means that they were furious, filled with wild, insane rage that controlled them completely.[3] They were totally closed-minded toward Jesus and His claim to be the Messiah and could no longer tolerate His presence in their midst.

b. An insane assault: To silence Jesus (v.29b).

The Nazarenes' insane rage caused them to attempt an assault against Jesus. The crazed mob drove God's Son out of town and were going to throw Him off a cliff! By killing Jesus, they would silence Him so that they would never have to be confronted with the truth again.

c. The insane behavior of the people failed (v.30).

Somehow Jesus was able to escape their assault. How? Scripture simply says that He passed through their midst—"He walked right through the crowd" (v.30 NIV). How could He so easily escape such an insane, enraged mob? It is reasonable to assume that something supernatural happened. Perhaps the people were stricken with a moment of confusion, a moment of shock, or some temporary blindness which enabled Him to quickly escape. It was not yet time for Him to die, so God somehow intervened.

The classic commentator Albert Barnes suggests that,

Jesus by divine power, by the force of a word or look, stilled their passions, arrested their purposes, and passed silently through them. That he had such a power over the spirits of men we learn from the occurrence in Gethsemane, when he said, "I am he; and they went backward and fell to the ground," (Jn.18:6).[4]

THOUGHT 1. The Lord will not continue to strive with a person, not forever. A person can go too far too often and face eternity without the presence of God. When confronted with the truth of their sinful condition, people need to surrender to the Spirit of God while there is still time.

> **Or do you presume on the riches of his kindness and forbearance and patience, not knowing that God's kindness is meant to lead you to repentance? But because of your hard and impenitent heart you are storing up wrath for yourself on the day of wrath when God's righteous judgment will be revealed. (Ro.2:4–5)**

> **Take care, brothers, lest there be in any of you an evil, unbelieving heart, leading you to fall away from the living God. But exhort one another every day, as long as it is called "today," that none of you may be hardened by the deceitfulness of sin. For we have come to share in Christ, if indeed we hold our original confidence firm to the end. (He.3:12–14)**

> **Then the Lord said, "My Spirit shall not abide in man forever, for he is flesh: his days shall be 120 years." (Ge.6:3)**

> **Blessed is the one who fears the Lord always, but whoever hardens his heart will fall into calamity. (Pr.28:14)**

---

3   *Practical Word Studies in the New Testament,* (Chattanooga, TN: Leadership Ministries Worldwide, 1998). Via Wordsearch digital edition.

4   Albert Barnes, *Barnes' Notes on the New Testament.* (Grand Rapids, MI: Kregel Classics, 1962). Via Wordsearch digital edition.

He who is often reproved, yet stiffens his neck, will suddenly be broken beyond healing. (Pr.29:1)

THOUGHT 2. A person or a group of people may wish to silence Jesus and His followers, but their efforts will be to no avail. The message of the gospel will never be silenced.

Simon Peter replied, "You are the Christ, the Son of the living God." . . . "And I tell you, you are Peter, and on this rock I will build my church, and the gates of hell shall not prevail against it." (Mt.16:16, 18)

Heaven and earth will pass away, but my words will not pass away. (Lu.21:33; see Mt.5:18)

Blessed be the LORD who has given rest to his people Israel, according to all that he promised. Not one word has failed of all his good promise, which he spoke by Moses his servant. (1 Ki.8:56)

So shall my word be that goes out from my mouth; it shall not return to me empty, but it shall accomplish that which I purpose, and shall succeed in the thing for which I sent it. (Is.55:11)

B. Jesus Ministers and Makes an Amazing Impact: A Day in the Life of Jesus, 4:31–44

(Mt.8:14–17; Mk.1:21–39)

1. **Jesus went down to Capernaum**

2. **Jesus taught in the Sabbath service with authority**

3. **Jesus delivered the most unclean**
   a. A man with an unclean spirit sat in worship

      1) Evil spirits acknowledged Jesus' deity

      2) Jesus rebuked the evil acknowledgement
      3) Jesus cast out the unclean spirit

   b. The people were amazed

   c. The people spread the news about Him everywhere they went [v.37]

4. **Jesus cured the most needful**
   a. So needful, a great fever
   b. So needful, could not speak or seek Jesus for herself

   c. So needful, could not even come to Jesus
   d. So needful, He came to her and healed her: She arose and ministered

5. **Jesus healed the diseases of those who sought Him out**

6. **Jesus rebuked the evil spirits, kept them from making a false profession**

7. **Jesus went to a solitary place to be in God's presence**

31 And he went down to Capernaum, a city of Galilee. And he was teaching them on the Sabbath,

32 and they were astonished at his teaching, for his word possessed authority.

33 And in the synagogue there was a man who had the spirit of an unclean demon, and he cried out with a loud voice,

34 "Ha! What have you to do with us, Jesus of Nazareth? Have you come to destroy us? I know who you are—the Holy One of God."

35 But Jesus rebuked him, saying, "Be silent and come out of him!" And when the demon had thrown him down in their midst, he came out of him, having done him no harm.

36 And they were all amazed and said to one another, "What is this word? For with authority and power he commands the unclean spirits, and they come out!"

37 And reports about him went out into every place in the surrounding region.

38 And he arose and left the synagogue and entered Simon's house. Now Simon's mother-in-law was ill with a high fever, and they appealed to him on her behalf.

39 And he stood over her and rebuked the fever, and it left her, and immediately she rose and began to serve them.

40 Now when the sun was setting, all those who had any who were sick with various diseases brought them to him, and he laid his hands on every one of them and healed them.

41 And demons also came out of many, crying, "You are the Son of God!" But he rebuked them and would not allow them to speak, because they knew that he was the Christ.

42 And when it was day, he departed and went into a desolate place. And the people sought him and came to him, and would have kept him from leaving them,

⁴³ but he said to them, "I must preach the good news of the kingdom of God to the other towns as well; for I was sent for this purpose."

⁴⁴ And he was preaching in the synagogues of Judea.

a. He tried to get alone
b. The people sought Him out and begged Him to stay

8. **Jesus persisted in His mission despite pressure to be sidetracked**

Division III

The Son of Man's Announced Mission and Public Ministry, 4:16–9:17

B. Jesus Ministers and Makes an Amazing Impact: A Day in the Life of Jesus, 4:31–44

(Mt.8:14–17; Mk.1:21–39)

4:31–44
Introduction

This is one of the most interesting passages in all of Scripture. It is a chronicle of one of the first days of Jesus' ministry. Luke paints the picture of a typical day so that we will have some idea of what a day was like in the life of Jesus. His report reveals just how busy and pressuring and tiring the day was, and it contains powerful lessons applicable to our lives. This is, *Jesus Ministers and Makes an Amazing Impact: A Day in the Life of Jesus*, 4:31-44.

1. Jesus went down to Capernaum (v.31).
2. Jesus taught in the Sabbath service with authority (v.32).
3. Jesus delivered the most unclean (vv.33-37).
4. Jesus cured the most needful (vv.38-39).
5. Jesus healed the diseases of those who sought Him out (v.40).
6. Jesus rebuked the evil spirits, kept them from making a false profession (v.41).
7. Jesus went to a solitary place to be in God's presence (v.42).
8. Jesus persisted in His mission despite pressure to be sidetracked (vv.43-44).

1 Jesus went down to Capernaum.

4:31

After being run out of Nazareth, Jesus went down to Capernaum, a city of Galilee. Capernaum became the *headquarters* of Jesus as He preached in the synagogues throughout the region (v.44). When His hometown rejected Him, He had to move somewhere. The city He chose as the center of His operations was Capernaum. Capernaum was the manufac-

³¹ And he went down to Capernaum, a city of Galilee. And he was teaching them on the Sabbath,

turing center of Palestine; therefore, it was strategically located, always flooded with traveling merchants. The major roads passed through its borders, roads which connected such metropolitan cities as Damascus, Jerusalem, and the great Syrian cities of Tyre and Sidon. The main caravan route leading to the Mediterranean Sea also ran through the city (see Is.9:1). It was both an ideal location for the spread of the gospel and for the Messiah to use as His base of operations (see note, *Capernaum*—Mt.4:12-13).

2 Jesus taught in the Sabbath service with authority.

Jesus' teaching was not ordinary, not the kind of teaching the people were used to hearing. They were astonished at His teaching, astounded by *how* He taught; He taught with unusual authority:

4:32

> His Word had authority, the authority of God's Spirit.
> His message had a commanding force to it.
> His message had the power of God's Spirit upon it, making the Word come alive to the hearts of the hearers (see note—Mt.7:29).

³² and they were astonished at his teaching, for his word possessed authority.

So Jesus answered them, "My teaching is not mine, but his who sent me. If anyone's will is to do God's will, he will know whether the teaching is from God or whether I am speaking on my own authority. The one who speaks on his own authority seeks his own glory; but the one who seeks the glory of him who sent him is true, and in him there is no falsehood." (Jn.7:16–18)

Do you not believe that I am in the Father and the Father is in me? The words that I say to you I do not speak on my own authority, but the Father who dwells in me does his works. (Jn.14:10)

4:33–37

3 Jesus delivered the most unclean.

As Jesus was in the synagogue, He had an encounter with a demon-possessed man—the most unclean of people. The demon revealed itself and boldly confronted Jesus—right in the house of God! Luke tells us what happened (see outline and notes—Mk.1:23-28).

³³ And in the synagogue there was a man who had the spirit of an unclean demon, and he cried out with a loud voice,
³⁴ "Ha! What have you to do with us, Jesus of Nazareth? Have you come to destroy us? I know who you are—the Holy One of God."
³⁵ But Jesus rebuked him, saying, "Be silent and come out of him!" And when the demon had thrown him down in their midst, he came out of him, having done him no harm.
³⁶ And they were all amazed and said to one another, "What is this word? For with authority and power he commands the unclean spirits, and they come out!"
³⁷ And reports about him went out into every place in the surrounding region.

a. **A man with an unclean spirit sat in worship (vv.33–35).** The man was "in the synagogue," actually attending the worship service; yet he was desperately unclean, as defiled as could be (v.33a). The man had the spirit "of an unclean demon." *Unclean* (Gk. akathartou, *ahk-ahth'-ar-too*) means that the man was both morally and ceremonially unclean, filthy within and without. He was trying to worship, but he was morally unclean and corrupt; his life was a sinful wreck.

As the man sat in God's house, the evil spirit within him could not remain silent. It "cried out with a loud voice," disrupting the service (v.33b). The evil spirit immediately *acknowledged* Jesus' deity. Imagine—people would not and will not believe and acknowledge who Jesus is, but demons do! The demon knew and acknowledged three realities (v.34; see note, pt.2—Mk.1:23-24 for detailed discussion):

> It had nothing to do with Jesus. It was unclean, dirty, and sinful in comparison with Jesus.
> It knew that it was to be destroyed by Jesus, that a day of judgment was coming.
> It knew that Jesus was "the Holy One of God." It knew and proclaimed that it stood face-to-face with the true Messiah, the Son of the living God.

THOUGHT 1. Every person without Christ is in desperate straits, just as this man was. Certainly, not all are demon-possessed as this man was, but they are nonetheless gripped by an evil force that keeps them separated from God. They cannot truly worship, for they have no relationship with God, no standing with Him. Because they have refused to repent, they face God's judgment.

You stiff-necked people, uncircumcised in heart and ears, you always resist the Holy Spirit. As your fathers did, so do you. (Ac.7:51)

They have turned to me their back and not their face. And though I have taught them persistently, they have not listened to receive instruction. (Je.32:33)

As for the word that you have spoken to us in the name of the LORD, we will not listen to you. (Je.44:16)

> But they refused to pay attention and turned a stubborn shoulder and stopped their ears that they might not hear. (Zec.7:11)

Jesus rebuked the evil spirit's acknowledgement (v.35a). This is a critical point: Jesus stopped the proclamation of the evil spirit, even though the spirit was acknowledging Jesus as God. Jesus would not have the evil spirit's witnessing to His deity. Why? Because it was a false witness, a profession only. The evil spirit was not confessing from the heart nor from the will to follow Jesus. He had not been born again. The *only confession* Jesus would accept was the confession of a person who made a deliberate decision to follow Him *as Lord* (see note—Mk.1:25-26).

> Because, if you confess with your mouth that Jesus is Lord and believe in your heart that God raised him from the dead, you will be saved. For with the heart one believes and is justified, and with the mouth one confesses and is saved. For the Scripture says, "Everyone who believes in him will not be put to shame." For there is no distinction between Jew and Greek; for the same Lord is Lord of all, bestowing his riches on all who call on him. For "everyone who calls on the name of the Lord will be saved." (Ro.10:9-13)

Jesus cast out the unclean spirit and saved the man (v.35b). How? By His Word, by simply telling the demon to be quiet and come out of him. The evil spirit threw the man down, but he came out of the man as Jesus commanded and did not hurt him (see note, pt.2—Mk.1:25-26 for detailed discussion). Note the great power of the Lord's Word.

> And Jesus came and said to them, "All authority in heaven and on earth has been given to me." (Mt.28:18)

> Since you have given him authority over all flesh, to give eternal life to all whom you have given him. (Jn.17:2)

b. The people were amazed (v.36).

The people were amazed, astonished, shocked, stunned by what they had witnessed. Note what amazed them: Jesus' *Word*—the authority and power of His Word to command demons and *cleanse* even the most unclean.

c. The people spread the news about Him everywhere they went (v.37).

The people spread Jesus' fame everywhere, witnessing to His cleansing and healing power. How could they not talk about Jesus, for they were witnessing a power never before seen.

THOUGHT 1. The Lord has the power to save and cleanse anyone who comes to Him, no matter how possessed by evil.

> Since you have given him authority over all flesh, to give eternal life to all whom you have given him. (Jn.17:2)

> Having the eyes of your hearts enlightened, that you may know what is the hope to which he has called you, what are the riches of his glorious inheritance in the saints, and what is the immeasurable greatness of his power toward us who believe, according to the working of his great might (Ep.1:18-19)

> I know that you can do all things, and that no purpose of yours can be thwarted. (Jb.42:2)

4 Jesus cured the most needful.

After the worship service in the synagogue, Jesus went to Peter's home. Peter's mother-in-law was critically ill. She is a picture of the most needful of people.

a. So needful, a great fever (v.38a).

The dear lady was desperately needful, overtaken with an extremely high fever. Her illness was so critical that it threatened her life.

38 And he arose and left the synagogue and entered Simon's house. Now Simon's mother-in-law was ill with a high fever, and they appealed to him on her behalf.

39 And he stood over her and rebuked the fever, and it left her, and immediately she rose and began to serve them.

b. So needful, could not speak or seek Jesus for herself (v.38b).

With such an extremely high fever, she was most likely delirious or perhaps even unconscious. She was so helpless she could not even speak to ask Jesus for help, so her family appealed to Jesus on her behalf, asking Him to help her.

c. So needful, could not even come to Jesus (v.39a).

The sick lady was so weakened she was unable to rise out of bed to seek the help of Jesus. Jesus came to where she was and stood over her.

d. So needful, He came to her and healed her: She arose and ministered (v.39b).

When Jesus rebuked the fever, it left her. Jesus healed this critically-ill woman by simply speaking the Word. Her recovery was immediate and complete: she arose and began to serve her family and their guests.

THOUGHT 1. Jesus is the great hope of the most needful. No matter how *desperate or helpless or weakened*—Jesus can speak the Word of healing. All that is needed is a believing heart and a willing mind.

Even if a person is so helpless that they are unable to speak verbally, that person can call upon the Lord by thought—in their hearts— and the Lord will still help them.

For "everyone who calls on the name of the Lord will be saved." (Ro.10:13)

"But that you may know that the Son of Man has authority on earth to forgive sins"—he then said to the paralytic—"Rise, pick up your bed and go home." (Mt.9:6)

4:40

⁴⁰ Now when the sun was setting, all those who had any who were sick with various diseases brought them to him, and he laid his hands on every one of them and healed them.

5 Jesus healed the diseases of those who sought Him out.

That same evening, a host of people with various diseases were brought to Jesus (see outline and notes—Mk.1:32–34 for detailed discussion). These people were totally helpless, unable to get to Jesus on their own. Thankfully, every one of them had someone who cared about them enough to bring them to the Lord. Their friends or loved ones waited until evening because it was the Sabbath. It would have been against the law for them to carry these people before the Sabbath had ended.

Jesus had been ministering rather extensively all day and was tired, yet He was approachable. He could be approached at all hours. There was never a closed door into His presence. The Lord healed the diseases of all those who sought Him out. He did not bypass or overlook a single one. He touched every one and healed every one. No matter the disease, they were healed.

THOUGHT 1. Note two challenging lessons.
1) The most helpless can come or be brought to Jesus. He is always available to help.
2) There is a strong challenge to us. We need to care enough to bring the helpless to Jesus.

So his fame spread throughout all Syria, and they brought him all the sick, those afflicted with various diseases and pains, those oppressed by demons, those having seizures, and paralytics, and he healed them. (Mt.4:24)

And they came, bringing to him a paralytic carried by four men. (Mk.2:3)

THOUGHT 2. No one, no matter how helpless, ever comes to Jesus that He does not help. Rich or poor, strong or weak, the Lord forbids no one.

That evening they brought to him many who were oppressed by demons, and he cast out the spirits with a word and healed all who were sick. This was to fulfill what was spoken by the prophet Isaiah: "He took our illnesses and bore our diseases." (Mt.8:16–17)

And Jesus answered them, "Those who are well have no need of a physician, but those who are sick. I have not come to call the righteous but sinners to repentance." (Lu.5:31–32)

How God anointed Jesus of Nazareth with the Holy Spirit and with power. He went about doing good and healing all who were oppressed by the devil, for God was with him. (Ac.10:38)

For you have been a stronghold to the poor, a stronghold to the needy in his distress, a shelter from the storm and a shade from the heat; for the breath of the ruthless is like a storm against a wall. (Is.25:4)

Surely he has borne our griefs and carried our sorrows; yet we esteemed him stricken, smitten by God, and afflicted. (Is.53:4)

6 Jesus rebuked the evil spirits, kept them from making a false profession.

4:41

In addition to healing the sick, Jesus also delivered many who were possessed by demons. As He cast the demons out of the oppressed, the evil spirits declared that Jesus is the Son of God. However, Jesus rebuked the evil spirits and would not allow them to make false professions. The Lord neither needed nor desired their testimony (see notes— Lu.4:33-37; Mk.1:25-26).

41 And demons also came out of many, crying, "You are the Son of God!" But he rebuked them and would not allow them to speak, because they knew that he was the Christ.

7 Jesus went to a solitary place to be in God's presence.

4:42

Jesus was exhausted and drained, spiritually as well as physically. Apparently, He had been ministering all day and night, that is, for almost twenty-four hours without a break. When the new day dawned, He went to a solitary place to be in God's presence.

42 And when it was day, he departed and went into a desolate place. And the people sought him and came to him, and would have kept him from leaving them,

a. **He tried to get alone.**

Jesus tried to get alone in an isolated place. He needed to be refreshed and revived in body and spirit. He wanted time to rest and be alone with God.

b. **The people sought Him out and begged Him to stay.**

The needy people would not let Jesus be alone. Desperate and helpless, they sought Him out and begged Him to stay.

THOUGHT 1. Note two great lessons.

1) We need to seek the renewal of our bodies and spirits in the Lord's presence.
2) We need to seek the Lord and beg for His help while He may be found. When Jesus was on the earth in an earthly, pre-resurrection body, He could help only those who surrounded Him. Now He is able to minister everywhere at once, but so few of us are seeking Him out. What an example these people were in seeking Him!

Come to me, all who labor and are heavy laden, and I will give you rest. (Mt.11:28)

Let us draw near with a true heart in full assurance of faith, with our hearts sprinkled clean from an evil conscience and our bodies washed with pure water. (He.10:22)

Seek the LORD and his strength; seek his presence continually! (1 Chr.16:11)

Seek the LORD while he may be found; call upon him while he is near. (Is.55:6)

8 Jesus persisted in His mission despite pressure to be sidetracked.

Jesus had to preach in other cities as well, so He could not stay with those of Capernaum who were pressuring Him. He had to fulfill His mission; He could not be sidetracked. Everyone had to hear the gospel. He had to give others the opportunity as well. He knew that the more people He could reach and disciple, the more others would hear and be reached (the principle of multiplication). So He set His face like a flint and moved on despite all who *tried to hinder Him*.

For the Son of Man came to seek and to save the lost. (Lu.19:10)

We must work the works of him who sent me while it is day; night is coming, when no one can work. (Jn.9:4)

4:43–44

⁴³ but he said to them, "I must preach the good news of the kingdom of God to the other towns as well; for I was sent for this purpose."

⁴⁴ And he was preaching in the synagogues of Judea.

CHAPTER 5

C. Jesus Calls His First Disciples: Steps to Calling People, 5:1–11

(Mt.4:18–22; Mk.1:16–20; Jn.1:35–51)

On one occasion, while the crowd was pressing in on him to hear the word of God, he was standing by the lake of Gennesaret,

2 and he saw two boats by the lake, but the fishermen had gone out of them and were washing their nets.

3 Getting into one of the boats, which was Simon's, he asked him to put out a little from the land. And he sat down and taught the people from the boat.

4 And when he had finished speaking, he said to Simon, "Put out into the deep and let down your nets for a catch."

5 And Simon answered, "Master, we toiled all night and took nothing! But at your word I will let down the nets."

6 And when they had done this, they enclosed a large number of fish, and their nets were breaking.

7 They signaled to their partners in the other boat to come and help them. And they came and filled both the boats, so that they began to sink.

8 But when Simon Peter saw it, he fell down at Jesus' knees, saying, "Depart from me, for I am a sinful man, O Lord."

9 For he and all who were with him were astonished at the catch of fish that they had taken,

10 and so also were James and John, sons of Zebedee, who were partners with Simon. And Jesus said to Simon, "Do not be afraid; from now on you will be catching men."

11 And when they had brought their boats to land, they left everything and followed him.

1. **The setting: Lake Gennesaret**
2. **Step 1: Seeing a vision of people who need to hear the Word of God**

3. **Step 2: Seizing resources**
   a. Jesus scanned the horizon for available resources
   b. Jesus saw a man, Simon, and led him to serve

4. **Step 3: Overcoming reluctance to willing obedience**

5. **Step 4: Demonstrating godly power**
   a. A great catch made, so great the nets broke
   b. A catch so great other help was needed
   c. A catch so great both boats were filled
   d. A catch so great the boats began to sink

6. **Step 5: Stirring a deep confession**
   a. Of sin
   b. Of Christ as Lord
   c. Of awe—reverence—fear [DS1]

7. **Step 6: Challenging people to discipleship, that is, to catch other people**[DS2]

8. **Step 7: Watching for the decision to surrender all**

Division III

The Son of Man's Announced Mission and Public Ministry, 4:16–9:17

C. Jesus Calls His First Disciples: Steps to Calling People, 5:1–11

(Mt.4:18–22; Mk.1:16–20; Jn.1:35–51)

5:1–11
Introduction

Jesus' mission is to seek and save the lost (Lu.19:10). Being all-powerful, our Lord can reach people however He chooses. He has chosen to involve His followers in seeking the lost that He might save them. He calls all who follow Him to participate with Him in the work of reaching others with the gospel and then training those who believe to reach others with the gospel (Mt.28:19–20).

On other occasions, our Lord describes the wonderful work of reaching others as sowing and reaping a harvest (Mt.9:37–38; 13:3–9, 18–23; Jn.4:35). Here, our Lord compares the work of winning the lost to fishing—fishing for and catching souls. This passage is a descriptive picture of how Jesus goes about calling people to join Him in the enormous task of reaching the world. It is critical for us to understand these steps if we are going to successfully make disciples who will, in turn, make disciples. This is, *Jesus Calls His First Disciples: Steps to Calling People*, 5:1-11.

1. The setting: Lake Gennesaret (v.1).
2. Step 1: Seeing a vision of people who need to hear the Word of God (v.1).
3. Step 2: Seizing resources (vv.2–3).
4. Step 3: Overcoming reluctance to willing obedience (vv.4–5).
5. Step 4: Demonstrating godly power (vv.6–7).
6. Step 5: Stirring a deep confession (vv.8–9).
7. Step 6: Challenging people to discipleship, that is, to catch other people (v.10).
8. Step 7: Watching for the decision to surrender all (v.11).

5:1a

On one occasion, while the crowd was pressing in on him to hear the word of God, he was standing by the lake of Gennesaret,

1 The setting: Lake Gennesaret.

Luke reports that the setting for Jesus' calling of His first disciples was the Lake of Gennesaret. This is simply another name for the Sea of Galilee. It was also known as "the sea of Tiberias" (Jn.6:1; 21:1) and, in Old Testament times, as the "sea of Chinnereth" (Nu.34:11; Jos.13:27).

5:1b

On one occasion, while the crowd was pressing in on him to hear the word of God, he was standing by the lake of Gennesaret,

2 Step 1: Seeing a vision of people who need to hear the Word of God.

The first step to calling people is seeing a vision of people—people who need the Word of God. The people were actually *pressing* (Gk. epikeisthai, *ep-ik-ace'-thigh*) in upon Jesus. They gathered and crowded around Him because they were hungry to hear the Word of God. They had a craving, a *hunger and thirst* for righteousness. Jesus satisfied their hunger; He spoke God's Word to them (vv.3–4). But He also foresaw the time when He would no longer be on this earth, and He called others to join Him in the great work of speaking God's Word to people (vv.4–11).

> **Blessed are those who hunger and thirst for righteousness, for they shall be satisfied. (Mt.5:6)**

> **But whoever drinks of the water that I will give him will never be thirsty again. The water that I will give him will become in him a spring of water welling up to eternal life. (Jn.4:14)**

> **On the last day of the feast, the great day, Jesus stood up and cried out, "If anyone thirsts, let him come to me and drink." (Jn.7:37)**

Like newborn infants, long for the pure spiritual milk, that by it you may grow up into salvation— if indeed you have tasted that the Lord is good. (1 Pe.2:2-3)

The Spirit and the Bride say, "Come." And let the one who hears say, "Come." And let the one who is thirsty come; let the one who desires take the water of life without price. (Re.22:17)

Come, everyone who thirsts, come to the waters; and he who has no money, come, buy and eat! Come, buy wine and milk without money and without price. (Is.55:1)

THOUGHT 1. If we are going to reach others with the gospel, we must go where people are. We cannot reach people if we live in isolation or ignore other people. Jesus loved and cared for people, and He was deeply concerned over their welfare. Therefore, He continually sought to be around them and to meet their needs. We need to follow His example.

Go therefore and make disciples of all nations, baptizing them in the name of the Father and of the Son and of the Holy Spirit, teaching them to observe all that I have commanded you. And behold, I am with you always, to the end of the age. (Mt.28:19-20)

And he said to them, "The harvest is plentiful, but the laborers are few. Therefore pray earnestly to the Lord of the harvest to send out laborers into his harvest." (Lu.10:2)

Do you not say, "There are yet four months, then comes the harvest"? Look, I tell you, lift up your eyes, and see that the fields are white for harvest. Already the one who reaps is receiving wages and gathering fruit for eternal life, so that sower and reaper may rejoice together. (Jn.4:35-36)

3 Step 2: Seizing resources.

5:2-3

a. **Jesus scanned the horizon for available resources (v.2).**

b. **Jesus saw a man, Simon, and led him to serve (v.3).**

² and he saw two boats by the lake, but the fishermen had gone out of them and were washing their nets.

³ Getting into one of the boats, which was Simon's, he asked him to put out a little from the land. And he sat down and taught the people from the boat.

The second step to calling people is seizing resources. Jesus had to find some way to handle the throng of people both then and later. The crowds were so large and their needs so many that He needed the help of others. He could not personally meet everyone's needs. Standing there and being confronted with the present problem, He scanned the horizon, looking for anything or anyone to help Him handle the situation.

As He looked around, He saw an opportunity and laid His plans. He saw a boat and a fisherman washing his nets outside the boat, and He could use both. The boat could be used as a platform from which to preach, and the man could become a disciple. He asked the man to let Him use the boat and to steer the boat out from land a short distance. The point is this: Jesus seized the resources available. He had the vision of people needing the Word of God, but He needed a platform and others to help, so He looked around and found both.

4 Step 3: Overcoming reluctance to willing obedience.

5:4-5

The third step to calling people is *overcoming their reluctance to obey what Christ commands.* As soon as Jesus finished His preaching, He wanted to bless Peter for helping Him. The Lord of heaven and earth was going to give Peter a bounty of fish, so he told Peter to row back out to sea and cast out his nets one more time. In addition, Jesus wanted to teach Peter a spiritual lesson and call him to a greater purpose in life. He wanted to win Peter's loyalty and discipleship. And, He wanted to show Peter that He, the Messiah, could look after and take care of him.

⁴ And when he had finished speaking, he said to Simon, "Put out into the deep and let down your nets for a catch."

⁵ And Simon answered, "Master, we toiled all night and took nothing! But at your word I will let down the nets."

Peter was reluctant to obey Jesus and objected to what Jesus asked. He was thoroughly *exhausted*, for he had "toiled all night" and had caught nothing. He had worked enough hours

133

already and had come back empty-handed. On top of that, he had stayed to help the Lord in His preaching by loaning his boat to Him when he needed to be home in bed.

Peter caught himself in the middle of his objection and obeyed. What caused the switch, the change from reluctance to willing obedience?

First, Peter was largely convinced that Jesus was who He claimed to be, the Messiah.

Second, Peter was drawn somewhat to follow Jesus. Therefore, when he began to object to Jesus' will, there was a prick of conscience, and he obeyed his conscience. He followed his heart . . .

- not his *mind*, thinking there were no fish
- not his *experience*, having already tried and failed to catch fish
- not his *body*, being too tired and exhausted, just incapable of going on

THOUGHT 1. Reluctance should always give in to obedience. We need to have a spirit that will *try* for God, no matter what the obstacles or how hopeless a situation may seem.

> Do not be slothful in zeal, be fervent in spirit, serve the Lord. (Ro.12:11)

> Therefore, my beloved brothers, be steadfast, immovable, always abounding in the work of the Lord, knowing that in the Lord your labor is not in vain. (1 Co.15:58)

> And let us not grow weary of doing good, for in due season we will reap, if we do not give up. (Ga.6:9)

> So that you may not be sluggish, but imitators of those who through faith and patience inherit the promises. (He.6:12)

> He who goes out weeping, bearing the seed for sowing, shall come home with shouts of joy, bringing his sheaves with him. (Ps.126:6)

THOUGHT 2. When a person is drawn to Christ, they desperately need to obey their heart and to obey it immediately.

> For he says, "In a favorable time I listened to you, and in a day of salvation I have helped you." Behold, now is the favorable time; behold, now is the day of salvation. (2 Co.6:2)

> Again he appoints a certain day, "Today," saying through David so long afterward, in the words already quoted, "Today, if you hear his voice, do not harden your hearts." (He.4:7)

> Seek the Lord while he may be found; call upon him while he is near. (Is.55:6)

5:6–7

⁶ And when they had done this, they enclosed a large number of fish, and their nets were breaking.
⁷ They signaled to their partners in the other boat to come and help them. And they came and filled both the boats, so that they began to sink.

5 Step 4: Demonstrating godly power.

a. **A great catch made, so great the nets broke (v.6).**

b. **A catch so great other help was needed (v.7a).**

c. **A catch so great both boats were filled (v.7b).**

d. **A catch so great the boats began to sink (v.7c).**

The fourth step to calling people is *demonstrating godly power*. Peter's obedience produced results; his obedience caught fish, and the catch was no ordinary catch. He caught so many fish that his nets broke (v.6). The catch was so great that he and his crew could not handle it, so they called for another boat to come and help them. The huge hoard of fish filled both boats. And these were not small fish; the weight of the fish was so heavy that the boats began to sink (v.7)!

The catch of fish was so tremendous that there was no question that Jesus was behind the miracle; Jesus was demonstrating the power of God. (Remember this was the very purpose of Jesus, to win Peter's loyalty and willingness to become a full-time disciple.) What happened is a little humorous when we remember what Jesus was doing with Peter, and Peter's reluctance and objection, weariness, and exhaustion. Peter thought he was tired, but he did not know what exhaustion was yet. The Lord must have stood to the side smiling to Himself. How our Lord loved this man Peter, even now! He was after Peter's loyalty, and He was going to get it even if He had to bring Peter to his knees (which is exactly what would happen, v.8). At any rate, there was some humor in what began to happen to this man who was so reluctant, moaning and groaning about his fatigue and his lack of previous success. Just imagine Peter already bone-weary, grumbling in his mind at this carpenter's telling him, the skilled fisherman, how to fish. Imagine Peter's exhaustion and weariness, reluctance and objection, and then all of a sudden a catch is made, a catch so great that he was going to have to work wearily for hours to handle it!

Jesus had His man! What else was Peter to do other than what followed? In all the humor of the situation, our Lord's heart was bound to be full of rejoicing because this rugged fisherman, flawed man though he was, was like a little child before Jesus. He was broken in humility before the Lord. His reluctance to obey the Lord was gone, and the experience was but the first of many experiences of brokenness yet to come.

I know that you can do all things, and that no purpose of yours can be thwarted. (Jb.42:2)

Also henceforth I am he; there is none who can deliver from my hand; I work, and who can turn it back? (Is.43:13)

6 Step 5: Stirring a deep confession.

The fifth step to calling people is *stirring a deep confession.* Peter knew exactly what had happened. He had been reluctant and objected to the Lord's request. But he was a skilled fisherman, and he knew that the great catch was no ordinary catch; it was a miracle of the Lord, a miracle which the Lord was using to teach him that he was to obey without reluctance and objection.

When Peter saw the miraculous catch of fish, he realized that he was in the presence of God. He raced over to Jesus, fell on his knees, and confessed His faith in Christ.

[8] But when Simon Peter saw it, he fell down at Jesus' knees, saying, "Depart from me, for I am a sinful man, O Lord."

[9] For he and all who were with him were astonished at the catch of fish that they had taken,

[10] and so also were James and John, sons of Zebedee, who were partners with Simon. And Jesus said to Simon, "Do not be afraid; from now on you will be catching men."

a. Of sin (v.8a).

First, Peter confessed his sin. His immediate sin was that of being reluctant to obey the Lord, of questioning the Lord's will and knowledge and power. But Peter's confession went far beyond his most recent sin: he freely admitted that he was "a sinful man"—he confessed his sinful condition. By saying, "Depart from me," Peter acknowledged that he was unworthy to stand in the Lord's presence.

b. Of Christ as Lord (v.8b).

Second, Peter confessed Jesus to be the *Lord.* Note that Peter had previously called Jesus *Master* (epistata, *ep-is-tah'-tah;* v.5), which is a word commonly used to address anyone in authority. But Peter had learned better. He now called Jesus *Lord* (kurie, *kur'-ih-eh*). He is the supreme One, the Lord who is holy and convicting, who must be obeyed and followed.

c. Of awe—reverence—fear (vv.9–10a).

Peter was *astonished* (thambos, *thahm'-bos*) at Christ's mighty power, as were all who were with him, including James (see DEEPER STUDY # 1) and John, his fishing partners. It was this amazement that led Peter to confess Jesus as Lord. His confession was one of awe and reverence—godly fear—toward Christ.

THOUGHT 1. Peter's confession is the confession of all who genuinely believe in Christ unto salvation. Like Peter, we must acknowledge our sinful condition and need of salvation. Then, we must confess Christ as Lord, fully trust in Him as the Source of our salvation.

Because, if you confess with your mouth that Jesus is Lord and believe in your heart that God raised him from the dead, you will be saved. For with the heart one believes and is justified, and with the mouth one confesses and is saved. (Ro.10:9-10)

If we confess our sins, he is faithful and just to forgive us our sins and to cleanse us from all unrighteousness. (1 Jn.1:9)

Abraham answered and said, "Behold, I have undertaken to speak to the Lord, I who am but dust and ashes." (Ge.18:27)

I had heard of you by the hearing of the ear, but now my eye sees you; therefore I despise myself, and repent in dust and ashes. (Jb.42:5–6)

And I said: "Woe is me! For I am lost; for I am a man of unclean lips, and I dwell in the midst of a people of unclean lips; for my eyes have seen the King, the LORD of hosts!" (Is.6:5)

DEEPER STUDY # 1

(5:10) **James:** there were two disciples named James. (1) The James mentioned in this passage, the brother of John, was the son of Zebedee. He along with Peter and his brother John formed an inner circle around the Lord (Mt.17:1; Mk.5:37; 9:2; 14:33). He is never mentioned apart from John. He was killed with the sword by Herod (Ac.12:2). (2) James the less was the son of Alphaeus (Mt.10:3). He was called *the less* because he was shorter of stature.

It should be noted that two other men named James are mentioned in the New Testament. (1) There is James the Lord's half-brother (Mt.13:55; Mk.6:3; Ga.1:19). He and the Lord's other brothers and sisters did not believe Jesus to be the Messiah until after Jesus' resurrection (Jn.7:5; Ac.1:14). James, however, became a great leader and pastor in the early church. He pastored the Jerusalem Church (Ac.12:17; 15:13; 21:18; Ga.1:19; 2:9, 12), and he wrote the Epistle of James. (2) There is also James who was the father of Judas (Lu.6:16; Ac.1:13).

5:10b

¹⁰ and so also were James and John, sons of Zebedee, who were partners with Simon. And Jesus said to Simon, "Do not be afraid; from now on you will be catching men."

7 Step 6: Challenging people to discipleship, that is, to catch other people.

The sixth step to calling people is *challenging them to discipleship,* that is, to *catch other people*—bring them to Christ. This is the challenge our Lord extended to Peter (see DEEPER STUDY # 2).

Jesus first said to Peter, *"Do not be afraid"* (mē phobou, may phah-boo'). This statement indicates that Peter was actually frightened. Jesus was calming him, telling him to trust and stop fearing. He, the Lord, was in charge and looking after everything.

Jesus then called Peter to "catch men." The word *catch* (zōgrōn, zoh-groan') means to *take alive* or to *catch for life.* The idea is that Peter was no longer to catch *fish* for the purpose of killing them, but he was to catch *people* for the purpose of giving life to them.

And he said to them, "Follow me, and I will make you fishers of men." (Mt.4:19)

And have mercy on those who doubt; save others by snatching them out of the fire; to others show mercy with fear, hating even the garment stained by the flesh. (Jude 22–23)

The fruit of the righteous is a tree of life, and whoever captures souls is wise. (Pr.11:30)

And I heard the voice of the Lord saying, "Whom shall I send, and who will go for us?" Then I said, "Here I am! Send me." (Is.6:8)

And those who are wise shall shine like the brightness of the sky above; and those who turn many to righteousness, like the stars forever and ever. (Da.12:3)

DEEPER STUDY # 2

(5:10) **Apostle—Witnessing:** see DEEPER STUDY # 5—Mt.10:2. See 2 Co.5:19–20; Jn.20:21; Ac.1:8.

8 Step 7: Watching for the decision to surrender all.

The seventh step to calling people is *watching for the decision to forsake all*. Peter, James, and John responded immediately to Jesus' call. They left everything—their businesses, their professions, and the biggest catch of fish they had ever seen—to follow Jesus. He was the Lord who had spoken, and they were to be His disciples who obeyed and followed.

And he said to all, "If anyone would come after me, let him deny himself and take up his cross daily and follow me." (Lu.9:23)

If anyone comes to me and does not hate his own father and mother and wife and children and brothers and sisters, yes, and even his own life, he cannot be my disciple. . . . So therefore, any one of you who does not renounce all that he has cannot be my disciple. (Lu.14:26, 33)

If anyone serves me, he must follow me; and where I am, there will my servant be also. If anyone serves me, the Father will honor him. (Jn.12:26)

11 And when they had brought their boats to land, they left everything and followed him.

D. Jesus Cleanses the Untouchable, 5:12–16

(Mt.8:1–4; Mk.1:40–45)

1. **Jesus was confronted by a desperate man, an untouchable**
   a. He was full of leprosy[DS1]
   b. He saw Jesus: Fell on his face and called Jesus "Lord," begging for cleansing
2. **Jesus cleansed the untouchable**
   a. Jesus touched him and said, "I am willing"
   b. The leper was cleansed
3. **Jesus charged the newly cleansed man**
   a. Tell nobody: Do not boast; watch being prideful[DS2]
   b. Rush to obey God: Worship and thank Him
4. **Jesus made an impact**
   a. His fame spread rapidly
   b. Crowds thronged to hear Him and to be healed by Him
   c. He withdrew into the wilderness to pray

¹² While he was in one of the cities, there came a man full of leprosy. And when he saw Jesus, he fell on his face and begged him, "Lord, if you will, you can make me clean."

¹³ And Jesus stretched out his hand and touched him, saying, "I will; be clean." And immediately the leprosy left him.

¹⁴ And he charged him to tell no one, but "go and show yourself to the priest, and make an offering for your cleansing, as Moses commanded, for a proof to them."

¹⁵ But now even more the report about him went abroad, and great crowds gathered to hear him and to be healed of their infirmities.

¹⁶ But he would withdraw to desolate places and pray.

Division III

The Son of Man's Announced Mission and Public Ministry, 4:16–9:17

D. Jesus Cleanses the Untouchable, 5:12–16

(Mt.8:1–4; Mk.1:40–45)

5:12–16
Introduction

Some individuals are treated by society as though they are untouchable. Some persons are so gripped and enslaved, so depraved and destitute, so different and derelict, so down and out, so helpless and hopeless, that they become untouchable to most people. But not to Jesus. And that is the driving message of this event. Jesus will touch the untouchable. He will accept and minister to the most despised and rejected. This is, *Jesus Cleanses the Untouchable*, 5:12–16.

1. Jesus was confronted by a desperate man, an untouchable (v.12).
2. Jesus cleansed the untouchable (v.13).
3. Jesus charged the newly cleansed man (v.14).
4. Jesus made an impact (vv.15–16).

1 Jesus was confronted by a desperate man, an untouchable.

Jesus was confronted by an untouchable individual. This man was so desperate that he violated all the restrictions the law and society placed on him and came to Jesus.

a. He was full of leprosy.

Luke specifies that the man was "full of leprosy." *Full* (Gk. plērēs, *play'-race*) means covered over or covered completely. The man's entire body was covered with sores and extremely disfigured (see DEEPER STUDY # 1).

> 12 While he was in one of the cities, there came a man full of leprosy. And when he saw Jesus, he fell on his face and begged him, "Lord, if you will, you can make me clean."

b. He saw Jesus: Fell on his face and called Jesus "Lord," begging for cleansing.

When this leper saw Jesus, he forgot all else . . .

- forgot all the people surrounding Jesus
- forgot the shame of his condition
- forgot the embarrassment
- forgot that the law forbade him to come within six feet of anyone

Nothing mattered but the *hope* he felt within, the possibility that Jesus would help him in his desperate condition. He rushed up to Jesus while people were scattering about for fear of catching his disease. He fell on his face and cried out to Jesus to cleanse him (see outline and notes—Mt.8:1-4; Mk.1:40-45 for additional discussion). In this one verse, Luke gives us four insights about this despised man.

First, he was determined. Nothing and no one was going to stop him from receiving Jesus' help, not even the fear and threats of people whom he would be frightening with the contagiousness of his disease.

Second, he was humble. He actually prostrated himself, falling on his face before Christ.

Third, he believed in Christ. The man confessed Christ as "Lord" (Kurie, *kur'-ee'-eh*; see notes—v.8). He fully believed—and confessed—that Jesus could heal him if He was willing to do so.

Fourth, he understood his condition—both physical and spiritual. The man's request was to be cleansed, not healed. He was asking for both spiritual and physical cleansing. He knew he was dirty and defiled both within and without.

And when Jesus heard it, he said to them, "Those who are well have no need of a physician, but those who are sick. I came not to call the righteous, but sinners." (Mk.2:17)

For we do not have a high priest who is unable to sympathize with our weaknesses, but one who in every respect has been tempted as we are, yet without sin. (He.4:15)

The LORD is near to the brokenhearted and saves the crushed in spirit. (Ps.34:18)

As for me, I am poor and needy, but the Lord takes thought for me. You are my help and my deliverer; do not delay, O my God! (Ps.40:17)

Wash me thoroughly from my iniquity, and cleanse me from my sin! (Ps.51:2)

The sacrifices of God are a broken spirit; a broken and contrite heart, O God, you will not despise. (Ps.51:17)

DEEPER STUDY # 1

(5:12) **Leprosy:** leprosy was the most terrible and greatly feared disease in Jesus' day. It was disfiguring and sometimes fatal. In the Bible leprosy is a type (picture) of sin.

1. The leper was considered *utterly unclean*—physically and spiritually. He could not approach within six feet of any person, including family members (Le.13:45).

2. The leper was judged as *dead—the living dead* and had to wear a black garment to be quickly recognized as from among the *dead*.

3. The leper was banished as an *outcast, totally ostracized* from society—considered without hope of going to heaven (Le.13:46). Such a person could not live within the walls of any city; the person's dwelling had to be outside the city gates.

4. The leper was thought to be *polluted, incurable* by any human means whatsoever. Leprosy could be cured by God and His power alone. (Note how Christ proves His Messiahship and deity by healing the leper.)

Imagine the anguish and heartbreak of the leper's being completely cut off from family and friends and society. Imagine the emotional and mental pain. The Gospels record other instances of lepers' being healed (see Mt.10:8; 11:5; Mk.1:40; Lu.7:22; 17:12; and perhaps Mt.26:6; see Mk.14:3).

5:13

2 Jesus cleansed the untouchable.

[13] And Jesus stretched out his hand and touched him, saying, "I will; be clean." And immediately the leprosy left him.

Deeply *moved with compassion* for the pitiful man (Mk.1:41), Jesus granted his plea for cleansing. The sight gripped Jesus' heart. The man's condition was wretched. Just imagine . . .

- his body full of sores
- his flesh eaten away
- his loneliness
- his alienation

- his emptiness
- his hopelessness
- his helplessness
- his desperation

a. Jesus touched him and said, "I am willing."

Jesus said, "I *will*—I will make you clean." The Savior reached out and touched the leper, an unheard-of act. The man was an untouchable, a man full of the most feared and dreaded and contagious disease known to the world of that day. Yet Jesus lowered Himself to touch the suffering man. No other person would. The man had been a leper for years, so many years that he was now full of leprosy, a very advanced stage. During all those years, no one would dare help him. He had not been touched by a human hand for so many years, he probably could not remember the comfort of a tender touch.

THOUGHT 1. Jesus wills for untouchables to be cleansed and fully restored, restored within their own hearts and restored within society. Jesus is willing to touch every person who has become untouchable.

> When he saw the crowds, he had compassion for them, because they were harassed and helpless, like sheep without a shepherd. (Mt.9:36)

> When he went ashore he saw a great crowd, and he had compassion on them and healed their sick. (Mt.14:14)

> As a father shows compassion to his children, so the LORD shows compassion to those who fear him. (Ps.103:13)

> In all their affliction he was afflicted, and the angel of his presence saved them; in his love and in his pity he redeemed them; he lifted them up and carried them all the days of old. (Is.63:9)

b. The leper was cleansed.

Jesus spoke the word of cleansing, "Be clean." Jesus saved the man spiritually, physically, and socially. The man was fully cleansed. But note how: he was cleansed by the *Word* of Jesus.

THOUGHT 1. The Lord's Word is sufficient, able to save and heal to the uttermost (He.7:25).

> How God anointed Jesus of Nazareth with the Holy Spirit and with power. He went about doing good and healing all who were oppressed by the devil, for God was with him. (Ac.10:38)

> Consequently, he is able to save to the uttermost those who draw near to God through him, since he always lives to make intercession for them. (He.7:25)

All these things my hand has made, and so all these things came to be, declares the LORD. But this is the one to whom I will look: he who is humble and contrite in spirit and trembles at my word. (Is.66:2)

3 Jesus charged the newly cleansed man.

Jesus gave two charges to the newly cleansed man (see note and DEEPER STUDY # 4—Mt.8:4; note—Mk.1:44 for additional discussion). The grateful man demonstrated his submission to Christ as his Lord by obeying Him.

> [14] And he charged him to tell no one, but "go and show yourself to the priest, and make an offering for your cleansing, as Moses commanded, for a proof to them."

a. **Tell nobody: Do not boast; watch being prideful.**

Jesus ordered the man not to tell anybody about his miracle.

The man had been saved from the depths and pit of defilement. He had been saved from so much, and he was now full of joy and rejoicing, bubbling over with happiness. He wanted to run all about telling the world, but Jesus, in His infinite wisdom, saw the danger in this, the danger . . .

- of pride and boasting within himself
- of jealousy and envy's arising within others toward him

b. **Rush to obey God: Worship and thank Him.**

Jesus instructed the man to rush to obey what God's law required of cured lepers (see DEEPER STUDY # 2). The man first needed to worship and offer thanks to God and to learn to obey God's Word before doing anything else.

> But declared first to those in Damascus, then in Jerusalem and throughout all the region of Judea, and also to the Gentiles, that they should repent and turn to God, performing deeds in keeping with their repentance. (Ac.26:20)

> Do your best to present yourself to God as one approved, a worker who has no need to be ashamed, rightly handling the word of truth. (2 Ti.2:15)

> Like newborn infants, long for the pure spiritual milk, that by it you may grow up into salvation— if indeed you have tasted that the Lord is good. (1 Pe.2:2–3)

DEEPER STUDY # 2

(5:14) **Leprosy:** in the unlikely event a leper was ever cured, there was a detailed list of laws and rituals the person had to go through. These rituals gave the priests time to confirm the cure and led the leper to make a thanksgiving offering to God (Le.14:1-32; see 13:38-59). Jesus was charging the man to make his offering to God and to receive the certificate confirming that he was cleansed.

4 Jesus made an impact.

a. **His fame spread rapidly (v.15a).**

b. **Crowds thronged to hear Him and to be healed by Him (v.15b).**

c. **He withdrew into the wilderness to pray (v.16).**

> [15] But now even more the report about him went abroad, and great crowds gathered to hear him and to be healed of their infirmities. [16] But he would withdraw to desolate places and pray.

By cleansing the leper, Jesus made an enormous impact on the region. In spite of Jesus' ordering the man to remain silent about his cleansing, the news traveled, and Jesus' fame spread rapidly. Multitudes thronged to hear Him and to be healed of their infirmities (v.15).

Jesus had both the message of salvation and the power to heal infirmities, but it was by Him and Him alone that both came. Jesus knew the source of His message and power: God and prayer. Therefore, He often withdrew to get alone with God and to seek His face and commune with Him (v.16).

E. Jesus Proves His Amazing Power to Forgive Sins, 5:17–26

(Mt.9:1–8; Mk.2:1–12)

1. An investigative committee visited Jesus
   a. They were representatives from everywhere
   b. They were to investigate Jesus' claims
   c. Jesus' power was set to face the opposition

2. The approach necessary for healing and forgiveness of sins
   a. Must seek help from others if necessary
   b. Must believe in Jesus' power
   c. Must be persistent[DS1]

   d. Must seek forgiveness

3. The power necessary to forgive sins: The power of God alone

4. The proof that Jesus can forgive sins, that He is the Son of Man[DS2]

   a. His Word: It works

   b. His claim: He is God, the Son of Man[DS3]
   c. His power: He saves and heals

   d. His impact
      1) Upon the man: The man was healed and praised God
      2) Upon the crowd: They were amazed and praised God and were filled with awe

17 On one of those days, as he was teaching, Pharisees and teachers of the law were sitting there, who had come from every village of Galilee and Judea and from Jerusalem. And the power of the Lord was with him to heal.

18 And behold, some men were bringing on a bed a man who was paralyzed, and they were seeking to bring him in and lay him before Jesus,

19 but finding no way to bring him in, because of the crowd, they went up on the roof and let him down with his bed through the tiles into the midst before Jesus.

20 And when he saw their faith, he said, "Man, your sins are forgiven you."

21 And the scribes and the Pharisees began to question, saying, "Who is this who speaks blasphemies? Who can forgive sins but God alone?"

22 When Jesus perceived their thoughts, he answered them, "Why do you question in your hearts?

23 Which is easier, to say, 'Your sins are forgiven you,' or to say, 'Rise and walk'?

24 But that you may know that the Son of Man has authority on earth to forgive sins"—he said to the man who was paralyzed—"I say to you, rise, pick up your bed and go home."

25 And immediately he rose up before them and picked up what he had been lying on and went home, glorifying God.

26 And amazement seized them all, and they glorified God and were filled with awe, saying, "We have seen extraordinary things today."

Division III

The Son of Man's Announced Mission and Public Ministry, 4:16–9:17

E. Jesus Proves His Amazing Power to Forgive Sins, 5:17–26

(Mt.9:1–8; Mk.2:1–12)

5:17–26
Introduction

The greatest need of every human being is forgiveness of sins. Many never recognize this need and never seek God's forgiveness. Consequently, they go through this life as a slave to their sins and the guilt sin brings, and they go out of this life into an eternity separated from God.

This particular passage of Scripture is critical because it deals with forgiveness of sins—the most important issue that ever confronts a person. Can our sins be forgiven, truly forgiven? If so, is Jesus Christ the One who has the power to forgive sins? This is, *Jesus Proves His Amazing Power to Forgive Sins, 5:17–26.*

1. An investigative committee visited Jesus (v.17).
2. The approach necessary for healing and forgiveness of sins (vv.18–20).
3. The power necessary to forgive sins: The power of God alone (v.21).
4. The proof that Jesus can forgive sins, that He is the Son of Man (vv.22–26).

1 An investigative committee visited Jesus.

5:17

A delegation of religious leaders came to where Jesus was teaching and ministering. Luke tells us who they were and why they were there.

¹⁷ On one of those days, as he was teaching, Pharisees and teachers of the law were sitting there, who had come from every village of Galilee and Judea and from Jerusalem. And the power of the Lord was with him to heal.

a. They were representatives from everywhere.
The committee was comprised of representatives from all over the country. Every major area was represented.

b. They were to investigate Jesus' claims.
The Pharisees and Scribes (teachers of the law) were the religious leaders of Israel (see Deeper Study # 1—Lu.6:2; Deeper Studies # 2, 3—Ac.23:8). The committee had come to *sit there* or *sit by*—to investigate, to observe Jesus, not to participate in services and ministry. They were "sitting by," not sitting at His feet and learning from Him.

c. Jesus' power was set to face the opposition.
Although tension was undoubtedly in the air, Jesus was unfazed by the religious leaders' presence. The power of God was upon Him, and He continued right on ministering. He did not let those who just *sat by* and were *critical* affect His preaching or ministry. He was immovable in His message and call.

THOUGHT 1. Note three critical observations.
1) There are always those who just *sit by*, who are just *spectators*, never really listening or learning, never becoming involved.
2) There are always those who are critical, who set themselves up as knowing best, who are censors and judges of what God's servants do. They listen and watch to make sure nothing is too different. If it is, they begin to criticize and judge.
3) God's servants must continue on in their call and ministry, remembering that they answer to God, not to their critics.

> Who are you to pass judgment on the servant of another? It is before his own master that he stands or falls. And he will be upheld, for the Lord is able to make him stand. (Ro.14:4)

But with me it is a very small thing that I should be judged by you or by any human court. In fact, I do not even judge myself. For I am not aware of anything against myself, but I am not thereby acquitted. It is the Lord who judges me. (1 Co.4:3–4)

Only let your manner of life be worthy of the gospel of Christ, so that whether I come and see you or am absent, I may hear of you that you are standing firm in one spirit, with one mind striving side by side for the faith of the gospel, and not frightened in anything by your opponents. This is a clear sign to them of their destruction, but of your salvation, and that from God. (Ph.1:27–28)

Do not be afraid of them, for I am with you to deliver you, declares the Lord. (Je.1:8)

5:18–20

¹⁸ And behold, some men were bringing on a bed a man who was paralyzed, and they were seeking to bring him in and lay him before Jesus,

¹⁹ but finding no way to bring him in, because of the crowd, they went up on the roof and let him down with his bed through the tiles into the midst before Jesus.

²⁰ And when he saw their faith, he said, "Man, your sins are forgiven you."

2 The approach necessary for healing and forgiveness of sins.

As the critical eyes of the religious leaders carefully examined every word Jesus spoke and every move He made, four men carried a paralyzed man to the Lord. These men of faith demonstrated the approach necessary to receive forgiveness of sins. The four steps they took in seeking forgiveness and healing from Jesus are the same four steps necessary for anyone to receive forgiveness of sins.

a. Must seek help from others if necessary (v.18a).

The paralyzed man had sought the help of his friends, and they were all seeking the help of Jesus. The man was unable to help himself, to get to Jesus to receive forgiveness and wholeness by himself. He had to have help, the help of Jesus and of friends. The same was true of all the friends of the man. They were unable to provide forgiveness and wholeness to the sick man. And none of them could carry their friend alone. They, too, knew that they needed the help of Jesus and of one another.

THOUGHT 1. It is always necessary to seek Jesus' help. And it is often necessary to seek the help of friends as well. We should seek spiritual help when we need it, and we should always be ready to assist those who need our help.

Bear one another's burdens, and so fulfill the law of Christ. (Ga.6:2)

b. Must believe in Jesus' power (v.18b).

These men *believed* and had confidence in Jesus' power to forgive sins and to heal. They believed that, if they came, Jesus had the power to help and that He loved and cared enough to help. Therefore, they came to Jesus. And note the inconvenience and difficulty they faced in coming. The man was bedridden. They would have to pick up his bed and carry it through the streets. Also, the crowds would be huge, perhaps making it impossible to get the bed through the throng of people. What belief! Such faith unlocks the help and blessings of God.

c. Must be persistent (v.19).

The men *persisted* despite enormous difficulty. Just as they had thought, the crowds were huge, much too large to get through to Jesus. But they did not give up. They went around to the side or back of the house and climbed up to the roof with the bed of the man (see DEEPER STUDY # 1). They removed some of the roof and used ropes to lower the man's bed below, right before the feet of Jesus. Of course, sitting there, Jesus observed the whole scene, perhaps as surprised as everyone else that people would be so bold and persistent. But as with any of us, the spirit of their bold persistence and the reason for such a spirit made all the difference in the world. They were desperate; their need was great, and they were helpless without Jesus. Such a spirit touched the Lord's heart and still touches His heart today.

d. Must seek forgiveness (v.20).

The man was definitely seeking forgiveness of sin as well as healing of body. The whole scene points to this fact. The man was paralyzed. There was the possibility that he had been injured or become diseased because of some foolish sin in the past. It was also the common belief of that day that suffering was due to sin. The man's mind was on his sin as the *cause* of his problem; therefore, he wanted Jesus to forgive his sins as well as heal him.

Jesus met the paralyzed man's greatest need and forgave His sins. Note three important observations.

First, Jesus saw "their faith," the faith of the friends as well as of the sick man. The faith of the friends played a part in the man's sins being forgiven. What a lesson to us, for our families and friends!

> But a Samaritan, as he journeyed, came to where he was, and when he saw him, he had compassion. He went to him and bound up his wounds, pouring on oil and wine. Then he set him on his own animal and brought him to an inn and took care of him. (Lu.10:33-34)

> We who are strong have an obligation to bear with the failings of the weak, and not to please ourselves. (Ro.15:1)

> And let us not grow weary of doing good, for in due season we will reap, if we do not give up. (Ga.6:9)

> I was eyes to the blind and feet to the lame. I was a father to the needy, and I searched out the cause of him whom I did not know. (Jb.29:15-16)

Second, Jesus saw a faith that believed and persisted against all kinds of obstacles, a faith that really believed and persisted. This is crucial to remember in seeking forgiveness.

> And I tell you, ask, and it will be given to you; seek, and you will find; knock, and it will be opened to you. For everyone who asks receives, and the one who seeks finds, and to the one who knocks it will be opened. (Lu.11:9-10)

> And without faith it is impossible to please him, for whoever would draw near to God must believe that he exists and that he rewards those who seek him. (He.11:6)

> But from there you will seek the LORD your God and you will find him, if you search after him with all your heart and with all your soul. (De.4:29)

> You will seek me and find me, when you seek me with all your heart. (Je.29:13)

Third, Jesus Himself forgave the man's sins. This is a critical fact to note. Jesus did not say that God the Father had forgiven the man's sins; He Himself granted forgiveness—and salvation—to the man. In doing so, Jesus was declaring that He is God.

> God exalted him at his right hand as Leader and Savior, to give repentance to Israel and forgiveness of sins. (Ac.5:31)

> Let it be known to you therefore, brothers, that through this man forgiveness of sins is proclaimed to you. (Ac.13:38)

> In him we have redemption through his blood, the forgiveness of our trespasses, according to the riches of his grace. (Ep.1:7)

DEEPER STUDY # 1

(5:19) **House:** many houses of Jesus' day had an outside stairway that climbed up to a second floor. The roof was easily reached from this stairway. Most roofs were flat and made of tile-like rocks matted together with a straw and clay-like substance. The roofs were sturdy enough for people to sit on and carry on conversations and other activities (see note—Mt.24:17). These men scooped out an opening through the roof. They were so sure of Jesus' power to help, nothing was going to prevent them from getting to Jesus—an unstoppable faith.

3 The power necessary to forgive sins: The power of God alone.

5:21

21 And the scribes and the Pharisees began to question, saying, "Who is this who speaks blasphemies? Who can forgive sins but God alone?"

Only God has the power to truly forgive sins. The religious leaders knew this; but they failed to see that Jesus Christ was One with God, the Son of God Himself—that He was One with God in being and nature, in exaltation and dominion, in love and compassion, in authority and power—all of which necessitated His coming to earth as the God in human flesh (see notes—Jn.1:1-2; note and DEEPER STUDY # 1—1:14; note—Ph.2:7). They were standing before Jesus thinking and reasoning, but not speaking aloud. In their minds they were saying He was guilty of blasphemy, but at this point they did not charge Him publicly.

THOUGHT 1. This is the very point over which so many people—including followers of religions—stumble: that Jesus Christ is God incarnate, God in human flesh, the Son of God who became a man to save the world.

> For God so loved the world, that he gave his only Son, that whoever believes in him should not perish but have eternal life. (Jn.3:16)

> Do you say of him whom the Father consecrated and sent into the world, "You are blaspheming," because I said, "I am the Son of God"? (Jn.10:36)

5:22-26

22 When Jesus perceived their thoughts, he answered them, "Why do you question in your hearts?
23 Which is easier, to say, 'Your sins are forgiven you,' or to say, 'Rise and walk'?
24 But that you may know that the Son of Man has authority on earth to forgive sins"—he said to the man who was paralyzed—"I say to you, rise, pick up your bed and go home."
25 And immediately he rose up before them and picked up what he had been lying on and went home, glorifying God.
26 And amazement seized them all, and they glorified God and were filled with awe, saying, "We have seen extraordinary things today."

4 The proof that Jesus can forgive sins, that He is the Son of Man.

Jesus knew the religious leaders' thoughts. His ability to read their minds was an immediate evidence of His deity. He proceeded to prove His deity, the fact that He had the right and power to forgive sins *because He was God*. The proofs He offered should be studied closely by all followers of religions and skeptics.

a. **His Word: It works (v.23).**
   The power of Jesus' Word proves His deity. In response to the Scribes' and Pharisees' brewing accusations of blasphemy, the Lord posed a test of God's power. He suggested that He merely *speak the Word*, "Rise and walk." The logic in His proposition was clear: *if His Word worked to heal the man, then His Word must work also to forgive sins* (see DEEPER STUDY # 2).

b. **His claim: He is God, the Son of Man (v.24a).**
   Jesus' claim to be God, the Son of Man also proves His deity (see DEEPER STUDY # 3). He was not afraid to put Himself to the test. He wanted all people to know and believe in Him, the Messiah, the Son of God who became the Son of Man; and He wanted all to know and believe that He had the authority to forgive sins. Therefore, He purposed to prove His power in the lives of those who seek forgiveness.

   > And I have seen and have borne witness that this is the Son of God. (Jn.1:34)

   > Jesus heard that they had cast him out, and having found him he said, "Do you believe in the Son of Man?" He answered, "And who is he, sir, that I may believe in him?" Jesus said to him, "You have seen him, and it is he who is speaking to you." (Jn.9:35-37)

   > Jesus said to her, "I am the resurrection and the life. Whoever believes in me, though he die, yet shall he live, and everyone who lives and believes in me shall never die. Do you believe this?" She said to him, "Yes, Lord; I believe that you are the Christ, the Son of God, who is coming into the world." (Jn.11:25-27)

c. **His power: He saves and heals (v.24b).**

Jesus proved His deity—and thereby His authority to save—by demonstrating His supernatural power: He healed the paralyzed man. Dramatically, Jesus spoke the Word, and the man arose. He was healed immediately. How? By the Word of the Lord. *God's Word* proved itself. When Jesus spoke the *Word of healing*, the man was healed, just as when Jesus spoke the *Word of forgiveness*, the man was forgiven.

> And Jesus came and said to them, "All authority in heaven and on earth has been given to me." (Mt.28:18)

> How God anointed Jesus of Nazareth with the Holy Spirit and with power. He went about doing good and healing all who were oppressed by the devil, for God was with him. (Ac.10:38)

d. **His impact (vv.25–26).**

The impact Jesus had on those present also proved His deity. The man glorified God (v.25). The people were utterly amazed. They glorified God and were filled with reverential awe (v.26).

THOUGHT 1. Jesus knows our thoughts, just what we are thinking, whether thoughts . . .

- of unbelief or belief
- of selfishness or unselfishness
- of worldliness or godliness
- of impurity or purity
- of deception or truth
- of wrong or right

> Knowing their thoughts, he said to them, "Every kingdom divided against itself is laid waste, and no city or house divided against itself will stand." (Mt.12:25)

> And I will strike her children dead. And all the churches will know that I am he who searches mind and heart, and I will give to each of you according to your works. (Re.2:23)

> Then hear from heaven your dwelling place and forgive and render to each whose heart you know, according to all his ways, for you, you only, know the hearts of the children of mankind. (2 Chr.6:30)

> You know when I sit down and when I rise up; you discern my thoughts from afar. (Ps.139:2)

THOUGHT 2. Four critical truths from these verses apply to people today.

1) Jesus is still *willing* to speak the Word of forgiveness and healing.
2) Jesus is the Son of Man and *purposes* to forgive the sins of all who are willing (see DEEPER STUDY # 3—Mt.8:20).
3) Jesus has both the power and will to speak the Word of forgiveness and healing to those who *seek* it.
4) The impact of Jesus' life on so many is evidence of His deity. The fact that some are genuinely glorifying God and serving Him in awe and reverence is *strong evidence* that Jesus has the power to forgive sins.

> God exalted him at his right hand as Leader and Savior, to give repentance to Israel and forgiveness of sins. (Ac.5:31)

> In him we have redemption through his blood, the forgiveness of our trespasses, according to the riches of his grace. (Ep.1:7)

DEEPER STUDY # 2

(5:23) **Sins—Forgiven:** the common belief of that day was that suffering was due to sin. Jesus' healing of the man was the proof that the man's sins were truly forgiven and that He had the power to forgive sins. The religionists could not logically deny this (see DEEPER STUDY # 4—Mt.26:28).

DEEPER STUDY # 3

(5:24) **Son of Man:** see DEEPER STUDY # 3—Mt.8:20.

F. Jesus Reveals His Great Mission: The Greatest Mission of All, 5:27–39

(Mt.9:9–17; Mk.2:13–22)

1. **The mission of calling outcasts**[DS1]
   a. He went out
   b. He saw the outcast
   c. He called the outcast
   d. The outcast left all and followed Jesus

   e. The outcast reached out to and shared his conversion with his friends

2. **The mission of calling sinners to repentance**
   a. The religionists questioned Jesus' associations
   b. Jesus' answer
      1) He illustrated His mission

      2) He stated His mission

3. **The mission of bringing real joy**
   a. The religionists questioned Jesus' behavior

   b. Jesus' answer: His presence brings joy and vitality to life

4. **The mission of dying**

5. **The mission of launching a new life and spiritual movement**
   a. Illustration 1: Not patching the old, but starting a new life

   b. Illustration 2: Not putting His teaching (wine) in old wineskins, but in new wineskins

   c. Illustration 3: The new is difficult to accept—it takes time

27 After this he went out and saw a tax collector named Levi, sitting at the tax booth. And he said to him, "Follow me."

28 And leaving everything, he rose and followed him.

29 And Levi made him a great feast in his house, and there was a large company of tax collectors and others reclining at table with them.

30 And the Pharisees and their scribes grumbled at his disciples, saying, "Why do you eat and drink with tax collectors and sinners?"

31 And Jesus answered them, "Those who are well have no need of a physician, but those who are sick.

32 I have not come to call the righteous but sinners to repentance."

33 And they said to him, "The disciples of John fast often and offer prayers, and so do the disciples of the Pharisees, but yours eat and drink."

34 And Jesus said to them, "Can you make wedding guests fast while the bridegroom is with them?"

35 "The days will come when the bridegroom is taken away from them, and then they will fast in those days."

36 He also told them a parable: "No one tears a piece from a new garment and puts it on an old garment. If he does, he will tear the new, and the piece from the new will not match the old.

37 And no one puts new wine into old wineskins. If he does, the new wine will burst the skins and it will be spilled, and the skins will be destroyed.

38 But new wine must be put into fresh wineskins.

39 And no one after drinking old wine desires new, for he says, 'The old is good.'"

Division III

The Son of Man's Announced Mission and Public Ministry, 4:16–9:17

F. Jesus Reveals His Great Mission: The Greatest Mission of All, 5:27-39

(Mt.9:9–17; Mk.2:13–22)

5:27-39
Introduction

The greatest life ever lived on earth was the life of Jesus Christ. The greatness of His life was due to the greatness of His Person: He was—and is—the holy Son of God who became a man, the perfect, ideal man. But the greatness of His life was also due to the greatness of His mission. No mission can ever compare with the mission which He was sent to do. The great mission of Christ was . . .

- a life-giving mission: to make people alive to God
- an eternal mission: to give people life forever
- a purposeful mission: to cause people to commit their lives to God unconditionally

Luke's very purpose in this passage is to reveal the great mission of Christ. He skillfully weaves several events together to spell out the great mission of the Lord. This is, *Jesus Reveals His Great Mission: The Greatest Mission of all*, 5:27-39.

1. The mission of calling outcasts (vv.27-29).
2. The mission of calling sinners to repentance (vv.30-32).
3. The mission of bringing real joy (vv.33-34).
4. The mission of dying (v.35).
5. The mission of launching a new life and spiritual movement (vv.36-39).

1 The mission of calling outcasts.

5:27-29

Jesus' great mission involved calling outcasts, those who are rejected by society (see notes—Mt.9:9; note and DEEPER STUDY # 1—Mk.2:14 for additional discussion). During Jesus' earthly ministry, nobody was more despised by the Jewish society than tax collectors.

> 27 After this he went out and saw a tax collector named Levi, sitting at the tax booth. And he said to him, "Follow me."
> 28 And leaving everything, he rose and followed him.
> 29 And Levi made him a great feast in his house, and there was a large company of tax collectors and others reclining at table with them.

a. **He went out (v.27a).**
There is deliberate purpose in this statement, "He went out." Jesus got up and left either the house (v.19) or the city. He went out for the specific purpose of seeking the outcast (see Lu.19:10; Jn.20:21).

b. **He saw the outcast (v.27b).**
Jesus "saw a tax collector named Levi [Matthew]." *Saw* (Gk. etheasato, *eh-theh-ah'-sah-tow*) means more than glanced or noticed. It means looked closely at, viewed attentively, contemplated or wondered about. This man was an outcast, the most hated of people among the public (see DEEPER STUDY # 1). Yet when Jesus saw him, He saw a man "named Levi [Matthew]," a sinner, a man who was hurting within, a man who needed redemption along with a new purpose for living. (see note—Mt.9:9 for detailed discussion).

c. **He called the outcast (v.27c).**
Very simply yet forcibly, Jesus called to this outcast, "Follow me." Note the Savior's great *love* and *compassion* for the outcast. The man was despised. By associating with such an outcast, Jesus was exposing Himself to criticism and rejection from Jewish society.

Note also the great humility of Christ. He stooped down to reach an outcast; this was the reason He came. He had come from heaven to earth to save sinners, those who were outcasts.

THOUGHT 1. Jesus' call is issued to all people, for we all are outcasts; none of us is worthy to enter heaven. However, there is a condition to becoming acceptable to God. We must humble ourselves before Jesus, just as Jesus humbled Himself before us.

> And said, "Truly, I say to you, unless you turn and become like children, you will never enter the kingdom of heaven." (Mt.18:3)

> For godly grief produces a repentance that leads to salvation without regret, whereas worldly grief produces death. (2 Co.7:10)

> And being found in human form, he humbled himself by becoming obedient to the point of death, even death on a cross. (Ph.2:8. See Ph.2:6–9.)

> The Lᴏʀᴅ is near to the brokenhearted and saves the crushed in spirit. (Ps.34:18)

> "Yet even now," declares the Lᴏʀᴅ, "return to me with all your heart, with fasting, with weeping, and with mourning." (Joel 2:12)

THOUGHT 2. The person who is truly an outcast of society, who is rejected and despised by people, can be saved and delivered from emptiness and loneliness. Jesus Christ will save that person. In fact, He longs to save and deliver all outcasts, the empty and lonely of the earth.

> Come to me, all who labor and are heavy laden, and I will give you rest. Take my yoke upon you, and learn from me, for I am gentle and lowly in heart, and you will find rest for your souls. For my yoke is easy, and my burden is light. (Mt.11:28–30)

> The Spirit and the Bride say, "Come." And let the one who hears say, "Come." And let the one who is thirsty come; let the one who desires take the water of life without price. (Re.22:17)

> Come now, let us reason together, says the Lᴏʀᴅ: though your sins are like scarlet, they shall be as white as snow; though they are red like crimson, they shall become like wool. (Is.1:18)

> Come, everyone who thirsts, come to the waters; and he who has no money, come, buy and eat! Come, buy wine and milk without money and without price. (Is.55:1)

d. The outcast left all and followed Jesus (v.28).

Matthew was very wealthy. Luke emphasizes words like "leaving everything" or "he left all." (Note also v.29 where Matthew made a "great feast" in his own house. The house itself must have been very large to hold so many people.)

This outcast left everything, his crooked profession and the ill-gained fruits of that profession, responding to Jesus immediately. How could a man such as Matthew give up so much to follow Jesus? Because money cannot buy happiness, peace, security, completeness, satisfaction, fulfillment, confidence, or assurance. Money can only buy things. Matthew had, as so many do, plenty of things: houses, land, clothes, food, furnishings. But he was *empty and restless* in heart, *incomplete and insecure* in spirit, *unfulfilled and dissatisfied* in life. When he confronted Jesus, he saw the possibility that Jesus could meet all his needs, truly meet them.

THOUGHT 1. Jesus said that it is hard for rich people to enter heaven, for they are attached to this material world. Matthew was one of the few who was willing to give up all in order to follow Jesus. In return, the kingdom of heaven will be his.

> And Jesus said to his disciples, "Truly, I say to you, only with difficulty will a rich person enter the kingdom of heaven. Again I tell you, it is easier for a camel to go through the eye of a needle than for a rich person to enter the kingdom of God." When the disciples heard this, they were greatly astonished, saying, "Who then can be saved?" But Jesus looked at them and said, "With man this is impossible, but with God all things are possible." (Mt.19:23–26; see Mt.19:16–26)

> For whoever would save his life will lose it, but whoever loses his life for my sake and the gospel's will save it. For what does it profit a man to gain the whole world and forfeit his soul? (Mk.8:35–36)

> So therefore, any one of you who does not renounce all that he has cannot be my disciple. (Lu.14:33)

e. The outcast reached out to and shared his conversion with his friends (v.29).

Matthew invited his friends—including the other tax collectors—to his house for a celebration of his conversion. This is a beautiful picture of the kind of witness every believer should be. Matthew's heart was filled immediately with the genuine joy for which he had ached. There was so much difference, so much love, joy, and peace; he just could not contain it. It burst forth. He had to tell his friends, but it would take so long to visit each one separately; he had to figure out a way to reach them sooner. How could he do it more quickly? Having a feast came to his mind. So, he held a feast for his friends to meet Jesus.

Matthew was excited about his faith. He knew the depth of emptiness from which he had come, and he was ever so appreciative and thankful. (Remember: Matthew, the outcast, was the one who wrote the *Gospel of Matthew*.) He wanted his friends to meet Jesus personally and to come to know the salvation given by Christ.

Jesus said to them again, "Peace be with you. As the Father has sent me, even so I am sending you." (Jn.20:21)

That is, in Christ God was reconciling the world to himself, not counting their trespasses against them, and entrusting to us the message of reconciliation. Therefore, we are ambassadors for Christ, God making his appeal through us. We implore you on behalf of Christ, be reconciled to God. (2 Co.5:19-20)

And what you have heard from me in the presence of many witnesses entrust to faithful men, who will be able to teach others also. (2 Ti.2:2)

DEEPER STUDY # 1

(5:27) **Tax Collector:** tax collectors were bitterly hated by the people for three reasons.

1. Tax collectors served the Roman conquerors. Most tax collectors were Jews, but in the people's eyes they had denied their Jewish heritage and betrayed their country. Therefore, they were ostracized, completely cut off from Jewish society and excommunicated from Jewish religion and privileges.

2. Tax collectors were cheats, dishonest and unjust men. Most tax collectors were extremely wealthy. The Roman government compensated tax collectors by allowing them to collect more than the percentage required for taxes. Tax collectors greedily abused their right, adding whatever amount they wished and felt could be collected (see DEEPER STUDY # 1—Ro.13:6). They took bribes from the wealthy who wanted to avoid taxes, fleeced the average citizen, and swindled the government when they could.

3. Tax collectors assumed rights that belonged only to God. God alone was King in the eyes of the Jews. This was a strong conviction of the Jews; therefore, God and the ruler He appointed were considered to be the head of Jewish government. God was their God, and they were His people. Taxes were to be paid only to Him and His government, which was centered only in the temple of Judaism. To pay taxes to earthly rulers was considered an abuse and a denial of God's rights. Therefore, tax collectors were excommunicated from Jewish religion and privileges. They were accursed, anathema.

2 The mission of calling sinners to repentance.

Jesus' reaching out to the outcasts revealed the heart of His great mission: calling sinners to repentance. He associated with the most sinful and despised of society because they needed Him most.

a. The religionists questioned Jesus' associations (v.30).

When Jesus attended Matthew's salvation celebration, the religious leaders questioned Jesus' association with

30 And the Pharisees and their scribes grumbled at his disciples, saying, "Why do you eat and drink with tax collectors and sinners?"

31 And Jesus answered them, "Those who are well have no need of a physician, but those who are sick.

32 I have not come to call the righteous but sinners to repentance."

tax collectors and sinners. They criticized and judged Him because He was associating with those who were not socially acceptable. Sinners and outcasts had rejected society. They had forsaken what was considered acceptable conduct. Why would Jesus associate with such outcasts and sinners who so clearly rebelled against society and its approved behavior?

In addition, Jesus was associating with those who were religiously and ceremonially unclean. Few, if any, had sought religious and ceremonial cleansing. They were guilty of breaking every law of religion and decency. Their behavior and uncleanness were bound to rub off, contaminating and misleading anyone associating with them, including Jesus.

b. Jesus' answer (vv.31–32).

Jesus answered their question by illustrating and stating His mission. The sick (sinners) are the ones who need a physician (Him, the Savior). The mission of Jesus was not to call the righteous to repentance; it was to call sinners to repentance.

THOUGHT 1. A person may be sick and not know it; therefore their sickness is never cured. Or one may be sick and not call the physician; therefore, their sickness is never cured. The righteous—those who determine to lead clean lives—either do not know or do not accept the fact that they need repentance. Sinners do know, but they may not accept the depth of their need nor turn from their sin in order to be saved by Jesus.

> For the Son of Man came to seek and to save the lost. (Lu.19:10)

> For God did not send his Son into the world to condemn the world, but in order that the world might be saved through him. (Jn.3:17)

> The thief comes only to steal and kill and destroy. I came that they may have life and have it abundantly. (Jn.10:10)

> If anyone hears my words and does not keep them, I do not judge him; for I did not come to judge the world but to save the world. (Jn.12:47)

> Behold, I stand at the door and knock. If anyone hears my voice and opens the door, I will come in to him and eat with him, and he with me. (Re.3:20)

5:33–34

³³ And they said to him, "The disciples of John fast often and offer prayers, and so do the disciples of the Pharisees, but yours eat and drink."
³⁴ And Jesus said to them, "Can you make wedding guests fast while the bridegroom is with them?"

3 The mission of bringing real joy.

When the Pharisees accused Jesus of failing to lead His disciples in the right way, He revealed another aspect of His mission. He came to bring joy—real joy—to people's lives.

a. The religionists questioned Jesus' behavior (v.33).

The religious leaders questioned Jesus' "loose behavior" and the fact that He was teaching His disciples the same behavior. Jesus' disciples were eating and drinking, actually feasting when they should have been fasting. By law, religious Jews fasted twice a week, every Monday and Thursday (Lu.18:12). Jesus was not only religious, He was a religious teacher, and even more, He was claiming to be the Messiah Himself. Why was He not fasting (see note—Mk.2:18–22 for detailed discussion)? Note something important. The Pharisees fasted as a ritual; their days for fasting were already determined. The ritual or the custom and tradition determined their fast. Their need for God, for a very special sense of God's presence, had nothing to do with fasting. Fasting was purely a matter of ritual and custom.

b. Jesus' answer: His presence brings joy and vitality to life (v.34).

Jesus' answer was revealing and of utmost importance. He claimed that He was the *Bridegroom*, and as long as He was with them, there was no need for them to fast. Now note what Jesus was saying (see note—Mt.9:15; Mk.2:19):
➤ His mission was that of a Bridegroom, to bring joy and vitality to life.
➤ His presence—not ritual and ceremonial demands—brought joy and vitality to life.

➤ There was no need to be fasting for a special sense of God's presence if the Bridegroom, the Son of God, was already present.

> These things I have spoken to you, that my joy may be in you, and that your joy may be full. (Jn.15:11)

> For the kingdom of God is not a matter of eating and drinking but of righteousness and peace and joy in the Holy Spirit. (Ro.14:17)

> Though you have not seen him, you love him. Though you do not now see him, you believe in him and rejoice with joy that is inexpressible and filled with glory. (1 Pe.1:8)

> You make known to me the path of life; in your presence there is fullness of joy; at your right hand are pleasures forevermore. (Ps.16:11)

> With joy you will draw water from the wells of salvation. (Is.12:3)

> I will greatly rejoice in the LORD; my soul shall exult in my God, for he has clothed me with the garments of salvation; he has covered me with the robe of righteousness, as a bridegroom decks himself like a priest with a beautiful headdress, and as a bride adorns herself with her jewels. (Is.61:10)

4 The mission of dying.

Jesus proceeded to reveal that His mission included dying. He said frankly that He—the Bridegroom—would be taken away from them. He meant that He was appointed to die. Dying on the cross was His primary mission for coming to earth. Note three significant truths about Christ's death.

> [35] "The days will come when the bridegroom is taken away from them, and then they will fast in those days."

First, His death enables His Spirit to be present with all believers around the world (Jn.14:16–18, 26; 15:26; 16:7, 13).

Second, His death brings sorrow to the heart of any who see and understand it. However, His death brings joy soon after, for there is the knowledge that Jesus lives forever (Jn.16:16–22; He.7:25; see Ep.1:19–23).

Third, His death and its cleansing power can be *forgotten* (2 Pe.1:9). The Lord's presence can fade from our consciousness. We can become so busy and preoccupied with the affairs of the world that we lose our sensitivity to the Lord's presence. At such times we need to get alone with God. Our concern for God's presence should be so great that neither food nor sleep matter. Nothing matters except regaining the consciousness of God's presence. We need to fast and pray and pray and fast.

THOUGHT 1. Christ's death caused the first disciples to fast. Consider three times it ought to cause us to fast and pray as well.

1) When we first learn of His death and what it really means.

> And said to them, "Thus it is written, that the Christ should suffer and on the third day rise from the dead." (Lu.24:46)

> For God so loved the world, that he gave his only Son, that whoever believes in him should not perish but have eternal life. (Jn.3:16)

> But God shows his love for us in that while we were still sinners, Christ died for us. (Ro.5:8)

> He himself bore our sins in his body on the tree, that we might die to sin and live to righteousness. By his wounds you have been healed. (1 Pe.2:24)

> For Christ also suffered once for sins, the righteous for the unrighteous, that he might bring us to God, being put to death in the flesh but made alive in the spirit. (1 Pe.3:18)

2) When we are reminded rather forcibly that Christ died for us. Such times should be heart-rending times, precious times of prayer and fasting.

3) When we allow His presence to slip out of our mind for some length of time. We need to get alone and meditate on His death, allowing nothing to interfere, including food.

> Watch and pray that you may not enter into temptation. The spirit indeed is willing, but the flesh is weak. (Mt.26:41)

And he told them a parable to the effect that they ought always to pray and not lose heart. (Lu.18:1)

Seek the Lord and his strength; seek his presence continually! (1 Chr.16:11)

If my people who are called by my name humble themselves, and pray and seek my face and turn from their wicked ways, then I will hear from heaven and will forgive their sin and heal their land. (2 Chr.7:14)

5:36–39

⁣³⁶ He also told them a parable: "No one tears a piece from a new garment and puts it on an old garment. If he does, he will tear the new, and the piece from the new will not match the old.
⁣³⁷ And no one puts new wine into old wineskins. If he does, the new wine will burst the skins and it will be spilled, and the skins will be destroyed.
⁣³⁸ But new wine must be put into fresh wineskins.
⁣³⁹ And no one after drinking old wine desires new, for he says, 'The old is good.'"

5 The mission of launching a new life and spiritual movement.

Finally, Jesus revealed that His mission was to launch a new life and a new spiritual movement. To make this truth clear, He gave three illustrations.

a. Illustration 1: Not patching the old, but starting a new life (v.36).

Jesus pointed out that a piece of new cloth is not used to patch an old garment because it does not match the old garment. Jesus was saying that He did not come to merely patch up the old life, but to start a new life and a new movement (see notes—Mt.9:16; Mk.2:21 for discussion).

b. Illustration 2: Not putting His teaching (wine) in old wineskins, but in new wineskins (v.37).

As a second illustration, Jesus remarked that new wine is not put into old bottles, for the new wine would burst the old bottles. Jesus says that He was not putting His teaching into the old life and movement, but He was launching a new life and movement for God, His Father (see notes—Mk.2:22).

c. Illustration 3: The new is difficult to accept—it takes time (vv.38–39).

Jesus concludes by making the point that new wine is difficult to accept if one has been drinking old wine. Jesus states that His new life and spiritual movement would be difficult to accept; it would take time. People were slow to give up the old, for they were too content with it (their religious ways and self-righteousness). Therefore, people would often refuse to even consider the new life and movement He was bringing.

Therefore, if anyone is in Christ, he is a new creation. The old has passed away; behold, the new has come. (2 Co.5:17)

To put off your old self, which belongs to your former manner of life and is corrupt through deceitful desires, and to be renewed in the spirit of your minds. (Ep.4:22–23)

And have put on the new self, which is being renewed in knowledge after the image of its creator. (Col.3:10)

He saved us, not because of works done by us in righteousness, but according to his own mercy, by the washing of regeneration and renewal of the Holy Spirit. (Tit.3:5)

Since you have been born again, not of perishable seed but of imperishable, through the living and abiding word of God. (1 Pe.1:23)

CHAPTER 6

G. Jesus Teaches That Need Supersedes Religion, 6:1–11

(Mt.12:1-13; Mk.2:23-28; 3:1-6)

On a Sabbath, while he was going through the grainfields, his disciples plucked and ate some heads of grain, rubbing them in their hands.

2 But some of the Pharisees said, "Why are you doing what is not lawful to do on the Sabbath?"

3 And Jesus answered them, "Have you not read what David did when he was hungry, he and those who were with him:

4 how he entered the house of God and took and ate the bread of the Presence, which is not lawful for any but the priests to eat, and also gave it to those with him?"

5 And he said to them, "The Son of Man is lord of the Sabbath."

6 On another Sabbath, he entered the synagogue and was teaching, and a man was there whose right hand was withered.

7 And the scribes and the Pharisees watched him, to see whether he would heal on the Sabbath, so that they might find a reason to accuse him.

8 But he knew their thoughts, and he said to the man with the withered hand, "Come and stand here." And he rose and stood there.

9 And Jesus said to them, "I ask you, is it lawful on the Sabbath to do good or to do harm, to save life or to destroy it?"

10 And after looking around at them all he said to him, "Stretch out your hand." And he did so, and his hand was restored.

11 But they were filled with fury and discussed with one another what they might do to Jesus.

1. **The setting: The Sabbath**
2. **Fact 1: Meeting people's real needs is more important than religion and ritual**
   a. The need: The disciples were hungry and picked grain
   b. The opposition: The religionists became upset because a religious rule was broken[DS1]
   c. The response given by Jesus: An illustration
      1) David and his companions were hungry
      2) David overrode the religious rules to meet their need [DS2]
   d. The point: The Son of Man[DS3] is greater than David—He is Lord of the Sabbath
3. **Fact 2: Doing good and saving life are more important than religion and ritual**
   a. The need: A man's right hand was shriveled
   b. The opposition by the religionists[DS4]
   c. The question and challenge given by Jesus
      1) He perceived their thoughts
      2) He challenged them to think honestly
      3) He healed the man—doing good
   d. The point: To do good and to save life supersedes rituals
   e. The religionists' insane anger

Division III

The Son of Man's Announced Mission and Public Ministry, 4:16–9:17

G. Jesus Teaches That Need Supersedes Religion, 6:1–11

(Mt.12:1-13; Mk.2:23–28; 3:1–6)

6:1–11
Introduction

People have the tendency to institutionalize religion, to make it full of form and ritual, rules and regulations, ceremonies and services. Religious leaders and laypeople alike are too often guilty of "having the appearance [a form] of godliness, but denying its power" (2 Ti.3:5). This is the very point Jesus is making in this passage. The power of godliness exists to meet people's needs. Yet too often, religion is placed before people and their needs. Maintaining the religious organization and form, keeping things the way they have always been, is considered more important than meeting people's needs. In this passage, Jesus confronts and refutes that idea. This is, *Jesus Teaches That Need Supersedes Religion, 6:1–11.*

1. The setting: The Sabbath (v.1).
2. Fact 1: Meeting people's real needs is more important than religion and ritual (vv.1–5).
3. Fact 2: Doing good and saving life are more important than religion and ritual (vv.6–11).

6:1

On a Sabbath, while he was going through the grainfields, his disciples plucked and ate some heads of grain, rubbing them in their hands.

1 The setting: The Sabbath.

Both of these events took place on the Sabbath (vv.1, 6). This fact is significant, for Jesus' actions directly challenged the Pharisees' Sabbath regulations.

6:1–5

On a Sabbath, while he was going through the grainfields, his disciples plucked and ate some heads of grain, rubbing them in their hands.
² But some of the Pharisees said, "Why are you doing what is not lawful to do on the Sabbath?"
³ And Jesus answered them, "Have you not read what David did when he was hungry, he and those who were with him:
⁴ how he entered the house of God and took and ate the bread of the Presence, which is not lawful for any but the priests to eat, and also gave it to those with him?"
⁵ And he said to them, "The Son of Man is lord of the Sabbath."

2 Fact 1: Meeting people's real needs is more important than religion and ritual.

Luke's purpose in this passage is to show that religion and ritual must never be put before people's needs (see Deeper Study # 1—Mt.12:1 for discussion). The first way Jesus demonstrated this was by permitting His disciples to pick grain on the Sabbath.

a. The need: The disciples were hungry and picked grain (v.1).

The disciples had a real need: they had not eaten since the day before and they were extremely hungry (Mt.12:1; Mk.2:23). As they were passing by a corn field, they began to pluck and eat some grain. They were not stealing the grain, for a hungry traveler was permitted by law to eat a few heads of grain when passing by a field (De.23:25). The crime was that the disciples *worked* by plucking the heads of grain *on the Sabbath day.*

b. The opposition: The religionists became upset because a religious rule was broken (v.2).

The Pharisees indignantly confronted Jesus about His disciples' actions (see Deeper Study # 1). Their picking grain was a serious offense to the orthodox Jews who had strict regulations for the Sabbath. Law after law was written to govern all activity on the Sabbath, laws which prevented a person from even contemplating any kind of work or activity. A good example of the legal restriction and the people's loyalty to it is seen in the women who witnessed Jesus' crucifixion. They would not even walk to His tomb to prepare His body for burial until the Sabbath was over (Mk.16:1f; Mt.28:1f).

It was a serious matter to break Sabbath law. A person was condemned, and if the offence were serious enough, the person was sentenced to die.

This practice may seem harsh to some, but when dealing with the Jewish nation, one must remember that it was their religion that held them together as a nation through centuries of exile. Their religion (in particular their beliefs about God's call to their nation), the temple, and the Sabbath became the *binding force* that kept Jews together and maintained their distinctiveness as a people. It protected them from alien beliefs and from being swallowed up by other nationalities through intermarriage. No matter where they were, they met and associated together and held on to their beliefs. A picture of this can be seen in the experience of Nehemiah when he led some Jews back to Jerusalem (Ne.13:15-22; see Je.17:19-27; Ezk.46:1-7).

With this background information in mind, we can understand to some degree why the religious leaders opposed Jesus with such hostility. Their problem was that they had allowed religion and ritual, ceremony and liturgy, position and security, recognition and livelihood to become more important than the basic essentials of human life: personal need and compassion, and the true worship and mercy of God. (See note and DEEPER STUDY # 1—Mt.12:10. This is an important note for this point.)

c. **The response given by Jesus: An illustration (vv.3-4).**

Jesus responded by challenging the Pharisees' customs. He used David's experience to illustrate His point. David had eaten the bread of the presence (showbread or consecrated bread) in the tabernacle when he was hungry, violating the law (see DEEPER STUDY # 2; Mk.2:25-27).

d. **The point: The Son of Man is greater than David—He is Lord of the Sabbath (v.5).**

Jesus declared that He, the Son of Man, has authority over the Sabbath. Christ pointed out that if David had the authority to suspend a Sabbath law, He did even more. He was greater, for He was the Son of Man—the Son of God who became a man (see DEEPER STUDY # 3). Therefore, He was, and is, the Lord over the Sabbath (see notes and thoughts—Mt.12:1-8; Mk.2:23-28 for detailed discussion).

> And Jesus came and said to them, "All authority in heaven and on earth has been given to me." (Mt.28:18)

> Let all the house of Israel therefore know for certain that God has made him both Lord and Christ, this Jesus whom you crucified. (Ac.2:36)

> God exalted him at his right hand as Leader and Savior, to give repentance to Israel and forgiveness of sins. (Ac.5:31)

> Yet for us there is one God, the Father, from whom are all things and for whom we exist, and one Lord, Jesus Christ, through whom are all things and through whom we exist. (1 Co.8:6)

> And he put all things under his feet and gave him as head over all things to the church. (Ep.1:22)

> Who has gone into heaven and is at the right hand of God, with angels, authorities, and powers having been subjected to him. (1 Pe.3:22)

THOUGHT 1. Christ shows that human needs are far more important than religious rituals and rules. However, two things must always be kept in mind.

1) The need must be a *real need* before religious rituals and rules are to be suspended. We are not to carelessly abuse, neglect, or ignore religious worship and ceremonies. Sometimes, however, a real need does arise that has to be taken care of immediately.

2) Jesus Christ is the Lord of the Sabbath; therefore, He should be the one who says when a need should supersede a religious ceremony. We must be living closely enough to Him in fellowship and worship, sacrifice and ministry, to sense what should be done.

> Even as the Son of Man came not to be served but to serve, and to give his life as a ransom for many. (Mt.20:28)

157

Jesus said to them again, "Peace be with you. As the Father has sent me, even so I am sending you." (Jn.20:21)

We who are strong have an obligation to bear with the failings of the weak, and not to please ourselves. (Ro.15:1)

Bear one another's burdens, and so fulfill the law of Christ. (Ga.6:2)

DEEPER STUDY # 1

(6:2) **Scribes—Scribal Law—Pharisees:** these Pharisees were probably Scribes. The Scribes were a profession of men sometimes called lawyers (see DEEPER STUDY # 1—Mt.22:35). They were some of the most devoted and committed men to religion in all of history and were of the sect known as the Pharisees. However, every Pharisee was not a Scribe. A Scribe was more of a scholar, more highly trained than the average Pharisee (see DEEPER STUDY # 3—Ac.23:8). The Scribes served two primary functions.

1. The Scribes copied the written law, the Old Testament Scriptures. They were strict copiers, meticulously keeping count of every letter in every word. This exactness was necessary, for God Himself had given the written law to the Jewish nation. Therefore, the law was not only the very Word of God, it was the greatest thing in the life of the Jewish nation. It was considered the most precious possession in all the world; consequently, the Jewish nation was committed to the preservation of the law (Ne.8:1-8). A young Jew could enter no greater profession than the profession of Scribes.

2. The Scribes studied, classified, and taught the moral law. This function brought about the Oral or Scribal Law that was so common in Jesus' day. It was the law of rules and regulations. There were, in fact, so many regulations that over fifty large volumes were required when they were finally put into writing. The great tragedy was that through the centuries, the Jews began to place the Oral Law over the Written Law (see note—Mt.12:1-8; note and DEEPER STUDY # 1—12:10; note—15:1-20).

The Scribes felt that the law was God's final word. Everything God wanted people to do could be deduced from it; therefore, they drew out of the law every possible rule they could and insisted that life was to be lived in conformity to these rules. Rules were to be a way of life, the preoccupation of a person's thoughts. At first these rules and regulations were taught by word of mouth; however, in the third century after Christ, they were put into certain writings.

The Halachoth: rules that were to govern the ritual of worship.

The Talmud: made up of two parts.
  ➤ The Mishnah: sixty-three discussions of various subjects of the law.
  ➤ Germara: the sacred legends of the people.

Midrashim: the commentaries on the writings.

Hagada: thoughts on the commentaries.

DEEPER STUDY # 2

(6:4) **Bread of the Presence—Showbread—Consecrated Bread:** the word means *the bread of the face*. It symbolized the *Presence of God* who is the Bread of Life. The showbread was twelve loaves of bread that were brought to the house of God as a symbolic offering to God. It was a thanksgiving offering expressing appreciation and praise to God for food. The loaves were to be taken to the Holy Place by the Priest and placed on the table before the Lord. The loaves symbolized an everlasting covenant between God and His people: He would always see to it that His people had whatever food was necessary to sustain them (see outline—Mt.6:25-34). The loaves were to be changed every week. The old loaves became food for the priests and were to be eaten by them alone.

(6:5) **Son of Man**: see Deeper Study # 3—Mt.8:20.

3 Fact 2: Doing good and saving life are more important than religion and ritual.

On a different Sabbath day, another situation arose that compelled Jesus to once again challenge the Pharisees' regulations. This time, He demonstrated that doing good and saving life are more important than religious rituals.

a. The need: A man's right hand was shriveled (v.6).

While Jesus was teaching in the synagogue, He noticed a man with a shriveled hand. The only thing we know about the man with the withered hand is just that: he had a withered hand. And it was his right hand, a significant detail because most people are right-handed. The Gospels say nothing else about him. However, a dramatic background is given by one of the books which was determined not to be inspired by the Holy Spirit, and, consequently, was never accepted into the New Testament: *The Gospel According to the Hebrews*. This book says that the man was a carpenter who made his living with his hands. It adds that the man pleaded with Jesus to heal him that he might be able to work and not have to beg for food in shame.

b. The opposition by the religionists (v.7).

The Scribes and Pharisees *watched* (Gk. paretērounto, *par-eh-tay-roon'-tah*) Jesus. The meaning is that they watched closely just as an animal examines its prey. Their purpose was to accuse Him. (See Deeper Study # 4 (note) and Deeper Study # 1—Mt.12:10. This is an important note for understanding why the religionists conflicted so much with Jesus.)

c. The question and challenge given by Jesus (vv.8–10a).

Jesus knew what the religious leaders' were thinking, that He was breaking the law by helping the disabled man. He asked them a carefully-crafted question: "Is it lawful on the Sabbath to do good or to do harm, to save life or to destroy it?" His point was clear: to not help somebody is to harm them. Is this what the law demands, to harm another person? The Lord challenged the religious leaders to contemplate the matter and to be honest in their conclusion. Note three worthy observations:

➤ Jesus knew their thoughts. This was evidence of His deity.
➤ Jesus was claiming to be the *Lord of good and the Lord of salvation*, the One who does good and the One who saves life.
➤ Jesus' love reached out even to those who opposed Him so violently, at least for a while, as long as there was some hope to reach them. He appealed to them to be open and honest, to think and reason, and to be willing to confess the truth. What He was doing was good and did save life. He was the Lord of good and the Lord of salvation.

d. The point: To do good and to save life supersedes rituals (v.10b).

Jesus' point was clear: to do good and to save life always supersedes religion and rituals. Picture the scene. Jesus stood there looking around where religionists stood; there was stone silence while He scanned His audience. He was awaiting their answer to His question (v.9). He longed

---

6 On another Sabbath, he entered the synagogue and was teaching, and a man was there whose right hand was withered.

7 And the scribes and the Pharisees watched him, to see whether he would heal on the Sabbath, so that they might find a reason to accuse him.

8 But he knew their thoughts, and he said to the man with the withered hand, "Come and stand here." And he rose and stood there.

9 And Jesus said to them, "I ask you, is it lawful on the Sabbath to do good or to do harm, to save life or to destroy it?"

10 And after looking around at them all he said to him, "Stretch out your hand." And he did so, and his hand was restored.

11 But they were filled with fury and discussed with one another what they might do to Jesus.

for them to answer honestly, to confess Him as the Lord of good and the Lord of salvation, but there was only stone silence. All of a sudden, His thunderous voice commanded, "Stretch out your hand!" When the man extended his hand, he discovered that it had been restored.

e. The religionists' insane anger (v.11).

The Scribes and Pharisees became insanely mad. They were filled with *fury* or *rage* (anoias, *ah-noy'-ahce*) which means insane rage, an intense anger that completely consumed them and caused them to act irrationally. According to Mark, they immediately stormed out of the synagogue and joined forces with the Herodians in plotting how to kill Jesus (see notes and thoughts—Mk.3:6).

THOUGHT 1. The man's life had to be saved; his hand had to be restored. The man might never stand before the Lord again. Now was the day of salvation, not tomorrow.

> For he says, "In a favorable time I listened to you, and in a day of salvation I have helped you." Behold, now is the favorable time; behold, now is the day of salvation. (2 Co.6:2)

THOUGHT 2. Doing good and saving life never abuses the Sabbath or Sunday. In fact, there is no better day to help and minister than on the Lord's Day.

If we do not help people—no matter the day, even on the Sabbath—then we are *withholding good and doing harm to our neighbor*.

> "Teacher, which is the great commandment in the Law?" And he said to him, "You shall love the Lord your God with all your heart and with all your soul and with all your mind. This is the great and first commandment. And a second is like it: You shall love your neighbor as yourself." (Mt.22:36–39)

> Love does no wrong to a neighbor; therefore love is the fulfilling of the law. (Ro.13:10)

> By this we know love, that he laid down his life for us, and we ought to lay down our lives for the brothers. But if anyone has the world's goods and sees his brother in need, yet closes his heart against him, how does God's love abide in him? Little children, let us not love in word or talk but in deed and in truth. By this we shall know that we are of the truth and reassure our heart before him. (1 Jn.3:16–19)

> He has told you, O man, what is good; and what does the LORD require of you but to do justice, and to love kindness, and to walk humbly with your God? (Mi.6:8)

DEEPER STUDY # 4

(6:7) Israel, History—Legalism: in understanding the Scribes and Pharisees it is helpful to understand that the Jews were above all else *a people of God's Law*. Their nation was based on the Ten Commandments and the first five books of the Old Testament, known as the Law or Pentateuch (*Genesis, Exodus, Leviticus, Numbers, Deuteronomy*). This fact alone, that the nation was based upon God's Law, makes Israel unique among the nations of the world.

There are several significant stages in Israel's history that show just how dominating a force the Law was in the nation's survival.

1. The Jews were a people created by God through one man, Abraham (Ge.12:1-3). Abraham believed he was called by God to be the father of a great nation, and he passed the belief down to his son, Isaac, who passed it down to his son, Jacob.

2. From the twelve sons of Jacob, the Jewish population grew immensely during the four hundred years of slavery in Egypt. They had been led to Egypt by Jacob's son Joseph to save the family during a life-threatening famine. Again, the significant fact was that the fathers passed on to their children the faith of Abraham: that they were the people of God, chosen to become the greatest of all nations.

3. The nation itself was officially formed at Mt. Sinai when God gave the Law to Moses. The nation was appointed for a spiritual purpose: to be the guardian of God's Law. This event was extremely significant, for Israel was appointed as the messenger of God to the

rest of the world, as the people who were to bear testimony to the only living and true God and to His Law. They were to be God's missionary force to the world.

4. The Jewish people had been conquered and scattered all over the world time after time. In Old Testament history they had been conquered and scattered by the Assyrians, Babylonians, and Persians; yet they had survived attempt after attempt to annihilate them as a people. The one thing that bound the people together, enabling them to survive was the Law of God and their belief and practice of it (see notes and DEEPER STUDY # 1—Mt.12:1-8, 10).

5. A small remnant of the Jewish people had been allowed to return to rebuild the capital, Jerusalem, and to start over again under the leadership of Nehemiah and Ezra.

It was at this point in Israel's history that the birth of the Scribes took place (about 450 B.C.). In a most dramatic moment in the nation's history, Ezra the Scribe took the Law (Genesis-Deuteronomy) and read it aloud to the handful of people who had returned. He then led the people to rededicate themselves to being the people of God's Law (Ne.8:1-8). The rededication was strong and meaningful. It had to be, for the nation had almost been wiped out, and there were but a few who had returned to begin the nation anew.

Therefore, the Law became the greatest thing in the people's lives, and the most honored profession became that of a Scribe who was made responsible to study, teach, and preserve the Law (see DEEPER STUDY # 1—Lu.6:2). Through the years the Scribes took the Law of God and attempted to define every key phrase and word of the Law. By so doing, they ended up with thousands and thousands of rules and regulations to govern the lives of people. The people would thereby become distinct from all other people and be protected from intermarriage and from being swallowed up by cultures of other nations. These rules and regulations became known as Scribal Law. Interestingly, when the Scribal Law was finally completed, it compiled more than fifty volumes.

The Pharisees originated as a group several hundred years later (about 175 B.C.). Antiochus Epiphanes of Syria marched against Jerusalem and captured the nation and made a deliberate attempt to destroy the Jewish people. To prevent the annihilation of their life and nation as a people, a group of men dedicated themselves at all cost to keep every detail of the Law (Scribal Law). The practice of Scribal Law by these men soon became a profession, for working to keep thousands and thousands of laws just left no time for anything else. Very simply stated, the practice of Scribal Law required more time than a man had; therefore, the profession of Pharisees was born—born to practice and preserve the Law. A Pharisee genuinely believed that by obeying the Law and imposing it upon the people, he was saving his people and their nation. It was the Law that made the Jewish people, their religion, and their nation, different from all other people. Therefore, the Pharisee had a consuming devotion to see that the Law was taught and practiced among the people.

These two things, *extreme legalism* and *extreme devotion*, were the two major traits of Pharisees. But the same two traits lying within a self-centered heart can lead to terrible abuse.

1. A person can become a stern legalist, laying burden after burden upon other people. Such legalism knows little of the mercy and forgiveness of God.

2. A person can become monastic, separate from the people.

3. A person can become *super-religious*, or *super-spiritual*, with a "holier than thou" attitude and air.

4. A person can become prideful because they belong to a certain profession and hold a particular place or position or title or because they are more disciplined in keeping rules. Thus, they feel more elevated than others, more honored, more religious, and more acceptable to God.

5. A person can become hypocritical. They claim to keep all the requirements of their religion when it is impossible to do so. There is just no way to keep thousands and thousands of rules and regulation; human nature prevents perfect obedience. In addition, a person becomes a hypocrite because they act and preach one thing publicly but practice another privately.

6. A person can become showy and ostentatious. Strict discipline and personal achievement instill a desire within a person to show their achievements and to seek recognition.

H. Jesus Chooses His Men: Whom He Chose and Why, 6:12–19

(Mk.3:13–19)

1. He chose them after prayerful consideration—after praying all night

2. He chose them from among His disciples
3. He chose them to be apostles
4. He chose diverse personalities

5. He chose them to minister with Him
   a. They ministered to two distinct groups
      1) To followers
      2) To the crowds
   b. They had a threefold ministry, Jn.20:21
      1) To preach
      2) To heal
      3) To encourage people to touch Jesus, to receive His power

¹² In these days he went out to the mountain to pray, and all night he continued in prayer to God.
¹³ And when day came, he called his disciples and chose from them twelve, whom he named apostles:
¹⁴ Simon, whom he named Peter, and Andrew his brother, and James and John, and Philip, and Bartholomew,
¹⁵ and Matthew, and Thomas, and James the son of Alphaeus, and Simon who was called the Zealot,
¹⁶ and Judas the son of James, and Judas Iscariot, who became a traitor.
¹⁷ And he came down with them and stood on a level place, with a great crowd of his disciples and a great multitude of people from all Judea and Jerusalem and the seacoast of Tyre and Sidon,
¹⁸ who came to hear him and to be healed of their diseases. And those who were troubled with unclean spirits were cured.
¹⁹ And all the crowd sought to touch him, for power came out from him and healed them all.

Division III

The Son of Man's Announced Mission and Public Ministry, 4:16–9:17

H. Jesus Chooses His Men: Whom He Chose and Why, 6:12–19

(Mk.3:13–19)

6:12–19
Introduction

"We are God's fellow workers" (1 Co.3:9). This simple statement is one of the most gratifying in the New Testament for believers who truly love the Lord and long to do something for Him. Jesus uses people to accomplish His mission—men, women, boys, and girls, who will carry His message of salvation to the world. What a privilege it is to be included in God's glorious, eternally-important work! This passage which records Jesus' choosing of His apostles shows how Jesus goes about selecting people to serve Him. This is, *Jesus Chooses His Men: Whom He Chose and Why, 6:12–19.*

1. He chose them after prayerful consideration—after praying all night (v.12).
2. He chose them from among His disciples (v.13).
3. He chose them to be apostles (v.13).
4. He chose diverse personalities (vv.14–16).
5. He chose them to minister with Him (vv.17–19).

1 He chose them after prayerful consideration—after praying all night.

Jesus chose His men after prayerful consideration. He had continued all night in prayer, discussing and sharing with God the Father. It was a momentous decision. Think about it. The destiny of the world and the fate of mankind was to rest upon the shoulders of these men. They were to carry the message of salvation to the world. Jesus needed to know exactly whom to choose. He needed to talk the matter over with His Father. He needed to be spiritually renewed; He needed His spirit and mind quick and sharp and full of God's presence as He made the *critical choices*. So, He not only prayed but also consulted with God *all night* in prayer. Note that He went to a mountain where He would be alone and not be disturbed.

6:12

12 In these days he went out to the mountain to pray, and all night he continued in prayer to God.

THOUGHT 1. In all honesty, how many minutes do we spend in prayer a day? Some say they pray all day as they go about their affairs. Praying as we walk throughout the day is good and commendable. We should "pray without ceasing" (1 Th.5:17). Christ did. But praying throughout the day by flickering our minds over to God for a moment here and there is not *concentrated prayer*, not the kind of prayer that really moves and causes things to happen. Thinking and talking to God here and there is *fellowship prayer*. Fellowship prayer is easy. It is very common to share with God as we walk through the day. But the kind of prayer that Jesus demonstrated here is *concentrated prayer*, a time set aside when we get alone with God and communicate with Him earnestly and intensely. Christ sets a dynamic example of *concentrated prayer* in this passage (see notes—Mt.6:9–13).

> And rising very early in the morning, while it was still dark, he departed and went out to a desolate place, and there he prayed. (Mk.1:35)
>
> And after he had taken leave of them, he went up on the mountain to pray. (Mk.6:46)
>
> But he would withdraw to desolate places and pray. (Lu.5:16)
>
> Now it happened that as he was praying alone, the disciples were with him. And he asked them, "Who do the crowds say that I am?" (Lu.9:18)
>
> And he withdrew from them about a stone's throw, and knelt down and prayed. (Lu.22:41)

2 He chose them from among His disciples.

6:13

Jesus chose those to whom He would entrust the responsibility of taking the gospel to the world from among His disciples. There were a large number of people following Jesus as disciples. A disciple was a learner. But a disciple in that day was much more than what we mean by a student who just studies a subject taught by a teacher. A disciple was a person who *attached* himself to his teacher and who followed his teacher wherever he went, studying and learning all he could from the teacher's life as well as from his word (see note—Mt.28:19–20 for detailed discussion and application).

13 And when day came, he called his disciples and chose from them twelve, whom he named apostles:

Note that Jesus called His disciples to Him; He called all those who had attached themselves to Him. (It would be interesting to know who all these were.) Out of these disciples, Jesus chose twelve to serve as His apostles and to join Him in His great mission and ministry. They were to serve with Him in a very, very special way (see vv.17–19; see outline—Lu.5:27–39).

THOUGHT 1. The Lord selects people for special service—areas of greater responsibility in His work—who are already actively and faithfully serving Him. When we prove ourselves faithful in smaller responsibilities, He will promote us to greater responsibilities.

> One who is faithful in a very little is also faithful in much, and one who is dishonest in a very little is also dishonest in much. If then you have not been faithful in the unrighteous wealth, who will entrust to you the true riches? (Lu.16:10–11)

And he said to him, "Well done, good servant! Because you have been faithful in a very little, you shall have authority over ten cities." (Lu.19:17)

And what you have heard from me in the presence of many witnesses entrust to faithful men, who will be able to teach others also. (2 Ti.2:2)

6:13

[13] And when day came, he called his disciples and chose from them twelve, whom he named apostles:

3 He chose them to be apostles.

Jesus designated these particular men as His apostles (see DEEPER STUDY # 5—Mt.10:2). The word *apostle* (Gk. apostolos) means one who is sent, a delegate. "The Lord chose [this] term to indicate the distinctive relation of the Twelve Apostles whom He chose to be His witnesses, because in Classical Greek the word was seldom used. . . . Therefore, it designates the office as instituted by Christ to witness of Him before the world (Jn.17:18). It also designates the authority which those called to this office possess."[1] These apostles were chosen directly by the Lord Himself or by the Holy Spirit (see Mt.10:1-2; Mk.3:13-14; Lu.6:13; Ac.9:6, 15; 13:2; 22:10, 14-15; Ro.1:1). They were men who had either seen or been a companion of the Lord Jesus.

Jesus called Himself an *apostle* (apesteilas, *ah-pes-tay'-las*, Jn.17:3), and He is called the *Apostle* and High Priest of our profession (He.3:1).

Others were also called apostles (Ac.14:4, 14, 17; Ro.16:7; 2 Co.8:23; Ga.1:19; Ph.2:25; 1 Th.2:6). However, there is a distinct difference between all these and the twelve whom Christ chose. The first twelve were . . .

- chosen by the Lord Himself while on earth
- chosen to *be with Him* during His earthly ministry (Mk.3:14)
- chosen to be trained by Him alone, personally
- chosen to be the eyewitnesses of His resurrection (Ac.1:22)
- chosen to be the ones who were to carry forth His message which had come from His very own mouth

There is a sense in which the gift of apostleship is still given and used in the ministry today (see DEEPER STUDY # 5—Mt.10:2).

THOUGHT 1. As believers we are ambassadors for Christ, ones who go forth representing Christ Himself both by life and word. We are to *reflect* the very life of Christ.

That is, in Christ God was reconciling the world to himself, not counting their trespasses against them, and entrusting to us the message of reconciliation. Therefore, we are ambassadors for Christ, God making his appeal through us. We implore you on behalf of Christ, be reconciled to God. (2 Co.5:19-20)

THOUGHT 2. The Lord does pick *a few* from among His followers (disciples) to serve Him in very special ways. Every church has to have its leaders; and every area, country, and generation has to have its leaders. God must have those who will go beyond in sacrificing and giving, serving and ministering in every place and generation.

There was a man sent from God, whose name was John. (Jn.1:6)

He said to him the third time, "Simon, son of John, do you love me?" Peter was grieved because he said to him the third time, "Do you love me?" and he said to him, "Lord, you know everything; you know that I love you." Jesus said to him, "Feed my sheep." (Jn.21:17)

Pay careful attention to yourselves and to all the flock, in which the Holy Spirit has made you overseers, to care for the church of God, which he obtained with his own blood. (Ac.20:28)

Shepherd the flock of God that is among you, exercising oversight, not under compulsion, but willingly, as God would have you; not for shameful gain, but eagerly. (1 Pe.5:2)

Draw near to me, hear this: from the beginning I have not spoken in secret, from the time it came to be I have been there. And now the Lord GOD has sent me, and his Spirit. (Is.48:16)

---

1 Spiros Zodhiates, ed., *The Complete Word Study Dictionary New Testament,* (Chattanooga, TN: AMG Publishers, 1992). Via Wordsearch digital edition.

4 He chose diverse personalities.

The men Jesus chose as apostles were from diverse backgrounds and walks of life. Peter, James, and John were fishermen with rather large businesses (Mk.1:19-20; Lu.5:2-3). One apostle was most likely wealthy: Matthew, the tax collector. His house must have been an estate, for it was large enough to handle a huge crowd for a large feast (Lu.5:27-29).

One was a political nationalist, an insurrectionist, Simon the Zealot. The Zealots pledged themselves to overthrow the Roman government and to assassinate as many Roman officials and Jewish cohorts as possible (Lu.6:15; Ac.1:13). One was evidently deeply religious: Nathanael (Jn.1:48). So far as is known, there was no outstanding official or famous citizen among the apostles.

> 14 Simon, whom he named Peter, and Andrew his brother, and James and John, and Philip, and Bartholomew,
> 15 and Matthew, and Thomas, and James the son of Alphaeus, and Simon who was called the Zealot,
> 16 and Judas the son of James, and Judas Iscariot, who became a traitor.

The men Jesus selected were a strange mixture of personalities. Matthew, being a tax collector and ostracized by the Jewish community, was bound to be a hard-crusted, non-religious individual (Mt.9:9). The fishermen James and John were of a rough breed with thundering personalities (Mk.3:17). Simon the Zealot was possessed with a fanatical, nationalistic spirit (Lu.6:15; Ac.1:13). Peter was apparently a rough fisherman with a loud, rough-hewn personality (Mk.14:71). The power of Christ to give purpose and meaning to life and to bring peace among people is clearly seen in His ability to bring so diverse a group together under one banner (see DEEPER STUDIES 4-15—Mk.3:16-19 for a discussion on each of the apostles).

> But God chose what is foolish in the world to shame the wise; God chose what is weak in the world to shame the strong; God chose what is low and despised in the world, even things that are not, to bring to nothing things that are, so that no human being might boast in the presence of God. (1 Co.1:27-29)

5 He chose them to minister with Him.

Jesus chose these men to carry out His mission with Him. Note that the twelve were now *with Him in a very special relationship*. Luke reports that Jesus came down from the mountain with them and they stood with Him to minister. The twelve were now to learn what their mission was to be.

> 17 And he came down with them and stood on a level place, with a great crowd of his disciples and a great multitude of people from all Judea and Jerusalem and the seacoast of Tyre and Sidon,
> 18 who came to hear him and to be healed of their diseases. And those who were troubled with unclean spirits were cured.
> 19 And all the crowd sought to touch him, for power came out from him and healed them all.

a. They ministered to two distinct groups (v.17).

Standing there, Jesus and the twelve were faced with a multitude of people. Their mission was to learn to minister to two distinct groups: "His disciples" and the multitude of people who needed Jesus' help—the works that can only be accomplished by Him and through His power.

b. They had a threefold ministry (vv.18-19).

The apostles needed to learn to carry out a threefold ministry:
➤ They were to preach to those "who came to hear" (v.18a).
➤ They were to minister to the sick and those with infirmities, both physical and spiritual (vv.17-18).
➤ They were to lead people to *touch Jesus* in order to receive His power (v.19). Later, after Jesus ascended back to heaven, they would lead people to receive a touch *from* Jesus. They were instruments of Jesus' power.

THOUGHT 1. The Lord's ministers are to preach and teach. They are to share with all those who come to hear about Jesus.

> Go therefore and make disciples of all nations, baptizing them in the name of the Father and of the Son and of the Holy Spirit, teaching them to observe all that I have commanded you. And behold, I am with you always, to the end of the age. (Mt.28:19-20)

> And he said to them, "Go into all the world and proclaim the gospel to the whole creation." (Mk.16:15)

In addition, the Lord's ministers are to minister to the diseased and brokenhearted of their community and world. In the name and power of Jesus, they are to help bring God's healing to the sick and mend the brokenhearted.

> How God anointed Jesus of Nazareth with the Holy Spirit and with power. He went about doing good and healing all who were oppressed by the devil, for God was with him. (Ac.10:38)

> He heals the brokenhearted and binds up their wounds. (Ps.147:3)

In order to be effective in these ministries, the Lord's servants must be instruments of Jesus' power. Jesus' power is to flow through His servant and flow outward to other people.

> And Jesus came and said to them, "All authority in heaven and on earth has been given to me." (Mt.28:18)

> But you will receive power when the Holy Spirit has come upon you, and you will be my witnesses in Jerusalem and in all Judea and Samaria, and to the end of the earth. (Ac.1:8)

> Now to him who is able to do far more abundantly than all that we ask or think, according to the power at work within us. (Ep.3:20)

> Preach the word; be ready in season and out of season; reprove, rebuke, and exhort, with complete patience and teaching. (2 Ti.4:2)

(Mt.5:3–12)

²⁰ And he lifted up his eyes on his disciples, and said: "Blessed are you who are poor, for yours is the kingdom of God.

²¹ Blessed are you who are hungry now, for you shall be satisfied. Blessed are you who weep now, for you shall laugh.

²² Blessed are you when people hate you and when they exclude you and revile you and spurn your name as evil, on account of the Son of Man!

²³ Rejoice in that day, and leap for joy, for behold, your reward is great in heaven; for so their fathers did to the prophets.

²⁴ But woe to you who are rich, for you have received your consolation.

²⁵ Woe to you who are full now, for you shall be hungry. Woe to you who laugh now, for you shall mourn and weep.

²⁶ Woe to you, when all people speak well of you, for so their fathers did to the false prophets."

1. **The promises to those who reject materialism**
   a. The poor: Will inherit the kingdom of God
   b. The hungry: Will be filled
   c. The sorrowful: Will laugh

   d. The persecuted: Will be rewarded
      1) The persecuted: Believers who are hated, ostracized, mocked and the rejected for Christ
      2) The attitude to have while being persecuted: Rejoicing
      3) The reward: Will be great

2. **The judgment of those who pursue materialism**
   a. The rich: Will have no future comfort
   b. The well-fed: Will hunger
   c. The merry: Will weep

   d. The prideful and compromising: Will have earthly approval only

Division III

The Son of Man's Announced Mission and Public Ministry, 4:16–9:17

I. Jesus Teaches the Perils of the Material World, 6:20–26

(Mt.5:3–12)

6:20–26
Introduction

The ways of Christ are the complete opposite of the ways of the world. What Jesus teaches in this passage is shocking to the world, for Jesus switches the world's values completely around. He rejects entirely the *materialism* (things) of the world and warns the worldly and materialistic that severe judgment is coming. This is, *Jesus Teaches the Perils of the Material World, 6:20–26.*

1. The promises to those who reject materialism (vv.20–23).
2. The judgment of those who pursue materialism (vv.24–26).

1 The promises to those who reject materialism.

Jesus contrasts those who live for the things of this world with those who focus on spiritual rather than material things. He speaks first to those who focus on the spiritual, promising them that they will be *blessed* (Gk. makarioi, *mah-kah'-rih-oy*)—know a depth of fulfillment and happiness and joy—that transcends anything this world has to offer.

²⁰ And he lifted up his eyes on his disciples, and said: "Blessed are you who are poor, for yours is the kingdom of God.
²¹ Blessed are you who are hungry now, for you shall be satisfied. Blessed are you who weep now, for you shall laugh.
²² Blessed are you when people hate you and when they exclude you and revile you and spurn your name as evil, on account of the Son of Man!
²³ Rejoice in that day, and leap for joy, for behold, your reward is great in heaven; for so their fathers did to the prophets."

a. The poor: Will inherit the kingdom of God (v.20).

Jesus first addresses the poor. This does not mean that a person must be poverty-stricken in order to be blessed. Hunger, nakedness, and slums are not pleasing to God, especially in a world of plenty. Jesus is not talking about material poverty. He means what Matthew adds in his Gospel: "poor in spirit" (see Mt.5:3). Being "poor in spirit" involves acknowledging three truths.

First, being poor in spirit is acknowledging our utter helplessness before God, our spiritual poverty, our spiritual need; acknowledging that we are solely dependent on God to meet our need.

Second, being poor in spirit is acknowledging our utter lack in facing life and eternity apart from God; acknowledging that the real blessings of life and eternity come only from a right relationship with God (see note—Ep.1:3; see Jn.10:10; Ga.5:22-23).

Third, being poor in spirit is acknowledging our utter lack of superiority before all others and our spiritual deadness before God; acknowledging that no matter what we have achieved in this world (fame, fortune, power), we are no better, no richer, no more superior than the next person. Our attitude toward others is not proud and haughty, not superior and overbearing. To be "poor in spirit" means acknowledging that every human being is a real person just like everyone else—a person who has a significant contribution to make to society and to the world. The person who is "poor in spirit" approaches life in humility and appreciation, not as though life owes us, but as though we owe life. We realize that we have been given the privilege of living; thus, we journey through life with a humble attitude, that is, with an attitude of being poor in spirit and contributing all we can out of a spirit of appreciation.

Two critical steps are taken by people who truly acknowledge their spiritual poverty:

➤ They turn their primary attention away from the things of this world, knowing possessions can never make them truly rich.
➤ They turn their primary attention to God and His kingdom, knowing that God alone can make them truly rich (see note—Ep.1:3).

The opposite of being "poor in spirit" is having a spirit that is full of self. There is a world of difference between these two spirits. There is the difference of thinking one is righteous versus acknowledging one has the need for righteousness. There is the difference of *having self-righteousness* versus having *another's righteousness*. We must have *another's righteousness*. Self-righteousness goes no further than self, that is, no further than death. *Another's righteousness*, that is, Christ's righteousness, lives forever (2 Co.5:21; Ph.3:9; see note—Ro.3:21-22; note and DEEPER STUDY # 1—Ga.2:15-16; outline and notes—Ro.10:4).

The promise to the *poor* is glorious. Note the exact words: "yours is the kingdom of God." The promise is not "yours shall be," but "yours is." The poor in spirit receive the kingdom of God *now* (see DEEPER STUDY # 3—Mt.19:23-24).

b. The hungry: Will be filled (v.21a).

Jesus continues, addressing the hungry. He is speaking of spiritual hunger, not physical hunger. Again, being physically hungry is not a blessing. It is often sad and tragic. Jesus is saying, "Blessed are they who hunger *spiritually*, who hunger after righteousness." It means to have a starving spirit, a spirit that craves righteousness and the things of God.

In the Bible, "righteousness" has two simple yet profound meanings. It means both *to be right and to do right* (see DEEPER STUDY # 5—Mt.5:6 for more discussion). Many people stress *being* righteous and neglect *doing* righteousness. This leads to two serious errors.

First, it leads to false security. It causes a person to think that they are saved and acceptable to God because they feel they have *made a profession of faith* in Jesus Christ. But they neglect doing good and living as they should. They neglect obeying God and serving others. Their lives do not agree with their profession, showing that their profession is false.

Second, it leads to loose living. It allows a person to go out and do pretty much as they desire. They feel secure and comfortable in their *professed* faith in Christ. They know that what they do may affect their fellowship with God and other believers, but they think their behavior will not affect their salvation. They think that no matter what they do, they are still acceptable to God.

The problem with this way of thinking is that it is a false righteousness. Again, righteousness in the Bible means *being righteous* and *doing righteousness*. The Bible knows nothing about being righteous without living righteously.

On the other hand, many people stress *doing righteousness* and neglect *being righteous*. This also leads to two serious errors.

First, it leads to self-righteousness and legalism. It causes a person to think that they are saved and acceptable to God because of their works—they do good. They work and behave morally and keep certain rules and regulations. They do the things a Christian should do by obeying the primary laws of God. But they neglect the most basic law: the law of love and acceptance—that God loves people and accepts them not because they do good but because they love and trust the righteousness of Christ (see note and DEEPER STUDY # 5—Mt.5:6).

Second, it leads to being judgmental and censorious. People who stress that they are righteous (acceptable to God) because they keep certain laws often judge and censor others. They feel that rules and regulations can be kept, for *they* keep them. Therefore, they judge those who fail to keep them.

The problem with this way of thinking is that it, too, is a false righteousness. Again, righteousness in the Bible is both *being righteous* and *doing righteousness*. The Bible knows nothing of being acceptable to God without *being made righteous in Christ Jesus* (see notes and DEEPER STUDY # 5—Mt.5:6; Ro.5:1 for more discussion; see 2 Co.5:21).

Note that Jesus does not say, "Blessed are the righteous," for no one is righteous (Ro.3:10). He says, "Blessed are those who *hunger and thirst* for righteousness" (Mt.5:6). Nobody is righteous, not perfectly righteous. Our chance to be righteous is gone. We have already come short and missed the mark. We are already imperfect. We have but one hope: that God will love us so much that He will somehow *count* us righteous. That is just what God does. God takes our faith in Jesus Christ and counts it as righteousness (see DEEPER STUDY # 2—Ro.4:22).

The Lord made a rich promise to those who hunger after righteousness: they will be satisfied or filled. They will be blessed with an abundant life of holiness, love, joy, peace, contentment, fulfillment, and effectiveness in the Lord's service.

c. The sorrowful: Will laugh (v.21b).

Jesus then speaks to the sorrowful, those who weep and mourn. The idea is a broken heart, a desperate, helpless weeping. It is weeping over sin; it is a broken heart over evil and suffering; it is a brokenness of self that comes from seeing Jesus on the cross and realizing that one's own sins put Him there (see Jas.4:9).

Who are those who mourn? Who are those so full of grief that they weep from deep within?

➢ The people who are desperately sorry for their sin and unworthiness before God. They have such a sensitivity to sin that their heart is completely broken (Lu.18:13).

➢ The people who genuinely feel the desperate plight and terrible suffering of others. The tragedies, the problems, the sinful behavior of others; the state, the condition, the lostness of the world—all weigh ever so heavily upon the heart of the mourner.

➢ The people who *experience* personal tragedy and intense trauma.

The promise to those who weep is that they will *laugh* (gelasete, *ghel-ah'-seh-teh*). The word means *loud laughter* that arises from a deep-seated joy and comfort. This laughter comes from seeing the end of sin and shame, sorrow and suffering, tragedy and trauma. In addition, it comes from *being comforted* (Mt.5:4; see note—2 Co.1:3). Note two glorious truths.

First, they receive a present comfort, a comfort in this life:
➢ A settled peace: a relief, a solace, a consolation within.
➢ An assurance of forgiveness and acceptance by God.
➢ A fullness of joy: a sense of God's presence, care and guidance (Jn.14:26); a sense of His sovereignty, of His working all things out for good to those who love Him (Ro.8:28; see Ps.16:11; Jn.10:10; 15:11; 2 Co.6:10).

Second, they receive an eternal comfort:
➢ A passing from death to life (Jn.3:16; Jn.5:24f).
➢ A wiping away of all tears (Is.25:8; Rev.7:17; 21:4).

d. The persecuted: Will be rewarded (vv.22–23).

The persecuted are those who endure suffering *for Christ*. Jesus spelled out what He meant by persecution. He meant being hated, ostracized, reproached, and having one's name spoken against.

Note the attitude we are to have while being persecuted. Jesus calls us to "rejoice" and "leap for joy" (v.23). How is this attitude possible? It is possible by keeping our eyes on the reward. Jesus promises the persecuted that they have a great reward awaiting them in heaven.

Believers are forewarned: we will suffer persecution (Jn.15:20; 16:4; Ph.1:29; 2 Ti.3:12; 1 Jn.3:13; 1 Pe.4:12f). Believers suffer persecution because we *are not of this world*. We are called out of the world. We are *in the world*, but we are not *of the world*. We are separated from the behavior of the world; therefore, the world reacts against us (Jn.15:19).

Believers also suffer persecution because we *strip away the world's cloak of sin*. We live and demonstrate a life of righteousness. When we live righteously, our lives expose—shine a light on—the sins of those who live unrighteously (Jn.15:21, 24; see 15:18; 2 Ti.3:12).

In addition, believers suffer persecution because the world does not know God or Christ. They want no God, no Lord other than themselves and their own imaginations. They want to do just what they want, to fulfill their own desires and not what another Lord wishes and demands (Jn.15:21; 16:3).

Then, believers suffer persecution because the world is deceived in its concept and belief of God. The world conceives God to be the Person who fulfills their earthly desires and lusts (Jn.16:2-3). The world's idea of God is that of a *Supreme Grandfather*. He protects, provides, and gives, no matter one's behavior, just so the behavior is not too far out. God (the Supreme Grandfather) will accept and work all things out in the final analysis. But the true believer teaches against this. God is love, but He is also just and demands righteousness. The world rebels against this concept of God (Jn.16:2-3).

Again, Jesus promises the persecuted that their reward is great in heaven, and they have the honor and joy of following in the footsteps (testimony) of the great prophets of the past. They will receive the kingdom of heaven eternally (He.11:35f; 1 Pe.4:12-13; see Deeper Study # 3—Mt.19:23-24). However, the persecuted also receive a great reward now:
➢ They experience a special honor (Ac.5:41).
➢ They experience a special consolation (2 Co.1:5).
➢ They are given a very special closeness, a glow of the Lord's presence (see note—1 Pe.4:14).
➢ They become a greater witness for Christ (2 Co.1:4-6).

2 The judgment of those who pursue materialism.

Jesus proceeds to speak to those who pursue materialism—the things of this world—as opposed to spiritual things. Note that they are the direct opposite of those who are poor, who hunger, who weep, and who are persecuted.

a. The rich: Will have no future comfort (v.24).

Jesus issues a strong warning to the rich. Who are the rich? Realistically, in comparison to what the vast majority of the world has, a rich person is anyone who has anything to put back beyond meeting the true needs of their own family. This is exactly what Christ and the Bible say time and again (see also Mk.12:41-44; Lu.21:1-4; Ac.4:34-35).

24 "But woe to you who are rich, for you have received your consolation.
25 Woe to you who are full now, for you shall be hungry. Woe to you who laugh now, for you shall mourn and weep.
26 Woe to you, when all people speak well of you, for so their fathers did to the false prophets."

Why are the rich warned? Because wealth pulls a person away from the kingdom of heaven. It is difficult for a rich person to enter heaven. Christ made this statement because of the things that *pulled* the rich young ruler away from heaven (Mk.10:17-25). There is a lure, an attraction, a force, a power, a pull, that reaches out and draws any of us who desire worldly wealth. There are pulls so forceful that they will enslave and doom any rich person who fails to turn and embrace God.

First, *wealth creates the big "I."* The wealthy are usually esteemed, honored, and envied. Wealth brings position, power, and recognition. It boosts *ego*, making a person self-sufficient and independent in this world. As a result, there is a tendency for the rich to feel they are truly self-sufficient, that they need nothing. And in such an atmosphere and world of thought, God is forgotten. The rich person tends to forget there are things that money cannot buy and events from which money cannot save. Peace, love, joy—all that really matter within the human spirit—can never be bought. Neither can money save one from disaster, disease, accident, and death.

Second, *wealth tends to make a person hoard.* The Bible lays down the principle of handling money for all people, even for the poor:

> And he said to him, "You shall love the Lord your God with all your heart and with all your soul and with all your mind. This is the great and first commandment. And a second is like it: You shall love your neighbor as yourself." (Mt.22:37-39)

> Let the thief no longer steal, but rather let him labor, doing honest work with his own hands, so that he may have something to share with anyone in need. (Ep.4:28)

The world reels in desperate need. People are starving, sick, unhoused, and unclothed by the millions; and teeming millions are spiritually lost and without God in this world and doomed to die without ever knowing Him. When any of us sit still and objectively look at the world in its desperate plight, how can we keep from asking: "How can any person hoard and not help—even to the last available penny? Why would anyone keep more than what they need for themselves and their family?"

As God looks at the rich, He is bound to ask the same questions. In fact, His questions are bound to be more pointed and forceful. This is exactly what Christ said to the rich young ruler:

> Jesus said to him, "If you would be perfect, go, sell what you possess and give to the poor, and you will have treasure in heaven; and come, follow me." (Mt.19:21)

Third, *riches tend to make a person selfish.* For some unexplainable reason, the more we get, the more we want. When we taste the things of this world and become comfortable, we tend to fear losing our possessions. We struggle to keep what we have and to get more. True, many are willing to make contributions, but only a certain amount, an amount that will not lower their overall estate or standing or level of comfort and possessions. There are few who give all they are and have to Christ to meet the needs of the world.

Again, Jesus said that it is difficult, very difficult for the rich to enter the kingdom of God (Lu.18:24). If we do not have compassion and take care of others when they are in desperate need, how can we expect God to have compassion and take care of us? The rich have the means to help and to save human life, *if they would.*

Fourth, *wealth attaches a person to the world.* Wealth enables people to buy things that . . .

- make them comfortable
- please their taste
- expand their experience
- stir their ego
- challenge their mental pursuit
- stimulate their flesh
- stretch their self-image

If people center their lives on the things of the world, their attention is on the world and not on God. They tend to become wrapped up in securing more and in protecting what they have. Too often, they give little if any time and thought to heavenly matters. Wealth and the things it can provide usually consume the rich.

The judgment of the rich is their wealth on earth. The word *received* (apechete, *ah-pekh'-eh-teh*) means a receipt in full. Their only *consolation* (paraklēsin, *pah-rah-clay'-sin:* help, aid, encouragement) is in this life—the wealth they have. There will be no consolation after this life—no help, no aid, no encouragement, no cheer. They are *paid in full* in the here and now. They choose this life, so all the good they will receive is the good they now experience.

> For we brought nothing into the world, and we cannot take anything out of the world. . . . But those who desire to be rich fall into temptation, into a snare, into many senseless and harmful desires that plunge people into ruin and destruction. (1 Ti.6:7, 9)

> Your gold and silver have corroded, and their corrosion will be evidence against you and will eat your flesh like fire. You have laid up treasure in the last days. (Jas.5:3)

> The possessions of his house will be carried away, dragged off in the day of God's wrath. (Jb.20:28)

> Surely a man goes about as a shadow! Surely for nothing they are in turmoil; man heaps up wealth and does not know who will gather! (Ps.39:6)

> I hated all my toil in which I toil under the sun, seeing that I must leave it to the man who will come after me. (Ec.2:18)

b. The well-fed: Will hunger (v.25a).

Jesus also issues a strong warning to the full. The full are the opposite of those who hunger for righteousness. The full are those who are filled with all that the world has to offer; in essence they are full of themselves, their own desires, urges, and cravings. They have no hunger for righteousness at all. Scripture identifies the full as those who . . .

- serve their own appetites and not the Lord Jesus Christ (Ro.16:18)
- indulge in the foods (things, sins) of the world (1 Co.6:13; see 6:9–13)
- make their bellies (appetites, desires) their god (Ph.3:19)
- "[are] filled with all manner of unrighteousness" (Ro.1:29–32)

The full will be judged by being made to hunger. This means they . . .

- will leave all that filled them behind when they die (Lu.12:20; 16:25)
- will have no desires filled after this life
- will have no delights throughout eternity
- will hunger for good (righteousness) and for the good things throughout eternity

> For you say, I am rich, I have prospered, and I need nothing, not realizing that you are wretched, pitiable, poor, blind, and naked. (Re.3:17)

> They close their hearts to pity; with their mouths they speak arrogantly. (Ps.17:10)

> Behold, this was the guilt of your sister Sodom: she and her daughters had pride, excess of food, and prosperous ease, but did not aid the poor and needy. (Ezk.16:49)

c. The merry: Will weep (v.25b).

The Lord proceeds to warn the merry—those who laugh now—strongly. Who are those who "laugh now?"

First, they are people who have no sense of sin, no sorrow or regret over evil and suffering, no brokenness over the cross and their own sin. Their joy is carnal and sensual.

Second, they are people who are laughing it up *in the world* with all its comfort and ease, pleasures and stimulations, recreations and pastimes. Their joy is the indulgence and entertaining of their flesh.

Third, they are people who pay little or no attention to the reality of the world, a world suffering under the weight of evil and disaster, greed and selfishness, sin and death. Their joy is found in denying and ignoring the truth of the world or in giving a pittance of time or money to help in order to ease their consciences.

Those who laugh now will be judged with mourning and weeping. They are doomed because they refused to face the reality of a world lost in sin and evil, a world that needed their attention and help. They refused to help the needy, those who suffered and wept so much in this world. Therefore, they will be left alone in the next world to mourn and weep over their great loss.

> **Draw near to God, and he will draw near to you. Cleanse your hands, you sinners, and purify your hearts, you double-minded. Be wretched and mourn and weep. Let your laughter be turned to mourning and your joy to gloom. Humble yourselves before the Lord, and he will exalt you. (Jas.4:8–10)**
>
> **That the exulting of the wicked is short, and the joy of the godless but for a moment? (Jb.20:5)**
>
> **Even in laughter the heart may ache, and the end of joy may be grief. (Pr.14:13)**
>
> **For as the crackling of thorns under a pot, so is the laughter of the fools; this also is vanity. (Ec.7:6)**
>
> **And joy and gladness are taken away from the fruitful field, and in the vineyards no songs are sung, no cheers are raised; no treader treads out wine in the presses; I have put an end to the shouting. (Is.16:10)**

d. The prideful and compromising: Will have earthly approval only (v.26).

Christ's last strong warning is to the prideful and compromising. These people are the opposite of those who are persecuted for Christ's sake. The worldly speak well of others who are worldly . . .

- who live as they live
- who speak as they speak
- who compromise
- who seek their company and approval
- who never point out the truth of sin and death, judgment and hell

Worldly people want attention and esteem, position and place, honor and praise, recognition and applause. The people of the world honor such ambitions and rewards. Therefore, they speak well of those who attain such. But note what Jesus said. He said that *false prophets* were those of whom the world spoke well, and this was their reward, all they would ever receive. They coveted worldly recognition and honor, and they received it, but at the expense of heavenly recognition and honor.

THOUGHT 1. We are not to be as false prophets, slapping people on the back, acknowledging and compromising with their worldliness. If we do, the world will speak well of us, but we will lose our reward. As believers, we need to tell the truth to all people: all need a Savior, and their eternal fate depends on their coming to Him for salvation, seeking His righteousness.

> **For the time is coming when people will not endure sound teaching, but having itching ears they will accumulate for themselves teachers to suit their own passions. (2 Ti.4:3)**
>
> **But false prophets also arose among the people, just as there will be false teachers among you, who will secretly bring in destructive heresies, even denying the Master who bought them, bringing upon themselves swift destruction. And many will follow their sensuality, and because of them the way of truth will be blasphemed. (2 Pe.2:1–2)**
>
> **I will not show partiality to any man or use flattery toward any person. (Jb.32:21)**
>
> **May the LORD cut off all flattering lips, the tongue that makes great boasts. (Ps.12:3)**
>
> **Whoever says to the wicked, "You are in the right," will be cursed by peoples, abhorred by nations. (Pr.24:24)**
>
> **A lying tongue hates its victims, and a flattering mouth works ruin. (Pr.26:28)**

J. Jesus Teaches the New Principles of Life, 6:27–38

(Mt.5:39, 43–48; 7:12)

1. The new principles
- a. Governing relationships
  - 1) Love your enemies
  - 2) Do good to the hateful
  - 3) Bless the curser
  - 4) Pray for the spiteful
  - 5) Offer the other cheek to the abuser
- b. Governing property
  - 1) Do not deprive others
  - 2) Give when needed
  - 3) Do not demand repayment of items taken by others
- c. Governing behavior toward others

2. The argument: A believer's behavior must surpass a sinner's
- a. In love
- b. In doing good

- c. In lending

3. The reward for living right
- a. You will receive a great reward
- b. You will be children of the Most High

- c. We will be merciful, just as God is merciful

4. The promise: Reciprocal behavior—you will receive what you give
- a. In relationships

- b. In property
- c. The principle: A person receives what they give

27 "But I say to you who hear, Love your enemies, do good to those who hate you,

28 bless those who curse you, pray for those who abuse you.

29 To one who strikes you on the cheek, offer the other also, and from one who takes away your cloak do not withhold your tunic either.

30 Give to everyone who begs from you, and from one who takes away your goods do not demand them back.

31 And as you wish that others would do to you, do so to them.

32 If you love those who love you, what benefit is that to you? For even sinners love those who love them.

33 And if you do good to those who do good to you, what benefit is that to you? For even sinners do the same.

34 And if you lend to those from whom you expect to receive, what credit is that to you? Even sinners lend to sinners, to get back the same amount.

35 But love your enemies, and do good, and lend, expecting nothing in return, and your reward will be great, and you will be sons of the Most High, for he is kind to the ungrateful and the evil.

36 Be merciful, even as your Father is merciful.

37 Judge not, and you will not be judged; condemn not, and you will not be condemned; forgive, and you will be forgiven;

38 give, and it will be given to you. Good measure, pressed down, shaken together, running over, will be put into your lap. For with the measure you use it will be measured back to you."

Division III

The Son of Man's Announced Mission and Public Ministry, 4:16–9:17

J. Jesus Teaches the New Principles of Life, 6:27–38

(Mt.5:39, 43–48; 7:12)

6:27–38
Introduction

As Jesus went on teaching, He continued to show that His ways are the exact opposite of the world's ways. He introduced a new set of principles by which we are to live that surely shocked His audience, just as they repulse people today. These radical standards go against every grain of society and every fiber of fallen human beings. People rebel by nature against what Jesus is saying. However, the people who choose to obey these principles will find that they are the salvation of society and the hope of humanity for life. This is, *Jesus Teaches the New Principles of Life, 6:27–38.*

1. The new principles (vv.27–31).
2. The argument: A believer's behavior must surpass a sinner's (vv.32–34).
3. The reward for living right (vv.35–36).
4. The promise: Reciprocal behavior—you will receive what you give (vv.37–38).

1 The new principles.

Jesus instituted new principles to govern our lives. Note that He was speaking to His disciples (v.20) and to those who would hear (v.27). He knew that all would not hear. Even if they were disciples, some just closed their ears if they did not like what they heard. And what Jesus was about to preach was a complete switch from the way people and society lived. He was about to say some things people had never heard or thought about. He knew some were going to shut their ears, so He warned them and encouraged them to guard against not listening.

27 "But I say to you who hear, Love your enemies, do good to those who hate you,
28 bless those who curse you, pray for those who abuse you.
29 To one who strikes you on the cheek, offer the other also, and from one who takes away your cloak do not withhold your tunic either.
30 Give to everyone who begs from you, and from one who takes away your goods do not demand them back.
31 And as you wish that others would do to you, do so to them."

a. Governing relationships (vv.27–29a).

Jesus began by instituting new principles to govern human relationships. He touched on five specific behaviors.

First, Jesus instructed His followers to *love all people, even enemies* (v.27a). Believers are to respect and honor all people (1 Pe.2:17). Every human being has something that is commendable, even if it is nothing more than the fact that he or she is a fellow human being with a soul to be reached for God.

New Testament Greek has different words for different types of love. There are specific words for affection, for the love we feel toward friends, and for romantic love. When Jesus commanded us to *love* our enemies, He chose the word *agapē*. It describes the highest possible form of love—greater than affection or friendship or romantic love and different from all of these. *Agapē* describes the love of God for sinful humanity, a self-sacrificing love, a love that is an act of the will, not merely a feeling or emotion. It is a love that seeks and does what is best for another, that does good for another, that even sacrifices for another—*regardless of how we feel about them.*

Loving our enemies is difficult because it goes against human nature. Our human nature is to *react against* our enemies: to hate, strike back, and wish hurt. At best, human nature treats enemies with coldness and distance. The root of human reaction against enemies is self and bitterness. (Self-preservation is not evil in itself. See note and DEEPER STUDY # 1—Mt.5:44. The section on *agapē* love points out that love is not complacent acceptance of wickedness and license.)

We ought to have mercy and compassion for our enemies. Those who are enemies may choose to remain antagonistic, but the believer can still forgive in mercy and compassion. In fact, if we do not have compassion for those who hate us, we have gained nothing of the spirit of Christ (v.36).

Second, Jesus taught us to do good to those who hate us (v.27b). Imagine the impact of these words to the world of Jesus' day. They were an enslaved people conquered and hated by the Romans, yet Jesus was saying, "Do good to them" (see note, *Love—Enemies*—Mt.5:44 for more discussion).

Doing good goes beyond words; it actually *acts* for the good of those who hate us. It reaches out to them through their family and friends, employment and business. It searches for ways to do good to them, realizing that they need to be reached for God. If no immediate way is found, then the Christian continues to bless them, ever waiting for the day when the hater will face one of the crises that comes to every human being. And then the believer goes and does good, ministering as Christ Himself ministered.

> To the contrary, "if your enemy is hungry, feed him; if he is thirsty, give him something to drink; for by so doing you will heap burning coals on his head." (Ro.12:20)

> See that no one repays anyone evil for evil, but always seek to do good to one another and to everyone. (1 Th.5:15)

> If you see the donkey of one who hates you lying down under its burden, you shall refrain from leaving him with it; you shall rescue it with him. (Ex.23:5)

> If your enemy is hungry, give him bread to eat, and if he is thirsty, give him water to drink. (Pr.25:21)

Third, Jesus told us to bless those who curse us (v.28a). People do curse, and sometimes they curse other people. When someone curses a believer, we are to bless that person, not rail back. We are to speak softly, using kind and reconciling words.

> Bless those who persecute you; bless and do not curse them. (Ro.12:14)

> Do not repay evil for evil or reviling for reviling, but on the contrary, bless, for to this you were called, that you may obtain a blessing. (1 Pe.3:9)

> A soft answer turns away wrath, but a harsh word stirs up anger. (Pr.15:1)

Fourth, we are to pray for those who mistreat us (v.28b). This command refers not only to those who speak evil of us but those whose behavior toward us is *spiteful*. It is speaking of those who attempt to shame and to hurt both our name and our being. Someone tries to shame, dishonor, disgrace and reproach us. And they go even farther; they misuse, mistreat, abuse, attack, and persecute us. What are we to do? Christ says, "Pray for them. When they mistreat you, pray for them." How should we pray for those who are spiteful toward us?
➤ Pray for God to forgive the persecutor.
➤ Pray for peace between one's self and the persecutor.
➤ Pray for the persecutor's salvation and correction.

> And Jesus said, "Father, forgive them, for they know not what they do." And they cast lots to divide his garments. (Lu.23:34)

> And falling to his knees he cried out with a loud voice, "Lord, do not hold this sin against them." And when he had said this, he fell asleep. (Ac.7:60)

Praying for those who mistreat us will greatly benefit *us*. It will keep us from becoming bitter, hostile, and reactionary.

Fifth, our Lord taught us to not retaliate against those who harm or injure us (v.29a). The word for *cheek* (Gk. siagona, *see-ah-gon'ah*) actually means the jaw or jawbone. A *strike* (tuptonti, *toop'-ton-tee*) is a strong blow, a blow that injures, a punch rather than merely a slap of contempt. Of course, there is contempt and bitterness, but there is also physical injury. Christ says that the believer is not to strike back, not to retaliate against . . .
• bitter insults or contempt
• bodily threats or injury

It is critical that what Jesus says here not be misconstrued through the lens of our modern day and time. Jesus is *not* saying that we should overlook or cover up wickedness or give evil people license to harm others. The ESV translates the Greek word rendered by other versions as *spitefully use* (NKJV) and *mistreat* (NASB, CSB, NIV) as *abuse* (v.28). When we hear the word, *abuse*, in our day, we usually think of child abuse or sexual abuse. A person who is a victim of such criminal abuses must not think Jesus is telling you that you are to accept this kind of treatment. While He commands you to pray for your abuser, you have a responsibility to report the abuser to the proper authorities for your protection and for the protection of others an abuser may harm. Some ministers and churches have even advised victims of such crimes to simply forgive the abuser, pray for them, and keep quiet about it. No spiritual leader should ever advise a victim to simply keep quiet or to cover up what has happened. To the contrary, spiritual leaders have a responsibility to God, to the laws of the land, and to other people to see to it that criminal abusers are stopped and brought to justice.

These commands speak to the spirit we should have toward those who mistreat us as the people of God—believers, followers of Christ. When suffering *for the gospel's sake*, for our personal testimony for Christ, the believer is to respond to mistreatment just as our Lord did. We are to demonstrate *moral strength through a quiet and meek spirit*, trusting God to touch the heart of our persecutors (see notes—Mt.5:38-39 for more discussion). This is what Jesus is talking about in these commands.

> And they spit on him and took the reed and struck him on the head. (Mt.27:30)

> When he had said these things, one of the officers standing by struck Jesus with his hand, saying, "Is that how you answer the high priest?" (Jn.18:22)

> Repay no one evil for evil, but give thought to do what is honorable in the sight of all. (Ro.12:17)

> But the fruit of the Spirit is love, joy, peace, patience, kindness, goodness, faithfulness, gentleness, self-control; against such things there is no law. (Ga.5:22-23)

> Correcting his opponents with gentleness. God may perhaps grant them repentance leading to a knowledge of the truth. (2 Ti.2:25)

> Do not say, "I will repay evil"; wait for the LORD, and he will deliver you. (Pr.20:22)

> Do not say, "I will do to him as he has done to me; I will pay the man back for what he has done." (Pr.24:29)

b. Governing property (vv.29b–30).

Jesus proceeded to give new principles governing personal property (possessions). Essentially, our Lord taught that we should be generous with our possessions, open-handed rather than closed-fisted. Christ-followers are to be marked by a generous spirit.

First, Jesus taught us not to deprive others (v.29b). This illustration is rooted in Jewish law governing the relationship between creditors and debtors. The Jews wore both an inner and an outer garment. Jewish law allowed the inner garment to be taken as a debt or pledge, but never the outer garment. A person might have several layers of underclothing, but only one outer garment (see Ex.22:26-27). However, if a creditor took the outer garment—an unlawful act—the believer was to offer their inner garment as well.

The principle Christ illustrates here is difficult to follow. We are not to be consumed with our rights and privileges in or out of court. We are to be focused on our duty as believers. We are to be consumed with living to the fullest for Christ and reaching out to a world lost and consumed with disputes and needing the peace which only God can bring (see note and thoughts—Mt.5:39-41 for additional discussion).

Second, Jesus taught us to give to others with needs (v.30a). We are to help those in need, and we are to help readily and willingly. Note that Christ allows no excuse. The picture is that the believer *gives and does not turn away* when a person asks. Note, however, the Bible does not say to give without discretion.

> It is well with the man who deals generously and lends; who conducts his affairs with justice. (Ps.112:5)

Third, Jesus teaches us to be patient with borrowers, to not demand repayment from others (v.30b). Often a person fails to pay back or return what they borrowed, whether tools, clothing, food, or money. We are not to demand them back, not if the person *needs* them and is going to be deprived and hurt if they are taken back. As believers, we have to consider two facts: first, the person's need; second, if the person has no need, the sin of allowing license—the freedom to act unjustly or do harm—and irresponsibility versus alienating and turning the person away from one's testimony of Christ. We must not allow license and irresponsibility, but we must be careful not to lose our chance of winning the person to Christ. No item, no amount of money is worth a soul.

> Give to the one who begs from you, and do not refuse the one who would borrow from you. (Mt.5:42)

THOUGHT 1. Two significant attitudes should control the believer's giving.

1) The believer is to live in readiness—a readiness to give and to lend (see 2 Co.8:11–15, esp. 11). We are not to live for this earth and world. We are to live for God and for heaven. Our citizenship is in heaven, from where we look for the Savior (Ph.3:20). Thus, our attachment to earthly things is only for meeting the necessities of life and for helping others. We are to help and to give.

> Sell your possessions, and give to the needy. Provide yourselves with moneybags that do not grow old, with a treasure in the heavens that does not fail, where no thief approaches and no moth destroys. (Lu.12:33)

> Contribute to the needs of the saints and seek to show hospitality. (Ro.12:13)

> So then, as we have opportunity, let us do good to everyone, and especially to those who are of the household of faith. (Ga.6:10)

> As for the rich in this present age, charge them not to be haughty, nor to set their hopes on the uncertainty of riches, but on God, who richly provides us with everything to enjoy. They are to do good, to be rich in good works, to be generous and ready to share. (1 Ti.6:17–18)

> Do not neglect to do good and to share what you have, for such sacrifices are pleasing to God. (He.13:16)

2) We are to work not only to provide our own necessities, but also to have enough to help those in need.

> In all things I have shown you that by working hard in this way we must help the weak and remember the words of the Lord Jesus, how he himself said, "It is more blessed to give than to receive." (Ac.20:35)

> Let the thief no longer steal, but rather let him labor, doing honest work with his own hands, so that he may have something to share with anyone in need. (Ep.4:28)

c. **Governing behavior toward others (v.31).**

Jesus summarized all these standards by giving the cardinal principle that should govern all of our behavior, the *golden rule* itself: we should treat others exactly how we want to be treated by others (see DEEPER STUDY # 1).

DEEPER STUDY # 1

(6:31) **Golden Rule—Righteousness—Justice:** the "golden rule" is probably the most well-known of Christ's teachings. It is the summit of ethics, of behavior, of righteousness, of godliness. It is a very practical statement of God's love; that is, God has done to us just as He wants us to do to Him. God has treated us just as He wants us to treat Him (and everyone else).

The golden rule reveals the heart of God. It shows us exactly how God's heart longs for us to live and act. It is a simple one-sentence statement revealing what love really is and what life in heaven (the perfect world) is to be like. It tells believers that, as citizens of both heaven and earth, we are to live as the golden rule dictates while still on the earth.

Four significant facts set the golden rule apart from all other teaching.

1. The golden rule is a simple one-sentence statement that embraces all human behavior. The fact that all of the law and all love can be stated in one simple sentence is

amazing. The simple statement of the golden rule includes all "the law and the prophets" (Mt.7:12).

2. The golden rule *demands true law and justice*. Note the wording; it is not negative and passive, yet it tells people how not to behave. It restrains us. For example, the golden rule teaches us not to lie, steal, cheat, or injure; and it teaches much more.

3. The golden rule is concerned with true love, that is, with positive, active behavior.
   a. It is more than not doing wrong (lying, stealing, cheating).
   b. It is more than just doing good (helping, caring, giving).
   c. It is *looking, searching, seeking for ways to do the good* that you want others to do to you; and then doing that good to others.

4. The golden rule teaches the whole law, for the whole law is contained in the words: "You shall love your neighbor as yourself" (Mt.22:39-40). Every human being would like to have all others treat them perfectly: to love and care for them to the ultimate degree and to express that love and care. The believer is to so love and care while still on earth. We are to give earth a taste of heaven before all things end. Lost people, being treated so supremely and getting a taste of heaven, might then turn to God.

2 The argument: A believer's behavior must surpass a sinner's.

a. In love (v.32).

b. In doing good (v.33).

c. In lending (v.34).

In these verses, Jesus presents a logical strong argument for us to live as He commands: our behavior should surpass a sinner's behavior. Obviously, the presence and power of Christ within us should compel us to go beyond the behavior of *sinners*—those who do not know the Lord.
➤ Sinners love those who love them.
➤ Sinners do good to those who do good to them.
➤ Sinners lend to secure an interest or favor or some gain.

³² "If you love those who love you, what benefit is that to you? For even sinners love those who love them.

³³ And if you do good to those who do good to you, what benefit is that to you? For even sinners do the same.

³⁴ And if you lend to those from whom you expect to receive, what credit is that to you? Even sinners lend to sinners, to get back the same amount."

Here Jesus bluntly points out a painful truth: believers who love and do good only to those who reciprocate are not making any more effort than sinners. The world sees virtue and goodness as love; they see doing good and lending as being neighborly. And it is good to love, to do good, and to lend. But loving, doing good, and lending are not enough for the believer. It is not what Christ did. Christ denied Himself in order to win the world. He loved His enemies and did good to those who hated Him. It might be said that He even loaned His life to the world.

> For while we were still weak, at the right time Christ died for the ungodly. . . . But God shows his love for us in that while we were still sinners, Christ died for us. . . . For if while we were enemies we were reconciled to God by the death of his Son, much more, now that we are reconciled, shall we be saved by his life. (Ro.5:6, 8, 10)

As Christ-followers, we are to do the very same as Christ: deny and sacrifice ourselves to win the world and offer others the privilege of being saved. It takes more than the virtue and goodness of love and doing good and lending to others to become a follower of Christ. It takes the denial and sacrifice of oneself for the sake of reaching the unlovely for Christ, those who are . . .

- enemies
- haters
- cursers
- borrowers
- persecutors
- thieves
- spiteful
- needful
- selfish

3 The reward for living right.

Jesus made a compelling promise to all who will *hear* Him (v.27)—who will listen and do what He is saying: *you will be rewarded.* The Lord sees all, and He will see your selfless, sacrificing, Christ-like living. He would be unrighteous if He did not reward you (He.6:10).

6:35-36

35 "But love your enemies, and do good, and lend, expecting nothing in return, and your reward will be great, and you will be sons of the Most High, for he is kind to the ungrateful and the evil.

36 Be merciful, even as your Father is merciful."

a. You will receive a great reward (v.35a).

If you live by these difficult principles, Jesus promises you a *great reward.* All that the believer suffers and loses on earth will be restored. But note: what we give up will not only be restored, we will *receive well beyond* what we have lost. We will receive an *enormous reward* for having obeyed the Lord and for having sacrificed in order to meet the needs of a dying world. What will the *great reward* be? It will be inheriting all that God the Father has.

> Then the King will say to those on his right, "Come, you who are blessed by my Father, inherit the kingdom prepared for you from the foundation of the world." (Mt.25:34; see DEEPER STUDY # 3—Mt.19:23-24)

> So that being justified by his grace we might become heirs according to the hope of eternal life. (Tit.3:7)

> Blessed be the God and Father of our Lord Jesus Christ! According to his great mercy, he has caused us to be born again to a living hope through the resurrection of Jesus Christ from the dead, to an inheritance that is imperishable, undefiled, and unfading, kept in heaven for you. (1 Pe.1:3-4)

Simply stated, the believer will receive *an inheritance* for having obeyed Christ and having served so sacrificially while on earth. The believer will have part in the glorious work of God that will be performed in the new heavens and earth, a work that will go on from glory to glory.

b. You will be children of the Most High (v.35b).

When we live by Jesus' challenging teaching, we will truly be the children of the Most High. *We will be like God,* for He is kind to the ungrateful and evil. His nature will be reproduced in us; we will bear a resemblance to Him, and others will recognize it. They will see that we are His children.

> So that you may be sons of your Father who is in heaven. For he makes his sun rise on the evil and on the good, and sends rain on the just and on the unjust. . . . You therefore must be perfect, as your heavenly Father is perfect. (Mt.5:45, 48)

> The Spirit himself bears witness with our spirit that we are children of God, and if children, then heirs—heirs of God and fellow heirs with Christ, provided we suffer with him in order that we may also be glorified with him. (Ro.8:16-17)

> But when the fullness of time had come, God sent forth his Son, born of woman, born under the law, to redeem those who were under the law, so that we might receive adoption as sons. And because you are sons, God has sent the Spirit of his Son into our hearts, crying, "Abba! Father!" (Ga.4:4-6)

c. We will be merciful, just as God is merciful (v.36).

Jesus further expounds the principle of likeness to our heavenly Father: when we are merciful to others, we are acting as God's child. What a privilege! The privilege of actually behaving as God behaves! The privilege of demonstrating and showing mercy! Note that this is a command from our Savior, a command to act as God acts, to be merciful as God is merciful. Obeying it will enrich our lives greatly. It will stir great assurance and confidence within, and it will make us a shining testimony to those who do not know the Lord.

> And now, little children, abide in him, so that when he appears we may have confidence and not shrink from him in shame at his coming. (1 Jn.2:28)

4 The promise: Reciprocal behavior—you will receive what you give.

God will be a debtor to no person. He will see to it that we are rewarded, both in this life and in eternity. Jesus made an extraordinary promise to the disciple who lives as He said—the promise of reciprocal behavior, of receiving back exactly what one gives.

a. In relationships (v.37).

Personal relationships are involved in reciprocal behavior. Jesus covered three specific behaviors: judging, condemning, and forgiving others. If we judge and condemn and are unforgiving of others, then both people and God will treat us the same. We will be judged, condemned, and unforgiven both on earth and in heaven. But if we do not judge and condemn others, but rather forgive them, then God and most people will not judge and condemn us; they will also be forgiving.

> [37] "Judge not, and you will not be judged; condemn not, and you will not be condemned; forgive, and you will be forgiven;
>
> [38] give, and it will be given to you. Good measure, pressed down, shaken together, running over, will be put into your lap. For with the measure you use it will be measured back to you."

b. In property (v.38a).

Property matters are involved in reciprocal behavior. The believer is to give and to possess a spirit of giving and not to be selfish and hoarding. If we give, we will receive back much more. In fact, our cup will be *running over*. God will pour all the good things of this earth into our life (lap or bosom).

c. The principle: A person receives what they give (v.38c).

The principle is clear and challenging: a person receives what they give. This is definitely true of God and usually true of other people. What a person puts into life is what they get out of life.

THOUGHT 1. People live on one of three levels . . .

- Satan's level—doing evil for good
- human level—doing good for good and evil for evil
- God's level—doing good for evil

Most—but by no means all—people live on the human level. They return good for good and evil for evil. Consequently, when we do good to others, most people will, in turn, do good to us. This is what Jesus is teaching here. We will usually receive from others what we first extend to them.

However, this outcome is not universally true. Some live on Satan's level and do evil to those who are good to them. When we do good to those who do evil to us, we live on God's level (vv.35–36). And when we continue to do good to them even after they offer evil for our good, God's power is released through, in, and to us. The undeserved love we extend to evildoers may be the very thing that turns them to the Lord. But regardless of how they respond, the Lord is keeping score, and His reward to us will be all the greater.

> For truly, I say to you, whoever gives you a cup of water to drink because you belong to Christ will by no means lose his reward. (Mk.9:41)
>
> But glory and honor and peace for everyone who does good, the Jew first and also the Greek. (Ro.2:10)
>
> Therefore, my beloved brothers, be steadfast, immovable, always abounding in the work of the Lord, knowing that in the Lord your labor is not in vain. (1 Co.15:58)
>
> Knowing that whatever good anyone does, this he will receive back from the Lord, whether he is a bondservant or is free. (Eph.6:8)
>
> For God is not unjust so as to overlook your work and the love that you have shown for his name in serving the saints, as you still do. (He.6:10)
>
> Is it not to share your bread with the hungry and bring the homeless poor into your house; when you see the naked, to cover him, and not to hide yourself from your own flesh? Then shall your light break forth like the dawn, and your healing shall spring up speedily; your righteousness shall go before you; the glory of the LORD shall be your rear guard. (Is.58:7-8)

K. Jesus Teaches His Rules for Discipleship: The Need to Watch, 6:39–45

(Mt.7:3–5, 17–18; 10:25; 12:35)

1. **Watch out for blind leaders and followers**
   a. They are both blind
   b. They both stumble and fall
2. **Watch the life of the Teacher (the Lord)**
   a. You must submit to Him
   b. Your goal is to be like Him
3. **Watch hypocrisy and criticism of others**
   a. You both have a problem
   b. You, the criticizer, have the bigger problem
   c. You, as a criticizer, are a hypocrite
   d. You are first to judge yourself: Will help you to see clearly how to help others

4. **Watch the fruit that a person brings forth**
   a. Every tree is known by its fruit
   b. Every tree reproduces after its nature or kind

   c. Every person reproduces what is in his or her heart

39 He also told them a parable: "Can a blind man lead a blind man? Will they not both fall into a pit?

40 A disciple is not above his teacher, but everyone when he is fully trained will be like his teacher.

41 Why do you see the speck that is in your brother's eye, but do not notice the log that is in your own eye?

42 How can you say to your brother, 'Brother, let me take out the speck that is in your eye,' when you yourself do not see the log that is in your own eye? You hypocrite, first take the log out of your own eye, and then you will see clearly to take out the speck that is in your brother's eye.

43 "For no good tree bears bad fruit, nor again does a bad tree bear good fruit,

44 for each tree is known by its own fruit. For figs are not gathered from thornbushes, nor are grapes picked from a bramble bush.

45 The good person out of the good treasure of his heart produces good, and the evil person out of his evil treasure produces evil, for out of the abundance of the heart his mouth speaks."

Division III

The Son of Man's Announced Mission and Public Ministry, 4:16–9:17

K. Jesus Teaches His Rules for Discipleship: The Need to Watch, 6:39–45

(Mt.7:3–5, 17–18; 10:25; 12:35)

6:39–45
Introduction

God cares about the quality of our lives. He wants each of us to have the fullest life that we possibly can. God also cares about our destiny, where we will spend eternity. Therefore, He has provided eternal life for us through His Son. He loves us so much that He gave His Son in order that we can have eternal life (Jn.3:16). Eternal life is both for the here and the hereafter. It is an abundant life that begins here on earth when we receive Christ and continues in the presence of God forever after we depart this life (Jn.10:10; 2 Co.5:8; Ph.1:21-23).

This is surely what our Lord had in mind as He taught the truths preserved in this passage. We need to watch how we live. Both the quality and future of our lives depend on it. Jesus gives us four rules to follow in order to enjoy the fullness of life that He died to provide for us, both here and in the hereafter. This is, *Jesus Teaches His Rules for Discipleship: The Need to Watch, 6:39-45.*

1. Watch out for blind leaders and followers (v.39).
2. Watch the life of the Teacher (the Lord) (v.40).
3. Watch hypocrisy and criticism of others (vv.41-42).
4. Watch the fruit that a person brings forth (vv.43-45).

1 Watch out for blind leaders and followers.

Jesus first warns us about following the wrong leaders. His thought-provoking question, "Can the blind lead the blind?" became a common saying that has continued throughout succeeding generations. What does this question mean? Note that Jesus is teaching through a *parable*; He is using something from the physical world to teach a spiritual lesson.

> [39] He also told them a parable: "Can a blind man lead a blind man? Will they not both fall into a pit?"

First, who are the blind? They are the leaders: the preachers, teachers, parents, business and governmental leaders—anyone who has influence or responsibility for anyone else. But observe a significant fact. Jesus also says that the blind are those who follow: the pupil, learner, listener, seeker, child—anyone who looks up to someone else for guidance.

Why are people blind? Consider the reasons people are blind physically and the correlation to spiritual life.

Of course, some people are born blind. They are born disabled, never having had the opportunity to see the *truth* of things, never having been exposed to the light.

People can also be blind due to an injury or disease. They used to be able to see and had every opportunity to see in the past, but now they are blind for various reasons:

➤ They injured themselves by some careless act. *They are guilty of blinding themselves.*
➤ They were blinded by someone else, either deliberately or carelessly. *Others led them astray, led them off into the darkness.*
➤ They were blinded by nature. *Circumstances, heritage, location kept them from ever having the opportunity to escape the darkness.*

Spiritually speaking, people can be blind because they want and choose to be in the dark. The darkness is their choice. They find the darkness to be enjoyable and comfortable; therefore, they refuse to come out into the light and to see the truth.

Then, some people are blind because they close their eyes or turn their head and look away. They simply refuse to see the light, the truth.

Jesus warned us about following blind leaders. He said doing so leads to two tragic results.

a. They are both blind.

When we follow blind leaders, we are blind as well. Both walk in darkness, both the leader and the follower. Being a leader does not guarantee that one walks in the light. A leader can be blind, and if the leader is blind, then the follower will remain blind. The leader must see and have his or her sight if the follower is to ever see. (Note the awesome responsibility upon leaders.)

b. They both stumble and fall.

When the leader is blind, both the leader and the follower stumble and fall. Being a leader does not guarantee that one will avoid falling. Spiritually blind people will stumble and fall no matter who they are, leaders or not. And note, leaders will especially stumble about and fall if they are on strange or unfamiliar terrain. The truth of Christ is totally unknown terrain to blind teachers, no matter their profession.

But if your eye is bad, your whole body will be full of darkness. If then the light in you is darkness, how great is the darkness! (Mt.6:23)

And this is the judgment: the light has come into the world, and people loved the darkness rather than the light because their works were evil. (Jn.3:19)

And even if our gospel is veiled, it is veiled to those who are perishing. In their case the god of this world has blinded the minds of the unbelievers, to keep them from seeing the light of the gospel of the glory of Christ, who is the image of God. (2 Co.4:3–4)

Now this I say and testify in the Lord, that you must no longer walk as the Gentiles do, in the futility of their minds. They are darkened in their understanding, alienated from the life of God because of the ignorance that is in them, due to their hardness of heart. (Ep.4:17–18)

Desiring to be teachers of the law, without understanding either what they are saying or the things about which they make confident assertions. (1 Ti.1:7)

For the time is coming when people will not endure sound teaching, but having itching ears they will accumulate for themselves teachers to suit their own passions, and will turn away from listening to the truth and wander off into myths. (2 Ti.4:3–4)

But false prophets also arose among the people, just as there will be false teachers among you, who will secretly bring in destructive heresies, even denying the Master who bought them, bringing upon themselves swift destruction. (2 Pe.2:1)

6:40

[40] "A disciple is not above his teacher, but everyone when he is fully trained will be like his teacher."

2 Watch the life of the Teacher (the Lord).

Second, Jesus exhorts us to watch the life of the Teacher, of the Lord Jesus Christ Himself. The way to keep from following blind (false) leaders is to keep our eyes on Christ. The goal of the Christian life is Christlikeness (Ro.8:29; 2 Co.3:18; Co.3:10). We will be *fully* or *perfectly* trained when we become like our Teacher or Master, the Lord Jesus Christ. The word *fully trained* (Gk. katertismenos, *kah-tare-tis-men'-os*) means to complete, render fit, mend. Katertismenos is a common word often used for mending, repairing, or restoring broken things such as nets (Mt.4:21) or people (Ga.6:1).

a. You must submit to Him.

The point is forceful: "a disciple is not above his Teacher" (see note, pt.1—Mt.10:24–25). We are not better than our Lord; therefore, we cannot expect to be treated better, nor can we expect to receive more in this world than our Lord received. As Christ's disciples, we cannot expect to be better by receiving more honor, praise, recognition, or esteem. We cannot expect to have more comfort, rest, or pleasure. The Lord suffered, humbled, and denied Himself for the sake of the world and its needs. As followers of the Lord, we are to do the same; we should deny ourselves in order to reach the world for our Lord (see note and DEEPER STUDY # 1—Lu.9:23). We are to submit to His Lordship in our lives by obeying His teaching and following His example.

It is enough for the disciple to be like his teacher, and the servant like his master. If they have called the master of the house Beelzebul, how much more will they malign those of his household. (Mt.10:25)

Then Jesus told his disciples, "If anyone would come after me, let him deny himself and take up his cross and follow me." (Mt.16:24)

Have this mind among yourselves, which is yours in Christ Jesus, who, though he was in the form of God, did not count equality with God a thing to be grasped, but emptied himself, by taking the form of a servant, being born in the likeness of men. And being found in human form, he humbled himself by becoming obedient to the point of death, even death on a cross. (Ph.2:5–8)

Looking to Jesus, the founder and perfecter of our faith, who for the joy that was set before him endured the cross, despising the shame, and is seated at the right hand of the throne of God. (He.12:2)

For to this you have been called, because Christ also suffered for you, leaving you an example, so that you might follow in his steps. (1 Pe.2:21)

b. Your goal is to be like Him.

The goal of the disciple is to "be like his Teacher." We are to seek to be like our Master: conformed, mended, repaired, restored (perfected) into His very image.

> For those whom he foreknew he also predestined to be conformed to the image of his Son, in order that he might be the firstborn among many brothers. (Ro.8:29)

> And we all, with unveiled face, beholding the glory of the Lord, are being transformed into the same image from one degree of glory to another. For this comes from the Lord who is the Spirit. (2 Co.3:18)

> That I may know him and the power of his resurrection, and may share his sufferings, becoming like him in his death. (Ph.3:10)

> "You are my witnesses," declares the LORD, "and my servant whom I have chosen, that you may know and believe me and understand that I am he. Before me no god was formed, nor shall there be any after me." (Is.43:10)

3 Watch hypocrisy and criticism of others.

The third rule given by our Lord is to watch hypocrisy and criticism of others. Jesus was speaking to everyone seated before Him. No matter how moral, decent, strong, religious, or free of visible sin, He was speaking to everyone seated in the audience. No one was exempt. Everyone was to watch out for hypocrisy and criticism of others. Why? To explain His point, Jesus used the illustration of having something in one's eye. Whatever is in a person's eye, even if it is only a speck, is serious. Even a speck causes the eye to water, squint, blink, and close. The speck hinders a person's sight (life, walk), holding them back from full sight and service. Note four truths Jesus taught in this parable.

> 41 "Why do you see the speck that is in your brother's eye, but do not notice the log that is in your own eye?
>
> 42 How can you say to your brother, 'Brother, let me take out the speck that is in your eye,' when you yourself do not see the log that is in your own eye? You hypocrite, first take the log out of your own eye, and then you will see clearly to take out the speck that is in your brother's eye."

a. You both have a problem (v.41a).

Both people, the one being criticized and the criticizer, have a problem. Both have a need to clean the dirt out of their eyes. Neither one is free of dirt. Not a single person serves in perfect obedience and ministry to the Lord. There is at least a speck in everyone's eye.

b. You, the criticizer, have the bigger problem (v.41b).

The criticizer has the bigger problem. This detail is usually overlooked. Criticism of others is a *log* (plank, beam). If one has only a *speck* in his eye, when he begins to criticize others, he immediately develops a *log* in his own eye. *Criticism is the tree that strikes the eye and blinds one to their own need*, their need for continued confession and repentance. Criticizers become blinded to their constant need for the righteousness of Jesus Christ.

> For whoever lacks these qualities is so nearsighted that he is blind, having forgotten that he was cleansed from his former sins. (2 Pe.1:9)

c. You, as a criticizer, are a hypocrite (v.42a).

Criticizers are hypocrites (see DEEPER STUDY # 2—Mt.23:13). They are merely human beings who are like all other human beings, full of ever so many faults and coming ever so short, yet they find fault with others. They criticize, grumble, gripe, condemn, judge, and censor others while they too are guilty of so much in so many other areas. And note: their greatest fault is that they set themselves up as the one who has the right to judge others.

d. You are first to judge yourself: Will help you to see clearly how to help others (v.42b).

As Christ's disciples, we are to examine ourselves first. We should be concerned about what is wrong in our own lives rather than others' shortcomings. Judging ourselves first will enable us to *see clearly* just how to help others. Simple honesty and thought say that a person must clean the dirt out of their own eye before they can see clearly enough to help others clean their eyesight. A rigid self-examination is required (Ps.51:1-13; 139:23-24).

> **Judge not, that you be not judged. (Mt.7:1)**

> **Who are you to pass judgment on the servant of another? It is before his own master that he stands or falls. And he will be upheld, for the Lord is able to make him stand. . . . Therefore let us not pass judgment on one another any longer, but rather decide never to put a stumbling block or hindrance in the way of a brother. (Ro.14:4, 13)**

> **Therefore do not pronounce judgment before the time, before the Lord comes, who will bring to light the things now hidden in darkness and will disclose the purposes of the heart. Then each one will receive his commendation from God. (1 Co.4:5)**

6:43-45

[43] "For no good tree bears bad fruit, nor again does a bad tree bear good fruit,
[44] for each tree is known by its own fruit. For figs are not gathered from thornbushes, nor are grapes picked from a bramble bush.
[45] The good person out of the good treasure of his heart produces good, and the evil person out of his evil treasure produces evil, for out of the abundance of the heart his mouth speaks."

4 Watch the fruit that a person brings forth.

Jesus draws one more word picture to teach a last lesson: watch the fruit that a person brings forth. While we are to judge ourselves and not others, we are to notice others' works—their words and deeds. Why? Because their works reveal what is truly in their hearts. This rule chiefly applies to discerning whom we should follow, especially spiritual leaders (see notes—v.39).

a. Every tree is known by its fruit (v.44a).

Every tree is known by its fruit, its nature. Good people are not judged by a bad piece of fruit here and there but by the good fruit they regularly bear. Every tree produces some bad fruit, yet the tree is not cast away. A tree is not rejected unless it *leans toward* bad fruit. When testing and examining people, we must not observe single acts here and there; rather, we need to consider the whole behavior of their lives. How important (see note—Mt.7:17 for detailed discussion)!

b. Every tree reproduces after its nature or kind (v.44b).

Jesus pointed out that every tree reproduces after its nature, after its kind. How can we tell if a person is false? There is one revealing mark: the fruit they gather. People are known by the fruit they feed on and the fruit they feed to others (see outlines and notes—Jn.15:1-8). If they feed themselves on thorns and thistles and not on grapes and figs, that is one way to tell. If they feed thorns and thistles to others instead of grapes and figs, that is another way to tell.

Thorns and thistles (bramble bush) represent false food, worldliness (see DEEPER STUDY # 3—Mt.13:7, 22). Grapes and figs are true food. There is only one true food for the human soul: the Lord Jesus Christ and His Word (see note—Jn.6:1-71; outlines and notes—Jn.6:30-36; 6:41-51; also see all outlines and notes 6:1-71; DEEPER STUDY # 4—Jn.17:17; see 5:24; 1 Pe.2:2-3.) We are to feed on and feed others the truth of the Lord and His Word. Any other source of food for the human soul is false food: it is thorn and thistle (worldliness). If eaten or served to others, it will choke the life out of the soul (Mt.13:7; see 1 Jn.2:15-16; Ro.12:1-2; 2 Co.6:17-18).

c. Every person reproduces what is in his or her heart (v.45).

People reproduce what is in their hearts. Note that Jesus is dealing specifically with a person's mouth, the *words* a person speaks. People speak what is in their heart. Their words expose their heart, the kind of person they are. The idea is that words come out of an overflowing heart: "Out of the abundance [overflow] of the heart the mouth speaks" (Mt.12:34). People's words expose five things about them:

➤ People's words expose their true nature: what they are really like beneath the surface.
➤ People's words expose what they are down deep within their heart: their motives, desires, ambitions, or the lack of initiative.
➤ People's words expose their true character: good or bad, kind or cruel.

➤ People's words expose their minds, what they think: pure or impure thoughts, dirty or clean thoughts.

➤ People's words expose their spirit, what they believe and pursue: legitimate or illegitimate, intelligent or ignorant, true or false, beneficial or wasteful.

So, every healthy tree bears good fruit, but the diseased tree bears bad fruit. (Mt.7:17)

Now the works of the flesh are evident: sexual immorality, impurity, sensuality, idolatry, sorcery, enmity, strife, jealousy, fits of anger, rivalries, dissensions, divisions, envy, drunkenness, orgies, and things like these. I warn you, as I warned you before, that those who do such things will not inherit the kingdom of God. But the fruit of the Spirit is love, joy, peace, patience, kindness, goodness, faithfulness, gentleness, self-control; against such things there is no law. (Ga.5:19–23)

So also faith by itself, if it does not have works, is dead. But someone will say, "You have faith and I have works." Show me your faith apart from your works, and I will show you my faith by my works. (Jas.2:17–18)

Keep your conduct among the Gentiles honorable, so that when they speak against you as evildoers, they may see your good deeds and glorify God on the day of visitation. (1 Pe.2:12)

L. Jesus Teaches Two Foundations of Life: Genuine vs. Counterfeit Discipleship, 6:46–49

(Mt.7:24–27)

1. **The true foundation of discipleship: Obedience**
2. **The true disciple: Lays a genuine foundation**
   a. He comes to Christ, hears and obeys
   b. He is like a builder
      1) He builds a house
      2) He digs deep
      3) He lays a rock foundation
   c. Result: It stands

3. **The false disciple: Lays a counterfeit foundation**
   a. He hears but does not obey
   b. He is like a builder
      1) He builds a house
      2) He does not dig
      3) He lays no foundation
   c. Result: There is a great fall

⁴⁶ "Why do you call me 'Lord, Lord,' and not do what I tell you? ⁴⁷ Everyone who comes to me and hears my words and does them, I will show you what he is like: ⁴⁸ he is like a man building a house, who dug deep and laid the foundation on the rock. And when a flood arose, the stream broke against that house and could not shake it, because it had been well built. ⁴⁹ But the one who hears and does not do them is like a man who built a house on the ground without a foundation. When the stream broke against it, immediately it fell, and the ruin of that house was great."

Division III

The Son of Man's Announced Mission and Public Ministry, 4:16–9:17

L. Jesus Teaches Two Foundations of Life: Genuine vs. Counterfeit Discipleship, 6:46–49

(Mt.7:24–27)

6:46–49
Introduction

As we approach this passage, it is helpful to keep in mind that Jesus was a carpenter by trade and profession. He knew houses; He knew the building trade. His personal knowledge and experience are the background for the parable He used to teach the spiritual truth of these verses.

Several important matters about building a house need to be noted here to fully grasp what Jesus is teaching and how it applies to building our lives. First, hearing instructions. This is critical. Knowing how to build is critical. Then, a person must hear and follow (obey) the instructions. And they must hear and build upon what they hear for the future. We are to always be building a sure foundation for the future (1 Ti.6:19).

Second, selecting the foundation. This, too, is critical. Selecting the site and material determine the future of the house. We must build our lives on a solid foundation. There is only one foundation on which to build: the rock (1 Co.3:11). An important part of that is making our call and choice to build certain (2 Pe.1:10). And we must be patient, persevering, and persistent; building on rock takes time and skill.

Third, counting the cost. This critical fact is brought out by Christ in another passage. Beginning and not finishing the house brings mockery and shame (Lu.14:28–30).

Every person has a house, a life to build. How you build your life determines your destiny, not just for this life, but for eternity. How you build your life makes all the difference between . . .

- success and failure
- life and death
- reward and loss
- acceptance and rejection
- standing and falling

There is only one solid foundation for every life: Jesus Christ (1 Co.3:11). He is the Rock upon which both individuals and churches are to build (Mt.16:18). Every individual either builds on the sinking sand of this world or on Christ the Solid Rock.

Jesus teaches that there are two kinds of builders: a wise builder hears and obeys His teaching (vv.47–48). A foolish builder hears but does not obey (v.49). This is, *Jesus Teaches Two Foundations of Life: Genuine vs. Counterfeit Discipleship*, 6:46–49.

1. The true foundation of discipleship: Obedience (v.46).
2. The true disciple: Lays a genuine foundation (vv.47–48).
3. The false disciple: Lays a counterfeit foundation (v.49).

1 The true foundation of discipleship: Obedience.

6:46

Jesus asks a probing question: "Why do you call me 'Lord, Lord,' and not do what I tell you?" The message is clear: the true foundation of discipleship is *obedience, doing the things which Jesus says*. There is no substitute. If a person is truly a follower of Jesus Christ, that person will do what Jesus says.

> [46] "Why do you call me 'Lord, Lord,' and not do what I tell you?"

Jesus directly confronts those sitting before Him who call Him "Lord" but do not practice His teachings. They acknowledge Him as Lord. They bear witness before others that He is Lord. They are known as followers of Jesus. But they do not obey Him.

Jesus is questioning their—and our—disobedience and disloyalty. He rebukes and warns anyone who calls Him Lord and does not do what He says. As Lord He is due allegiance and expects loyalty from all, especially those who call Him Lord.

A profession of words is not enough. Even repeating one's profession, "Lord, Lord," is not enough. A person can cry before the world and still be questioned and warned by Christ: "Why do you not do what I tell you?"

We are cheating ourselves if we profess Jesus as our Lord and do not obey Him. Profession without obedience gives a false security; it makes us feel like we are acceptable to God when we are not. Christ says that the only foundation to true discipleship is to do the things which Christ says. Those who do not obey Christ are counterfeit disciples. Their profession is false, and they are not acceptable to God because their faith is not genuine.

2 The true disciple: Lays a genuine foundation.

6:47–48

True disciples—genuine Christ-followers—*lay a genuine foundation*. They build their lives on obedience to Jesus Christ.

> [47] "Everyone who comes to me and hears my words and does them, I will show you what he is like:
> [48] he is like a man building a house, who dug deep and laid the foundation on the rock. And when a flood arose, the stream broke against that house and could not shake it, because it had been well built."

a. He comes to Christ, hears and obeys (v.47).

True disciples come to Christ. They hear what Christ says and do what He says. All three steps—coming, hearing, and doing—are essential to being a genuine disciple.

b. He is like a builder (v.48a).

True disciples are like a builder building a house. Every person has a house to build, a life to build. Having been born into this world, we cannot escape the fact. We are building our lives, and how we build our lives determines our eternal destiny.

God's own Son instructs us how to build. We either *hear and follow* (obey) the instructions or *hear and reject* (disobey) the instructions and build our own way. The instructions, the words of Christ, are the materials which determine the structure and future of our lives. Our lives and our destiny depend on how we respond to the teachings of Christ.

The disciple digs deep to lay the foundation (footing). This is critical to note. The ground is not soil, it is rock. Great effort and energy are demanded. The most expensive and costly thing to a builder is *hitting rock*, yet rock is by far the best foundation.

➤ This builder chose the rock for his foundation. He did not just hit it while digging for his footing; he knew the rock was there and chose it as the right foundation for his house. He deliberately chose *the most sure and secure* foundation available.

➤ This builder *dug deep*. He took no chances. He wanted to be absolutely sure and secure, as sure and secure as possible. So he *dug* as deep as possible.

➤ This builder was willing to put both the *time and effort and cost* into digging rock. It was difficult, exhausting, and expensive; yet he did it. Why? Because it was *his house,* and he wanted to be absolutely sure and secure.

This is a picture of genuine followers of Christ. They lay the foundation upon the rock. Christ is the only solid foundation upon which we can build and structure our lives. "No one can lay a foundation than that which is laid, which is Jesus Christ" (1 Co.3:11; see Ep.2:20; 1 Pe.2:4–5).

THOUGHT 1. The Lord is not a lifeless rock, but "a living stone" (1 Pe.2:4). When we come to Him and recognize Him "as a living stone," we are "built up as a spiritual house" (1 Pe.2:5).

> Like newborn infants, long for the pure spiritual milk, that by it you may grow up into salvation— if indeed you have tasted that the Lord is good. As you come to him, a living stone rejected by men but in the sight of God chosen and precious, you yourselves like living stones are being built up as a spiritual house, to be a holy priesthood, to offer spiritual sacrifices acceptable to God through Jesus Christ. (1 Pe.2:2–5)

c. **Result: It stands (v.48b).**

True disciples stand; the houses (lives) they build stand against the storms of life and eternity. Now note: they are not exempt from the storms of life. Just because they built on the rock does not mean storms will not come. In fact, it is because storms do come that they built on the rock. This person (the true disciple) knows that it rains "on the just and on the unjust" (Mt.5:45). All kinds of storms will come, the storms of . . .

- sickness
- sin
- temptation
- suffering
- disappointment
- tension

- death
- accidents
- complaints
- mistreatments
- abuse
- hospitalization

THOUGHT 1. A person must build on Jesus Christ. There is no other foundation that can withstand the coming storms of trouble, problems, afflictions, evil, and death.

> Jesus said to them, "Have you never read in the Scriptures: 'The stone that the builders rejected has become the cornerstone; this was the Lord's doing, and it is marvelous in our eyes'?" (Mt.21:42)

> For no one can lay a foundation other than that which is laid, which is Jesus Christ. (1 Co.3:11)

> Built on the foundation of the apostles and prophets, Christ Jesus himself being the cornerstone. (Ep.2:20)

> Thus storing up treasure for themselves as a good foundation for the future, so that they may take hold of that which is truly life. (1 Ti.6:19)

> For it stands in Scripture: "Behold, I am laying in Zion a stone, a cornerstone chosen and precious, and whoever believes in him will not be put to shame." (1 Pe.2:6)

THOUGHT 2. When the storms come, those who have built their lives on Christ will not fall.

1) God accepts us in Christ; He adopts us as a child of His.

> But when the fullness of time had come, God sent forth his Son, born of woman, born under the law, to redeem those who were under the law, so that we might receive adoption as sons. And because you are sons, God has sent the Spirit of his Son into our hearts, crying, "Abba! Father!" (Ga.4:4-6)

> He predestined us for adoption to himself as sons through Jesus Christ, according to the purpose of his will, to the praise of his glorious grace, with which he has blessed us in the Beloved. (Ep.1:5-6)

2) God promises to provide the necessities of life.

> But seek first the kingdom of God and his righteousness, and all these things will be added to you. (Mt.6:33; see Mt.6:25-34)

3) God promises to work out all things (all storms) for good to those who build wisely.

> And we know that for those who love God all things work together for good, for those who are called according to his purpose. (Ro.8:28)

4) God blesses those who "hear the Word of God and keep it."

> But he said, "Blessed rather are those who hear the word of God and keep it!" (Lu.11:28)

5) Christ promises joy to those who hear and receive the things He said.

> These things I have spoken to you, that my joy may be in you, and that your joy may be full. (Jn.15:11; see Jn.13:17)

3 The false disciple: Lays a counterfeit foundation.

Those who do not obey Christ are false disciples. They are not genuine Christ-followers, not genuine believers. They *lay a counterfeit foundation* for their lives, a foundation built on a mere profession of Christ, but not a genuine belief in Jesus Christ as their Lord (Ro.10:9-11). Note the clear contrast Christ presents between the true disciple and the false disciple.

[49] "But the one who hears and does not do them is like a man who built a house on the ground without a foundation. When the stream broke against it, immediately it fell, and the ruin of that house was great."

a. He hears but does not obey.

False disciples hear Christ's words but *do not do* what Christ says. They ignore what Christ says and go on living as they always have. Some are too busy, too wrapped up in the things of this world to fully follow Christ. They are deceived, thinking that they are saved by the profession of their mouths alone. They do not think about the consequences of their disobedience and what it reveals: Jesus Christ is not their Lord.

b. He is like a builder.

False disciples are also like a builder. They build houses (lives), but note a very critical point. They hear the instructions of the Master Builder, Jesus Christ (through church, parents, radio, books, friends, television or the Internet). They have been told how to build, and they know where to build; therefore, they are expected to build according to Christ's instructions. In fact, it is shocking if they do not build a solid house (note the question and shock of Christ in v.46).

However, they do not build on the foundation of rock. How foolish! Here is the depth of humanity's foolishness well-illustrated. Why do they not dig?

➢ Getting to the rock is too time-consuming and demanding.
➢ They fail to look ahead, to consider the future.
➢ They want to be doing something else.

Consequently, they lay no foundation, no footing. What a tragedy! They know better, but they ignore the Master Builder's instructions. The false disciples hear what the prophets and righteous men of old desired to hear (Mt.13:17; 1 Pe.1:10). What a privilege they have! And how they abuse that privilege! Week after week, day after day, year after year they hear; yet, they never follow the instructions on how to build their lives.

c. Result: There is a great fall.

False disciples *fall*. The houses (lives) they build collapse against the storms of life and eternity. Floods of trials do come. They cannot be stopped; houses without a foundation cannot stand. Note: "Immediately it fell; and the *ruin of that house was great.*"

Every person's work—the life they have built—will become evident. Our work is to be tested in this life through many, many trials, and in the next life by Christ at the Day of Judgment. Lives not built on Christ will suffer tremendous collapse. All who built their house on sand *must face* Christ in that day (He.9:27).

THOUGHT 1. The person who builds on sand clings to a *false trust*. Their faith and trust are in the wrong things.

> Whoever trusts in his riches will fall, but the righteous will flourish like a green leaf. (Pr.11:28)

> Whoever trusts in his own mind is a fool, but he who walks in wisdom will be delivered. (Pr.28:26)

> You felt secure in your wickedness; you said, "No one sees me"; your wisdom and your knowledge led you astray, and you said in your heart, "I am, and there is no one besides me." (Is.47:10)

> Thus says the LORD: "Cursed is the man who trusts in man and makes flesh his strength, whose heart turns away from the LORD." (Je.17:5)

> Say to those who smear it with whitewash that it shall fall! There will be a deluge of rain, and you, O great hailstones, will fall, and a stormy wind break out. (Ezk.13:11)

THOUGHT 2. The person who builds on the sands of this world of sin will fall.

> For you yourselves are fully aware that the day of the Lord will come like a thief in the night. While people are saying, "There is peace and security," then sudden destruction will come upon them as labor pains come upon a pregnant woman, and they will not escape. (1 Th.5:2-3; see 2 Pe.3:4, 9-13)

> How shall we escape if we neglect such a great salvation? It was declared at first by the Lord, and it was attested to us by those who heard. (He.2:3)

> There the evildoers lie fallen; they are thrust down, unable to rise. (Ps.36:12)

> The righteousness of the blameless keeps his way straight, but the wicked falls by his own wickedness. (Pr.11:5)

> "Were they ashamed when they committed abomination? No, they were not at all ashamed; they did not know how to blush. Therefore they shall fall among those who fall; at the time that I punish them, they shall be overthrown," says the LORD. (Je.6:15)

CHAPTER 7

M. Jesus Finds Great Faith in a Soldier: What Great Faith Involves, 7:1–10

(Mt.8:5–13)

After he had finished all his sayings in the hearing of the people, he entered Capernaum.

² Now a centurion had a servant who was sick and at the point of death, who was highly valued by him.

³ When the centurion heard about Jesus, he sent to him elders of the Jews, asking him to come and heal his servant.

⁴ And when they came to Jesus, they pleaded with him earnestly, saying, "He is worthy to have you do this for him,

⁵ for he loves our nation, and he is the one who built us our synagogue."

⁶ And Jesus went with them. When he was not far from the house, the centurion sent friends, saying to him, "Lord, do not trouble yourself, for I am not worthy to have you come under my roof.

⁷ Therefore I did not presume to come to you. But say the word, and let my servant be healed.

⁸ For I too am a man set under authority, with soldiers under me: and I say to one, 'Go,' and he goes; and to another, 'Come,' and he comes; and to my servant, 'Do this,' and he does it."

⁹ When Jesus heard these things, he marveled at him, and turning to the crowd that followed him, said, "I tell you, not even in Israel have I found such faith."

¹⁰ And when those who had been sent returned to the house, they found the servant well.

1. **Great faith cares deeply for people, even the lowly**
   a. Jesus returned to Capernaum
   b. Jesus was approached regarding a centurion's servant who was very sick and highly valued

2. **Great faith feels unworthy in approaching Jesus Christ**

3. **Great faith seeks God in Jesus Christ Himself**

4. **Great faith is centered in Jesus Christ**
   a. In Jesus as Sovereign Lord

   b. In Jesus' supreme power and Word, His authority

5. **Great faith stirs the mighty power of Jesus Christ**
   a. Jesus marveled at the soldier's great faith
   b. Jesus commended the soldier
   c. Jesus healed the servant

193

Division III

The Son of Man's Announced Mission and Public Ministry, 4:16–9:17

M. Jesus Finds Great Faith in a Soldier: What Great Faith Involves, 7:1–10

(Mt.8:5–13)

7:1–10
Introduction

Jesus is willing to meet all people's needs—Gentile or Jew, rich or poor, leader or follower, ruler or slave. He bridges the gaps, prejudices, and divisions between different people or groups of people. The one essential for securing His help is faith. We must have faith in Christ and His power. This truth is clearly demonstrated in what happened between this soldier and Jesus, whose faith the Lord described as "such faith" or "great faith." What is "great faith?" How can we have it? What will we do when we have it? This is, *Jesus Finds Great Faith in a Soldier: What Great Faith Involves,* 7:1–10.

1. Great faith cares deeply for people, even the lowly (v.1).
2. Great faith feels unworthy in approaching Jesus Christ (v.3).
3. Great faith seeks God in Jesus Christ Himself (vv.4–5).
4. Great faith is centered in Jesus Christ (vv.6–8).
5. Great faith stirs the mighty power of Jesus Christ (vv.9–10).

7:1–2

After he had finished all his sayings in the hearing of the people, he entered Capernaum. ² Now a centurion had a servant who was sick and at the point of death, who was highly valued by him.

1 Great faith cares deeply for people, even the lowly.

Luke introduces us to the unlikely man whom Jesus said had "great faith." He reveals the first quality that moved Jesus to describe Him in such an honored way: he cared deeply for people, even his lowliest servants.

a. **Jesus returned to Capernaum (v.1).**

After Jesus finished teaching, He returned to Capernaum. Capernaum was His headquarters where He now lived (see note—Lu.4:31).

b. **Jesus was approached regarding a centurion's servant who was very sick and highly valued (v.2).**

Upon returning to Capernaum, Jesus became acquainted with a certain centurion. A *centurion* was a Roman army official who led a battalion of one hundred men (see DEEPER STUDY # 1—Ac.23:23). Centurions were the officers who directly commanded the soldiers. They trained them, drilled them, inspected them, and ordered them from day to day. They were tough, hardened men.

This particular centurion, however, was a man who cared deeply for people. One of his servants was gravely ill, and he sought Jesus' help for his highly-valued employee. The Greek word translated in verse 2 as *Highly valued* or *dear* (entimos, *en'-tih-mos*) speaks of something or someone esteemed, honored, precious, prized. In the society of that day, a slave was nothing, only a tool or a possession to be used as the owner wished. Slaves had no rights whatsoever, not even the right to life. An owner could mistreat and kill a slave without even having to give an account. But this soldier loved his slave. This fact reveals a deep concern and care for people. It would have been much less bother to dispose of the slave or to ignore him and just let him die, but this centurion could not do that. He cared about his servant. Note how he *personally* looked after the slave, an individual who meant nothing to the rest of society. But his arms and love were wide open to do all he could to help this helpless person. This alone, helping a person who meant nothing to society, was bound to affect Christ dramatically.

And he said to him, "You shall love the Lord your God with all your heart and with all your soul and with all your mind. This is the great and first commandment. And a second is like it: You shall love your neighbor as yourself." (Mt.22:37–39)

This is my commandment, that you love one another as I have loved you. (Jn.15:12)

Let love be genuine. Abhor what is evil; hold fast to what is good. (Ro.12:9)

And may the Lord make you increase and abound in love for one another and *for* all, as we do for you. (1 Th.3:12)

If you really fulfill the royal law according to the Scripture, "You shall love your neighbor as yourself," you are doing well. (Jas.2:8)

2 Great faith feels unworthy in approaching Jesus Christ.

This centurion, the man of great faith, was a man who had heard about Jesus. He had either been where news of Jesus was being broadcast, or someone had personally told him about the Lord and His marvelous works. He had heard the message of hope, and he did not close his mind to it or ignore it. He believed what he had heard about Christ, believed that He could help his dying servant.

³ When the centurion heard about Jesus, he sent to him elders of the Jews, asking him to come and heal his servant.

The centurion, however, felt unworthy to approach Jesus himself. Why would he feel this way?

➢ He was a Roman, not a Jew.
➢ He was a Roman soldier, and an officer at that. Most Jews despised the Roman soldiers.
➢ He was a soldier, trained to take life and probably guilty of having taken life. What he had heard about Jesus was the message of love and brotherhood.
➢ He was a sinner, a terrible sinner, a Roman heathen, *totally unworthy* and rejected in the eyes of most. He felt that Jesus, too, would count him unworthy and reject him.

Therefore, the centurion requested help from others. He asked them to intercede for him. He did not allow his sense of unworthiness and rejection to defeat him; neither was he too proud to ask for help, despite his superior position.

At this point, it is important to address the fact that Luke's account of this episode differs from Matthew's. Luke says the centurion sent some religious leaders to approach Jesus, whereas Matthew says that the centurion approached Jesus. There is no contradiction here; in a dictatorial society, whatever a leader commands others to do is counted as his act, as he himself having done it. The leader's representatives act for him; thus, he is said to have done it.

THOUGHT 1. People must be exposed to the gospel, be where the gospel is proclaimed, or be witnessed to personally before they can believe in Him. It is our responsibility to share the good news of Christ with them.

And he said to them, "Go into all the world and proclaim the gospel to the whole creation." (Mk.16:15)

How then will they call on him in whom they have not believed? And how are they to believe in him of whom they have never heard? And how are they to hear without someone preaching? (Ro.10:14)

All this is from God, who through Christ reconciled us to himself and gave us the ministry of reconciliation (2 Co.5:18)

THOUGHT 2. We need to humble ourselves before the Lord if we wish to receive the Lord's blessings, just as this centurion did. This does not mean that we should be afraid to approach the Lord; the centurion could have approached Christ personally, and the Lord would have no doubt received him. But we need to have the same spirit of humility, the same feeling of unworthiness.

For by the grace given to me I say to everyone among you not to think of himself more highly than he ought to think, but to think with sober judgment, each according to the measure of faith that God has assigned. (Ro.12:3)

But he gives more grace. Therefore it says, "God opposes the proud but gives grace to the humble.... Humble yourselves before the Lord, and he will exalt you." (Jas.4:6, 10)

For though the LORD is high, he regards the lowly, but the haughty he knows from afar. (Ps.138:6)

For thus says the One who is high and lifted up, who inhabits eternity, whose name is Holy: "I dwell in the high and holy place, and also with him who is of a contrite and lowly spirit, to revive the spirit of the lowly, and to revive the heart of the contrite." (Is.57:15)

7:4-5

⁴ And when they came to Jesus, they pleaded with him earnestly, saying, "He is worthy to have you do this for him,
⁵ for he loves our nation, and he is the one who built us our synagogue."

3 Great faith seeks God in Jesus Christ Himself.

When the Jewish leaders approached Jesus on the centurion's behalf, they told the Lord that he was worthy of His help (v.4). He loved the Jewish nation, so much so that he had even built a synagogue for their worship of Jehovah (v.5). He was not a superficial follower of religion. He had heard about the God of Israel and accepted Him, rejecting the gods of Rome. This he did despite the hostility and rejection of the Jews. He was so drawn to God that he evidently was going to let nothing stop him from discovering the truth. This soldier, the man of great faith, was a man who sought God. Even more, he sought the power of God in Jesus Christ.

The point is, he was a man of faith (v.9), a man who loved God. The very reason he would love the Jewish nation (a people who despised him) and build a synagogue for them was because of his genuine love for God. It was most unusual for a Gentile, especially a Gentile official, to care for the Jews. Anti-Semitism was the prevailing attitude among Roman military brass. Jew and Gentile had virtually no dealings with one another (see notes—Mt.15:26-27; Mk.7:25; DEEPER STUDY # 1—7:27). Note how far the centurion went to serve God: he *loved* those who had formerly rejected and despised him, and he did what he could to edify and enhance the worship of God's people by building a synagogue. His love and faith were so strong and evident that those who had despised him now felt close to him—close enough to intercede for him.

That they should seek God, and perhaps feel their way toward him and find him. Yet he is actually not far from each one of us. (Ac.17:27)

For I am not ashamed of the gospel, for it is the power of God for salvation to everyone who believes, to the Jew first and also to the Greek. (Ro.1:16)

But now the righteousness of God has been manifested apart from the law, although the Law and the Prophets bear witness to it—the righteousness of God through faith in Jesus Christ for all who believe.... (Ro.3:21-22)

And without faith it is impossible to please him, for whoever would draw near to God must believe that he exists and that he rewards those who seek him. (He.11:6)

And the people of Nineveh believed God. They called for a fast and put on sackcloth, from the greatest of them to the least of them. (Jon.3:5)

7:6-8

⁶ And Jesus went with them. When he was not far from the house, the centurion sent friends, saying to him, "Lord, do not trouble yourself, for I am not worthy to have you come under my roof.
⁷ Therefore I did not presume to come to you. But say the word, and let my servant be healed.
⁸ For I too am a man set under authority, with soldiers under me: and I say to one, 'Go,' and he goes; and to another, 'Come,' and he comes; and to my servant, 'Do this,' and he does it."

4 Great faith is centered in Jesus Christ.

Great faith is not merely faith in God; it is centered in Jesus Christ. Jesus is the way, the truth, and the life. Nobody can come to God apart from Him (Jn.14:6). In reality, this centurion's faith was even greater than that of the Jewish leaders to whom he appealed. They rejected Christ, but he believed in God's Son.

a. In Jesus as Sovereign Lord (v.6).

Note that the centurion called Jesus "Lord." Great faith is believing that Christ is the sovereign Lord. All power is subject to Him.

b. In Jesus' supreme power and Word, His authority (vv.7–8).

Great faith is believing that Christ rewards those who seek Him (He.11:6). He will use His power on behalf of those who seek Him. The centurion believed that Jesus could and would help his beloved dying servant. In fact, he was so convinced of Jesus' power that he believed the Lord could heal his servant *from a distance.* Jesus did not even need come into the man's house; He could simply speak the Word of healing, and the gravely-ill servant would be healed (v.7).

Note that the centurion had diligently sought Jesus, believing Jesus could meet his need. Many believers diligently seek the Lord, but the centurion's faith was so much greater than most believers. Why? Because he believed that *the Word of Christ was all that was needed.* He believed that Jesus did not even have to be present for the need to be met. He explained that, as a centurion, he had authority over other men. All he had to do was issue an order and it was carried out, whether he was present or not. He was a sovereign commander (v.8). He was saying, "How much more are you, Lord. Merely speak the word, and my need will be met." What a forceful and powerful lesson on faith for all!

> And Jesus came and said to them, "All authority in heaven and on earth has been given to me." (Mt.28:18)

> Commit your way to the LORD; trust in him, and he will act. (Ps.37:5)

> It is better to take refuge in the LORD than to trust in man. (Ps.118:8)

> Trust in the LORD forever, for the LORD GOD is an everlasting rock. (Is.26:4)

> Seek the LORD while he may be found; call upon him while he is near. (Is.55:6)

5 Great faith stirs the mighty power of Jesus Christ.

When Jesus heard the centurion's faith-filled statement, He was stirred to action. Great faith stirs the matchless power of Jesus Christ.

⁹ When Jesus heard these things, he marveled at him, and turning to the crowd that followed him, said, "I tell you, not even in Israel have I found such faith."

¹⁰ And when those who had been sent returned to the house, they found the servant well.

a. Jesus marveled at the soldier's great faith (v.9a).

Only twice is Jesus said to have marveled at people: at the centurion, and at the people in Nazareth because of their unbelief (Mk.6:6). What an impact this man made upon Jesus! And what a contrast between him—a Gentile—and the unbelieving people of Nazareth, Jesus' own people.

b. Jesus commended the soldier (v.9b).

Jesus embraced and commended the centurion. He embraced him for his faith, not for who he was or for what he had done as a soldier. *Believing,* that is, true faith, is a rare thing. Not many truly believe; yet belief in Christ is one of the greatest qualities of human life—a quality ignored, neglected, and in some cases denied.

Moreover, Jesus commended the centurion before others. There are times when recognition and commendation are to be given, but note what it was for which Jesus commended the centurion. It was for spiritual graces, for his spiritual strength.

c. Jesus healed the servant (v.10).

When the centurion's messengers returned to his house, the servant who was dying when they left was now well! Jesus had healed the servant, and His power to meet the centurion's request proved His Messiahship—that He is truly the Son of God.

THOUGHT 1. Jesus Christ has the power to meet our needs; however, there is one prerequisite: faith. We must believe that Jesus Christ *can* meet our needs.

> And Jesus answered them, "Have faith in God. Truly, I say to you, whoever says to this mountain, 'Be taken up and thrown into the sea,' and does not doubt in his heart, but believes

that what he says will come to pass, it will be done for him. Therefore I tell you, whatever you ask in prayer, believe that you have received it, and it will be yours." (Mk.11:22–24)

But even now I know that whatever you ask from God, God will give you. (Jn.11:22)

Consequently, he is able to save to the uttermost those who draw near to God through him, since he always lives to make intercession for them. (He.7:25)

N. Jesus Raises a Widow's Son:
Showing Great Compassion and Power, 7:11–17

11 Soon afterward he went to a town called Nain, and his disciples and a great crowd went with him.

12 As he drew near to the gate of the town, behold, a man who had died was being carried out, the only son of his mother, and she was a widow, and a considerable crowd from the town was with her.

13 And when the Lord saw her, he had compassion on her and said to her, "Do not weep."

14 Then he came up and touched the bier, and the bearers stood still. And he said, "Young man, I say to you, arise."

15 And the dead man sat up and began to speak, and Jesus gave him to his mother.

16 Fear seized them all, and they glorified God, saying, "A great prophet has arisen among us!" and "God has visited his people!"

17 And this report about him spread through the whole of Judea and all the surrounding country.

1. **The great attraction of Jesus**
   a. He entered Nain with His disciples
   b. He attracted a large crowd
2. **The great compassion of Jesus: He was touched**
   a. By death, that of an only son
   b. By a mother's broken heart
   c. By a loving, caring woman, beloved by others
   d. By a need: The Lord saw and had compassion[DS1]

3. **The great power of Jesus**
   a. To bypass traditional beliefs
   b. To stop the death processional
   c. To raise the dead

4. **The great awe of the people**
   a. They praised God
   b. They believed Jesus to be a prophet
   c. They acknowledged God's dealing with them (Israel) again
   d. They bore witness

Division III

The Son of Man's Announced Mission and Public Ministry, 4:16–9:17

N. Jesus Raises a Widow's Son: Showing Great Compassion and Power, 7:11–17

7:11–17
Introduction

The most phenomenal event in all history—and the most difficult to believe—is the resurrection of the dead. Whether it is the fact of Jesus Himself being resurrected, or the promise of believers being raised someday, or of Jesus raising the dead, some people just have enormous difficulty believing such claims. Luke knew this, so he wanted to help unbelieving minds. In this event, Luke shared the great compassion and power of Jesus to raise the dead. This is, *Jesus Raises a Widow's Son: Showing Great Compassion and Power,* 7:11-17.

1. The great attraction of Jesus (v.11).
2. The great compassion of Jesus: He was touched (vv.12-13).
3. The great power of Jesus (vv.14-15).
4. The great awe of the people (vv.16-17).

1 The great attraction of Jesus.

As Christ's ministry expanded, so did the crowd of people following Him. There was—and is—a great attraction about Jesus. People were—and still are—drawn to Him (Jn.12:32).

7:11

¹¹ Soon afterward he went to a town called Nain, and his disciples and a great crowd went with him.

a. He entered Nain with His disciples.

The day after Jesus healed the centurion's servant, He entered Nain. This is the only time this town is named in the Bible. It was only about six miles from Nazareth and a day's journey from Capernaum. It is the same area where Elisha raised the son of the Shunammite woman (2 Ki.4:18–37). As we see in Luke 7, this obscure village became an area where the great compassion and power of God would be manifested.

b. He attracted a large crowd.

Many people witnessed the great conquest of death that occurred that day. Many of Jesus' disciples were present, and there were multitudes of unbelievers there as well. The unbelievers were following Jesus for any number of reasons, including . . .

- curiosity
- neighborly fellowship
- a belief in His ethics
- a need for help

- admiration
- a desire for something to do
- being impressed with His teaching
- thinking Him to be a great prophet

7:12–13

¹² As he drew near to the gate of the town, behold, a man who had died was being carried out, the only son of his mother, and she was a widow, and a considerable crowd from the town was with her.
¹³ And when the Lord saw her, he had compassion on her and said to her, "Do not weep."

2 The great compassion of Jesus: He was touched.

A somber scene touched the heart of God's Son as He neared the gate into Nain. A dead man was being carried out of the city, accompanied by his grieving mother. He was all she had. The great compassion of Jesus was evident to all who watched Him minister to the hurting woman that day.

a. By death, that of an only son (v.12a).

Jesus is always touched by death and how it impacts loved ones. The fact that we die is what brought Him to earth. It may be that the whole scene of sin and death flashed across His mind—the scene of . . .

- humanity's sin and death (Ro.5:12; 6:23; He.9:27)
- the great cost of sin and death, that is, His own death in bearing the sins and death of the world (1 Pe.2:24; 1 Jn.2:1-2)

   For to this end Christ died and lived again, that he might be Lord both of the dead and of the living. (Ro.14:9)

b. By a mother's broken heart (v.12b).

Here Jesus was touched by the broken heart of a devastated mother. Note her situation. She was a widow, apparently somewhat up in years with only one child, a grown son. He had just died, and now she was all alone in the world—a world that was harsh and rough on women, offering them little chance for earning a living and little help on a permanent basis. Hereafter, the woman would be without any permanent companion, provider, or protector; and there was no one to carry on the family line. The family name would die out with her death. She was brokenhearted, full of desperation and pain, without understanding and hope. When Jesus saw all this, He was moved with compassion.

c. By a loving, caring woman, beloved by others (v.12c).

Jesus was touched by how much other people loved this grieving woman. A large crowd of her friends and neighbors accompanied her, indicating that she had been a woman who had *loved and cared* for others throughout the years. Now, others were showing love and care for her. Jesus is always touched and moved to help those who have helped others (Lu.6:38).

> **Blessed are the merciful, for they shall receive mercy. (Mt.5:7)**

Note a curious observation: in this particular need, no one asked Jesus for help. He initiated the help Himself, acted purely out of His own compassion. Why did He not always do this? Perhaps it was that this grieving mother was so obviously filled with love and care for others that she stood out as a glorious example of what love for God is all about (Mt.22:38-39; Jn.13:34-35; 1 Jn.4:7).

d. By a need: The Lord saw and had compassion (v.13).

The Lord saw the woman's need, and, having compassion, spoke words of assurance to her (see DEEPER STUDY # 1). "Do not weep," Jesus said tenderly. Note that Luke says it was "the Lord" who saw her. This is the first time Luke uses the title "the Lord" by itself, and it is striking. The point Luke is making is that "the Lord," the sovereign power of the universe, saw this woman who was utterly heartbroken. "The Lord" of all actually saw her.

What a heartwarming, comforting fact! The Lord of the universe actually felt compassion for a simple woman. He is not just the sovereign power of a vast universe who is *off in outer space somewhere*, unattached and disinterested in this earth and its inhabitants. Contrariwise, He is vitally interested, interested enough to be looking and seeing, and He is concerned about what He sees. Here He is full of compassion for one heartbroken woman (see note—Lu.7:13). Luke is definitely stressing the staggering thought that "the Lord" is vitally interested in the affairs of human beings, even in the tragic plight of a simple woman. Truly, He bears our griefs and carries our sorrows (Is.53:4).

> **Who shall separate us from the love of Christ? Shall tribulation, or distress, or persecution, or famine, or nakedness, or danger, or sword? (Ro.8:35)**

> **Casting all your anxieties on him, because he cares for you. (1 Pe.5:7)**

> **As a father shows compassion to his children, so the LORD shows compassion to those who fear him. (Ps.103:13)**

> **But the steadfast love of the LORD is from everlasting to everlasting on those who fear him, and his righteousness to children's children. (Ps.103:17)**

> **In all their affliction he was afflicted, and the angel of his presence saved them; in his love and in his pity he redeemed them; he lifted them up and carried them all the days of old. (Is.63:9)**

> **The steadfast love of the LORD never ceases; his mercies never come to an end. (Lam.3:22)**

DEEPER STUDY # 1

(7:13) **Compassion** (Gk. esplagchnisthe, *es-plahgkh-nis'-thay*): to be moved inwardly, to yearn with tender mercy, affection, pity, empathy, compassion. It is the very seat of a person's affections. It is the deepest movement of emotions possible; being moved within the deepest part of one's being. Bible teacher Warren Wiersbe effectively defines compassion as "your hurt in my heart."

3 The great power of Jesus.

Immediately prior to leaving this earth and ascending to heaven, Jesus announced that He has power or authority over all things (Mt.28:18). His great power over all, including death, is seen here in three surprising, authoritative acts.

7:14–15

¹⁴ Then he came up and touched the bier, and the bearers stood still. And he said, "Young man, I say to you, arise."

¹⁵ And the dead man sat up and began to speak, and Jesus gave him to his mother.

a. To bypass traditional beliefs (v.14a).

First, Jesus touched the bier or open coffin. The people of that day believed that a person became polluted by touching a corpse. According to the law, the person became ceremonially unclean, unacceptable to God (Nu.19:11, 16). By touching the bier, Jesus was showing that He possessed the right and power to override traditional religious laws and beliefs. He was the sovereign power even over religious beliefs and over death and life.

b. To stop the death processional (v.14b).

When Jesus touched the bier, the processional came to a sudden halt. The pallbearers stopped; they "stood still." They obeyed the authority of the Lord.

THOUGHT 1. Willingness and obedience on the part of the pallbearers and the mother were essential for Jesus to raise the dead son. We, too, must be willing and obedient if we wish to experience the miraculous power of Christ, including one day being raised from the dead. We must obey the gospel, repenting of our sins and genuinely believing in Jesus Christ.

> Jesus said to her, "I am the resurrection and the life. Whoever believes in me, though he die, yet shall he live." (Jn.11:25)

> That by any means possible I may attain the resurrection from the dead. (Ph.3:11; see Ph.3:7–11)

> For since we believe that Jesus died and rose again, even so, through Jesus, God will bring with him those who have fallen asleep. For this we declare to you by a word from the Lord, that we who are alive, who are left until the coming of the Lord, will not precede those who have fallen asleep. For the Lord himself will descend from heaven with a cry of command, with the voice of an archangel, and with the sound of the trumpet of God. And the dead in Christ will rise first. (1 Th.4:14–16)

c. To raise the dead (v.14c–15).

Jesus spoke the brief command to the dead young man, "I say to you, arise." The words *I say* testify to the authority and power of Jesus Christ over death and, in essence, His power over all things. It was the command, the powerful *Word* of *Jesus*, the Son of God and God the Son, that raised the dead.

> Truly, truly, I say to you, whoever hears my word and believes him who sent me has eternal life. He does not come into judgment, but has passed from death to life. Truly, truly, I say to you, an hour is coming, and is now here, when the dead will hear the voice of the Son of God, and those who hear will live. For as the Father has life in himself, so he has granted the Son also to have life in himself. And he has given him authority to execute judgment, because he is the Son of Man. Do not marvel at this, for an hour is coming when all who are in the tombs will hear his voice and come out, those who have done good to the resurrection of life, and those who have done evil to the resurrection of judgment. (Jn.5:24–29)

> For this reason the Father loves me, because I lay down my life that I may take it up again. No one takes it from me, but I lay it down of my own accord. I have authority to lay it down, and I have authority to take it up again. This charge I have received from my Father. (Jn.10:17–18)

> For he must reign until he has put all his enemies under his feet. The last enemy to be destroyed is death. (1 Co.15:25–26)

> When I saw him, I fell at his feet as though dead. But he laid his right hand on me, saying, "Fear not, I am the first and the last, and the living one. I died, and behold I am alive forevermore, and I have the keys of Death and Hades." (Re.1:17–18)

He will swallow up death forever; and the Lord GOD will wipe away tears from all faces, and the reproach of his people he will take away from all the earth, for the LORD has spoken. (Is.25:8)

7:11–17

4 The great awe of the people.

A sense of fear swept over the people who witnessed Jesus raise the young man from the dead. The word *fear* (phobos, *phoh'-bos*) speaks of reverence and of awe. Seeing the dead man sit up and speak struck the fear of God in their hearts. They responded in four ways.

> [16] Fear seized them all, and they glorified God, saying, "A great prophet has arisen among us!" and "God has visited his people!"
> [17] And this report about him spread through the whole of Judea and all the surrounding country.

a. They praised God (v.16a).

First, they glorified God (edoxazon ton theon, *eh-dox'-ah-zon tahn theh'-on*). The tense in the Greek is imperfect active and means that they *began* to glorify God at that point and *continued* to glorify God.

b. They believed Jesus to be a prophet (v.16b).

Second, the awestruck people declared that Jesus was "a *great* prophet" (De.18:15; Jn.1:21). Their statement was no doubt rooted in the fact that they had just witnessed Jesus perform a miracle nearly identical to one performed by Elijah, the greatest and most powerful of Israel's prophets (1 Ki.17:19–24). However, what they *did not* say is as significant as what they said. They stopped short of saying that Jesus was the Messiah.

c. They acknowledged God's dealing with them (Israel) again (v.16c).

Although the people did not acknowledge Jesus as the Messiah, they did acknowledge the fact that God was moving in Israel once again. Revival fires were blazing throughout all Israel. For four hundred years, there had been no word, no moving from the Lord. But things were changing drastically and dramatically. The message of John the Baptist had been heard by multitudes, and Jesus was affecting the lives of scores of people. The people recognized that God was now visiting and dealing with Israel once again.

d. They bore witness (v.17).

Finally, the people bore witness of what they had seen. As the story of the dead man's raising spread far and wide, so did the fame of and curiosity about this Man named Jesus.

> By this my Father is glorified, that you bear much fruit and so prove to be my disciples. (Jn.15:8)

> Through him then let us continually offer up a sacrifice of praise to God, that is, the fruit of lips that acknowledge his name. (He.13:15)

> But you are a chosen race, a royal priesthood, a holy nation, a people for his own possession, that you may proclaim the excellencies of him who called you out of darkness into his marvelous light. (1 Pe.2:9)

> You who fear the LORD, praise him! All you offspring of Jacob, glorify him, and stand in awe of him, all you offspring of Israel! (Ps.22:23)

> Then my tongue shall tell of your righteousness and of your praise all the day long. (Ps.35:28)

O. Jesus Answers John the Baptist's Question: Is Jesus the Messiah? 7:18–28

(Mt.11:1–15)

1. **John, in prison, heard of Jesus' loving works**
   a. John was puzzled: Pictured a conquering Messiah
   b. John sent two disciples to question whether Jesus was the Messiah

2. **The ministry and message of Jesus proved He is the Messiah**
   a. He demonstrated the power and works of the Messiah
   b. He fulfilled the prophecies of the Messiah[DS1]
   c. He preached the gospel of the Messiah

   d. He promised both the blessing and judgment of the Messiah

3. **The forerunner, John himself, proved Jesus is the Messiah**
   a. His conviction and staunchness

   b. His self-denial and discipline

   c. His prophetic mission

   d. His identity as the true forerunner

4. **The kingdom of God proves Jesus is the Messiah**

---

18 The disciples of John reported all these things to him. And John,

19 calling two of his disciples to him, sent them to the Lord, saying, "Are you the one who is to come, or shall we look for another?"

20 And when the men had come to him, they said, "John the Baptist has sent us to you, saying, 'Are you the one who is to come, or shall we look for another?'"

21 In that hour he healed many people of diseases and plagues and evil spirits, and on many who were blind he bestowed sight.

22 And he answered them, "Go and tell John what you have seen and heard: the blind receive their sight, the lame walk, lepers are cleansed, and the deaf hear, the dead are raised up, the poor have good news preached to them.

23 And blessed is the one who is not offended by me."

24 When John's messengers had gone, Jesus began to speak to the crowds concerning John: "What did you go out into the wilderness to see? A reed shaken by the wind?

25 What then did you go out to see? A man dressed in soft clothing? Behold, those who are dressed in splendid clothing and live in luxury are in kings' courts.

26 What then did you go out to see? A prophet? Yes, I tell you, and more than a prophet.

27 This is he of whom it is written, 'Behold, I send my messenger before your face, who will prepare your way before you.'

28 I tell you, among those born of women none is greater than John. Yet the one who is least in the kingdom of God is greater than he."

Division III

The Son of Man's Announced Mission and Public Ministry, 4:16–9:17

O. Jesus Answers John the Baptist's Question: Is Jesus the Messiah? 7:18–28

(Mt.11:1–15)

7:18–28
Introduction

At times, even faithful believers question their faith. Is there really a God? Is the Bible really true? Is Jesus Christ really God's Son? Occasionally, these questions are asked in moments of rebellion, but such doubts usually arise in moments of weakness and despair. What we need to remember is that *honest* questions never disappoint God; only rebellion is judged by Him. God will meet and answer any honest question posed by a hurting or needful person.

John the Baptist had a moment of wondering, a moment of doubt, a moment of questioning. In presenting John's question and Jesus' response, this passage gives the final proof of Jesus' Messiahship. This is, *Jesus Answers John the Baptist's Question: Is Jesus the Messiah?*, 7:18-28.

1. John, in prison, heard of Jesus' loving works (vv.18-20).
2. The ministry and message of Jesus proved He is the Messiah (vv.21-23).
3. The forerunner, John himself, proved Jesus is the Messiah (vv.24-27).
4. The kingdom of God proves Jesus is the Messiah (v.28).

1 John, in prison, heard of Jesus' loving works.

7:18-20

John's doubts arose while he was in prison. His faithfulness to the truth had cost him his freedom, and it would soon cost him his life (see Lu.3:19-20; 9:9). Apparently, his disciples were allowed to visit him and brought him word about Jesus' loving works. He was eager to hear about Jesus and the Messianic movement, so they related the wonderful miracles and teachings of Jesus. However, their report included nothing about eliminating injustices nor freeing people from the tyranny and rule of others. They said nothing about the fulfillment of the Jews' hope for the great Messiah who

> [18] The disciples of John reported all these things to him. And John,
> [19] calling two of his disciples to him, sent them to the Lord, saying, "Are you the one who is to come, or shall we look for another?"
> [20] And when the men had come to him, they said, "John the Baptist has sent us to you, saying, 'Are you the one who is to come, or shall we look for another?'"

was to take over the world and rule in righteousness, executing judgment on all evil people and nations. In fact, the very opposite seemed to be taking place; for when the people were stirred to exalt Jesus as their king, He withdrew and discouraged their actions (Lu.5:16). Unjustly imprisoned and awaiting execution from the oppressive government he had expected Jesus to overthrow, John began to question whether Jesus was the Messiah.

a. **John was puzzled: Pictured a conquering Messiah (v.18).**
What John heard puzzled him, for Jesus seemed to be fulfilling only half of the prophecies concerning the Messiah, the half dealing with ministry. The prophecies dealing with a conquering Messiah who would bring righteousness and judgment were not being fulfilled (see notes—Mt.11:1-6).

b. **John sent two disciples to question whether Jesus was the Messiah (vv.19-20).**
John needed assurance, so he sent two disciples to ask Jesus if He was indeed the promised Messiah, or should God's people be looking for someone else (v.19). The faithful messengers asked Jesus the question exactly as John had posed it (v.20).

2 The ministry and message of Jesus proved He is the Messiah.

Jesus answered John's question by pointing to His ministry and message. He gave His faithful forerunner four assurances that proved His Messiahship beyond question.

²¹ In that hour he healed many people of diseases and plagues and evil spirits, and on many who were blind he bestowed sight.

²² And he answered them, "Go and tell John what you have seen and heard: the blind receive their sight, the lame walk, lepers are cleansed, and the deaf hear, the dead are raised up, the poor have good news preached to them.

²³ And blessed is the one who is not offended by me."

a. He demonstrated the power and works of the Messiah (v.21).

Note what Jesus did when John's disciples approached Him and told Him that John needed assurance. Our loving Lord turned and gave the two disciples a demonstration of what His ministry involved. They had only heard about His ministry; now they were to see for themselves. He cured many who were sick and demon-possessed, and He gave sight to many who were blind. Apparently, He ministered for about an hour.

The point was, Jesus was telling John not only to *hear* His claims of Messiahship but also to *look at* His works and judge Him by what He did for people. He did not just profess to be the Messiah, He was proving it. He was proving it by ministering to people in *the power of God*. In particular, Jesus demonstrated two glorious truths:

➤ He demonstrated that God truly exists and that He is sovereign. He is above and beyond nature, and He has the power to override the laws of nature by miraculously healing the sick.

➤ He demonstrated that God loves and cares for people and has planned a way for humanity to be saved and delivered forever.

b. He fulfilled the prophecies of the Messiah (v.22a).

After ministering to the people, Jesus turned to John's disciples and told them to go tell John what they had *seen* and *heard*. Tell him about the miracles they had *personally* witnessed. These miracles fulfilled the prophecies about the Messiah.

Again, John was questioning Jesus' Messiahship. The reports he had heard said nothing about Jesus' mobilizing the people into a great army. Jesus was not plotting the strategy to free Israel from Roman domination and to set up the kingdom of God. John had heard nothing about the Day of the Lord, about the Messianic fire of judgment, about cities' falling and sinners' being judged. And his time was running out. He would be tried and executed soon. The answer Jesus sent back to John was a totally new concept of Messiahship. It was God's idea of Messiahship, radically different from man's idea. It was a demonstration and proclamation of salvation, of God's care and love for people. (See notes—Lu.3:24-31; Deeper Study # 3—Jn.1:45 for discussion. Also see notes—Mt.1:1; Deeper Study # 2—1:18; Deeper Study # 3—3:11; notes—11:1-6; 11:2-3; Deeper Study # 1—11:5; Deeper Study # 2—11:6; Deeper Study # 1—12:16; note—22:42.)

Jesus was saying that His power and concern (love) were the power and concern *predicted* for the Messiah, and both were unlimited (see Deeper Study # 1; see note, pt.2—Mt.11:4-6 for detailed discussion).

c. He preached the gospel of the Messiah (v.22b).

In addition to performing the works of the Messiah, Jesus preached the gospel of the Messiah. The "poor" referred to those who were "poor in spirit," those who had need and acknowledged their need (6:20; Mt.5:3). God's heart and compassion reached out to any who came and brought their need to Him. It was these, the poor in spirit, to whom He preached the good news (see note, pt.4—Mt.11:4-6 for more discussion).

d. He promised both the blessing and judgment of the Messiah (v.23).

Jesus promised John that he would be blessed if he was not *offended* at Jesus; that is, if he did not stumble over his expectations of the Messiah and stop believing in Jesus, if he held fast to his faith in Christ. He was seeing the blessing of the Messiah, and the Messiah's judgment would come in God's perfect time and according to His perfect plan (see Deeper Study # 2—Mt.11:6). Note the two facets of what Jesus promised—the two areas of work predicted about the Messiah:

➤ The area of blessing, of the Spirit, of salvation, of God's care and love for people. This is the area Christ covered here. Today is the day of blessing.

> **And Jesus answered them, "Go and tell John what you hear and see: the blind receive their sight and the lame walk, lepers are cleansed and the deaf hear, and the dead are raised up, and the poor have good news preached to them." (Mt.11:4-5)**

> **For God so loved the world, that he gave his only Son, that whoever believes in him should not perish but have eternal life. For God did not send his Son into the world to condemn the world, but in order that the world might be saved through him. (Jn.3:16-17)**

> **If anyone hears my words and does not keep them, I do not judge him; for I did not come to judge the world but to save the world. (Jn.12:47)**

> **And the grace of our Lord overflowed for me with the faith and love that are in Christ Jesus. The saying is trustworthy and deserving of full acceptance, that Christ Jesus came into the world to save sinners, of whom I am the foremost. (1 Ti.1:14-15)**

➤ The area of fire, of wrath, of judgment. The Messiah will fulfill the judgment of God when He returns (see Deeper Study # 2—Mt.1:18; Deeper Study # 3—3:11; notes—11:1-6; 11:2-3; Deeper Study # 2—11:6; Deeper Study # 1—12:16; note—22:42 for discussion).

Deeper Study # 1

(7:22) **Messiah, False Concepts:** Jesus was referring to Scripture in this verse. He was telling John that His actions were prophesied by the prophets (Is.35:5-6; 61:1-2; see Ps.72:2; 146:8; Zec.11:11). Note, however, that Jesus stressed the personal ministry and not the political. He omitted the phrases of Is.61:1 that could be interpreted that He was to be a political leader: "proclaiming liberty to the captives, and the opening of the prisons." He needed to get John's attention away from the wrong concept of the Messiah. He was reaching out in the power of the Spirit to individuals, saving and restoring them, not reaching out to mobilize people for the deliverance of Israel from the Roman enslavement.

3 The forerunner, John himself, proved Jesus is the Messiah.

7:24-27

As soon as John's disciples were gone, Jesus turned His attention to the crowd. This was necessary, for the people had heard all that had happened and their opinion of John had been negatively affected. By all appearances, John had wavered in his faith. If the people were allowed to think this, they would soon question if John were really the prophet who was to pave the way for the Messiah. Then, following on the heels of this question, would be the questioning of Jesus' being the true Messiah. If this kind of talk and questioning got started, it would affect not only the crowd but also those who had already believed. It would be devastating to the Lord's mission. Note something in all this: how fickle people really are and how easily people forget a prophet's true calling and strength and relish in the news of his weak moment.

[24] When John's messengers had gone, Jesus began to speak to the crowds concerning John: "What did you go out into the wilderness to see? A reed shaken by the wind?
[25] What then did you go out to see? A man dressed in soft clothing? Behold, those who are dressed in splendid clothing and live in luxury are in kings' courts.
[26] What then did you go out to see? A prophet? Yes, I tell you, and more than a prophet.
[27] This is he of whom it is written, 'Behold, I send my messenger before your face, who will prepare your way before you.'"

Out of love for and loyalty to John, as well as out of concern for His own ministry, Jesus reprimanded the crowd. He vindicated John and his mission. He reminded the forgetful and fickle that John *was* the prophesied forerunner, proving that He, Jesus, was the true Messiah (see outline and notes—Mt.11:7-15 for detailed discussion).

a. His conviction and staunchness (v.24).

Jesus wanted the people to know that John's momentary doubts were not a true representation of whom he really was. John was a man of conviction and staunchness. He was not like a reed shaken by the wind. John's steadfastness and firm adherence to his convictions proved that he was indeed the prophesied forerunner, and, therefore, the One he proclaimed—Christ—was indeed the Messiah.

➤ John's conviction that he was the forerunner proves Jesus is the Messiah.
➤ John's conviction that the Messiah was coming proves Jesus is the Messiah.
➤ John's conviction that He (Jesus) was the Lamb of God proves Jesus is the Messiah.
➤ John's staunchness in standing up to the religionists proves Jesus is the Messiah.
➤ John's staunchness in standing up to Herod proves Jesus is the Messiah.

> Therefore, my beloved brothers, be steadfast, immovable, always abounding in the work of the Lord, knowing that in the Lord your labor is not in vain. (1 Co.15:58)

> But test everything; hold fast what is good. (1 Th.5:21)

> Let us hold fast the confession of our hope without wavering, for he who promised is faithful. (He.10:23)

b. His self-denial and discipline (v.25).

Jesus reminded the people that John was a man of self-denial and sacrifice. He was not a man clothed in luxurious, fashionable clothing. He denied himself and sacrificed the things of the world in order to carry out the work of God.

> So therefore, any one of you who does not renounce all that he has cannot be my disciple. (Lu.14:33)

> Indeed, I count everything as loss because of the surpassing worth of knowing Christ Jesus my Lord. For his sake I have suffered the loss of all things and count them as rubbish, in order that I may gain Christ. (Ph.3:8)

c. His prophetic mission (v.26).

John was a prophet, a man sent on a prophetic mission. He proclaimed the Word of God, and his proclamation could not be denied. But Jesus informed the people that John was *more* than a prophet. His purpose, mission, and importance far exceeded that of any other prophet. He was the subject of prophecy as well as the messenger of it (Mal.3:1). He was the foreordained herald who brought the message to the world that *the Lord had come*. In this, John excelled over all other prophets. They only *foresaw* the Messiah's coming, but John *saw* Him come.

d. His identity as the true forerunner (v.27).

Jesus erased any remaining doubts by stating plainly and unequivocally that John was the true forerunner of the Messiah, the messenger predicted by the Scripture. At the same time, Jesus was *claiming* to be the Messiah before whom John prepared the way. The logic is clear: if John was the true forerunner, then the one he identified as the Messiah was indeed the true Messiah.

> In those days John the Baptist came preaching in the wilderness of Judea, "Repent, for the kingdom of heaven is at hand." For this is he who was spoken of by the prophet Isaiah when he said, "The voice of one crying in the wilderness: 'Prepare the way of the Lord; make his paths straight.'" (Mt.3:1–3)

> And he will go before him in the spirit and power of Elijah, to turn the hearts of the fathers to the children, and the disobedient to the wisdom of the just, to make ready for the Lord a people prepared. (Lu.1:17)

> And you, child, will be called the prophet of the Most High; for you will go before the Lord to prepare his ways. (Lu.1:76)

> A voice cries: "In the wilderness prepare the way of the LORD; make straight in the desert a highway for our God." (Is.40:3)

> Behold, I send my messenger, and he will prepare the way before me. And the Lord whom you seek will suddenly come to his temple; and the messenger of the covenant in whom you delight, behold, he is coming, says the LORD of hosts. (Mal.3:1)

4 The kingdom of God proves Jesus is the Messiah.

Jesus exalted John as the greatest man ever born *up to that time*. He then pointed out that He Himself had ushered in a new era, a new age, the age of the kingdom of God. This too proves that He was the Messiah.

Jesus' entrance into human history divided time and the ages. The period of history before Jesus came into the world is known as the age of promise. But since Jesus' coming, people have been living in the time and age of God's kingdom. John lived much of his life in the age of promise, whereas followers of Jesus live in the kingdom of God. Therefore, the least in the kingdom is greater than the greatest of prophets who lived in the age of promise. *Jesus Christ is the reason*: knowing Him personally makes all the difference in the privileges of a person. The citizens of God's kingdom know the presence of Christ within their bodies in the Person of the Holy Spirit, and they know the *active* rule and reign of God in life (1 Co.6:19-20; see Jn.14:16-18, 20, 23). However, those who lived in the age of promise only had the *hope* of the promise (Ro.8:16-17; Ga.4:4-6; see note—Mt.11:11 for more discussion).

7:28

²⁸ "I tell you, among those born of women none is greater than John. Yet the one who is least in the kingdom of God is greater than he."

> Blessed be the God and Father of our Lord Jesus Christ! According to his great mercy, he has caused us to be born again to a living hope through the resurrection of Jesus Christ from the dead, to an inheritance that is imperishable, undefiled, and unfading, kept in heaven for you. (1 Pe.1:3-4)

> Though you have not seen him, you love him. Though you do not now see him, you believe in him and rejoice with joy that is inexpressible and filled with glory, obtaining the outcome of your faith, the salvation of your souls. Concerning this salvation, the prophets who prophesied about the grace that was to be yours searched and inquired carefully, inquiring what person or time the Spirit of Christ in them was indicating when he predicted the sufferings of Christ and the subsequent glories. It was revealed to them that they were serving not themselves but you, in the things that have now been announced to you through those who preached the good news to you by the Holy Spirit sent from heaven, things into which angels long to look. (1 Pe.1:8-12; see also vv.13-16)

> May grace and peace be multiplied to you in the knowledge of God and of Jesus our Lord. His divine power has granted to us all things that pertain to life and godliness, through the knowledge of him who called us to his own glory and excellence, by which he has granted to us his precious and very great promises, so that through them you may become partakers of the divine nature, having escaped from the corruption that is in the world because of sinful desire. (2 Pe.1:2-4)

P. Jesus Reveals God's Verdict on This Generation and Age, 7:29–35

(Mt.11:16–27)

1. Reactions to John
  a. The common people and tax collectors whom John baptized: Acknowledged God's way
  b. The religionists who were not baptized: Rejected God's purpose

  c. Jesus warned His generation and age

2. An age of childishness

3. An age of escapism: Seeking to avoid responsibility
  a. Accused John of being too extreme in denying self
  b. Accused Jesus of being too loose, of indulgence and license

4. An age with only a few wise toward God

29 (When all the people heard this, and the tax collectors too, they declared God just, having been baptized with the baptism of John,

30 but the Pharisees and the lawyers rejected the purpose of God for themselves, not having been baptized by him.)

31 "To what then shall I compare the people of this generation, and what are they like?

32 They are like children sitting in the marketplace and calling to one another, 'We played the flute for you, and you did not dance; we sang a dirge, and you did not weep.'

33 For John the Baptist has come eating no bread and drinking no wine, and you say, 'He has a demon.'

34 The Son of Man has come eating and drinking, and you say, 'Look at him! A glutton and a drunkard, a friend of tax collectors and sinners!'

35 Yet wisdom is justified by all her children."

Division III

The Son of Man's Announced Mission and Public Ministry, 4:16–9:17

P. Jesus Reveals God's Verdict on This Generation and Age, 7:29–35

(Mt.11:16–27)

7:29-35
Introduction

John the Baptist's question about Jesus revealed more about the people than about him. After answering John's question and sending John's disciples on their way, Jesus addressed the crowd who had witnessed the scene. He ended up pronouncing the verdict on the spiritual condition of His generation. In so doing, He gave a glimpse of God's verdict on every generation of people (see outline and notes—Mt.11:16–27 for more discussion). This is, *Jesus Reveals God's Verdict on This Generation and Age,* 7:29–35.

1. Reactions to John (vv.29–31).
2. An age of childishness (v.32).

3. An age of escapism: Seeking to avoid responsibility (vv.33–34).

4. An age with only a few wise toward God (v.35).

1 Reactions to John.

The reaction of the people to John was twofold. The common people and tax collectors affirmed John and his ministry, but the religious leaders rejected him. By accepting John and his ministry, they "acknowledged that God's way was right" (NIV).

> [29] (When all the people heard this, and the tax collectors too, they declared God just, having been baptized with the baptism of John,
> [30] but the Pharisees and the lawyers rejected the purpose of God for themselves, not having been baptized by him.)
> [31] "To what then shall I compare the people of this generation, and what are they like?"

a. The common people and tax collectors whom John baptized: Acknowledged God's way (v.29).

The common people and the tax collectors responded positively to what Jesus had said. The tax collectors were set apart from the people themselves. This was because they were so despised and ostracized. They were actually treated in a class all by themselves, a class of betrayers (usually wealthy) who had forsaken the common people. The tax collectors, of course, felt the sting of rejection and in some cases sensed their sin and the need for repentance. These responded to John.

Many common people had also repented and been baptized by John. Sensing their need for forgiveness, they turned from their sins and believed John's message that the Messiah was coming.

The people who repented declared that God is just in all His ways. By repenting and being baptized, they vindicated John's ministry. They proclaimed that God is just and righteous and that they owed their lives to Him. Their repentance proved itself through changed lives and also proved that God was just and that John's message was true.

b. The religionists who were not baptized: Rejected God's purpose (v.30).

The religionists (Pharisees and lawyers) rejected the counsel of God. The evidence was clearly seen in what they failed to do: they did not repent and were not baptized by John. Being the religious leaders, they were the very ones who should have responded, but they did not. And what a surprise! The Pharisees were the practitioners of religion, a whole sect of men who had given their lives to live out the law—even to the most minute detail (see DEEPER STUDY # 3 Ac.23:8). The lawyers (Scribes) were those who gave their lives to study and learn the law to the fullest extent possible (see DEEPER STUDY # 1—Lu.6:2; DEEPER STUDY # 1—Mt.22:35).

c. Jesus warned His generation and age (v.31).

Jesus warned His generation—particularly the Scribes and Pharisees—of the error of their ways and their rebellion against God and His plan. They were a religious generation . . .

- that should have known and been prepared for the prophet of God and his message
- that had God's Word, yet ignored it
- that had the worship of God and the ordinances of God, yet neglected them
- to whom God sent His prophet, yet they rejected him
- to whom God sent His Son, yet they rejected Him
- that was smug in its own adequacy and sufficiency

2 An age of childishness.

Trying to get across the truth about His own generation, Jesus sought a way to describe them. The most accurate illustration which came to His mind was that of children (see note—Mt.11:16-19). He was saying that His own generation was a *childish generation*. By saying they were "like children," He meant they were *perverse*—stubborn, delinquent, rebellious, and corrupt. His generation was perverse. They turned

> [32] "They are like children sitting in the marketplace and calling to one another, 'We played the flute for you, and you did not dance; we sang a dirge, and you did not weep.'"

away from that which was right and good to that which was corrupt; they acted contrary to the evidence; they were opposed to that which was right, reasonable, and acceptable; and they were obstinate in their opposition—appearing mindless and contrary. They did not want the truth, so they made excuses for not receiving the truth.

Jesus' illustration was clearly understood. It may have been that children were playing in the marketplace as He spoke. Imagine that a few begin to play wedding music on their pipes and cry out to others, "Let's play wedding." The others shout back, "No. We don't want to dance around today." So the first group, still wanting to play, begins to play funeral music and shouts back, "Well, let's play funeral." "No. We don't want to play funeral either. We don't feel like acting sad."

Every generation is alike in that it has its privileges. The privileges are used by some and ignored and abused by others. Since the coming of Christ, God's very own Son, the greatest privilege in all the world has been the privilege of knowing Him personally and of being brought into a right relationship with God. As with all privileges, some have come to know Him personally, but the vast majority have ignored and abused Him, just as the religious leaders and so many people of His day did.

> But I, brothers, could not address you as spiritual people, but as people of the flesh, as infants in Christ. I fed you with milk, not solid food, for you were not ready for it. And even now you are not yet ready. (1 Co.3:1-2)

> When I was a child, I spoke like a child, I thought like a child, I reasoned like a child. When I became a man, I gave up childish ways. (1 Co.13:11)

> So that we may no longer be children, tossed to and fro by the waves and carried about by every wind of doctrine, by human cunning, by craftiness in deceitful schemes. (Ep.4:14)

> For though by this time you ought to be teachers, you need someone to teach you again the basic principles of the oracles of God. You need milk, not solid food. (He.5:12)

> For my people are foolish; they know me not; they are stupid children; they have no understanding. They are "wise"—in doing evil! But how to do good they know not. (Je.4:22)

7:33-34

[33] "For John the Baptist has come eating no bread and drinking no wine, and you say, 'He has a demon.'
[34] The Son of Man has come eating and drinking, and you say, 'Look at him! A glutton and a drunkard, a friend of tax collectors and sinners!'"

3 An age of escapism: Seeking to avoid responsibility.

Jesus continued describing His generation. They were a generation of escapism, always seeking an excuse to escape *personal* responsibility. The generation was contrary and mindless; they were faultfinders who could not be pleased. The people found fault with whatever was suggested. They just could not accept anything that made them responsible for their actions. They found fault with a separatist approach to the gospel, and they also found fault with a sociable approach to the gospel.

a. Accused John of being too extreme in denying self (v.33).
They accused John of being too conservative and too self-denying. John came neither eating nor drinking; he was a separatist. He was from the desert; and he lived a strict, austere, highly disciplined life. He did not associate with people; he did not make friends. He simply isolated himself, cut himself off from everyone and withdrew from society. His message was a gospel of repentance and of separation from the things of the world. Therefore, they accused him of having a "demon," of being mad and insane for choosing to live that way.

b. Accused Jesus of being too loose, of indulgence and license (v.34).
In total contrast, they accused Jesus of indulgence and license, of being too loose. Jesus was the very opposite of John. He lived and preached a gospel of liberty, eating and drinking with people. He was with them in their social moments; and He moved among all sorts of people—mixing, being friendly and open and accessible to all, no matter how terrible they were thought to be. Therefore, He was accused of being a sinner Himself: a glutton, a drunkard, and an immoral companion of sinners.

God clearly used both approaches (see 1 Co.12:6–7). Jesus did not condemn John's approach, and John did not condemn Jesus' approach. They supported each other, but the majority of people rejected any attempt to restrict their *own play* (remember the comparison to children). They wished to continue doing their own thing: seeking pleasure, intellectual pursuit, secular interest, or religious commitment. Most were willing to go only so far in restricting their own desires, wills, and way. Just like today, few were willing to deny self completely (see note and Deeper Study # 1—Lu.9:23).

> But exhort one another every day, as long as it is called "today," that none of you may be hardened by the deceitfulness of sin. (He.3:13)

> But these, like irrational animals, creatures of instinct, born to be caught and destroyed, blaspheming about matters of which they are ignorant, will also be destroyed in their destruction, suffering wrong as the wage for their wrongdoing. They count it pleasure to revel in the daytime. They are blots and blemishes, reveling in their deceptions, while they feast with you. They have eyes full of adultery, insatiable for sin. They entice unsteady souls. They have hearts trained in greed. Accursed children! Forsaking the right way, they have gone astray. They have followed the way of Balaam, the son of Beor, who loved gain from wrongdoing. (2 Pe.2:12–15)

> So I spoke to you, and you would not listen; but you rebelled against the command of the LORD and presumptuously went up into the hill country. (De.1:43)

> He who is often reproved, yet stiffens his neck, will suddenly be broken beyond healing. (Pr.29:1)

> For thus said the Lord GOD, the Holy One of Israel, "In returning and rest you shall be saved; in quietness and in trust shall be your strength." But you were unwilling. (Is.30:15)

4 An age with only a few wise toward God.

7:35

Jesus summed up His generation as having only a few who were wise toward God. Specifically, Jesus said, "Wisdom is justified by all her children." What does this statement mean?

35 "Yet wisdom is justified by all her children."

First, wisdom does have children, wise children.

Second, wise children will justify what is wise and right; they will declare wisdom.

Third, the wise will declare that both John and Jesus were right in their different approaches. The way they lived and preached, the separated approach versus the social approach, are both right. They were both of God, one the forerunner and the other the Messiah, the Son of God (see note, pt.2—Mt.11:16–19 and Deeper Study # 1—Mt.11:19 for a different understanding of this verse).

Fourth, the wise (children of wisdom) are the non-critical, the saved who know that God sent both John (the separated) and Jesus (the Messiah). Very simply, the wise are the few who accept the ministry of both John and Jesus, both of whom fulfilled the *prophetic Word of God*.

> And because of him you are in Christ Jesus, who became to us wisdom from God, righteousness and sanctification and redemption. (1 Co.1:30; see 1 Co.1:24)

> In whom are hidden all the treasures of wisdom and knowledge. (Col.2:3; see Is.11:2)

> And he said to man, "Behold, the fear of the Lord, that is wisdom, and to turn away from evil is understanding." (Jb.28:28; see Ho.14:9)

Q. Jesus Contrasts the Attitudes of the Repentant and the Self-Righteous, 7:36–50

1. **The setting: Simon, a Pharisee, invited Jesus to dinner, and Jesus accepted**

2. **The attitude of the repentant: A female prostitute**
   a. She sensed a desperate need

   b. She approached the Lord openly, despite all
   c. She surrendered to the Lord in utter humility
   d. She loved much, giving her most precious possession

3. **The attitude of the self-righteous: A religionist**
   a. He was a considerate man, but self-righteous
   b. He considered himself better than others
   c. He sensed no need for forgiveness

4. **The two attitudes illustrated: The parable of two debtors**

   a. One debtor owed a man much, the other owed little

   b. The lender freely forgave both debtors
   c. The piercing question: Which debtor appreciated and loved the lender more?
   d. The begrudging answer: The debtor who owed more loved more

5. **The need of the self-righteous: To really see Jesus, who the repentant say He is**
   a. He is the one who deserves more than common courtesies
      1) A common vs. a worshipful respect
      2) A common vs. a humble greeting

      3) A common vs. a sacrificial gift

---

³⁶ One of the Pharisees asked him to eat with him, and he went into the Pharisee's house and reclined at table.

³⁷ And behold, a woman of the city, who was a sinner, when she learned that he was reclining at table in the Pharisee's house, brought an alabaster flask of ointment,

³⁸ and standing behind him at his feet, weeping, she began to wet his feet with her tears and wiped them with the hair of her head and kissed his feet and anointed them with the ointment.

³⁹ Now when the Pharisee who had invited him saw this, he said to himself, "If this man were a prophet, he would have known who and what sort of woman this is who is touching him, for she is a sinner."

⁴⁰ And Jesus answering said to him, "Simon, I have something to say to you." And he answered, "Say it, Teacher."

⁴¹ "A certain moneylender had two debtors. One owed five hundred denarii, and the other fifty.

⁴² When they could not pay, he cancelled the debt of both. Now which of them will love him more?"

⁴³ Simon answered, "The one, I suppose, for whom he cancelled the larger debt." And he said to him, "You have judged rightly."

⁴⁴ Then turning toward the woman he said to Simon, "Do you see this woman? I entered your house; you gave me no water for my feet, but she has wet my feet with her tears and wiped them with her hair.

⁴⁵ You gave me no kiss, but from the time I came in she has not ceased to kiss my feet.

⁴⁶ You did not anoint my head with oil, but she has anointed my feet with ointment.

⁴⁷ Therefore I tell you, her sins, which are many, are forgiven—for she loved much. But he who is forgiven little, loves little."

⁴⁸ And he said to her, "Your sins are forgiven."

⁴⁹ Then those who were at table with him began to say among themselves, "Who is this, who even forgives sins?"

⁵⁰ And he said to the woman, "Your faith has saved you; go in peace."

b. He is the one who has the power to forgive sins

c. He is the one whom people need to ask about

d. He is the one who saves the repentant

Division III

The Son of Man's Announced Mission and Public Ministry, 4:16–9:17

Q. Jesus Contrasts the Attitudes of the Repentant and the Self-Righteous, 7:36–50

7:36–50
Introduction

A beautiful, sacrificial act of gratitude shone a glaring light on the contrast between the attitudes of the repentant and the self-righteous who refused to repent. It needs to be studied carefully, for self-righteousness is a serious sin, one that is both common and condemning. This is, *Jesus Contrasts the Attitudes of the Repentant and the Self-Righteous, 7:36–50.*

1. The setting: Simon, a Pharisee, invited Jesus to dinner, and Jesus accepted (v.36).
2. The attitude of the repentant: A female prostitute (vv.37–38).
3. The attitude of the self-righteous: A religionist (v.39).
4. The two attitudes illustrated: The parable of two debtors (vv.40–43).
5. The need of the self-righteous: To really see Jesus, who the repentant say He is (vv.44–50).

1 The setting: Simon, a Pharisee, invited Jesus to dinner, and Jesus accepted.

7:36

One of the Pharisees, Simon, invited Jesus to his house for dinner, and Jesus accepted his invitation. However, Simon did not extend to Jesus the common courtesies usually shown to guests (vv.44–46). Bluntly stated, he was rude to the Lord. He was not even sure Jesus was a prophet, much

³⁶ One of the Pharisees asked him to eat with him, and he went into the Pharisee's house and reclined at table.

less the Messiah (v.39). Why then did he invite Jesus to his house? We do not know; nothing is said as to why. One speculation is that Simon enjoyed the company of popular public figures, and he had heard so much about Jesus that he wanted to meet and talk with Him on an informal basis. There is also the chance that, after hearing Jesus' convicting and condemning verdict against the Pharisees, he was under genuine conviction and wanted to learn more about—and from—Jesus. However, the way he intentionally treated Jesus favors the assumption that he, a Pharisee, had evil motives.

Jesus ate with both sinners and the religious—the Pharisees (Lu.5:29–30). No one was excluded from His attention or love, even when they lacked the common everyday courtesies and respect (vv.44–46). The Savior sought every person, regardless of who or what they were (Lu.19:10).

Simon was no doubt a wealthy man. The houses of the rich most often had an open courtyard, usually in the center of the house. Sometimes the host would allow the public to stand around in the courtyard and listen to the discussions, in particular when a rabbi or some popular public figure was the chief guest.

7:37-38

2 The attitude of the repentant: A female prostitute.

³⁷ And behold, a woman of the city, who was a sinner, when she learned that he was reclining at table in the Pharisee's house, brought an alabaster flask of ointment,

³⁸ and standing behind him at his feet, weeping, she began to wet his feet with her tears and wiped them with the hair of her head and kissed his feet and anointed them with the ointment.

After learning that Jesus was at Simon's house, an uninvited woman entered the courtyard. When she saw Jesus' unwashed feet, she showered the respect and courtesy on Him that His host had neglected. She washed the Lord's tired, dirty feet with her tears and anointed them with perfume—an extremely valuable commodity.

What made the scene even more dramatic was the fact that this woman was known to be a sinner, a prostitute. She demonstrated what all sinners have to do in coming to Jesus.

a. She sensed a desperate need (v.37).

The woman was well aware of her desperate need for Jesus' help. She was either convicted of her sin while hearing Jesus or else she had heard Him before and came under heavy conviction. His plea for men and women to repent and prepare for the kingdom of God pierced her heart. She knew she was a sinner: unclean, lost, condemned. The guilt and weight of her sin was more than she could bear. She ached for forgiveness and cleansing, for freedom and liberty.

b. She approached the Lord openly, despite all (v.38a).

The immoral woman knew that the public scorned and gossiped about her, and the so-called decent people wanted nothing to do with her. She knew that if she were recognized, the Pharisee might throw her out of the house, for he knew about her (v.39). But what would Jesus do—He who said, "Come to me all who labor and are heavy laden, and I will give you rest" (Mt.11:28)?

As she thought about the situation, her thinking turned into hope, and her hope into belief. Surely He who offered such an invitation would receive her. Before anyone could stop her, she rushed to Jesus and stood behind Him at His feet. (Remember, in the Ancient Middle East, people reclined to eat. They rested on their left arm facing each other around the table with their body and feet extending out away from the table.) Though she could probably think of many reasons why she should not put herself in such a vulnerable position, she entered the Pharisee's house anyway and approached Jesus.

c. She surrendered to the Lord in utter humility (v.38b).

Standing there a captive to her sin and shame, the repentant woman was overcome with conviction and emotion. She fell at Jesus' feet weeping—so broken that tears poured from her eyes. She unwound her hair and wiped and kissed Jesus' feet. Seldom has such love and devotion been shown Jesus.

Now note: there was only one thing that could make a prostitute enter a Pharisee's home— desperation. She was gripped with a sense of lostness, of helplessness, of urgency. The letting down of her hair (to wipe Jesus' feet) was forbidden of women in public. She must have been so desperate that she was totally oblivious to the onlookers. The point is, she was surrendering her heart and life to the Lord, begging Him to forgive her. She was so broken she was unable to speak, but Jesus knew her heart; words were not necessary (vv.47-48).

d. She loved much, giving her most precious possession (v.38c).

After bathing the Lord's feet with her tears, the woman anointed them with perfume she brought in an alabaster jar. Perfume was highly treasured by women of that day (see note—Mt.26:8-9). Apparently, by describing the perfume as he does, Luke emphasizes the perfume's monetary value and the great sacrifice she was making. It was probably the most costly possession she had, so she was giving it to her Lord. However, the more important detail is that she anointed her Lord; she anointed His feet in a supreme act of humility and love and surrender (see note—Lu.7:44-50).

THOUGHT 1. The person who comes to Christ must come with a broken and contrite heart. He receives those who are broken by the weight and guilt of their sin.

> **Come to me, all who labor and are heavy laden, and I will give you rest. (Mt.11:28)**

> **For we do not have a high priest who is unable to sympathize with our weaknesses, but one who in every respect has been tempted as we are, yet without sin. Let us then with confidence draw near to the throne of grace, that we may receive mercy and find grace to help in time of need. (He.4:15-16)**

> **The LORD is near to the brokenhearted and saves the crushed in spirit. (Ps.34:18)**

> **For thus says the One who is high and lifted up, who inhabits eternity, whose name is Holy: "I dwell in the high and holy place, and also with him who is of a contrite and lowly spirit, to revive the spirit of the lowly, and to revive the heart of the contrite." (Is.57:15)**

> **All these things my hand has made, and so all these things came to be, declares the LORD. But this is the one to whom I will look: he who is humble and contrite in spirit and trembles at my word. (Is.66:2)**

3 The attitude of the self-righteous.

7:39

Simon reacted to the sinful woman's act of worship with a typical Pharisee attitude. Sadly, his self-righteous attitude is prevalent among many pious believers today. His behavior reveals several tragic traits.

> [39] Now when the Pharisee who had invited him saw this, he said to himself, "If this man were a prophet, he would have known who and what sort of woman this is who is touching him, for she is a sinner."

a. He was a considerate man, but self-righteous.

Simon was unquestionably self-righteous, but he tried to be considerate. Note, he only thought these things; he would not say them publicly lest he embarrass his guests. Picture the pious Pharisee reclining at the table, puffed up with his feelings of superiority, yet remaining silent, thinking that by holding his tongue he was showing himself to be even more righteous.

b. He considered himself better than others.

Simon considered himself better than other people. He felt he was better than the sinful woman, so he would never allow her to touch *him*. He would keep his distance, ignore her, and have nothing to do with her. But note something else. He considered his judgment and knowledge, opinions and behavior, to be better than others. He expected others (Jesus) to judge and act as he did. He thought that if Jesus only knew who the woman was, then He would reject her.

THOUGHT 1. Many do live self-righteously. They feel that they live and act better than others. They feel and act superior because they have . . .

- a better house
- a better profession or job
- a better education
- a better religion
- a better child
- a better heritage
- a better income
- a better discipline
- a better position
- more ability
- more success
- more recognition
- better skills
- a better life

c. He sensed no need for forgiveness.

Simon sensed no need for forgiveness and repentance. He thought of himself as *good enough*. He felt his *religion* made him good enough. He was a Pharisee, a man who had given his life to practice religion. If anyone were ever *good enough,* he should have been—because of his devotion to his religion (see Deeper Study # 3—Ac.23:8).

In addition, he felt his *behavior* made him *good enough.* He was decent and moral, just and equitable, respected and highly esteemed. In his mind, not only was he moral, he would have nothing to do with anyone who was immoral. He had not and never would commit a sin that would be publicly condemned. Therefore, he felt as though he had done nothing for which he needed forgiveness.

> Not everyone who says to me, "Lord, Lord," will enter the kingdom of heaven, but the one who does the will of my Father who is in heaven. (Mt.7:21)

> And he said to them, "Well did Isaiah prophesy of you hypocrites, as it is written, 'This people honors me with their lips, but their heart is far from me.'" (Mk.7:6)

> Not that we dare to classify or compare ourselves with some of those who are commending themselves. But when they measure themselves by one another and compare themselves with one another, they are without understanding. (2 Co.10:12)

> They profess to know God, but they deny him by their works. They are detestable, disobedient, unfit for any good work. (Tit.1:16)

THOUGHT 1. Jesus captured the attitude of the Pharisees in a convicting parable:

> I tell you, this man went down to his house justified, rather than the other. For everyone who exalts himself will be humbled, but the one who humbles himself will be exalted. (Lu.18:14)

We need to look carefully in the mirror of God's Word as we read this parable. If we see ourselves at all in the attitude of the Pharisees, we should repent and pray for God's Spirit to transform us, humble us, and help us to remember that we are but sinners saved by God's grace.

> Little children, let us not love in word or talk but in deed and in truth. (1 Jn.3:18)

> Many a man proclaims his own steadfast love, but a faithful man who can find? (Pr.20:6)

> There are those who are clean in their own eyes but are not washed of their filth. (Pr.30:12)

7:40-43

⁴⁰ And Jesus answering said to him, "Simon, I have something to say to you." And he answered, "Say it, Teacher."
⁴¹ "A certain moneylender had two debtors. One owed five hundred denarii, and the other fifty.
⁴² When they could not pay, he cancelled the debt of both. Now which of them will love him more?"
⁴³ Simon answered, "The one, I suppose, for whom he cancelled the larger debt." And he said to him, "You have judged rightly."

4 The two attitudes illustrated: The parable of two debtors.

a. **One debtor owed a man much, the other owed little (v.41).**

b. **The lender freely forgave both debtors (v.42a).**

c. **The piercing question: Which debtor appreciated and loved the lender more (v.42b)?**

d. **The begrudging answer: The debtor who owed more loved more (v.43).**

Simon questioned silently whether Jesus was truly a prophet. However, Jesus was a prophet and much more—He was the Son of God; therefore, He not only knew the people who were sitting around Him, He knew their every thought. Simon had never said a word about Jesus' not knowing who the woman was nor about his own question about Jesus' being a prophet. Simon had only been thinking these thoughts within himself (v.39).

Jesus needed to address what Simon was thinking. *He announced* that He had something to say, indicating that He was about to say something critically important (v.40). Undivided attention was needed. Every self-righteous person needs to listen and listen closely.

To make His point, Jesus related a parable. The parable and its meaning are strikingly clear. A glance at the verses and points in our corresponding outline show this. Note how clearly the parable illustrates the grace of God in freely forgiving sin and giving salvation (see Ep.1:7; 2:8-9; 1 Jn.1:9; 2:1-2).

THOUGHT 1. Jesus is the Son of God; therefore, what a person thinks pales into insignificance when facing the one who knows all thoughts, including what a person really thinks and feels *within*. Jesus knows the truth of every thought and feeling within us. If we are self-righteous, Jesus knows it. If we are repentant, truly repentant, Jesus knows it. Nobody hides anything, no feeling, no thought from Him.

> And they prayed and said, "You, Lord, who know the hearts of all, show which one of these two you have chosen." (Ac.1:24)

> And I will strike her children dead. And all the churches will know that I am he who searches mind and heart, and I will give to each of you according to your works. (Re.2:23)

> And you, Solomon my son, know the God of your father and serve him with a whole heart and with a willing mind, for the Lord searches all hearts and understands every plan and thought. If you seek him, he will be found by you, but if you forsake him, he will cast you off forever. (1 Chr.28:9)

> If we had forgotten the name of our God or spread out our hands to a foreign god, would not God discover this? For he knows the secrets of the heart. (Ps.44:20–21)

5 The need of the self-righteous: To really see Jesus, who the repentant say He is.

Self-righteous people need to really see Jesus as those who are repentant see Him. Note what Jesus asked Simon, "Do you see this woman" (v.44)? The repentant woman had much to teach the self-righteous about Jesus. The repentant *really see* Jesus, *who* He really is and *as* He really is.

a. He is the one who deserves more than common courtesies (vv.44–46).

Simon had withheld the most common courtesies from Jesus. A host usually showed respect by providing water for guests to wash their dusty, sandaled feet (v.44). The kiss was the accepted greeting among friends (v.45), and oil was usually given for honored guests to refresh themselves after traveling under the hot sun (v.46). It was expensive, so it was usually reserved for honored guests. In stinging contrast to self-righteous Simon, the sinful woman had given Jesus all these courtesies *and more.*

44 Then turning toward the woman he said to Simon, "Do you see this woman? I entered your house; you gave me no water for my feet, but she has wet my feet with her tears and wiped them with her hair.
45 You gave me no kiss, but from the time I came in she has not ceased to kiss my feet.
46 You did not anoint my head with oil, but she has anointed my feet with ointment.
47 Therefore I tell you, her sins, which are many, are forgiven—for she loved much. But he who is forgiven little, loves little."
48 And he said to her, "Your sins are forgiven."
49 Then those who were at table with him began to say among themselves, "Who is this, who even forgives sins?"
50 And he said to the woman, "Your faith has saved you; go in peace."

Her heartfelt adoration of Jesus showed that He deserves *more* than the courtesies commonly shown to others.

First, Jesus deserved more than a common *respect* (water); He deserved a worshipful respect (v.44). He was seen as Lord and was respected as Lord by the repentant woman. He was the one who alone could meet the needs of the human heart; therefore, He was the one who was to be worshiped. The self-righteous needed to learn this.

Second, Jesus deserved more than a common *greeting*; He deserved a humble, broken-hearted greeting (v.45). The repentant woman approached Jesus with a sense of unworthiness and humility. She saw the worthiness of Jesus and grasped something of His awesomeness as the Son of God and as the sovereign Lord of the universe; therefore, He is the one to whom all people owe their allegiance, the one who alone has the power to forgive and accept the sinful. The repentant woman also saw Jesus as the one who alone could help her, the one who alone had the power to help, so she approached Jesus and greeted Him with a deep sense of humility and unworthiness. The self-righteous needed to learn this.

Third, Jesus deserved more than a common *gift*; He deserved a sacrificial gift (v.46). The repentant woman saw Jesus as the hope and Savior of one's life, so she gave Jesus her life, all she was and had. She surrendered her life and gave the most precious gift she had to anoint her Lord. The self-righteous needed to learn this.

b. He is the one who has the power to forgive sins (vv.47–48).

Not only is Jesus the one who deserves more than the courtesies commonly expressed to other people, He is the one who has the power to forgive sins. The woman's sins were many. Jesus did not overlook her sins, nor the seriousness of them. After all it was her sins and the sins of others that brought about *His humiliation*, His having to come to this sinful world and to die for the human race. However, He forgave her sins despite their awfulness. Every sinner should note this carefully.

Jesus' parable had clearly conveyed a powerful, piercing point: self-righteousness senses the need for *little* forgiveness; therefore, the self-righteous love little. The self-righteous Pharisee had only a formal, distant relationship with God. His relationship was cold, having only a small sense of sin and feeling only a slight need for forgiveness. It was enough to have Jesus present at his table (the table was about the only place many acknowledged Christ's presence). He wanted nothing more, no true relationship with Jesus as his Savior and Lord.

THOUGHT 1. The self-righteous approach to God . . .

- has only a little sense of sin; therefore senses only a little need for forgiveness
- is blinded to humanity's *state of sin*, to our true being, that of coming short of God's glory (Ro.3:23)
- has little sense of the need for special mercy and grace, is blinded to God's sovereign majesty and person
- has only a formal, distant relationship with God, has little personal relationship with God
- gives little honor to God, makes little sacrifice for God

THOUGHT 2. The fact of forgiveness, the very knowledge that millions have been truly forgiven, is proof that Christ is the Son of God, the one to whom people are to go for forgiveness. What Jesus said to the repentant woman is what He says to every repentant sinner who falls at His feet in repentance and faith: "Your sins are forgiven" (v.48).

> In him we have redemption through his blood, the forgiveness of our trespasses, according to the riches of his grace. (Ep.1:7)

> And you, who were dead in your trespasses and the uncircumcision of your flesh, God made alive together with him, having forgiven us all our trespasses. (Col.2:13)

> I am writing to you, little children, because your sins are forgiven for his name's sake. (1 Jn.2:12)

> I acknowledged my sin to you, and I did not cover my iniquity; I said, "I will confess my transgressions to the Lord," and you forgave the iniquity of my sin. Selah (Ps.32:5)

> I, I am he who blots out your transgressions for my own sake, and I will not remember your sins. (Is.43:25)

c. He is the one whom people need to ask about (v.49).

The other dinner guests muttered among themselves, wondering who this Man was, this Man who forgave sins. Their reaction makes a vital point: Jesus is the one whom people need to ask about. People need to know about the only one who has the authority to forgive sins.

THOUGHT 1. The very fact that Jesus claimed the right and power to forgive sins should cause every person to sit up, take notice, and ask, "Who is this?"

> God exalted him at his right hand as Leader and Savior, to give repentance to Israel and forgiveness of sins. (Ac.5:31)

> Let it be known to you therefore, brothers, that through this man forgiveness of sins is proclaimed to you. (Ac.13:38)

> But with you there is forgiveness, that you may be feared. (Ps.130:4)

> I have blotted out your transgressions like a cloud and your sins like mist; return to me, for I have redeemed you. (Is.44:22)

Let the wicked forsake his way, and the unrighteous man his thoughts; let him return to the LORD, that he may have compassion on him, and to our God, for he will abundantly pardon. (Is.55:7)

I will cleanse them from all the guilt of their sin against me, and I will forgive all the guilt of their sin and rebellion against me. (Je.33:8)

d. He is the one who saves the repentant (v.50).

Jesus assured the repentant woman that she had been saved, saved by His grace and through her *faith* (Ep.2:8). The woman believed Christ to be the Savior, the one who could forgive her sins. She came to Him with a heart that was genuinely repentant. Therefore, Christ saved her, just as He promises to save all repentant, believing sinners.

For God so loved the world, that he gave his only Son, that whoever believes in him should not perish but have eternal life. (Jn.3:16)

Jesus said to him, "I am the way, and the truth, and the life. No one comes to the Father except through me." (Jn.14:6)

Because, if you confess with your mouth that Jesus is Lord and believe in your heart that God raised him from the dead, you will be saved. For with the heart one believes and is justified, and with the mouth one confesses and is saved. (Ro.10:9–10)

The saying is trustworthy and deserving of full acceptance, that Christ Jesus came into the world to save sinners, of whom I am the foremost. (1 Ti.1:15)

CHAPTER 8

R. Jesus and the Women Who Supported Him, 8:1-3

1. **They supported Jesus' ministry of preaching**[DS1, 2]
   a. A ministry that reached out
   b. A ministry that was true to the gospel
2. **They supported Jesus' ministry of discipleship**
3. **They supported Jesus' ministry of salvation and deliverance**
   a. Mary Magdalene: A woman with a dark past[DS3]
   b. Joanna: A lady of the king's court[DS4]
   c. Susanna:[DS5] An unnoticed follower
   d. Many others: Unknown[DS6]

Soon afterward he went on through cities and villages, proclaiming and bringing the good news of the kingdom of God. And the twelve were with him,

2 and also some women who had been healed of evil spirits and infirmities: Mary, called Magdalene, from whom seven demons had gone out,
3 and Joanna, the wife of Chuza, Herod's household manager, and Susanna, and many others, who provided for them out of their means.

Division III

The Son of Man's Announced Mission and Public Ministry, 4:16–9:17

R. Jesus and the Women Who Supported Him, 8:1–3

8:1–3
Introduction

Ministry requires money. The work of the ministry itself involves expenses, and those who minister have the same needs every other person has. The Lord has ordained that those who proclaim the gospel should earn their living from the gospel (1 Co.9:13–14). Many people do not realize that Jesus received financial support for His ministry. As Luke reports in this passage, there were some women who supported Him and His disciples. Imagine the great blessing and privilege of giving financially to the personal ministry of Jesus Christ! Yet, when we give our tithes and offerings today, we have the same blessing and privilege. This is, *Jesus and the Women Who Supported Him, 8:1-3.*

1. They supported Jesus' ministry of preaching (v.1).
2. They supported Jesus' ministry of discipleship (v.1).
3. They supported Jesus' ministry of salvation and deliverance (vv.2–3).

8:1a

Soon afterward he went on through cities and villages, proclaiming and bringing the good news of the kingdom of God. And the twelve were with him,

1 They supported Jesus' ministry of preaching.

When these women supported Jesus, they supported a preaching ministry. Preaching was Jesus' business; it was what He came to do, His primary call and mission (see DEEPER STUDY # 1). Note the word *afterward* (en toi kathexēs, *en toy kah-thex-ace'*). The combination of Greek words translated *afterward* in this verse suggests events happening one after the other, an orderly, successive step or progression. The suggestion is that right after the banquet at Simon's home, Jesus went about His primary task of preaching and proclaiming the gospel. He did not linger in fellowship or in any other pursuits, no matter their legitimacy or enjoyment. He was faithful and consistent in preaching and proclaiming the gospel. The point is, the women supported a solid preaching ministry. They supported the Lord because He *preached* and was faithful to His call to preach.

a. A ministry that reached out.

These women supported a ministry that reached out to people. Jesus did not sit back and expect people to come to Him; He went through every city and village, preaching the gospel. He had an ache, a compassion for all, not willing that any should perish. He sought everyone *within His reach*. Note that He did not just seek the limelight of the cities. He went out into the villages of the countryside as well. He had been sent to preach, and He preached anywhere and everywhere He could reach. The whole thrust of His being was to reach people for God, to reach everyone He could. This was the kind of ministry the women supported.

> Even as the Son of Man came not to be served but to serve, and to give his life as a ransom for many. (Mt.20:28)

> The Spirit of the Lord is upon me, because he has anointed me to proclaim good news to the poor. He has sent me to proclaim liberty to the captives and recovering of sight to the blind, to set at liberty those who are oppressed, to proclaim the year of the Lord's favor. (Lu.4:18-19)

> But he said to them, "I must preach the good news of the kingdom of God to the other towns as well; for I was sent for this purpose." (Lu.4:43)

> For the Son of Man came to seek and to save the lost. (Lu.19:10)

> Then Pilate said to him, "So you are a king?" Jesus answered, "You say that I am a king. For this purpose I was born and for this purpose I have come into the world—to bear witness to the truth. Everyone who is of the truth listens to my voice." (Jn.18:37)

b. A ministry that was true to the gospel.

These women supported a ministry that was *true* to the gospel, a ministry that was *centered on* the gospel, a ministry that proclaimed the glad tidings of the kingdom of God (see DEEPER STUDY # 2; DEEPER STUDY # 3—Mt.19:23-24). Note that Jesus did not preach religion and ritual, ceremony and ordinance, laws and rules, works and deeds, mind and spirit, soul and body, thinking and reasoning. He touched on all these, but they were not His primary message. His message was the *good news*—the gospel of salvation.

> For God so loved the world, that he gave his only Son, that whoever believes in him should not perish but have eternal life. For God did not send his Son into the world to condemn the world, but in order that the world might be saved through him. Whoever believes in him is not condemned, but whoever does not believe is condemned already, because he has not believed in the name of the only Son of God. (Jn.3:16-18)

> Truly, truly, I say to you, whoever hears my word and believes him who sent me has eternal life. He does not come into judgment, but has passed from death to life. (Jn.5:24)

> And this is his commandment, that we believe in the name of his Son Jesus Christ and love one another, just as he has commanded us. (1 Jn.3:23)

DEEPER STUDY # 1

(8:1) **Preach—Preaching** (kerussŏn, *kay-roos'-own*): to proclaim, to publish, to be a herald, to preach the gospel as a herald.

DEEPER STUDY # 2

(8:1) **Bringing the Good News or Glad Tidings** (euaggelizomenos, *yoo-ang-ghel-iz-om'-en-os*): to preach glad tidings, to announce glad tidings, to declare good news, to proclaim the gospel of Jesus Christ. Note the Greek word, how it resembles the word *evangelism*. The English word *evangelism* comes from it. By the very nature of their work, preachers are evangelists. They are heralds who come in the name of the King, representing the King (see 2 Co.5:20). They proclaim *only* the message of the King; they have no message of their own. If and when they begin to proclaim their own message, they are no longer the representative or the spokesperson of the King.

8:1b

Soon afterward he went on through cities and villages, proclaiming and bringing the good news of the kingdom of God. And the twelve were with him,

2 They supported Jesus' ministry of discipleship.

When these generous women supported Jesus' ministry, they invested in a ministry of discipleship. Note that our Lord stressed the critical importance of discipleship by His own life and practice. Making disciples of others was what He was doing with the twelve, and it was soon to be the *Great Commission* to all His followers. The support of the women in this ministry was critical, for it is doubtful that the disciples could have given their *full time* to Jesus without financial support (see note—Mt.28:19-20 for detailed discussion).

> Go therefore and make disciples of all nations, baptizing them in the name of the Father and of the Son and of the Holy Spirit, teaching them to observe all that I have commanded you. And behold, I am with you always, to the end of the age. (Mt.28:19–20)

> Jesus said to them again, "Peace be with you. As the Father has sent me, even so I am sending you." (Jn.20:21)

> And what you have heard from me in the presence of many witnesses entrust to faithful men, who will be able to teach others also. (2 Ti.2:2)

8:2–3

[2] and also some women who had been healed of evil spirits and infirmities: Mary, called Magdalene, from whom seven demons had gone out, [3] and Joanna, the wife of Chuza, Herod's household manager, and Susanna, and many others, who provided for them out of their means.

3 They supported Jesus' ministry of salvation and deliverance.

a. **Mary Magdalene: A woman with a dark past (v.2).**

b. **Joanna: A lady of the king's court (v.3a).**

c. **Susanna: An unnoticed follower (v.3b).**

d. **Many others: Unknown (v.3c).**

These women supported Jesus' ministry out of devotion; they were grateful for what He had done for them. Each of them had been *reached and healed, saved and delivered* by Jesus. They had received a very special touch from Him, and as a result they provided for Jesus' and His disciples' needs from their own finances and possessions. Note the women who ministered to the Lord in this tangible, necessary way (see DEEPER STUDIES 3-6).

DEEPER STUDY # 3

(8:2) **Mary Magdalene:** she was delivered from seven demons (Lu.8:2), was one of Jesus' primary financial supporters (Lu.8:3), was among the women who courageously stood at the cross (Mt.27:55-56), and was one to whom Jesus appeared after His resurrection (Mt.28:1; Mk.16:1; Lu.24:10; see Jn.20:11).

DEEPER STUDY # 4

(8:3) **Joanna:** her husband, Herod's household manager or steward, was the court official who looked after the king's estate and financial interests. The very nature of his job shows that he had to be a most-trusted official and was no doubt compensated generously (see Lu.24:10).

DEEPER STUDY # 5

(8:3) **Susanna:** there is no other reference to Susanna. She represents the prominent disciple who is known by everyone but serves in a capacity that few ever notice. But note: she was such a devoted servant in giving, and her name is known.

DEEPER STUDY # 6

(8:3) **Many others:** these represent the unknown and quiet, but all-important, followers of the Lord. They serve completely in the background, never up front; therefore, they are totally unknown. But note: they are faithful and do serve, consistently and faithfully. Their names are not known on earth, but rest assured, they are well-known in heaven.

S. Jesus Teaches the Sure Fate of the Word: How People Receive the Word, 8:4–15

(Mt.13:1-23; Mk.4:1-20)

1. Crowds thronged Jesus—came from every town

2. The parable: A farmer sowed seed
 a. Some fell by the path
  1) Was trampled
  2) Was devoured
 b. Some fell upon rock
  1) Was withered and scorched
  2) Had no moisture or depth
 c. Some fell among thorns: Was choked out

 d. Some fell on good ground: Was fruitful

3. The reason Jesus spoke in parables

 a. To reveal the truth so that hearts might be opened
 b. To conceal the truth from closed minds

4. The interpretation
 a. The seed is the Word of God
 b. Some are by the path
  1) They hear the Word
  2) The devil snatches the Word away

 c. Some are on rock
  1) They hear the Word
  2) They have no root: When tempted, they fall away

 d. Some are among thorns
  1) They hear the Word
  2) They are choked out by materialism and pleasure

 e. Some are on rich soil
  1) They keep the Word
  2) They have honest and good hearts
  3) They bear fruit

⁴ And when a great crowd was gathering and people from town after town came to him, he said in a parable,
⁵ "A sower went out to sow his seed. And as he sowed, some fell along the path and was trampled underfoot, and the birds of the air devoured it.
⁶ And some fell on the rock, and as it grew up, it withered away, because it had no moisture.
⁷ And some fell among thorns, and the thorns grew up with it and choked it.
⁸ And some fell into good soil and grew and yielded a hundredfold." As he said these things, he called out, "He who has ears to hear, let him hear."
⁹ And when his disciples asked him what this parable meant,
¹⁰ he said, "To you it has been given to know the secrets of the kingdom of God, but for others they are in parables, so that 'seeing they may not see, and hearing they may not understand.'
¹¹ Now the parable is this: The seed is the word of God.
¹² The ones along the path are those who have heard; then the devil comes and takes away the word from their hearts, so that they may not believe and be saved.
¹³ And the ones on the rock are those who, when they hear the word, receive it with joy. But these have no root; they believe for a while, and in time of testing fall away.
¹⁴ And as for what fell among the thorns, they are those who hear, but as they go on their way they are choked by the cares and riches and pleasures of life, and their fruit does not mature.
¹⁵ As for that in the good soil, they are those who, hearing the word, hold it fast in an honest and good heart, and bear fruit with patience."

Division III

The Son of Man's Announced Mission and Public Ministry, 4:16–9:17

S. Jesus Teaches the Sure Fate of the Word: How People Receive the Word, 8:4–15
(Mt.13:1–23; Mk.4:1–20)

8:4–15
Introduction

Revival was sweeping the country. It began with John the Baptist and continued with Jesus, the Messiah. Multitudes of people were flocking to Jesus and being challenged to repent and follow God. The whole nation was charged with expectation, for the carpenter from Nazareth was not only claiming to be the Messiah, He was backing up His claims with a supernatural demonstration of power—the power of God. But as Scripture says, "the Lord knew all people" (Jn.2:25). He knew that many were not really sincere. They lacked . . .

- a real spirit of repentance
- a changed life
- an honest commitment

- a genuine faith
- a willingness to sacrifice
- a consistent obedience

Jesus knew that many were following Him not because they wanted to know God, not because they were genuine and sincere, but because of . . .

- family and friends
- fellowship with others
- social identification

- good feelings
- needs being met

The insincerity of so many, of course, cut to the heart of Jesus—but He still wanted to warn and reach as many people as possible. This is what the parable of the sower and the seed is all about. Jesus wanted people to know that *hearing* the Word of God is not enough. The hearing of the Word and supposed receiving of the Word must be accompanied by the bearing of fruit. Those who truly receive the Word, who genuinely repent and believe, will bear fruit.

Note how the parable speaks to every person. It is a *warning* to all hearers of the Word, especially to those who are not genuine followers of Christ, those who make a profession without truly believing (Ro.10:9–10). It gives great *assurance* to genuine believers: they will definitely bear fruit. It is a great encouragement to the preacher and teacher and to the lay witness. The seed we sow will bear *some* fruit; our labor for the Lord is not in vain (see outline and notes—Mt.13:1–9; Mk.4:1–20 for more discussion). This is, *Jesus Teaches the Sure Fate of the Word: How People Receive the Word*, 8:4–15.

1. Crowds thronged Jesus—came from every town (v.4).
2. The parable: A farmer sowed seed (vv.5–8).
3. The reason Jesus spoke in parables (vv.9–10).
4. The interpretation (vv.11–15).

1 Crowds thronged Jesus—came from every town.

Thousands were now flocking to Jesus from every town. We can estimate the numbers on the basis of His having fed five thousand *men* on one occasion. This does not count the women and children, each of which would outnumber the men by far. We are probably safe to say, as we can with every generation, that more women followed Jesus than men, and that most families were larger than the average family today. We can reasonably estimate the crowd as being well over twenty thousand.

⁴ And when a great crowd was gathering and people from town after town came to him, he said in a parable,

2 The parable: A farmer sowed seed.

Jesus drew His parable from something the people were well-acquainted with in everyday life. He spoke about a sower, a farmer, who went out to sow seed. In sharing the parable, Jesus named four distinct things that happened to the seed once it was sown.

8:5-8

⁵ "A sower went out to sow his seed. And as he sowed, some fell along the path and was trampled underfoot, and the birds of the air devoured it.
⁶ And some fell on the rock, and as it grew up, it withered away, because it had no moisture.
⁷ And some fell among thorns, and the thorns grew up with it and choked it.
⁸ And some fell into good soil and grew and yielded a hundredfold." As he said these things, he called out, "He who has ears to hear, let him hear."

a. **Some fell by the path (v.5).**
Some seed fell by the wayside, off to the side, out of the field upon the walking paths and roads. The paths and roads, of course, were trodden down and the soil was hard; therefore, the seed just lay on top and the birds came and devoured it.

b. **Some fell upon rock (v.6).**
Some seed fell upon rock, that is, a large layer of rock right beneath the surface dirt. This seed, of course, grew quickly because water collected on the rock right after a rain. But it soon withered away because the water rapidly evaporated, leaving nothing but dry soil. Consequently, the sun scorched the young plant.

c. **Some fell among thorns: Was choked out (v.7).**
Some seed fell among thorns. This seed sprouted, but the plants were soon choked to death by thorns.

d. **Some fell on good ground: Was fruitful (v.8).**
Other seed fell on good ground. This seed sprang up, established deep roots, and was very fruitful, bearing a hundredfold.

Immediately upon finishing the parable, Jesus *called out* or *cried* (Gk. ephonei, *eh-phon'-ay*) with a loud shout: "He who has ears to hear, let him hear." The Lord stressed the importance of understanding and heeding the parable.

THOUGHT 1. Note: the farmer did go out, and he did sow. How many *do not* go out? Of those who do, how many really sow the seed of the Word? It is so easy for the minister and believer . . .

- to sit in the comfort of the home or office and rest and work administratively instead of going out and sowing the seed of the gospel
- to visit and care for the flock in their needs instead of going out into the fields to sow

> Go therefore and make disciples of all nations, baptizing them in the name of the Father and of the Son and of the Holy Spirit, teaching them to observe all that I have commanded you. And behold, I am with you always, to the end of the age. (Mt.28:19–20)

> And he said to them, "Go into all the world and proclaim the gospel to the whole creation." (Mk.16:15)

> And when Paul had seen the vision, immediately we sought to go on into Macedonia, concluding that God had called us to preach the gospel to them. (Ac.16:10)

> But the Lord said to me, "Do not say, 'I am only a youth'; for to all to whom I send you, you shall go, and whatever I command you, you shall speak." (Je.1:7)

8:9-10

⁹ And when his disciples asked him what this parable meant,
¹⁰ he said, "To you it has been given to know the secrets of the kingdom of God, but for others they are in parables, so that 'seeing they may not see, and hearing they may not understand.'"

3 The reason Jesus spoke in parables.

Later, when Jesus and the disciples were all alone, the disciples asked Him to explain the parable (v.9). But Jesus used the occasion, first, to explain why He was now beginning to teach by parables. Up until now He had been teaching by direct statement and clear illustration, using few parables. But from this point forward, His primary method would be the parable. Why? Jesus gave two reasons.

a. To reveal the truth so that hearts might be opened (v.10a).

Jesus wanted people with *open hearts*, those who were truly seeking God, to learn all they could about the *secrets* or *mysteries* of the kingdom of God. Simply stated, people with open hearts were sincerely seeking truth. Parables required considerable thought among listeners in order for them to grasp the meaning. People who really sought after God would seek, strive, think, and ask until they found the meaning of the parable. And then they would chew on the meaning, drawing all the meaning they could out of the parable so that they could learn everything possible about the truth the Lord was teaching.

b. To conceal the truth from closed minds (v.10b).

Many who flocked to hear Jesus had *closed minds*. Closed minds are hardened and unwilling to consider the *secrets* or *mysteries* of the kingdom of God. Simply stated, closed minds have no real interest in truth, and, when exposed to the truth, their hearts are closed to it. Sitting there in the audience, closed-minded people heard and understood the words and the pictures that the words painted. But these people had little interest in searching into the hidden meaning (secrets or mysteries) of the parable. They found Jesus and His message interesting, for He was a very capable preacher, full of charisma and practical help for living. But when it came to committing one's life totally to His cause and commandments, as far as denying self completely and sacrificing all one is and has, it was not worth it to them. They were not willing to change their lives as Jesus commanded so they were certainly not willing to take the time or effort required to search out the meaning of the parable. Jesus actually said that He wanted the meaning hidden from the closed minded.

Note something else as well. The closed-minded, hardhearted, and carnal often *react* to the truth (instead of learning from it) when the truth points a finger at them and their wrong thinking and behavior (see outline and notes—Mt.13:10-17 for a full outline on why Jesus spoke in parables).

THOUGHT 1. What Christ said about seeking the truth is especially true of those who already know God personally. However, it is also true of the crowd, of any who are genuine in their search for God but have not yet found Him. Christ longs to reach any who are truly seeking Him. The parable is an excellent method to stir interest and curiosity among people. Of course, if people are sincere in knowing *the truth*, they will search out the meaning (truth), no matter how much time and effort are required.

> If anyone's will is to do God's will, he will know whether the teaching is from God or whether I am speaking on my own authority. (Jn.7:17)

> Having the eyes of your hearts enlightened, that you may know what is the hope to which he has called you, what are the riches of his glorious inheritance in the saints. (Ep.1:18)

> Therefore do not be foolish, but understand what the will of the Lord is. (Ep.5:17)

> Blessed is the one who finds wisdom, and the one who gets understanding. (Pr.3:13)

> And he said, "Go, and say to this people: 'Keep on hearing, but do not understand; keep on seeing, but do not perceive.' Make the heart of this people dull, and their ears heavy, and blind their eyes; lest they see with their eyes, and hear with their ears, and understand with their hearts, and turn and be healed." (Is.6:9-10)

4 The interpretation.

Jesus proceeded to give His disciples the interpretation of the parable. He explained that the sower represents all who sow the Word into people's hearts and minds (Mk.4:14). This would include the Lord Jesus Christ and His servants who obey His Great Commission (Mt.28:18-20; Mk.16:15). Whether ministers or laypeople, we who sow the seed of the Word are "God's fellow workers" (1 Co.3:9).

8:11-15

¹¹ "Now the parable is this: The seed is the word of God.

¹² The ones along the path are those who have heard; then the devil comes and takes away the word from their hearts, so that they may not believe and be saved.

¹³ And the ones on the rock are those who, when they hear the word, receive it with joy. But these have no root; they believe for a while, and in time of testing fall away.

¹⁴ And as for what fell among the thorns, they are those who hear, but as they go on their way they are choked by the cares and riches and pleasures of life, and their fruit does not mature.

¹⁵ As for that in the good soil, they are those who, hearing the word, hold it fast in an honest and good heart, and bear fruit with patience."

a. The seed is the Word of God (v.11).

The seed is the Word of God. It is called the "imperishable" or "incorruptible seed" (1 Pe.1:23), and "the Word of the truth, the gospel which . . . is bearing fruit" (Col.1:5-6).

The ground upon which the seed is sown is the heart of the hearer. Jesus gave two significant truths about the ground:

➤ There are different ways to hear and receive the Word (seed).

➤ The fate of the Word, how well it grows, depends on the hearer.

THOUGHT 1. The success of the seed depends on one thing alone; the condition of the soil (heart) to receive the seed (Word). If the ground (heart) is soft and rich, being full of the right minerals (spiritual qualities) and cleared of all junk and brush, plowed and turned over, then it is ready to receive the seed.

> They are darkened in their understanding, alienated from the life of God because of the ignorance that is in them, due to their hardness of heart. (Ep.4:18)

> Take care, brothers, lest there be in any of you an evil, unbelieving heart, leading you to fall away from the living God. (He.3:12)

> Oh that they had such a heart as this always, to fear me and to keep all my commandments, that it might go well with them and with their descendants forever! (De.5:29)

> And I will give them one heart, and a new spirit I will put within them. I will remove the heart of stone from their flesh and give them a heart of flesh. (Ezk.11:19)

b. Some are by the path (v.12).

Those along the path or by the wayside do hear the Word of God. They are present, but they are off to the side, out of the way, not involved. They may even respect the message and the one sharing the Word with them. However, they let their minds wander and think little and involve themselves even less. They pay little attention to the warnings and promises of the Word.

Note what happens. Before such a person believes, the devil comes and snatches the Word away. It is taken from the person; the person never applies the Word to his or her life, never lets the Word of God sink into their hearts and minds (see Judas Iscariot, and see Herod who enjoyed listening to John the Baptist, Mk.6:20).

> For this people's heart has grown dull, and with their ears they can barely hear, and their eyes they have closed; lest they should see with their eyes and hear with their ears and understand with their heart and turn, and I would heal them. (Ac.28:27)

> But because of your hard and impenitent heart you are storing up wrath for yourself on the day of wrath when God's righteous judgment will be revealed. (Ro.2:5)

> But exhort one another every day, as long as it is called "today," that none of you may be hardened by the deceitfulness of sin. (He.3:13)

> Blessed is the one who fears the LORD always, but whoever hardens his heart will fall into calamity. (Pr.28:14)

> He who is often reproved, yet stiffens his neck, will suddenly be broken beyond healing. (Pr.29:1)

c. Some are on rock (v.13).

Some seed falls on rocky ground. This image speaks of those who hear the Word and become excited over it. They receive the Word, profess belief in Christ, and make a profession of faith before the world. But they fail to count the cost, to consider the commitment, the self-denial, the sacrifice, the study, the learning, the hours and effort required. They do not apply themselves to *learn Christ*; therefore, they do not become rooted and grounded in the Word. They are only superficial believers.

Note what happens: when trials and temptations come, they fall away. Their profession is scorched and consumed, burned up by the heat of the trial and temptation (see John Mark who at first failed to endure [Ac.13:13] and the men who discovered that following Christ cost too much [Lu.9:57–62]).

> But the one who hears and does not do them is like a man who built a house on the ground without a foundation. When the stream broke against it, immediately it fell, and the ruin of that house was great. (Lu.6:49)

> Jesus said to him, "No one who puts his hand to the plow and looks back is fit for the kingdom of God." (Lu.9:62)

> But now that you have come to know God, or rather to be known by God, how can you turn back again to the weak and worthless elementary principles of the world, whose slaves you want to be once more? (Ga.4:9)

> But my righteous one shall live by faith, and if he shrinks back, my soul has no pleasure in him. (He.10:38)

> For if, after they have escaped the defilements of the world through the knowledge of our Lord and Savior Jesus Christ, they are again entangled in them and overcome, the last state has become worse for them than the first. For it would have been better for them never to have known the way of righteousness than after knowing it to turn back from the holy commandment delivered to them. What the true proverb says has happened to them: "The dog returns to its own vomit, and the sow, after washing herself, returns to wallow in the mire." (2 Pe.2:20–22)

> But I have this against you, that you have abandoned the love you had at first. Remember therefore from where you have fallen; repent, and do the works you did at first. If not, I will come to you and remove your lampstand from its place, unless you repent. (Re.2:4–5)

d. Some are among thorns (v.14).

Some seed falls among thorns. This illustration speaks of people whose hearts are consumed by the love of this world and the things of this world. They receive the Word and *honestly try* (profess) to live for Christ. Christ and His followers and the church and its activities appeal to them. So they join right in, even professing Christ as they go about their daily affairs. But there is one problem: the thorns or worldliness. They are unwilling to cut completely loose from the world, unwilling to separate themselves from the world and worldly people (2 Co.6:17–18). They lead double lives, trying to live for Christ and yet still fit in with the world. They keep right on growing in the midst of the thorns, giving their minds and attention to the *cares* and *riches* and *pleasures* of this world.

Note what happens: they bear fruit. Fruit does appear, but it never ripens; it is never able to be plucked. The thorns choke the life out of it. It never lives to be used (see account of the rich young ruler [Lu.18:18f], Ananias and Sapphira [Ac.5:1f], and Demas [2 Ti.4:10]).

THOUGHT 1. Note the three types of thorns that choke the spiritual life out of people and the fruit they bear.

1) The cares of this life

> Therefore I tell you, do not be anxious about your life, what you will eat or what you will drink, nor about your body, what you will put on. Is not life more than food, and the body more than clothing? (Mt.6:25)

> But watch yourselves lest your hearts be weighed down with dissipation and drunkenness and cares of this life, and that day come upon you suddenly like a trap. (Lu.21:34)

> Do not be anxious about anything, but in everything by prayer and supplication with thanksgiving let your requests be made known to God. (Ph.4:6)

Casting all your anxieties on him, because he cares for you. (1 Pe.5:7)

It is in vain that you rise up early and go late to rest, eating the bread of anxious toil; for he gives to his beloved sleep. (Ps.127:2)

2) The riches of this life

And Jesus said to his disciples, "Truly, I say to you, only with difficulty will a rich person enter the kingdom of heaven." (Mt.19:23)

For we brought nothing into the world, and we cannot take anything out of the world. . . . But those who desire to be rich fall into temptation, into a snare, into many senseless and harmful desires that plunge people into ruin and destruction. (1 Ti.6:7, 9)

Your gold and silver have corroded, and their corrosion will be evidence against you and will eat your flesh like fire. You have laid up treasure in the last days. (Jas.5:3)

And when your herds and flocks multiply and your silver and gold is multiplied and all that you have is multiplied, then your heart be lifted up, and you forget the LORD your God, who brought you out of the land of Egypt, out of the house of slavery. (De.8:13–14)

Like the partridge that gathers a brood that she did not hatch, so is he who gets riches but not by justice; in the midst of his days they will leave him, and at his end he will be a fool. (Je.17:11)

3) The pleasures of this life

And I will say to my soul, "Soul, you have ample goods laid up for many years; relax, eat, drink, be merry." (Lu.12:19)

But she who is self-indulgent is dead even while she lives. (1 Ti.5:6)

But understand this, that in the last days there will come times of difficulty. For people will be lovers of self, lovers of money, proud, arrogant, abusive, disobedient to their parents, ungrateful, unholy, treacherous, reckless, swollen with conceit, lovers of pleasure rather than lovers of God. (2 Ti.3:1–2, 4)

For we ourselves were once foolish, disobedient, led astray, slaves to various passions and pleasures, passing our days in malice and envy, hated by others and hating one another. (Tit.3:3)

You have lived on the earth in luxury and in self-indulgence. You have fattened your hearts in a day of slaughter. (Jas.5:5)

Now therefore hear this, you lover of pleasures, who sit securely, who say in your heart, "I am, and there is no one besides me; I shall not sit as a widow or know the loss of children": These two things shall come to you in a moment, in one day; the loss of children and widowhood shall come upon you in full measure, in spite of your many sorceries and the great power of your enchantments. (Is.47:8–9)

e. Some are on rich soil (v.15).

Unlike the first three Jesus mentions, some seed falls on good ground. The good ground represents those who have "honest" or "noble and good hearts." Therefore, when they hear the Word, they hold it fast and bear fruit. Note what Jesus specifically says about them.

First, their hearts are *honest* or *noble* (Gk. kalē, *kah-lay'*). This word means fair and just. It has the idea of holding fast. These people are honest and fair; they are noble in listening and considering the Word. They honestly seek to learn and know the truth.

Now these Jews were more noble than those in Thessalonica; they received the word with all eagerness, examining the Scriptures daily to see if these things were so. (Ac.17:11)

And we also thank God constantly for this, that when you received the word of God, which you heard from us, you accepted it not as the word of men but as what it really is, the word of God, which is at work in you believers. (1 Th.2:13)

Second, their hearts are *good* (agathē, *ah-gah-thay'*), meaning devoted, committed, given over to the truth. Once they know the truth, they hold fast to it.

But thanks be to God, that you who were once slaves of sin have become obedient from the heart to the standard of teaching to which you were committed. (Ro.6:17)

Oh that they had such a heart as this always, to fear me and to keep all my commandments, that it might go well with them and with their descendants forever! (De.5:29)

> This day the Lord your God commands you to do these statutes and rules. You shall therefore be careful to do them with all your heart and with all your soul. (De.26:16)

> This Book of the Law shall not depart from your mouth, but you shall meditate on it day and night, so that you may be careful to do according to all that is written in it. For then you will make your way prosperous, and then you will have good success. (Jos.1:8)

Third, they hold the Word fast; they keep the Word. They do not let the devil snatch it, nor the trials and temptations of life scorch it, nor the cares and riches and pleasures of this life choke it out.

> Truly, truly, I say to you, if anyone keeps my word, he will never see death. (Jn.8:51)

> Jesus answered him, "If anyone loves me, he will keep my word, and my Father will love him, and we will come to him and make our home with him." (Jn.14:23)

> I have manifested your name to the people whom you gave me out of the world. Yours they were, and you gave them to me, and they have kept your word. (Jn.17:6)

> And by this we know that we have come to know him, if we keep his commandments. (1 Jn.2:3)

> I know your works. Behold, I have set before you an open door, which no one is able to shut. I know that you have but little power, and yet you have kept my word and have not denied my name. (Re.3:8)

Fourth, they bear fruit with *patience* (hupomonē, hoo-pom-on-ay')—endurance, perseverance, steadfastness in difficult circumstances. They endure and study, grow and serve more and more. They constantly water the plant and pluck the weeds and thorns, and they continue to do so until the fruit is fully grown and harvested and *taken home* to the Master of the house.

> I am the vine; you are the branches. Whoever abides in me and I in him, he it is that bears much fruit, for apart from me you can do nothing. (Jn.15:5)

> Filled with the fruit of righteousness that comes through Jesus Christ, to the glory and praise of God. (Ph.1:11)

> So as to walk in a manner worthy of the Lord, fully pleasing to him: bearing fruit in every good work and increasing in the knowledge of God. (Col.1:10)

> They are planted in the house of the Lord; they flourish in the courts of our God. They still bear fruit in old age; they are ever full of sap and green. (Ps.92:13–14)

> He who goes out weeping, bearing the seed for sowing, shall come home with shouts of joy, bringing his sheaves with him. (Ps.126:6)

T. Jesus Teaches Three Fundamental Principles of Life, 8:16–18

(Mt.5:15-16; 10:26-27; 13:12; Mk.4:21-23; Lu.11:33-36)

1. **A lamp (life) is for the purpose of giving light**[DS1]
   a. It has to be lit
   b. It is not to be covered
   c. It is to be conspicuous
   d. It is to be seen
2. **Secrecy is impossible: All things will be found out**

3. **Truth is very narrow**
   a. A person must listen carefully, discerning the truth
   b. The reason: Truth will be rewarded, but the *seemingly* true will be stripped away

16 "No one after lighting a lamp covers it with a jar or puts it under a bed, but puts it on a stand, so that those who enter may see the light.

17 For nothing is hidden that will not be made manifest, nor is anything secret that will not be known and come to light.
18 Take care then how you hear, for to the one who has, more will be given, and from the one who has not, even what he thinks that he has will be taken away."

Division III

The Son of Man's Announced Mission and Public Ministry, 4:16–9:17

T. Jesus Teaches Three Fundamental Principles of Life, 8:16–18

(Mt.5:15–16; 10:26–27; 13:12; Mk.4:21–23; Lu.11:33–36)

8:16–18
Introduction

We are saved for a purpose. In the previous passage, Jesus described that purpose as bearing fruit. The person who truly receives the Word—who genuinely believes and is truly born again—will bear fruit for the Lord. In this passage, Jesus describes that purpose as giving light. The genuine believer's life will be a light to others. The principles Jesus gave here speak clearly to all believers, both laypeople and ministers. This is, *Jesus Teaches Three Fundamental Principles of Life*, 8:16-18.
1. A lamp (life) is for the purpose of giving light (v.16).
2. Secrecy is impossible: All things will be found out (v.17).
3. Truth is very narrow (v.18).

8:16

16 "No one after lighting a lamp covers it with a jar or puts it under a bed, but puts it on a stand, so that those who enter may see the light."

1 A lamp (life) is for the purpose of giving light.

In Jesus' illustration, the lamp represents our lives. We do not purchase it or earn it. The lamp (life) is a gift from God. We have it, but we have to use it for it to be of any benefit. A lamp (representative of life) exists for the purpose of giving light. It can still be used for other purposes such as a beautiful decoration or ornament. When a lamp is merely a decoration, it serves a purpose, but it fails to fulfill its *primary* function, the very purpose for which it was made and formed: to give light.

a. It has to be lit.

The lamp needs to be lit. Until it is lit, it merely exists; it is not fulfilling its purpose. We are the ones who must take the initiative to have our candle lit. We have to come to Christ, the Light of the World, and receive the enlivening spark of His light. We have to reach out for the light that is Jesus Christ. Christ is the Light, but we have to put the lamp of our life up to the light of Christ in order to be lit (Jn.1:9; 8:12; 11:9–10; 12:36, 46; Ep.5:8).

b. It is not to be covered.

Once a lamp has been lit, *no one* covers it with a jar or puts it under a bed. To do so would be foolish. All the energy and effort as well as the purpose for lighting the lamp are wasted if it is hidden under a bed or covered. The lamp and its light are useless, of no purpose. Jesus' point is clear: just as the seed sown in good soil bears fruit (v.15), the lamp—person—who has been lit with the light of Christ—genuinely born again, born spiritually—will shine their light for God's glory and for the good of others (Mt.5:16).

> For whoever is ashamed of me and of my words in this adulterous and sinful generation, of him will the Son of Man also be ashamed when he comes in the glory of his Father with the holy angels. (Mk.8:38)

> For God gave us a spirit not of fear but of power and love and self-control. Therefore do not be ashamed of the testimony about our Lord, nor of me his prisoner, but share in suffering for the gospel by the power of God. (2 Ti.1:7–8)

c. It is to be conspicuous.

The lamp is to be conspicuous, placed high on a lampstand where it can be easily seen. Every genuine believer has had their lamp ignited; they have touched Christ, the Light of the World, and Christ has given them light. Therefore, they burn and give off light. The only question is, how brightly do they shine? Their light may be bright or dim, strong or weak, flickering or flaming, blinking or flooding, smoking or clear. Christ says it is foolish to have light and it not be displayed, openly giving off light.

> As it is my eager expectation and hope that I will not be at all ashamed, but that with full courage now as always Christ will be honored in my body, whether by life or by death. (Ph.1:20)

> Yet if anyone suffers as a Christian, let him not be ashamed, but let him glorify God in that name. (1 Pe.4:16)

> And now, little children, abide in him, so that when he appears we may have confidence and not shrink from him in shame at his coming. (1 Jn.2:28)

> Then I shall not be put to shame, having my eyes fixed on all your commandments. (Ps.119:6)

> But the Lord GOD helps me; therefore I have not been disgraced; therefore I have set my face like a flint, and I know that I shall not be put to shame. (Is.50:7)

d. It is to be seen.

The lamp is to be seen by all who enter. This is the critical point. This is the very purpose of the lamp, *to provide light*. And light does numerous things (see DEEPER STUDY # 1).

> You are the light of the world. A city set on a hill cannot be hidden. Nor do people light a lamp and put it under a basket, but on a stand, and it gives light to all in the house. In the same way, let your light shine before others, so that they may see your good works and give glory to your Father who is in heaven. (Mt.5:14–16)

> For we cannot but speak of what we have seen and heard. (Ac.4:20)

> That you may be blameless and innocent, children of God without blemish in the midst of a crooked and twisted generation, among whom you shine as lights in the world. (Ph.2:15)

> And your life will be brighter than the noonday; its darkness will be like the morning. (Jb.11:17)

> Come and hear, all you who fear God, and I will tell what he has done for my soul. (Ps.66:16)

(8:16) **Light—Purpose:** Christ said, "I am the Light of the world" (Jn.8:12; 9:5). Here He says His disciples are to be like Him—"the light of the world." Therefore, the disciples are to undergo a radical transformation. We are to *become like Christ* more and more and *to reflect the light* of Christ (2 Co.3:18; 4:6-7). Light is and does a number of things.

1. Light is clear and pure. It is clean, that is, good, right, and true (Ep.5:8f).
2. Light penetrates. It cuts through and eliminates darkness.
3. Light enlightens. It enlarges one's vision and knowledge of an area.
4. Light reveals. It opens up the truth of an area, a whole new world, and it clears the way so that a person can see the truth and the life (Jn.14:6).
5. Light guides (Jn.12:36, 46). It directs the way to go and leads along the right path.
6. Light strips away (Jn.3:19-20). It unclothes the darkness that blackens life.
7. Light defeats chaos (see Ge.1:2-3). It brings peace to the disturbance caused by walking in pitch darkness.
8. Light discriminates between the right way and the wrong way (see note—Ep.5:10; see 5:8-10).
9. Light warns. It warns of dangers that lie ahead in one's path.

8:17

[17] "For nothing is hidden that will not be made manifest, nor is anything secret that will not be known and come to light."

2 Secrecy is impossible: All things will be found out.

Jesus said that nothing can be truly hidden; it will be made manifest or revealed. Commentators have various opinions of what Jesus was talking about in this statement. The immediate context seems to suggest that Jesus was saying that a person who truly has the light of Jesus Christ cannot keep it hidden. A genuine believer cannot keep it secret; they cannot hide their light. They must let it shine before others. Just as the seed sown in good soil *will* bear fruit (v.15), the person whose lamp (life) has been ignited with the light of Christ *will* let it be known. It cannot be hidden; it will be evident.

So also good works are conspicuous, and even those that are not cannot remain hidden. (1 Ti.5:25)

By this it is evident who are the children of God, and who are the children of the devil: whoever does not practice righteousness is not of God, nor is the one who does not love his brother. (1 Jn.3:10)

There is also a practical application of what Jesus is saying here. Everything that people try to hide will be found out, uncovered. It is impossible to keep something secret forever. People try to hide things. They try to keep some things secret. Consider the following examples:

➤ They try to hide sin and shame. They sin in the dark and behind closed doors, when out and away from home and friends, or by keeping secret books or bank accounts.
➤ They try to hide possessions lest they have to give or spend more.
➤ They try to hide abilities and talents, lest they have to serve and use them. They prefer the ease and comfort of complacency and plenty instead of the rigors and sacrifice required to meet the needs of a suffering world.
➤ They try to hide the light and the truth they have come to know. They are lazy, complacent, embarrassed, apprehensive and fearful; or else they lack the vision, willingness, commitment, initiative, and endurance to set the light and truth out before other people. They just keep quiet within their own world, unwilling to sacrifice and deny themselves in order *to go* and share with those in darkness and ignorance.

People who hide things are deceived: they think they will never be found out. They think their secrets will be hid forever and never discovered . . .

- not by mom or dad
- not by friend or acquaintance
- not by preacher or God
- not by wife or children
- not by society or organization

Therefore, they feel they are safe with their secret. They feel bad consequences will never happen to them; suffering and punishment, bad and evil will never fall upon them. They will be able to keep their secret hid forever and escape punishment.

However, Christ said nothing—not a single thing—will be hid forever. Every secret thing will be revealed and opened up. The thing hidden is seen, if not by other people then by God, and it will be revealed. God will reveal the truth in the Day of Judgment if not before. The deceptions, the cloaks, the disguises, the secrets, the hidden things of all people will be stripped away and unveiled; then all will see (Ro.2:2, 6, 11, 16).

> **On that day when, according to my gospel, God judges the secrets of men by Christ Jesus. (Ro.2:16)**

> **Therefore do not pronounce judgment before the time, before the Lord comes, who will bring to light the things now hidden in darkness and will disclose the purposes of the heart. Then each one will receive his commendation from God. (1 Co.4:5)**

> **But if you will not do so, behold, you have sinned against the LORD, and be sure your sin will find you out. (Nu.32:23)**

> **For God will bring every deed into judgment, with every secret thing, whether good or evil. (Ec.12:14)**

> **I the LORD search the heart and test the mind, to give every man according to his ways, according to the fruit of his deeds. (Je.17:10)**

> **Can a man hide himself in secret places so that I cannot see him? declares the LORD. Do I not fill heaven and earth? declares the LORD. (Je.23:24)**

3 Truth is very narrow.

8:18

Jesus made the point that truth is very narrow. This verse is a severe warning. It is referring back to the seed or the Word of God and the hearers. Very simply, Christ warns that we must hear and use what we hear if we want to be given more from God. If we do not use what we hear, then what we have will be taken away.

> [18] "Take care then how you hear, for to the one who has, more will be given, and from the one who has not, even what he thinks that he has will be taken away."

a. **A person must listen carefully, discerning the truth.**
We must take heed *how* we hear. We can hear but hear wrongly. We can think and guess and suppose we know what we hear, but it is false and counterfeit and will be stripped away. Note that we must "take care" or "take heed," discern what we hear. We must make sure we have the truth (see DEEPER STUDY # 1—Jn.1:9; DEEPER STUDY # 1—8:32; DEEPER STUDY # 2—14:6).

b. **The reason: Truth will be rewarded, but the** *seemingly* **true will be stripped away**
The reason we need to guard how we hear is strikingly clear: the truth will be rewarded, but the *seemingly true* will be stripped away. If we use what we hear, we will be given more; if we do not use what we have, the truth we have received will be taken away. Those who *hear* the truth must *apply* and *practice* the truth. This is a serious warning, both to unbelievers and false believers—"the one who has not" but "thinks that he has." Jesus is referring to people who profess to be saved but never bear fruit nor shine their light. They merely "think" that they have salvation, but they do not truly have it. What they "think" they have will be taken away.

As an application, there is also a lesson here about stewardship. Consider the fact that seekers and achievers do receive and get more. The non-dreamer and complacent receive little and get less.

It is the law of nature. The early get and survive. As is often said, the early bird gets the worm; the late get little and suffer. This, of course, is a human law. People reward energy and effort, production and results. They threaten and often take away from the lazy and inactive. Those who labor and practice and are diligent and persistent will always see and hear and get. They are in a position to get more and more and to be given more and more. But the lazy and idle, the neglectful and unfaithful, will always lose.

All through life, a person either gains or loses. They seldom, if ever, stand still. It all depends on the dreams, the effort, and the energy they are willing to exert.

Most significantly, *it is the law of God.* God has ordained that we get what we give, that we sow what we reap. Both now and in eternity, we are either rewarded or judged according to our works.

> Blessed are those who hunger and thirst for righteousness, for they shall be satisfied. (Mt.5:6)

> But seek first the kingdom of God and his righteousness, and all these things will be added to you. (Mt.6:33)

> Ask, and it will be given to you; seek, and you will find; knock, and it will be opened to you. For everyone who asks receives, and the one who seeks finds, and to the one who knocks it will be opened. (Mt.7:7-8)

> One who is faithful in a very little is also faithful in much, and one who is dishonest in a very little is also dishonest in much. (Lu.16:10)

> The LORD your God will make you abundantly prosperous in all the work of your hand, in the fruit of your womb and in the fruit of your cattle and in the fruit of your ground. For the LORD will again take delight in prospering you, as he took delight in your fathers. (De.30:9)

THOUGHT 1. This verse is both a great encouragement and a realistic warning.

1) It is a great encouragement to the . . .
- faithful
- diligent
- steadfast
- committed
- determined
- consistent
- unwavering
- persistent
- hardworking
- obedient
- self-starter and finisher
- achiever

2) It is a realistic and understandable threat to the . . .
- lazy
- idle
- complacent
- inconsistent
- closed-minded
- indifferent
- unconcerned
- self-satisfied
- inactive
- negligent
- shiftless
- purposeless
- half-hearted
- preoccupied
- unfocused
- careless

> Do not be slothful in zeal, be fervent in spirit, serve the Lord. (Ro.12:11; see Mt.25:24-27)

> For even when we were with you, we would give you this command: If anyone is not willing to work, let him not eat. For we hear that some among you walk in idleness, not busy at work, but busybodies. Now such persons we command and encourage in the Lord Jesus Christ to do their work quietly and to earn their own living. (2 Th.3:10-12)

> And we desire each one of you to show the same earnestness to have the full assurance of hope until the end, so that you may not be sluggish, but imitators of those who through faith and patience inherit the promises. (He.6:11-12)

> Because you did not serve the LORD your God with joyfulness and gladness of heart, because of the abundance of all things, therefore you shall serve your enemies whom the LORD will send against you, in hunger and thirst, in nakedness, and lacking everything. And he will put a yoke of iron on your neck until he has destroyed you. (De.28:47-48)

> Go to the ant, O sluggard; consider her ways, and be wise. Without having any chief, officer, or ruler, she prepares her bread in summer and gathers her food in harvest. How long will you lie there, O sluggard? When will you arise from your sleep? A little sleep, a little slumber, a little folding of the hands to rest, and poverty will come upon you like a robber, and want like an armed man. (Pr.6:6-11)

> The soul of the sluggard craves and gets nothing, while the soul of the diligent is richly supplied. (Pr.13:4)

(Mt.12:46-50; Mk.3:31-35)

---

19 Then his mother and his brothers came to him, but they could not reach him because of the crowd.
20 And he was told, "Your mother and your brothers are standing outside, desiring to see you."
21 But he answered them, "My mother and my brothers are those who hear the word of God and do it."

1. **Jesus' family sought to see Him but were unable to get through the crowd**

2. **True kinship is not based upon biological relationships**
3. **True kinship is based upon hearing and obeying the Word of God**

Division III

The Son of Man's Announced Mission and Public Ministry, 4:16-9:17

U. Jesus Teaches the Basis of True Kinship, 8:19-21

(Mt.12:46-35; Mk.3:31-35)

8:19-21
Introduction

The immediate family is generally thought to be the closest bond on earth. Sometimes it is; sometimes it is not. It should always be very, very close. However, in this passage, Christ teaches that there is a closer tie than the family, the tie that binds Him and His followers together. This is, *Jesus Teaches the Basis of True Kinship,* 8:19-21 (see outline and notes—Mt.12:46-50; Mk.3:31-35 for more discussion).

1. Jesus' family sought to see Him but were unable to get through the crowd (vv.19-20).
2. True kinship is not based upon biological relationships (v.21).
3. True kinship is based upon hearing and obeying the Word of God (v.21).

1 Jesus' family sought to see Him but were unable to get through the crowd.

8:19-20

Jesus' family came to where He was ministering to see Him. However, they were not able to get to Him because of the crowd (v.19), so they sent word by someone else for Him to come outside to them (Mt.12:47; Mk.3:31). Apparently, they were too embarrassed for one of them to try to reach Him.

It is interesting to observe what Jesus' relatives were *not* doing. They were not making a social call. It was not a friendly visit, not family members visiting family members.

19 Then his mother and his brothers came to him, but they could not reach him because of the crowd.
20 And he was told, "Your mother and your brothers are standing outside, desiring to see you."

Jesus was preaching and holding a service, yet His family interrupted Him right in the middle of the service. However, Jesus did not stop preaching; He continued right on. In fact, He used the occasion to teach a great spiritual truth.

Nor were they visiting Jesus to hear Him preach or to learn from Him. This is known from the fact that His brothers did not believe in Him and the fact that the family did not enter the service. Note also that the family was late for the service; they arrived while He was already preaching.

Why, then, was Jesus' family seeking Him? Several facts need to be considered in answering the question.

First, when Jesus began His ministry, some of the family supported Him and followed His leadership. They went with Him and His disciples on one of His first evangelistic tours to Capernaum and remained with Him for a long time, apparently helping out in both practical and ministerial duties (Jn.2:12).

Second, the family witnessed two *unbelievable events* at the beginning of Jesus' ministry when He visited their hometown, Nazareth. They heard Jesus claim to be the Messiah, the very One who was the fulfillment of the Holy Scripture. Imagine the shock of hearing one's own brother claiming to be Messiah, the Savior of the world. Then they witnessed their own hometown neighbors reject and attempt to kill Jesus. They actually saw their closest neighbors and dearest friends become insanely violent against their brother. Again, imagine the shock and the fear for Jesus' welfare and the embarrassment as they walked among their friends throughout the coming days and weeks. It would be very difficult to live and face one's neighbors and community after such an incident (Lu.4:16-31).

Third, the family was under constant pressure from friends to bring Jesus home—friends who counted themselves trusted enough to advise the family. The friends thought Jesus was *insane* by going about making the claims He was making, claims which included being the Son of God. Apparently, the family at some point gave permission for some friends to go bring Jesus home (Mk.3:21).

Fourth, Jesus' brothers neither supported nor believed in Him. In fact, their disbelief eventually declined into ridicule. This is seen happening about six months before the crucifixion (Jn.7:5). As a point of interest, the brothers never believed in Him until after His resurrection.

What seems to have been happening was that Mary and the family were coming to take Jesus home. The brothers had become convinced that Jesus was either insane or else caught up in the frenzy and honor of the people, and Mary feared for His life and welfare. Acting out of a mother's love and concern, she wanted to be a responsible mother and bring Him home to help Him all she could (see notes—Mt.12:46-50; Mk.3:31-35).

8:21

21 But he answered them, "My mother and my brothers are those who hear the word of God and do it."

2 True kinship is not based upon biological relationships.

Picture the scene. Jesus was standing before the crowd preaching, and all of a sudden He was interrupted, being told that His mother and brothers were outside *desiring to see Him*. Of course, Jesus knew why they had come, and in this event He saw a unique opportunity to teach a profound truth, the truth that *true kinship* is not based on human relationships. There is a relationship that is greater than the biological family relationship.

THOUGHT 1. A true family, a true kinship does not exist just because some people have common blood and genetic traits. This is clearly seen in the pages of family histories every day. Too many families are in turmoil, divided and being torn apart. Too many families are in constant conflict ranging from mild verbal attacks to murderous assaults. Obviously, God does not intend it to be this way, but the sinful human nature is so depraved that many people hate and harm their blood relatives. There is . . .

- parent against child
- child against parent
- brother against brother
- sister against sister
- relative against relative
- husband against wife

But to all who did receive him, who believed in his name, he gave the right to become children of God, who were born, not of blood nor of the will of the flesh nor of the will of man, but of God. (Jn.1:12-13)

Since you have been born again, not of perishable seed but of imperishable, through the living and abiding word of God. (1 Pe.1:23)

3 True kinship is based upon hearing and obeying the Word of God.

Jesus made a shocking statement: His true family was those who heard and obeyed God's Word. True kinship is based on the Word of God—hearing it and doing it. The emphasis, of course, is on doing the Word of God. The person who is closest to God is the person who obeys God, who takes His Word seriously. Any honest person knows that the child who obeys is the child closest to his or her parent's heart.

> 21 But he answered them, "My mother and my brothers are those who hear the word of God and do it."

The deepest relationships in life are not determined by blood, but by hearts and minds being knit together. The deepest relationships are founded on common purposes and cares and behavior. However, Christian believers have something even beyond this: they have the very *Word of God Himself*. When the believer hears and obeys the Word, that is, the will of God, five things happen.

First, God takes the believer's heart and life and welds them together with the hearts and lives of other believers—spiritually and supernaturally. They become the adopted children of God; therefore, people who hear the Word of God and obey it are spiritually bound together in the family of God.

➢ Adoption by redemption

But to all who did receive him, who believed in his name, he gave the right to become children of God. (Jn.1:12)

For you did not receive the spirit of slavery to fall back into fear, but you have received the Spirit of adoption as sons, by whom we cry, "Abba! Father!" The Spirit himself bears witness with our spirit that we are children of God, and if children, then heirs—heirs of God and fellow heirs with Christ, provided we suffer with him in order that we may also be glorified with him. (Ro.8:15–17)

But when the fullness of time had come, God sent forth his Son, born of woman, born under the law, to redeem those who were under the law, so that we might receive adoption as sons. And because you are sons, God has sent the Spirit of his Son into our hearts, crying, "Abba! Father!" (Ga.4:4–6)

For through him we both have access in one Spirit to the Father. So then you are no longer strangers and aliens, but you are fellow citizens with the saints and members of the household of God. (Ep.2:18–19)

➢ Adoption by separation

Therefore go out from their midst, and be separate from them, says the Lord, and touch no unclean thing; then I will welcome you, and I will be a father to you, and you shall be sons and daughters to me, says the Lord Almighty. (2 Co.6:17–18)

For he who sanctifies and those who are sanctified all have one source. That is why he is not ashamed to call them brothers. (He.2:11)

For you are a people holy to the LORD your God, and the LORD has chosen you to be a people for his treasured possession, out of all the peoples who are on the face of the earth. (De.14:2)

Second, believers become a people who search God's Word out, absorb it into their lives, and obey it. His Word becomes their life and behavior. Believers obey the three basic commandments:

➢ The commandment of God

And this is his commandment, that we believe in the name of his Son Jesus Christ and love one another, just as he has commanded us. (1 Jn.3:23)

➢ The commandment of Christ

Truly, truly, I say to you, whoever hears my word and believes him who sent me has eternal life. He does not come into judgment, but has passed from death to life. (Jn.5:24)

➢ The greatest commandment

"Teacher, which is the great commandment in the Law?" And he said to him, "You shall love the Lord your God with all your heart and with all your soul and with all your mind. This is the great and first commandment. And a second is like it: You shall love your neighbor as yourself. On these two commandments depend all the Law and the Prophets." (Mt.22:36–40)

Third, believers live obediently in a very special relationship to God and Christ.

Whoever has my commandments and keeps them, he it is who loves me. And he who loves me will be loved by my Father, and I will love him and manifest myself to him. (Jn.14:21)

> Like newborn infants, long for the pure spiritual milk, that by it you may grow up into salvation— if indeed you have tasted that the Lord is good. (1 Pe.2:2-3)

Fourth, believers act together and live together in *fellowship* within the church and society. They are knitted together by God's Word and God's true family (see DEEPER STUDY # 3—Ac.2:42 for more discussion).

> And they devoted themselves to the apostles' teaching and the fellowship, to the breaking of bread and the prayers. (Ac.2:42)

> So we, though many, are one body in Christ, and individually members one of another. (Ro.12:5)

> Because there is one bread, we who are many are one body, for we all partake of the one bread. (1 Co.10:17)

> For just as the body is one and has many members, and all the members of the body, though many, are one body, so it is with Christ. For in one Spirit we were all baptized into one body—Jews or Greeks, slaves or free—and all were made to drink of one Spirit. (1 Co.12:12-13)

> Now you are the body of Christ and individually members of it. (1 Co.12:27)

> Until we all attain to the unity of the faith and of the knowledge of the Son of God, to mature manhood, to the measure of the stature of the fullness of Christ. (Ep.4:13)

Fifth, believers become God's new community, new society, new nation of people. They become His church, His new creation—spiritually and supernaturally born again—who comprise the true family of God (see DEEPER STUDY # 8—Mt.21:43; note—Mk.3:34-35; DEEPER STUDY # 1—Jn.4:22; notes—Ep.2:11-18; pt.4—Ep.2:14-15; 2:15; 4:17-19; see 1 Pe.2:9-10; Re.21:1f for discussion).

> For through him we both have access in one Spirit to the Father. So then you are no longer strangers and aliens, but you are fellow citizens with the saints and members of the household of God, built on the foundation of the apostles and prophets, Christ Jesus himself being the cornerstone, in whom the whole structure, being joined together, grows into a holy temple in the Lord. In him you also are being built together into a dwelling place for God by the Spirit. (Ep.2:18-22)

(Mt.8:23-27; Mk.4:35-41)

²² One day he got into a boat with his disciples, and he said to them, "Let us go across to the other side of the lake." So they set out,

²³ and as they sailed he fell asleep. And a windstorm came down on the lake, and they were filling with water and were in danger.

²⁴ And they went and woke him, saying, "Master, Master, we are perishing!" And he awoke and rebuked the wind and the raging waves, and they ceased, and there was a calm.

²⁵ He said to them, "Where is your faith?" And they were afraid, and they marveled, saying to one another, "Who then is this, that he commands even winds and water, and they obey him?"

1. **Jesus' humanity: He was definitely a man**
   a. He needed and requested others' help

   b. He became tired and slept
2. **Jesus' confidence in His men: He entrusted His life to them**

3. **Jesus' power and sovereignty: He was definitely God**
   a. The disciples despaired
   b. Jesus calmed the storm

4. **Jesus' faith in God**
   a. He questioned the disciples' faith
   b. He stirred the disciples to question who He was

Division III

The Son of Man's Announced Mission and Public Ministry, 4:16–9:17

V. Jesus Calms a Storm: Jesus' Deity and Sovereignty, 8:22–25

(Mt.8:23–27; Mk.4:35–41)

8:22-25
Introduction

Jesus did not merely claim to be God; He *demonstrated* the fact. Our Lord's calming of the storm is a clear demonstration of His deity and sovereignty. It also displays something else: the sovereign power of Christ to calm the storms that arise in our lives. This is, *Jesus Calms a Storm: Jesus' Deity and Sovereignty,* 8:22-25.

1. Jesus' humanity: He was definitely a man (vv.22-23).
2. Jesus' confidence in His men: He entrusted His life to them (v.23).
3. Jesus' power and sovereignty: He was definitely God (v.24).
4. Jesus' faith in God (v.25).

1 Jesus' humanity: He was definitely a man.

When studying Jesus' deity, it helps to see His humanity, the fact that He was fully man. Seeing Jesus as man helps tremendously in understanding God, for Jesus' humanity highlights God even more.

First, Christ's humanity, His having to suffer through life as a man, shows us the great love of God. In Christ, God identifies

²² One day he got into a boat with his disciples, and he said to them, "Let us go across to the other side of the lake." So they set out,

²³ and as they sailed he fell asleep. And a windstorm came down on the lake, and they were filling with water and were in danger.

with the human race, and He identifies fully in every way and in everything. He knows how we feel and suffer because He was fully human. He knows all the trials and experiences and routines of day-to-day life; therefore, He is able to save us from the depths to the uttermost (He.7:25).

> For surely it is not angels that he helps, but he helps the offspring of Abraham. Therefore he had to be made like his brothers in every respect, so that he might become a merciful and faithful high priest in the service of God, to make propitiation for the sins of the people. For because he himself has suffered when tempted, he is able to help those who are being tempted. (He.2:16-18)

> For we do not have a high priest who is unable to sympathize with our weaknesses, but one who in every respect has been tempted as we are, yet without sin. Let us then with confidence draw near to the throne of grace, that we may receive mercy and find grace to help in time of need. (He.4:15-16)

Second, Christ's humanity shows us the great power of God. It shows God's power to actually become a man, to bring about the Incarnation. Standing before us as flesh and blood, Jesus Christ is a powerful demonstration of God's great sovereignty. He can do anything, even become a man. By partaking of flesh and blood, Jesus Christ shows the enormous power (sovereignty) of God.

> Now the birth of Jesus Christ took place in this way. When his mother Mary had been betrothed to Joseph, before they came together she was found to be with child from the Holy Spirit. And her husband Joseph, being a just man and unwilling to put her to shame, resolved to divorce her quietly. But as he considered these things, behold, an angel of the Lord appeared to him in a dream, saying, "Joseph, son of David, do not fear to take Mary as your wife, for that which is conceived in her is from the Holy Spirit. She will bear a son, and you shall call his name Jesus, for he will save his people from their sins." All this took place to fulfill what the Lord had spoken by the prophet: "Behold, the virgin shall conceive and bear a son, and they shall call his name Immanuel" (which means, God with us). (Mt.1:18-23)

> And the Word became flesh and dwelt among us, and we have seen his glory, glory as of the only Son from the Father, full of grace and truth. (Jn.1:14)

> Paul, a servant of Christ Jesus, called to be an apostle, set apart for the gospel of God, which he promised beforehand through his prophets in the holy Scriptures, concerning his Son, who was descended from David according to the flesh and was declared to be the Son of God in power according to the Spirit of holiness by his resurrection from the dead, Jesus Christ our Lord. (Ro.1:1-4)

> For God has done what the law, weakened by the flesh, could not do. By sending his own Son in the likeness of sinful flesh and for sin, he condemned sin in the flesh. (Ro.8:3)

> But emptied himself, by taking the form of a servant, being born in the likeness of men. (Ph.2:7)

> Great indeed, we confess, is the mystery of godliness: He was manifested in the flesh, vindicated by the Spirit, seen by angels, proclaimed among the nations, believed on in the world, taken up in glory. (1 Ti.3:16)

> Since therefore the children share in flesh and blood, he himself likewise partook of the same things, that through death he might destroy the one who has the power of death, that is, the devil. (He.2:14)

> By this you know the Spirit of God: every spirit that confesses that Jesus Christ has come in the flesh is from God. (1 Jn.4:2)

> For many deceivers have gone out into the world, those who do not confess the coming of Jesus Christ in the flesh. Such a one is the deceiver and the antichrist. (2 Jn.7)

> Therefore the Lord himself will give you a sign. Behold, the virgin shall conceive and bear a son, and shall call his name Immanuel (Is.7:14)

> For to us a child is born, to us a son is given; and the government shall be upon his shoulder, and his name shall be called Wonderful Counselor, Mighty God, Everlasting Father, Prince of Peace. (Is.9:6)

Christ's humanity shows God's power to control physical events. When Jesus the carpenter calms a storm and multiplies food, the power and sovereignty of God are stressed—stressed much more than when some mystical force or freak accident happens to intervene in physical events. When Jesus Christ stands and works a miracle before people's very eyes, *God's power is clearly seen*. It is visible, and there is no question about it. The presence and power, the very being and sovereignty of God, are acting for all to see; and *only a hard and foolish heart would deny it*.

The union of Jesus' deity and humanity is a profound truth. It is truly remarkable how both aspects of His person function simultaneously. As Christ's divine authority over the forces of nature is demonstrated, two evidences of His humanity are also displayed.

a. He needed and requested others' help (v.22).

First, Jesus needed and requested the disciples' help. He wanted to cross the lake. He could have walked around the lake; it was only a mile's journey, but He wanted to go by boat in order to get away from the crowd. The people had been pressing in on Him most of the day now, demanding and needing help. The *pressure and physical strain* had gotten to Jesus, wearing Him down. He needed time away from the crowds. If He walked, they would follow Him, so He requested the seamanship skills of the disciples to cross the lake. As they were sailing, He could get alone someplace on the boat, away even from the disciples.

b. He became tired and slept (v.23).

In addition, Jesus was tired and needed sleep. He was fully human, flesh and blood; therefore, He sometimes suffered exhaustion just as any hardworking person does. In fact, He was so exhausted that He slept through a raging storm (vv.23-24).

2 Jesus' confidence in His men: He entrusted His life to them.

8:23

Jesus demonstrated a very striking point: He had utter confidence in His men. He entrusted His life to them, which means He laid the completion of His mission into their hands. His enormous confidence is seen in the fact that He slept soundly, remaining asleep even through the fiercest storm. Even when the boat was filling with water and danger abounded, Jesus slept on.

> 23 and as they sailed he fell asleep. And a windstorm came down on the lake, and they were filling with water and were in danger.

Note that Jesus was present but not actively engaged in this particular task. The disciples had the natural skill to handle this work, so they were expected to do it themselves. And note: the task was difficult, demanding all the seafaring skills they had.

> **Therefore, having this ministry by the mercy of God, we do not lose heart. (2 Co.4:1)**
>
> **I thank him who has given me strength, Christ Jesus our Lord, because he judged me faithful, appointing me to his service. (1 Ti.1:12)**

3 Jesus' power and sovereignty: He was definitely God.

8:24

Along with Jesus' humanity, His power and sovereignty are clearly seen in this event. He was definitely God, just as He was definitely man.

> 24 And they went and woke him, saying, "Master, Master, we are perishing!" And he awoke and rebuked the wind and the raging waves, and they ceased, and there was a calm.

a. The disciples despaired.

The disciples came to Jesus crying out, "Master, Master, we are perishing!" They had no problem realizing and acknowledging their need, and they believed and were sure that Jesus could save them.

It was their cry—a desperate, fervent cry—that awakened the Lord and brought about the calm. He awakened to their need, and their danger and fear were relieved. The calm and stillness came because they cried in all earnestness.

b. Jesus calmed the storm.

Jesus rebuked the raging wind and surging water by simply speaking. It was His Word that removed the threat and that brought calm both within nature and within the disciples' fearful hearts (see Ps.89:9; Ph.4:6-7). Jesus' mastery over the sea was absolute, clearly showing (revealing) that He is the sovereign Lord of the universe. Moreover, Jesus' mastery over the fear of the human heart was absolute, clearly showing that He is the loving God so desperately needed by troubled humanity.

THOUGHT 1. Christ can calm the storms that so often confront us, the storms of . . .

- suffering
- bankruptcy
- temptation
- loss
- hatred
- passion

- lust
- trouble
- trial
- anger
- grief
- persecution

THOUGHT 2. Bringing calm to the storms of life involves doing as the disciples did: coming to Christ.

1) Acknowledging that we are perishing.
2) Believing that Jesus can save us.
3) Crying out for Jesus to save us.

> Come to me, all who labor and are heavy laden, and I will give you rest. (Mt.11:28)

> Do not be anxious about anything, but in everything by prayer and supplication with thanksgiving let your requests be made known to God. And the peace of God, which surpasses all understanding, will guard your hearts and your minds in Christ Jesus. (Ph.4:6–7)

> Casting all your anxieties on him, because he cares for you. (1 Pe.5:7)

> This poor man cried, and the Lord heard him and saved him out of all his troubles. (Ps.34:6)

THOUGHT 3. God's Word is the source and power that brings calmness to the storms of life.

> And Jesus came and said to them, "All authority in heaven and on earth has been given to me." (Mt.28:18)

> Peace I leave with you; my peace I give to you. Not as the world gives do I give to you. Let not your hearts be troubled, neither let them be afraid. (Jn.14:27)

> I have said these things to you, that in me you may have peace. In the world you will have tribulation. But take heart; I have overcome the world. (Jn.16:33)

> The Lord will rescue me from every evil deed and bring me safely into his heavenly kingdom. To him be the glory forever and ever. Amen. (2 Ti.4:18)

> Fear not, for I am with you; be not dismayed, for I am your God; I will strengthen you, I will help you, I will uphold you with my righteous right hand. (Is.41:10)

> Call to me and I will answer you, and will tell you great and hidden things that you have not known. (Je.33:3)

8:25

[25] He said to them, "Where is your faith?" And they were afraid, and they marveled, saying to one another, "Who then is this, that he commands even winds and water, and they obey him?"

4 Jesus' faith in God.

Jesus' purpose throughout the storm was to challenge the disciples, to test their faith and to stir them to question who He was. His own faith in God the Father is demonstrated in this verse. Look carefully at Jesus' question, "Where is *your* faith?" He was contrasting His confidence with their confidence. He was trusting God (as Man); why were they not trusting God?

Jesus was stressing the absolute necessity for His people to have faith in God. He demonstrated faith perfectly by sleeping in the midst of a storm. His life was in the hands of God; He had put it there. Therefore, His destiny was under God's control and at God's disposal. This was the lesson Christ wanted to teach His disciples.

a. He questioned the disciples' faith.

Jesus was rebuking the disciples for their fear and lack of faith. They need not have been terrified and distrusting; instead, they should have labored on against the storm knowing that He was nearby and would never have let them perish. They should have known that their lives and destiny were in His hands and under His love and care and power.

Note a crucial lesson: the disciples' faith was to be exercised during the storm, not lying dormant within their hearts doing nothing. Faith existed for the purpose of struggling against the storm.

THOUGHT 1. The lesson is clear. The very time for us to use our faith is when the storms of life come. It is against the storms that our faith is to be stirred and exercised.

> He said to them, "Because of your little faith. For truly, I say to you, if you have faith like a grain of mustard seed, you will say to this mountain, 'Move from here to there,' and it will move, and nothing will be impossible for you." (Mt.17:20)

> And Jesus said to him, " 'If you can'! All things are possible for one who believes." (Mk.9:23)

> In all circumstances take up the shield of faith, with which you can extinguish all the flaming darts of the evil one. (Ep.6:16)

> And without faith it is impossible to please him, for whoever would draw near to God must believe that he exists and that he rewards those who seek him. (He.11:6)

> If any of you lacks wisdom, let him ask God, who gives generously to all without reproach, and it will be given him. But let him ask in faith, with no doubting, for the one who doubts is like a wave of the sea that is driven and tossed by the wind. (Jas.1:5–6)

> And they rose early in the morning and went out into the wilderness of Tekoa. And when they went out, Jehoshaphat stood and said, "Hear me, Judah and inhabitants of Jerusalem! Believe in the LORD your God, and you will be established; believe his prophets, and you will succeed." (2 Chr.20:20)

b. **He stirred the disciples to question who He was.**

When Jesus rebuked the storm, the disciples feared as those who stand in the presence of God Himself. They did not, of course, fully understand the Person of Christ. But they knew they stood in the presence of One who deserved the same fearful reverence due God. This is seen in three responses:

➢ They were *afraid*—stricken with awe and reverence.

➢ They *marveled* at Jesus' enormous power and sovereignty.

➢ They asked, *"Who is this?"* This was just the question Jesus wanted them to ask. They needed to be thinking about who He was.

> And do not fear those who kill the body but cannot kill the soul. Rather fear him who can destroy both soul and body in hell. (Mt.10:28)

> And his mercy is for those who fear him from generation to generation. (Lu.1:50)

> But in every nation anyone who fears him and does what is right is acceptable to him. (Ac.10:35)

> And now, Israel, what does the LORD your God require of you, but to fear the LORD your God, to walk in all his ways, to love him, to serve the LORD your God with all your heart and with all your soul. (De.10:12)

> Oh, how abundant is your goodness, which you have stored up for those who fear you and worked for those who take refuge in you, in the sight of the children of mankind! (Ps.31:19)

> Let all the earth fear the LORD; let all the inhabitants of the world stand in awe of him! (Ps.33:8)

W. Jesus Casts Out Demons in Gadara: Power to Free People from Evil Spirits, 8:26–39

(Mt.8:28–34; Mk.5:1–20)

1. **The very face of evil—evil spirits—is confronted and overcome**
   a. The character of evil spirits
      1) Possessed a man
      2) Caused a man to lose his sense of shame and self-respect
      3) Caused alienation
      4) Stripped a man of his necessities
      5) Became enraged against the Lord
         • Knew Him
         • Opposed Him
         • Feared Him

      6) Seized a man
      7) Hated restraint, v.31

      8) Were numerous, formidable

      9) Desired a body to inhabit for the purpose of working evil
      10) Were subject to the Lord's command and power
   b. The power of Christ to deliver people from evil

2. **The reaction of a covetous people**

   a. Saw a great deliverance and the good that had been done: Feared the strange event, what they could not understand

   b. Feared the great loss of property

26 Then they sailed to the country of the Gerasenes, which is opposite Galilee.
27 When Jesus had stepped out on land, there met him a man from the city who had demons. For a long time he had worn no clothes, and he had not lived in a house but among the tombs.

28 When he saw Jesus, he cried out and fell down before him and said with a loud voice, "What have you to do with me, Jesus, Son of the Most High God? I beg you, do not torment me."
29 For he had commanded the unclean spirit to come out of the man. (For many a time it had seized him. He was kept under guard and bound with chains and shackles, but he would break the bonds and be driven by the demon into the desert.)
30 Jesus then asked him, "What is your name?" And he said, "Legion," for many demons had entered him.
31 And they begged him not to command them to depart into the abyss.
32 Now a large herd of pigs was feeding there on the hillside, and they begged him to let them enter these. So he gave them permission.
33 Then the demons came out of the man and entered the pigs, and the herd rushed down the steep bank into the lake and drowned.
34 When the herdsmen saw what had happened, they fled and told it in the city and in the country.
35 Then people went out to see what had happened, and they came to Jesus and found the man from whom the demons had gone, sitting at the feet of Jesus, clothed and in his right mind, and they were afraid.
36 And those who had seen it told them how the demon-possessed man had been healed.

³⁷ Then all the people of the surrounding country of the Gerasenes asked him to depart from them, for they were seized with great fear. So he got into the boat and returned.

³⁸ The man from whom the demons had gone begged that he might be with him, but Jesus sent him away, saying,

³⁹ "Return to your home, and declare how much God has done for you." And he went away, proclaiming throughout the whole city how much Jesus had done for him.

1) Rejected Jesus
2) Feared Him and feared more loss

3. The spirit of a delivered man
  a. He desired to be a disciple

  b. He was commissioned as a disciple—to his own hometown

Division III

The Son of Man's Announced Mission and Public Ministry, 4:16–9:17

W. Jesus Casts Out Demons in Gadara: Power to Free People from Evil Spirits, 8:26–39

(Mt.8:28–34; Mk.5:1–20)

8:26–39
Introduction

Evil spirits are demons. There is only one devil (see DEEPER STUDY # 1—Re.12:9). However, there are many evil or unclean spirits or demons, and the New Testament has much to say about them.

The following characteristics of demons, in addition to those given in the outline of this passage, are revealed in Scripture:

1. They are spirits (Mt.12:43–45).
2. They are Satan's emissaries (Mt.12:26–27).
3. They know their fate is to be eternal doom (Mt.8:29; Lu.8:31).
4. They affect people's health (Mt.12:22; 17:15–18; Lu.13:16). Apparently, demon-possession is to be distinguished from mental illness.
5. They seduce people to a false religion of asceticism—extreme self-denial (1 Ti.4:1–3).
6. They seduce people to depart from the faith (1 Ti.4:1).
7. They are cast out of people in the name of Jesus Christ (Ac.16:18).
8. They will participate in the apocalyptic judgment which is coming upon the earth (Re.9:1–11, 20).

Evil spirits are enemies of Christ and of people. As such, they oppress, possess, and obsess people.
  ➤ They delude the world and blind people from Christ (Ep.2:2).
  ➤ They attack theology (1 Ti.4:1–3).
  ➤ They attack society (Re.9:3, 20–21).
  ➤ They attack individuals (Lu.8:29).
  ➤ They influence people to commit the sins of devil-worship, idolatry, sorcery, fornication, theft, murder, and much more (Re.9:20–21).

Our defense against demons is the Lord. We must pray and fast and put on the armor of God in order to stand against their tremendous, enslaving power (Mt.17:21; Ep.6:12f).

This passage is excellent for studying the character of evil spirits and the Lord's power to deliver people from them. This is, *Jesus Casts Out Demons in Gadara: Power to Free People from Evil Spirits*, 8:26-39.

1. The very face of evil—evil spirits—is confronted and overcome (vv.26-33).
2. The reaction of a covetous people (vv.34-37).
3. The spirit of a delivered man (vv.38-39).

8:26-33

26 Then they sailed to the country of the Gerasenes, which is opposite Galilee.

27 When Jesus had stepped out on land, there met him a man from the city who had demons. For a long time he had worn no clothes, and he had not lived in a house but among the tombs.

28 When he saw Jesus, he cried out and fell down before him and said with a loud voice, "What have you to do with me, Jesus, Son of the Most High God? I beg you, do not torment me."

29 For he had commanded the unclean spirit to come out of the man. (For many a time it had seized him. He was kept under guard and bound with chains and shackles, but he would break the bonds and be driven by the demon into the desert.)

30 Jesus then asked him, "What is your name?" And he said, "Legion," for many demons had entered him.

31 And they begged him not to command them to depart into the abyss.

32 Now a large herd of pigs was feeding there on the hillside, and they begged him to let them enter these. So he gave them permission.

33 Then the demons came out of the man and entered the pigs, and the herd rushed down the steep bank into the lake and drowned.

1 The very face of evil—evil spirits—is confronted and overcome.

In these verses, Luke describes a terrifying scene. It sounds like the storyline of a horror movie, but it is not a story; it is not fiction. It is the real account of a pack of demons and a man under their control. In it, the very face of evil—evil spirits—is confronted and overcome.

a. The character of evil spirits (vv.27–33a).

Evil spirits are enemies of human beings. Their vile, destructive character is displayed in this passage. At least ten traits of demons are seen (see notes—Mt.8:28-31; Mk.5:2-5 for more discussion and thoughts for application).

First, evil spirits can possess a person for long periods of time (v.27a). They take hold of people, controlling their faculties and causing them to act abnormally, hurting both themselves and others.

Second, evil spirits cause people to lose their sense of shame and self-respect (v.27b). This man was driven to run around naked. The point is, evil spirits destroy people's sense of modesty, privacy, intimacy, and respect. Evil spirits cause people to enjoy the attention of public exposure and the embarrassment of others.

Third, evil spirits cause alienation, the loss of all friends and social life (v.27c). They lead a person to be ostracized from others. They often force people to withdraw into themselves and away from others, including immediate family, or they compel people to live in such a way that society shuns them, forcing them to live alone or with others like themselves. This is seen in this man's being forced to live among the tombs of the dead.

Fourth, evil spirits strip people of the necessities of life (v.27d). This possessed man neither wore clothes nor lived in a house.

Fifth, evil spirits are enraged against the Lord (v.28). Note that they knew Jesus was the Son of the Most High God and screamed viciously at Him (see the Holy One of God, Mk.4:34). They also opposed Him and feared Him, begging Him not to torment them (see note—Mk.1:23-24; 5:6-7; see Mt.8:31-32; Jas.2:19).

Sixth, evil spirits seize people (v.29a). Their influence and unrestrained nature seem to come and go, to lie calm and then to break forth in violence.

Seventh, evil spirits hate restraint and cause people to mistreat and oppose others (v.29b). They drive people to struggle against morality and justice and against being governed, restricted, controlled, and disciplined. They drive people to live wild and loose lives, to do as they please. They cause people to become unclean, sullen, violent, and malicious (see Mt.8:28; 9:33; 10:1; 12:43; Mk.1:23; 5:3-5; 9:17-20; Lu.6:18; 9:39). In addition, they deprive people of purpose, meaning, and significance. They destroy their self-image and their public image.

Note that Christ asked the man what his name was (v.30a). The Lord was stirring within the man fond memories of who he was before he had become demon-possessed.

Eighth, evil spirits are numerous and formidable (v.30b). The evil spirit cried out within the man that his name was *Legion*. The legion refers to the Roman military legion which included over six thousand men. This definitely indicates that the man's case was desperate; the evil spirits in him were formidable, just as a military legion was formidable. (See Mary Magdalene who had been possessed by seven devils, Mk.16:9. Note how a specific number was known. See also Mk.5:9, "many.")

Ninth, evil spirits desire a body to inhabit for the purpose of working evil (v.32a). They desire to be malicious, violent, and destructive. The evil spirits are said to be the ones who are speaking here. They recognized Jesus' sovereignty. Note how the demons thought and worked:

➢ They were indwelling and hurting this man physically, mentally, and spiritually.
➢ They wished (if exorcised from the human body) to hurt other people by damaging and destroying their property (the pigs).
➢ They wished (if exorcised) to keep other people from Christ by destroying property and having them blame God for the devastation and loss.

Tenth, evil spirits are subject to the Lord's command and power (v.32b). They begged Jesus to allow them to let them enter the pigs (see DEEPER STUDY # 1).

b. The power of Christ to deliver people from evil (v.33).

Christ's power is greater than the power of demons. As seen here, demons submit to the powerful Word of Jesus Christ. The devil's power may be great, but the Word of Christ is omnipotent (all powerful), for all power belongs to Him.

> What then shall we say to these things? If God is for us, who can be against us? (Ro.8:31f. Read this whole passage for a beautiful and powerful description of the Lord's love and might.)

> Little children, you are from God and have overcome them, for he who is in you is greater than he who is in the world. (1 Jn.4:4)

Note the result of Jesus' mighty Word: the man was saved; the evil spirits were cast out of him. Christ had the power to deliver and save. All He had to do was say, "Go," and whatever evil indwelt the man departed. The man was delivered completely from the evil: its presence, guilt, and consequences. The man was "saved to the uttermost" (He.7:25)—completely saved, wholly and entirely delivered (see note—Mk.5:8-13 for more discussion and thoughts for application).

> And Jesus came and said to them, "All authority in heaven and on earth has been given to me." (Mt.28:18)

> How God anointed Jesus of Nazareth with the Holy Spirit and with power. He went about doing good and healing all who were oppressed by the devil, for God was with him. (Ac.10:38)

> Consequently, he is able to save to the uttermost those who draw near to God through him, since he always lives to make intercession for them. (He.7:25)

> I know that you can do all things, and that no purpose of yours can be thwarted. (Jb.42:2)

DEEPER STUDY # 1

(8:33) **Swine:** a question is often asked about the swine which were killed. This is discussed in Matthew (see DEEPER STUDY # 2—Mt.8:32).

2 The reaction of a covetous people.

The herdsmen of the swine no doubt feared being held responsible for the loss of the herd. They fled the scene and told others what had happened throughout the city and the surrounding country-side. People rushed to see for themselves what had taken place. Tragically, they reacted according to their covetous nature. The healing of the demoniac had cost them a lot of money (see DEEPER STUDY # 2—Mt.8:32; Mk.5:14–17 for more discussion and application).

8:34-37

34 When the herdsmen saw what had happened, they fled and told it in the city and in the country.
35 Then people went out to see what had happened, and they came to Jesus and found the man from whom the demons had gone, sitting at the feet of Jesus, clothed and in his right mind, and they were afraid.
36 And those who had seen it told them how the demon-possessed man had been healed.
37 Then all the people of the surrounding country of the Gerasenes asked him to depart from them, for they were seized with great fear. So he got into the boat and returned.

a. **Saw a great deliverance and the good that had been done: Feared the strange event, what they could not understand (v.35).**

The people saw the great deed done, the marvelous deliverance of the demon-possessed man. However, their response was not one of rejoicing; it was fear—fear of Christ's power. They had known the demon-possessed man, how desperately hopeless his condition had been; and here he sat, delivered and made whole. They could not understand what Christ had done, and instead of believing in Him, they were afraid of Him.

b. **Feared the great loss of property (vv.36–37).**

Overwhelmed by the fear of Jesus, the people rejected Him and asked Him to leave their area. Most likely, they were gripped with a sense of judgment because of their swine's being killed. They were also bound to be wondering if the proclaimed Messiah had come to judge them ahead of time or to destroy more of their property. The Jewish people who were among those raising swine definitely knew they were breaking the law of God (see Lev.11:7; Is.65:3–4; 66:17). Because of this sin and other sins and their callousness toward this healed demon-possessed man, they were intensely afraid of God's Son. They were unwilling to repent of their sins and to begin living for God. Thus, they could feel nothing else but fear.

Jesus did exactly what they asked. He left them. They chose the *swine of the world* over the joy and salvation of Christ.

> For what will it profit a man if he gains the whole world and forfeits his soul? Or what shall a man give in return for his soul? (Mt.16:26)

> For whoever is ashamed of me and of my words in this adulterous and sinful generation, of him will the Son of Man also be ashamed when he comes in the glory of his Father with the holy angels. (Mk.8:38)

> Do not love the world or the things in the world. If anyone loves the world, the love of the Father is not in him. For all that is in the world—the desires of the flesh and the desires of the eyes and pride of life—is not from the Father but is from the world. (1 Jn.2:15-16)

> He who loves money will not be satisfied with money, nor he who loves wealth with his income; this also is vanity. (Ec.5:10)

8:38-39

38 The man from whom the demons had gone begged that he might be with him, but Jesus sent him away, saying,
39 "Return to your home, and declare how much God has done for you." And he went away, proclaiming throughout the whole city how much Jesus had done for him.

3 The spirit of a delivered man.

The man whom Jesus had delivered had a different spirit. He serves as a dynamic example of what every person whom Christ has saved should be.

a. **He desired to be a disciple (v.38).**

As soon as the demon-possessed man was delivered, he begged Jesus to let him go with Him. He wanted to follow Christ, to travel with Him as one of His disciples. He was *on fire* for the Lord and wanted to commit himself to the ministry.

b. **He was commissioned as a disciple—to his own hometown (v.39).**

But note what Christ did: He redirected the man. He commissioned him to go to his own hometown. The people of Gadara had rejected Christ, and they needed to be reached. This was where the Lord needed this man to minister. These people needed to be constantly reminded of what Jesus had done for this man, to see this walking testimony of Jesus' divinity and power.

THOUGHT 1. Christ often redirects our fervor and willingness. He knows where we can best serve Him and the cause of His kingdom.

THOUGHT 2. Every person, when saved, should become a dynamic witness for the Lord and be willing to go wherever He sends them.

THOUGHT 3. We should never let a redirection or a call to go elsewhere kill our fervor.

> In the same way, let your light shine before others, so that they may see your good works and give glory to your Father who is in heaven. (Mt.5:16)

> Go therefore and make disciples of all nations, baptizing them in the name of the Father and of the Son and of the Holy Spirit, teaching them to observe all that I have commanded you. And behold, I am with you always, to the end of the age. (Mt.28:19–20)

> And he said to them, "Go into all the world and proclaim the gospel to the whole creation." (Mk.16:15)

> But you will receive power when the Holy Spirit has come upon you, and you will be my witnesses in Jerusalem and in all Judea and Samaria, and to the end of the earth. (Ac.1:8)

> Now those who were scattered went about preaching the word. (Ac.8:4)

> But in your hearts honor Christ the Lord as holy, always being prepared to make a defense to anyone who asks you for a reason for the hope that is in you; yet do it with gentleness and respect. (1 Pe.3:15)

X. Jesus Raises Jairus' Daughter and Heals a Woman: The Reward of True Faith, 8:40–56

(Mt.9:18–26; Mk.5:21–43)

1. The Gerasenes had rejected Jesus, but the Galileans welcomed Him

2. The faith of a desperate ruler
   a. His rank: A religious ruler
   b. His approach: He forgot pride and position—humbled himself
   c. His faith: He believed Jesus could save his daughter
   d. His reward: Jesus went to help him

3. The faith of an embarrassed and hopeless woman
   a. Her despair

   b. Her shame: Ceremonially unclean and socially outcast
   c. Her unusual *touch of faith*: Many touched Jesus, but only she was healed
   d. Her fearful reverence and honest trust

   e. Her reward: Jesus' undivided attention and healing

4. The faith of determined but helpless parents
   a. The parents' helplessness: Their daughter died
   b. The parents' need: An unwavering conviction[DS1]

⁴⁰ Now when Jesus returned, the crowd welcomed him, for they were all waiting for him.

⁴¹ And there came a man named Jairus, who was a ruler of the synagogue. And falling at Jesus' feet, he implored him to come to his house,

⁴² for he had an only daughter, about twelve years of age, and she was dying. As Jesus went, the people pressed around him.

⁴³ And there was a woman who had had a discharge of blood for twelve years, and though she had spent all her living on physicians, she could not be healed by anyone.

⁴⁴ She came up behind him and touched the fringe of his garment, and immediately her discharge of blood ceased.

⁴⁵ And Jesus said, "Who was it that touched me?" When all denied it, Peter said, "Master, the crowds surround you and are pressing in on you!"

⁴⁶ But Jesus said, "Someone touched me, for I perceive that power has gone out from me."

⁴⁷ And when the woman saw that she was not hidden, she came trembling, and falling down before him declared in the presence of all the people why she had touched him, and how she had been immediately healed.

⁴⁸ And he said to her, "Daughter, your faith has made you well; go in peace."

⁴⁹ While he was still speaking, someone from the ruler's house came and said, "Your daughter is dead; do not trouble the Teacher any more."

⁵⁰ But Jesus on hearing this answered him, "Do not fear; only believe, and she will be well."

⁵¹ And when he came to the house, he allowed no one to enter with him, except Peter and John and James, and the father and mother of the child.

⁵² And all were weeping and mourning for her, but he said, "Do not weep, for she is not dead but sleeping."

⁵³ And they laughed at him, knowing that she was dead.

⁵⁴ But taking her by the hand he called, saying, "Child, arise."

⁵⁵ And her spirit returned, and she got up at once. And he directed that something should be given her to eat.

⁵⁶ And her parents were amazed, but he charged them to tell no one what had happened.

c. The parents' strong faith: They followed Jesus despite the mockery

d. The parents' reward: Jesus' undivided attention and resurrection power

e. The parents' amazement: Jesus' unusual command

Division III

The Son of Man's Announced Mission and Public Ministry, 4:16–9:17

X. Jesus Raises Jairus' Daughter and Heals a Woman:
The Reward of True Faith, 8:40–56

(Mt.9:18–26; Mk.5:21–43)

8:40–56
Introduction

Again and again in His Word, God promises to reward true faith. In reporting on a busy day in Jesus' ministry, Luke tells the exciting stories of two people whose unwavering faith was richly rewarded by the Lord. These people serve as vital examples for all who face situations that seem hopeless. This is, *Jesus Raises Jairus' Daughter and Heals a Woman: The Reward of True Faith,* Mt.8:40–56.

1. The Gerasenes had rejected Jesus, but the Galileans welcomed Him (v.40).
2. The faith of a desperate ruler (vv.41–42).
3. The faith of an embarrassed and hopeless woman (vv.43–48).
4. The faith of determined but helpless parents (vv.49–56).

1 The Gerasenes had rejected Jesus, but the Galileans welcomed Him.

8:40

The Gerasenes (Gadarenes) and the Galileans stand as prime examples of the two possible responses to the Lord Jesus Christ. The Gerasenes rejected Jesus and ran Him out of town. The Galileans received Him and welcomed Him enthusiastically. One people drove Him away; the other hoped in Him. One country was closed to Him; the other was open to Him.

⁴⁰ Now when Jesus returned, the crowd welcomed him, for they were all waiting for him.

Note a crucial observation. When Jesus was rejected by a people . . .

• He did not retaliate, strike back

- He did not begin to moan, grumble, or gripe
- He did not slip into discouragement or depression
- He did not quit

What did Jesus do when rejected? He immediately left the people, the country of those who rejected Him, and continued His ministry elsewhere.

8:41–42

41 And there came a man named Jairus, who was a ruler of the synagogue. And falling at Jesus' feet, he implored him to come to his house,

42 for he had an only daughter, about twelve years of age, and she was dying. As Jesus went, the people pressed around him.

2 The faith of a desperate ruler.

One of the individuals waiting for Jesus was a man named Jairus. He was desperate to see Jesus, for his precious twelve-year-old daughter was dying.

a. His rank: A religious ruler (v.41a).

Jairus was a religious ruler, probably the highest-ranking official in the area. He was the head of the synagogue, the very center of Jewish life in the city. Evidently, he was well-to-do and highly esteemed among the people.

b. His approach: He forgot pride and position—humbled himself (v.41b).

Jairus approached Jesus with a willingness to pay whatever price necessary to help his daughter. He laid his position on the line in order to secure Jesus' help. The Jewish religious leaders were now opposing Jesus with a fierceness seldom seen, and they were attacking Him publicly. By coming to Jesus, Jairus risked provoking the hostility of his peers and losing his position.

Nevertheless, Jairus forgot self-interests and humbled himself completely, laying all pride aside. He ran up to Jesus and fell down at Jesus' feet begging for help (see note and DEEPER STUDY # 1—Lu.9:23).

> For whoever would save his life will lose it, but whoever loses his life for my sake will save it. For what does it profit a man if he gains the whole world and loses or forfeits himself? For whoever is ashamed of me and of my words, of him will the Son of Man be ashamed when he comes in his glory and the glory of the Father and of the holy angels. (Lu.9:24–26)

> But he gives more grace. Therefore it says, "God opposes the proud but gives grace to the humble." . . . Humble yourselves before the Lord, and he will exalt you. (Jas.4:6, 10)

c. His faith: He believed Jesus could save His daughter (v.42a).

Jairus was running the risk of losing everything for the sake of someone else: his twelve-year-old daughter. She was his only child, and she was dying. Note Jairus' faith. He begged Jesus to help. He believed with all his heart that Jesus could save his daughter—if He would only come to his house.

> When he calls to me, I will answer him; I will be with him in trouble; I will rescue him and honor him. (Ps.91:15)

> Then you shall call, and the LORD will answer; you shall cry, and he will say, "Here I am." If you take away the yoke from your midst, the pointing of the finger, and speaking wickedness. (Is.58:9)

> Call to me and I will answer you, and will tell you great and hidden things that you have not known. (Je.33:3)

d. His reward; Jesus went to help him (v.42b).

Jairus' faith was immediately rewarded: "Jesus went." He answered Jairus' plea by turning and heading to Jairus' house. Jairus' strong faith, coupled with his selfless humility, compelled Jesus to meet his desperate need.

> And whatever you ask in prayer, you will receive, if you have faith. (Mt.21:22)

> If you ask me anything in my name, I will do it. (Jn.14:14)

3 The faith of an embarrassed and hopeless woman.

As Jesus tried to make his way to Jairus' house, the people continued to throng Him (v.42). An embarrassed and hopeless woman managed to break through the crushing crowd to make contact with Jesus. Like Jairus, she was a person of great faith.

a. Her despair (v.43).

For twelve years (interestingly, the age of Jairus' daughter), this woman had been suffering from a discharge of blood. She had spent every penny she had on doctors, all of whom could do nothing to help her. Imagine the depths of her despair, broke and broken by an affliction that had ruined every aspect of her life.

b. Her shame: Ceremonially unclean and socially outcast (v.44).

The afflicted woman was ashamed, extremely embarrassed over her problem. She was considered ceremonially unclean; that is, she was cut off from society and religious worship (Le.15:19-33). Most likely, she had even been divorced, for her husband would have been considered unclean because he lived with her (Le.15:25-27). Imagine a woman's having to live with the shame of being divorced—and the loss of her husband and security—because of a medical problem. The humiliating stigma of her disease made her hesitant about letting anyone know about her condition. Her hemorrhaging was a personal, intimate matter for her, something she did not want to be known and discussed publicly.

> **43** And there was a woman who had had a discharge of blood for twelve years, and though she had spent all her living on physicians, she could not be healed by anyone.
> **44** She came up behind him and touched the fringe of his garment, and immediately her discharge of blood ceased.
> **45** And Jesus said, "Who was it that touched me?" When all denied it, Peter said, "Master, the crowds surround you and are pressing in on you!"
> **46** But Jesus said, "Someone touched me, for I perceive that power has gone out from me."
> **47** And when the woman saw that she was not hidden, she came trembling, and falling down before him declared in the presence of all the people why she had touched him, and how she had been immediately healed.
> **48** And he said to her, "Daughter, your faith has made you well; go in peace."

c. Her unusual *touch of faith*: Many touched Jesus, but only she was healed (vv.44-45).

This pitiable woman acted *in faith*, touching just the fringe of Jesus' garment. "The 'border' [fringe] of the Lord's garment was one of the four tassels that were always a part of the Jewish mantle. When worn, the garment was so arranged that one of the tassels hung down over the shoulder at the back."[1] Note that the woman did not touch *Jesus* Himself, only the tassel on His garment. To touch Jesus would have been considered contamination and was against the law.

Many needy people were thronging Jesus and touching Him, but only one touched Him in faith. The woman had an *expectant, believing attitude*. She believed that if she could only touch Him she would be made whole (v.47; see Mt.9:21). And she was: her hemorrhaging stopped immediately.

> **And Jesus said to him, " 'If you can'! All things are possible for one who believes." (Mk.9:23)**

> **Oh, how abundant is your goodness, which you have stored up for those who fear you and worked for those who take refuge in you, in the sight of the children of mankind! (Ps.31:19)**

> **Commit your way to the LORD; trust in him, and he will act. (Ps.37:5)**

d. Her fearful reverence and honest trust (vv.45-47).

Jesus knew what had happened. He had felt the power go out of Him when the woman touched Him and asked, "Who touched Me" (v.45)? Note what Jesus was doing. He did not ask who touched Him because He did not know; He wanted the woman to testify of what He had done for her. He had allowed the woman to be healed in order to help her in her embarrassment.

---

1 John Phillips, *Exploring the Gospel of Luke: An Expository Commentary* (The John Phillips Commentary Series), (Grand Rapids, MI: Kregel Academic & Professional, 2005). Via Wordsearch digital edition.

However, secret discipleship was impossible. He wanted her to make a public confession of her deliverance.

> So everyone who acknowledges me before men, I also will acknowledge before my Father who is in heaven. (Mt.10:32)

> And I tell you, everyone who acknowledges me before men, the Son of Man also will acknowledge before the angels of God. (Lu.12:8)

> Because, if you confess with your mouth that Jesus is Lord and believe in your heart that God raised him from the dead, you will be saved. For with the heart one believes and is justified, and with the mouth one confesses and is saved. (Ro.10:9–10)

Serving and helping others cost Jesus, and cost Him dearly. Spiritual power had flowed out from His being into the woman (v.46). It was that power which healed her. Note that the disciples were unaware of what it cost Jesus to minister. They were insensitive to the spiritual energy He was exerting, oblivious to what Jesus was doing:

➤ He was taking our infirmities upon Himself and bearing our sicknesses.

> This was to fulfill what was spoken by the prophet Isaiah: "He took our illnesses and bore our diseases." (Mt.8:17; see Is.53:4)

➤ He was teaching that public confession of Him was essential (Ro.10:9–10).

When the woman realized that she had been discovered, she gave a glowing testimony of what Jesus had done for her (v.47). She knew that He who had such power knew who had touched Him, so she came as all should come in approaching the Lord: "trembling and falling down before Him," confessing all. Her fearful reverence and honest trust of Jesus were evident to everyone.

THOUGHT 1. It is spiritual power that flows into and delivers any of us, the spiritual power of Christ.

> In the same way, let your light shine before others, so that they may see your good works and give glory to your Father who is in heaven. (Mt.5:16)

> And all the crowd sought to touch him, for power came out from him and healed them all. (Lu.6:19)

e. **Her reward: Jesus' undivided attention and healing (v.48).**
The woman's faith was glorious rewarded with Jesus' undivided attention and healing. Her faith moved Jesus to meet her face to face; her faith wrought some wonderful blessings for her:
➤ She was called, "Daughter." This was the only time Jesus ever called a woman "Daughter." What a distinct privilege! It meant she had become a child of God.

> The Spirit himself bears witness with our spirit that we are children of God, and if children, then heirs—heirs of God and fellow heirs with Christ, provided we suffer with him in order that we may also be glorified with him. (Ro.8:16–17)

> But when the fullness of time had come, God sent forth his Son, born of woman, born under the law, to redeem those who were under the law, so that we might receive adoption as sons. And because you are sons, God has sent the Spirit of his Son into our hearts, crying, "Abba! Father!" (Ga.4:4–6)

➤ She was assured that she was whole permanently. Her deliverance would last.
➤ She was given peace (see note—Jn.14:27).

> Do not be anxious about anything, but in everything by prayer and supplication with thanksgiving let your requests be made known to God. And the peace of God, which surpasses all understanding, will guard your hearts and your minds in Christ Jesus. (Ph.4:6–7)

> Peace I leave with you; my peace I give to you. Not as the world gives do I give to you. Let not your hearts be troubled, neither let them be afraid. (Jn.14:27)

> I have said these things to you, that in me you may have peace. In the world you will have tribulation. But take heart; I have overcome the world. (Jn.16:33)

4 The faith of determined but helpless parents.

While Jesus was still speaking to the newly-healed woman, news came to Jairus that his daughter had died. As this suspenseful scene plays out, the determined faith of the dead girl's parents and the power of Jesus over death stand out.

a. The parents' helplessness: their daughter died (v.49).

Jairus' faith had been sorely tried. His daughter was critically ill, and he was forced to wait while Jesus ministered to another needy person. What he surely feared had happened. Jesus was too late; Jairus's daughter had died.

The messenger from Jairus' household pulled him off to the side and told him not to bother the Lord any more. The messenger felt there was no need to trouble Jesus any further since Jairus's daughter was now dead. Note that Jesus' power was thought to be limited and ineffective in the face of death. So, the messenger suggested that Jairus could now go home. The point is, Jairus was totally helpless, and the thought that Jesus' power would be effective in dealing with the dead never crossed this gloomy messenger's mind.

b. The parents' need: An unwavering conviction (v.50).

Before Jairus even had a chance to respond, Jesus spoke forcibly. He encouraged the devastated father to stay steadfast in his faith, to have an unwavering conviction in the providence, power, and promise of Christ. Specifically, the Lord made three statements to the dead girl's father:

> *Do not fear*: do not be gripped with terror, dread, fear, anxiety.
> *Only believe* (see notes—Mk.11:22-23; Deeper Study # 2—Jn.2:24; note—Ro.10:16-17; Deeper Study # 1—He.10:38).
> *And she will be well* (sothēsetai, *so-thay'-seh-tigh*): restored, made alive, saved.

c. The parents' strong faith: They followed Jesus despite the mockery (vv.51-53).

Imagine the strong faith required to believe simply because of Jesus' Word, because of what He said! Yet such was the faith of Jarius. He ignored the gloomy messenger and walked on with Jesus back to his house.

Upon arrival, Jesus took only the parents and His inner circle into the house (v.51). The parents and daughter would need quiet and time to be reunited and to regain their joyful composure before seeing people. The inner circle would give enough witness to verify and record the incident for all generations. The faithless would not have the privilege of witnessing the greatest of all miracles—the raising of the dead.

The mourners who scorned Jesus probably included relatives, friends, neighbors, and professional mourners (v.52). Professional mourners were a custom in the East. When Jesus said the girl was sleeping, these mourners mocked and ridiculed Him openly (v.53).

Some readers and skeptics stumble on Jesus' words, "she is not dead, but sleeping," insisting that the girl was actually still alive. But that is not what Jesus was saying; the girl *was* definitely dead. Her spirit had left her body (v.55). In describing death as sleep, Jesus was teaching spiritual truths about death (see Deeper Study # 1).

d. The parents' reward: Jesus' undivided attention and resurrection power (vv.54-55).

The parents' stubborn faith was richly rewarded. Their strong faith caused Jesus to give the matter His full attention, to save their daughter and actually raise her up from the dead. When Jesus gently commanded her to arise, the dead girl's spirit returned to her body and she arose.

---

⁴⁹ While he was still speaking, someone from the ruler's house came and said, "Your daughter is dead; do not trouble the Teacher any more."

⁵⁰ But Jesus on hearing this answered him, "Do not fear; only believe, and she will be well."

⁵¹ And when he came to the house, he allowed no one to enter with him, except Peter and John and James, and the father and mother of the child.

⁵² And all were weeping and mourning for her, but he said, "Do not weep, for she is not dead but sleeping."

⁵³ And they laughed at him, knowing that she was dead.

⁵⁴ But taking her by the hand he called, saying, "Child, arise."

⁵⁵ And her spirit returned, and she got up at once. And he directed that something should be given her to eat.

⁵⁶ And her parents were amazed, but he charged them to tell no one what had happened.

Jesus commanded that food be given to her. This activity would help her mother handle the emotion of the moment and help to strengthen the daughter.

THOUGHT 1. Parents specifically need *stubborn faith* in behalf of their children. However, note what must precede stubborn faith: a desperate, determined, and unwavering faith that forgets and denies oneself, seeking Jesus no matter the cost. Difficult cases require both a desperate faith and a determined faith. It is such faith that receives the *great* reward.

> He said to them, "Because of your little faith. For truly, I say to you, if you have faith like a grain of mustard seed, you will say to this mountain, 'Move from here to there,' and it will move, and nothing will be impossible for you." (Mt.17:20; see Mt.21:21)

> And Jesus answered them, "Have faith in God. Truly, I say to you, whoever says to this mountain, 'Be taken up and thrown into the sea,' and does not doubt in his heart, but believes that what he says will come to pass, it will be done for him. Therefore I tell you, whatever you ask in prayer, believe that you have received it, and it will be yours." (Mk.11:22–24)

> But let him ask in faith, with no doubting, for the one who doubts is like a wave of the sea that is driven and tossed by the wind. For that person must not suppose that he will receive anything from the Lord; he is a double-minded man, unstable in all his ways. (Jas.1:6–8)

e. The parents' amazement: Jesus' unusual command (v.56).

Seeing the parents' amazement, Jesus then gave them an unusual command: to tell no one about the miracle. The Lord gave them no explanation, no reason for this command. But the parents did not question Him. It is safe to assume that this faith-filled couple obeyed Jesus' puzzling instruction without needing to understand the reason for it.

DEEPER STUDY # 1

(8:50) **Death—Sleep:** some argue that this girl was actually alive and that Jesus knew it. But note several facts (see DEEPER STUDY # 1—Jn.11:13 for more discussion).

1. Jesus and the Bible speak of death as nothing more than sleep. But sleep means *rest and comfort in God* (Mt.27:52; Ac.7:60; 1 Th.4:13–18). Many within the world think of death as annihilation or ceasing to exist. Jesus drew the contrast in order to say that death is not annihilation. Believers continue to exist, resting in the life and comfort of God.

2. Jesus knew the girl was physically dead, but not spiritually (v.52). He clearly said so, although the people did not understand what He was saying.

3. Note the words "her spirit returned." The point is this: her spirit had left her body, and upon the command of Jesus, her spirit returned. Her life returned to the body immediately.

CHAPTER 9

Y. Jesus Commissions His Disciples, 9:1–9

(Mt.9:35–10:42; Mk.6:7–13)

And he called the twelve together and gave them power and authority over all demons and to cure diseases,

2 and he sent them out to proclaim the kingdom of God and to heal.

3 And he said to them, "Take nothing for your journey, no staff, nor bag, nor bread, nor money; and do not have two tunics.

4 And whatever house you enter, stay there, and from there depart.

5 And wherever they do not receive you, when you leave that town shake off the dust from your feet as a testimony against them."

6 And they departed and went through the villages, preaching the gospel and healing everywhere.

7 Now Herod the tetrarch heard about all that was happening, and he was perplexed, because it was said by some that John had been raised from the dead,

8 by some that Elijah had appeared, and by others that one of the prophets of old had risen.

9 Herod said, "John I beheaded, but who is this about whom I hear such things?" And he sought to see him.

1. **Their call: To come together for ministry**
2. **Their resources: Power and authority from Jesus**
3. **Their mission: To preach and minister (heal)**
4. **Their method**
   a. Not to seek success through personal appearance and materialism
   b. To minister in the homes, to the interested and the hospitable[DS1]
   c. To warn rejecters
5. **Their obedience: They went out preaching and ministering (healing)**
6. **Their impact**
   a. Herod was disturbed by their message
   b. The people speculated about Jesus' identity
   c. Herod desired to know Jesus' identity

Division III

The Son of Man's Announced Mission and Public Ministry, 4:16–9:17

Y. Jesus Commissions His Disciples, 9:1–9

(Mt.9:35–10:42; Mk.6:7–13)

9:1–9
Introduction

The event detailed in this passage is significant, for it foreshadows Jesus' giving of the Great Commission (Mt.28:18–20). Here, Luke relates the first time Jesus sent His disciples out alone to minister. The instructions the Lord gave to the early disciples are needed by every generation of believers. Just as He sent the Twelve, He has sent us all to proclaim the gospel to the world. This is, *Jesus Commissions His Disciples*, 9:1–9.

1. Their call: To come together for ministry (v.1).
2. Their resources: Power and authority from Jesus (v.1).
3. Their mission: To preach and minister (heal) (v.2).
4. Their method (vv.3–5).
5. Their obedience: They went out preaching and ministering (healing) (v.6).
6. Their impact (vv.7–9).

9:1

And he called the twelve together and gave them power and authority over all demons and to cure diseases,

1 Their call: To come together for ministry.

Jesus had to call His disciples back *together*. Note the word *together* (Gk. sugkalesamenos, *soog-kah-les-ahm'-en-os*), which indicates that the Twelve had been apart. As people read the Gospels, many presume that Jesus and the disciples were together all the time, every day. However, that was not the case. The disciples had families and responsibilities. We tend to glamorize the disciples and Jesus, forgetting the disciples were ordinary men with day-to-day duties. They were not with the Lord at this time. They had to spend some time at home taking care of their families and whatever other duties they had. No doubt they did spend most of their time with Jesus as traveling evangelists, but at certain times, they returned home in order to tend to family affairs.

The basic ingredient for ministry is *togetherness*. Note the words, "called . . . together." These words point to the necessity of *coming together* as Jesus intended.

> Little children, yet a little while I am with you. You will seek me, and just as I said to the Jews, so now I also say to you, "Where I am going you cannot come." A new commandment I give to you, that you love one another: just as I have loved you, you also are to love one another. (Jn.13:33–34)

> Only let your manner of life be worthy of the gospel of Christ, so that whether I come and see you or am absent, I may hear of you that you are standing firm in one spirit, with one mind striving side by side for the faith of the gospel. (Ph.1:27)

The purpose for which Jesus called the Twelve together was to minister. Jesus was completing His Galilean ministry. He was now ready to make His way to Jerusalem (Lu.9:51). His ministry had been successful. Multitudes knew of His coming to earth; many had been helped, and some did believe. Now, before He left the area, He wanted to reach out one more time to those who were close to believing and to more deeply root and ground those who already believed.

> **THOUGHT 1.** The coming together of the disciples is a picture of believers coming together regularly in local churches (He.10:25). We are called to gather in the Lord's presence, and then we are called to go out and share the gospel with and minister to others in our daily lives.
>
> > And they worshiped him and returned to Jerusalem with great joy, and were continually in the temple blessing God. (Lu.24:52–53)
> >
> > And day by day, attending the temple together and breaking bread in their homes, they received their food with glad and generous hearts. (Ac.2:46)
> >
> > Not neglecting to meet together, as is the habit of some, but encouraging one another, and all the more as you see the Day drawing near. (He.10:25)
> >
> > But you shall seek the place that the Lord your God will choose out of all your tribes to put his name and make his habitation there. There you shall go. (De.12:5)

2 Their resources: Power and authority from Jesus.

Jesus sent His disciples out with everything they needed to be successful in the field: power and the authority to use that power. *Power* (dunamin, *doo'-nah-min*) is the *gift*, the necessary resource to minister; *authority* (exousian, *ex-ooh-see'-ahn*) is the *right* to minister. The disciple has to decide when and where to exercise the Lord's power (resource). The awesome responsibility for being entrusted with such power should help to keep Christ's servants on our faces before God, acknowledging our total dependence on Him. It should also help us seek a closeness with God, a true sensitivity to the Spirit of God.

Jesus gave the disciples power and authority over "all demons." *All* means that the disciple was to have power over all kinds of evil, no matter how evil and enslaving, strong and fierce, subtle and undetected. It also points to the glorious purpose of Jesus. He had come to defeat and conquer the evil forces of this world, to rout and triumph over "all" of them.

> Now is the judgment of this world; now will the ruler of this world be cast out. (Jn.12:31)

> For we do not wrestle against flesh and blood, but against the rulers, against the authorities, against the cosmic powers over this present darkness, against the spiritual forces of evil in the heavenly places. (Ep.6:12)

> He has delivered us from the domain of darkness and transferred us to the kingdom of his beloved Son, in whom we have redemption, the forgiveness of sins. (Col.1:13-14)

> He disarmed the rulers and authorities and put them to open shame, by triumphing over them in him. (Col.2:15)

> Since therefore the children share in flesh and blood, he himself likewise partook of the same things, that through death he might destroy the one who has the power of death, that is, the devil, and deliver all those who through fear of death were subject to lifelong slavery. (He.2:14-15)

> Whoever makes a practice of sinning is of the devil, for the devil has been sinning from the beginning. The reason the Son of God appeared was to destroy the works of the devil. (1 Jn.3:8)

Jesus also gave the disciples power and authority to "cure diseases." This would demonstrate the great compassion of the Lord and draw people to Him (Jn.12:32). It would also help tremendously in confirming the faith of some.

THOUGHT 1. Think how little power is really seen in the lives and ministry of believers, lay and minister alike! This lack of power reveals just how *displaced* or *misplaced* so many believers are. The *authority* to minister (where and when) has not been used as it should. The face of the Lord has not been sought, not to the point that a true closeness to His Spirit has directed our authority. We have taken the authority, the right to minister where we wish, into our own hands. The evidence: after 2000 years so much of the world still has not heard the gospel.

> But you will receive power when the Holy Spirit has come upon you, and you will be my witnesses in Jerusalem and in all Judea and Samaria, and to the end of the earth. (Ac.1:8)

> And with great power the apostles were giving their testimony to the resurrection of the Lord Jesus, and great grace was upon them all. (Ac.4:33)

> And my speech and my message were not in plausible words of wisdom, but in demonstration of the Spirit and of power. (1 Co.2:4)

> And God is able to make all grace abound to you, so that having all sufficiency in all things at all times, you may abound in every good work. (2 Co.9:8)

> Now to him who is able to do far more abundantly than all that we ask or think, according to the power at work within us. (Ep.3:20)

> Because our gospel came to you not only in word, but also in power and in the Holy Spirit and with full conviction. You know what kind of men we proved to be among you for your sake. (1 Th.1:5)

3 Their mission: To preach and minister (heal).

The disciples were sent on the very same mission as Christ. First, they were to preach the kingdom of God (see DEEPER STUDY # 3—Mt.19:23-24). Preaching met the spiritual needs of the human soul. Then, they were to heal the sick. Healing met the physical needs of the human body.

² and he sent them out to proclaim the kingdom of God and to heal.

> Even as the Son of Man came not to be served but to serve, and to give his life as a ransom for many. (Mt.20:28)

When the crowds learned it, they followed him, and he welcomed them and spoke to them of the kingdom of God and cured those who had need of healing. (Lu.9:11)

For the Son of Man came to seek and to save the lost. (Lu.19:10)

Jesus said to them again, "Peace be with you. As the Father has sent me, even so I am sending you." (Jn.20:21)

9:3-5

³ And he said to them, "Take nothing for your journey, no staff, nor bag, nor bread, nor money; and do not have two tunics.
⁴ And whatever house you enter, stay there, and from there depart.
⁵ And wherever they do not receive you, when you leave that town shake off the dust from your feet as a testimony against them."

4 Their method.

The Lord was greatly concerned about the testimony of the gospel and of His disciples. Therefore, He gave them specific instructions as to their method of ministering and their conduct while ministering.

a. Not to seek success through personal appearance and materialism (v.3).

The disciples were not to seek success through personal appearance and materialism. They were to live in utter simplicity and humility. This was the point of Christ's telling them to not take some specific items (see note—Mk.6:8-13 for more discussion). The Lord was saying three things to the disciples:

➢ The need and the hour were urgent. Concentrate on preaching and ministering. Do not get sidetracked.

Set your minds on things that are above, not on things that are on earth. (Col.3:2)

➢ Learn to believe and trust God day by day. Become a living example of what is being preached: faith in God. Do not begin to trust in the things of the world. Learn to trust God daily, and then others can learn what is meant by "believing" and "trusting" God through your example.

But seek first the kingdom of God and his righteousness, and all these things will be added to you. (Mt.6:33)

➢ Avoid the very appearance of evil. Having your mind on the things of this world will distract from God and from people's needs and from the ministry. Become attached to God and to His kingdom alone; not to money, houses, lands, cars, clothes, hairstyles, appearance, food, buying, selling, and accumulating. Be heavenly-minded and ministry-centered, so that people may know there is a far better life than what this earth offers.

For those who live according to the flesh set their minds on the things of the flesh, but those who live according to the Spirit set their minds on the things of the Spirit. For to set the mind on the flesh is death, but to set the mind on the Spirit is life and peace. (Ro.8:5-6)

These all died in faith, not having received the things promised, but having seen them and greeted them from afar, and having acknowledged that they were strangers and exiles on the earth. For people who speak thus make it clear that they are seeking a homeland. If they had been thinking of that land from which they had gone out, they would have had opportunity to return. But as it is, they desire a better country, that is, a heavenly one. Therefore God is not ashamed to be called their God, for he has prepared for them a city. (He.11:13-16)

By faith Moses, when he was grown up, refused to be called the son of Pharaoh's daughter, choosing rather to be mistreated with the people of God than to enjoy the fleeting pleasures of sin. He considered the reproach of Christ greater wealth than the treasures of Egypt, for he was looking to the reward. (He.11:24-26)

b. To minister in the homes, to the interested and the hospitable (v.4).

Jesus instructed the disciples to minister in the homes to the interested and the hospitable families (see DEEPER STUDY # 1). They were to remain in one home until they left the area. Two wise reasons can be seen for this command. First, to keep from offending their hosts who might think the disciples were not satisfied with their accommodations and hospitality. Second, to prevent the community from thinking they might be trying to take advantage of as many people as possible.

c. To warn rejecters (v.5).

If a community or city did not receive their witness and if a home could not be found that would receive them, then the disciples were to leave. They were neither to force the issue or create a bad situation either for the rejecters or for themselves. There was to be no tongue-lashing, accusation, or divisiveness created. They were simply to leave; and as they left, they were to give a silent testimony against those who rejected them. Jesus told them to shake the dust from their feet. This was a strong warning and a symbol of serious judgment. It meant that not even the dust of that place was worthy of the gospel of God, much less the people. The place and its people were *left* to themselves just as they had wished. They were left *without God* and His glorious news of salvation, so they were to be left alone to govern their own lives just as they had willed. God would *abandon* them to their own way and choice of life.

DEEPER STUDY # 1

(9:4) **Church, in Homes:** the method Christ chose for evangelizing was the method of home evangelism (see 10:5f). Note this, for it should speak loudly and clearly to us. The disciple was to carefully investigate and search out a receptive family and home. He was to make that home the center for ministry. Note several things about this method.

1. It emphasizes the family, making it the very hub of ministry.

2. It stresses stability and security. Nothing on earth is to be any more secure and stable than the family. By placing the center of ministry in the home, the kingdom of God becomes secure and stable.

3. It centers preaching and ministering in the community right where people live and walk. It makes the presence of Christ visible to all in day-to-day living.

4. It serves as the center from which the message can move out in an ever-widening circle, spreading from family to family.

> **THOUGHT 1.** The most ideal form of evangelism is probably this method given by Christ: a selected home and family serving as the center of witness within a community or town. The early church was definitely centered in the homes of committed believers (Ac.5:42; 12:12; 16:40; 20:20; 1 Co.16:19; Col.4:15; Phm.2).
>
> > And every day, in the temple and from house to house, they did not cease teaching and preaching that the Christ is Jesus. (Ac.5:42)
> >
> > How I did not shrink from declaring to you anything that was profitable, and teaching you in public and from house to house. (Ac.20:20)
> >
> > The churches of Asia send you greetings. Aquila and Prisca, together with the church in their house, send you hearty greetings in the Lord. (1 Co.16:19)
> >
> > And Apphia our sister and Archippus our fellow soldier, and the church in your house. (Phm.2)

5 Their obedience: They went out preaching and ministering (healing).

9:6

The disciples did exactly what Christ had commissioned them to do. They did not fail in the least. They went out preaching and ministering. Note three details:

⁶ And they departed and went through the villages, preaching the gospel and healing everywhere.

➢ They *departed*. There was no hesitation, no question, no condition, no hanging back, no slowness to move.

➢ They *went through the villages* or *towns*. They reached a home and ministered to its surrounding community, ever moving farther and farther out into the whole town. Then they moved on to another town to bear witness to its people as well.

➢ They *preached and ministered everywhere*. They had an extensive ministry, very successful in its outreach, ministering to both soul (preaching) and body (healing).

Go and stand in the temple and speak to the people all the words of this Life. (Ac.5:20)

Now those who were scattered went about preaching the word. (Ac.8:4)

Preach the word; be ready in season and out of season; reprove, rebuke, and exhort, with complete patience and teaching. (2 Ti.4:2)

9:7–9

⁷ Now Herod the tetrarch heard about all that was happening, and he was perplexed, because it was said by some that John had been raised from the dead,
⁸ by some that Elijah had appeared, and by others that one of the prophets of old had risen.
⁹ Herod said, "John I beheaded, but who is this about whom I hear such things?" And he sought to see him.

6 Their impact.

The disciples' ministry had a tremendous impact on the entire region. The impact of the message and ministry reached far and wide during these days (see outline and notes—Mt.14:1-14; Mk.6:14-29 for detailed discussion).

a. Herod was disturbed by their message (v.7).

The message and ministry of Jesus and His apostles reached even into the halls of government. Herod became disturbed. He had murdered John the Baptist, and some were saying that Jesus was John the Baptist risen from the dead. Of course, Herod's conscience was bothering him, just as all people are at some point nagged by the reality of the hereafter and the consequences of their sins.

b. The people speculated about Jesus' identity (v.8).

As stated, people were speculating about Jesus' identity, wondering if Jesus might be a resurrected John the Baptist (see outline and notes—Jn.7:37-53). Others suggested that He was Elijah or one of the other Old Testaments prophets who had come back from the dead.

c. Herod desired to know Jesus' identity (v.9).

Herod thought he had gotten rid of John's convicting preaching. Was it possible that John had arisen from the dead or that another like John had come on the scene? Haunted by anxiety and fear, Herod had to know who Jesus was, so he tried to see this miracle worker for himself.

Z. Jesus Teaches How to Minister, 9:10–17

(Mt.14:15-21; Mk.6:30-44; Jn.6:1-14)

10 On their return the apostles told him all that they had done. And he took them and withdrew apart to a town called Bethsaida.

11 When the crowds learned it, they followed him, and he welcomed them and spoke to them of the kingdom of God and cured those who had need of healing.

12 Now the day began to wear away, and the twelve came and said to him, "Send the crowd away to go into the surrounding villages and countryside to find lodging and get provisions, for we are here in a desolate place."

13 But he said to them, "You give them something to eat." They said, "We have no more than five loaves and two fish—unless we are to go and buy food for all these people."

14 For there were about five thousand men. And he said to his disciples, "Have them sit down in groups of about fifty each."

15 And they did so, and had them all sit down.

16 And taking the five loaves and the two fish, he looked up to heaven and said a blessing over them. Then he broke the loaves and gave them to the disciples to set before the crowd.

17 And they all ate and were satisfied. And what was left over was picked up, twelve baskets of broken pieces.

1. **Jesus demonstrated the need for privacy and rest**
   a. The apostles returned and reported to Jesus
   b. Jesus sought privacy with the disciples
2. **Jesus allowed the needy to interrupt their much-needed privacy and rest**
3. **Jesus met both spiritual and physical needs**

4. **Jesus challenged the apostles to meet the people's needs**
   a. The wrong attitude: Let the people take care of themselves

   b. The right attitude: Let the apostles meet the peoples' needs
   c. The problem: Inadequate resources

5. **Jesus approached needs in an orderly fashion**

6. **Jesus looked to God to meet the needs**
   a. He thanked God for what He had
   b. He broke and gave what He had

   c. The needs of all were met

Division III

The Son of Man's Announced Mission and Public Ministry, 4:16–9:17

Z. Jesus Teaches How to Minister, 9:10–17

(Mt.14:15–21; Mk.6:30–44; Jn.6:1–14)

9:10–17
Introduction

Jesus once said that He did not come to be served, but to serve—to minister (Mk.10:45). So it is with the Lord's disciples. But *how* we minister is of vital concern, for how we serve determines people's eternal fate and the success or failure of the Lord's mission. As in all things, our Lord prepares and instructs us as to how we should minister. This is, *Jesus Teaches How to Minister*, 9:10–17 (see outlines and notes—Mt.14:15–21; Mk.6:30–44 for more discussion and applications).

1. Jesus demonstrated the need for privacy and rest (v.10).
2. Jesus allowed the needy to interrupt their much needed privacy and rest (v.11).
3. Jesus met both spiritual and physical needs (v.11).
4. Jesus challenged the apostles to meet the people's needs (vv.12-13).
5. Jesus approached needs in an orderly fashion (vv.14-15).
6. Jesus looked to God to meet the needs (vv.16-17).

9:10

¹⁰ On their return the apostles told him all that they had done. And he took them and withdrew apart to a town called Bethsaida.

1 Jesus demonstrated the need for privacy and rest.

Jesus demonstrated and taught the need for times of privacy and rest. When the disciples returned from their mission, Jesus took them to an isolated, private place. He had never needed time with them as much as He did now, for He was closing out His Galilean ministry. In fact, there would be little public ministry hereafter. From this point forward, He would concentrate primarily on His disciples, giving them intensive training (see notes—Mt.16:13-20; 16:21-28; 17:1-13; 17:22; 17:24-27; 20:17; 20:20-28 to see the emphasis on this intensive training).

a. **The apostles returned and reported to Jesus.**
   The Twelve returned from their mission and reported what had happened. Jesus needed to discuss their witnessing tour with them. As they reported, He needed to point out both their strengths and weaknesses of how they went about it. Because they needed to learn to minister in the most effective way possible, an evaluation session was needed.

b. **Jesus sought privacy with the disciples.**
   The disciples needed to evaluate themselves; but they needed to do it away from the crowds, in the presence of God alone. They were physically exhausted, and their spirits were drained; they needed a break in order to restore both their spirits and bodies.
   What did Jesus do? He took them to a private place near the town of Bethsaida. Its quietness and privacy are mentioned, which indicates that they did not actually stay in the city (v.12).
   The point was clearly demonstrated for the disciples. There is a time for ministry and for evaluating oneself and one's ministry; there is also a time for renewing one's spirit and body.

   Come to me, all who labor and are heavy laden, and I will give you rest. (Mt.11:28)

   And he said to them, "Come away by yourselves to a desolate place and rest a while." For many were coming and going, and they had no leisure even to eat. (Mk.6:31)

   And he said, "My presence will go with you, and I will give you rest." (Ex.33:14)

Six days you shall work, but on the seventh day you shall rest. In plowing time and in harvest you shall rest. (Ex.34:21; see Ex.23:12; 31:15; 35:2)

Six days shall work be done, but on the seventh day is a Sabbath of solemn rest, a holy convocation. You shall do no work. It is a Sabbath to the Lᴏʀᴅ in all your dwelling places. (Le.23:3)

2 Jesus allowed the needy to interrupt their much-needed privacy and rest.

The people so craved Jesus' ministry that they followed Him and the disciples. They were interrupting the disciples' need for privacy, rest, and spiritual renewal. The disciples had been ministering, doing all they could, yet here the people were demanding more. Luke emphasized the contrast between Jesus and the disciples. The disciples became irritated (vv.12-13). Jesus, on the other hand, was filled with compassion for the people, and He welcomed them (see Mk.6:34). The disciples had a much needed lesson to learn, and they needed to learn the lesson more than they needed rest. The lesson was simple but dramatic: while one is resting, the multitudes are still lost. People still have needs. Christ's followers must often put other people's needs above our own. We must be careful about taking *too much* time off. Too many are lost and hurting.

> ¹¹ When the crowds learned it, they followed him, and he welcomed them and spoke to them of the kingdom of God and cured those who had need of healing.

Do you not say, "There are yet four months, then comes the harvest"? Look, I tell you, lift up your eyes, and see that the fields are white for harvest. (Jn.4:35)

We must work the works of him who sent me while it is day; night is coming, when no one can work. (Jn.9:4)

For we cannot but speak of what we have seen and heard. (Ac.4:20)

Preach the word; be ready in season and out of season; reprove, rebuke, and exhort, with complete patience and teaching. (2 Ti.4:2)

Whatever your hand finds to do, do it with your might, for there is no work or thought or knowledge or wisdom in Sheol, to which you are going. (Ec.9:10)

3 Jesus met both spiritual and physical needs.

The people did not need preaching alone; they also needed help physically. Both body and soul needed to be saved and restored. So, Jesus ministered to both their spiritual and physical needs.

> ¹¹ When the crowds learned it, they followed him, and he welcomed them and spoke to them of the kingdom of God and cured those who had need of healing.

First, Jesus preached the kingdom of God—of which God is the ruler and humanity is the subject, of which the Word of God is law and the people's obedience is required.

Second, Jesus healed the people that "had need of healing." This is always true. A believer who really *needs healing* is healed. But note: *the need of healing is not always a person's greatest need*. Only God, in His infinite wisdom and good purpose for our lives, truly knows what we *need*. God sometimes uses the physical need to meet that which is far more important: the spiritual need and the glory of God. Therefore, not all believers are always healed, not in this life. Sometimes the believer needs to learn love, joy, peace, endurance, prayer, trust, faith, and hope through their suffering (see Dᴇᴇᴘᴇʀ Sᴛᴜᴅʏ # 3—Mt.8:1-4 for detailed discussion).

How God anointed Jesus of Nazareth with the Holy Spirit and with power. He went about doing good and healing all who were oppressed by the devil, for God was with him. (Ac.10:38)

4 Jesus challenged the apostles to meet the people's needs.

The people had been listening to Jesus for hours. Sundown was soon to come. The people would be caught out in the desert in the dark, unable to get food before the next day. Some had already gone most of the day without food. It was time for Jesus to stop and let the people go; however, He gave no sign of stopping. So the disciples suggested He dismiss the crowd. But Jesus challenged them to meet the people's needs.

9:12-13

¹² Now the day began to wear away, and the twelve came and said to him, "Send the crowd away to go into the surrounding villages and countryside to find lodging and get provisions, for we are here in a desolate place."
¹³ But he said to them, "You give them something to eat." They said, "We have no more than five loaves and two fish—unless we are to go and buy food for all these people."

a. **The wrong attitude: Let the people take care of themselves (v.12).**

The disciples suggested that Jesus let the people go and take care of their own needs. Keep in mind that the crowd was not welcomed by the disciples, not this day. It was to have been a day of rest and spiritual renewal for them. The point is, the disciples had not sensed any personal responsibility for the *hunger* (physical or spiritual) of the crowd. They were willing, even wanting the crowd to go away, no matter the difficulty the people would have in fending for themselves.

b. **The right attitude: Let the apostles meet the peoples' needs (v.13a).**

In response, Jesus emphatically said, "You give them something to eat." The "you" is emphatic in the Greek. Jesus was stressing that it was the disciples' responsibility to take care of the people's needs. They were to "feed" the people *both* spiritually *and* physically. The people were not to be left to themselves. Under the circumstances, they could not provide food for themselves.

Note something else: it was more important for the people to be hearing God's Word and receiving ministry than to be out seeking something to eat (Mt.4:4). It is, of course, necessary to seek bread in order to survive, but seeking spiritual food is absolutely essential. Seeking spiritual food must be interrupted only when necessary.

> But the Lord answered her, "Martha, Martha, you are anxious and troubled about many things, but one thing is necessary. Mary has chosen the good portion, which will not be taken away from her." (Lu.10:41-42)

> Jesus said to them, "I am the bread of life; whoever comes to me shall not hunger, and whoever believes in me shall never thirst." (Jn.6:35)

> I am the living bread that came down from heaven. If anyone eats of this bread, he will live forever. And the bread that I will give for the life of the world is my flesh. (Jn.6:51)

c. **The problem: Inadequate resources (v.13b).**

The disciples readily confessed that they had too little to meet the overwhelming need of so many people. Just think about the enormity of the situation for a moment. The crowd was huge; the task was *impossible*. There was no possibility the disciples could meet the need of the people. So they did exactly what needed to be done:
➤ They told Jesus exactly what they did have.
➤ They did the best thinking they could, giving the best solution they could.

What the disciples had was inadequate, but they did lay what they had before Jesus and discussed the only solution they knew—to go and buy food.

9:14-15

¹⁴ For there were about five thousand men. And he said to his disciples, "Have them sit down in groups of about fifty each."
¹⁵ And they did so, and had them all sit down.

5 Jesus approached needs in an orderly fashion.

The crowd was massive. Over five thousand men alone were there, not counting the women and children. The need was so great that it could only be met by an orderly, highly-organized approach. Jesus instructed the disciples to divide the people into groups of fifty. Some groups consisted of double rows of fifty each (Mk.6:40).

> **THOUGHT 1.** The feeding of this massive crowd is a picture of distributing the bread of life—the gospel of Jesus Christ—to the world. The task is enormous. It can be met only by an orderly, organized approach.

6 Jesus looked to God to meet the needs.

Standing there with five loaves of bread and two fish and fifteen thousand or more people to feed, Jesus looked to God to meet the need. Note exactly what Jesus did.

> [16] And taking the five loaves and the two fish, he looked up to heaven and said a blessing over them. Then he broke the loaves and gave them to the disciples to set before the crowd.
> [17] And they all ate and were satisfied. And what was left over was picked up, twelve baskets of broken pieces.

a. He thanked God for what He had (v.16a).
Jesus looked up to heaven, giving thanks to God for what He did have. This is what is meant by the *blessing*.

b. He broke and gave what He had (v.16b).
Jesus broke the bread and fish and gave them to the disciples to distribute to the people. Note the crucial point. Jesus was doing what He could: looking up to God, giving thanks and then using what He had. He could do no more.

c. The needs of all were met (v.17).
Miraculously, there was plenty to feed all the people. In fact, there was more than enough. The disciples picked up twelve baskets of leftovers. Twelve disciples, twelve baskets: perhaps a basket for each disciple. Or, the leftovers may have been used for another need.

> **THOUGHT 1.** The lesson is clear for every believer. Once we do our part, God will multiply our resources. God will enable us to meet people's needs—if we will only confess our inadequate resources, give thanks for what we have, and then give what we have.
>
> > But seek first the kingdom of God and his righteousness, and all these things will be added to you. (Mt.6:33)
> >
> > The earth is the LORD's and the fullness thereof, the world and those who dwell therein. (Ps.24:1)
> >
> > Whoever brings blessing will be enriched, and one who waters will himself be watered. (Pr.11:25)
> >
> > Whoever has a bountiful eye will be blessed, for he shares his bread with the poor. (Pr.22:9)
> >
> > Whoever gives to the poor will not want, but he who hides his eyes will get many a curse. (Pr.28:27)
> >
> > The silver is mine, and the gold is mine, declares the LORD of hosts. (Hag.2:8)

IV. THE SON OF MAN'S INTENSIVE PREPARATION OF HIS DISCIPLES FOR JERUSALEM AND DEATH, 9:18–50

A. The First Prediction of His Death: Who Jesus Really Is, 9:18–22

(Mt.16:13–23; Mk.8:27–33)

1. **The people's belief: Jesus was only a great man**
   a. Jesus was praying alone
   b. Jesus asked the disciples, "Who do people say I am?"
   c. The disciples listed several theories

2. **The disciples' conviction: Jesus was the Messiah**

3. **The full meaning of the conviction**

   a. The significance was not yet grasped
   b. The ultimate truth: Jesus was the suffering and conquering Savior[DS1]

18 Now it happened that as he was praying alone, the disciples were with him. And he asked them, "Who do the crowds say that I am?"

19 And they answered, "John the Baptist. But others say, Elijah, and others, that one of the prophets of old has risen."

20 Then he said to them, "But who do you say that I am?" And Peter answered, "The Christ of God."

21 And he strictly charged and commanded them to tell this to no one,

22 saying, "The Son of Man must suffer many things and be rejected by the elders and chief priests and scribes, and be killed, and on the third day be raised."

Division IV

The Son of Man's Intensive Preparation of His Disciples for Jerusalem and Death, 9:18–50

A. The First Prediction of His Death: Who Jesus Really Is, 9:18–22

(Mt.16:13–23; Mk.8:27–33)

9:18–22
Introduction

The most critical question of life is the question Jesus asked the disciples in this passage: "Who do you say that I am?" (v.20). Sometime later, Jesus would ask this same question of the Pharisees, only phrasing it, "What do you think about the Christ?" (Mt.22:42).

Every human being must be confronted with this question. The answer has serious implications in this life. But it is far more significant for the life to come, for it determines whether a person spends eternity in God's presence or totally separated from God in hell. This is, *The First Prediction of His Death: Who Jesus Really Is,* 9:18–22.

1. The people's belief: Jesus was only a great man (vv.18–19).
2. The disciples' conviction: Jesus was the Messiah, promised by God (v.20).
3. The full meaning of the conviction (vv.21–22).

1 The people's belief: Jesus was only a great man.

Luke establishes the setting for Jesus' great question and Peter's great confession. Mark adds that it happened while they were on their way to Caesarea Philippi. The scene was that of Jesus being off to the side, away from the disciples and all alone. He was seeking the face of God and agonizing in prayer. Then all of a sudden, He quit praying, walked over to the disciples, and asked them two probing questions.

a. Jesus was praying alone (v.18a).

As the group traveled, Jesus sensed a deep need for prayer, so He went off by Himself to pray. Perhaps He needed personal strength, for He had "set His face to go to Jerusalem," which means that He was setting His face toward the cross where He was to die for the sins of the human race (v.51). The days ahead would hold excruciating suffering for Him.

> **18** Now it happened that as he was praying alone, the disciples were with him. And he asked them, "Who do the crowds say that I am?"
>
> **19** And they answered, "John the Baptist. But others say, Elijah, and others, that one of the prophets of old has risen."

b. Jesus asked the disciples, "Who do people say I am?" (v.18b).

The disciples also had to face the issue of the cross, that the Messiah had to die for the sins of the world in order that people could be saved. This was a radically different concept of the Messiah than the popular concept. The popular concept said that the Messiah was to be the Son of David, the promised King who was to come and free Israel from her enemies and set up the kingdom of God over all nations of the earth (see note—Mt.16:21-28).

The disciples also had an immediate need, the need for a very special *revelation* into Christ's person. It was time for them to grasp and confess without any hesitation that He was the Messiah, the very Son of God. Perhaps Jesus paused to pray for them as well. He was now ready to examine their hearts and convictions about Him, so He asked the disciples, "Who do the crowds say that I am?"

The disciples' concept of the Messiah needed to be corrected and established. Their concept was the popular concept that saw the Messiah only as the greatest of men. They desperately needed to grasp and understand to the fullest measure who Jesus was. The very destiny of the world rested in their hands. People were doomed and lost forever unless the disciples fully understood. Therefore, Jesus had to examine them to make sure they were thinking for themselves and rejecting the false ideas of Messiahship held by the people of the day.

THOUGHT 1. Three important lessons on prayer can be gleaned from what Christ was doing.

1) We need to pray before momentous events.

> **Ask, and it will be given to you; seek, and you will find; knock, and it will be opened to you. (Mt.7:7)**

> **Is anyone among you suffering? Let him pray. Is anyone cheerful? Let him sing praise. (Jas.5:13)**

> **Call to me and I will answer you, and will tell you great and hidden things that you have not known. (Je.33:3)**

2) We are to pray for others, that they might have special insight and the power of the Spirit on their lives.

> **Praying at all times in the Spirit, with all prayer and supplication. To that end, keep alert with all perseverance, making supplication for all the saints. (Ep.6:18)**

3) We must pray for strength to withstand severe trials and temptations, that we might be enabled to bear whatever cross lies ahead.

> **Watch and pray that you may not enter into temptation. The spirit indeed is willing, but the flesh is weak. (Mt.26:41)**

> **Likewise the Spirit helps us in our weakness. For we do not know what to pray for as we ought, but the Spirit himself intercedes for us with groanings too deep for words. (Ro.8:26)**

When he calls to me, I will answer him; I will be with him in trouble; I will rescue him and honor him. (Ps.91:15)

When the poor and needy seek water, and there is none, and their tongue is parched with thirst, I the LORD will answer them; the God of Israel will not forsake them. (Is.41:17)

c. **The disciples listed several theories (v.19).**

While there were certainly exceptions, the people in general believed that Jesus was only a great man. Some, the disciples answered, thought Jesus was John the Baptist, that is, the fore-runner of the Messiah (Mal.4:5). Both John and Jesus were doing a unique and great work for God. Both were divinely chosen and gifted by God, and both proclaimed the kingdom of God and prepared people for it. Therefore, when some looked at Jesus and His ministry, they thought Jesus was not the Messiah Himself, but the promised forerunner of the Messiah (Mal.4:5).

Others were professing Jesus to be the greatest prophet and teacher of all time. Elijah was so considered, and Elijah was also predicted to be the forerunner of the coming Messiah (Mal.4:5). Even today the Jews expect Elijah to return before the Messiah. In celebrating the Passover, they leave a chair vacant for him to occupy. Elijah had also been used by God to miraculously feed a widow woman and her son (1 Ki.17:14). The people connected Elijah's miracle and Jesus' feeding of the multitude.

Still others speculated Jesus was one of the other prophets of old. These were professing Jesus to be a great prophet sent for their day and time. He was thought to be one of the great prophets brought back to life or one in whom the spirit of a great prophet dwelt (see De.18:15, 18).

The popular opinion of the Messiah was wrong. Most of the people honored Jesus highly, very highly. They saw Him as a great man; in fact, they saw Him as one of the greatest of men. However, such a concept would spell doom for the world if it were not corrected. Jesus had to make sure the people's idea had not influenced and corrupted the thinking of the disciples.

THOUGHT 1. Note that the same false confessions about Christ exist in every generation.
1) He was only a great man of righteousness, martyred for His faith. As such He leaves us a great example of how to live and stand up for what we believe.
2) He was one of the greatest teachers and prophets of all time.
3) He was a great man who revealed some very important things to us about God and religion. As such He can make a significant contribution to every person in their search for God.
4) He was a great man and prophet sent to the people (Jews) of His day; however, we can learn a great deal that will help us by studying His life.

"Is not this the carpenter, the son of Mary and brother of James and Joses and Judas and Simon? And are not his sisters here with us?" And they took offense at him. (Mk.6:3)

He was in the world, and the world was made through him, yet the world did not know him. He came to his own, and his own people did not receive him. (Jn.1:10–11)

Who is the liar but he who denies that Jesus is the Christ? This is the antichrist, he who denies the Father and the Son. No one who denies the Son has the Father. Whoever con-fesses the Son has the Father also. (1 Jn.2:22–23)

And every spirit that does not confess Jesus is not from God. This is the spirit of the anti-christ, which you heard was coming and now is in the world already. (1 Jn.4:3)

9:20

[20] Then he said to them, "But who do you say that I am?" And Peter answered, "The Christ of God."

2 The disciples' conviction: Jesus was the Messiah.

Jesus sat and listened closely to what the disciples had to say about the people's ideas regarding the Messiah. Now He was ready to ask the second probing question . . .

- the question whose answer determines a person's eter-nal salvation
- the question that is the most significant question ever asked

"But who do you say that I am?" The "you" is emphatic. Jesus stressed the *personal*, the importance of a personal response: "But *you*, who do *you* say that I am?"

The answer was immediate and forceful: *the Christ of God*. Peter was the spokesman for all the disciples, and he emphatically declared that Jesus was *the Christ of God*. It was a powerful statement—a statement profound in its meaning, for Jesus was "the Christ," that is, "the Messiah," *the anointed One of God* (see DEEPER STUDY # 2—Mt.1:18). This title conveys three truths:

➤ Jesus was sent on a deliberate mission, the mission of saving humanity (Lu.19:10).
➤ Jesus was *sent and qualified* by God to carry out that mission (Jn.3:16; 4:34; 5:23-24, 30, 36-38; 6:29, 38-40, 44, 57; 7:16, 18, 28-29; 8:16, 18, 26, 29, 42; 9:4; 10:36; 11:42; 12:45, 49; 14:24; 15:21; 16:5; 17:3, 18, 21, 23, 25; 20:21; 1 Jn.4:9-10, 14).
➤ Jesus was the fulfillment of all the prophecies which promised the coming of the Messiah for the salvation of mankind.

The question was very personal. It might have even offended some of the disciples. However, Jesus meant the question to be personal. It had to be, for an individual's eternal destiny and fate is determined by their answer. Jesus was not just a man as the popular idea of Him declared. He was more, much more. He was *the Christ of God*. Every person's life, death, and eternal fate hinges on how they see and confess Christ.

> So everyone who acknowledges me before men, I also will acknowledge before my Father who is in heaven, but whoever denies me before men, I also will deny before my Father who is in heaven. (Mt.10:32-33)

> For whoever is ashamed of me and of my words in this adulterous and sinful generation, of him will the Son of Man also be ashamed when he comes in the glory of his Father with the holy angels. (Mk.8:38)

> And I tell you, everyone who acknowledges me before men, the Son of Man also will acknowledge before the angels of God. (Lu.12:8)

> He first found his own brother Simon and said to him, "We have found the Messiah" (which means Christl).... Philip found Nathanael and said to him, "We have found him of whom Moses in the Law and also the prophets wrote, Jesus of Nazareth, the son of Joseph." (Jn.1:41, 45)

> Nathanael answered him, "Rabbi, you are the Son of God! You are the King of Israel!" (Jn.1:49)

> Come, see a man who told me all that I ever did. Can this be the Christ? (Jn.4:29)

> And we have believed, and have come to know, that you are the Holy One of God. (Jn.6:69)

> She said to him, "Yes, Lord; I believe that you are the Christ, the Son of God, who is coming into the world." (Jn.11:27)

> Thomas answered him, "My Lord and my God!" (Jn.20:28)

> Because, if you confess with your mouth that Jesus is Lord and believe in your heart that God raised him from the dead, you will be saved. For with the heart one believes and is justified, and with the mouth one confesses and is saved. (Ro.10:9-10)

> No one who denies the Son has the Father. Whoever confesses the Son has the Father also. (1 Jn.2:23)

> Whoever confesses that Jesus is the Son of God, God abides in him, and he in God. (1 Jn.4:15)

3 The full meaning of the conviction.

Upon Peter's great confession—a confession made on behalf of the group—Jesus gave the disciples a strange order. He strictly warned them not to tell this to anyone (v.21). Why would the Lord say such a thing?

²¹ And he strictly charged and commanded them to tell this to no one,
²² saying, "The Son of Man must suffer many things and be rejected by the elders and chief priests and scribes, and be killed, and on the third day be raised."

a. The significance was not yet grasped (v.22).

The disciples did not yet grasp the full meaning of the Messiah. The disciples were yet to experience the death and resurrection of Jesus Christ. The prophecies of the Messiah which stuck out in their minds were those dealing with His exaltation, sovereignty, power, and glory. They saw His ruling and reigning over the earth and subjecting people to

God by force. Their idea of the Messiah was that of an earthly rule within the bounds of the physical and material world. They had little if any idea of the spiritual world; therefore, they were not ready to share the truth of the Messiah (see note—Ep.1:3). They would be sharing an incomplete message, a false message; so Jesus had to charge them to tell nobody, not yet, not until they understood the real meaning of the spiritual salvation which He was bringing. Note the importance of understanding the full meaning of the Messiah. Jesus charged them and then commanded them to say nothing until they did understand.

b. **The ultimate truth: Jesus was the suffering and conquering Savior (v.22).**

Jesus began to clearly reveal that the Messiah had to be both a *suffering* and a conquering Savior. For some time, Jesus had been telling His disciples about His death and resurrection, but they had not understood. Why?

➤ The idea of a suffering Messiah differed radically from their own idea of the Messiah (see notes—Mt.1:1; Deeper Study # 2—1:18; Deeper Study # 3—3:11; notes—11:1-6; 11:2-3; Deeper Study # 1—11:5; Deeper Study # 2—11:6; Deeper Study # 1—12:16; note—Lu.7:21-23).

➤ The revelation had been hidden in pictures and symbols.

Jesus answered them, "Destroy this temple, and in three days I will raise it up." (Jn.2:19)

And as Moses lifted up the serpent in the wilderness, so must the Son of Man be lifted up. (Jn.3:14)

I am the living bread that came down from heaven. If anyone eats of this bread, he will live forever. And the bread that I will give for the life of the world is my flesh. (Jn.6:51)

The difference now was that Jesus no longer spoke in pictures and symbols, but He told them in simple and direct words (Mt.20:18-20; Lu.18:31-33). A new stage in the revelation of God's plan for the world was now taking place: God's Son was to be rejected by the Jewish leaders and die and be raised again for the sins of the world (see Deeper Study # 1). God's plan for saving the world was to take place through a suffering Messiah, not a conquering Messiah who was going to deliver a *materialistic* world into the hands of His followers. His death was to usher in the kingdom of God, making it possible for His followers to live eternally in the very presence of God Himself (see Deeper Study # 3—Mt.19:23-24; see Jn.3:16; 5:24f).

Note the word *must* (dei, *day*). It is strong; it means a constraint, an imperative, a necessity was laid upon Him. He had no choice. His death and resurrection had been planned and willed by God through all eternity. The prophets had foretold it. He must fulfill the will of God, for God had ordained His death (see Deeper Study # 3—Ac.2:23 for more discussion; see Mt.26:54).

Was it not necessary that the Christ should suffer these things and enter into his glory? (Lu.24:26)

And said to them, "Thus it is written, that the Christ should suffer and on the third day rise from the dead, and that repentance for the forgiveness of sins should be proclaimed in his name to all nations, beginning from Jerusalem." (Lu.24:46-47)

DEEPER STUDY # 1

(9:22) **Jesus Christ, Opposition:** note the three Jewish groups who were to take the lead in killing Jesus. These were the three groups who made up the Sanhedrin, the supreme court of Jewish justice. It was comprised of seventy members (see the historical basis for this structure, 2 Chr.19:5-11).

1. The elders: these were the older, respected men of a community. The elders were judges of the civil courts, of temporal affairs (Ex.3:29; 12:21; 24:9; Nu.11:25; 1 S.16:4; Ezr.10:14; Mt.27:12).

2. The chief priests: these were primarily leaders from among the Sadducees who held most of the high offices of Jewish government under Roman rule (see note—Ac.23:8). The chief priests were judges of religious affairs.

3. The Scribes: these were Pharisees who held the teaching positions of the nation (see Deeper Study # 1—Lu.6:2).

(Mt.16:24-28; Mk.8:34-9:1)

²³ And he said to all, "If anyone would come after me, let him deny himself and take up his cross daily and follow me.

²⁴ For whoever would save his life will lose it, but whoever loses his life for my sake will save it. ²⁵ For what does it profit a man if he gains the whole world and loses or forfeits himself? ²⁶ For whoever is ashamed of me and of my words, of him will the Son of Man be ashamed when he comes in his glory and the glory of the Father and of the holy angels. ²⁷ But I tell you truly, there are some standing here who will not taste death until they see the kingdom of God."

1. **The terms of discipleship**
   a. Must deny yourself
   b. Must take up your cross daily[DS1]
   c. Must follow Jesus
2. **A warning to the self-serving**
   a. Do not save your life for yourself
   b. Spend your life for Christ
3. **A question for the self-serving: What do you profit if you gain the whole world but lose your life?**[DS2]
4. **The judgment of the self-serving**
   a. The reason: Is ashamed of Jesus and His Words
   b. The judgment: Counted unsuitable for glory
5. **The disciple's reward: God's kingdom**

Division IV

The Son of Man's Intensive Preparation of His Disciples for Jerusalem and Death, 9:18–50

B. The Terms of Discipleship, 9:23–27

(Mt.16:24–28; Mk.8:34–9:1)

9:23-27
Introduction

Jesus had just told His disciples plainly that He was going to be executed (v.22). Now, He was issuing a challenge to His disciples, and, in doing so, He revealed *how* He would die: by crucifixion. Just as He would bear His cross, all who wish to follow Him must bear their cross as well. There is no option; discipleship requires it. This is, *The Terms of Discipleship, 9:23-27*.

1. The terms of discipleship (v.23).
2. A warning to the self-serving (v.24).
3. A question for the self-serving: What do you profit if you gain the whole world and lose your life? (v.25).
4. The judgment of the self-serving (v.26).
5. The disciple's reward: God's kingdom (v.27).

1 The terms of discipleship.

All twelve of the men with Jesus had decided to commit their lives to following Him. But, when they made the decision, did they really understand what discipleship means? Jesus frankly explained what is required of those who want to follow Him.

9:23

²³ And he said to all, "If anyone would come after me, let him deny himself and take up his cross daily and follow me."

a. Must deny yourself.

First, we must deny ourselves. Our tendency is to indulge ourselves and do exactly what we desire; but Christ-followers are not to indulge themselves, their comfort and ease, appetites and urges, thoughts and feelings, deceptions and enticements, plots and intrigues, pride and boastings, reactions and disturbances. We are to deny ourselves by discipline and control and by loving and caring, sacrificing and giving, helping and ministering. We are not to live for our desires, pleasure, and comfort. We are to *die to self.*

b. Must take up your cross daily.

Second, we must take up our cross and do it daily. The command to take up the cross is directly tied to the command to deny self; it is dying to self (see DEEPER STUDY # 1). But it is also a command to identify with Christ. It "means to be identified with Him in surrender, suffering, and sacrifice."[1] *The Bible Knowledge Commentary* provides this excellent explanation:

"When the Roman Empire crucified a criminal or captive, the victim was often forced to carry his cross part of the way to the crucifixion site. Carrying his cross through the heart of the city was supposed to be a tacit admission that the Roman Empire was correct in the sentence of death imposed on him, an admission that Rome was right and he was wrong. So when Jesus enjoined His followers to carry their crosses and follow Him, He was referring to a public display before others that Jesus was right and that the disciples were following Him even to their deaths."[2]

c. Must follow Jesus.

Third, we must follow Jesus. However, our tendency is to follow *someone else* and to give our first allegiance to *something else.* Within the world, there are many things available for a person to serve and to put first. There are . . .

- service organizations
- humanitarian needs
- religion (institutional)
- family
- recreation
- hobby
- education
- profession
- houses
- business
- clubs
- fame/honor
- comfort
- social acceptance
- pleasure
- health
- appearance
- sports

But when we follow Christ, we put Him first. He becomes the first priority in our lives, the Lord of our lives.

Following Christ also means walking in His steps, living as He lived, following His example, loving and serving people as He loved and served people, adopting His mission, imitating His holiness, laying down our lives as He laid down His life. To follow Christ, we must stay close to Christ. We cannot follow Christ from a distance. If we are to walk in His footsteps, we must be close enough to Him to see those footsteps clearly.

Following Christ involves suffering. We can expect to be hated and mistreated just as He was hated and mistreated (Jn.15:18-20; 1 Pe.2:20-21). You cannot follow Christ faithfully without being persecuted (2 Ti.3:12).

> **My sheep hear my voice, and I know them, and they follow me. I give them eternal life, and they will never perish, and no one will snatch them out of my hand. My Father, who has given them to me, is greater than all, and no one is able to snatch them out of the Father's hand. (Jn.10:27-29)**

> **If anyone serves me, he must follow me; and where I am, there will my servant be also. If anyone serves me, the Father will honor him. (Jn.12:26)**

---

1 Warren W. Wiersbe, *The Bible Exposition Commentary,* (Colorado Springs, CO: David C. Cook, 2008). Via Wordsearch digital edition.

2 John Walvoord and Roy B. Zuck, eds., *The Bible Knowledge Commentary New Testament: An Exposition of the Scriptures by Dallas Seminary Faculty,* (Colorado Springs, CO: David C. Cook, 1983).

Therefore be imitators of God, as beloved children. And walk in love, as Christ loved us and gave himself up for us, a fragrant offering and sacrifice to God. (Ep.5:1-2)

Therefore, as you received Christ Jesus the Lord, so walk in him. (Col.2:6)

For to this you have been called, because Christ also suffered for you, leaving you an example, so that you might follow in his steps. (1 Pe.2:21)

DEEPER STUDY # 1

(9:23) **Cross—Discipleship:** people in Jesus' day knew what it meant to "take up" a cross. They saw scores of criminals bear the cross to the place where they were to be executed, and they witnessed scores of crucifixions, some even by the sides of the roads that led in and out of the cities.

"Taking up one's cross" does not mean merely bearing one's particular hardship in life, such as poor health, abuse, unemployment, declining parents, an unsaved spouse, a way-ward child. The cross is always an instrument of death, not just an object to carry or bear. The Christian is to die mentally and actively. We are to deny ourselves daily. We are to let the mind of Christ, the mind of humbling ourselves to the point of death, be in us and fill our thoughts every day (Ph.2:5-8; 2 Co.10:3-5). We are to put our will, our desires, our wants, our ambitions to death. In their stead, we are to follow Jesus and to do His will all day long. Note this is not negative, passive behavior. It takes positive, active behavior to *will*, to *deny self*, to *take up* one's *cross*, to *follow* Christ. We have to act, work, get to it, be diligent, consistent, and enduring in order to die to self.

There are several ways the believer dies to self. Romans 6:11-13 spells out the ways as clearly as they can be explained.

So you also must consider yourselves dead to sin and alive to God in Christ Jesus. Let not sin therefore reign in your mortal body, to make you obey its passions. Do not present your members to sin as instruments for unrighteousness, but present yourselves to God as those who have been brought from death to life, and your members to God as instruments for righteousness. (Ro.6:11-13; see Ro.6:2-10)

1. We count ourselves crucified with Christ.

We know that our old self was crucified with him in order that the body of sin might be brought to nothing, so that we would no longer be enslaved to sin. (Ro.6:6)

So you also must consider yourselves dead to sin. . . . (Ro.6:11ª)

I have been crucified with Christ. It is no longer I who live, but Christ who lives in me. And the life I now live in the flesh I live by faith in the Son of God, who loved me and gave himself for me. (Ga.2:20)

And those who belong to Christ Jesus have crucified the flesh with its passions and desires. (Ga.5:24)

2. We count ourselves dead to sin, but alive to God.

So you also must consider yourselves dead to sin and alive to God in Christ Jesus. (Ro.6:11)

So as to live for the rest of the time in the flesh no longer for human passions but for the will of God. (1 Pe.4:2)

3. We do not let sin reign in our bodies.

Let not sin therefore reign in your mortal body, to make you obey its passions. (Ro.6:12)

Put to death therefore what is earthly in you: sexual immorality, impurity, passion, evil desire, and covetousness, which is idolatry. (Col.3:5)

4. We do not yield any parts of our bodies as instruments of sin.

Do not present your members to sin as instruments for unrighteousness, . . . (Ro.6:13ª)

For if you live according to the flesh you will die, but if by the Spirit you put to death the deeds of the body, you will live. (Ro.8:13)

5. We yield ourselves to God—as much as those who are alive from the dead are yielded to God.

> . . . but present yourselves to God as those who have been brought from death to life, . . . (Ro.6:13ᵇ)

> I appeal to you therefore, brothers, by the mercies of God, to present your bodies as a living sacrifice, holy and acceptable to God, which is your spiritual worship. (Ro.12:1)

> But put on the Lord Jesus Christ, and make no provision for the flesh, to gratify its desires. (Ro.13:14)

6. We yield every part of our bodies as an instrument of righteousness.

> . . . present . . . your members to God as instruments for righteousness. (Ro.6:13ᶜ)

> But I say, walk by the Spirit, and you will not gratify the desires of the flesh. (Ga.5:16)

It should be noted that one's hardship or burden can bring a person to the place where the Lord can deal with them. It is then that the hardship becomes the cross and denial of self that Jesus is talking about. With an act of self-denial, the Christian can then count himself or herself alive to God (Ro.6:13) and can then follow Jesus. This is an act which can be described as committing all that one is and has to Christ. It is an act that needs to be repeated every day (see Mt.10:38; see outlines and notes—Mt.19:21–30).

9:24

²⁴ "For whoever would save his life will lose it, but whoever loses his life for my sake will save it."

2 A warning to the self-serving.

Jesus issues a strong warning to all who live for themselves. Note the word *life* (Gk. psuchēn, *soo-cane'*). In this context it means the natural life; the earthly life that quickly passes away; the fading, aging, decaying, corruptible life of the earth. The warning is twofold (see note—Mt.16:25–28 for more discussion).

a. Do not save your life for yourself.

Those who *save* their life, that is, work to please themselves on this earth, will lose their life eternally. God does not give people life . . .

- to indulge themselves: getting all they can of the comforts and pleasures and interests of life
- to hoard life: keeping all the good things of life and seldom becoming involved in giving and sacrificing to help those who do not have life's necessities

> And as for what fell among the thorns, they are those who hear, but as they go on their way they are choked by the cares and riches and pleasures of life, and their fruit does not mature. (Lu.8:14)

> And I will say to my soul, "Soul, you have ample goods laid up for many years; relax, eat, drink, be merry." But God said to him, "Fool! This night your soul is required of you, and the things you have prepared, whose will they be?" So is the one who lays up treasure for himself and is not rich toward God. (Lu.12:19–21)

> But she who is self-indulgent is dead even while she lives. (1 Ti.5:6)

> All the toil of man is for his mouth, yet his appetite is not satisfied. (Ec.6:7)

b. Spend your life for Christ.

People who *lose* their life, that is, who spend their life serving and pleasing Christ on this earth, will save their life. They will find true life, an abundant life, a quality of life unparalleled by anything this world can offer.

➤ It is a life spent knowing God and fellowshipping with God.

> That which we have seen and heard we proclaim also to you, so that you too may have fellowship with us; and indeed our fellowship is with the Father and with his Son Jesus Christ. (1 Jn.1:3)

"You are my witnesses," declares the LORD, "and my servant whom I have chosen, that you may know and believe me and understand that I am he. Before me no god was formed, nor shall there be any after me." (Is.43:10)

➤ It is a life spent in healthy relationships and fellowship with other people.

And they devoted themselves to the apostles' teaching and the fellowship, to the breaking of bread and the prayers. (Ac.2:42)

But if we walk in the light, as he is in the light, we have fellowship with one another, and the blood of Jesus his Son cleanses us from all sin. (1 Jn.1:7)

I am a companion of all who fear you, of those who keep your precepts. (Ps. 119:63)

Two are better than one, because they have a good reward for their toil. For if they fall, one will lift up his fellow. But woe to him who is alone when he falls and has not another to lift him up! (Ec.4:9–10)

Then those who feared the LORD spoke with one another. The LORD paid attention and heard them, and a book of remembrance was written before him of those who feared the LORD and esteemed his name. (Mal.3:16)

➤ It is a life spent helping save a world lost in sin and shame and suffering.

Even as the Son of Man came not to be served but to serve, and to give his life as a ransom for many. (Mt.20:28)

For the Son of Man came to seek and to save the lost. (Lu.19:10)

Jesus said to them again, "Peace be with you. As the Father has sent me, even so I am sending you." (Jn.20:21)

We who are strong have an obligation to bear with the failings of the weak, and not to please ourselves. (Ro.15:1)

3 A question for the self-serving: What do you profit if you gain the whole world but lose your life?

²⁵ "For what does it profit a man if he gains the whole world and loses or forfeits himself?"

Christ asks one question of the self-serving, but the question has two components or pictures: If a person gains the world but loses their life, what do they gain? The Lord challenges all who seek to save their life, who live to please themselves, to think honestly (see note—Mt.16:25–28 for more discussion).

First, Christ paints the picture of gaining the *whole* world. Note that Christ did not say this: what if a man could gain and own all the land of Texas, or all the wealth of Africa. He said what if a man could gain the *whole world*. Scripture defines exactly what the *whole world* is:

For all that is in the world—the desires of the flesh and the desires of the eyes and pride of life—is not from the Father but is from the world. (1 Jn.2:16)

"All that is in the world"—the *whole world*—consists of . . .
- everything the flesh can desire: all the pleasures in the world
- everything the eyes can desire: all the possessions in the world
- everything human pride can desire: all the power, prestige, positions, and popularity in the world

Imagine for a moment: What if a person could gain *all* of this? No individual can or will gain it all; but many pursue and some do gain a great deal of land, wealth, honor, pleasure, prestige, power, and fleshly satisfaction.

Second, Jesus presents the picture of losing self, of forfeiting oneself. Note that this is a stated fact, an inevitable and sure result. Those who seek to please themselves are doomed to "lose" or "destroy" themselves and to "forfeit" themselves or be "lost" (see DEEPER STUDY # 2). They tried to *find themselves* here on earth, but they never did. They *lost themselves*. They lost the greatest things in all the world: certainty, assurance, confidence, and satisfaction of knowing that they are eternally secure and destined to live and serve God forever.

I tell you, many will come from east and west and recline at table with Abraham, Isaac, and Jacob in the kingdom of heaven, while the sons of the kingdom will be thrown into the outer darkness. In that place there will be weeping and gnashing of teeth. (Mt.8:11–12)

And he said to him, "Friend, how did you get in here without a wedding garment?" And he was speechless. Then the king said to the attendants, "Bind him hand and foot and cast him into the outer darkness. In that place there will be weeping and gnashing of teeth." (Mt.22:12–13)

And cast the worthless servant into the outer darkness. In that place there will be weeping and gnashing of teeth. (Mt.25:30)

But watch yourselves lest your hearts be weighed down with dissipation and drunkenness and cares of this life, and that day come upon you suddenly like a trap. (Lu.21:34)

DEEPER STUDY # 2

(9:25) **Forfeit or Lost** (zēmiōtheis, *zay-me-oh-thace'*): to suffer the loss of, to lose what is of greatest value, to be punished by forfeiting and losing (see 1 Co.3:15).

9:26

26 "For whoever is ashamed of me and of my words, of him will the Son of Man be ashamed when he comes in his glory and the glory of the Father and of the holy angels."

4 The judgment of the self-serving.

The self-serving suffer a tragic end: they will be judged by God. They did not have to suffer the judgment of God, but they chose the world and its things and pleasures over Christ. Why will the self-serving be judged?

a. **The reason: Is ashamed of Jesus and His Words.**

There is basically one reason: the self-serving person is ashamed of *Jesus and His Words*. This person is embarrassed and ashamed by such things as . . .

- being known as a true believer
- following and obeying Christ completely
- witnessing and standing up for Christ and what is right
- living less extravagantly than others
- having less because of giving so much
- associating with the needy to help them

- driving a cheaper car
- living in a less expensive home
- not socializing with the worldly
- not compromising and going along
- not having the things others have
- not joining in off-colored talk and jokes

Simply stated, the self-serving loved the acceptance and recognition of society, the comfort and pleasure of the world too much—they loved it all too much to give up their life and bear the reproach of Christ. They misjudged, counting the few years of plenty on this earth as worth the unending years of the new earth and heavens.

b. **The judgment: counted unsuitable for glory.**

Judgment is the most tragic event imaginable in the life of the self-serving. They will be as counted unsuitable for glory. Second Thessalonians 1:7–10 expounds what Jesus was saying here:

And to grant relief to you who are afflicted as well as to us, when the Lord Jesus is revealed from heaven with his mighty angels in flaming fire, inflicting vengeance on those who do not know God and on those who do not obey the gospel of our Lord Jesus. They will suffer the punishment of eternal destruction, away from the presence of the Lord and from the glory of his might, when he comes on that day to be glorified in his saints, and to be marveled at among all who have believed, because our testimony to you was believed. (2 Th.1:7–10)

The Lord is coming. It is stated without equivocation. It is definite, even fixed. Jesus said He will come, and He is coming in a threefold glory:

➤ His own glory, exalted as the Messiah, the Christ of God (Ph.2:9–11)
➤ The glory of God in all the brilliance and splendor of His person (1 Ti.6:16; 1 Jn.1:5; Re.22:15)

➤ The glory of the angels in their magnificence of being and brightness. They will accompany Jesus when He returns to judge the earth.

The point is clear: when Jesus comes in His glory, self-serving people will not join Him. They will not be welcomed into the glory of the Lord. Why? Christ will be *ashamed* of them because they were ashamed of Him and His Word. They rejected Christ and His message because they loved themselves. They chose to spend their lives satisfying themselves rather than serving Christ. The Lord will be ashamed of them because they are . . .

- not properly dressed (with the righteousness of God)
- not employed (in the things of God)
- too dirty (morally and righteously)
- too poor (spiritually)
- too immoral (not repenting)
- too unjust (not changing)
- too different (from the children of God)
- too unlearned (in the things of God)

The self-serving refuse to acknowledge Christ by repenting of their sinfulness and believing in Him as their Lord and Savior. Therefore, on that day when He comes as Lord of all, He will not acknowledge them as His children, as His followers, for they are not. They made their choice to live for themselves rather than by the Words of Jesus. They forfeited themselves for the pursuit of selfish pleasures, possessions, and pride.

And then will I declare to them, "I never knew you; depart from me, you workers of lawlessness." (Mt.7:23)

But he answered, "Truly, I say to you, I do not know you." (Mt.25:12)

But the one who denies me before men will be denied before the angels of God. (Lu.12:9)

But he will say, "I tell you, I do not know where you come from. Depart from me, all you workers of evil!" (Lu.13:27)

5 The disciple's reward: God's kingdom.

9:27

The disciple—the person who chooses to live for Christ rather than for self—receives a rich reward: the kingdom of God. The believer enters the kingdom of God immediately upon believing (see Deeper Study # 3—Mt.19:23-24). "This kingdom came when he was exalted on the cross, when he was glorified in the resurrection, and when he was enthroned in the ascension. This kingdom came when Pentecost brought previously unknown kingdom power to bear on earth and reaped an unprecedented harvest into kingdom membership."[3] Standing there in the crowd before Christ, some were to be eyewitnesses of the death and resurrection of Christ and the coming of the Holy Spirit. They were to taste and experience the kingdom of God in this life—before they died. Since that day, untold millions have been saved and have experienced the kingdom of God before experiencing *physical death* (see Jn.3:16; 5:24; 8:52; He.2:9, 14-15).

[27] "But I tell you truly, there are some standing here who will not taste death until they see the kingdom of God."

---

3 Trent Butler, Max Anders (ed.), *Holman New Testament Commentary: Luke*, (Nashville, TN: Holman Reference, 2000). Via Wordsearch digital edition.

C. The Events of the Transfiguration: A Glimpse into Glory, 9:28–36

(see Mt.17:1–13; Mk.9:2–13)

1. **Event 1: Jesus went up a mountain to pray**
   a. He took three disciples with Him

   b. He prayed
2. **Event 2: The countenance and clothing of Jesus were changed—became as bright as lightning**
3. **Event 3: Two men appeared and talked with Jesus**
   a. Moses, the lawgiver; Elijah, the great prophet
   b. The men discussed Jesus' imminent death

4. **Event 4: The three disciples witnessed the event**
   a. They were awakened by the glory

   b. They wanted to memorialize the experience

5. **Event 5: A cloud overshadowed them all**

6. **Event 6: The voice of God spoke to them**

7. **Event 7: The glorious experience ended**

28 Now about eight days after these sayings he took with him Peter and John and James and went up on the mountain to pray.
29 And as he was praying, the appearance of his face was altered, and his clothing became dazzling white.

30 And behold, two men were talking with him, Moses and Elijah,

31 who appeared in glory and spoke of his departure, which he was about to accomplish at Jerusalem.
32 Now Peter and those who were with him were heavy with sleep, but when they became fully awake they saw his glory and the two men who stood with him.
33 And as the men were parting from him, Peter said to Jesus, "Master, it is good that we are here. Let us make three tents, one for you and one for Moses and one for Elijah"—not knowing what he said.
34 As he was saying these things, a cloud came and overshadowed them, and they were afraid as they entered the cloud.
35 And a voice came out of the cloud, saying, "This is my Son, my Chosen One; listen to him!"
36 And when the voice had spoken, Jesus was found alone. And they kept silent and told no one in those days anything of what they had seen.

Division IV

*The Son of Man's Intensive Preparation of His
Disciples for Jerusalem and Death, 9:18–50*

C. The Events of the Transfiguration: A Glimpse into Glory, 9:28–36

(see Mt.17:1–13; Mk.9:2–13)

9:28–36
Introduction

Surely, as Peter, James, and John accompanied Jesus that day up a mountain to pray, they could never have imagined what they were about to see. Approximately thirty years later, Peter briefly, yet brilliantly, recalled that the blessed three were "eyewitnesses of His majesty" (2 Pe.1:16). For a thrilling moment, they saw Jesus in His gleaming glory. Their hearts must have leapt in their chests when God the Father spoke from heaven saying, "This is my beloved Son, with whom I am well pleased" (Mt.17:5; 2 Pe.1:17).

Why did this most marvelous of earthly sights occur? What were the reasons for the transfiguration of Jesus? At least seven reasons can be discerned.

1. Jesus needed a very special strength to face the pressure of the cross. In the transfiguration and in the Garden of Gethsemane, God is shown strengthening His Son in a marvelous way. Jesus was enabled to become the sin-bearer for the world (2 Co.5:21).

2. The disciples needed their faith strengthened to face what lay ahead. Therefore, God gave them a glimpse of the glory of Jesus, showing them exactly who Jesus was—and is (He.1:3).

3. The disciples needed the energizing power and insight of God's Spirit, for Jesus was to be killed (Mt.16:21; see Mt.17:1-2). After the resurrection, the disciples' memory would need to be *enlightened* to understand the spiritual significance of the cross. They would thereby become dynamic witnesses for Him. Remembering the transfiguration would stir their conviction.

4. The disciples needed to know that Jesus was more than a great lawgiver and a great prophet. In fact, He was the very Son of God who fulfilled all the Law and the Prophets (the Old Testament). He was the one who was to usher in the New Testament or covenant between God and humanity (see outline and notes—Mt.5:17-18; 2 Co.3:6-18; see Mt.9:16-17).

5. The disciples needed to see into the glory of the spiritual world and into the reality of life after death. They needed to understand God's purpose in Christ: to save people eternally and to make it possible for people to be transferred from this world into the next at the moment of death. The Messiah of the cross was God's way, not a messiah of power and dominion.

6. The disciples would need to be reminded of the glory of Christ in the future, for the cross was an ugly sight because of the blood and suffering and sin and death. But it was also a glorious event planned by God, through which He revealed His love and grace and through which He saves the world (see outline and notes—Mt.16:21-28).

7. The disciples needed a glimpse into the glory that all believers will experience when we are raised and transformed into the Lord's image. By seeing Moses and Elijah, the disciples saw two Old Testament believers who were *still living*, and they were living in a glorious state (vv.30-31). They also knew that Christ had power over life and death. He could raise whom He wished from the dead to be in glory with Him.

The transfiguration was an unparalleled event, an event that intrigues people yet today. But, as has already been seen, intrigue was not its purpose. We should learn from the transfiguration, learn more about who Jesus really is and more about the life we are to live. This is, *The Events of the Transfiguration: A Glimpse into Glory,* 9:28–36.

1. Event 1: Jesus went up a mountain to pray (v.28).
2. Event 2: The countenance and clothing of Jesus were changed—became as bright as lightning (v.29).
3. Event 3: Two men appeared and talked with Jesus (vv.30–31).

4. Event 4: The three disciples witnessed the event (vv.32–33).
5. Event 5: A cloud overshadowed them all (v.34).
6. Event 6: The voice of God spoke to them (v.35).
7. Event 7: The glorious experience ended (v.36).

9:28–29a

28 Now about eight days after these sayings he took with him Peter and John and James and went up on the mountain to pray.
29 And as he was praying, the appearance of his face was altered, and his clothing became dazzling white.

1 Event 1: Jesus went up a mountain to pray.

As He so often did, Jesus separated Himself from others in order to spend time with the Father in prayer. This time, however, He chose to not go entirely alone.

a. He took three disciples with Him (v.28).

Jesus called Peter, James, and John—His inner circle—to accompany Him up a mountain to pray (see DEEPER STUDY # 1—Mk.9:2). Why did the Lord take only these three disciples? Why did He leave the other nine behind? Why did He not allow all twelve to see what was about to occur? The answer is not given. Perhaps it was for the same reason that leaders sometimes need to be alone with only a few of their closest friends.

➤ There is the need for supportive companionship and prayer because of severe pressure.
➤ There is the need to guard what is happening from spreading out into the public before it should.

The leader knows that the fewer witnesses to an event, the less likely something will spread. In Jesus' case, He was under severe pressure, and the transfiguration and the glory of His person could not be understood until after the cross and the resurrection. He had to keep the matter quiet for now (see v.36).

b. He prayed (v.29a).

Jesus went up into the mountain for the express purpose of praying (v.28). And pray He did. What drove Jesus to pray on *this* occasion, at *this* particular time?

One reason is, the cross lay right before Him. The *weight* of bearing the sin of the world was bearing down on Him, and the pressure was almost more than He could stand. The terrifying strain and pressure are seen in three significant events that lay just ahead: the need for Moses and Elijah to talk with Him about His death; the excruciating pressure of Gethsemane; and the terrifying cry on the cross (Mt.26:36-46; see note—Mt.27:46-49).

Another reason is, the disciples had much to learn—and time was short. Jesus faced a tremendous problem: how to make them understand that God's way was not the way of earthly power and might (see notes—Mt.1:1; DEEPER STUDY # 2—1:18; DEEPER STUDY # 3—3:11; notes—11:1-6; 11:2-3; DEEPER STUDY # 1—11:5; DEEPER STUDY # 2—11:6; DEEPER STUDY # 1—12:16; note—Lu.7:21-23), but the way of spiritual and eternal salvation (Jn.3:16; 2 Co.5:21; 1 Pe.2:24; 3:18).

With such pressure and responsibility bearing down on Him, Jesus was compelled to seek God and trust God to meet His need, and God did—in a most remarkable and encouraging way. The transfiguration was a spectacular event that met the special needs of Jesus Christ. While He met Jesus' need, God the Father also met the needs of the three disciples who accompanied Him.

THOUGHT 1. God will always meet the needs of the person who prays and seeks His help.

And I tell you, ask, and it will be given to you; seek, and you will find; knock, and it will be opened to you. For everyone who asks receives, and the one who seeks finds, and to the one who knocks it will be opened. (Lu.11:9-10)

If you abide in me, and my words abide in you, ask whatever you wish, and it will be done for you. (Jn.15:7)

And whatever we ask we receive from him, because we keep his commandments and do what pleases him. (1 Jn.3:22)

When he calls to me, I will answer him; I will be with him in trouble; I will rescue him and honor him. (Ps.91:15)

When the poor and needy seek water, and there is none, and their tongue is parched with thirst, I the LORD will answer them; I the God of Israel will not forsake them. (Is.41:17)

Call to me and I will answer you, and will tell you great and hidden things that you have not known. (Je.33:3)

2 Event 2: The countenance and clothing of Jesus were changed— became as bright as lightning.

As Jesus was praying, something spectacular happened, something miraculous, something unforgettable. The appearance of Jesus' face was altered. He looked different than His disciples had ever seen Him before. "His face shone like the sun" (Mt.17:2). Imagine being as bright as the sun!

²⁹ And as he was praying, the appearance of his face was altered, and his clothing became dazzling white.

In addition, Jesus' clothing was altered, becoming a dazzling or glistening white. The word *dazzling* or *glistening* (Gk. exastraptōn, *ex-ahs-trahp'-tone*) means to flash like lightning, to gleam, to be radiant.

> And he was transfigured before them, and his face shone like the sun, and his clothes became white as light. (Mt.17:2)

> And his clothes became radiant, intensely white, as no one on earth could bleach them. (Mk.9:3)

Again, Jesus was praying when these changes took place. Apparently, He was concentrating so intensely and was so wrapped up in God that God transformed Him, that is, allowed His Godly nature to shine right through Him.

THOUGHT 1. Note several lessons.
1) The divine nature of Christ is seen in this event. God is showing that Christ is definitely His Son. As a result, there is no excuse for unbelief.
2) The need of Christ was desperate, so God the Father was meeting His need in a very special way. When our need is desperate, God will meet our need in a very special way if we will come to Him in intense prayer.

THOUGHT 2. It is when a genuine believer prays with intensity that heaven opens and God manifests His glory. We can never know what will happen when we pray, but we can be sure that we will never see the glory of God if we do not pray. In addition, the glory of God may be reflected in our countenance because, through intense prayer, we have been in His presence. The glow of glory may radiate from *our* faces.

> And we all, with unveiled face, beholding the glory of the Lord, are being transformed into the same image from one degree of glory to another. For this comes from the Lord who is the Spirit. (2 Co.3:18)

> When Moses came down from Mount Sinai, with the two tablets of the testimony in his hand as he came down from the mountain, Moses did not know that the skin of his face shone because he had been talking with God. (Ex.34:29)

> Those who look to him are radiant, and their faces shall never be ashamed. (Ps.34:5)

> And those who are wise shall shine like the brightness of the sky above; and those who turn many to righteousness, like the stars forever and ever. (Da.12:3)

3 Event 3: Two men appeared and talked with Jesus.

The splendid altering of Jesus' appearance was not the only heavenly wonder displayed that unforgettable day. Two men appeared in glory with Jesus and carried on a conversation with Him.

9:30-31

³⁰ And behold, two men were talking with him, Moses and Elijah,

³¹ who appeared in glory and spoke of his departure, which he was about to accomplish at Jerusalem.

a. Moses, the lawgiver; Elijah, the great prophet (v.30).

The "two men" were, amazingly, men who had lived and walked the earth centuries earlier: Moses and Elijah. Moses was the great lawgiver and Elijah was the greatest of the prophets. These two men were honoring and ministering to Jesus. By such they were symbolizing that the law and the prophets found their fulfillment in Jesus. Jesus was the one of whom the law and the prophets spoke; He was the one to whom they pointed (see Lu.24:26-27; 1 Pe.1:11).

b. The men discussed Jesus' imminent death (v.31).

Through Luke, the Holy Spirit revealed a detail not included in the accounts of the other Gospel authors: Moses and Elijah were talking with Jesus about His impending death. Jesus was feeling extreme pressure in thinking about His death, and the subject probably never left His mind. Death for Him meant so much more than the death of ordinary people. He was going to die for the sins of all people of all generations, and God was going to separate Himself from Jesus. The pressure and suffering were to be unbearable (see note—Mt.20:19; Mk.10:33). He desperately needed to be strengthened—inwardly and spiritually—to bear the suffering of the cross.

Apparently, Jesus needed a very special kind of encouragement, an encouragement from two Old Testament believers—believers who had lived in the faith and expectation of His coming to save them. Sharing their love for Him and their trust and hope in His dying for them, Moses and Elijah would stir Jesus to continue on for the sake of mankind. It must have been a precious moment for all three. At first glance, it seems that we are left only to speculate about what they said. However, a deeper look yields glorious insight into what Moses and Elijah said to Jesus on the "holy mountain" (2 Pe.1:18). Specifically, two Greek words used by Luke give some hint of this.

The Greek word Luke used for "departure" or "decease" is *exodon*—Exodus! There stood Moses sharing how God had so miraculously saved and delivered the children of Israel out of bondage and how the Exodus (deliverance) was only a picture of the marvelous deliverance that He, God's Son, was to accomplish for humanity. Jesus was to accomplish a new exodus, a new *saving deliverance*, except this time it was to be for all people. People of every generation, every nation, every race were to be delivered from the bondage of sin and death, from the devil and hell—delivered into the glorious liberty of God and life, both abundant and eternal life. Jesus' dying was to be well worth it, Moses and Elijah stressed.

Elijah's emphasis was surely the many prophecies concerning the sufferings of Jesus and the glory that should follow. Again, Luke hints at this in the word *accomplish* (plēroun, *play-roon'*) which means to fulfill or to bring to fulfillment.

> And taking the twelve, he said to them, "See, we are going up to Jerusalem, and everything that is written about the Son of Man by the prophets will be accomplished." (Lu.18:31. See Lu.12:50; 22:37.)

> Concerning this salvation, the prophets who prophesied about the grace that was to be yours searched and inquired carefully, inquiring what person or time the Spirit of Christ in them was indicating when he predicted the sufferings of Christ and the subsequent glories. (1 Pe.1:10-11)

It is significant to note that the very encouragement that our Lord needed as Man was given by two who had believed and hoped in His coming. Being reminded of the marvelous deliverance (exodus) that had happened so long ago was bound to strengthen and lift the heart of Christ. Just seeing Moses and Elijah stand there, two who had trusted and believed and hoped, surely caused the Lord's spirit to rise. He was greatly encouraged and knew He could not fail these men who had trusted and hoped in Him so much. Far more important, He could not fail His Father, who sent Him for this express purpose.

THOUGHT 1. Our faith and hope are realized and fulfilled in Christ. He is our Deliverer or Exodus out of the grip of sin and death, the devil and hell. We can be free in Christ, free to live abundantly and eternally.

> Truly, truly, I say to you, whoever hears my word and believes him who sent me has eternal life. He does not come into judgment, but has passed from death to life. (Jn.5:24)

> There is therefore now no condemnation for those who are in Christ Jesus. For the law of the Spirit of life has set you free in Christ Jesus from the law of sin and death. For God has done what the law, weakened by the flesh, could not do. By sending his own Son in the likeness of sinful flesh and for sin, he condemned sin in the flesh, in order that the righteous requirement of the law might be fulfilled in us, who walk not according to the flesh but according to the Spirit. (Ro.8:1-4)

> Who gave himself for our sins to deliver us from the present evil age, according to the will of our God and Father. (Ga.1:4)

> Who gave himself for us to redeem us from all lawlessness and to purify for himself a people for his own possession who are zealous for good works. (Tit.2:14)

> Since therefore the children share in flesh and blood, he himself likewise partook of the same things, that through death he might destroy the one who has the power of death, that is, the devil, and deliver all those who through fear of death were subject to lifelong slavery. (He.2:14-15)

> And from Jesus Christ the faithful witness, the firstborn of the dead, and the ruler of kings on earth. To him who loves us and has freed us from our sins by his blood (Re.1:5)

THOUGHT 2. We should not fear death nor discussing death, not if we are genuine believers. Sharing what God says about death with other believers will encourage us in our faith and hope.

> So we are always of good courage. We know that while we are at home in the body we are away from the Lord, for we walk by faith, not by sight. Yes, we are of good courage, and we would rather be away from the body and at home with the Lord. (2 Co.5:6-8)

> For to me to live is Christ, and to die is gain. . . . I am hard pressed between the two. My desire is to depart and be with Christ, for that is far better. (Ph.1:21, 23)

> But we do not want you to be uninformed, brothers, about those who are asleep, that you may not grieve as others do who have no hope. For since we believe that Jesus died and rose again, even so, through Jesus, God will bring with him those who have fallen asleep. For this we declare to you by a word from the Lord, that we who are alive, who are left until the coming of the Lord, will not precede those who have fallen asleep. For the Lord himself will descend from heaven with a cry of command, with the voice of an archangel, and with the sound of the trumpet of God. And the dead in Christ will rise first. Then we who are alive, who are left, will be caught up together with them in the clouds to meet the Lord in the air, and so we will always be with the Lord. Therefore encourage one another with these words. (1 Th.4:13-18)

> And I heard a voice from heaven saying, "Write this: Blessed are the dead who die in the Lord from now on." "Blessed indeed," says the Spirit, "that they may rest from their labors, for their deeds follow them!" (Re.14:13)

> Precious in the sight of the Lord is the death of his saints. (Ps.116:15)

4 Event 4: The three disciples witnessed the event.

9:32-33

Peter, James, and John were "eyewitnesses of [the] majesty" of Jesus Christ when He appeared in His glory at the transfiguration (2 Pe.1:16). Again, the transfiguration was for their benefit as well as for Jesus'.

a. They were awakened by the glory (v.32).
The three disciples had fallen asleep, as they were prone to do when Jesus was praying (Mt.26:40, 43, 45).

³² Now Peter and those who were with him were heavy with sleep, but when they became fully awake they saw his glory and the two men who stood with him.

³³ And as the men were parting from him, Peter said to Jesus, "Master, it is good that we are here. Let us make three tents, one for you and one for Moses and one for Elijah"—not knowing what he said.

Suddenly, something woke them—more than likely the brilliance of the light, the Shekinah glory upon Christ. The three were *tasting glory*. They were in the very presence of God Himself and were sampling some of heaven's perfection: joy, peace, security, fulfillment. They did not want to leave this hallowed ground.

b. They wanted to memorialize the experience (v.33).

Peter offered to build three *tents* or *tabernacles* for Jesus and the two prophets. By this act he hoped to extend the stay of the heavenly guests and the glorious experience. The *tents* (skēnas, *skay'-nahs*) offered were booths or shelters made of branches and grass which could be built quickly, the kind often built by travelers on their stops along the road by night.

Note that Peter said, "Let us." Even in a moment as glorious as this, Peter would not act against His Lord's will. Imagine the devotion and loyalty.

THOUGHT 1. There is always a pull to live in the glory and forget the human need, to experience the high and neglect the low. We must always remember it is the discipline of serving where there is need and ministering to the low that results in glory and the experiencing of highs.

> In all things I have shown you that by working hard in this way we must help the weak and remember the words of the Lord Jesus, how he himself said, "It is more blessed to give than to receive." (Ac.20:35)

> We who are strong have an obligation to bear with the failings of the weak, and not to please ourselves. (Ro.15:1)

> Bear one another's burdens, and so fulfill the law of Christ. (Ga.6:2)

> Remember those who are in prison, as though in prison with them, and those who are mistreated, since you also are in the body. (He.13:3)

> Religion that is pure and undefiled before God the Father is this: to visit orphans and widows in their affliction, and to keep oneself unstained from the world. (Jas.1:27)

> Is it not to share your bread with the hungry and bring the homeless poor into your house; when you see the naked, to cover him, and not to hide yourself from your own flesh? (Is.58:7)

9:34

5 Event 5: A cloud overshadowed them all.

³⁴ As he was saying these things, a cloud came and overshadowed them, and they were afraid as they entered the cloud.

Peter, James, and John had already seen extraordinarily marvelous things: the dazzling brilliance of Jesus' glory and two men from centuries past. But there was more to come. As Peter was speaking, a cloud moved across the mountain and engulfed them. As the cloud swept them into its midst, they were paralyzed with fear.

Matthew reports that the cloud was "a bright cloud" (Mt.17:5). It was the Shekinah glory, the cloud that symbolized God's presence. It was the cloud that guided Israel out of Egypt and that rested upon the tabernacle and above the Mercy Seat in the Most Holy Place (Ex.13:20; 40:34-38). It was the cloud that filled the temple at its dedication to the Lord (2 Chr.5:14). It was the cloud that departed from the temple in Ezekiel's vision (Ezk.10:4, 18).

God dwells in unapproachable light upon which no person has looked or can look (1 Ti.6:16). A mere fragment of this overwhelming light illuminated the cloud that conveyed God's presence. Peter later called it "the Majestic" or "Excellent Glory" (2 Pe.1:17). This "bright cloud" overshadowing Christ was a sharp contrast to the dark and threatening cloud that overshadowed the giving of the old covenant to Moses, that is, the Law (Ex.19:18; 20:21). There is a point to be made here. The Law (old covenant) was dark and threatening (see notes—Ga.3:10). The new covenant (the love of Christ) is bright: it is given to save and bless, not to threaten and condemn (He.12:18-24; He.8:6-13).

6 Event 6: The voice of God spoke to them.

As if what the disciples had already seen and heard was not glorious enough, they then heard the voice of God the Father Himself thunder out of the cloud. The message was clear: God audibly declared that Jesus is His Son. Then, God gave the three disciples a command: "Listen to" or "hear Him." According to *The Bible Knowledge Commentary*: "Those familiar with the Old Testament, as the disciples were, doubtless immediately recognized the reference (in the words 'listen to Him') to Deuteronomy 18:15 with its messianic prediction of a Prophet greater than Moses. The people were to listen to (i.e., obey) the Prophet."[1] God was both telling and warning the disciples to listen to Christ:

9:35

[35] And a voice came out of the cloud, saying, "This is my Son, my Chosen One; listen to him!"

> ➤ He was God's Son, the beloved and chosen One.
> ➤ He was "the Prophet" of whom Moses spoke, the Messiah (Ac.3:22).
> ➤ What He spoke was the truth, even when He predicted His death and resurrection.

The cloud and the voice of God terrified the disciples and caused them to fall immediately upon their faces, prostrate and unable to look up (Mt.17:6). As mortal men, they were crouched in fear, paralyzed in terror.

THOUGHT 1. God warns every living human being to listen to Christ. He is God's Son, the Messiah and Savior of the world. His words are the truth. All who do not listen to Him will be destroyed, eternally separated from God in hell (Ac.3:23).

> **Whoever does not love me does not keep my words. And the word that you hear is not mine but the Father's who sent me. (Jn.14:24)**
>
> **For I have given them the words that you gave me, and they have received them and have come to know in truth that I came from you; and they have believed that you sent me. (Jn.17:8)**
>
> **Moses said, "The Lord God will raise up for you a prophet like me from your brothers. You shall listen to him in whatever he tells you. And it shall be that every soul who does not listen to that prophet shall be destroyed from the people." (Ac.3:22–23)**
>
> **If we receive the testimony of men, the testimony of God is greater, for this is the testimony of God that he has borne concerning his Son. Whoever believes in the Son of God has the testimony in himself. Whoever does not believe God has made him a liar, because he has not believed in the testimony that God has borne concerning his Son. And this is the testimony, that God gave us eternal life, and this life is in his Son. Whoever has the Son has life; whoever does not have the Son of God does not have life. (1 Jn.5:9–12)**

7 Event 7: The glorious experience ended.

After the Father spoke, the transfiguration ended, and Jesus stood there all alone. Matthew and Mark report that Jesus instructed Peter, James, and John to tell nobody about what they had witnessed until after His resurrection (Mt.17:9; Mk.9:10). The three obeyed the Lord and kept silent about what they had been privileged to see and hear.

9:36

[36] And when the voice had spoken, Jesus was found alone. And they kept silent and told no one in those days anything of what they had seen.

THOUGHT 1. Imagine how difficult it was to obey Jesus' command. Like any of us, the three disciples itched to tell others about what they had seen and heard. Yet, they obeyed the Lord. What an example for us to follow when obeying Christ is not easy!

---

1 John Walvoord and Roy B. Zuck, eds., *The Bible Knowledge Commentary New Testament: An Exposition of the Scriptures by Dallas Seminary Faculty*, (Colorado Springs, CO: David C. Cook, 1983). Via Wordsearch digital edition.

But he answered them, "My mother and my brothers are those who hear the word of God and do it." (Lu.8:21)

As obedient children, do not be conformed to the passions of your former ignorance (1 Pe.1:14)

For this is the love of God, that we keep his commandments. And his commandments are not burdensome. (1 Jn.5:3)

And Samuel said, "Has the Lord as great delight in burnt offerings and sacrifices, as in obeying the voice of the Lord? Behold, to obey is better than sacrifice, and to listen than the fat of rams." (1 Sa.15:22)

(Mt.17:14–23; Mk.9:14–32)

37 On the next day, when they had come down from the mountain, a great crowd met him.

38 And behold, a man from the crowd cried out, "Teacher, I beg you to look at my son, for he is my only child.

39 And behold, a spirit seizes him, and he suddenly cries out. It convulses him so that he foams at the mouth, and shatters him, and will hardly leave him.

40 And I begged your disciples to cast it out, but they could not."

41 Jesus answered, "O faithless and twisted generation, how long am I to be with you and bear with you? Bring your son here."

42 While he was coming, the demon threw him to the ground and convulsed him. But Jesus rebuked the unclean spirit and healed the boy, and gave him back to his father.

43 And all were astonished at the majesty of God.

44 "Let these words sink into your ears: The Son of Man is about to be delivered into the hands of men."

45 But they did not understand this saying, and it was concealed from them, so that they might not perceive it. And they were afraid to ask him about this saying.

1. **The setting: The day after the transfiguration**
   a. Jesus was met by a crowd
   b. A man cried out in desperation for his only son

   1) The 1st problem: An evil spirit possessed the boy[DS1]

   2) The 2nd problem: The disciples were powerless to help
2. **Rebuke 1: The people's unbelief and perverse hearts[DS2, 3]**

3. **Rebuke 2: The disciples' lack of power**
   a. Jesus rebuked the evil spirit through His own act of healing

   b. The people were amazed at God's greatness
4. **Rebuke 3: The disciples' slowness to grasp the Messiah's death**

Division IV

The Son of Man's Intensive Preparation of His Disciples for Jerusalem and Death, 9:18–50

D. The Second Prediction of Death: A Rebuke of the Present Generation, 9:37–45

(Mt.17:14–23; Mk.9:14–32)

9:37–45
Introduction

The unlimited power and unshakeable promises of God call for but one response from us. That response is *faith*. God calls us to have faith in Him. Without faith, we cannot please Him (He.11:6).

Our Lord's displeasure at faithlessness is clearly seen in this passage where Jesus rebukes His generation for their lack of faith (v.41). Frankly, they deserved His rebuke, as do we, when we live and try to serve Him faithlessly. This is, *The Second Prediction of Death: A Rebuke of the Present Generation,* 9:37–45.

1. The setting: The day after the transfiguration (vv.37–40).
2. Rebuke 1: The people's unbelief and perverse heart (v.41).
3. Rebuke 2: The disciples' lack of power (vv.42–43).
4. Rebuke 3: The disciples' slowness to grasp the Messiah's death (vv.44–45).

9:37–40

37 On the next day, when they had come down from the mountain, a great crowd met him.
38 And behold, a man from the crowd cried out, "Teacher, I beg you to look at my son, for he is my only child.
39 And behold, a spirit seizes him, and he suddenly cries out. It convulses him so that he foams at the mouth, and shatters him, and will hardly leave him.
40 And I begged your disciples to cast it out, but they could not."

1 The setting: The day after the transfiguration.

a. Jesus was met by a crowd (v.37).

b. A man cried out in desperation for his only son (v.38). The day after the transfiguration, Jesus, Peter, James, and John were coming down after spending the night on the mountain (v.37). A huge crowd ran to meet Jesus, and a man broke through the crowd, elbowing his way up to Jesus (Mt.17:14; Mk.9:15).

The man cried out to Jesus in desperation, begging Jesus to *look at* his son (v.38). The words *cried* and *beg* or *implore* are strong; he shouted and begged persistently for Jesus to meet his need.

The Greek term for *look at* or *on* (epiblepsai epi, *ep-ee-blep'-sigh ep-ee*) is a medical term. It means to carefully examine a patient and to have pity on that person. This man's son was possessed by an evil spirit that was abusing him physically (v.39; see Deeper Study # 1).

The disciples were powerless in helping the man's son, despite his desperate need (v.40). This was critical, for it meant that the power of God had left them. They had just demonstrated the power to cast out demons on their preaching tour (Lu.9:1–6, 10), but now they had no power. There was something wrong in their lives, some sin or shortcoming that was blocking the power of God. Jesus later told them they had not been praying and fasting as they should (Mt.17:21).

Deeper Study # 1

(9:39) **Evil Spirits:** the son's illness seemed to have been both physical and spiritual. Mark's description of the illness suggests symptoms associated with epilepsy combined with demon-possession (Mt.17:15; Mk.9:17–18). The demon-possession in particular seems to have heightened and aggravated the condition, perhaps causing some suicidal tendencies (Mt.17:15; Mk.9:22). Throughout the Gospels this seems to be one of the major works of evil spirits: to *heighten and aggravate* existing conditions.

9:41

41 Jesus answered, "O faithless and twisted generation, how long am I to be with you and bear with you? Bring your son here."

2 Rebuke 1: The people's unbelief and perverse hearts.

Jesus was grieved by the disciples' powerlessness to deal with the evil spirit. He rebuked them for their lack of faith and wayward hearts. However, the Lord was not speaking only to the disciples; He was speaking to the whole generation. What the disciples lacked was lacked by all. Their sins were the sins of all, the sins of *being faithless and twisted* or *perverse* (see Deeper Studies 2, 3).

Jesus said two things to the faithless disciples and their generation: His presence would not always be available, and He would not be patient with people's unbelief forever. This particular generation had actually seen the power of God. They had seen the miraculous works of the Lord with their own eyes. Still, they did not believe. They viewed Jesus only as a great prophet and minister . . .

- not as the very presence of God in their midst
- not as the true Messiah before whom a person must repent
- not as the Christ to whom a person owed their life and service

Because of this, the generation of people living during Christ's ministry were walking around faithless and perverse before God, as powerless and helpless as ever.

He said to them, "Why are you so afraid? Have you still no faith?" (Mk.4:40)

"If you are the Christ, tell us." But he said to them, "If I tell you, you will not believe." (Lu.22:67)

Truly, truly, I say to you, we speak of what we know, and bear witness to what we have seen, but you do not receive our testimony. (Jn.3:11)

So the Jews gathered around him and said to him, "How long will you keep us in suspense? If you are the Christ, tell us plainly." Jesus answered them, "I told you, and you do not believe. The works that I do in my Father's name bear witness about me." (Jn.10:24–25)

Though he had done so many signs before them, they still did not believe in him. (Jn.12:37)

And without faith it is impossible to please him, for whoever would draw near to God must believe that he exists and that he rewards those who seek him. (He.11:6)

DEEPER STUDY # 2

(9:41) **Faithless** (Gk. apistos, *ah'-pis-tos*): disbelieving; being without faith; being outside of faith; not keeping faith, unbelieving (see Tit.1:15).

DEEPER STUDY # 3

(9:41) **Twisted or Perverse** (diestrammenē, *dee-es-trahm-men'-ay*): having been distorted, twisted, turned aside or away, or corrupted (see Ac.20:30; Ph.2:15).

And from among your own selves will arise men speaking twisted things, to draw away the disciples after them. (Ac.20:30)

That you may be blameless and innocent, children of God without blemish in the midst of a crooked and twisted generation, among whom you shine as lights in the world. (Ph.2:15)

And constant friction among people who are depraved in mind and deprived of the truth, imagining that godliness is a means of gain. (1 Ti.6:5)

3 Rebuke 2: The disciples' lack of power.

9:42–43

After rebuking the faithless disciples and their generation verbally, Jesus did what they could not. His powerful act served as a silent but stinging rebuke of their lack of power.

a. Jesus rebuked the evil spirit through His own act of healing (v.42).

In a brazen act of evil daring, the demon presented itself, throwing the helpless boy down to the ground with a violent seizure. Jesus immediately rebuked the evil spirit and healed the boy of his infirmity (see DEEPER STUDY # 2—Mk.9:17–18 for more discussion). Note three observations about our Lord's deliverance of this boy:

42 While he was coming, the demon threw him to the ground and convulsed him. But Jesus rebuked the unclean spirit and healed the boy, and gave him back to his father.

43 And all were astonished at the majesty of God.

➤ Jesus brought healing at the boy's very worst moment, while he was under attack by the evil spirit. The Lord's power was clearly demonstrated.

> **"But that you may know that the Son of Man has authority on earth to forgive sins"—he then said to the paralytic—"Rise, pick up your bed and go home." (Mt.9:6)**

> **And Jesus came and said to them, "All authority in heaven and on earth has been given to me." (Mt.28:18)**

> **For nothing will be impossible with God. (Lu.1:37)**

> **How God anointed Jesus of Nazareth with the Holy Spirit and with power. He went about doing good and healing all who were oppressed by the devil, for God was with him. (Ac.10:38)**

> **I know that you can do all things, and that no purpose of yours can be thwarted. (Jb.42:2)**

➤ Jesus rebuked the spirit, broke the devil's power by *His Word*. Satan could not stand before the Lord's Word. Jesus had purposed to triumph over Satan's evil forces.

> **Now is the judgment of this world; now will the ruler of this world be cast out. (Jn.12:31)**

> **He has delivered us from the domain of darkness and transferred us to the kingdom of his beloved Son, in whom we have redemption, the forgiveness of sins. (Col.1:13-14)**

> **He disarmed the rulers and authorities and put them to open shame, by triumphing over them in him. (Col.2:15)**

> **Since therefore the children share in flesh and blood, he himself likewise partook of the same things, that through death he might destroy the one who has the power of death, that is, the devil, and deliver all those who through fear of death were subject to lifelong slavery. (He.2:14-15)**

> **Whoever makes a practice of sinning is of the devil, for the devil has been sinning from the beginning. The reason the Son of God appeared was to destroy the works of the devil. (1 Jn.3:8)**

➤ Jesus showed tenderness for people. He demonstrated this by delivering the boy to his father.

b. The people were amazed at God's greatness (v.43).

The people were all *astonished* or *amazed* at the *majesty* of God. The Greek word for "majesty" (megaleiotēti, *meh-gah-lay-aah'-tay-tee*) is used to describe greatness, superbness, magnificence. Note that Jesus brought honor to God, not to Himself.

THOUGHT 1. Powerlessness is inexcusable. Why? Because Christ has revealed how we can possess the power and strength of God.

> **He said to them, "Because of your little faith. For truly, I say to you, if you have faith like a grain of mustard seed, you will say to this mountain, 'Move from here to there,' and it will move, and nothing will be impossible for you." (Mt.17:20-21)**

> **I am the vine; you are the branches. Whoever abides in me and I in him, he it is that bears much fruit, for apart from me you can do nothing. (Jn.15:5)**

> **But you will receive power when the Holy Spirit has come upon you, and you will be my witnesses in Jerusalem and in all Judea and Samaria, and to the end of the earth. (Ac.1:8; see outline—Ro.8:1-17)**

> **Not that we are sufficient in ourselves to claim anything as coming from us, but our sufficiency is from God. (2 Co.3:5)**

9:44-45

⁴⁴ "Let these words sink into your ears: The Son of Man is about to be delivered into the hands of men."

⁴⁵ But they did not understand this saying, and it was concealed from them, so that they might not perceive it. And they were afraid to ask him about this saying.

4 Rebuke 3: The disciples' slowness to grasp the Messiah's death.

Jesus used the occasion to drill the truth of His impending death into the disciples' minds. The power of God Jesus demonstrated may have directed their thoughts to His conquering the earth and subjecting all people to Himself. Their hopes may have been stirred at the prospect of His earthly reign.

While the disciples were yet marveling at Christ's wondrous works (v.43), He rebuked their slowness to grasp the reality of His death (v.44). He again had to show them that God's Messiah had to die in order to save the world.

Jesus exhorted them strongly, saying, "Let these words sink into your ears." Give special attention to them. Take definite action to firmly establish them in your minds.

Jesus then told the disciples directly that He would soon be *delivered* (paradidosthai, *pah-rah-dih'-dos-thigh*) into the hands of His executioners. This verb is in the passive voice, indicating that this action was being performed on Him by another. Jesus may have been referring to His betrayal by Judas; or, He may have been emphasizing that His death was ordained and predetermined in the counsel and plan of God (see note—Mt.17:22).

> This Jesus, delivered up according to the definite plan and foreknowledge of God, you crucified and killed by the hands of lawless men. (Ac.2:23)

> He who did not spare his own Son but gave him up for us all, how will he not also with him graciously give us all things? (Ro.8:32)

Even after this direct, clear statement, the disciples still did not grasp the Messiah's death. They just did not understand. Note why: it was hidden from them, so that they could not perceive it.

Why was it concealed from them? Certainly not because of God. The reason had to be because of their unbelief and perverseness. They just refused to see it. They were spiritually dull, lacking a sensitivity to spiritual truth.

> And he said to them, "O foolish ones, and slow of heart to believe all that the prophets have spoken!" (Lu.24:25)

> Why do you not understand what I say? It is because you cannot bear to hear my word. (Jn.8:43)

> For this people's heart has grown dull, and with their ears they can barely hear, and their eyes they have closed; lest they should see with their eyes and hear with their ears and understand with their heart and turn, and I would heal them. (Ac.28:27)

> The natural person does not accept the things of the Spirit of God, for they are folly to him, and he is not able to understand them because they are spiritually discerned. (1 Co.2:14)

> I will instruct you and teach you in the way you should go; I will counsel you with my eye upon you. Be not like a horse or a mule, without understanding, which must be curbed with bit and bridle, or it will not stay near you. (Ps.32:8–9)

> But they do not know the thoughts of the LORD; they do not understand his plan, that he has gathered them as sheaves to the threshing floor. (Mi.4:12)

E. The Way of Greatness: Humility, 9:46–50

(Mt.18:1-4; Mk.9:33-41)

1. **The desire for greatness: Wanting position, recognition, and power**
2. **The picture of greatness: Jesus illustrated through a little child**

3. **The right concept of greatness**
   a. Welcoming a child in Jesus' name
   b. The reward
      1) Will receive Jesus
      2) Will receive God
      3) Will be the greatest
4. **The right to greatness: Not an exclusive right**

⁴⁶ An argument arose among them as to which of them was the greatest.
⁴⁷ But Jesus, knowing the reasoning of their hearts, took a child and put him by his side
⁴⁸ and said to them, "Whoever receives this child in my name receives me, and whoever receives me receives him who sent me. For he who is least among you all is the one who is great."

⁴⁹ John answered, "Master, we saw someone casting out demons in your name, and we tried to stop him, because he does not follow with us."
⁵⁰ But Jesus said to him, "Do not stop him, for the one who is not against you is for you."

Division IV

The Son of Man's Intensive Preparation of His Disciples for Jerusalem and Death, 9:18–50

E. The Way of Greatness: Humility, 9:46–50

(Mt.18:1–4; Mk.9:33–41)

9:46–50
Introduction

To some degree, all people are interested in greatness. It is enough for some people to simply be accepted and approved by friends and neighbors; that is enough greatness for them. Others want more: to be elevated to a particular position, to be known and admired, to accumulate great wealth and possessions—they want something that gives them greater recognition and greater prestige. They crave for more greatness than others. Some crave the greatness of authority and rule, of power and fame, of position and wealth. They want prestige and honor and recognition far above the ordinary.

Jesus' disciples were no different than other people. Their arguing over which of them should be the greatest provided the perfect opportunity for Him to teach them—and us—what true greatness is and how we can achieve it. This is, *The Way of Greatness: Humility*, 9:46–50.

1. The desire for greatness: Wanting position, recognition, and power (v.46).
2. The picture of greatness: Jesus illustrated through a little child (v.47).
3. The right concept of greatness (v.48).
4. The right to greatness: Not an exclusive right (vv.49-50).

1 The desire for greatness: Wanting position, recognition, and power.

Jesus' disciples were arguing over the highest positions in the Lord's kingdom. They were maneuvering for positions of leadership. Later, James and John would even manipulate their mother into asking Jesus to give them the highest positions.

The disciples were thinking of an earthly kingdom, a physical and material messianic rule right here on earth. Their desire was for worldly position, name, recognition, honor, authority, challenge, duties, pleasure, and wealth. They were not thinking in terms of goodness or character. They did not mean the greatest in love and care, in ministry and help, but in position and rule, name and recognition.

46 An argument arose among them as to which of them was the greatest.

The Twelve did not understand what the kingdom of heaven was. They still saw an earthly and temporal kingdom and not a spiritual and eternal kingdom. They still thought in terms of getting all they could for a few short years while on this earth. They had not grasped the hope and reality of the spiritual world, of eternal life and blessings (see DEEPER STUDY # 3—Mt.19:23-24; Ep.1:3 for more discussion).

Just as all people are, the disciples were full of self. They were thinking of self, not of others, not how they could be great in helping others. They were not even thinking of Jesus. And remember, He had just revealed that He was to give His life for the salvation of the world (v.44; see Mk.9:33-34). Their thoughts should have been on Jesus and the meaning of what He had said. They should have been seeking to encourage Him and to learn all they could from Him. Instead they were so full of self, they could think of no one but themselves.

THOUGHT 1. It is difficult to admit that we are full of self, that is, self-centered, selfish. The fact hurts; we revolt against it. But before we can become what we *should be,* we have to face the truth as to what we *are.*

Whoever exalts himself will be humbled, and whoever humbles himself will be exalted. (Mt.23:12)

How can you believe, when you receive glory from one another and do not seek the glory that comes from the only God? (Jn.5:44)

For by the grace given to me I say to everyone among you not to think of himself more highly than he ought to think, but to think with sober judgment, each according to the measure of faith that God has assigned. . . . Live in harmony with one another. Do not be haughty, but associate with the lowly. Never be wise in your own sight. (Ro.12:3, 16)

Do nothing from selfish ambition or conceit, but in humility count others more significant than yourselves. Let each of you look not only to his own interests, but also to the interests of others. (Ph.2:3–4)

For the wicked boasts of the desires of his soul, and the one greedy for gain curses and renounces the LORD. (Ps.10:3)

2 The picture of greatness: Jesus illustrated through a little child.

As the self-centered disciples bickered, Jesus picked up a child and set the child by His side. What was Jesus doing?

47 But Jesus, knowing the reasoning of their hearts, took a child and put him by his side

Very simply, Jesus was showing the disciples what greatness is. A person is great when he or she takes a child and brings that child to Jesus. Greatness surrounds Christ and children, children who are *willing* to be brought to Christ.

The child Jesus lifted to His side represents people of all ages. True greatness is setting the people of the world by Christ's side, beside the one who can meet all their needs. Greatness is bringing people to the one who can give them freedom from the bondages of this world. Imagine how great the person is who shows people how to be liberated from . . .

- sin
- guilt
- drunkenness
- immorality
- oppression

- loneliness
- suffering
- lying
- stealing
- emptiness

- death
- laziness
- cursing
- selfishness
- hatred

True greatness is bringing people to the one who can give them abundant life now and eternally when this life is over.

> Truly, truly, I say to you, whoever hears my word and believes him who sent me has eternal life. He does not come into judgment, but has passed from death to life. (Jn.5:24)

> So that being justified by his grace we might become heirs according to the hope of eternal life. (Tit.3:7)

> And this is the testimony, that God gave us eternal life, and this life is in his Son. Whoever has the Son has life; whoever does not have the Son of God does not have life. I write these things to you who believe in the name of the Son of God, that you may know that you have eternal life. (1 Jn.5:11–13)

> The fruit of the righteous is a tree of life, and whoever captures souls is wise. (Pr.11:30)

> And those who are wise shall shine like the brightness of the sky above; and those who turn many to righteousness, like the stars forever and ever. (Da.12:3)

9:48

[48] and said to them, "Whoever receives this child in my name receives me, and whoever receives me receives him who sent me. For he who is least among you all is the one who is great."

3 The right concept of greatness.

Jesus explained the right concept of greatness. It is not achieving power, position, or possessions. It is *receiving* (Gr. dexētai, *dex'-ay-tigh*)—welcoming, accepting, taking—others. Jesus is talking about loving, ministering to, and helping others.

a. Welcoming a child in Jesus' name.

Greatness is *receiving* or welcoming a child, that is, a person, in the name of Jesus. To receive a child means at least three things.

First, it means doing just what Jesus did: *reaching out and welcoming and accepting* a person into our arms. This sounds easy—taking a child into our arms—but it is not always so. Sometimes a person . . .
- is unkempt, dirty, even filthy
- is acting ugly, mean, misbehaving
- is disliked, rejected, unacceptable to others

And there is always the threat that receiving a person will cause our own friends to withdraw their friendship because the person is unacceptable to them.

Second, it means sharing the best news that we have: the *good news of God's kingdom*. Jesus did not say that greatness is *just* receiving a child. He added that the child must be received *in His name*. The name of Jesus has to be shared with the person. The person is to be told and shown that we act in the name and cause of Jesus. The kingdom of God is to be shared with the child (the person received).

Third, it means helping the person in every way possible, no matter the cost. We do our best to meet their . . .
- physical and mental needs
- material and social needs
- spiritual and godly needs

> Even as the Son of Man came not to be served but to serve, and to give his life as a ransom for many. (Mt.20:28)

> In all things I have shown you that by working hard in this way we must help the weak and remember the words of the Lord Jesus, how he himself said, "It is more blessed to give than to receive." (Ac.20:35)

We who are strong have an obligation to bear with the failings of the weak, and not to please our-selves. (Ro.15:1)

Bear one another's burdens, and so fulfill the law of Christ. (Ga.6:2)

b. The reward.

The Lord then revealed what the reward will be for receiving people in His name. This reward stresses the importance of receiving people. It is close to Jesus' heart, the very purpose for which He came to earth (Mt.20:28). It is the thing His followers are to be doing, the very thing to which we are to commit our lives. Therefore, He wants to challenge His followers to get to it. There is no better challenge than to lay the reward out in front of them. The reward is threefold for the individual who receives persons *in the name of Jesus Christ.*

First, the person who receives others in Jesus' name receives *Him.* When we receive or welcome others, we are welcoming Christ. When we minister to others, we are ministering to Christ (Mt.25:40). Another way to see what Christ is saying is . . .

- receiving our neighbor *equals* receiving Christ
- loving our neighbor *equals* loving Christ

If anyone says, "I love God," and hates his brother, he is a liar; for he who does not love his brother whom he has seen cannot love God whom he has not seen. (1 Jn.4:20; see Mt.22:36–39)

Second, we receive God. Welcoming others is welcoming Christ, and welcoming Christ is welcoming God the Father.

But love your enemies, and do good, and lend, expecting nothing in return, and your reward will be great, and you will be sons of the Most High, for he is kind to the ungrateful and the evil. Be merciful, even as your Father is merciful. (Lu.6:35–36)

Third, we will be truly great. Note that Jesus did not say *greatest;* He said "great." Everyone who serves by bringing people to Christ, by receiving others *in the name of Christ* will be *great.*

Note a crucial point. Reaching and receiving others is evidence that we have received Christ. To open one's heart to Christ is to open one's heart to others. There is no such thing as an open heart to God and a closed hand to other people. A person acts according to what is in their heart. If their heart belongs to God, then their hand (life) belongs to other people. They will do all they can to love and help people, receiving and welcoming every person who will be brought to Christ. That person is "great."

And whoever gives one of these little ones even a cup of cold water because he is a disciple, truly, I say to you, he will by no means lose his reward. (Mt.10:42)

Then the righteous will shine like the sun in the kingdom of their Father. He who has ears, let him hear. (Mt.13:43)

His master said to him, "Well done, good and faithful servant. You have been faithful over a little; I will set you over much. Enter into the joy of your master." (Mt.25:23)

If anyone serves me, he must follow me; and where I am, there will my servant be also. If anyone serves me, the Father will honor him. (Jn.12:26)

But glory and honor and peace for everyone who does good, the Jew first and also the Greek. (Ro.2:10)

For you had compassion on those in prison, and you joyfully accepted the plundering of your property, since you knew that you yourselves had a better possession and an abiding one. (He.10:34)

4 The right to greatness: Not an exclusive right.

John knew that the apostles had just done what Christ had demonstrated they should not do. They had just failed to receive a man; in fact, they had rejected the man. And to top it off, the man was ministering in the name of Christ, but he was not a part of their group. John wanted to find out if they

⁴⁹ John answered, "Master, we saw someone casting out demons in your name, and we tried to stop him, because he does not follow with us."

⁵⁰ But Jesus said to him, "Do not stop him, for the one who is not against you is for you."

were right in forbidding others to preach in Jesus' name. John felt there were bound to be limits to what Jesus was saying.

What Jesus said is pointed and clear, yet it is difficult for some to accept. He instructed the disciples to allow the man to continue to minister because, even though he was not a part of the disciples' group, he was not against them. He was not working against them; He was working for the same purpose as they were. Therefore, Jesus concluded, he was *for* them. The twelve disciples did not have an exclusive right to greatness, an exclusive right to minister in Jesus' name.

THOUGHT 1. We are to receive all who minister in Jesus' name sincerely and according to the truth. No individual, church, denomination, or group has a monopoly on the truth nor on the ministry of Christ (see outline and notes—Mk.9:38–41 for detailed discussion).

And whatever town or village you enter, find out who is worthy in it and stay there until you depart. As you enter the house, greet it. And if the house is worthy, let your peace come upon it, but if it is not worthy, let your peace return to you. And if anyone will not receive you or listen to your words, shake off the dust from your feet when you leave that house or town. Truly, I say to you, it will be more bearable on the day of judgment for the land of Sodom and Gomorrah than for that town. (Mt.10:11–15)

And I have other sheep that are not of this fold. I must bring them also, and they will listen to my voice. So there will be one flock, one shepherd. (Jn.10:16)

Some indeed preach Christ from envy and rivalry, but others from good will. The latter do it out of love, knowing that I am put here for the defense of the gospel. The former proclaim Christ out of selfish ambition, not sincerely but thinking to afflict me in my imprisonment. What then? Only that in every way, whether in pretense or in truth, Christ is proclaimed, and in that I rejoice. Yes, and I will rejoice. (Ph.1:15–18)

V. THE SON OF MAN'S GREAT JOURNEY TO JERUSALEM (STAGE 1): HIS MISSION AND PUBLIC CHALLENGE, 9:51–13:21

A. The Son of Man's Mission: Jesus' Mission Misunderstood, 9:51–56

51 When the days drew near for him to be taken up, he set his face to go to Jerusalem.

52 And he sent messengers ahead of him, who went and entered a village of the Samaritans, to make preparations for him.
53 But the people did not receive him, because his face was set toward Jerusalem.
54 And when his disciples James and John saw it, they said, "Lord, do you want us to tell fire to come down from heaven and consume them?"
55 But he turned and rebuked them.
56 And they went on to another village.

1. **Jesus' mission: To secure salvation**
   a. By His ascension[DS1]
   b. By His death: He set His face toward Jerusalem
2. **Jesus' mission misunderstood**
   a. He sent forerunners to prepare the way

   b. He was rejected by the Samaritans

   c. The disciples reacted against the Samaritans

3. **Jesus' mission explained:** He did not come to destroy people but to save them

Division V

The Son of Man's Great Journey to Jerusalem (Stage I): His Mission and Public Challenge, 9:51–13:21

A. The Son of Man's Mission: Jesus' Mission Misunderstood, 9:51–56

9:51–19:28
Division Overview

This passage marks a significant turning point in Jesus' ministry. Luke 9:51–19:28 has no parallel in the other Gospels. Most of the events are recorded by Luke alone. The thrust of the passage is that Jesus' face is set—it is fixed toward Jerusalem.

Luke divides this journey of Jesus into three stages. Each stage begins by strongly emphasizing Jesus' journey toward Jerusalem (Lu.9:51, 53; 13:22; 17:11). Several other passages hint of or mention the journey (Lu.9:53, 57; 10:1, 38; 13:33; 14:25; 18:31; 19:11, 28).

9:51–56
Introduction

When Jesus set His face toward Jerusalem, He was setting His face toward death. This was one of the turning points of His life. As He launched forth in this new direction, the first subject covered is His mission. The mission of the Son of Man is seen in terms so clear that the genuine follower of the Lord should not miss the meaning. Tragically, many did, and still do. This is, *The Son of Man's Mission: Jesus' Mission Misunderstood*, 9:51–56.

1. Jesus' mission: To secure salvation (v.51).
2. Jesus' mission misunderstood (vv.52–54).
3. Jesus' mission explained: He did not come to destroy people but to save them (vv.55–56).

9:51

[51] When the days drew near for him to be taken up, he set his face to go to Jerusalem.

1 Jesus' mission: To secure salvation.

Jesus knew why He had come to earth. His mission was to secure salvation for all who would believe in Him. Now, He was fully aware that the appointed time had come for Him to accomplish that mission once for all (He.10:10).

a. By His ascension.

Luke writes that the time was approaching for Jesus to be "taken" or "received up." This phrase is a reference to our Lord's ascension back to heaven (Ac.2:1–11; see Deeper Study # 1). Christ's ascension would testify that He had fully finished the work the Father sent Him to do, that His mission was accomplished. It would be God's stamp of confirmation that salvation had been secured for the fallen human race.

b. By His death: He set His face toward Jerusalem.

Christ's mission—to bring salvation—could only be accomplished through His sacrificial death. Therefore, the Savior "set His face to go to Jerusalem."

What is so significant about Jerusalem? Very simply, it was in Jerusalem that Jesus was to die for the salvation of fallen humanity and be taken up, that is, ascend into heaven (vv.22, 31). When Jesus "set His face to go to Jerusalem," Jerusalem symbolized the death, resurrection, and ascension of our Lord. He was going to Jerusalem for the express purpose of dying. It was in Jerusalem that He secured salvation through His death, resurrection, and ascension.

> But God shows his love for us in that while we were still sinners, Christ died for us. (Ro.5:8)

> He has delivered us from the domain of darkness and transferred us to the kingdom of his beloved Son, in whom we have redemption, the forgiveness of sins. (Col.1:13–14)

> This is good, and it is pleasing in the sight of God our Savior, who desires all people to be saved and to come to the knowledge of the truth. For there is one God, and there is one mediator between God and men, the man Christ Jesus, who gave himself as a ransom for all, which is the testimony given at the proper time. (1 Ti.2:3–6)

> But we see him who for a little while was made lower than the angels, namely Jesus, crowned with glory and honor because of the suffering of death, so that by the grace of God he might taste death for everyone. (He.2:9)

> He himself bore our sins in his body on the tree, that we might die to sin and live to righteousness. By his wounds you have been healed. (1 Pe.2:24; see 1 Pe.3:18)

> But he was pierced for our transgressions; he was crushed for our iniquities; upon him was the chastisement that brought us peace, and with his wounds we are healed. (Is.53:5)

DEEPER STUDY # 1

(9:51) **Jesus Christ, Ascension**: *taken* or *received up* (Gk. analēmpseōs, *ahn-ah-lame'-pseh-ohce*) refers to the ascension of Christ (see analambanō, *ahn-ah-lahm-bah'-no*, Ac.1:2, 11, 22; 1 Ti.3:16). Salvation was to be secured by the ascension of Christ. How? The ascended Lord testifies of at least four vital truths.

1. It testifies of the *risen Lord*. The ascension means that Christ arose from the dead. If He had remained in the grave, He would still be there in the form of dust. He could not have ascended. If He were to be "taken up," He had to be *raised up* from the dead. Therefore, to speak of the ascension is to mean that Christ is risen. Death is conquered; people can now be saved from death.

But the words "it was counted to him" were not written for his sake alone, but for ours also. It will be counted to us who believe in him who raised from the dead Jesus our Lord, who was delivered up for our trespasses and raised for our justification. (Ro.4:23–25)

Now if Christ is proclaimed as raised from the dead, how can some of you say that there is no resurrection of the dead? But if there is no resurrection of the dead, then not even Christ has been raised. And if Christ has not been raised, then our preaching is in vain and your faith is in vain. We are even found to be misrepresenting God, because we testified about God that he raised Christ, whom he did not raise if it is true that the dead are not raised. For if the dead are not raised, not even Christ has been raised. And if Christ has not been raised, your faith is futile and you are still in your sins. Then those also who have fallen asleep in Christ have perished. If in Christ we have hope in this life only, we are of all people most to be pitied. But in fact Christ has been raised from the dead, the firstfruits of those who have fallen asleep. For as by a man came death, by a man has come also the resurrection of the dead. For as in Adam all die, so also in Christ shall all be made alive. But each in his own order: Christ the firstfruits, then at his coming those who belong to Christ. Then comes the end, when he delivers the kingdom to God the Father after destroying every rule and every authority and power. (1 Co.15:12–24)

But emptied himself, by taking the form of a servant, being born in the likeness of men. And being found in human form, he humbled himself by becoming obedient to the point of death, even death on a cross. Therefore God has highly exalted him and bestowed on him the name that is above every name. (Ph.2:7–9)

2. It testifies of the *advocate* or *representative Lord*. On earth Christ lived a perfect life; He was without sin (Jn.8:46; 2 Co.5:21; He.4:15; 1 Pe.1:19; 2:22). Because He was obedient to the death of the cross, God has highly exalted Him (Ph.2:8–9). He is sitting at the right hand of God the Father (Col.3:1). He is "Jesus Christ the righteous"; therefore, He is our "advocate with the Father" (1 Jn.2:1). He is able to represent us before God because He has lived on earth and secured a perfect righteousness. He is the *ideal man* (see note— Mt.5:17–18), our advocate, the one who is qualified to plead our case before God and see to it that we are saved.

Consequently, he is able to save to the uttermost those who draw near to God through him, since he always lives to make intercession for them. (He.7:25)

3. It testifies of the *priestly* or *intercessory Lord*. Every person suffers while on earth: suffers pain, trial, need, want, temptation, loss, illness, and eventually death. We are incapable of even knowing how to pray as we ought in order to secure the help we need. But Christ knows and understands. He has been to earth and suffered just as we suffer. Therefore, He knows how to intercede for us and how to deliver us.

Who shall bring any charge against God's elect? It is God who justifies. Who is to condemn? Christ Jesus is the one who died—more than that, who was raised—who is at the right hand of God, who indeed is interceding for us. (Ro.8:33–34)

For surely it is not angels that he helps, but he helps the offspring of Abraham. Therefore he had to be made like his brothers in every respect, so that he might become a merciful and faithful high priest in the service of God, to make propitiation for the sins of the people. For because he himself has suffered when tempted, he is able to help those who are being tempted. (He.2:16–18)

Since then we have a great high priest who has passed through the heavens, Jesus, the Son of God, let us hold fast our confession. For we do not have a high priest who is unable to sympathize with our weaknesses, but one who in every respect has been tempted as we are, yet without sin. Let us then with confidence draw near to the throne of grace, that we may receive mercy and find grace to help in time of need. (He.4:14–16)

4. It testifies of the *exalted Lord*. Christ has ascended to be exalted, to rule and reign over the universe. There is a great day of judgment coming upon the world, a day when all people will bow the knee and acknowledge that Jesus is Lord, the Son of the living God.

Then comes the end, when he delivers the kingdom to God the Father after destroying every rule and every authority and power. For he must reign until he has put all his enemies under his feet. The last enemy to be destroyed is death. (1 Co.15:24–26)

And what is the immeasurable greatness of his power toward us who believe, according to the working of his great might that he worked in Christ when he raised him from the dead and seated him at his right hand in the heavenly places, far above all rule and authority and power and dominion, and above every name that is named, not only in this age but also in the one to come. And he put all things under his feet and gave him as head over all things to the church, which is his body, the fullness of him who fills all in all. (Ep.1:19–23)

Therefore God has highly exalted him and bestowed on him the name that is above every name, so that at the name of Jesus every knee should bow, in heaven and on earth and under the earth, and every tongue confess that Jesus Christ is Lord, to the glory of God the Father. (Ph.2:9–11)

9:52–54

⁵² And he sent messengers ahead of him, who went and entered a village of the Samaritans, to make preparations for him.

⁵³ But the people did not receive him, because his face was set toward Jerusalem.

⁵⁴ And when his disciples James and John saw it, they said, "Lord, do you want us to tell fire to come down from heaven and consume them?"

2 Jesus' mission misunderstood.

Jesus' route to Jerusalem included passing through a Samaritan village. However, the chilly reception the Samaritan gave Him is a glaring example of just how misunderstood Jesus' mission was.

a. He sent forerunners to prepare the way (v.52).

Jesus sent some disciples to run ahead of Him and prepare the way for His coming. Apparently, this was the method Christ used to let people in a certain area know He was coming their way. Those who had interest could thereby be prepared for His coming.

b. He was rejected by the Samaritans (v.53).

However, when the Samaritans heard Jesus was headed their way, they refused to receive Him; He was not welcome in their village. Why did the Samaritans reject Jesus? Because He was heading for Jerusalem, going to a place they despised. Jews were unacceptable to them; therefore, they would have nothing to do with Jesus if He were going to minister in Jerusalem. Jerusalem had its own worship and priests, and the Samaritans had theirs. If Jesus would be theirs alone, they would gladly receive Him; if not, then He was not welcome in their circles (see Deeper Study # 2—Lu.10:33 for more detailed discussion).

c. The disciples reacted against the Samaritans (v.54).

James and John were enraged over the Samaritans' treatment of the Lord. They reacted furiously, asking Jesus if they should call fire down from heaven to destroy the village and its people. Note two crucial observations:

➤ Their strong faith in Jesus: they believed without question that Jesus had the authority to control the power of heaven, either through Himself or through them.

➤ Their misunderstanding of Jesus' mission: They thought in terms of a messianic ruler on earth, subjecting people to Himself and forcing them to worship and serve God. They saw the Messiah's judging those who rejected Him.

By reacting as they did, James and John were guilty of the very same error that the Samaritans had just committed. They were full of bitterness, wrath, and vengeance, reacting against the Samaritans just as the Samaritans had reacted against them. They wanted to destroy the Samaritans because the Samaritans were not willing to worship (Jesus) and live as James and John wished.

For God did not send his Son into the world to condemn the world, but in order that the world might be saved through him. (Jn.3:17)

If anyone hears my words and does not keep them, I do not judge him; for I did not come to judge the world but to save the world. (Jn.12:47)

3 Jesus' mission explained: He did not come to destroy people but to save them.

Jesus rebuked James and John for their vengeful, misdirected wrath. Jesus' mission was not to destroy people, but to save them. This truth is repeated time and time again. The Savior refused to let the Samaritan's rejection detour, delay, or discourage Him. He pressed on toward Jerusalem, on toward the place where His mission would be accomplished.

For the Son of Man came to seek and to save the lost. (Lu.19:10)

Truly, truly, I say to you, whoever hears my word and believes him who sent me has eternal life. He does not come into judgment, but has passed from death to life. (Jn.5:24)

[55] But he turned and rebuked them. [56] And they went on to another village.

The thief comes only to steal and kill and destroy. I came that they may have life and have it abundantly. (Jn.10:10)

The saying is trustworthy and deserving of full acceptance, that Christ Jesus came into the world to save sinners, of whom I am the foremost. (1 Ti.1:15)

THOUGHT 1. Note two observations.

1) By refusing to judge the unbelieving Samaritans, Christ proclaimed that today is the day of salvation, and He proclaimed it loudly and clearly.

For he says, "In a favorable time I listened to you, and in a day of salvation I have helped you." Behold, now is the favorable time; behold, now is the day of salvation. (2 Co.6:2)

Behold, I stand at the door and knock. If anyone hears my voice and opens the door, I will come in to him and eat with him, and he with me. (Re.3:20)

2) Scripture pronounces that judgment is *to come*. The death of every person is appointed, followed by an appointment with judgment.

And just as it is appointed for man to die once, and after that comes judgment. (He.9:27)

B. The Great Cost of Discipleship, 9:57–62

(Mt.8:18–22)

1. A person must count the cost
   a. A man offered to follow Christ

   b. Jesus offered no luxury, no material comfort: He offered only self-denial and sacrifice[DS1]

2. A person must follow Christ immediately
   a. Jesus invited another man
   b. The man had divided attention
   c. Jesus' demand
      1) A sense of urgency
      2) Go now and preach

3. A person must not look back
   a. Another man offered to follow Christ:
   b. The man's dual loyalty
   c. Jesus' judgment: Looking back disqualifies a person

57 As they were going along the road, someone said to him, "I will follow you wherever you go."
58 And Jesus said to him, "Foxes have holes, and birds of the air have nests, but the Son of Man has nowhere to lay his head."
59 To another he said, "Follow me." But he said, "Lord, let me first go and bury my father."

60 And Jesus said to him, "Leave the dead to bury their own dead. But as for you, go and proclaim the kingdom of God."
61 Yet another said, "I will follow you, Lord, but let me first say farewell to those at my home."
62 Jesus said to him, "No one who puts his hand to the plow and looks back is fit for the kingdom of God."

Division V

The Son of Man's Great Journey to Jerusalem (Stage I): His Mission and Public Challenge, 9:51–13:21

B. The Great Cost of Discipleship, 9:57–62

(Mt.8:18–22)

9:57–62
Introduction

Luke tells here the stories of three different men who had the same opportunity, the opportunity to follow Christ. However, something stood between each of them and being a fully-devoted, totally-committed disciple. Their three cases are combined in Scripture to teach one critical truth: discipleship demands a great cost. Only those who put Christ first above everything and everybody else can be His disciple.

Many stumble over what Jesus said to these men because they do not fully understand what Jesus said, especially to the two who put family obligations or affections ahead of following Him. When studying this passage, it is important to keep the following in mind:

➤ Do not be distracted or discouraged by what Jesus did *not* say. He was not saying that we are to neglect the care of our aged parents; nor was He saying that we should abandon family ties or not own homes or have any of life's comforts.

➤ When Jesus was dealing with these men about discipleship, His time was short. He was already on His way to Jerusalem to die. Literally, there was no time for these men to delay.

➤ Jesus knew these men's hearts. He could see what we cannot see.

In each of these men's stories, there is one thing Luke does not tell us: what they ultimately decided. We do not know whether or not they chose to follow Christ in the end. Perhaps we are left asking, "What did they do?" in order to stir us to ask ourselves, "What will *I* do?" This is, *The Great Cost of Discipleship*, 9:57–62.

1. A person must count the cost (vv.57–58).
2. A person must follow Christ immediately (vv.59–60).
3. A person must not look back (vv.61–62).

1 A person must count the cost.

It is an honorable thing to desire to follow Christ, but our Lord wants us to know exactly what being His disciple requires. Many set out to follow Christ but quickly turn back because they do not grasp what true discipleship requires; they do not count the cost.

[57] As they were going along the road, someone said to him, "I will follow you wherever you go."
[58] And Jesus said to him, "Foxes have holes, and birds of the air have nests, but the Son of Man has nowhere to lay his head."

a. A man offered to follow Christ (v.57).

A man offered to become a follower of Jesus, and he made what he thought to be a noble promise: he would follow Jesus wherever He led. Why was following Christ desirable to this man? Perhaps for the same reasons so many are attracted to the Lord:

➤ He enjoyed the presence of the Lord and His followers.
➤ He was motivated by the Lord's wisdom and teaching.
➤ He appreciated the good the Lord did.

b. Jesus offered no luxury, no material comfort: He offered only self-denial and sacrifice (v.58).

Jesus' to-the-point reply no doubt startled the man. Instead of welcoming him, the Lord warned him: following Him would mean a life of sacrifice. The man had to count the cost, for Jesus offered no luxury and no material comfort—only self-denial (see note—Mt.8:19-20 for more discussion).

Jesus pointed out that He Himself was the prime example of self-denial and sacrifice. He denied Himself completely. He sacrificed and gave all, both Himself and all He had. He did not even have a home, no place to lay His head. The animals of the world did; the birds had their nests, and the foxes had their holes, but Jesus had no place. He sacrificed all to meet the needs of a dying and desperate world.

Jesus told the man to count the cost of *true* discipleship. A profession was not enough. Being willing to follow was not enough. The man must *deny himself completely* and be willing to sacrifice to meet the needs of a lost and desperate world (see note and DEEPER STUDY # 1—Lu.9:23 for discussion).

Note that Jesus called Himself the *Son of Man* (see DEEPER STUDY # 1). This title pictures exactly who He is. This man was to follow Jesus, accepting Him as the Son of Man. He was to accept Jesus as the *ideal servant* of mankind, the *ideal man* who loved and ministered to all, and who did it perfectly.

THOUGHT 1. Some people are willing and determined to go to the ends of the earth. However Jesus said that *He—the Son of Man, His pattern of life*—must be accepted.

Many are committed, but their commitments are *self-centered commitments*, not Christ-centered commitments. We must realize that self-commitments can arise from (1) strong wills, (2) strong determinations, and (3) strong discipline. And the person can follow through in a great way. But self-commitment is not enough for Christ. There has to be a total commitment to the Son of Man, abandoning all of self and all of the world.

> **And he said to all, "If anyone would come after me, let him deny himself and take up his cross daily and follow me." (Lu.9:23)**

For we who live are always being given over to death for Jesus' sake, so that the life of Jesus also may be manifested in our mortal flesh. (2 Co.4:11)

For you know the grace of our Lord Jesus Christ, that though he was rich, yet for your sake he became poor, so that you by his poverty might become rich. (2 Co.8:9)

Have this mind among yourselves, which is yours in Christ Jesus, who, though he was in the form of God, did not count equality with God a thing to be grasped, but emptied himself, by taking the form of a servant, being born in the likeness of men. And being found in human form, he humbled himself by becoming obedient to the point of death, even death on a cross. (Ph.2:5–8)

For to this you have been called, because Christ also suffered for you, leaving you an example, so that you might follow in his steps. (1 Pe.2:21)

DEEPER STUDY # 1

(9:58) **Son of Man:** Jesus was not only what an ordinary person is, a son of man; but Jesus was what every person ought to be, the Son of Man Himself. As such, He has become the *ideal man*, the *representative man*, the *perfect man*, the *pattern*, the *embodiment* of everything we ought to be (see DEEPER STUDY # 3—Mt.1:16). Jesus Christ is the *perfect picture* of a human being. Everything God wants us to be is seen perfectly in Jesus Christ (see Jn.1:14; Col.2:9-10; He.1:3). The title, *Son of Man*, also indicates that Christ is the *ideal servant* of humanity. It stresses His sympathy for the poor, the brokenhearted, the captives, the blind, the bruised, the outcasts, the bereaved (see Lu.4:18). Jesus is the pattern, the model, the perfect example of concern and caring. He served just like every person ought to serve others.

Jesus called Himself "the Son of Man" about eighty times. It was His favorite title for Himself. The title *Son of Man* is probably based on the Son of Man of Daniel 7:13-14. There is a picture of Jesus as the heavenly Son of Man contrasted with Adam as the earthly man in 1 Corinthians 15:45-47. Each served as a representative of mankind in God's plan for world history.

9:59-60

⁵⁹ To another he said, "Follow me." But he said, "Lord, let me first go and bury my father." ⁶⁰ And Jesus said to him, "Leave the dead to bury their own dead. But as for you, go and proclaim the kingdom of God."

2 A person must follow Christ immediately.

Luke proceeds to tell of another man's confrontation with discipleship. The first man's story emphasizes the self-denial and sacrifice involved with following Christ. This man's story stresses the requirement of immediate obedience to Christ's call.

a. **Jesus invited another man (v.59a).**

This man stands in contrast to the previously-mentioned man (vv.57-58). The first man offered to follow Jesus; this man, however, was invited or called by Jesus to follow Him. There was something very special within the man that caught Jesus' eye, and Jesus moved to call him. In fact, the *specialness* within the man was of such quality that Jesus stayed after the man even after the man hesitated. The man was of too much value to let go, so Jesus pleaded and even commanded him to proclaim or preach the gospel (v.60).

b. **The man had divided attention (v.59b).**

The call of Christ came to this man, yet he hesitated (see note—Mt.8:21). He wanted to delay following Christ until after his father died.

The man's problem was *divided attention*. When he felt God's call, he looked at his situation and did not yield immediately. What happened to him is what often happens. His circumstances were not ideal, so he wanted to wait until they changed. As soon as circumstances changed, he would leave and follow Jesus.

Peter began to say to him, "See, we have left everything and followed you." Jesus said, "Truly, I say to you, there is no one who has left house or brothers or sisters or mother or father or children or lands, for my sake and for the gospel, who will not receive a hundredfold now in this time, houses and brothers and sisters and mothers and children and lands, with persecutions, and in the age to come eternal life." (Mk.10:28-30)

If anyone comes to me and does not hate his own father and mother and wife and children and brothers and sisters, yes, and even his own life, he cannot be my disciple. Whoever does not bear his own cross and come after me cannot be my disciple. (Lu.14:26-27)

And what you have heard from me in the presence of many witnesses entrust to faithful men, who will be able to teach others also. Share in suffering as a good soldier of Christ Jesus. No soldier gets entangled in civilian pursuits, since his aim is to please the one who enlisted him. (2 Ti.2:2-4)

As for you, always be sober-minded, endure suffering, do the work of an evangelist, fulfill your ministry. (2 Ti.4:5)

c. Jesus' demand (v.60).

Jesus demanded that the man act now and not wait. Jesus saw through the man's partial commitment. He saw through the man's lack of trust in God. Jesus expects us to take care of our parents (1 Ti.5:3-8), but, at the same time, He calls us to follow His will for our lives. For some, His call requires continual travel in His service or relocating to another region. Either way, they are faced with leaving family behind to follow Christ's calling. Obeying Christ must be our first priority, and we must obey Him immediately. Note the details of Jesus' call.

First, the call of Christ includes a sense of urgency. Many people misunderstand this verse, thinking that the man's father had died and Jesus would not even allow the man to remain behind long enough for the funeral. This interpretation is inaccurate, for such an idea is totally contrary to the loving character of Christ. Actually, the man's father was not yet dead, and the man wanted to wait until *after his father had died* to obey Christ's call (perhaps out of a sincere heart or perhaps in order to receive an inheritance). This was unacceptable to Christ, because the need was urgent. The need is so great, and people are dying every hour *without Christ*. If we hesitate, for whatever reason, some whom we might have reached will die and be doomed. The point is forceful: the work to which Christ calls us is urgent. We must not delay or hesitate.

And Jesus said to them, "Follow me, and I will make you become fishers of men." And immediately they left their nets and followed him. (Mk.1:17-18)

We must work the works of him who sent me while it is day; night is coming, when no one can work. (Jn.9:4)

Besides this you know the time, that the hour has come for you to wake from sleep. For salvation is nearer to us now than when we first believed. The night is far gone; the day is at hand. So then let us cast off the works of darkness and put on the armor of light. (Ro.13:11-12)

This is what I mean, brothers: the appointed time has grown very short. From now on, let those who have wives live as though they had none. (1 Co.7:29)

Making the best use of the time, because the days are evil. (Ep.5:16)

So teach us to number our days that we may get a heart of wisdom. (Ps.90:12)

Second, Christ's call is to *go* (Mt.28:19; Mk.16:15; Ac.1:8), and we must go wherever Christ calls us. For many, Christ's call means leaving home and family behind, just as it did for this man. Others, like the maniac of Gadara, are called to share the gospel in their homeland (Mk.5:18-19).

In addition, Jesus' call is to proclaim or preach the kingdom of God. Christ tells His messengers what to preach, yet many do not declare the real message of God's kingdom (see note— Mt.19:23-24). Note that the Lord continued to call the man even after he had offered his excuse for not going at that time. The Lord's call on the man did not change with the man's hesitation.

THOUGHT 1. Note two important points.

1) Every person is of extreme value to Jesus. Therefore, the Spirit stays after us as long as we allow Him, despite our selfishness.

2) Every person who is called by Christ to preach must respond immediately. The Lord's call is to be the first priority of a person's life.

> **For we cannot but speak of what we have seen and heard. (Ac.4:20)**
>
> **When Silas and Timothy arrived from Macedonia, Paul was occupied with the word, testifying to the Jews that the Christ was Jesus. (Ac.18:5)**
>
> **For if I preach the gospel, that gives me no ground for boasting. For necessity is laid upon me. Woe to me if I do not preach the gospel! (1 Co.9:16)**
>
> **Preach the word; be ready in season and out of season; reprove, rebuke, and exhort, with complete patience and teaching. (2 Ti.4:2)**
>
> **If I say, "I will not mention him, or speak any more in his name," there is in my heart as it were a burning fire shut up in my bones, and I am weary with holding it in, and I cannot. (Je.20:9)**
>
> **The lion has roared; who will not fear? The Lord GOD has spoken; who can but prophesy? (Am.3:8)**

9:61–62

⁶¹ Yet another said, "I will follow you, Lord, but let me first say farewell to those at my home." ⁶² Jesus said to him, "No one who puts his hand to the plow and looks back is fit for the kingdom of God."

3 A person must not look back.

Luke tells about a third man and his encounter with discipleship. This man would not move forward in following Christ because he could not stop looking back at what he was leaving behind.

a. Another man offered to follow Christ (v.61a).

Like the first man, this man offered himself to Jesus. He was *willing* to follow Jesus. Perhaps something about the Lord touched his heart, or maybe the Lord's teaching and ministry appealed to him. It may be that he had seen the enormous benefit of Christ's ministry to people and to society. Whatever the case, he made a decision to follow Jesus. He was *willing*.

b. The man's dual loyalty (v.61b).

Note the words *but* and *first*. This man set a condition for his discipleship. He had a *double allegiance*. He had thought through his decision and concluded that he was willing to follow Christ, *but* he *first* wanted to spend more time with his family. He may have wanted his family's counsel and advice, to see how they felt about his decision. Perhaps he felt their approval was needed. Then again, he could have been putting his love for family before his love for Christ. Perhaps he was attached to his family more than he was attached to Christ.

This man represents all who put something else ahead of Christ: a family matter, business affairs, employment, finances, a home, pleasures, possessions—some other concern that takes priority over Christ's call on our lives. As is the case with so many, we see in this man a dual loyalty, a loyalty to someone or something else over Christ.

THOUGHT 1. Family is important, as Scripture so clearly teaches. By no means is Christ suggesting that it is not. However, family should be our *first* attachment *after* our attachment to Christ. Next to our commitment to Christ, it is the most important commitment in our lives. Christ is to be first in our lives, then family, then other obligations and interests.

> **But seek first the kingdom of God and his righteousness, and all these things will be added to you. (Mt.6:33)**
>
> **So therefore, any one of you who does not renounce all that he has cannot be my disciple. (Lu.14:33)**
>
> **No servant can serve two masters, for either he will hate the one and love the other, or he will be devoted to the one and despise the other. You cannot serve God and money. (Lu.16:13)**
>
> **And now, Israel, what does the LORD your God require of you, but to fear the LORD your God, to walk in all his ways, to love him, to serve the LORD your God with all your heart and with all your soul. (De.10:12)**

Has the Lord as great delight in burnt offerings and sacrifices, as in obeying the voice of the Lord? Behold, to obey is better than sacrifice, and to listen than the fat of rams. (1 Sa.15:22)

And Elijah came near to all the people and said, "How long will you go limping between two different opinions? If the Lord is God, follow him; but if Baal, then follow him." And the people did not answer him a word. (1 Ki.18:21)

c. Jesus' judgment: Looking back disqualifies a person (v.62).

Jesus stated His judgment on the man's conditional discipleship in a way that is hard to forget: no person who puts their hand to the plow—sets out to follow Christ—and then looks back . . . is fit for the kingdom of God. The man got the point, and it is doubtful he ever forgot it. Christ's directive more than likely pricked his conscience and disturbed him continually as the saying flashed across his mind. He had willed to follow Christ, but he had "looked back." He longed for what he was leaving behind; in this case, his family. He could not leave that which tugged at his heart more than the call of Christ did. Therefore, he was not fit for the kingdom of God.

Grasp the meaning of Christ's illustration and how it applies to following Christ. Those who begin to plow and then look back . . .

- plow a crooked row—no row is ever straight, not like it should be (the work is not done right)
- plow an inconsistent field: the field is never matured; it never receives consistent work
- plow without total commitment: they may turn away at any time, leaving a job unfinished
- plow but allow distractions and disruptions which affect the crops (the plants are not cared for)

THOUGHT 1. Many people never go forward in the service of Christ because they cannot leave someone or something behind. For some it is a successful career or a good-paying job. For some it is a lifestyle. For some it is family, or friends, or a romantic interest who is not committed to Christ. For some it is the sins of the old life: some long for the sinful pleasures they enjoyed before they came to Christ.

Jesus is clear: those who look back are not fit for His kingdom. We must let go of the past and its pull on us in order that we can serve Jesus Christ wholeheartedly (Ph.3:13–14).

But now that you have come to know God, or rather to be known by God, how can you turn back again to the weak and worthless elementary principles of the world, whose slaves you want to be once more? (Ga.4:9)

Brothers, I do not consider that I have made it my own. But one thing I do: forgetting what lies behind and straining forward to what lies ahead, I press on toward the goal for the prize of the upward call of God in Christ Jesus. (Ph.3:13–14)

But my righteous one shall live by faith, and if he shrinks back, my soul has no pleasure in him. (He.10:38)

Draw near to God, and he will draw near to you. Cleanse your hands, you sinners, and purify your hearts, you double-minded. (Jas.4:8)

For if, after they have escaped the defilements of the world through the knowledge of our Lord and Savior Jesus Christ, they are again entangled in them and overcome, the last state has become worse for them than the first. (2 Pe.2:20)

But I have this against you, that you have abandoned the love you had at first. Remember therefore from where you have fallen; repent, and do the works you did at first. If not, I will come to you and remove your lampstand from its place, unless you repent. (Re.2:4–5)

CHAPTER 10

C. The Seventy Sent Out: Great Purpose, 10:1–16

(Mt.10)

1. **First, obey the Lord's call to labor**

2. **Second, pray for more laborers**

3. **Third, go into an antagonistic world**

4. **Fourth, trust God and sense the hour's urgency**

5. **Fifth, guard the message—do not force it on people**

6. **Sixth, accept compensation, but do not seek luxury**

7. **Seventh, be accommodating and adaptable**
   a. Identify with people
   b. Minister to people
   c. Proclaim the kingdom of God

8. **Eighth, walk away from rejecters**
   a. Any town and people who reject

      1) Symbolize God's rejection by wiping off the very dust of the city
      2) Reason: The kingdom of God came near, but they rejected it
      3) Judgment: Shall be greater than Sodom's

   b. Any who only profess to be God's people[DS1]
      1) Illustrated: By two Jewish cities
      2) The reason: The works of Christ were seen, yet He was rejected

After this the Lord appointed seventy-two others and sent them on ahead of him, two by two, into every town and place where he himself was about to go. ² And he said to them, "The harvest is plentiful, but the laborers are few. Therefore pray earnestly to the Lord of the harvest to send out laborers into his harvest. ³ Go your way; behold, I am sending you out as lambs in the midst of wolves. ⁴ Carry no moneybag, no knapsack, no sandals, and greet no one on the road. ⁵ Whatever house you enter, first say, 'Peace be to this house!' ⁶ And if a son of peace is there, your peace will rest upon him. But if not, it will return to you. ⁷ And remain in the same house, eating and drinking what they provide, for the laborer deserves his wages. Do not go from house to house. ⁸ Whenever you enter a town and they receive you, eat what is set before you. ⁹ Heal the sick in it and say to them, 'The kingdom of God has come near to you.' ¹⁰ But whenever you enter a town and they do not receive you, go into its streets and say, ¹¹ 'Even the dust of your town that clings to our feet we wipe off against you. Nevertheless know this, that the kingdom of God has come near.' ¹² I tell you, it will be more bearable on that day for Sodom than for that town. ¹³ Woe to you, Chorazin! Woe to you, Bethsaida! For if the mighty works done in you had been done in Tyre and Sidon, they would have repented long ago, sitting in sackcloth and ashes.

14 But it will be more bearable in the judgment for Tyre and Sidon than for you.

15 And you, Capernaum, will you be exalted to heaven? You shall be brought down to Hades.

16 The one who hears you hears me, and the one who rejects you rejects me, and the one who rejects me rejects him who sent me."

3) The judgment: To be more terrible than Tyre and Sidon

c. Any who receive a constant witness but still reject: To receive the greatest judgment—hell

9. Ninth, know that the Christian laborer represents the Lord

Division V

The Son of Man's Great Journey to Jerusalem (Stage I): His Mission and Public Challenge, 9:51–13:21

C. The Seventy Sent Out: Great Purpose, 10:1–16

(Mt.10)

10:1–16
Introduction

A challenging truth is presented clearly in this passage: Jesus does not only call preachers or ministers to proclaim the gospel. They are not solely responsible for kingdom work. To the contrary, He calls what we refer to as laypeople—those who do not have a special call to preach God's Word—to join Him in the greatest of all works. The seventy or seventy-two appointed by Christ in this passage symbolize the laypeople of the church. Every believer has the opportunity to be a fellow laborer with God (1 Co.3:9). Here, our Lord instructs Christian laborers as to how we are to serve Him in this desperately needy world. These are His instructions to us, the ones to whom He has given the Great Commission and the ministry of reconciliation (Mt.28:18–20; Mk.16:15; Ac.1:8; 2 Co.5:18). This is, *The Seventy Sent Out: Great Purpose,* 10:1-16.

1. First, obey the Lord's call to labor (v.1).
2. Second, pray for more laborers (v.2).
3. Third, go into an antagonistic world (v.3).
4. Fourth, trust God and sense the hour's urgency (v.4).
5. Fifth, guard the message—do not force it on people (vv.5–6).
6. Sixth, accept compensation, but do not seek luxury (v.7).
7. Seventh, be accommodating and adaptable (vv.8–9).
8. Eighth, walk away from rejecters (vv.10–15).
9. Ninth, know that the Christian laborer represents the Lord (v.16).

1 First, obey the Lord's call to labor.

10:1

Jesus appointed seventy (or seventy-two) disciples to prepare the way for Him. Trustworthy manuscripts differ on this detail, and there is textual evidence for each number. The number seventy is significant throughout the Bible, and Jesus' appointment of these seventy (or seventy-two)

After this the Lord appointed seventy-two others and sent them on ahead of him, two by two, into every town and place where he himself was about to go.

witnesses is seen as symbolic, just as the appointment of twelve apostles is said to be symbolic. The twelve apostles are said to symbolize . . .

- the twelve patriarchs
- the twelve tribes of Israel
- the twelve leaders of the tribes

The seventy are said to symbolize . . .

- the nations of the world (see Ge.10 where seventy names are listed; seventy-two in the Septuagint Greek Version of the Old Testament); the point being made in the symbolism is that the gospel is to go into all the world
- the seventy elders who saw the glory of God (Ex.24:1, 9)
- the seventy elders of Israel (Nu.11:16f)
- the seventy palm trees at Elim (Ex.15:27); there were also twelve wells of water at Elim said to represent the twelve apostles
- the great Sanhedrin, the ruling body of the Jews, which had seventy members

This verse establishes that Jesus had many more disciples than just the twelve who were specially chosen. At least seventy others followed Jesus so closely that He could send them out as witnesses for Him. Peter spoke of the witnesses as the "men who have accompanied us during all the time that the Lord Jesus went in and out among us" (Ac.1:21; see 1:15). They were people who were willing to go, people who obeyed the Lord's call to labor for Him. When the Lord appointed them, they accepted the responsibility He was giving them and carried it out faithfully.

Jesus saw a tremendous need, a need so great that a large corps of witnesses was needed. He sent them out two by two for mutual encouragement and help. Note that they served as forerunners; they went to the places where He was headed to prepare the people for His coming.

THOUGHT 1. How many of us follow Christ so closely that He can send us out as witnesses for Him? Our task mirrors the task of these witnesses. Jesus is coming to this world again; He has appointed us to go into all the world, sharing God's saving grace and transforming power in order that people will be prepared for His coming (Tit.2:11–13). Like these seventy, we need to obey the call of Christ to labor in the fields of the world, to sow the seed of the gospel and harvest souls for His kingdom.

Therefore you also must be ready, for the Son of Man is coming at an hour you do not expect. (Mt.24:44)

For the grace of God has appeared, bringing salvation for all people, training us to renounce ungodliness and worldly passions, and to live self-controlled, upright, and godly lives in the present age, waiting for our blessed hope, the appearing of the glory of our great God and Savior Jesus Christ. (Tit.2:11–13)

And now, little children, abide in him, so that when he appears we may have confidence and not shrink from him in shame at his coming. (1 Jn.2:28)

10:2

² And he said to them, "The harvest is plentiful, but the laborers are few. Therefore pray earnestly to the Lord of the harvest to send out laborers into his harvest."

2 Second, pray for more laborers.

As Jesus sent these witnesses out, He instructed them to pray for more laborers (see outline and notes—Mt.9:37-38 for more discussion). This was their very first duty. Jesus gave four reasons why more laborers were needed.

First, a great harvest of precious souls was waiting to be reached with the gospel. The number of people in the world even then was staggering, and the vast majority were without Jesus, reeling to and fro under the weight of the problems of a sinful and dying world.

Second, the laborers were few, very few. The seventy (or seventy-two) along with the twelve were not nearly enough laborers to reap the harvest of souls waiting for the good news of Christ.

Third, the need was urgent: the crop was ripe, ready for *harvest* (Jn.4:35-36). Many wanted the *gospel*, the answer to life. They were actually ready to be reaped, wanting purpose, meaning, and significance in their lives. They might not have known what was causing the longing and aching within their hearts; they might not have known how to identify it, but they were ready to listen and grab hold of the answer. And Jesus was the answer.

Fourth, God was the one who had to send laborers. He was the source of laborers, and Jesus called His disciples to pray for God to send more out.

THOUGHT 1. Jesus' instruction to these disciples is for us as well: we must always be praying diligently for laborers to take the gospel to the world. The need is even greater than it was in Jesus' day, for the population of the world has increased exponentially as the centuries have rolled by. The laborers are still few, and the need is still urgent. Many are waiting to hear the good news that Jesus is the answer to the longing and aching within their hearts.

Note a crucial point. A generation's concern determines how well that generation gets along under God's care. A generation that longs for God—that seeks after God to send forth laborers—will have laborers and see a good deal of righteousness prevail during its life. A generation that ignores God reaps a harvest of immorality and ungodliness, injustice and evil. The answer to a solid generation, to a moral and just generation is prayer—prayer for laborers to be sent out to reap the precious harvest of souls. If voices are not proclaiming love and morality and justice, then sin and death will reign.

> But when the grain is ripe, at once he puts in the sickle, because the harvest has come. (Mk.4:29)

> Do you not say, "There are yet four months, then comes the harvest"? Look, I tell you, lift up your eyes, and see that the fields are white for harvest. Already the one who reaps is receiving wages and gathering fruit for eternal life, so that sower and reaper may rejoice together. (Jn.4:35-36)

> And let us not grow weary of doing good, for in due season we will reap, if we do not give up. (Ga.6:9)

> Those who sow in tears shall reap with shouts of joy! He who goes out weeping, bearing the seed for sowing, shall come home with shouts of joy, bringing his sheaves with him. (Ps.126:5-6)

> Sow for yourselves righteousness; reap steadfast love; break up your fallow ground, for it is the time to seek the LORD, that he may come and rain righteousness upon you. (Ho.10:12)

3 Third, go into an antagonistic world.

10:3

Jesus warned the witnesses that they were going into an antagonistic world (see note, pt.2—Mt.10:16 for more discussion). The threat of persecution was real. Jesus said that they would be like lambs in the midst of wolves; some people they encountered would be like *wolves* . . .

3 "Go your way, behold, I am sending you out as lambs in the midst of wolves."

- protecting their territory, snarling and putting down the messenger of God, trying to scare him or her away from trying to tame the world
- growling and threatening the believer who opposes the way of the world
- hungry and ready to hunt down, attack, and consume

By describing the witnesses as lambs, Jesus was not just emphasizing their vulnerability; He was also describing the spirit or attitude they were to display. They were to be as a sheep: meek, harmless, and noncombative. Jesus Himself would display this spirit when He was arrested and nailed to the cross (Is.53:7).

THOUGHT 1. As we grow ever closer to the return of Christ, the world grows increasingly hostile to Christ and the gospel. If we are faithful to the Lord's command to proclaim the gospel to all people, we should expect to be opposed and persecuted. Jesus' command to these witnesses is to us as well: we are to be like sheep, displaying the same attitude Jesus instructed these seventy witnesses to display and the same attitude He later displayed on the cross.

> I have said all these things to you to keep you from falling away. They will put you out of the synagogues. Indeed, the hour is coming when whoever kills you will think he is offering service to God. And they will do these things because they have not known the Father, nor me. But I have said these things to you, that when their hour comes you may remember that I told them to you. I did not say these things to you from the beginning, because I was with you. (Jn.16:1-4)

Pay careful attention to yourselves and to all the flock, in which the Holy Spirit has made you overseers, to care for the church of God, which he obtained with his own blood. I know that after my departure fierce wolves will come in among you, not sparing the flock; and from among your own selves will arise men speaking twisted things, to draw away the disciples after them. Therefore be alert, remembering that for three years I did not cease night or day to admonish every one with tears. (Ac.20:28-31)

For it has been granted to you that for the sake of Christ you should not only believe in him but also suffer for his sake. (Ph.1:29)

That no one be moved by these afflictions. For you yourselves know that we are destined for this. (1 Th.3:3)

Indeed, all who desire to live a godly life in Christ Jesus will be persecuted. (2 Ti.3:12)

Beloved, do not be surprised at the fiery trial when it comes upon you to test you, as though something strange were happening to you. But rejoice insofar as you share Christ's sufferings, that you may also rejoice and be glad when his glory is revealed. If you are insulted for the name of Christ, you are blessed, because the Spirit of glory and of God rests upon you. But let none of you suffer as a murderer or a thief or an evildoer or as a meddler. Yet if anyone suffers as a Christian, let him not be ashamed, but let him glorify God in that name. (1 Pe.4:12-16)

Do not fear what you are about to suffer. Behold, the devil is about to throw some of you into prison, that you may be tested, and for ten days you will have tribulation. Be faithful unto death, and I will give you the crown of life. (Re.2:10)

10:4

⁴ "Carry no moneybag, no knapsack, no sandals, and greet no one on the road."

4 Fourth, trust God and sense the hour's urgency.

Jesus' instructed these disciples not to carry a *moneybag* (a purse or wallet), a *knapsack* (Gk. pēran, *pay'-rahn*)—a bag carried by travelers for food and provisions—or two pair of sandals. They were to trust God for what they needed, not worrying about money for food, housing, or clothing (Mt.6:24-34). Worrying about such things would be cumbersome, taking away precious time that should be spent in ministering. Also, they were preaching a message of faith and trust in God. They needed to live what they were preaching and become a living picture of the dependency that God wants from every person.

But seek first the kingdom of God and his righteousness, and all these things will be added to you. (Mt.6:33)

Not that I am speaking of being in need, for I have learned in whatever situation I am to be content. I know how to be brought low, and I know how to abound. In any and every circumstance, I have learned the secret of facing plenty and hunger, abundance and need. I can do all things through him who strengthens me. (Ph.4:11-13)

Trust in the Lord, and do good; dwell in the land and befriend faithfulness. . . . Commit your way to the Lord; trust in him, and he will act. (Ps.37:3, 5)

You keep him in perfect peace whose mind is stayed on you, because he trusts in you. Trust in the Lord forever, for the Lord God is an everlasting rock. (Is.26:3-4)

In addition, Jesus instructed these witnesses that they were not to waste time by stopping along the way and carrying on needless conversation. They were to sense the urgency of their mission and to their appointed place as quickly as possible. Their time to minister was short, and the need of the lost was overwhelming. They were to stay focused on the work Jesus was sending them to do.

THOUGHT 1. The Lord's servants must stay focused on the work Christ has appointed us to do. Time is short and the need is urgent. We must be careful not to become so involved and engrossed in the things of this life and this world that we fail to please the one who has called us to His service (2 Ti.2:4).

We must work the works of him who sent me while it is day; night is coming, when no one can work. (Jn.9:4)

Besides this you know the time, that the hour has come for you to wake from sleep. For salvation is nearer to us now than when we first believed. (Ro.13:11)

This is what I mean, brothers: the appointed time has grown very short. From now on, let those who have wives live as though they had none. (1 Co.7:29)

Making the best use of the time, because the days are evil. (Ep.5:16)

So teach us to number our days that we may get a heart of wisdom. (Ps.90:12)

5 Fifth, guard the message—do not force it on people.

The Lord's witnesses were to maintain peace wherever they went. They were to never be contentious or to create conflict by forcing their message on people. Their message, of course, was the message of peace (v.5; Ro.10:15; Ep.2:13-17; 6:15; see note, *Peace*—Jn.14:27 for discussion) . . .

- peace with God (Ro.5:1)
- the peace of God dwelling within a person's heart (Ph.4:8)
- peace with others (Mk.9:50; Ro.12:18; He.12:14)

[5] "Whatever house you enter, first say, 'Peace be to this house!'

[6] And if a son of peace is there, your peace will rest upon him. But if not, it will return to you."

If the head of the household was peaceful toward the witnesses and their mission, then the message of peace was to be continued (v.6). But if the message of peace was not accepted, then it was to be taken away. The disciple was to guard the message, to avoid proclaiming the message of peace to anyone who was not willing to receive it. They were to force neither themselves nor their message on anyone.

Note that the method Christ used was *house evangelism* (see DEEPER STUDY # 1—Lu.9:4 for discussion). The witnesses were to take their message to the people, in their homes (Ac.20:20).

As you enter the house, greet it. And if the house is worthy, let your peace come upon it, but if it is not worthy, let your peace return to you. And if anyone will not receive you or listen to your words, shake off the dust from your feet when you leave that house or town. Truly, I say to you, it will be more bearable on the day of judgment for the land of Sodom and Gomorrah than for that town. (Mt.10:12-15)

Therefore, since we have been justified by faith, we have peace with God through our Lord Jesus Christ. (Ro.5:1)

And how are they to preach unless they are sent? As it is written, "How beautiful are the feet of those who preach the good news!" (Ro.10:15)

If possible, so far as it depends on you, live peaceably with all. (Ro.12:18)

But now in Christ Jesus you who once were far off have been brought near by the blood of Christ. For he himself is our peace, who has made us both one and has broken down in his flesh the dividing wall of hostility by abolishing the law of commandments expressed in ordinances, that he might create in himself one new man in place of the two, so making peace, and might reconcile us both to God in one body through the cross, thereby killing the hostility. And he came and preached peace to you who were far off and peace to those who were near. (Ep.2:13-17)

And, as shoes for your feet, having put on the readiness given by the gospel of peace. (Ep.6:15)

6 Sixth, accept compensation, but do not seek luxury.

Jesus gave His laborers permission to graciously accept whatever was provided to them. They were to accept compensation without feeling self-conscious or embarrassed in receiving payment for their labor.

[7] "And remain in the same house, eating and drinking what they provide, for the laborer deserves his wages. Do not go from house to house."

However, they were to remain in the same house the entire time they were in a certain place. They were not to seek luxury, going from house to house and person to person seeking more and more of the better things of life. *The laborer was to live in simplicity, focusing on others rather than themselves.* They were to seek to meet people's needs, not to accumulate things of this world. What a contrast of value: things vs. people. How mixed up people allow their values to become!

For those who live according to the flesh set their minds on the things of the flesh, but those who live according to the Spirit set their minds on the things of the Spirit. For to set the mind on the flesh is death, but to set the mind on the Spirit is life and peace. (Ro.8:5-6)

If then you have been raised with Christ, seek the things that are above, where Christ is, seated at the right hand of God. Set your minds on things that are above, not on things that are on earth. (Col.3:1–2)

These all died in faith, not having received the things promised, but having seen them and greeted them from afar, and having acknowledged that they were strangers and exiles on the earth. For people who speak thus make it clear that they are seeking a homeland. If they had been thinking of that land from which they had gone out, they would have had opportunity to return. But as it is, they desire a better country, that is, a heavenly one. Therefore God is not ashamed to be called their God, for he has prepared for them a city. (He.11:13–16)

By faith Moses, when he was grown up, refused to be called the son of Pharaoh's daughter, choosing rather to be mistreated with the people of God than to enjoy the fleeting pleasures of sin. He considered the reproach of Christ greater wealth than the treasures of Egypt, for he was looking to the reward. (He.11:24–26)

Jesus made a critical point that the church must always remember and embrace: the Lord's servants are worthy of their wages. Therefore, they should be compensated fairly and taken care of adequately (1 Ti.5:18). Actually, Scripture says the laborer is worth double compensation, and such appreciation should be expressed to them (1 Ti.5:17). They are never to be taken advantage of. They are to be looked after by seeing that they have all the necessities of life.

In the same way, the Lord commanded that those who proclaim the gospel should get their living by the gospel. (1 Co.9:14)

Let the one who is taught the word share all good things with the one who teaches. (Ga.6:6)

Yet it was kind of you to share my trouble. (Ph.4:14)

For the Scripture says, "You shall not muzzle an ox when it treads out the grain," and, "The laborer deserves his wages." (1 Ti.5:18)

10:8–9

⁸ "Whenever you enter a town and they receive you, eat what is set before you.
⁹ Heal the sick in it and say to them, 'The kingdom of God has come near to you.'"

7 Seventh, be accommodating and adaptable.

The Lord ordered His servants to be accommodating and to adapt to what was provided for them. They were to graciously accept the hospitality offered to them, whatever it was.

a. Identify with people (v.8).

The Lord wanted His messengers to identify with the people they were trying to reach. Jesus made this point by using the most basic thing—food—as an example (v.8). If necessary, God's messengers were to change their customs and habits to reach the people. They were to accommodate and adapt to the people they were trying to reach, even down to the food eaten. The people needed to see that the Lord's servants considered themselves no better than they were, that they accepted and received them into their life and heart.

The second is this: "You shall love your neighbor as yourself." There is no other commandment greater than these. (Mk.12:31; see Ga.5:14; Jas.2:8)

But hospitable, a lover of good, self-controlled, upright, holy, and disciplined. (Tit.1:8)

Let brotherly love continue. Do not neglect to show hospitality to strangers, for thereby some have entertained angels unawares. (He.13:1–2)

Show hospitality to one another without grumbling. (1 Pe.4:9)

b. Minister to people (v.9a).

The Lord defined precisely what His laborers were to do. First, they were to minister to the people by meeting their physical needs, even to the point of healing the sick by the power of Christ.

Even as the Son of Man came not to be served but to serve, and to give his life as a ransom for many. (Mt.20:28)

Jesus said to them again, "Peace be with you. As the Father has sent me, even so I am sending you." (Jn.20:21)

How God anointed Jesus of Nazareth with the Holy Spirit and with power. He went about doing good and healing all who were oppressed by the devil, for God was with him. (Ac.10:38)

In all things I have shown you that by working hard in this way we must help the weak and remember the words of the Lord Jesus, how he himself said, "It is more blessed to give than to receive." (Ac.20:35)

We who are strong have an obligation to bear with the failings of the weak, and not to please our-selves. (Ro.15:1)

Bear one another's burdens, and so fulfill the law of Christ. (Ga.6:2)

c. Proclaim the kingdom of God (v.9b).

In addition, they were to proclaim the kingdom of God. They were to let people know that the kingdom was near them, right before them. The opportunity to receive the kingdom was pres-ent, right then and there (see DEEPER STUDY # 3—Mt.19:23-24 for discussion). Note that the message was given by Christ; it was not created in the mind of the messenger. The witnesses were to proclaim *Christ's* message, not their own.

From that time Jesus began to preach, saying, "Repent, for the kingdom of heaven is at hand." (Mt.4:17)

But he said to them, "I must preach the good news of the kingdom of God to the other towns as well; for I was sent for this purpose." (Lu.4:43)

Soon afterward he went on through cities and villages, proclaiming and bringing the good news of the kingdom of God. And the twelve were with him. (Lu.8:1)

He presented himself alive to them after his suffering by many proofs, appearing to them during forty days and speaking about the kingdom of God. (Ac.1:3)

But when they believed Philip as he preached good news about the kingdom of God and the name of Jesus Christ, they were baptized, both men and women. (Ac.8:12)

When they had appointed a day for him, they came to him at his lodging in greater numbers. From morning till evening he expounded to them, testifying to the kingdom of God and trying to con-vince them about Jesus both from the Law of Moses and from the Prophets. (Ac.28:23)

8 Eighth, walk away from rejecters.

Jesus instructed His witnesses clearly about what they should do when they and their message were rejected: they should simply walk away. Again, they were not to be conten-tious, nor were they to force their message on people. This, of course, protected the messengers from harm, at least to some degree. It also served as an immediate warning to any who rejected them, perhaps causing them to think about the matter more deeply and changing their minds and hearts toward Jesus. Jesus discussed three groups of rejecters.

a. Any town and people who reject (vv.10–12).

First, Jesus warned His laborers that some communities would reject them (v.10). The messengers were to respond by shaking the dust of the town off their feet, symboliz-ing God's rejection of them (v.11a). This was a silent testi-mony that God was doing just what they wanted, leaving them alone to walk through life as they desired (see note, pt.3—Lu.9:3-5 for more discussion).

10 "But whenever you enter a town and they do not receive you, go into its streets and say,
11 'Even the dust of your town that clings to our feet we wipe off against you. Nevertheless know this, that the kingdom of God has come near.'
12 I tell you, it will be more bearable on that day for Sodom than for that town.
13 Woe to you, Chorazin! Woe to you, Beth-saida! For if the mighty works done in you had been done in Tyre and Sidon, they would have repented long ago, sitting in sackcloth and ashes.
14 But it will be more bearable in the judg-ment for Tyre and Sidon than for you.
15 And you, Capernaum, will you be exalted to heaven? You shall be brought down to Hades."

The reason for God's judgment was that they rejected the kingdom of God. The kingdom came near them; the opportunity was there, but they rejected it (v.11b). They shut their doors to God. Their judgment was, therefore, to be greater than Sodom's (v.12; see DEEPER STUDY # 4—Mt.10:15; DEEPER STUDY # 4—11:23 for more discussion).

b. Any who only profess to be God's people (vv.13–14).

Second, Jesus informed His servants about those who *only profess* to be God's people, pronounc-ing *woe* upon them (see DEEPER STUDY # 1). These were illustrated by *Chorazin* and *Bethsaida*, two towns that were heavily populated by Jewish people who professed to be the people of God. Yet they *only professed*. They rejected God's Son, despite seeing the mighty works He had done among them. Their profession was profession only, not genuine faith. Therefore, they were to be judged by God, and their judgment was to be greater than the judgment which was to come upon the heathen. Why? Because they had the opportunity to accept Christ, an opportunity that the heathen never had (Tyre and Sidon). Note that the Lord is teaching degrees of judgment here (see outline and notes—Mt.11:20-24; Ro.2:11-15 for more discussion).

c. Any who receive a constant witness but still reject: To receive the greatest judgment—hell (v.15).

Third, Jesus spoke of those who had received a constant witness but still rejected Him, specifically, *Capernaum*. Capernaum was the *chosen* city and headquarters of Christ (Mt.9:1), yet the people rejected Christ. They were to receive the greatest judgment of all, hell itself (see outline and notes—Mt.11:20-24 for more discussion).

THOUGHT 1. Judgment is definitely coming, and everyone who rejects the Lord Jesus Christ will be condemned to eternal separation from Him.

> And this is the judgment: the light has come into the world, and people loved the darkness rather than the light because their works were evil. (Jn.3:19)

> But because of your hard and impenitent heart you are storing up wrath for yourself on the day of wrath when God's righteous judgment will be revealed. (Ro.2:5)

> And to grant relief to you who are afflicted as well as to us, when the Lord Jesus is revealed from heaven with his mighty angels in flaming fire, inflicting vengeance on those who do not know God and on those who do not obey the gospel of our Lord Jesus. (2 Th.1:7-8)

> It was also about these that Enoch, the seventh from Adam, prophesied, saying, "Behold, the Lord comes with ten thousands of his holy ones, to execute judgment on all and to convict all the ungodly of all their deeds of ungodliness that they have committed in such an ungodly way, and of all the harsh things that ungodly sinners have spoken against him." (Jude 14-15)

> And now, because you have done all these things, declares the LORD, and when I spoke to you persistently you did not listen, and when I called you, you did not answer, therefore I will do to the house that is called by my name, and in which you trust, and to the place that I gave to you and to your fathers, as I did to Shiloh. And I will cast you out of my sight, as I cast out all your kinsmen, all the offspring of Ephraim. (Je.7:13-15)

> The soul who sins shall die. The son shall not suffer for the iniquity of the father, nor the father suffer for the iniquity of the son. The righteousness of the righteous shall be upon himself, and the wickedness of the wicked shall be upon himself. (Ezk.18:20)

DEEPER STUDY # 1

(10:13) **Woe:** not a call for vengeance, but an expression of deep regret, of warning (see 6:24).

10:16

[16] "The one who hears you hears me, and the one who rejects you rejects me, and the one who rejects me rejects him who sent me."

9 Ninth, know that the Christian laborer represents the Lord.

Finally, Jesus encouraged His laborers by reminding them that they represented Him. Those who rejected them were rejecting Him, and, in turn, the one who sent Him—God the Father.

Jesus was teaching His messengers that their position and message were of the highest value. They represented Christ and should be given the most serious hearing possible. When they spoke, it was counted as though Christ Himself were speaking. Consequently, rejecting the messenger was the most serious offense. It was counted as the rejection of God Himself.

> Whoever receives you receives me, and whoever receives me receives him who sent me. (Mt.10:40)

> Whoever receives one such child in my name receives me. (Mt.18:5)

> And the King will answer them, "Truly, I say to you, as you did it to one of the least of these my brothers, you did it to me." . . . Then he will answer them, saying, "Truly, I say to you, as you did not do it to one of the least of these, you did not do it to me." And these will go away into eternal punishment, but the righteous into eternal life. (Mt.25:40, 45-46)

> But Saul, still breathing threats and murder against the disciples of the Lord, went to the high priest and asked him for letters to the synagogues at Damascus, so that if he found any belonging to the Way, men or women, he might bring them bound to Jerusalem. Now as he went on his way, he approached Damascus, and suddenly a light from heaven shone around him. And falling to the ground, he heard a voice saying to him, "Saul, Saul, why are you persecuting me?" (Ac.9:1-4)

¹⁷ The seventy-two returned with joy, saying, "Lord, even the demons are subject to us in your name!"

¹⁸ And he said to them, "I saw Satan fall like lightning from heaven.

¹⁹ Behold, I have given you authority to tread on serpents and scorpions, and over all the power of the enemy, and nothing shall hurt you.

²⁰ Nevertheless, do not rejoice in this, that the spirits are subject to you, but rejoice that your names are written in heaven."

1. **Christ's laborers have power over Satan**
   a. The disciples returned
   b. The disciples had great results
   c. Jesus foresaw the total defeat of Satan

2. **Christ's laborers have authority over all enemies: Perfect security**

3. **Christ's laborers are to rejoice in their salvation, not in their power**

Division V

The Son of Man's Great Journey to Jerusalem (Stage I): His Mission and Public Challenge, 9:51–13:21

D. The Seventy Return (Part I): Great Power, 10:17–20

10:17–20
Introduction

Christ gives great power to everyone who sincerely labors for Him (Ac.1:8; Ep.3:20). The presence of God's power in His servants' lives is a wonderful thing; however, it is something that can be misunderstood and abused. When the seventy (or seventy-two) appointed laborers returned, Jesus used the occasion to teach a much-needed lesson about the power of God in our lives. This is, *The Seventy Return (Part I): Great Power, 10:17–20.*

1. Christ's laborers have power over Satan (v.18).
2. Christ's laborers have authority over all enemies: Perfect security (v.19).
3. Christ's laborers are to rejoice in their salvation, not in their power (v.20).

1 Christ's laborers have power over Satan.

10:17–18

After Jesus called and prepared seventy (or seventy-two) for a special mission (see note—10:1 for discussion), they went out in obedience to their Lord to sow the seed of the gospel. Just as Scripture promises, they returned with shouts of joy, bringing their sheaves with them (Ps.126:6). Their testimony has significant lessons for every generation of Christian laborers.

¹⁷ The seventy-two returned with joy, saying, "Lord, even the demons are subject to us in your name!"

¹⁸ And he said to them, "I saw Satan fall like lightning from heaven."

a. The disciples returned (v.17a).

The laborers returned with *joy* (Gk. charas, *kah-rahce,'* meaning joy and rejoicing, a heart full of gladness). Frankly, their spirit was different from what so many express after a period of arduous ministry. They were not sharing and reveling in . . .
- how much they had done for Christ
- how taxing the work had been
- how strong the opposition and enemy had fought

The very opposite was true. They were rejoicing in Christ over the phenomenal power of Christ's name and over the thrill of being vessels through whom His power was displayed.

b. The disciples had great results (v.17b).

The disciples' labors for Christ had been blessed with astounding results—results that were wrought through the name of Christ. They seemed surprised when they reported, "Lord, even the demons are subject to us." Note two observations that every Christian laborer needs to remember:

➢ The power for effective ministry comes *through Christ's name*.

> **And there is salvation in no one else, for there is no other name under heaven given among men by which we must be saved. (Ac.4:12)**

➢ Powerful results in ministry should lead to a confession of our own weakness and nothingness before Christ. The seventy knew and readily confessed that the power to do the work had not come from them. Only the name of Christ can give genuine power and results.

> **Now to him who is able to do far more abundantly than all that we ask or think, according to the power at work within us, to him be glory in the church and in Christ Jesus throughout all generations, forever and ever. Amen. (Ep.3:20–21)**

Indeed, the laborers returned, giving glory to Christ. They praised Him for the glorious experience He had granted them in His name. They were not in any sense drawing attention to themselves. They were lifting up Christ and praising Him. Even demons were subject to them in *Christ's name*.

These disciples returned, having ministered to both body and soul. People were physically healed (v.9) and spiritually freed when forces of evil were cast out of their lives (see outline and notes—Mt.8:28–34 for more discussion and thoughts).

c. Jesus foresaw the total defeat of Satan (v.18).

With a powerful statement that every servant of Christ needs to keep constantly in mind, Jesus responded to the seventy's surprise at the demons' subjection to them: "I saw Satan fall like lightning from heaven." The key to understanding this statement is understanding the verb *saw* (etheōroun, *eh-theh-oh'-roon*). The Greek verb is in the imperfect tense and active voice. It is translated most literally as "I was seeing." Of the most commonly used Bible versions, the *New American Standard Bible* translates it most accurately, rendering it "I was watching . . ." When placed in context with the previous verse (v.17), Jesus seems to be saying, "While you were ministering and demons were submitting to you in My name, I was seeing Satan fall from heaven." Satan "falling from heaven" means falling from the height and the summit of power. Christ envisioned Satan's falling from his summit of power as the *god and prince* of this world (see DEEPER STUDY # 1—Re.12:9). The idea is that Jesus saw the seventy's victorious mission as an indication that the total defeat of Satan was now beginning.

➢ Jesus saw Satan defeated in the people's souls.

> **And you were dead in the trespasses and sins in which you once walked, following the course of this world, following the prince of the power of the air, the spirit that is now at work in the sons of disobedience. (Ep.2:1–2; see vv.3–10)**

> **He has delivered us from the domain of darkness and transferred us to the kingdom of his beloved Son, in whom we have redemption, the forgiveness of sins. (Col.1:13–14)**

➢ Jesus saw Satan defeated through the spread of the gospel.

> **Now is the judgment of this world; now will the ruler of this world be cast out. And I, when I am lifted up from the earth, will draw all people to myself. (Jn.12:31–32)**

> **Nevertheless, I tell you the truth: it is to your advantage that I go away, for if I do not go away, the Helper will not come to you. But if I go, I will send him to you. And when he comes, he will convict the world concerning sin and righteousness and judgment: concerning sin, because they do not believe in me; concerning righteousness, because I go to the Father, and you will see me no longer; concerning judgment, because the ruler of this world is judged. (Jn.16:7–11)**

> **In their case the god of this world has blinded the minds of the unbelievers, to keep them from seeing the light of the gospel of the glory of Christ, who is the image of God. (2 Co.4:4)**

> Jesus saw Satan defeated in the daily strategies and struggles which he wages against the individual believer (see note—Ro.8:2-4).

Finally, be strong in the Lord and in the strength of his might. Put on the whole armor of God, that you may be able to stand against the schemes of the devil. For we do not wrestle against flesh and blood, but against the rulers, against the authorities, against the cosmic powers over this present darkness, against the spiritual forces of evil in the heavenly places. (Ep.6:10-12; see vv.13-18)

Whoever makes a practice of sinning is of the devil, for the devil has been sinning from the beginning. The reason the Son of God appeared was to destroy the works of the devil. (1 Jn.3:8)

> Jesus saw Satan defeated in His power over death.

The last enemy to be destroyed is death. (1 Co.15:26)

> Jesus saw Satan defeated through His death on the cross.

He disarmed the rulers and authorities and put them to open shame, by triumphing over them in him. (Col.2:15)

He himself bore our sins in his body on the tree, that we might die to sin and live to righteousness. By his wounds you have been healed. (1 Pe.2:24; see Jn.12:32)

> Jesus saw Satan defeated in the end of the world, at the conclusion of the ages and time, and at the outset of eternity (see outlines and notes—Re.20:1-3; 20:7-10).

And the devil who had deceived them was thrown into the lake of fire and sulfur where the beast and the false prophet were, and they will be tormented day and night forever and ever. (Re.20:10)

THOUGHT 1. As we labor in the powerful name of Jesus, we need to see the reality that Jesus saw: Satan is a defeated foe. Through His atoning death and victorious resurrection, our Lord has disarmed the forces of evil and triumphed mightily over them (Col.2:15). We minister from a position of victory, not of defeat. Therefore, we ought to "be strong in the Lord and in the strength or power of His might" (Ep.6:10). We must serve boldly and with confidence, resisting the spirit of fear and timidity and embracing the spirit of power and love and controlled thinking (2 Ti.1:7). We need to "see" the power of God in the same way that Christ "saw" it. God's power is manifested for the purpose of defeating Satan, of delivering people from the power of Satan.

2 Christ's laborers have authority over all enemies: Perfect security.

As Christ's laborers, we have *authority* (exousian, *ex-ooh-sih'*-ahn) over all enemies; we have perfect security in the Lord. Christ said that He had given His servants "authority to tread or trample on serpents and scorpions"—venomous creatures. Are these words to be taken literally or figuratively (see Mk.16:15-18.)?

[19] "Behold, I have given you authority to tread on serpents and scorpions, and over all the power of the enemy, and nothing shall hurt you."

There is a literal application to Jesus' statement. If it is God's purpose to continue using His servant, then God will protect His servant no matter the threat or injury, whether by shipwreck (Ac.28:14f) or snake bite (Ac.28:3-5). The life of a genuine believer is in the hands of God every moment of that person's life, and God looks after the believer. Whatever befalls the believer is under God's will and care (Ro.8:28f). (See 2 Co.11:23-30 for a descriptive picture of what does befall God's servant and a picture of how God delivers until He is ready to take His servant home.)

But note a crucial point. We are not to test God; we should never presume on the power of God. The true servants of God do not put themselves in *harm's way* where they will be threatened. Such a person is busy at the wrong thing. The servant is to be busy reaching people for Christ, not proving their ability with animals or their immunity to their bites (see notes—Mk.16:17-18 for discussion).

There is also a spiritual meaning, as revealed by the rest of Jesus' statement: "and over all the *power* (dunamin, *doo'-nah-min*) of the enemy." Christ gives us authority over the power of the enemy (Satan). The seventy had experienced this authority when the demons had been subject to them in Jesus' name (v.18). Note five truths.

First, the enemy does have power; the idea is that he has enormous power.

For we do not wrestle against flesh and blood, but against the rulers, against the authorities, against the cosmic powers over this present darkness, against the spiritual forces of evil in the heavenly places. (Ep.6:12)

Second, the Lord's power is greater, much greater.

What then shall we say to these things? If God is for us, who can be against us? (Ro.8:31)

Little children, you are from God and have overcome them, for he who is in you is greater than he who is in the world. Since therefore the children share in flesh and blood, he himself likewise partook of the same things, that through death he might destroy the one who has the power of death, that is, the devil, and deliver all those who through fear of death were subject to lifelong slavery. Whoever makes a practice of sinning is of the devil, for the devil has been sinning from the beginning. The reason the Son of God appeared was to destroy the works of the devil. (1 Jn.4:4; He.2:14–15; 1 Jn.3:8)

Third, the Lord gives His power to His laborers.

And he called the twelve together and gave them power and authority over all demons and to cure diseases. (Lu.9:1)

For God gave us a spirit not of fear but of power and love and self-control. (2 Ti.1:7)

Fourth, the laborer's power is over *all* the power of the enemy.

And what is the immeasurable greatness of his power toward us who believe, according to the working of his great might (Ep.1:19)

Now to him who is able to do far more abundantly than all that we ask or think, according to the power at work within us. (Ep.3:20)

Fifth, Christ's laborers are *perfectly secure* against all enemies. No spiritual power will by any means be able to touch them. They are secure in the hands of God.

My Father, who has given them to me, is greater than all, and no one is able to snatch them out of the Father's hand. (Jn.10:29; see Ep.6:10–18)

And I am sure of this, that he who began a good work in you will bring it to completion at the day of Jesus Christ. (Ph.1:6)

But the Lord is faithful. He will establish you and guard you against the evil one. (2 Th.3:3)

Which is why I suffer as I do. But I am not ashamed, for I know whom I have believed, and I am convinced that he is able to guard until that day what has been entrusted to me. (2 Ti.1:12)

The Lord will rescue me from every evil deed and bring me safely into his heavenly kingdom. To him be the glory forever and ever. Amen. (2 Ti.4:18)

Who by God's power are being guarded through faith for a salvation ready to be revealed in the last time. (1 Pe.1:5)

20 "Nevertheless, do not rejoice in this, that the spirits are subject to you, but rejoice that your names are written in heaven."

3 Christ's laborers are to rejoice in their salvation, not in their power.

Jesus taught His servants that we are not to rejoice in the authority and power He has given us over the forces of evil, but in the fact that our names are written in heaven—that we have been saved. The real basis for joy is not power or authority, but salvation. The great privilege of believers is not our work and ministry, but the fact that we are the children of God and have been given eternal life.

➤ We have been adopted as a son or daughter of God.

Therefore go out from their midst, and be separate from them, says the Lord, and touch no unclean thing; then I will welcome you, and I will be a father to you, and you shall be sons and daughters to me, says the Lord Almighty. (2 Co.6:17–18)

But when the fullness of time had come, God sent forth his Son, born of woman, born under the law, to redeem those who were under the law, so that we might receive adoption as sons. And because you are sons, God has sent the Spirit of his Son into our hearts, crying, "Abba! Father!" (Ga.4:4–6)

➤ We have received the Spirit of adoption which gives us open access into the very presence of God.

For you did not receive the spirit of slavery to fall back into fear, but you have received the Spirit of adoption as sons, by whom we cry, "Abba! Father!" (Ro.8:15)

Likewise the Spirit helps us in our weakness. For we do not know what to pray for as we ought, but the Spirit himself intercedes for us with groanings too deep for words. (Ro.8:26)

➢ We have been made heirs of God and, unbelievably, equal heirs with Christ.

The Spirit himself bears witness with our spirit that we are children of God, and if children, then heirs—heirs of God and fellow heirs with Christ, provided we suffer with him in order that we may also be glorified with him. (Ro.8:16–17)

So that being justified by his grace we might become heirs according to the hope of eternal life. (Tit.3:7)

Blessed be the God and Father of our Lord Jesus Christ! According to his great mercy, he has caused us to be born again to a living hope through the resurrection of Jesus Christ from the dead, to an inheritance that is imperishable, undefiled, and unfading, kept in heaven for you. (1 Pe.1:3–4)

➢ Our names are written down in heaven (see Re.13:8; 17:8; 20:12; 22:19).

Yes, I ask you also, true companion, help these women, who have labored side by side with me in the gospel together with Clement and the rest of my fellow workers, whose names are in the book of life. (Ph.4:3)

But you have come to Mount Zion and to the city of the living God, the heavenly Jerusalem, and to innumerable angels in festal gathering, and to the assembly of the firstborn who are enrolled in heaven, and to God, the judge of all, and to the spirits of the righteous made perfect. (He.12:22–23)

The one who conquers will be clothed thus in white garments, and I will never blot his name out of the book of life. I will confess his name before my Father and before his angels. (Re.3:5)

But nothing unclean will ever enter it, nor anyone who does what is detestable or false, but only those who are written in the Lamb's book of life. (Re.21:27)

"But now, if you will forgive their sin—but if not, please blot me out of your book that you have written." But the LORD said to Moses, "Whoever has sinned against me, I will blot out of my book." (Ex.32:32–33)

At that time shall arise Michael, the great prince who has charge of your people. And there shall be a time of trouble, such as never has been since there was a nation till that time. But at that time your people shall be delivered, everyone whose name shall be found written in the book. (Da.12:1)

E. The Seventy Return (Part II): Great Privileges, 10:21–24

(Mt.11:25-27)

1. **Jesus rejoiced**
2. **Privilege 1: The spiritual insight into truth**
   a. God hides truth from the wise and learned
   b. God reveals truth to babes

3. **Privilege 2: The knowledge of God and of His only Son**
   a. God's Son is supreme: All things are entrusted to Him
   b. God and the Son alone know one another
   c. The Son reveals God to some
4. **Privilege 3: The insight and privilege of learning about God's great salvation**
   a. The disciples were privileged
   b. The prophets and kings of old longed to see and hear the Messiah

21 In that same hour he rejoiced in the Holy Spirit and said, "I thank you, Father, Lord of heaven and earth, that you have hidden these things from the wise and understanding and revealed them to little children; yes, Father, for such was your gracious will. 22 All things have been handed over to me by my Father, and no one knows who the Son is except the Father, or who the Father is except the Son and anyone to whom the Son chooses to reveal him."

23 Then turning to the disciples he said privately, "Blessed are the eyes that see what you see! 24 For I tell you that many prophets and kings desired to see what you see, and did not see it, and to hear what you hear, and did not hear it."

Division V

The Son of Man's Great Journey to Jerusalem (Stage I): His Mission and Public Challenge, 9:51–13:21

E. The Seventy Return (Part II): Great Privileges, 10:21–24

(Mt.11:25–27)

10:21–24
Introduction

In addition to great power, Christ's laborers have great privileges. Christ taught us not to rejoice in the power we have been given, but in the privileges we have been given through our salvation. As Jesus thought of these glorious privileges, He was filled with such joy that He broke out in spontaneous praise to God. Truly, the Lord longs to share these privileges with every individual. This is, *The Seventy Return (Part II): Great Privileges*, 10:21-24.

1. Jesus rejoiced (v.21).
2. Privilege 1: The spiritual insight into truth (v.21).
3. Privilege 2: The knowledge of God and of His only Son (v.22).
4. Privilege 3: The insight and privilege of learning about God's great salvation (vv.23-24).

1 Jesus rejoiced.

This passage begins with a statement that touches our hearts and reveals Jesus' heart: Jesus *"rejoiced* (ēgalliasato, *ay-gall-ih-ah'-sah-tow*) in the Holy Spirit." The Greek word is much stronger than the English word *rejoice*, and it is much stronger than the Greek word normally used for *rejoice* (chairo, *kigh'-row*; v.20). *Ēgalliasato* speaks of great joy and exultation, an exceeding measure of ecstatic joy. It means to be overflowing with joy or thrilled with joy. In verse 21, the idea is *victorious joy* because of the glorious triumph over the arch-enemy Satan (vv.18–20).

> [21] In that same hour he rejoiced in the Holy Spirit and said, "I thank you, Father, Lord of heaven and earth, that you have hidden these things from the wise and understanding and revealed them to little children; yes, Father, for such was your gracious will."

This abundant joy comes only from the Spirit; it cannot be worked up. It is a joy of confidence and assurance that arises from down deep within—a confidence and assurance that all is well with God and the victory is won over evil. This was the joy experienced by Christ when the seventy returned. Souls had been snatched from the grip of sin and death, for the power of God over evil had been exercised by people. Satan's fall was assured. God would be victorious throughout the world as the gospel was carried forth by His servants. Therefore, the Spirit of God stirred Jesus to rejoice greatly over the victory won.

> Looking to Jesus, the founder and perfecter of our faith, who for the joy that was set before him endured the cross, despising the shame, and is seated at the right hand of the throne of God. (He.12:2)

2 Privilege 1: The spiritual insight into truth.

The first privilege of the Lord's servants is spiritual insight into truth. Christ's laborers are able to grasp "these things"—spiritual truth. The term "these things" refers to the gospel of the Lord Jesus Christ. More specifically, however, it refers to the truth which the seventy had learned (vv.19–20); that is, that God is active in the world. God saves people and cares for people, giving them power over the forces of evil and writing their names in heaven. Note an important fact: knowing "these things" is the greatest knowledge in all the world. No other knowledge could ever surpass knowing God in such a personal way, knowing . . .

> [21] In that same hour he rejoiced in the Holy Spirit and said, "I thank you, Father, Lord of heaven and earth, that you have hidden these things from the wise and understanding and revealed them to little children; yes, Father, for such was your gracious will."

- that He has saved us
- that He cares and looks after us
- that He delivers us from the power of evil
- that He infuses us with assurance and confidence and perfect security

a. God hides truth from the wise and learned.

God hides "these things" from the wise and understanding or prudent. Such people are those who think themselves wise and intelligent. They are the self-sufficient, the proud, the wise of this world (1 Co.1:21, 25–29; 2:14). However, they are blind to the Lord of heaven and earth and to the truth. The proud and self-sufficient by their very nature sense no need for help and refuse to receive it. Instead, they rest in their own ability and achievements.

Jesus' statement is clear and alarming: spiritual truth is *hidden*. Where? In God. God has done the logical thing. He has taken spiritual truth and locked it up in Himself. The only access to truth is *through* God. The only key to spiritual truth is faith and trust *in* God.

Individuals who consider themselves wise and intelligent and sufficient enough *without* God never come *to* God. Therefore, they never experience a personal relationship *with* God. The self-sufficient person never comes to know God, nor the spiritual truth *hidden in* God (Ro.1:18–22). God and His presence and His plan for the ages are foreign to the self-sufficient. They do not believe God—not enough to come to Him. Therefore, the things of the Spirit and of the gospel and of the kingdom are hidden from them. However, God's heart and truths are open to the ones who come in dependency and trust.

Note a crucial point: Christ is not condemning intelligence and wisdom, but rather intellectual pride and self-sufficiency. God made us to think and reason and seek and search in order to discover and build, but God expects us not to think of ourselves too highly (Ro.12:3; see Ph.2:3-4). We are to walk humbly during our short stay on earth, knowing from whom we have come and to whom we are ultimately going. We are to trust God, putting our time and destiny in God's hands.

God will not reveal truth to those who consider themselves wise, intelligent, and self-sufficient. Why? Because they *rest* in their own ability and achievements and *sense no need* beyond themselves. They sense no need for God. They . . .

- keep God out of their lives
- push God away
- deny God's existence
- question the value of God
- believe they have no need for God, not now
- believe God is irrelevant in a scientific, technological world

God is not the author of people's self-sufficiency and pride. It is people who make themselves their own *god* and create the religion of humanism (that human beings are sufficient unto themselves, Ro.1:21-25). As a result, God leaves such persons to themselves. God does not force people to worship Him, for forced behavior would be making people like robots. And God wants to be loved and worshiped by people because they *choose* to worship Him. Therefore, people's sin becomes their punishment; their rejection becomes harder and harder, and they are removed farther and farther away from God—exactly what they had desired (Jn.12:39-40; Ro.1:18-32; see also Ac.28:26-27; Ro.11:7-8).

In addition, God hides the truth from such persons because their *evil hearts* would only corrupt the truth. They would mix the truth with their own *rationalized and humanistic ideas*. Note another fact: if the self-sufficient knew the truth, they would be honored as the creators of the truth. They would lift man up as the source of truth. Unfortunately, this is exactly the claim made by so many. However, God will not share the honor due His Son with anyone. His Son, the only Son He has, is to receive all the honor and praise of this earth. Why? Because He is the one who has loved perfectly, loved so much that He laid down His life to save the world.

If a person honors God with what they have (their intelligence, abilities, and achievements), God will give "these things" to that person. But if the person takes what they have and claims to be self-sufficient, then God will hide "these things" from their understanding.

> He also told this parable to some who trusted in themselves that they were righteous, and treated others with contempt. (Lu.18:9)

> Therefore they could not believe. For again Isaiah said, "He has blinded their eyes and hardened their heart, lest they see with their eyes, and understand with their heart, and turn, and I would heal them." (Jn.12:39-40)

> For his invisible attributes, namely, his eternal power and divine nature, have been clearly perceived, ever since the creation of the world, in the things that have been made. So they are without excuse. For although they knew God, they did not honor him as God or give thanks to him, but they became futile in their thinking, and their foolish hearts were darkened. Claiming to be wise, they became fools. (Ro.1:20-22; see vv.18-32)

> For the word of the cross is folly to those who are perishing, but to us who are being saved it is the power of God. For it is written, "I will destroy the wisdom of the wise, and the discernment of the discerning I will thwart." Where is the one who is wise? Where is the scribe? Where is the debater of this age? Has not God made foolish the wisdom of the world? For since, in the wisdom of God, the world did not know God through wisdom, it pleased God through the folly of what we preach to save those who believe. (1 Co.1:18-21; see 1 Co.3:19-21)

> Be not wise in your own eyes; fear the LORD, and turn away from evil. (Pr.3:7)

> Woe to those who are wise in their own eyes, and shrewd in their own sight! (Is.5:21)

b. **God reveals truth to babes.**

God reveals "these things" to *little children* or *babes* (see DEEPER STUDY # 4—Mk.10:14). Jesus uses this term to describe those who are humble before God, those who do not consider themselves wise and understanding and self-sufficient, those who acknowledge . . .

- that this world is not all there is
- that a few short years of life are not all there is
- that they are inadequate in solving the problem of sin and death in the world
- that God exists, and that He is their Father
- that God exists, and that He rewards those who diligently seek Him (He.11:6)

The *little children* or *babes* are those who look up to God as their Father because they are . . .
- open and receptive within their spirits
- dependent and trusting spiritually
- responsive and submissive to spiritual truth
- teachable and obedient to God
- loving and forgiving toward others (Mt.22:36-40; 1 Jn.4:20-21; Mt.6:14-15)

To reveal spiritual truth to people who are humble and dependent on God is His *gracious will*. It pleases God enormously that He is able to reveal *these things* to trusting, teachable people.

> So Jesus said to the Jews who had believed him, "If you abide in my word, you are truly my disciples, and you will know the truth, and the truth will set you free." (Jn.8:31-32)

> You are my friends if you do what I command you. No longer do I call you servants, for the servant does not know what his master is doing; but I have called you friends, for all that I have heard from my Father I have made known to you. (Jn.15:14-15)

> And we impart this in words not taught by human wisdom but taught by the Spirit, interpreting spiritual truths to those who are spiritual. The natural person does not accept the things of the Spirit of God, for they are folly to him, and he is not able to understand them because they are spiritually discerned. (1 Co.2:13-14)

> Like newborn infants, long for the pure spiritual milk, that by it you may grow up into salvation— if indeed you have tasted that the Lord is good. (1 Pe.2:2-3)

3 Privilege 2: The knowledge of God and of His only Son.

The second privilege of the Lord's servants is knowing God and Christ in a very personal way. Through the prophet Jeremiah, the Lord emphasizes what a rich privilege this is:

> Thus says the Lord: "Let not the wise man boast in his wisdom, let not the mighty man boast in his might, let not the rich man boast in his riches, but let him who boasts boast in this, that he understands and knows me, that I am the Lord who practices steadfast love, justice, and righteousness in the earth. For in these things I delight, declares the Lord." (Je.9:23-24)

Here, Jesus reveals three truths about the knowledge of God.

22 "All things have been handed over to me by my Father, and no one knows who the Son is except the Father, or who the Father is except the Son and anyone to whom the Son chooses to reveal him."

a. God's Son is supreme: All things are entrusted to Him.

In His sovereignty, God has chosen to give all things to His Son, for all things were made for God's Son (Col.1:16-17). Jesus Christ is the supreme authority over the universe; therefore, He is to oversee and rule the universe. However, His Lordship is not seen, not right now, not by the vast majority of people. Jesus was neither understood nor accepted by the people of His day, nor is He understood and accepted by most people today (Jn.1:10-11). But the truth of Christ's Lordship will be obvious someday, for the day is coming when the Son of God will be revealed to the world in His glory and power.

> Because he has fixed a day on which he will judge the world in righteousness by a man whom he has appointed; and of this he has given assurance to all by raising him from the dead (Ac.17:31)

> Then comes the end, when he delivers the kingdom to God the Father after destroying every rule and every authority and power. For he must reign until he has put all his enemies under his feet. (1 Co.15:24-25)

And being found in human form, he humbled himself by becoming obedient to the point of death, even death on a cross. Therefore God has highly exalted him and bestowed on him the name that is above every name, so that at the name of Jesus every knee should bow, in heaven and on earth and under the earth, and every tongue confess that Jesus Christ is Lord, to the glory of God the Father. (Ph.2:8-11)

And to grant relief to you who are afflicted as well as to us, when the Lord Jesus is revealed from heaven with his mighty angels in flaming fire, inflicting vengeance on those who do not know God and on those who do not obey the gospel of our Lord Jesus. They will suffer the punishment of eternal destruction, away from the presence of the Lord and from the glory of his might, when he comes on that day to be glorified in his saints, and to be marveled at among all who have believed, because our testimony to you was believed. (2 Th.1:7-10)

Only God the Father and God the Son have perfect knowledge. Therefore, a complete knowledge of God can be grasped only by the Son, and a complete knowledge of the Son can be grasped only by God the Father.

So Jesus proclaimed, as he taught in the temple, "You know me, and you know where I come from. But I have not come of my own accord. He who sent me is true, and him you do not know. I know him, for I come from him, and he sent me." (Jn.7:28-29)

Jesus answered, "If I glorify myself, my glory is nothing. It is my Father who glorifies me, of whom you say, 'He is our God.' But you have not known him. I know him. If I were to say that I do not know him, I would be a liar like you, but I do know him and I keep his word." (Jn.8:54-55)

Just as the Father knows me and I know the Father; and I lay down my life for the sheep. (Jn.10:15)

O righteous Father, even though the world does not know you, I know you, and these know that you have sent me. (Jn.17:25)

God is Spirit (Jn.4:24). He is of another dimension of being entirely. If a person is to know the spiritual world, then God must reveal that spiritual world and the things of that world to that person.

b. God and the Son alone know one another.

Jesus is profoundly claiming that He and God alone know each other. His statement is simple and clear: "no one knows who the Son is except the Father, or who the Father is except the Son."

c. The Son reveals God to some.

However, Jesus chooses to reveal the Father, who is Spirit, to some, and they too share in the knowledge of God. Passages such as this show that the persons chosen to receive this revelation are the humble who truly seek God and trust the Son's testimony (see outline and notes—1 Co.2:6-13; 2:14-3:4; Jn.4:23-24).

Yet among the mature we do impart wisdom, although it is not a wisdom of this age or of the rulers of this age, who are doomed to pass away. But we impart a secret and hidden wisdom of God, which God decreed before the ages for our glory. None of the rulers of this age understood this, for if they had, they would not have crucified the Lord of glory. (1 Co.2:6-8)

The natural person does not accept the things of the Spirit of God, for they are folly to him, and he is not able to understand them because they are spiritually discerned. The spiritual person judges all things, but is himself to be judged by no one. "For who has understood the mind of the Lord so as to instruct him?" But we have the mind of Christ. (1 Co.2:14-16)

The people chosen to receive this revelation are those Jesus speaks of in the previous verse. They are humble people who look to God and trust Him, those whom Jesus compared to *little children* or *babes* (v.21).

10:23-24

²³ Then turning to the disciples he said privately, "Blessed are the eyes that see what you see!
²⁴ For I tell you that many prophets and kings desired to see what you see, and did not see it, and to hear what you hear, and did not hear it."

4 Privilege 3: The insight and privilege of learning about God's great salvation.

The third privilege of the Lord's servants is seeing and learning God's full revelation, the full understanding of salvation. Jesus shared this point with His disciples alone, for only those who are genuinely saved can truly understand and appreciate the greatness of salvation.

a. The disciples were privileged (v.23).

Jesus told the disciples that they were *blessed* to see the things they were seeing. God had favored them by giving them the full revelation of His salvation. Greek scholar A.T. Robertson refers to this statement from Jesus as "a beatitude of privilege."[1]

b. The prophets and kings of old longed to see and hear the Messiah (v.24).

Jesus' disciples were favored over the prophets and kings of old who had longed for the Messiah. He himself was the great salvation which God's servants of old had desired to see and hear. Again, Jesus says that His disciples were highly privileged to know Him, to see and hear Him and the truth which He reveals. He is the Messiah, the Son of the Living God. He is the one promised by God down through the ages (see Is.53:1f.)

> And now I stand here on trial because of my hope in the promise made by God to our fathers, to which our twelve tribes hope to attain, as they earnestly worship night and day. And for this hope I am accused by Jews, O king! Why is it thought incredible by any of you that God raises the dead? (Ac.26:6–8)

> Which was not made known to the sons of men in other generations as it has now been revealed to his holy apostles and prophets by the Spirit. (Ep.3:5)

> Concerning this salvation, the prophets who prophesied about the grace that was to be yours searched and inquired carefully, inquiring what person or time the Spirit of Christ in them was indicating when he predicted the sufferings of Christ and the subsequent glories. It was revealed to them that they were serving not themselves but you, in the things that have now been announced to you through those who preached the good news to you by the Holy Spirit sent from heaven, things into which angels long to look. (1 Pe.1:10–12)

> I wait for your salvation, O Lord. (Ge.49:18)

---

1   A.T. Robertson, *Word Pictures in the New Testament*, (Nashville, TN: Broadman Press, 1930). Via Wordsearch digital edition.

F. The Parable of the Good Samaritan: Two Supreme Questions of Life, 10:25–37

(see Mt.22:34–40; Mk.12:28–34)

1. **Question 1: How do I inherit eternal life?**[DS1]
   a. A lawyer tested Jesus: Asked how to inherit eternal life
   b. Jesus responded: Asked the lawyer to interpret the law
      1) First, love God supremely
      2) Second, love your neighbor as yourself

   c. Jesus affirmed the response: Obey and you will live

2. **Question 2: Who is my neighbor?**

   a. The traveler: Was foolish and irresponsible
      1) Traveled a dangerous road alone
      2) Was robbed
      3) Was assaulted and left half-dead
   b. The priest: Passed by without helping the man
      1) Saw the injured traveler
      2) Rushed by him
   c. The Levite: Passed by without helping the man
      1) Saw the traveler
      2) Passed by at a distance
   d. The Samaritan:[DS2] Placed compassion before prejudice and opinion
      1) Gave of himself, from the heart
      2) Sacrificed his work, time, energy, goods, and money

      3) Provided for continued care for the injured traveler

   e. The Lord's commission: Go and do likewise

²⁵ And behold, a lawyer stood up to put him to the test, saying, "Teacher, what shall I do to inherit eternal life?"

²⁶ He said to him, "What is written in the Law? How do you read it?"
²⁷ And he answered, "You shall love the Lord your God with all your heart and with all your soul and with all your strength and with all your mind, and your neighbor as yourself."
²⁸ And he said to him, "You have answered correctly; do this, and you will live."
²⁹ But he, desiring to justify himself, said to Jesus, "And who is my neighbor?"
³⁰ Jesus replied, "A man was going down from Jerusalem to Jericho, and he fell among robbers, who stripped him and beat him and departed, leaving him half dead.
³¹ Now by chance a priest was going down that road, and when he saw him he passed by on the other side.

³² So likewise a Levite, when he came to the place and saw him, passed by on the other side.

³³ But a Samaritan, as he journeyed, came to where he was, and when he saw him, he had compassion.
³⁴ He went to him and bound up his wounds, pouring on oil and wine. Then he set him on his own animal and brought him to an inn and took care of him.
³⁵ And the next day he took out two denarii and gave them to the innkeeper, saying, 'Take care of him, and whatever more you spend, I will repay you when I come back.'
³⁶ Which of these three, do you think, proved to be a neighbor to the man who fell among the robbers?"
³⁷ He said, "The one who showed him mercy." And Jesus said to him, "You go, and do likewise."

Division V

The Son of Man's Great Journey to Jerusalem (Stage I): His Mission and Public Challenge, 9:51–13:21

F. The Parable of the Good Samaritan: Two Supreme Questions of Life, 10:25-37

(see Mt.22:34–40; Mk.12:28–34)

10:25-37
Introduction

From any perspective, life is extremely complex. Yet, Jesus reduced all of life to two simple questions, as seen in this passage. There are two supreme questions of life, and if people would ask these questions and then heed their answers, it would revolutionize the world. This is, *The Parable of the Good Samaritan: Two Supreme Questions of Life*, 10:25-37.

1. Question 1: How do I inherit eternal life? (vv.25-28).
2. Question 2: Who is my neighbor? (vv.29-37).

1 Question 1: How do I inherit eternal life?

10:25-28

The first supreme question of life is, how do we inherit eternal life (see DEEPER STUDY # 1)? As Solomon wrote by inspiration of the Holy Spirit, God has put eternity in the human heart (Ec.3:11). Every person knows that there is more than this life, that there is something that awaits us when our earthly life has come to an end. Many deny it; many are deceived about it; many refuse to face it. But a person's reaction to it does not change the fact of it: God has naturally revealed the truth of eternity to every human being.

²⁵ And behold, a lawyer stood up to put him to the test, saying, "Teacher, what shall I do to inherit eternal life?"

²⁶ He said to him, "What is written in the Law? How do you read it?"

²⁷ And he answered, "You shall love the Lord your God with all your heart and with all your soul and with all your strength and with all your mind, and your neighbor as yourself."

²⁸ And he said to him, "You have answered correctly; do this, and you will live."

a. **A lawyer tested Jesus: Asked how to inherit eternal life (v.25).**
The individual who asked Jesus about eternal life on this occasion had more than natural revelation about eternity; He had the special revelation of God's Word. He was a lawyer, a Scribe, one whose profession was studying God's law (see DEEPER STUDY # 1—Mt.22:35). However, this lawyer was not seeking the truth. His question was not sincere; He was not really seeking the way to God. His purpose was to *test* Jesus, to trip Him up, to lead Jesus to discredit Himself by giving some unusual answer that would incite the people against Him.

Note that the lawyer's question stressed *works*. He asked, "What shall I *do*?" To him, salvation was through works. God was going to accept him because he was or could become *good enough*. He had no concept of the part that God's love and grace play in salvation (see Ep.2:8-8; Tit.3:5-7 for a description of what he failed to see).

b. **Jesus responded: Asked the lawyer to interpret the law (vv.26-27).**
Too wise to be trapped, Jesus answered the scheming lawyer's question with a question: "What does the law say?" (v.26). Note how clearly Jesus led the conversation to spell out the steps to eternal life.

God's Word (law) has the answer to all our questions about eternal life. If a person desires eternal life, he or she must look into the Word of God (2 Ti.3:15). Jesus asked the lawyer for his interpretation of what God's law said about eternal life. Again, studying God's law was this man's profession; he was one of the Jewish experts on God's Word. The lawyer quoted two verses in his answer to Jesus (De.6:5; Le.19:18).

First, the lawyer correctly answered that God's law requires people to love Him supremely (v.27a; De.6:5). "Love the Lord your God." Love God as *your* very own God. This is a personal relationship, not a distant relationship. God is not impersonal, not far out in space someplace, distant, and removed. God is personal, ever so close, and we are to be personally involved with God as though face to face. The command is to *"love the Lord your God."* Loving God is alive and active, not dead and inactive. We are, therefore, to maintain a personal relationship with God that is alive and active.

Furthermore, God's law requires people to love Him with all of our being, all of our nature, everything we are. Jesus breaks our being into three parts: the heart, the soul, and the mind (see notes—Mk.12:29-31 for more discussion). In addition, we are commanded to love God with all of our *strength* (ischus, *is-koos'*)—"with every amount of physical strength, force, vigor, or energy that a person can exert."[1]

> **May the Lord direct your hearts to the love of God and to the steadfastness of Christ. (2 Th.3:5)**

> **Keep yourselves in the love of God, waiting for the mercy of our Lord Jesus Christ that leads to eternal life. (Jude 21)**

> **You shall love the LORD your God with all your heart and with all your soul and with all your might. (De.6:5)**

> **And now, Israel, what does the LORD your God require of you, but to fear the LORD your God, to walk in all his ways, to love him, to serve the LORD your God with all your heart and with all your soul. (De.10:12)**

> **You shall therefore love the LORD your God and keep his charge, his statutes, his rules, and his commandments always. (De.11:1)**

> **Only be very careful to observe the commandment and the law that Moses the servant of the LORD commanded you, to love the LORD your God, and to walk in all his ways and to keep his commandments and to cling to him and to serve him with all your heart and with all your soul. (Jos.22:5)**

Second, the lawyer answered that God's law requires us to love our neighbor as ourselves (v.27b; Le.19:18). If a person desires eternal life, he or she has to love their *neighbor*. The first commandment, "Love God," is abstract; it cannot be seen or understood standing by itself. There has to be a *demonstration, an act, something done* for love to be seen and understood. A profession of love without demonstration is empty. It is profession only. Love is not known unless it is first shown. We demonstrate our love for God by loving our neighbor as ourselves. Two important truths about this commandment need to be emphasized at this point:

➤ Love is an active experience, not inactive and dormant. This is the point Jesus is making. Love for God *acts*. Love acts by showing and demonstrating itself. It is inaccurate and foolish for a person to say, "I love God," and then be inactive and dormant, doing nothing for God. If people truly love God, they will *do things* for God. Any person who loves does things for the one loved.

➤ The *primary thing* God wants from us is to love our neighbor, not to do religious works. Doing religious deeds is good, but it is not the first thing God wants. God wants us to make loving our neighbor the first order of our lives. To do religious deeds is only dealing with things such as rituals, observances, ordinances, laws. Such things are lifeless, unfeeling and unresponsive. They are not helped by our doing them. Only we are helped. They make us feel good and religious, which provides some benefit to our growth. However, religious works are not what demonstrate our love for God. Loving our neighbor is what proves our love for God. People may say they love God, but if they hate and act unkindly toward their neighbor, everyone knows their religion is but a mere profession; it is not genuine (see note—Mt.22:39 for more discussion).

> **The second is this: "You shall love your neighbor as yourself." There is no other commandment greater than these. (Mk.12:31)**

> **A new commandment I give to you, that you love one another: just as I have loved you, you also are to love one another. By this all people will know that you are my disciples, if you have love for one another. (Jn.13:34-35)**

> **This is my commandment, that you love one another as I have loved you. (Jn.15:12)**

---

1 *Practical Word Studies in the New Testament,* (Chattanooga, TN: Leadership Ministries Worldwide, 1998). Via Wordsearch digital edition

> Owe no one anything, except to love each other, for the one who loves another has fulfilled the law. For the commandments, "You shall not commit adultery, You shall not murder, You shall not steal, You shall not covet," and any other commandment, are summed up in this word: "You shall love your neighbor as yourself." Love does no wrong to a neighbor; therefore love is the fulfilling of the law. (Ro.13:8-10)
>
> For the whole law is fulfilled in one word: "You shall love your neighbor as yourself." (Ga.5:14)
>
> If you really fulfill the royal law according to the Scripture, "You shall love your neighbor as yourself," you are doing well. (Jas.2:8)

c. Jesus affirmed the response: Obey and you will live (v.28).

Jesus affirmed that the man's answer was correct, according to God's law. If he obeyed these commands, he would *live*—live eternally, inherit eternal life.

The problem this man had—and the problem every human being has—is that *nobody* can "do this"; *nobody* can obey these commands, not *perfectly*. If we can inherit eternal life by what we "do," if we can earn it or receive it by works, we must keep God's law *perfectly*. To do so is impossible. We have all sinned and come short of what God expects from us (Ro.3:10, 19-30; Ga.2:16; 3:10-12). This was the purpose of the law, to show us that we cannot live up to God's standards, that we cannot keep God's law, not perfectly. The purpose of the law is to teach us that we need a Savior, and, consequently, bring us to faith in Christ (Ga.3:19-24).

THOUGHT 1. God has given us the answer to eternal life in clear terms—so clear we are left without excuse.

1) He has given us the answer in written words. It is in black and white, certain and unmistakable.
2) He has given us the answer in the life of Christ Himself. God has caused the words to be lived out in a human life, giving us the example of the Ideal Life (see DEEPER STUDY #1—Jn.1:1-5).

DEEPER STUDY #1

(10:25) **Eternal Life**: see DEEPER STUDY # 2—Jn.1:4; DEEPER STUDY # 1—Jn.10:10; DEEPER STUDY # 1—Jn.17:2-3.

---

2 Question 2: Who is my neighbor?

The second supreme question of life is, who is my neighbor? Note the lawyer felt the need to "justify himself" (v.29) He sensed that Jesus was saying that he had not kept the law; he had failed to love his neighbor. So, he asked the logical question, "Who is my neighbor?" Jesus answered and drove the point home to the human heart by doing what He had so often done—He gave an illustration. "Jesus did not say that this story was a parable, so it could well be the report of an actual occurrence."[2]

a. The traveler: Was foolish and irresponsible (v.30).

Jesus related the experience of a foolish and irresponsible traveler. He was foolish because he traveled an extremely dangerous road alone. The twenty-one-mile road between Jerusalem and Jericho was known for its perils. It was a rugged, rocky pass much of the way through wild country. It had become such a favorite habitat for violent thieves that it earned the nickname, *the Way of Blood*. Wise travelers never journeyed there alone. They always traveled

---

2 Warren W. Wiersbe, *The Bible Exposition Commentary—New Testament*, (Colorado Springs, CO: David C. Cook, 2004). Via Wordsearch digital edition.

[29] But he, desiring to justify himself, said to Jesus, "And who is my neighbor?"
[30] Jesus replied, "A man was going down from Jerusalem to Jericho, and he fell among robbers, who stripped him and beat him and departed, leaving him half dead.
[31] Now by chance a priest was going down that road, and when he saw him he passed by on the other side.
[32] So likewise a Levite, when he came to the place and saw him, passed by on the other side.
[33] But a Samaritan, as he journeyed, came to where he was, and when he saw him, he had compassion.
[34] He went to him and bound up his wounds, pouring on oil and wine. Then he set him on his own animal and brought him to an inn and took care of him.
[35] And the next day he took out two denarii and gave them to the innkeeper, saying, 'Take care of him, and whatever more you spend, I will repay you when I come back.'
[36] Which of these three, do you think, proved to be a neighbor to the man who fell among the robbers?"
[37] He said, "The one who showed him mercy." And Jesus said to him, "You go, and do likewise."

with caravans. Therefore, this traveler was irresponsible, foolish, and reckless. Some would even argue that such foolishness was undeserving of help.

This foolhardy man met with the fate he should have expected: he was attacked by robbers. The vicious criminals stripped him of everything he had, beat him severely, and left him half dead, indicating that he was most likely unconscious.

THOUGHT 1. How many are foolish and reckless in life, exposing and destroying their bodies by going where they should not and by doing what they should not?

> The prudent sees danger and hides himself, but the simple go on and suffer for it. (Pr.22:3)

> Whoever is wise, let him understand these things; whoever is discerning, let him know them; for the ways of the LORD are right, and the upright walk in them, but transgressors stumble in them. (Ho.14:9)

b. The priest: Passed by without helping the man (v.31).

A priest was traveling the same road and saw the injured traveler lying helpless. This man was a religious leader, and he did not even make a move toward helping the suffering man. He "passed by on the other side" which means he rushed away. Perhaps the priest was hurrying to meet his evening religious duties. The trip was a day's journey, and he would have to rush to make it. There was also a religious rule that made a person unclean for seven days after touching a dead body. If the man was dead, it would cause the priest to forfeit his turn of duty at the temple. The priest was not about to sacrifice his primary work and privilege for a possibly dead man. Whatever the reason, the priest had no compassion on the severely wounded man and left him for dead.

THOUGHT 1. How many put work, even religious service, and *busyness* before helping others?

THOUGHT 2. How many put their church and its ceremony and ritual before the needs of desperate people? How much less would be invested in buildings and facilities if people were seen as half-dead travelers who need our compassion and help?

> Then he will say to those on his left, "Depart from me, you cursed, into the eternal fire prepared for the devil and his angels. For I was hungry and you gave me no food, I was thirsty and you gave me no drink, I was a stranger and you did not welcome me, naked and you did not clothe me, sick and in prison and you did not visit me." (Mt.25:41–43)

> And that servant who knew his master's will but did not get ready or act according to his will, will receive a severe beating. (Lu.12:47)

> So whoever knows the right thing to do and fails to do it, for him it is sin. (Jas.4:17)

> He has told you, O man, what is good; and what does the LORD require of you but to do justice, and to love kindness, and to walk humbly with your God? (Mi.6:8)

c. The Levite: Passed by without helping the man (v.32).

A Levite also passed by without helping the victim. A servant of the temple, the Levite was most likely traveling with the priest. As with the priest, we can only speculate about his reasons for coldly leaving the man to die. Perhaps he feared that the robbers might still be lurking behind the shadows of the surrounding cliffs. Perhaps he felt that meddling with the poor soul was just too much bother to undergo. Since a higher-ranking religious figure had decided not to help the man, perhaps he felt that neither should he. Whatever he was thinking, this religious man had no compassion for this traveler who had been attacked so brutally and, like the priest, left him for dead.

> What good is it, my brothers, if someone says he has faith but does not have works? Can that faith save him? If a brother or sister is poorly clothed and lacking in daily food, and one of you says to them, "Go in peace, be warmed and filled," without giving them the things needed for the body, what good is that? (Jas.2:14–16)

But if anyone has the world's goods and sees his brother in need, yet closes his heart against him, how does God's love abide in him? Little children, let us not love in word or talk but in deed and in truth. (1 Jn.3:17-18)

For he did not remember to show kindness, but pursued the poor and needy and the broken-hearted, to put them to death. He loved to curse; let curses come upon him! He did not delight in blessing; may it be far from him! (Ps.109:16-17)

Whoever closes his ear to the cry of the poor will himself call out and not be answered. (Pr.21:13)

Rescue those who are being taken away to death; hold back those who are stumbling to the slaughter. If you say, "Behold, we did not know this," does not he who weighs the heart perceive it? Does not he who keeps watch over your soul know it, and will he not repay man according to his work? (Pr.24:11-12)

The weak you have not strengthened, the sick you have not healed, the injured you have not bound up, the strayed you have not brought back, the lost you have not sought, and with force and harshness you have ruled them. (Ezk.34:4; see vv.5-10)

d. The Samaritan: Placed compassion before prejudice and opinion (vv.33-35).

Later, a *Samaritan* passed by (see DEEPER STUDY # 2). In stunning contrast to the priest and the Levite, the Samaritan helped the critically-injured man (v.33). He placed compassion before everything: prejudice, opinion, work, time, energy, and money. The good Samaritan gave of himself. From his heart, he gave his compassion—his all—in order to help the desperate man.

The fact that the compassionate man is a Samaritan makes the story even more dramatic. Bible teacher Warren Wiersbe infers that this detail suggests Jesus is describing an actual occurrence. "For Jesus to tell a story that made the Jews look bad and the Samaritans look good would either be dangerous or self-defeating."[3] The injured man was a Jew. The Samaritan and the Jew were of different races—races who hated and despised each other. No prejudice has ever run any deeper than the prejudice between these two ethnic groups (see note—Lu.10:33). Yet the Samaritan had a sense of *common humanity*. He was a man who saw another man—not as a Jew, and not as an enemy. This was most strange, for the Jews cursed the Samaritans, and there was the likelihood that the injured Jew would curse the Samaritan when he had recovered. However, despite all, the Samaritan saw a fellow human being in desperate need, and he was moved with compassion for him.

The good Samaritan gave up his work, time, and energy to help the man (v.34). Note what he did. Each step is significant in showing how we are to love our neighbors.

➢ He went to him: reached out personally to help.
➢ He bound up his wounds: eased his pain.
➢ He took care of him: nursed, looked after him personally.
➢ He poured oil and wine into his wounds: gave of his own goods.
➢ He set him on his own animal: sacrificed his own comfort.
➢ He provided a place for him to recover and paid for his care.

Note the time, energy, and money involved in this. Showing love to one's neighbor is putting love into action; and putting love into action requires time, energy, and money. Love is not just an idea or a feeling toward God. It is *practical acts and commitment* to help any who need help.

The good Samaritan saw to it that continued compassion and care were given (v.35). *Two denarii* amounted to somewhere between twenty-four to forty-eight days of room and board, a considerable sum. And note: the Samaritan said that if it cost more, he would pay it when he returned. The good Samaritan saw a desperate need and did *all he could* to help.

e. The Lord's commission: go and do likewise (vv.36-37).

Note a striking point: Christ still did not answer the lawyer (v.36). There was no need. The answer was strikingly clear. This man now knew who his neighbor was: it was any person who needed mercy, whether a friend or just an acquaintance or even an enemy. The lawyer

---

3 Ibid.

was forced to admit this (v.37). However, more than just confession was needed. Love was needed.

THOUGHT 1. What Jesus said to the lawyer He says also to all of us: "Go and do likewise." We need to demonstrate love as we go about our daily affairs. We must help our neighbors—all those around us who hurt, have needs, and are suffering.

"For I was hungry and you gave me food, I was thirsty and you gave me drink, I was a stranger and you welcomed me, I was naked and you clothed me, I was sick and you visited me, I was in prison and you came to me." Then the righteous will answer him, saying, "Lord, when did we see you hungry and feed you, or thirsty and give you drink? And when did we see you a stranger and welcome you, or naked and clothe you? And when did we see you sick or in prison and visit you?" And the King will answer them, "Truly, I say to you, as you did it to one of the least of these my brothers, you did it to me." (Mt.25:35-40)

In all things I have shown you that by working hard in this way we must help the weak and remember the words of the Lord Jesus, how he himself said, "It is more blessed to give than to receive." (Ac.20:35)

To the contrary, "if your enemy is hungry, feed him; if he is thirsty, give him something to drink; for by so doing you will heap burning coals on his head." (Ro.12:20)

Bear one another's burdens, and so fulfill the law of Christ. (Ga.6:2)

Remember those who are in prison, as though in prison with them, and those who are mistreated, since you also are in the body. (He.13:3)

If you meet your enemy's ox or his donkey going astray, you shall bring it back to him. (Ex.23:4)

If your brother becomes poor and cannot maintain himself with you, you shall support him as though he were a stranger and a sojourner, and he shall live with you. (Le.25:35)

For the LORD your God is God of gods and Lord of lords, the great, the mighty, and the awesome God, who is not partial and takes no bribe. He executes justice for the fatherless and the widow, and loves the sojourner, giving him food and clothing. Love the sojourner, therefore, for you were sojourners in the land of Egypt. (De.10:17-19)

Do not rejoice when your enemy falls, and let not your heart be glad when he stumbles. (Pr.24:17)

Is not this the fast that I choose: to loose the bonds of wickedness, to undo the straps of the yoke, to let the oppressed go free, and to break every yoke? Is it not to share your bread with the hungry and bring the homeless poor into your house; when you see the naked, to cover him, and not to hide yourself from your own flesh? (Is.58:6-7)

DEEPER STUDY # 2

(10:33) **Samaritans:** Samaria was the central part of Palestine. Palestine was a small province of the Roman Empire, reaching only one hundred twenty miles from north to south. The province was divided into three sections:
> Judea, the southern section
> Galilee, the northern section
> Samaria, the central section, lying right between the two

There was bitter hatred between the Jews and the Samaritans. Two things in particular caused this hatred.
1. The Samaritans were biracial or half-Jews. Centuries before (about 720 B.C.), the King of Assyria had captured the ten tribes of Israel and deported a large number of the people, scattering them throughout Media (see 2 K.17:6-41). He then took people from all over the Assyrian empire and transplanted them into Samaria to repopulate the land. The result was only natural. Intermarriage took place, and the people had biracial children. This infuriated the strict Jews who held to a pure race.
2. The Samaritans mixed pagan religions with Judaism. The transplanted heathen, of course, brought their gods with them. The God of Israel eventually won out, but the

religion of the Samaritans never became pure Judaism. Three things happened to cause this.

a. When Ezra led the Jews back from exile in Babylon, the first thing the Jews did was to start rebuilding their temple. The Samaritans offered to help them but the Jews rejected their help, declaring that the Samaritans, through intermarriage and worship of false gods, had lost their purity and forfeited their right to worship the only true God. This severe denunciation, of course, embittered the Samaritans against the Jews in Jerusalem.

b. The Samaritans built a rival temple on Mount Gerizim to stand in competition with the Jewish temple at Jerusalem (see Jn.4:20-21).

c. The Samaritans twisted both Scripture and history to favor their own people and nation.

➤ They twisted Scripture by accepting only the first five books of the Bible, the Pentateuch. Just imagine! They missed all the richness and depth of the Psalms and prophets.

➤ They twisted history by claiming that three great events took place on Mt. Gerizim, events that set it apart as a place of worship. They taught it was the place where Abraham offered Isaac, where Melchizedek met Abraham, and where Moses built his first altar after leading Israel out of Egyptian bondage.

1. **Jesus entered a village and met two women of strong character**
   a. Martha's character
      1) Welcoming and generous
      2) Courageous
      3) Caring and loving
   b. Mary's character
      1) Loving and humble
      2) Gripped with a spiritual hunger
2. **Martha's problem**
   a. She was distracted by serving

   b. She was distracted by temporal things

3. **Martha's one need: To sit quietly and listen to Jesus' words as Mary had chosen to do**

38 Now as they went on their way, Jesus entered a village. And a woman named Martha welcomed him into her house.

39 And she had a sister called Mary, who sat at the Lord's feet and listened to his teaching.

40 But Martha was distracted with much serving. And she went up to him and said, "Lord, do you not care that my sister has left me to serve alone? Tell her then to help me."

41 But the Lord answered her, "Martha, Martha, you are anxious and troubled about many things,

42 but one thing is necessary. Mary has chosen the good portion, which will not be taken away from her."

Division V

The Son of Man's Great Journey to Jerusalem (Stage I): His Mission and Public Challenge, 9:51–13:21

G. The One Thing Needed: To Sit at Jesus' Feet, 10:38–42

10:38–42
Introduction

This event is chronologically out of sequence in Luke's Gospel, for Mary and Martha lived in Bethany, a suburb two to three miles outside of Jerusalem. Why then does Luke place it here on Jesus' journey to Jerusalem? Perhaps he feared the story of the Good Samaritan might be construed to teach salvation by works. Mary and Martha's experience teaches that waiting and sitting at Jesus' feet is much more important than running to and fro, trying to work one's way into God's favor. There is one basic essential in life, and that is sitting at Jesus' feet and hearing His Word. This is, *The One Thing Needed: To Sit at Jesus' Feet, 10:38–42*.

1. Jesus entered a village and met two women of strong character (vv.38–39).
2. Martha's problem (vv.40–41).
3. Martha's one need: To sit quietly and listen to Jesus' words as Mary had chosen to do (v.42).

10:38–39

38 Now as they went on their way, Jesus entered a village. And a woman named Martha welcomed him into her house.

39 And she had a sister called Mary, who sat at the Lord's feet and listened to his teaching.

1 Jesus entered a village and met two women of strong character.

The scene Luke describes revolves around two women of strong character, Martha and her sister, Mary. Along with their brother, Lazarus, these ladies were among Jesus' dearest friends and most devoted followers. Because of their outstanding qualities, they stand as shining examples to every believer. However, rather than patterning our lives after one or the other, we should strive to incorporate the strong qualities of each into our lives, as will be seen.

a. Martha's character (v.38).

Martha's character is highly commendable. Scripture says that "Jesus loved Martha" (Jn.11:5). It is important to see the strong points of her character and to see what it was that caused such a strong person to fall short in one critical area.

First, Martha was a *welcoming and generous* person, a *giving* person. Note that she owned a house so large she could provide lodging to Jesus and His apostles. Taking care of so many was expensive, yet she willingly entertained them. The following two traits also show how giving she was.

Second, Martha was a *courageous* person. It was now dangerous to associate too closely with Jesus, especially around Jerusalem. The authorities were seeking some way to kill Jesus (see Jn.7:25, 30, 32). Many of His own disciples had forsaken Him (Jn.6:66), and others were now speaking against Him (Jn.7:20, 43–44). Even His own family had rejected Him (Jn.7:3–5). Nevertheless, Martha welcomed Jesus regardless of the circumstances; she was willing to let the world know of her devotion to Him.

Third, Martha was a *caring and loving* person. She loved and cared for her sister Mary. Apparently, Mary was living with Martha, and her brother Lazarus was also living there (Jn.11:1f). For some unknown reason, Martha was taking care of them both. She felt a deep devotion for her family, loving and caring for them very much. This was apparent even in the midst of the agitation she felt toward Mary (v.40).

b. Mary's character (v.39).

Mary's character was also commendable. She was *loving and humble*. Note how she loved Jesus; she attached herself to Him. Her love and devotion ran deep, so deep that nothing else mattered except being right next to Him. Note also her humility. She *sat* at His feet, not by His side and not in front of Him. The room or courtyard was spacious enough to entertain a large crowd, so she could have chosen to sit elsewhere. Mary definitely had a devoted love and a sense of humility toward her Lord.

In addition, Mary had a *spiritual hunger* for the Word of the Lord: she gave her full attention to Jesus' teaching. She sat there, fixing her eyes on Him. She centered her mind on what He said, listening and concentrating, devouring every word—not taking Jesus' message lightly. She hungered for the Word of Christ, absorbing His words and taking them to heart. This means that she had . . .

- a spiritual hunger
- a readiness to hear
- a desire to surrender
- a willingness to obey

2 Martha's problem.

In spite of her gracious yet bold character, Martha developed a problem: she became distracted. The word *distracted* (periespato, *per-ees-pah'-tow*) is used in the New Testament only this once and literally means to be drawn around, to be twisted. The idea is that Martha was drawn around and twisted with anxiety and worry. She was distracted from the *main thing*, running here and there, being drawn by things going on around her. Martha's distraction can be viewed and applied to our lives in two ways.

[40] But Martha was distracted with much serving. And she went up to him and said, "Lord, do you not care that my sister has left me to serve alone? Tell her then to help me."
[41] But the Lord answered her, "Martha, Martha, you are anxious and troubled about many things,"

a. She was distracted by serving (v.40).

She was distracted with "much serving"—all that she had to do in hosting a large group of people. Simply stated, she was preoccupied with her cares and responsibilities.[1] She loved

---

1 Spiros Zodhiates, ed., *The Complete Word Study Dictionary: New Testament*, (Chattanooga, TN: AMG Publishers, 1992). Via Wordsearch digital edition.

others, so she ministered to them, helping whomever and wherever she could, even using her own home as a center for caring. But Martha had a problem. She became so burdened down, so tired and fatigued, so pressured and tense . . .

- that she lost sight of the foremost priority
- that she became agitated and critical of those who were not helping her

b. She was distracted by temporal things (v.41).

Martha could also be distracted by temporal things, by things associated with *this* life such as food and necessities and cares of this world. Martha was wealthy to some degree, which is indicated by her entertaining Jesus and His large group. Apparently, she was very active, possessing initiative and some management ability. She had much to look after, including a brother and sister who lived with her. It was the things of this world—food, necessities, cares, and social entertaining—that had distracted her.

As any gracious hostess would do, Martha felt a keen responsibility for taking care of her guests and meeting their needs. When Jesus and His large group arrived, she naturally expected her sister to help with the preparation of the meals and lodging. The problem in her mind was that Jesus did not even suggest that Mary help. Martha was disturbed with Jesus as well as with Mary.

Martha had a legitimate complaint, and that legitimacy points out the importance of sitting at Jesus' feet and hearing His Word (v.39). No matter *how* important anything else is, sitting at Jesus' feet is the one thing that is to be given priority.

The fact that Martha opened her home to others and took care of her sister shows that Martha was loving and concerned about people. The fact that she invited Jesus and His large group to her home for a meal reveals that she loved and wanted to serve the Lord. But evidently, she had become *too* busy. Perhaps her wealth, initiative, hospitality, social status, and management ability were the things that had priority in her mind and life. As good as they were, they were not enough, for they did not meet the one basic essential in life: having her spiritual hunger fed with the Word of Christ Himself.

THOUGHT 1. People need food and necessities and some social entertainment, but we must not be distracted by these. We must guard against letting the cares and things of this life choke the Word out of our lives.

> And as for what fell among the thorns, they are those who hear, but as they go on their way they are choked by the cares and riches and pleasures of life, and their fruit does not mature. (Lu.8:14)

> And do not seek what you are to eat and what you are to drink, nor be worried. (Lu.12:29)

> But watch yourselves lest your hearts be weighed down with dissipation and drunkenness and cares of this life, and that day come upon you suddenly like a trap. (Lu.21:34)

> No soldier gets entangled in civilian pursuits, since his aim is to please the one who enlisted him. (2 Ti.2:4)

THOUGHT 2. We should seek out opportunities to serve, working to meet the needs of others and of a desperate world. Sadly, in most churches, a small percentage of the people do the lion's share of the work. It is easy for the faithful laborers to become resentful toward the many who simply sit and receive and do little in return. We have to guard against becoming burdened down to the point . . .

- that the pressure of our responsibilities gets to us
- that we become critical of others

> Jesus answered them, "Do not grumble among yourselves." (Jn.6:43)

> Nor grumble, as some of them did and were destroyed by the Destroyer. (1 Co.10:10)

> Do all things without grumbling or disputing, that you may be blameless and innocent, children of God without blemish in the midst of a crooked and twisted generation, among whom you shine as lights in the world. (Ph.2:14–15)

> Then I considered all that my hands had done and the toil I had expended in doing it, and behold, all was vanity and a striving after wind, and there was nothing to be gained under the sun. (Ec.2:11)

3 Martha's one need: To sit quietly and listen to Jesus' words as Mary had chosen to do.

Jesus loved Martha and addressed her issue tenderly. This gentleness is seen in His softly saying to her, "Martha, Martha" (see Lu.22:31; Ac.9:4 for other places where Jesus tenderly addresses people by name twice). Jesus was deeply concerned for this selfless lady who served Him and others so conscientiously. She was bowing under the stress and pressure of her responsibilities. So many people had moved in on her, and she was trying her best to meet the needs of all. The Lord's tender heart went out to her, wanting to ease her stress and her frustration with her sister.

> 42 "but one thing is necessary. Mary has chosen the good portion, which will not be taken away from her."

Jesus lovingly admonished Martha because she was anxious and troubled about "many things" (v.41). The word *anxious* (merimnas, *mer-im-nahce'*) means worried, overwhelmed with care. It has the idea of being inwardly torn and divided in two, of being distracted from what one's mind and heart and life should be focused on. The word *troubled* (thorubazē, *thor-ooh-bah'-zay*) means disturbed, agitated, in turmoil, stirred up, ruffled. Martha sought to please Jesus with her service and ministering, but two things were weighing her down:

➤ She was looking after "many things," too many. She was trying to do *too much* for too many.
➤ She had become anxious and troubled.

Jesus counseled Martha that only "one thing" is necessary (v.42). What is that one thing? The Lord clearly said that it was the *good portion* or *part* which Mary chose. Mary sat at Jesus' feet and listened to His Word (v.39). Martha's mistake was neglecting to do what Mary did. She let "many things" distract her from spending time in the Lord's presence, from sitting at His feet and hearing His Word. Note what Jesus meant by the "many things" that distracted Martha from spending time with the Lord:

- giving lodging and food to those who needed such
- preparing the food for those who needed it
- serving the hungry
- making others comfortable

(Remember that Jesus was poor in worldly goods, having no place to lay His head, and apparently, He sometimes had no money for food. Yet, He still stressed the spiritual over the physical.)

Jesus said that what Mary had chosen, the hunger and thirst after righteousness (God's Word), would be filled and never taken away. (Mt.5:6).

THOUGHT 1. Our devotion to Christ is a daily affair (Lu.9:23). Therefore, spending time at His feet and hearing His Word is to be a daily experience. Every believer should have what is commonly called *daily devotions*, a time set aside every day when we get alone with God and sit at the Lord's feet to bathe in His presence and hear His Word.

And rising very early in the morning, while it was still dark, he departed and went out to a desolate place, and there he prayed. (Mk.1:35)

And then as a widow until she was eighty-four. She did not depart from the temple, worshiping with fasting and prayer night and day. (Lu.2:37)

Now these Jews were more noble than those in Thessalonica; they received the word with all eagerness, examining the Scriptures daily to see if these things were so. (Ac.17:11)

This Book of the Law shall not depart from your mouth, but you shall meditate on it day and night, so that you may be careful to do according to all that is written in it. For then you will make your way prosperous, and then you will have good success. (Jos.1:8)

But his delight is in the law of the LORD, and on his law he meditates day and night. He is like a tree planted by streams of water that yields its fruit in its season, and its leaf does not wither. In all that he does, he prospers. (Ps.1:2–3)

O LORD, in the morning you hear my voice; in the morning I prepare a sacrifice for you and watch. (Ps.5:3)

CHAPTER 11

H. The Great Subject of Prayer, 11:1–13

(Mt.6:5-15; Mk.11:20-26)

1. Jesus prayed
   a. The disciples asked Jesus to teach them how to pray
   b. John had taught his disciples to pray

2. Jesus' model prayer
   a. Thank God
      1) For being your Father
      2) For heaven
   b. Praise His name
   c. Pray
      1) For His kingdom
      2) For daily bread
      3) For forgiveness
      4) For deliverance

3. Your part in prayer[DS1]
   a. The illustration: You are to persevere and endure in prayer

   b. The point: When you persevere and endure in prayer, you receive what you request

   c. The exhortation
      1) Ask—will be given
      2) Seek—will find
      3) Knock—will be opened
   d. The answer assured

4. God's part in prayer
   a. The illustration: Even an earthly (sinful) father gives good—not evil—to his children

   b. The point: God is even more willing to give the very best—the Holy Spirit—to His children who ask

Now Jesus was praying in a certain place, and when he finished, one of his disciples said to him, "Lord, teach us to pray, as John taught his disciples."

² And he said to them, "When you pray, say: Father, hallowed be your name. Your kingdom come.

³ Give us each day our daily bread,

⁴ and forgive us our sins, for we ourselves forgive everyone who is indebted to us. And lead us not into temptation."

⁵ And he said to them, "Which of you who has a friend will go to him at midnight and say to him, 'Friend, lend me three loaves,

⁶ for a friend of mine has arrived on a journey, and I have nothing to set before him';

⁷ and he will answer from within, 'Do not bother me; the door is now shut, and my children are with me in bed. I cannot get up and give you anything'?

⁸ I tell you, though he will not get up and give him anything because he is his friend, yet because of his impudence he will rise and give him whatever he needs.

⁹ And I tell you, ask, and it will be given to you; seek, and you will find; knock, and it will be opened to you.

¹⁰ For everyone who asks receives, and the one who seeks finds, and to the one who knocks it will be opened.

¹¹ What father among you, if his son asks for a fish, will instead of a fish give him a serpent;

¹² or if he asks for an egg, will give him a scorpion?

¹³ If you then, who are evil, know how to give good gifts to your children, how much more will the heavenly Father give the Holy Spirit to those who ask him!"

Division V

The Son of Man's Great Journey to Jerusalem (Stage I):
His Mission and Public Challenge, 9:51–13:21

H. The Great Subject of Prayer, 11:1–13

(Mt.6:5–15; Mk.11:20–26)

11:1–13
Introduction

The nineteenth century British poet Alfred Lord Tennyson wrote, "More things are wrought by prayer than this world dreams of." Scripture says, *"You do not have because you do not ask"* (Jas.4:2). We can only wonder if, in heaven someday, God will show us all He would have done for us, if we had but asked.

Of the Gospel authors, Luke gives the most comprehensive account of Jesus' teaching on prayer. In fact, this passage is one of the most thorough passages in all of Scripture dealing with prayer. It is a passage that should be studied time and again. As we approach it, we should pray along with the disciples, "Lord, teach us to pray" (v.1). This is, *The Great Subject of Prayer,* 11:1-13.

1. Jesus prayed (v.1).
2. Jesus' model prayer (vv.2–4).
3. Your part in prayer (vv.5–10).
4. God's part in prayer (vv.11–13).

1 Jesus prayed.

In a messianic psalm, David prophesied that Jesus would give Himself to prayer (Ps.109:4). Indeed, our Lord was always praying (see Introduction, Special Features, pt.8 for a complete list of Jesus' recorded prayer times).

> Now Jesus was praying in a certain place, and when he finished, one of his disciples said to him, "Lord, teach us to pray, as John taught his disciples."

- ➤ He prayed at His baptism (Lu.3:21).
- ➤ He prayed during His temptation (Lu.5:16).
- ➤ He continued all night in prayer (Lu.6:12).
- ➤ He was alone praying (Lu.9:18).
- ➤ He went up into a mountain to pray (Lu.9:28).
- ➤ He was now praying in a certain place (Lu.11:1).

a. The disciples asked Jesus to teach them how to pray.

While Jesus prayed, something caught the eye and ear of the disciples. Apparently, they were off to the side someplace but within sight and hearing. Two things stirred them to ask Jesus to teach them to pray.

First, they had often heard Jesus pray, and they had heard Him repeatedly emphasize prayer as one of the greatest needs of human life. Jesus always insisted that prayer was the source of His strength in living and serving God. Because of Jesus' example, the disciples were inspired to hunger after the same strength for life and service.

Second, the disciples were inspired by the *way* Jesus prayed. The Lord prayed as a Son to His Father, and such intimacy stirred the disciples to want the same kind of relationship with God. Therefore, they asked Jesus to teach them to pray.

b. John had taught his disciples to pray.

It was a common practice for a teacher to instruct his disciples in prayer. John the Baptist had taught his disciples to pray, and Jesus' disciples used this as the basis to ask Him to teach them to pray.

2 Jesus' model prayer.

Without hesitation, our Lord granted His disciples' request. Naturally, Jesus will teach anyone to pray—anyone who is sincere and wants to pray effectively. Note what Jesus did. He said, *"When you pray, say. . . ."* or *"Pray like this."* He was giving a model prayer on which we are to base our praying. It is a guide, a pattern for us to follow, the points of which are to be prayed through. The Lord did not intend for us to pray *these exact words*, but to adopt this sample prayer as an outline for our prayers, making it personal and specific according to our individual needs (see note—Mt.6:9-13 for more discussion).

11:2-4

² And he said to them, "When you pray, say: Father, hallowed be your name. Your kingdom come.
³ Give us each day our daily bread,
⁴ and forgive us our sins, for we ourselves forgive everyone who is indebted to us. And lead us not into temptation."

a. Thank God (v.2a).

Jesus instructed us to begin our prayers by acknowledging who God is and where He is. This acknowledgement should naturally flow into expressing our gratitude to Him.

First, we should thank God for being our "Father." This title expresses that we have a personal relationship with God, a family relationship, the relationship of a child to a parent. It is a family relationship formed through a person's being born again (Jn.1:12-13; 2 Co.6:17-18; see also Ga.4:4-7). We need to thank God for being our Father, for creating the family of God, and allowing us to be a part of so glorious a family, for making a way for us to have a relationship with Him through His Son, Jesus Christ (Ga.3:26). This relationship is the basis for our approaching God, the creator and sovereign power of the universe.

Second, we are praying to our Father who is in heaven.[1] Heaven is the spiritual dimension of being; it is a real, literal place, incorruptible and undefiled, and it does not fade away (1 Pe.1:4). More importantly, it is where God is, and it is where we will be. We should thank God for heaven, that He is there and that we will be in heaven with Him (Jn.14:2-3).

b. Praise His name (v.2b).

As we pray, we should praise God for the holiness of His name. His name is *hallowed* (Gk. hagiasthētō, *ha-ghee-ahs-thay'-tow*)—set apart, holy, undefiled and to be held in reverence (Ps.111:9). God is holy, righteous, pure, loving, kind, merciful, gracious. Therefore, we are to praise God for who He is.

c. Pray (vv.2c-4).

In its purest form, prayer is simply *asking* (Mt.7:7-8, 11; 21:22; Jn.14:14; 16:24; Jas.4:2). Jesus taught us to request four things in particular. But note: these should be prayed for only after we have thanked and praised God.

First, we should pray for God's kingdom to come (v.2c). Christ needs to be enthroned, His rule and reign established on earth. His will needs to be done in all of our lives just as it is done in heaven. We need to pray for such to come (see DEEPER STUDY # 3—Mt.19:23-24 for a discussion of the kingdom that shows items for which we should pray).

Ultimately, our prayers for the coming of the Lord's kingdom will be answered by the return of Jesus Christ. "Faith looks forward to that time when the Lord shall come the second time and deliver His own from all the distracting conditions that now prevail. . . . Then indeed the will of God will be done on earth as it is now done in heaven."[2]

Second, Jesus instructed us to pray for the provision of life's necessities, as represented by "our daily bread" (v.3). We are to depend on God to provide our needs (Mt.6:25-34). People are

---

1 While the manuscripts from which the ESV and many other modern Bible translations originate do not include the words "in heaven," and "your will be done," they do include them in Matthew's account of this same event (Mt.6:9-10). They are included here in the manuscripts from which the KJV and NKJV are translated.

2 H. A. Ironside, *Ironside Expository Commentaries: Luke*, (Grand Rapids, MI: Kregel Academic, 2007). Via Wordsearch digital edition.

hungry, starving both physically and spiritually. We all need to be fed both without and within. We need to pray *daily* for the nourishment of our bodies and our spirits.

Third, we need to pray for forgiveness (v.4a). We should pray for the Father to forgive our sins, and we need to take some time in discussing the matter with our Father. But note the word "our." We are to ask God to forgive "our sins," the sins of our family, neighbors, city, state, nation, and world. Sin is a shame, an affront to God. Sin is the most serious matter and most tragic event to ever occur in the universe. It is to be discussed with the Father every day—not just our own sins, but the world's sins. Intercessory prayer for the sinners of the world is to be a daily event in the life of every believer.

But note a crucial fact: old sins that have been confessed and covered by the blood of Christ are not to be brought back up to God. They are already forgiven, hid and cast away by God. He does not want them remembered anymore. They are too painful and hurtful. However, new sins are committed every day, so many within our hearts and throughout the world that it would stagger the human mind. We are ever so short of God's glory—*unconformed* to the image of Christ, undeveloped and immature—so far short of what we should be. Believers need to come to God every day, begging for a fresh experience of forgiveness both for themselves and for the world.

Note there is a condition for asking for God's forgiveness (v.4b). We must forgive those who sin against us. We sin and sin often against God. If we expect God to forgive us, we have to forgive those who sin against us.

> **For if you forgive others their trespasses, your heavenly Father will also forgive you, but if you do not forgive others their trespasses, neither will your Father forgive your trespasses. (Mt.6:14-15)**

> **And whenever you stand praying, forgive, if you have anything against anyone, so that your Father also who is in heaven may forgive you your trespasses. (Mk.11:25)**

Fourth, we are to pray for deliverance (v.4c). The idea of God's leading people into temptation does not agree with the overall teaching of Scripture. Scripture plainly states that God does not tempt anyone to do evil (Jas.1:13), so Jesus is not saying that God actually leads people into temptation. What Jesus *is* saying is that we should pray for God to deliver us from temptation and from the evil one, Satan (see Lu.22:40; 1 Co.10:13). We are to ask God to lead us *away from* temptation.

3 Your part in prayer.

After giving a model prayer, Jesus proceeded to teach what our part—our responsibility—is in prayer. No clearer explanation of our duty in prayer could be given than what our Lord taught here.

a. The illustration: You are to persevere and endure in prayer (vv.5-7).

Jesus illustrates very simply what our part in prayer is. It is to persevere and endure in prayer. Just as the man in the story persisted to appeal to his neighbor until his neighbor met his need, we are to keep on praying until the Lord meets our needs.

b. The point: When you persevere and endure in prayer, you receive what you request (v.8).

Jesus drove the point home: when you persevere in prayer, you will receive what you request. We will receive what we ask for if we will not leave the throne of God, if we will have the faith and endurance to keep asking until our need is met.

5 And he said to them, "Which of you who has a friend will go to him at midnight and say to him, 'Friend, lend me three loaves,

6 for a friend of mine has arrived on a journey, and I have nothing to set before him';

7 and he will answer from within, 'Do not bother me; the door is now shut, and my children are with me in bed. I cannot get up and give you anything'?

8 I tell you, though he will not get up and give him anything because he is his friend, yet because of his impudence he will rise and give him whatever he needs.

9 And I tell you, ask, and it will be given to you; seek, and you will find; knock, and it will be opened to you.

10 For everyone who asks receives, and the one who seeks finds, and to the one who knocks it will be opened."

The whole point is that we must be sincere, fervent, constant, persistent, persevering, and enduring in seeking the face of God for what we need (see DEEPER STUDY # 1).

c. The exhortation (v.9).

Just in case some do not grasp the point of the illustration, Jesus states it directly. The story is an exhortation, a mini-sermon, to persevere and endure in prayer. We are to . . .

- *ask* God for what we need, and it will be given to us
- *seek* God in prayer, and we will find Him
- *knock*, and God will open the door to us

The Greek verbs for ask, seek, and knock are all *continuous action*. This is the key to understanding what Jesus is saying. We are to keep on asking and seeking and knocking, ever beseeching God to hear us until our prayers are answered. The point is, we must mean what we pray, and the way we show God our fervency and sincerity is by continuing to ask for what we need.

d. The answer assured (v.10).

Jesus assures us that our prayers will be answered. Believers always receive what we *need* from God (Mt.6:32-33; Ph.4:19). In the illustration shared by Jesus, the friend was occupied with a very needed and worthy matter—he was rejuvenating his body with sleep. The point is this: most have experienced being disturbed while sleeping (whether by a crying child or some other noise) and being slow to arise. Few arise unless the beckoning call persists. But one always arises if the child coughs or cries enough or the noise repeats itself enough. Persistence proves one's sincerity and the depth of the need. There are certain requests that need a "continual coming" to God (Lu.18:5; see note and DEEPER STUDY # 1—Mt.7:7).

> **And he told them a parable to the effect that they ought always to pray and not lose heart. (Lu.18:1)**

> **Praying at all times in the Spirit, with all prayer and supplication. To that end, keep alert with all perseverance, making supplication for all the saints. (Ep.6:18)**

> **Continue steadfastly in prayer, being watchful in it with thanksgiving. (Col.4:2)**

> **Pray without ceasing. (1 Th.5:17)**

> **But from there you will seek the LORD your God and you will find him, if you search after him with all your heart and with all your soul. (De.4:29)**

> **I love those who love me, and those who seek me diligently find me. (Pr.8:17)**

> **You will seek me and find me, when you seek me with all your heart. (Je.29:13)**

DEEPER STUDY # 1

(11:5-10) **Prayer—Fellowship:** Why does God not always answer our prayers immediately? Why is it necessary for us to ask and to seek and to knock and to keep on asking and seeking and knocking? Why do we need to ask at all when God knows our needs even before we ask?

There are at least four reasons.

1. Prayer teaches us to communicate and fellowship with God and to trust and seek after God more and more. When God holds back the answer, we keep coming to talk and share with Him more and more. Just as a human father longs for such fellowship and trust, our heavenly Father longs for such fellowship and trust.

2. Prayer teaches us both patience and hope in God and His promises. When God does not answer immediately, we patiently (enduringly) keep coming into His presence, waiting for and hoping in what He has promised us (Mt.21:22; Jn.14:26; 1 Jn.5:14-15).

3. Prayer teaches us to love God as our Father more and more. Knowing that what we ask is indeed coming yet having to wait on it causes us to draw closer and closer to God and His gifts. And then when the answer is given, our hearts are endeared ever so much more to Him.

4. Prayer demonstrates how deeply we trust God and how much we love and depend on Him. Those who really trust God—who really know that what they ask is going to be received—will bring more and more to God. They will come to God in prayer more and more. But the person who is not quite sure about receiving will only occasionally come, usually only in emergencies. God easily sees in our prayer life how much we really love and trust Him.

4 God's part in prayer.

Here Jesus teaches what God's part—God's responsibility—is in prayer. Jesus' explanation of God's part in prayer is just as clear as His explanation of our part; no clearer explanation could be given.

> **11** "What father among you, if his son asks for a fish, will instead of a fish give him a serpent;
> **12** or if he asks for an egg, will give him a scorpion?
> **13** If you then, who are evil, know how to give good gifts to your children, how much more will the heavenly Father give the Holy Spirit to those who ask him!"

a. The illustration: Even an earthly (sinful) father gives good—not evil—to his children (vv.11-12).

As with our part in prayer, Jesus illustrates what God's part is. Earthly fathers, who are all *evil*—sinful human beings—are good to their children. They give their children what they need. When their children are hungry and ask for food, they do not give them something they cannot eat.

b. The point: God is even more willing to give the very best—the Holy Spirit—to His children who ask (v.13).

God is not evil; He is not sinful. If sinful earthly fathers are good to their children, *how much more* will the holy, righteous God be good to His children! God is most willing to give.

Men are evil, full of selfishness and sin, yet they give their children what they need. Note the enormous contrast being made between sinful humans and God, who is perfectly good. If evil people give, it is impossible that God, who is good, would not give.

Our heavenly Father not only gives, He gives us the very best, the Source of all good things, the Holy Spirit Himself. Just imagine the very presence of God dwelling within our hearts and bodies! If He dwells within us, then every good thing is assured. Once we have the Holy Spirit, we do not have to pray to God who is *way off* in outer space somewhere. We do not have to wait for what we need spiritually to arrive; what we need is *within* us. We have His presence within . . .

• to accompany and be with us

   Nevertheless, I tell you the truth: it is to your advantage that I go away, for if I do not go away, the Helper will not come to you. But if I go, I will send him to you. (Jn.16:7)

• to look after and care for us

   But the fruit of the Spirit is love, joy, peace, patience, kindness, goodness, faithfulness, gentleness, self-control; against such things there is no law. (Ga.5:22-23)

• to direct and guide us

   When the Spirit of truth comes, he will guide you into all the truth, for he will not speak on his own authority, but whatever he hears he will speak, and he will declare to you the things that are to come. (Jn.16:13)

   For all who are led by the Spirit of God are sons of God. (Ro.8:14)

• to assure and comfort us

   But the Helper, the Holy Spirit, whom the Father will send in my name, he will teach you all things and bring to your remembrance all that I have said to you. (Jn.14:26)

   For you did not receive the spirit of slavery to fall back into fear, but you have received the Spirit of adoption as sons, by whom we cry, "Abba! Father!" The Spirit himself bears witness with our spirit that we are children of God, and if children, then heirs—heirs of God and fellow heirs with Christ, provided we suffer with him in order that we may also be glorified with him. (Ro.8:15-17)

- to pray and intercede for us

Likewise the Spirit helps us in our weakness. For we do not know what to pray for as we ought, but the Spirit himself intercedes for us with groanings too deep for words. (Ro.8:26)

THOUGHT 1. God is a loving, generous Father who is most willing to give. As children of God, we can rest assured that when the circumstances of life become hard, God will give us the presence and power of the Holy Spirit to see us through.

Note another fact: God is not only willing to answer, He is *most willing* to answer. He loves and cares for us in all your needs. We need to always remember this when immersed in difficult circumstances. Note something else: God always answers our prayers, but sometimes the answer has to be "no." Why? Because what we asked is not always for our good—it is not what we *need*—and God is always going to do what is best for us.

And whatever you ask in prayer, you will receive, if you have faith. (Mt.21:22)

Therefore I tell you, whatever you ask in prayer, believe that you have received it, and it will be yours. (Mk.11:24)

Whatever you ask in my name, this I will do, that the Father may be glorified in the Son. If you ask me anything in my name, I will do it. (Jn.14:13–14)

If you abide in me, and my words abide in you, ask whatever you wish, and it will be done for you. (Jn.15:7)

Until now you have asked nothing in my name. Ask, and you will receive, that your joy may be full. (Jn.16:24)

If any of you lacks wisdom, let him ask God, who gives generously to all without reproach, and it will be given him. But let him ask in faith, with no doubting, for the one who doubts is like a wave of the sea that is driven and tossed by the wind. (Jas.1:5–6)

And whatever we ask we receive from him, because we keep his commandments and do what pleases him. (1 Jn.3:22)

And this is the confidence that we have toward him, that if we ask anything according to his will he hears us. And if we know that he hears us in whatever we ask, we know that we have the requests that we have asked of him. (1 Jn.5:14–15)

If my people who are called by my name humble themselves, and pray and seek my face and turn from their wicked ways, then I will hear from heaven and will forgive their sin and heal their land. (2 Chr.7:14)

When he calls to me, I will answer him; I will be with him in trouble; I will rescue him and honor him. (Ps.91:15)

When the poor and needy seek water, and there is none, and their tongue is parched with thirst, I the LORD will answer them; I the God of Israel will not forsake them. (Is.41:17)

Before they call I will answer; while they are yet speaking I will hear. (Is.65:24)

Call to me and I will answer you, and will tell you great and hidden things that you have not known. (Je.33:3)

And I will put this third into the fire, and refine them as one refines silver, and test them as gold is tested. They will call upon my name, and I will answer them. I will say, "They are my people"; and they will say, "The LORD is my God." (Zec.13:9)

(Mt.12:22-30; Mk.3:22-30)

14 Now he was casting out a demon that was mute. When the demon had gone out, the mute man spoke, and the people marveled.

15 But some of them said, "He casts out demons by Beelzebul, the prince of demons,"

16 while others, to test him, kept seeking from him a sign from heaven.

17 But he, knowing their thoughts, said to them, "Every kingdom divided against itself is laid waste, and a divided household falls.

18 And if Satan also is divided against himself, how will his kingdom stand? For you say that I cast out demons by Beelzebul."

19 And if I cast out demons by Beelzebul, by whom do your sons cast them out? Therefore they will be your judges.

20 But if it is by the finger of God that I cast out demons, then the kingdom of God has come upon you.

21 When a strong man, fully armed, guards his own palace, his goods are safe;

22 but when one stronger than he attacks him and overcomes him, he takes away his armor in which he trusted and divides his spoil.

23 Whoever is not with me is against me, and whoever does not gather with me scatters.

24 When the unclean spirit has gone out of a person, it passes through waterless places seeking rest, and finding none it says, 'I will return to my house from which I came.'

25 And when it comes, it finds the house swept and put in order.

26 Then it goes and brings seven other spirits more evil than itself, and they enter and dwell there. And the last state of that person is worse than the first."

1. **Jesus proves He is the Messiah: He casts a demon out of a man**
   a. The people were amazed: Who was Jesus?
   b. Some accused Him of being a deceiver, of Beelzebul or Beelzebub

   c. Some tested Him: Sought a sign

2. **Illust.1—a kingdom and a house: Jesus claims to be of another kingdom and house than Satan's kingdom and house**

3. **Illust.2—the religious exorcists: Jesus claims the right to be respected, at least as much as other ministers**
4. **Illust.3—the finger of God: Jesus claims to possess the power to usher in the kingdom of God**
5. **Illust.4—a stronger man: Jesus claims to be stronger than Satan, to conquer him and take away his defenses**

6. **Illust.5—a shepherd and a flock: Jesus claims that a person must follow Him, not try to be neutral**
7. **Illust.6—an empty house: Jesus claims that a person must not only reform their life (cast out evil) but also be filled with His very presence**

8. Conclusion—the necessary thing: To hear the Word of God and keep it

²⁷ As he said these things, a woman in the crowd raised her voice and said to him, "Blessed is the womb that bore you, and the breasts at which you nursed!" ²⁸ But he said, "Blessed rather are those who hear the word of God and keep it!"

Division V

The Son of Man's Great Journey to Jerusalem (Stage I): His Mission and Public Challenge, 9:51–13:21

I. The Proof that Jesus Is the Messiah, 11:14–28

(Mt.12:22–30; Mk.3:22–30)

11:14–28
Introduction

When Jesus came to earth as a man, many rejected, denied, and cursed Him. Throughout the centuries since, this has always been the case, and it continues to be so today. So many refuse to believe that Jesus is God's Son, the only Savior, and Lord of all. Yet there is enormous evidence that He is exactly who He claimed to be. Jesus Himself presents some of the indisputable evidence in this passage. This is, *The Proof that Jesus Is the Messiah,* 11:14–28.

1. Jesus proves He is the Messiah: He casts a demon out of a man (vv.14–16).
2. Illust.1—a kingdom and a house: Jesus claims to be of another kingdom and house than Satan's kingdom and house (vv.17–18).
3. Illust.2—the religious exorcists: Jesus claims the right to be respected, at least as much as other ministers (v.19).
4. Illust.3—the finger of God: Jesus claims to possess the power to usher in the kingdom of God (v.20).
5. Illust.4—a stronger man: Jesus claims to be stronger than Satan, to conquer him and take away his defenses (vv.21–22).
6. Illust.5—a shepherd and a flock: Jesus claims that a person must follow Him, not try to be neutral (v.23).
7. Illust.6—an empty house: Jesus claims that a person must not only reform their life (cast out evil) but also be filled with His very presence (vv.24–26).
8. Conclusion—the necessary thing: To hear the Word of God and keep it (vv.27–28).

11:14–16

¹⁴ Now he was casting out a demon that was mute. When the demon had gone out, the mute man spoke, and the people marveled.
¹⁵ But some of them said, "He casts out demons by Beelzebul, the prince of demons,"
¹⁶ while others, to test him, kept seeking from him a sign from heaven.

1 Jesus proves He is the Messiah: He casts a demon out of a man.

Jesus saw a man held in the grip of evil by some demonic spirit that made him *mute* (unable to speak) and *blind* (see Mt.12:22). Jesus' compassionate heart went out to the man, and He cast out the evil spirit and healed the man. In doing so, He demonstrates to all that He is the true Messiah, the one who possesses the power of God perfectly. He shows that He has come to destroy the works of the devil (1 Jn.3:8). In casting out demons, He wages war against the evil spiritual forces of this world (Ep.6:12). The people's response is threefold.

a. The people were amazed: Who was Jesus (v.14)?

The people who witnessed Jesus' power over demons were amazed and astonished, wondering just who Jesus might be. Matthew adds that some speculated that Jesus might be the Son of David (Mt.12:23).

b. Some accused Him of being a deceiver, of Beelzebul or Beelzebub (v.15).

Others immediately rejected Jesus. But note they did not question His power. They had to admit He possessed the power to do marvelous things. The tragedy of their rejection was that they said the power was of Beelzebul or Beelzebub, the ruler of the demons (see DEEPER STUDY # 1—Mk.3:22 for more discussion).

c. Some tested Him: Sought a sign (v.16).

Others sought a supernatural sign that would satisfy their fleshly desires. To confess Christ would cost them everything they had, both wealth and friends (see note and DEEPER STUDY # 1—Lu.9:23; note—Mt.19:16–22). There was already plenty of evidence that Jesus was the true Messiah; they were simply unwilling to deny themselves to meet the needs of a desperate world and to be ridiculed and abused by the world (see note—Mt.16:2–4). Therefore, they demanded a sign—a sign so great that all people would believe. If everyone and everything could be miraculously converted all at once, then heaven would be on earth and all of people's carnal desires would be met (see outline and notes—Jn.6:22–30, esp. vv.26–27, 30). A sign from heaven, would convince all people that Jesus was who He claimed to be. (Note: if God did this, it would be treating us as robots, eliminating our freedom of choice and will.)

Jesus knew what the unbelievers standing there were thinking. Therefore, He gave six illustrations that delivered a crushing blow to their carnal thoughts and unbelief.

THOUGHT 1. People think that if they had a spectacular sign, then all people would believe and two things would happen.

1) There would be no abuse, ridicule, or persecution by friends or neighbors or anyone else.
2) The whole world would be converted. The kingdom of God would come to earth, and there would be plenty for everyone. There would be no need to protect what one has nor to fear the selfishness and evil of others. This, of course, is untrue, for people are by nature *selfish and self-centered*, seeking to improve their own lives. People would still disbelieve and distrust God and would still choose to do what they desired instead of doing God's will.

> **The heart is deceitful above all things, and desperately sick; who can understand it? (Je.17:9)**

2 Illustration 1—a kingdom and a house: Jesus claims to be of another kingdom and house than Satan's kingdom and house.

17 But he, knowing their thoughts, said to them, "Every kingdom divided against itself is laid waste, and a divided household falls. 18 And if Satan also is divided against himself, how will his kingdom stand? For you say that I cast out demons by Beelzebul."

In these verses, Jesus uses a very simple illustration to make His claim that His power is not of Satan—the illustration of *a divided kingdom and a house* (v.17). It is an illustration that is clearly understood because everyone knows of kingdoms and houses that are divided and that crumble every day.

Jesus acknowledges the existence of Satan and his kingdom, both of which struggle against righteousness and good. He does not deny Satan's existence, nor does He try to correct people's mistaken notions about the devil and his kingdom. Why? Because the devil and his kingdom are not *mistaken notions*. They are very, very real (see DEEPER STUDY # 1—Re.12:9).

Jesus points out the logical fact that Satan is not divided against himself (v.18). The devil is not going to do good, nor is he going to do something that builds up God's kingdom. The very opposite is true. Satan is going to build his own kingdom, his own rule and reign. He desires to oppose and exalt himself against God. He wants people to follow him and his way of evil and consequently cut the heart of God. He wants God to hurt, and he knows that God hurts when a person goes astray and turns from God's kingdom (see Deeper Study # 3—Mt.19:23–24). Therefore, Satan seeks to lead people into evil by enticing them through the carnal desires of the sinful human nature. Satan knows that sin leads to disease and to the destruction of the human body and family. He knows that such destruction causes great pain and hurt and suffering for God, which apparently is his ultimate motive.

The point is clear: Satan is not going to cast out evil. By casting out an evil spirit, Jesus is doing good. Therefore, His power has to be of God. He, the Messiah, is of God's kingdom and house, not of Satan's kingdom and house.

> Whoever believes in him is not condemned, but whoever does not believe is condemned already, because he has not believed in the name of the only Son of God. (Jn.3:18)

> Do you say of him whom the Father consecrated and sent into the world, "You are blaspheming," because I said, "I am the Son of God"? If I am not doing the works of my Father, then do not believe me; but if I do them, even though you do not believe me, believe the works, that you may know and understand that the Father is in me and I am in the Father. (Jn.10:36–38)

> How much worse punishment, do you think, will be deserved by the one who has trampled underfoot the Son of God, and has profaned the blood of the covenant by which he was sanctified, and has outraged the Spirit of grace? (He.10:29)

11:19

¹⁹ "And if I cast out demons by Beelzebul, by whom do your sons cast them out? Therefore they will be your judges."

3 Illustration 2—religious exorcist: Jesus claims the right to be respected, at least as much as other ministers.

Jesus' second illustration revolves around *the religious exorcists* of the day. Here, Jesus claims the right to be respected, at least as much as other ministers. This is a simple argument. There were Jewish exorcists, sons of the Jewish nation, who tried to cast out devils in the name of God, usually unsuccessfully. Jesus argues that they were not accused of hellish power. Why is He being accused? The question is pointed and instructive, for Jesus always heals and is always successful in casting out evil. Certainly, He should be respected as much if not more than other ministers.

THOUGHT 1. The mistake of the Jews was that they exalted priests (ministers) and religion above God. Many do the same today. They read, quote, and use other ministers as their source much more than they use Jesus and the Holy Scripture.

THOUGHT 2. Jesus Christ should be exalted as the Messiah, the Son of God who alone can cast out evil. Therefore, He ought to be read, quoted, and preached day in and day out. Jesus Christ should be honored by every person.

> That all may honor the Son, just as they honor the Father. Whoever does not honor the Son does not honor the Father who sent him. Truly, truly, I say to you, whoever hears my word and believes him who sent me has eternal life. He does not come into judgment, but has passed from death to life. (Jn.5:23–24)

> You search the Scriptures because you think that in them you have eternal life; and it is they that bear witness about me. (Jn.5:39; see vv.40–47)

> Simon Peter answered him, "Lord, to whom shall we go? You have the words of eternal life." (Jn.6:68)

> The officers answered, "No one ever spoke like this man!" (Jn.7:46)

> Ascribe to the LORD the glory due his name; worship the LORD in the splendor of holiness. (Ps.29:2)

> O LORD, you are my God; I will exalt you; I will praise your name, for you have done wonderful things, plans formed of old, faithful and sure. (Is.25:1)

4 Illustration 3—the finger of God: Jesus claims to possess the power to usher in the kingdom of God.

Jesus uses the *finger of God* as His third illustration. Either He casts out demons by the power of Satan or by the finger (power) of God. The finger of God is the same as the Spirit of God (see Mt.12:28). The power that casts out devils is the power of God. It comes from God and from no one else (see note, pt.3—Lu.11:17-18).

Now note something of crucial importance. Jesus essentially says, "If I possess the power of God, then I possess the power to bring the kingdom of God to you. Wherever the power of God is, there is the kingdom of God, for the power of God is used to bring about the rule and reign of God. Therefore, the kingdom of God is come upon you and is

20 "But if it is by the finger of God that I cast out demons, then the kingdom of God has come upon you."

beginning in this day and age. The power of evil is now being cast out." Jesus is, of course, urging that no one miss the kingdom of God. He is ushering the kingdom in, but it has to be accepted (see DEEPER STUDY # 3—Mt.19:23-24).

> Now after John was arrested, Jesus came into Galilee, proclaiming the gospel of God, and saying, "The time is fulfilled, and the kingdom of God is at hand; repent and believe in the gospel." (Mk.1:14-15)

> The Law and the Prophets were until John; since then the good news of the kingdom of God is preached, and everyone forces his way into it. (Lu.16:16)

> Being asked by the Pharisees when the kingdom of God would come, he answered them, "The kingdom of God is not coming in ways that can be observed, nor will they say, 'Look, here it is!' or 'There!' for behold, the kingdom of God is in the midst of you." (Lu.17:20-21)

5 Illustration 4: a stronger man: Jesus claims to be stronger than Satan, to conquer him and take away his defenses.

Jesus uses a fourth illustration of *a stronger man* to prove His Messiahship. In these verses, He claims to be stronger than Satan. Grasp the meaning of the different parts of this metaphor:

21 "When a strong man, fully armed, guards his own palace, his goods are safe;
22 but when one stronger than he attacks him and overcomes him, he takes away his armor in which he trusted and divides his spoil."

> ➤ Satan is the *strong man* (v.21a). Note he is armed.
> ➤ Satan's "palace" is his kingdom, and his "goods" are people who are subjected to him: people who follow the way of the world, that is, selfishness, the rejection of God, and rebellion against righteousness (v.21b).
> ➤ Satan works to keep his palace (kingdom) and goods (people) "safe" or "in peace," that is, under his rule and reign (v.21c). There is some *peace and comfort* in Satan's realm. Satan will give pleasures to secure a person in his kingdom. But note, it is only for a season (He.11:25; 9:27).
> ➤ The *stronger* Man is Jesus Christ (v.22a).
> ➤ Jesus Christ attacks or comes upon Satan (v.22b).

> Since therefore the children share in flesh and blood, he himself likewise partook of the same things, that through death he might destroy the one who has the power of death, that is, the devil, and deliver all those who through fear of death were subject to lifelong slavery. (He.2:14-15)

> Whoever makes a practice of sinning is of the devil, for the devil has been sinning from the beginning. The reason the Son of God appeared was to destroy the works of the devil. (1 Jn.3:8)

> ➤ Jesus Christ overcomes Satan (v.22c).

> He has delivered us from the domain of darkness and transferred us to the kingdom of his beloved Son, in whom we have redemption, the forgiveness of sins. (Col.1:13-14)

> He disarmed the rulers and authorities and put them to open shame, by triumphing over them in him. (Col.2:15)

> ➤ Jesus Christ takes away Satan's armor, his defenses: delivers the people who are controlled by his strategies (v.22d).

Finally, be strong in the Lord and in the strength of his might. Put on the whole armor of God, that you may be able to stand against the schemes of the devil. (Ep.6:10–11; see vv.12–18)

➢ Jesus Christ divides Satan's spoils: the spoils of a clear mind, clean body, pure heart, and the gifts of the Spirit (v.22d).

Therefore it says, "When he ascended on high he led a host of captives, and he gave gifts to men." (In saying, "He ascended," what does it mean but that he had also descended into the lower regions, the earth? He who descended is the one who also ascended far above all the heavens, that he might fill all things.) And he gave the apostles, the prophets, the evangelists, the shepherds and teachers. (Ep.4:8–11; see Ga.5:22–23)

11:23

²³ "Whoever is not with me is against me, and whoever does not gather with me scatters."

6 Illustration 5—a shepherd and a flock: Jesus claims that a person must follow Him, not try to be neutral.

Jesus' contrasts the actions of gathering and scattering in His fifth illustration, that of *a shepherd and a flock*. A shepherd gathers his flock. Here, Christ is pictured as the shepherd. The person who does not stand with Christ does not gather but instead scatters the flock. Jesus Christ is the decisive figure of history that determines a person's destiny (see note—Lu.7:28). Where a person stands in relation to Jesus Christ determines the success and impact of his or her life.

There is *no neutrality* with Christ: a person is either with Him or against Him. A person either fights against evil or against righteousness, either fights for the kingdom of God or for the kingdom of evil. Standing still is impossible, for standing still is doing nothing for God. Not gathering is scattering: standing still, being neutral, is working for evil by allowing evil to continue and to grow without opposition. A voice of silence is a voice for evil. There is no middle road, no neutral position.

No servant can serve two masters, for either he will hate the one and love the other, or he will be devoted to the one and despise the other. You cannot serve God and money. (Lu.16:13)

You cannot drink the cup of the Lord and the cup of demons. You cannot partake of the table of the Lord and the table of demons. (1 Co.10:21)

He is a double-minded man, unstable in all his ways. (Jas.1:8)

Draw near to God, and he will draw near to you. Cleanse your hands, you sinners, and purify your hearts, you double-minded. (Jas.4:8)

I call heaven and earth to witness against you today, that I have set before you life and death, blessing and curse. Therefore choose life, that you and your offspring may live. (De.30:19)

And Elijah came near to all the people and said, "How long will you go limping between two different opinions? If the Lᴏʀᴅ is God, follow him; but if Baal, then follow him." And the people did not answer him a word. (1 Ki.18:21)

11:24–26

²⁴ "When the unclean spirit has gone out of a person, it passes through waterless places seeking rest, and finding none it says, 'I will return to my house from which I came.'
²⁵ And when it comes, it finds the house swept and put in order.
²⁶ Then it goes and brings seven other spirits more evil than itself, and they enter and dwell there. And the last state of that person is worse than the first."

7 Illustration 6—an empty house or life: Jesus claims that a person must not only reform their life (cast out evil) but also be filled with His very presence.

To prove His deity, Jesus pictures *an empty house or life* in His sixth illustration. Here Jesus claims that a person must turn from self-reformation to Him and be indwelled with His very presence. Note the explanation of this illustration.

Jesus described what happens when an evil spirit is cast out of a person's life:

➢ The spirit wanders through many "waterless" or "dry places," seeking rest but finding none (v.24a).

➢ It says, "I will return to my house" (v.24b). Note the words, "to my house," the place that was so comfortable, the place where the demon was at home and at ease.

Now note what happens when the evil spirit returns to the house—the person it has formerly possessed:

➤ The spirit finds the house swept—clean and put in order and available to be occupied (v.25). The person had removed all rubbish and swept out all the dirt. All of this has to do with reforming and cleaning up one's life. Here, the person cleans the house (their life), but does not invite a new *tenant* (i.e., the Lord Jesus Christ) to move in and occupy the premises.

➤ Finding the house unoccupied, the evil spirit swarms in with more force than ever (v.26). It brings seven other spirits with it, and the person is now worse than ever before with multiplied evil now dwelling within. It is unlikely the person will ever be free again.

Again, the illustration makes the point that it is not enough for people to reform or clean up their lives. They must believe in Christ, receive Him into their lives, be filled with His presence. If they are not, the evil that previously held them captive will return.

> And because lawlessness will be increased, the love of many will grow cold. (Mt.24:12)

> Formerly, when you did not know God, you were enslaved to those that by nature are not gods. But now that you have come to know God, or rather to be known by God, how can you turn back again to the weak and worthless elementary principles of the world, whose slaves you want to be once more? You observe days and months and seasons and years! (Ga.4:8-10)

> While evil people and impostors will go on from bad to worse, deceiving and being deceived. (2 Ti.3:13)

> For if, after they have escaped the defilements of the world through the knowledge of our Lord and Savior Jesus Christ, they are again entangled in them and overcome, the last state has become worse for them than the first. For it would have been better for them never to have known the way of righteousness than after knowing it to turn back from the holy commandment delivered to them. (2 Pe.2:20-21)

THOUGHT 1. The answer to being indwelled with the presence of Christ is not *reformation*—not the changing of the outside or the external—but the *transformation* or *regeneration* of our hearts. Filling our hearts with the Spirit of Christ Himself transforms us into new people.

> Therefore, if anyone is in Christ, he is a new creation. The old has passed away; behold, the new has come. (2 Co.5:17)

> Paul, an apostle of Christ Jesus by the will of God, To the saints who are in Ephesus, and are faithful in Christ Jesus: Grace to you and peace from God our Father and the Lord Jesus Christ. Blessed be the God and Father of our Lord Jesus Christ, who has blessed us in Christ with every spiritual blessing in the heavenly places, even as he chose us in him before the foundation of the world, that we should be holy and blameless before him. In love he predestined us for adoption to himself as sons through Jesus Christ, according to the purpose of his will. (Ep.1:1-5)

> And to put on the new self, created after the likeness of God in true righteousness and holiness. (Ep.4:24)

> By which he has granted to us his precious and very great promises, so that through them you may become partakers of the divine nature, having escaped from the corruption that is in the world because of sinful desire. (2 Pe.1:4)

8 Conclusion—the necessary thing: To hear the Word of God and keep it.

Luke is the only Gospel writer to mention the incident reported in these verses. Apparently, a woman in the crowd was caught up in Jesus' teaching and presence. She spontaneously exclaimed that a woman who could give birth to one like Jesus was to be blessed. But note what Jesus says in verse 28. There is a greater blessing than what even Mary had. Imagine! A greater blessing than being able to testify that one had given birth to Jesus! What is it? "Blessed are those who hear the Word of God and keep it"!

²⁷ As he said these things, a woman in the crowd raised her voice and said to him, "Blessed is the womb that bore you, and the breasts at which you nursed!"
²⁸ But he said, "Blessed rather are those who hear the word of God and keep it!"

> Whoever has my commandments and keeps them, he it is who loves me. And he who loves me will be loved by my Father, and I will love him and manifest myself to him. (Jn.14:21)

But the one who looks into the perfect law, the law of liberty, and perseveres, being no hearer who forgets but a doer who acts, he will be blessed in his doing. (Jas.1:25)

And whatever we ask we receive from him, because we keep his commandments and do what pleases him. (1 Jn.3:22)

Now therefore, if you will indeed obey my voice and keep my covenant, you shall be my treasured possession among all peoples, for all the earth is mine. (Ex.19:5)

Oh that they had such a heart as this always, to fear me and to keep all my commandments, that it might go well with them and with their descendants forever! (De.5:29)

If they listen and serve him, they complete their days in prosperity, and their years in pleasantness. (Jb.36:11)

(Mt.5:14–16; 12:38–42; Mk.4:21–22; Lu.8:16)

29 When the crowds were increasing, he began to say, "This generation is an evil generation. It seeks for a sign, but no sign will be given to it except the sign of Jonah."

30 For as Jonah became a sign to the people of Nineveh, so will the Son of Man be to this generation.

31 The queen of the South will rise up at the judgment with the men of this generation and condemn them, for she came from the ends of the earth to hear the wisdom of Solomon, and behold, something greater than Solomon is here.

32 The men of Nineveh will rise up at the judgment with this generation and condemn it, for they repented at the preaching of Jonah, and behold, something greater than Jonah is here.

33 No one after lighting a lamp puts it in a cellar or under a basket, but on a stand, so that those who enter may see the light.

34 Your eye is the lamp of your body. When your eye is healthy, your whole body is full of light, but when it is bad, your body is full of darkness.

35 Therefore be careful lest the light in you be darkness.

36 If then your whole body is full of light, having no part dark, it will be wholly bright, as when a lamp with its rays gives you light."

1. **The crowds thronged Jesus**
   a. Jesus charged: This is an evil generation
   b. The reason: They sought a sign

2. **The one and only sign to be given: The sign of Jonah, that is, the resurrection of Jesus Christ**

3. **The sign's (resurrection) effect: It will condemn this evil generation**
   a. Because they did not seek Christ (as the queen sought wisdom)

   b. Because they did not repent at hearing Christ's preaching (as Nineveh repented)

4. **The sign's (resurrection) visibility: It is as clearly seen as a shining lamp**
   a. A fact: A shining lamp is not hid but is placed where it gives light
   b. A choice: To see the sign (resurrection) with a healthy eye or a diseased eye

   c. A warning: Beware of a diseased eye, of a body full of darkness
   d. A promise: A healthy eye will give great light

Division V

The Son of Man's Great Journey to Jerusalem (Stage I): His Mission and Public Challenge, 9:51–13:21

J. The Ultimate Proof that Jesus is the Messiah: The Resurrection, 11:29–36

(Mt.5:14–16; 12:38–42; Mk.4:21–22; Lu.8:16)

11:29–36
Introduction

Among the abundant evidence that Jesus Christ is truly the Messiah, the Son of the living God, one proof stands head and shoulders above the rest. The most powerful proof that Jesus is the Messiah—the decisive argument—is the resurrection. People may seek for other evidence and other signs, but God has given this one supreme sign. It is *the* sign that Jesus Christ is who He claims to be. No other sign will ever be given. The resurrection of Jesus Christ leaves people without excuse. This is, *The Ultimate Proof that Jesus is the Messiah: The Resurrection*, 11:29-36.

1. The crowds thronged Jesus (v.29).
2. The one and only sign to be given: The sign of Jonah, that is, the resurrection of Jesus Christ (vv.29–30).
3. The sign's (resurrection) effect: It will condemn this evil generation (vv.31-32).
4. The sign's (resurrection) visibility: It is as clearly seen as a shining lamp (vv.33-36).

11:29

²⁹ When the crowds were increasing, he began to say, "This generation is an evil generation. It seeks for a sign, but no sign will be given to it except the sign of Jonah."

1 The crowds thronged Jesus.

As Jesus taught and ministered, the crowd continued to grow. The Lord had a strong message for those who were thronging him, a message He delivered frankly and to the point.

a. Jesus charged: This is an evil generation.

The Lord leveled a serious charge against His generation: "This is an evil generation." Why would He make such a harsh statement?

b. The reason: They sought a sign.

Jesus judged the present generation as evil because they sought a sign. What is wrong with seeking some proof that Jesus is who He claims to be? Nothing. There is nothing wrong with seeking evidence that Jesus is the Son of God. The problem is not in seeking evidence; the problem is in seeking *more and more* evidence. God had given abundant evidence that Jesus is His Son, but the people would not accept it. It was not enough to convince them; they wanted something *sensational*. Think for a moment.

What greater evidence could God give than to *reveal Himself* to humanity? The greatest sign in all the world was to have God's very own Son stand in the people's presence so they could see and touch Him.

> And the Word became flesh and dwelt among us, and we have seen his glory, glory as of the only Son from the Father, full of grace and truth. (John bore witness about him, and cried out, "This was he of whom I said, 'He who comes after me ranks before me, because he was before me.'") For from his fullness we have all received, grace upon grace. (Jn.1:14–16)

> That which was from the beginning, which we have heard, which we have seen with our eyes, which we looked upon and have touched with our hands, concerning the word of life— the life was made manifest, and we have seen it, and testify to it and proclaim to you the eternal life, which was with the Father and was made manifest to us— that which we have seen and heard we proclaim also to you, so that you too may have fellowship with us; and indeed our fellowship is with the Father and with his Son Jesus Christ. (1 Jn.1:1–3)

In addition, what greater evidence could God give that Jesus is His Son than to meet all the needs of people while Jesus was among them? The greatest evidence in all the world was seeing Jesus demonstrate the love and power of God . . .

- by feeding the hungry
- by calming both nature and people's fear of nature
- by preaching and teaching as no other man has ever done
- by healing all sorts of sicknesses and infirmities
- by casting out evil spirits
- by raising the dead

> **Blessed are those who hunger and thirst for righteousness, for they shall be satisfied. (Mt.5:6)**

> **But whoever drinks of the water that I will give him will never be thirsty again. The water that I will give him will become in him a spring of water welling up to eternal life. (Jn.4:14)**

> **On the last day of the feast, the great day, Jesus stood up and cried out, "If anyone thirsts, let him come to me and drink." (Jn.7:37)**

> **And my God will supply every need of yours according to his riches in glory in Christ Jesus. (Ph.4:19)**

> **They feast on the abundance of your house, and you give them drink from the river of your delights. (Ps.36:8; see Ps.23:1f)**

> **And the LORD will guide you continually and satisfy your desire in scorched places and make your bones strong; and you shall be like a watered garden, like a spring of water, whose waters do not fail. (Is.58:11)**

As if that were not enough, what greater evidence could God give that He was bringing salvation to mankind than to send His Son into the world to personally save people? What greater evidence could God give than. . . .

- to have His Son live as a Man, living a perfect and sinless life, and, by His perfection, to secure righteousness for all who would believe
- to have His Son die for sinners
- to raise His Son from the dead

People were and are totally unjustified in seeking additional signs. God has given the greatest evidence that could ever be given. If people reject the proofs already given, they will reject any sign, no matter what the sign might be. Needing signs and evidence is not the problem. The problem of unbelievers is twofold.

First, people do not believe simply because they do not want to believe. They want to live as they desire, to do their own thing. They want no Lord over them, certainly not one who demands total commitment. The unbelieving heart is hard, and people are obstinate in their unbelief (see notes—Lu.10:21; DEEPER STUDY # 4—Mt.12:24; note—12:31-32).

Second, those who will not believe do not understand the love and the faith of God, that is, what God is truly all about. They fail to see what God is after and has always been after: faith and love, not signs and works. God wants people to simply believe and love Him because of who He is and because of what He does for them. The true religion of God is not a religion of works and signs, but of faith and love in Christ Jesus, His own Son (see DEEPER STUDY # 2—Jn.2:24; DEEPER STUDY # 1—4:22; note—4:48-49; DEEPER STUDY # 1—Ro.4:1-25; note—4:4-5; see Ac.2:22).

2 The one and only sign to be given: The sign of Jonah, that is, the resurrection of Jesus Christ.

Jesus said that the one and only sign verifying His Messiahship would be given (v.29). He referred to that sign as "the sign of Jonah," who was brought back from the belly of the huge fish. The "sign of Jonah" points to Jesus' resurrection from the dead (see note—Mt.12:38-40). The resurrection is the *great proof* that Jesus is the Messiah, the Savior of the world. Christ's resurrection declares that He is the Son of God *in* or *with power* (Gk. dunamei, *doo-nah'-may*)—with explosive force (Ro.1:4).

> [29] When the crowds were increasing, he began to say, "This generation is an evil generation. It seeks for a sign, but no sign will be given to it except the sign of Jonah.
>
> [30] For as Jonah became a sign to the people of Nineveh, so will the Son of Man be to this generation."

Here Jesus claims to be greater than Jonah (v.32). He claims to be the greatest messenger who has ever come, the Messiah Himself. Since His coming, all people are definitely without excuse. The worst sinners in history repented at the preaching of a mere man, the prophet Jonah. Now the Messiah Himself, God's own Son, has come. And He has preached and announced that the kingdom of God itself is at hand. Every person is now, beyond question, without excuse.

11:31–32

31 "The queen of the South will rise up at the judgment with the men of this generation and condemn them, for she came from the ends of the earth to hear the wisdom of Solomon, and behold, something greater than Solomon is here.

32 The men of Nineveh will rise up at the judgment with this generation and condemn it, for they repented at the preaching of Jonah, and behold, something greater than Jonah is here."

3 The sign's (resurrection) effect: It will condemn this evil generation.

Jesus declares that the sign of His Messiahship—His resurrection—would condemn this evil generation. Two witnesses from the Old Testament—the Queen of Sheba and the people of Nineveh—would also condemn them at their judgment. These two witnesses illustrate the two reasons the unbelieving generation will be judged.

a. Because they did not seek Christ (as the queen sought wisdom) (v.31).

This evil generation did not seek Jesus, the one who is the truth. In verse 31, Jesus gives a prime example in referencing the Queen of Sheba (see 1 Ki.10:1f; 2 Chr.9:1f). The Queen of Sheba demonstrates how a person is to seek the truth and how important it is to seek Christ. In going to Jerusalem to hear the wisdom of Solomon, she had to seek as diligently and go through as much as anyone ever has in seeking the truth. Note the circumstances that made her search difficult.

First, she had a long and perilous search. She had to travel from "the ends of the earth" to seek the truth.

Second, she had heavy responsibilities. She was a queen with demanding duties and a busy schedule as the head of state. As with all heads of state, she had much demanding her time and presence and depending on her care, yet she let nothing stop her search for the truth.

Third, she had a high level of uncertainty associated with her search. In many ways, her search was a gamble. She could not be absolutely certain that Solomon was as wise in the truth as he was said to be. Reputations become exaggerated when spread by word of mouth, and she knew this. In addition, she had no personal invitation to visit Solomon. She could not be sure he would see her or grant much time to her.

Fourth, she had to bear terrible prejudice. She was a woman in a man's world. In her day women were nothing more than chattel, possessed and used by men for their own pleasure as they so desired.

The Queen of Sheba's diligent seeking will stand in the day of judgment as a testimony against all who fail to seek after Christ. Her seeking will leave all without excuse. There is no distance too far, no road too perilous, no responsibility so important, no question so weighty, no prejudice or opposition so strong that it should keep a person from seeking after Christ. The Queen of Sheba faced all this, yet despite all, she sought the truth. It was the foremost priority of her life; therefore, her example leaves everyone without excuse.

> But seek first the kingdom of God and his righteousness, and all these things will be added to you. (Mt.6:33)

> And I tell you, ask, and it will be given to you; seek, and you will find; knock, and it will be opened to you. For everyone who asks receives, and the one who seeks finds, and to the one who knocks it will be opened. (Lu.11:9–10; see vv.5–8)

> And he made from one man every nation of mankind to live on all the face of the earth, having determined allotted periods and the boundaries of their dwelling place, that they should seek God, and perhaps feel their way toward him and find him. Yet he is actually not far from each one of us. (Ac.17:26–27)

> But from there you will seek the LORD your God and you will find him, if you search after him with all your heart and with all your soul. (De.4:29)

Yes, if you call out for insight and raise your voice for understanding, if you seek it like silver and search for it as for hidden treasures, then you will understand the fear of the LORD and find the knowledge of God. (Pr.2:3–5)

Seek the LORD while he may be found; call upon him while he is near. (Is.55:6)

In verse 31, Jesus makes the point that He is greater than Solomon. The Queen of Sheba overcame her extreme circumstances to meet with Solomon, yet the people of Jesus' day had the one greater than Solomon in their midst. He is the way, the truth, and the life. Imagine! He is *life* itself (Jn.14:6). He is the one whom all people must seek and find or else face condemnation.

Since Christ's coming, all people are definitely without excuse. The most improbable person (the Queen of Sheba) went to the farthest extremes possible to seek after the truth from a mere man, Solomon. Now the Messiah, who is *the truth* Himself, has come and revealed the truth of God. Beyond question, every person is now without excuse.

And the Word became flesh and dwelt among us, and we have seen his glory, glory as of the only Son from the Father, full of grace and truth. (Jn.1:14)

Jesus said to him, "I am the way, and the truth, and the life. No one comes to the Father except through me." (Jn.14:6)

Jesus said to him, "Have I been with you so long, and you still do not know me, Philip? Whoever has seen me has seen the Father. How can you say, 'Show us the Father'? Do you not believe that I am in the Father and the Father is in me? The words that I say to you I do not speak on my own authority, but the Father who dwells in me does his works. Believe me that I am in the Father and the Father is in me, or else believe on account of the works themselves." (Jn.14:9–11)

But as it is, Christ has obtained a ministry that is as much more excellent than the old as the covenant he mediates is better, since it is enacted on better promises. (He.8:6)

And to Jesus, the mediator of a new covenant, and to the sprinkled blood that speaks a better word than the blood of Abel. See that you do not refuse him who is speaking. For if they did not escape when they refused him who warned them on earth, much less will we escape if we reject him who warns from heaven. (He.12:24–25)

b. **Because they did not repent at hearing Christ's preaching (as Nineveh repented) (v.32).**
Jesus uses the people of Nineveh to contrast with this evil generation's refusal to repent upon hearing Jesus' preaching. The Ninevites stand as a prime example of *repentance* and just how essential repentance is. People must repent, or else they will be condemned.

The truth of God's Word is tells us a day of judgment awaits us in the future. Note the words, "at" or "in the judgment." There is a definite day of judgment.

The Ninevites' repentance will be used as a testimony in the day of judgment. The people of Nineveh are the prime example of people's turning to God from the depth of sin. They had fallen into the pit of sin, as deep as a people can fall. Yet, they repented at the preaching of Jonah.

Jesus teaches that the Ninevites' repentance leaves all without excuse. Why? There is no one who has fallen any deeper into sin than they did, yet they repented. They show that anyone can turn to God from sin no matter how terrible their sin is. No person has an excuse for not turning to God.

As with Solomon, Jesus declares that He is greater than Jonah. The people of Nineveh repented at the preaching of a mere man, yet this evil generation refused to repent when God's own Son preached to them.

No, I tell you; but unless you repent, you will all likewise perish. (Lu.13:3)

And Peter said to them, "Repent and be baptized every one of you in the name of Jesus Christ for the forgiveness of your sins, and you will receive the gift of the Holy Spirit." (Ac.2:38)

Repent therefore, and turn back, that your sins may be blotted out. (Ac.3:19)

The times of ignorance God overlooked, but now he commands all people everywhere to repent. (Ac.17:30)

If my people who are called by my name humble themselves, and pray and seek my face and turn from their wicked ways, then I will hear from heaven and will forgive their sin and heal their land. (2 Chr.7:14)

Let the wicked forsake his way, and the unrighteous man his thoughts; let him return to the LORD, that he may have compassion on him, and to our God, for he will abundantly pardon. (Is.55:7)

365

4 The sign's (resurrection) visibility: It is as clearly seen as a shining lamp.

The resurrection of Jesus Christ stands as a sign that is clearly visible to the world. It is like a lamp shining brightly in the darkness of the world's sin and unbelief. However, that light—the light that brilliantly beams the truth about God's Son—must be viewed with a healthy eye.

11:33-36

[33] "No one after lighting a lamp puts it in a cellar or under a basket, but on a stand, so that those who enter may see the light. [34] Your eye is the lamp of your body. When your eye is healthy, your whole body is full of light, but when it is bad, your body is full of darkness. [35] Therefore be careful lest the light in you be darkness. [36] If then your whole body is full of light, having no part dark, it will be wholly bright, as when a lamp with its rays gives you light."

a. **A fact: A shining lamp is not hid but is placed where it gives light (v.33).**

Just as nobody hides a shining lamp, Jesus says that the resurrection would not take place in secret nor would it be a secret. Jesus was resurrected openly and publicly so that all could "see the light" and be convinced that He is the true Messiah.

b. **A choice: to see the sign (resurrection) with a healthy eye or a diseased eye (v.34).**

A person must decide how they view Christ's resurrection, with a healthy eye or diseased eye. The healthy or good eye concentrates on seeing the light, the way of God and righteousness. The bad eye focuses on the world and material things, the flesh and passion, pleasure and stimulation, self and wealth. Such an eye refuses to see the obvious sign of Christ's deity and lordship.

Remember, the one sign God has given of who Jesus is—the resurrection—is dramatically clear. God has not kept the sign a secret nor has He hidden it. The sign can be seen just as clearly as a searchlight in the dark of midnight. The only conceivable thing that can prevent a person from seeing it is a bad or unhealthy eye; and if a person's eye is bad, their whole body is full of darkness, that is, full of evil and, ultimately, eternal death.

c. **A warning: beware of a diseased eye, of a body full of darkness (v.35).**

Every person thinks that what they see, even with a diseased eye, is the truth. Jesus' warning is clear: make sure that you are looking through a healthy eye, and make sure that what is in you is light and not darkness. The resurrection is the light of God. *Seeing any other light is darkness.* It is looking for light and truth with a diseased eye.

d. **A promise: a healthy eye will give great light (v.36).**

Very simply, if a person is "full of light" from having seen the resurrection and allows no part of darkness (doubt, unbelief, false belief) to enter, then their whole being will be full of light. It will be like a lamp shining directly and brightly on them, and it will transform their lives radically.

THOUGHT 1. Jesus Christ is the Light of the world; He is the Light to which people must open the door of their dark hearts. He is the Light which people must take into their sinful lives and world of darkness.

> In him was life, and the life was the light of men. . . . The true light, which gives light to everyone, was coming into the world. (Jn.1:4, 9)

> Again Jesus spoke to them, saying, "I am the light of the world. Whoever follows me will not walk in darkness, but will have the light of life." (Jn.8:12)

> I have come into the world as light, so that whoever believes in me may not remain in darkness. (Jn.12:46)

> For God, who said, "Let light shine out of darkness," has shone in our hearts to give the light of the knowledge of the glory of God in the face of Jesus Christ. (2 Co.4:6)

> The people who walked in darkness have seen a great light; those who dwelt in a land of deep darkness, on them has light shone. (Is.9:2)

K. The Severe Charges Against Religionists, 11:37–54

(Mt.23:13–36; Mk.12:38–40)

³⁷ While Jesus was speaking, a Pharisee asked him to dine with him, so he went in and reclined at table.

³⁸ The Pharisee was astonished to see that he did not first wash before dinner.

³⁹ And the Lord said to him, "Now you Pharisees cleanse the outside of the cup and of the dish, but inside you are full of greed and wickedness.

⁴⁰ You fools! Did not he who made the outside make the inside also?

⁴¹ But give as alms those things that are within, and behold, everything is clean for you.

⁴² But woe to you Pharisees! For you tithe mint and rue and every herb, and neglect justice and the love of God. These you ought to have done, without neglecting the others.

⁴³ Woe to you Pharisees! For you love the best seat in the synagogues and greetings in the marketplaces.

⁴⁴ Woe to you! For you are like unmarked graves, and people walk over them without knowing it."

⁴⁵ One of the lawyers answered him, "Teacher, in saying these things you insult us also."

⁴⁶ And he said, "Woe to you lawyers also! For you load people with burdens hard to bear, and you yourselves do not touch the burdens with one of your fingers.

⁴⁷ Woe to you! For you build the tombs of the prophets whom your fathers killed.

⁴⁸ So you are witnesses and you consent to the deeds of your fathers, for they killed them, and you build their tombs.

⁴⁹ Therefore also the Wisdom of God said, 'I will send them prophets and apostles, some of whom they will kill and persecute,'

1. **A Pharisee invited Jesus to dine**
   a. Jesus accepted the invitation

   b. Jesus was questioned about ceremonial cleanliness, then made seven severe charges against religionists

2. **Charge 1: Religionists are ceremonially clean, but inwardly unclean**
   a. They clean the outside but not the inside
   b. God made both the outside and the inside (the hearts) of people
   c. The giving of one's heart cleanses everything

3. **Charge 2: Religionists obey God in tithing but ignore justice and love**

4. **Charge 3: Religionists crave prominence and honor**

5. **Charge 4: Religionists mislead others, causing them to become unclean**

6. **Charge 5: Religionists burden people with rules and regulations**

   a. A lawyer's (an expert in the law) spiritual blindness
   b. Jesus' charge: They too were guilty

7. **Charge 6: Religionists honor the true prophets of God—as long as they are dead**
   a. They honor the past servants of God whom their forefathers killed

   b. They reject the present servants of God

c. The judgment to be required of them[DS1, 2]

8. Charge 7: Religionists have substituted the truth about God (Scriptures) with their own rules and ideas

9. Conclusion: A reaction of hostility and opposition toward Jesus

[50] so that the blood of all the prophets, shed from the foundation of the world, may be charged against this generation,

[51] from the blood of Abel to the blood of Zechariah, who perished between the altar and the sanctuary. Yes, I tell you, it will be required of this generation.

[52] Woe to you lawyers! For you have taken away the key of knowledge. You did not enter yourselves, and you hindered those who were entering."

[53] As he went away from there, the scribes and the Pharisees began to press him hard and to provoke him to speak about many things,

[54] lying in wait for him, to catch him in something he might say.

Division V

The Son of Man's Great Journey to Jerusalem (Stage I): His Mission and Public Challenge, 9:51–13:21

K. The Severe Charges Against Religionists, 11:37–54

(Mt.23:13–36; Mk.12:38–40)

11:37–54
Introduction

Most people feel they are religious to some degree. For that reason, the religious person needs to pay close attention to what Jesus says in this passage. There is great danger in religion, for it deceives people into thinking they are right when they are not. Every person adhering to religion needs to examine their hearts and lives to make sure their religion is true and that what they are following is right. As seen in this passage, Jesus was severe in His charges against false religionists (see outline and notes—Mt.23:1-36; Lu.15:25-32; 18:9-12; Ro.2:17-29 for more discussion and application).

What is meant by the term "religionist?" Broadly stated, a religionist is someone who strictly adheres to a man-made system of worship or teachings. Many man-made religions are totally foreign to God's Word. Many others, however, start with God's Word and deviate from it. The specific religionists to whom Jesus addresses here are the Pharisees and Scribes. While the details Jesus mentions may not apply to all who adhere to a religion, the principles taught do. This is, *The Severe Charges Against Religionists*, 11:37-54.

1. A Pharisee invited Jesus to dine (vv.37–38).
2. Charge 1: Religionists are ceremonially clean, but inwardly unclean (vv.39–41).
3. Charge 2: Religionists obey God in tithing, but ignore justice and love (v.42).
4. Charge 3: Religionists crave prominence and honor (v.43).
5. Charge 4: Religionists mislead others, causing them to become unclean (v.44).
6. Charge 5: Religionists burden people with rules and regulations (vv.45-46).
7. Charge 6: Religionists honor the true prophets of God—as long as they are dead (vv.47-51).
8. Charge 7: Religionists have substituted the truth about God (Scriptures) with their own rules and ideas (v.52).
9. Conclusion: A reaction of hostility and opposition toward Jesus (vv.53-54).

1 A Pharisee invited Jesus to dine.

As Jesus was speaking about the evil generation that refused to believe, a Pharisee invited Him to dine with him. Most likely, this Pharisee was in the audience listening to Jesus. For some reason, He wanted to talk personally with Jesus, so he invited Him to a meal.

a. Jesus accepted the invitation (v.37).

Jesus accepted the man's invitation. When He entered the man's home, the Lord went straight to the table and sat down to eat without washing His hands.

37 While Jesus was speaking, a Pharisee asked him to dine with him, so he went in and reclined at table.
38 The Pharisee was astonished to see that he did not first wash before dinner.

b. Jesus was questioned about ceremonial cleanliness, then made seven severe charges against religionists (v.38).

Jesus' failure to wash astonished the Pharisee, for it was a serious violation of religious law. The requirement to wash had nothing to do with cleanliness, but with ceremonial purity. The religious leaders taught that a person's hands had been in contact with a sinful world; therefore, the person needed to wash hands before eating to prevent evil from entering the body. The Pharisee (religionist) was thinking to himself that Jesus had seriously violated this law. Jesus, of course, knew His thoughts and began to reply. His reply was in the form of seven severe charges against those who adhere strictly to a religion.

2 Charge 1: Religionists are ceremonially clean, but inwardly unclean.

Jesus' first charge was that the religionists were clean ceremonially but unclean within. Their religion was merely outward. They kept their religious rituals, but they did nothing about their wicked hearts.

39 And the Lord said to him, "Now you Pharisees cleanse the outside of the cup and of the dish, but inside you are full of greed and wickedness.
40 You fools! Did not he who made the outside make the inside also?
41 But give as alms those things that are within, and behold, everything is clean for you."

a. They clean the outside but not the inside (v.39).

Jesus illustrates this point by describing a person washing dishes. The person washes the outside of the cup and dish but leaves the inside dirty. The Pharisees were like these half washed dishes. Outwardly, they were clean, but their hearts were filthy and full of *greed* (Gk. harpagēs, *har-pah-ghace'*)—plunder, extortion, robbery, taking by force—and *wickedness*.

Note that Jesus said the Pharisees' hearts were *full* of plunder and wickedness. What did Jesus mean? Religionists—those who adhere to man-made traditions and teachings rather than God's Word—are *plundering* the way of God, trying to *seize* God's kingdom their own way instead of following God's way. They are committing extortion against God by robbing God of the salvation He has set up. Their wickedness is that of disobeying God and refusing to follow Jesus, who is the only way of righteousness established by God (Ro.10:3-4; Ph.3:9). Instead of coming to God by Jesus Christ, religionists try to come to God through their own righteousness. They try to make themselves clean by keeping their religious ceremonies and rituals (see note—Mt.23:25-26 for more discussion and a different explanation).

THOUGHT 1. Note two critical lessons that must be heeded by all religionists.

1) Jesus Christ is God's righteousness.

> But now the righteousness of God has been manifested apart from the law, although the Law and the Prophets bear witness to it— the righteousness of God through faith in Jesus Christ for all who believe. For there is no distinction: for all have sinned and fall short of the glory of God, and are justified by his grace as a gift, through the redemption that is in Christ Jesus, whom God put forward as a propitiation by his blood, to be received by faith. This was to show God's righteousness, because in his divine forbearance he had passed over former sins. (Ro.3:21-25)

> For, being ignorant of the righteousness of God, and seeking to establish their own, they did not submit to God's righteousness. For Christ is the end of the law for righteousness to everyone who believes. For Moses writes about the righteousness that is based on the law, that the person who does the commandments shall live by them. (Ro.10:3-5)

> And be found in him, not having a righteousness of my own that comes from the law, but that which comes through faith in Christ, the righteousness from God that depends on faith. (Ph.3:9)

2) No person, religious or non-religious, can establish their own righteousness. They cannot make themselves clean enough to approach God: not by works, nor by religious ceremony and worship, nor by cleaning up their lives outwardly.

> For I tell you, unless your righteousness exceeds that of the scribes and Pharisees, you will never enter the kingdom of heaven. (Mt.5:20)

> On that day many will say to me, "Lord, Lord, did we not prophesy in your name, and cast out demons in your name, and do many mighty works in your name?" And then will I declare to them, "I never knew you; depart from me, you workers of lawlessness." (Mt.7:22-23)

> For by works of the law no human being will be justified in his sight, since through the law comes knowledge of sin. (Ro.3:20)

> Yet we know that a person is not justified by works of the law but through faith in Jesus Christ, so we also have believed in Christ Jesus, in order to be justified by faith in Christ and not by works of the law, because by works of the law no one will be justified. (Ga.2:16)

> For by grace you have been saved through faith. And this is not your own doing; it is the gift of God, not a result of works, so that no one may boast. (Ep.2:8-9)

> But when the goodness and loving kindness of God our Savior appeared, he saved us, not because of works done by us in righteousness, but according to his own mercy, by the washing of regeneration and renewal of the Holy Spirit, whom he poured out on us richly through Jesus Christ our Savior, so that being justified by his grace we might become heirs according to the hope of eternal life. (Tit.3:4-7)

b. God made both the outside and the inside (the hearts) of people (v.40).

Jesus says the outside is not all that is unclean. The inside—the heart—is also unclean and must be cleansed to become acceptable to God. Note that He calls religionists "fools." God made the whole person, the heart as well as the body. An outward righteousness is not enough; in fact, it is no righteousness at all.

THOUGHT 1. The heart is the source of evil; therefore, it has to be cleansed by Christ.

> For from within, out of the heart of man, come evil thoughts, sexual immorality, theft, murder, adultery. (Mk.7:21)

> Take care, brothers, lest there be in any of you an evil, unbelieving heart, leading you to fall away from the living God. (He.3:12)

> This is an evil in all that is done under the sun, that the same event happens to all. Also, the hearts of the children of man are full of evil, and madness is in their hearts while they live, and after that they go to the dead. (Ec.9:3)

> The heart is deceitful above all things, and desperately sick; who can understand it? (Je.17:9)

c. The giving of one's heart cleanses everything (v.41).

In verse 41, Jesus describes the giving of one's heart to God in terms the Pharisees would easily understand: He compared it to giving money. The Pharisees were quite conscientious about giving tithes precisely, and they boasted in doing so (v.42; 18:11-12). They also boasted in giving alms to the poor (Mt.6:1-4). Jesus told the Pharisees that they needed to give what was *within* them the same way they gave alms. If we will give our hearts to God, then we will become clean in all things. A cleansed heart results in a cleansed life.

THOUGHT 1. Christ changes a person from the inside out; He cleanses the heart. When our hearts are changed, a change in our outward actions will follow.

As for that in the good soil, they are those who, hearing the word, hold it fast in an honest and good heart, and bear fruit with patience. (Lu.8:15)

But thanks be to God, that you who were once slaves of sin have become obedient from the heart to the standard of teaching to which you were committed, and, having been set free from sin, have become slaves of righteousness. For when you were slaves of sin, you were free in regard to righteousness. But what fruit were you getting at that time from the things of which you are now ashamed? For the end of those things is death. But now that you have been set free from sin and have become slaves of God, the fruit you get leads to sanctification and its end, eternal life. For the wages of sin is death, but the free gift of God is eternal life in Christ Jesus our Lord. (Ro.6:17-18, 20-23)

Because, if you confess with your mouth that Jesus is Lord and believe in your heart that God raised him from the dead, you will be saved. For with the heart one believes and is justified, and with the mouth one confesses and is saved. (Ro.10:9-10)

Let us draw near with a true heart in full assurance of faith, with our hearts sprinkled clean from an evil conscience and our bodies washed with pure water. Let us hold fast the confession of our hope without wavering, for he who promised is faithful. (He.10:22-23)

3 Charge 2: Religionists obey God in tithing but ignore justice and love.

The Pharisees took tithing very seriously. Tithing is the command of God and is meant to be a joyful experience (De.14:22-23; Lev.27:30). The Pharisees wanted to make sure they did exactly what God commanded, so they went beyond what God actually required. They tithed of every little thing, even the plants of their gardens and the small potted plants they might have in their homes (see DEEPER STUDY # 6—Mt.23:23 for more discussion.)

42 "But woe to you Pharisees! For you tithe mint and rue and every herb, and neglect justice and the love of God. These you ought to have done, without neglecting the others."

Jesus does not say that going beyond the tithe is wrong. Jesus is not discussing tithing; He simply uses the tithe to illustrate His point. The point is that the Pharisees stressed outward duties such as tithing and ceremony, ritual and ordinances, works and form; but they neglected the inward duties such as *justice and love of God.*

➢ *Justice* has to do with the way we treat others. Religionists and their organizations are the recipients of the tithe and offerings of God's people. The monies and gifts are too often coveted for themselves and the building of their organization more than for ministering to the poor, the oppressed, and the lost. Too often monies are kept for extravagant buildings and livelihoods and personal comfort—monies that God wants used to feed the hungry, clothe the naked, house orphans, care for widows and reach the lost. Such extravagance and misuse of the tithe reveals an unjust heart. It is cheating the needy of the world. It is as Jesus said, neglecting or bypassing justice. It is overlooking what is right and just in a world that reels under the weight of millions who are in desperate need.

➢ *The love of God* is both the love He has given us in Christ and the love we are to have for Him and others.

And a second is like it: You shall love your neighbor as yourself. (Mt.22:39)

Let love be genuine. Abhor what is evil; hold fast to what is good. (Ro.12:9)

Masters, treat your bondservants justly and fairly, knowing that you also have a Master in heaven. (Col.4:1)

Justice, and only justice, you shall follow, that you may live and inherit the land that the LORD your God is giving you. (De.16:20)

Give justice to the weak and the fatherless; maintain the right of the afflicted and the destitute. (Ps.82:3)

To do righteousness and justice is more acceptable to the LORD than sacrifice. (Pr.21:3)

Thus says the LORD of hosts, Render true judgments, show kindness and mercy to one another, do not oppress the widow, the fatherless, the sojourner, or the poor, and let none of you devise evil against another in your heart. (Zec.7:9-10)

4 Charge 3: Religionists crave prominence and honor.

Jesus' third charge against religionists is that of craving prominence and honor. The Pharisees loved the most prominent positions and seats. They sat at the front of the synagogues, facing the congregation. Many churches have individuals who, like the Pharisees, seek prominent positions and seats.

11:43

⁴³ "Woe to you Pharisees! For you love the best seat in the synagogues and greetings in the marketplaces."

In addition, they loved the "greetings in the marketplaces"—being called by titles that honored and recognized them. In Jesus' day it was "Rabbi." In our day they are the various titles we give to honor a person above others. However, Jesus did not say that having a position or title is wrong. It is the *love* of these that is condemned, the pride that relishing in such titles reveals.

THOUGHT 1. We need to always be open with ourselves and search our hearts honestly for pride.

> How can you believe, when you receive glory from one another and do not seek the glory that comes from the only God? (Jn.5:44)

> I have written something to the church, but Diotrephes, who likes to put himself first, does not acknowledge our authority. (3 Jn.9)

> Man in his pomp will not remain; he is like the beasts that perish. This is the path of those who have foolish confidence; yet after them people approve of their boasts. Selah. (Ps.49:12–13)

> For when he dies he will carry nothing away; his glory will not go down after him. (Ps.49:17)

> Therefore Sheol has enlarged its appetite and opened its mouth beyond measure, and the nobility of Jerusalem and her multitude will go down, her revelers and he who exults in her. (Is.5:14)

11:44

⁴⁴ "Woe to you! For you are like unmarked graves, and people walk over them without knowing it."

5 Charge 4: Religionists mislead others, causing them to become unclean.

Jesus' fourth charge against the Pharisees is that they misled others and made them unclean and corrupt. In verse 44, Jesus uses one of the religionists' ceremonial regulations to illustrate His point. According to pharisaical law, a person was considered to be unclean if they walked over a grave. Note exactly what Jesus says in this verse. The Pharisees were like unmarked graves. People who walked over unmarked graves did not know they were doing something that made them unclean. In the same way, the Pharisees misled the people. The people did not realize that their religious leaders were corrupting them (see note—Mt.23:27–28 for more discussion). They did not realize they were doing wrong by following them.

> So you also outwardly appear righteous to others, but within you are full of hypocrisy and lawlessness. (Mt.23:28)

> In the meantime, when so many thousands of the people had gathered together that they were trampling one another, he began to say to his disciples first, "Beware of the leaven of the Pharisees, which is hypocrisy. Nothing is covered up that will not be revealed, or hidden that will not be known." (Lu.12:1–2)

> For it is shameful even to speak of the things that they do in secret. (Ep.5:12)

> They profess to know God, but they deny him by their works. They are detestable, disobedient, unfit for any good work. (Tit.1:16)

6 Charge 5: Religionists burden people with rules and regulations.

As to be expected, the Pharisees and Scribes present were becoming enraged as Jesus presented these charges. One spoke up, and our Lord responded with the fifth charge: the religionists burdened people with overwhelming rules and regulations.

a. A lawyer's (an expert in the law) spiritual blindness (v.46a).

A lawyer present seems to have excluded himself and his profession from Jesus' charges—until something clicked in his mind. Apparently, he had been applying all of Jesus' charges to someone else. It never dawned on him that Jesus could be talking to him! All of a sudden, something struck the lawyer's mind, and he felt Jesus was including his profession. Jesus proceeded to leave no doubt in anyone's mind. He was speaking to all who put religion, ritual, ceremony, heritage, or anything else before God. Every person's duty, including those of religionists, is to turn their heart and being over to God.

> [45] One of the lawyers answered him, "Teacher, in saying these things you insult us also."
> [46] And he said, "Woe to you lawyers also! For you load people with burdens hard to bear, and you yourselves do not touch the burdens with one of your fingers."

b. Jesus' charge: They too were guilty (v.46b).

Jesus now charged the religionist with creating rules and regulations beyond what God required. Jesus was speaking of the Scribal law (see DEEPER STUDY # 1—Lu.6:2). The Scribal law was considered even more important than the Word of God itself. In the minds of the religionists, the law of God was sometimes hard to understand, but their rules and regulations were not. Therefore, any breaking of the Scribal law was considered deliberate and much more serious than violating God's law! Jesus also charged the religionists with failing to lift one finger to help a person in keeping the law. Instead, they condemned those who erred or struggled.

Jesus makes it clear that the Law, the Word of God, is adequate by itself. People do not have to add rules and regulations to it (see note—Mt.23:4 for more discussion).

> And everyone who hears these words of mine and does not do them will be like a foolish man who built his house on the sand. And the rain fell, and the floods came, and the winds blew and beat against that house, and it fell, and great was the fall of it. (Mt.7:26-27)

> And that servant who knew his master's will but did not get ready or act according to his will, will receive a severe beating. (Lu.12:47)

> You then who teach others, do you not teach yourself? While you preach against stealing, do you steal? (Ro.2:21)

> So whoever knows the right thing to do and fails to do it, for him it is sin. (Jas.4:17)

7 Charge 6: Religionists honor the true prophets of God—as long as they are dead.

Jesus' sixth charge is that religionists honored the true prophets of God—as long as they were dead. However, they rejected *the* Prophet (De.18:15, 18) and the one greater than all the prophets, Jesus Christ, God's own Son.

a. They honor the past servants of God whom their forefathers killed (v.48).

The religionists honored the past. They showed great respect for the prophets of old—renovating, adorning, and looking after their tombs and relics. They took great pride in their roots.

> Bear fruits in keeping with repentance. And do not begin to say to yourselves, "We have Abraham as our father." For I tell you, God is able from these stones to raise up children for Abraham. (Lu.3:8)

> [47] "Woe to you! For you build the tombs of the prophets whom your fathers killed.
> [48] So you are witnesses and you consent to the deeds of your fathers, for they killed them, and you build their tombs.
> [49] Therefore also the Wisdom of God said, 'I will send them prophets and apostles, some of whom they will kill and persecute,'
> [50] so that the blood of all the prophets, shed from the foundation of the world, may be charged against this generation,
> [51] from the blood of Abel to the blood of Zechariah, who perished between the altar and the sanctuary. Yes, I tell you, it will be required of this generation."

They answered him, "We are offspring of Abraham and have never been enslaved to anyone. How is it that you say, 'You will become free'?" . . . They answered him, "Abraham is our father." Jesus said to them, "If you were Abraham's children, you would be doing the works Abraham did." (Jn.8:33, 39)

And they reviled him, saying, "You are his disciple, but we are disciples of Moses." (Jn.9:28)

b. They reject the present servants of God (v.49).

The religionists, however, *rejected* the teaching and godly lives of the prophets and apostles whom God presently sent. They revered the past—Abraham and Moses, Jeremiah and Zechariah—but they rejected God's very own Son. In rejecting Him, they bore witness that they were just as their fathers were: murderers (v.48). Their ancestors had persecuted and killed the prophets of old, and they were persecuting—and would ultimately kill—God's Son.

The Pharisees went out and immediately held counsel with the Herodians against him, how to destroy him. (Mk.3:6)

And the chief priests and the scribes heard it and were seeking a way to destroy him, for they feared him, because all the crowd was astonished at his teaching. (Mk.11:18)

It was now two days before the Passover and the Feast of Unleavened Bread. And the chief priests and the scribes were seeking how to arrest him by stealth and kill him, for they said, "Not during the feast, lest there be an uproar from the people." (Mk.14:1-2)

c. The judgment to be required of them (vv.50–51).

The religionists of Jesus' generation would face an even harsher judgment than their ancestors. The blood of all the prophets, ranging from Abel to Zechariah, would fall on their heads (see DEEPER STUDIES 1, 2). Why the blood of all? Because Jesus' generation had the greatest privilege and opportunity ever known to mankind. God's Son Himself, the summit of the prophets, now stood before the world, in particular before the religionists. To reject Him was to reject all the prophets. He was *the one prophet* who exceeded all prophets, the one to whom all prophets had looked (see notes—Mt.23:29-33; 23:34-36; DEEPER STUDIES 10, 11—23:35; DEEPER STUDY # 12—23:36).

For the Son of Man is going to come with his angels in the glory of his Father, and then he will repay each person according to what he has done. (Mt.16:27)

But because of your hard and impenitent heart you are storing up wrath for yourself on the day of wrath when God's righteous judgment will be revealed. He will render to each one according to his works. (Ro.2:5-6)

And if you call on him as Father who judges impartially according to each one's deeds, conduct yourselves with fear throughout the time of your exile. (1 Pe.1:17)

If you say, "Behold, we did not know this," does not he who weighs the heart perceive it? Does not he who keeps watch over your soul know it, and will he not repay man according to his work? (Pr.24:12)

I the LORD search the heart and test the mind, to give every man according to his ways, according to the fruit of his deeds. (Je.17:10)

Great in counsel and mighty in deed, whose eyes are open to all the ways of the children of man, rewarding each one according to his ways and according to the fruit of his deeds. (Je.32:19)

DEEPER STUDY # 1

(11:51) **Zechariah:** see DEEPER STUDY # 11—Mt.23:35.

DEEPER STUDY # 2

(11:51) **Abel:** see Ge.4:8.

8 Charge 7: Religionists have substituted the truth about God (Scriptures) with their own rules and ideas.

Jesus' seventh charge is also directed to the lawyers of that time and anyone who stresses religion over repentance. The religionists of that time had taken away the key that unlocked the Scriptures and the way to God. They stressed the external, the ceremony, their religious formalities over the heart and repentance, the Scripture and obedience. In doing so, they turned people away from Scripture to their own ideas and thoughts, rules and regulations.

> [52] "Woe to you lawyers! For you have taken away the key of knowledge. You did not enter yourselves, and you hindered those who were entering."

> But Jesus answered them, "You are wrong, because you know neither the Scriptures nor the power of God." (Mt.22:29)

> For we are not, like so many, peddlers of God's word, but as men of sincerity, as commissioned by God, in the sight of God we speak in Christ. (2 Co.2:17)

> As he does in all his letters when he speaks in them of these matters. There are some things in them that are hard to understand, which the ignorant and unstable twist to their own destruction, as they do the other Scriptures. (2 Pe.3:16)

Note that some persons were entering into the truth until the religionists got hold of them. The religionists stopped them from fully believing and following the truth.

> But woe to you, scribes and Pharisees, hypocrites! For you shut the kingdom of heaven in people's faces. For you neither enter yourselves nor allow those who would enter to go in. (Mt.23:13)

> For the lips of a priest should guard knowledge, and people should seek instruction from his mouth, for he is the messenger of the Lord of hosts. But you have turned aside from the way. You have caused many to stumble by your instruction. You have corrupted the covenant of Levi, says the Lord of hosts. (Mal.2:7-8)

9 Conclusion: A reaction of hostility and opposition toward Jesus.

Jesus had told the religionists the truth about themselves without watering it down in any way, shape, or form. The Scribes and Pharisees could not tolerate the truth and were enraged. They reacted with hostility and furious opposition toward God's Son. From this point forward, they tried to trap Jesus so they could arrest Him and stop Him from continuing to expose their sins.

> [53] As he went away from there, the scribes and the Pharisees began to press him hard and to provoke him to speak about many things,
> [54] lying in wait for him, to catch him in something he might say.

CHAPTER 12

L. The Things People Should Guard Against and Fear, 12:1–12

1. **Thousands of people gathered around Jesus**
2. **Message 1: Guard against hypocrisy**[DS1]

   a. Deeds will be exposed

   b. Words will be exposed

3. **Message 2: What to fear and what not to fear**[DS2]

   a. Do not fear people, but fear God and God alone
     1) Because He is more powerful than man
     2) Because He cares for you

   b. Fear the spirit of disloyalty, of denying Christ

   c. Fear the unpardonable sin: Blasphemy against the Holy Spirit

   d. Do not fear persecution or trials: The Holy Spirit will empower you

In the meantime, when so many thousands of the people had gathered together that they were trampling one another, he began to say to his disciples first, "Beware of the leaven of the Pharisees, which is hypocrisy. ² Nothing is covered up that will not be revealed, or hidden that will not be known. ³ Therefore whatever you have said in the dark shall be heard in the light, and what you have whispered in private rooms shall be proclaimed on the housetops. ⁴ I tell you, my friends, do not fear those who kill the body, and after that have nothing more that they can do. ⁵ But I will warn you whom to fear: fear him who, after he has killed, has authority to cast into hell. Yes, I tell you, fear him! ⁶ Are not five sparrows sold for two pennies? And not one of them is forgotten before God. ⁷ Why, even the hairs of your head are all numbered. Fear not; you are of more value than many sparrows. ⁸ And I tell you, everyone who acknowledges me before men, the Son of Man also will acknowledge before the angels of God, ⁹ but the one who denies me before men will be denied before the angels of God. ¹⁰ And everyone who speaks a word against the Son of Man will be forgiven, but the one who blasphemes against the Holy Spirit will not be forgiven. ¹¹ And when they bring you before the synagogues and the rulers and the authorities, do not be anxious about how you should defend yourself or what you should say, ¹² for the Holy Spirit will teach you in that very hour what you ought to say."

Division V

The Son of Man's Great Journey to Jerusalem (Stage I):
His Mission and Public Challenge, 9:51–13:21

L. The Things People Should Guard Against and Fear, 12:1–12

12:1–12
Introduction

Luke 12 begins with Jesus speaking to His disciples, covering what they *should* fear and what they should *not* fear. Our Lord's message had a view to the future, after He had died, risen from the dead, and ascended back to heaven. The Jewish religious leaders would exert crushing pressure on them, persecuting them severely and even killing them if they did not compromise their faith and teaching (v.11). They must not cave in to the Pharisees' demands. They must fear God more than the authorities.

Jesus did discuss some particular things that His disciples needed to fear, things that need to be feared by everyone. This is, *The Things People Should Guard Against and Fear,* 12:1-12.

1. Thousands of people gathered around Jesus (v.1).
2. Message 1: Guard against hypocrisy (vv.1–3).
3. Message 2: What to fear and what not to fear (vv.4–12).

1 Thousands of people gathered around Jesus.

12:1

A huge crowd now gathered around Jesus, a crowd so large it was beyond numbering accurately. The Greek word for *many thousands* or *innumerable* (muriadōn, *mur-ih-ahd'-own*) is the source of our English word *myriad*. It usually refers to ten thousand or more (Mt.18:24; 1 Co.14:19; Jude 1:14; Re.9:16). It is also used of a quantity too large to number (1 Co.4:15; He.12:22). Picture a crowd at a modern-day major athletic event. So many people had gathered that they were pushing and trampling on each other. They were so eager to hear Jesus that they were trying to get as close as possible.

> In the meantime, when so many thousands of the people had gathered together that they were trampling one another, he began to say to his disciples first, "Beware of the leaven of the Pharisees, which is hypocrisy."

THOUGHT 1. What a lesson for people today—to be so hungry for the Word of God that we flock to His preaching and struggle to get up front!

2 Message 1: Guard against hypocrisy.

12:1-3

Jesus warned His disciples to guard against hypocrisy. Whether He was addressing the Twelve or all of His followers is unclear. He referred to hypocrisy as "the leaven of the Pharisees" (see DEEPER STUDY # 3—Mt.16:12; note and DEEPER STUDIES 1, 2—Mk.8:15 for more discussion and application).

The Pharisees, surprisingly, were the ones who were guilty of hypocrisy, that is, saying one thing and doing another (see DEEPER STUDY # 2—Mt.23:13). They claimed to be followers of God, to lead people to God . . .

- in their ceremony and ritual
- in their form of worship and teaching
- in their doctrine and preaching

> In the meantime, when so many thousands of the people had gathered together that they were trampling one another, he began to say to his disciples first, "Beware of the leaven of the Pharisees, which is hypocrisy.
> [2] Nothing is covered up that will not be revealed, or hidden that will not be known.
> [3] Therefore whatever you have said in the dark shall be heard in the light, and what you have whispered in private rooms shall be proclaimed on the housetops."

However, Jesus said that what the Pharisees were doing was hypocrisy, for religious formalities and rituals are not God's way of salvation. And it was like leaven (yeast), spreading and penetrating through the people (see Deeper Study # 1).

> You hypocrites! Well did Isaiah prophesy of you, when he said: "This people honors me with their lips, but their heart is far from me; in vain do they worship me, teaching as doctrines the commandments of men." (Mt.15:7-9)

> But woe to you, scribes and Pharisees, hypocrites! For you shut the kingdom of heaven in people's faces. For you neither enter yourselves nor allow those who would enter to go in. . . . So you also outwardly appear righteous to others, but within you are full of hypocrisy and lawlessness. (Mt.23:13, 28)

> Why do you see the speck that is in your brother's eye, but do not notice the log that is in your own eye? How can you say to your brother, "Brother, let me take out the speck that is in your eye," when you yourself do not see the log that is in your own eye? You hypocrite, first take the log out of your own eye, and then you will see clearly to take out the speck that is in your brother's eye. For no good tree bears bad fruit, nor again does a bad tree bear good fruit. (Lu.6:41-43)

> You hypocrites! You know how to interpret the appearance of earth and sky, but why do you not know how to interpret the present time? And why do you not judge for yourselves what is right? (Lu.12:56-57)

Again, Jesus' disciples were the ones whom He warned to fear hypocrisy. Why? Because they—particularly the Twelve—were the teachers, the preachers of righteousness. They were both to proclaim the truth and live the truth. They needed to fear and guard against becoming like the Pharisees.

a. Deeds will be exposed (v.2).

Jesus warned that every person's *deeds* will be exposed. There is nothing covered or hidden that will remain so. Every act—whether done behind closed doors, in the dark, placed in a file or deposit box, or written in a book, pamphlet or letter—will be revealed and known. If Jesus' disciples became like the Pharisees—insincere in their ministry, two-faced, teaching one thing and living another—they would be exposed.

b. Words will be exposed (v.3).

In addition, every person's *words* were to be exposed. There is no word that will not be heard and proclaimed for all to hear. Every word—whether spoken in the dark or whispered in the ear of someone or just conceived in the mind—will come to light.

> For nothing is hidden that will not be made manifest, nor is anything secret that will not be known and come to light. (Lu.8:17)

> Therefore do not pronounce judgment before the time, before the Lord comes, who will bring to light the things now hidden in darkness and will disclose the purposes of the heart. Then each one will receive his commendation from God. (1 Co.4:5)

> But they will not get very far, for their folly will be plain to all, as was that of those two men. (2 Ti.3:9)

> But if you will not do so, behold, you have sinned against the Lord, and be sure your sin will find you out. (Nu.32:23)

> For his eyes are on the ways of a man, and he sees all his steps. (Jb.34:21)

> For my eyes are on all their ways. They are not hidden from me, nor is their iniquity concealed from my eyes. (Je.16:17)

DEEPER STUDY # 1

(12:1) **Leaven:** leaven (yeast) is inserted in dough, and once it is, it does at least four things.

1. Leaven penetrates, seeps, and works its way through the dough. It cannot be seen, but it still works.

2. Leaven spreads. It spreads slowly, but once it is inserted, it cannot be stopped. It continues to spread until the whole dough is leavened.

3. Leaven swells the dough. It puffs dough up, making dough look much larger than it really is. Note: it does not add to the dough. It only changes its appearance.

4. Leaven ferments and sours the dough. It changes the dough's very nature.

3 Message 2: What to fear and what not to fear.

Jesus continued teaching His disciples, calling them his "friends" (Jn.15:13-15). He challenged them specifically about what they should fear and what they should not fear. It is important to keep in mind that the Lord was preparing them for the future, when they would be persecuted for their faith.

a. Do not fear people, but fear God and God alone (vv.4-5).

Jesus told His disciples not to fear other people. The same people who would soon kill Him would seek to kill them too. But they should not be afraid of their persecutors. They should stand fast in the Lord, fearing Him rather than those who sought to harm them. The reason is logical: humans can only kill the body. God, on the other hand, has the authority to cast both body and soul "into hell" (see DEEPER STUDY # 2; note and DEEPER STUDY # 1—Mt.10:28; DEEPER STUDY # 2—5:22). God is far more powerful than man. Other humans can only affect us in this life. God has the power to condemn us eternally.

But Jesus taught His disciples that they should fear God for an even greater reason: He cares for each of us personally and deeply (vv.6-7). Jesus expressed God's care for His children by pointing to His care for sparrows, the most common and least valuable of birds according to human perception. Note the word "forgotten" (v.6). Not a single sparrow is forgotten before God. How much more, then, will God remember us, remember our need of His protection and provision? How much more valuable are God's dear children to Him, the ones for whom He gave His only begotten Son? If God cares so deeply for the sparrow, how much more does He care for us? The Lord never forgets His own, no matter the circumstance. There is something very precious here, yet there is a revelation of God's power as well:

> 4 "I tell you, my friends, do not fear those who kill the body, and after that have nothing more that they can do.
> 5 But I will warn you whom to fear: fear him who, after he has killed, has authority to cast into hell. Yes, I tell you, fear him!
> 6 Are not five sparrows sold for two pennies? And not one of them is forgotten before God.
> 7 Why, even the hairs of your head are all numbered. Fear not; you are of more value than many sparrows.
> 8 And I tell you, everyone who acknowledges me before men, the Son of Man also will acknowledge before the angels of God,
> 9 but the one who denies me before men will be denied before the angels of God.
> 10 And everyone who speaks a word against the Son of Man will be forgiven, but the one who blasphemes against the Holy Spirit will not be forgiven.
> 11 And when they bring you before the synagogues and the rulers and the authorities, do not be anxious about how you should defend yourself or what you should say,
> 12 for the Holy Spirit will teach you in that very hour what you ought to say."

➤ Precious is the thought that every sparrow, no matter how common or disregarded by humans, is very dear to God.

➤ God's power is revealed in the truth that He knows every single sparrow on the earth, and not a single one falls that He is unaware about its injury (Mt.10:29). The idea is that injury to the sparrow causes pain and hurt that God feels.

In this simple, heartwarming statement about sparrows, our Lord taught four assuring truths about God. First, Jesus taught about God's providence. God sees, knows, cares, and oversees all the events and happenings on earth—even for the little sparrow that is so common and of little human value.

> Therefore I tell you, do not be anxious about your life, what you will eat or what you will drink, nor about your body, what you will put on. Is not life more than food, and the body more than clothing? Look at the birds of the air: they neither sow nor reap nor gather into barns, and yet your heavenly Father feeds them. Are you not of more value than they? (Mt.6:25-26)

> Casting all your anxieties on him, because he cares for you. (1 Pe.5:7)

Second, Jesus pointed out God's knowledge (omniscience). God knows every little happening and all that is, even to the most minute detail. He knows when a single sparrow falls to the ground. He knows every hair of a person's head, even the number of hairs—a constantly changing number.

> Do not be like them, for your Father knows what you need before you ask him. (Mt.6:8)

> For all the nations of the world seek after these things, and your Father knows that you need them. (Lu.12:30)

You know when I sit down and when I rise up; you discern my thoughts from afar. (Ps.139:2)

Have you not known? Have you not heard? The LORD is the everlasting God, the Creator of the ends of the earth. He does not faint or grow weary; his understanding is unsearchable. (Is.40:28)

Third, Jesus alluded to God's power (omnipotence). God is able to control the events that happen to the believer, no matter how detailed and minute. He can control and work them out for good to such an extent that there is no need for the believer to fear.

And we know that for those who love God all things work together for good, for those who are called according to his purpose. (Ro.8:28)

For this light momentary affliction is preparing for us an eternal weight of glory beyond all comparison. (2 Co.4:17)

But he said to me, "My grace is sufficient for you, for my power is made perfect in weakness." Therefore I will boast all the more gladly of my weaknesses, so that the power of Christ may rest upon me. (2 Co.12:9)

Fourth, Jesus spoke of God's love. If God loves the little sparrow, how much more does He love us? If He loved us so much that He would give His Son for us, is there anything He would not do for us (Ro.8:32)? Nothing can separate us from the love of Christ and of God.

Who shall separate us from the love of Christ? Shall tribulation, or distress, or persecution, or famine, or nakedness, or danger, or sword? . . . For I am sure that neither death nor life, nor angels nor rulers, nor things present nor things to come, nor powers, nor height nor depth, nor anything else in all creation, will be able to separate us from the love of God in Christ Jesus our Lord. (Ro.8:35, 38–39)

b. Fear the spirit of disloyalty, of denying Christ (vv.8–9).

The conjunction *and* or *also* (Gk. de, *deh*) at the beginning of verse 8 connects the proceeding thought to the previous one (v.7). Because God cares so intimately and deeply for us, we should fearlessly acknowledge or confess Him before other people, especially those who persecute us for our faith. We must never deny Him. If there is anything we should fear, it is the spirit of disloyalty, of denying Christ.

Jesus encourages us to stand boldly for Him by reminding us that we will be judged for our faithfulness or unfaithfulness to Him. We will be judged before the angels of God. Angels will witness the Lord either acknowledge us or deny us. *Deny* (aparneomai, *ah-par-neh'-om-eye*) means to utterly reject or disown.

This statement raises some critical questions: Is Jesus saying that God will disown His children who, in a momentary failure of faith, deny Christ? Will they be cast into hell (v.5)? Is it possible for a true believer to deny Christ?

Peter's experience reveals that the answer to the last question is, "Yes." Gripped by fear for his life, Peter's faith failed, and he denied Christ (Lu.22:34, 57). However, Jesus did not disown Peter. To the contrary, Jesus restored Peter and recommissioned him to both service and leadership (Jn.21:15–19).

What, then, was Jesus saying in this verse? Commentator Richard C.H. Lenski explains: "Jesus uses the . . . aorist participle to designate the man who denied him; and this aorist is not past in time but constative, summing up into one the life course of the denier."[1] The *New American Commentary* adds, "Luke 12:9, however, is a clear instance of apostasy by a member of the Christian community."[2]

Writing to Timothy about the subject of persecution, Paul appears to quote Christ, saying, "If we deny Him, He also will deny us" (2 Ti.2:12). Then, Paul adds, "If we are faithless, He remains faithful; He cannot deny Himself" (2 Ti.2:13). The *Bible Knowledge Commentary* explains these statements as follows:

"If we disown Him, He will also disown us [NIV] speaks of the possibility of apostasy (cf. 1 Tim.4:1; Heb.10:38–39; 2 John 9) and the Lord's ultimate rejection of those who professed Christ only temporarily

---

1 Richard C. H. Lenski, *The Interpretation of St. Luke's Gospel (Commentary on the New Testament)*, (Minneapolis, MN: Augsburg Fortress Press, 2008). Via Wordsearch digital edition.

2 Robert H. Stein, *The New American Commentary (Luke, Vol.24): An Exegetical and Theological Exposition of Holy Scripture*, (Nashville, TN: Holman Reference, 1993). Via Wordsearch digital edition.

(cf. Matt.10:33). Instead of identifying with Christ, the apostate finally dissociates himself with Christ. . . . **If we are faithless, He will remain faithful** *speaks not of the apostate, but of a true child of God who nevertheless proves unfaithful (cf. 2 Tim.1:15). Christ* **cannot disown Himself;** *therefore He will not deny even unprofitable members of His own body. True children of God cannot become something other than children, even when disobedient and weak. Christ's faithfulness to Christians is not contingent on their faithfulness to Him."[3]*

To summarize, Jesus seems to be speaking not of believers who, in a moment of intense fear and utter faithlessness deny Him and subsequently repent, as Peter did; but of professing believers who continually deny Him and ultimately depart from the faith—apostates. Such were never genuinely saved from the outset. Consequently, Christ will deny them on the Day of Judgment, and God will cast them into hell (v.4).

> **Not everyone who says to me, "Lord, Lord," will enter the kingdom of heaven, but the one who does the will of my Father who is in heaven. On that day many will say to me, "Lord, Lord, did we not prophesy in your name, and cast out demons in your name, and do many mighty works in your name?" And then will I declare to them, "I never knew you; depart from me, you workers of lawlessness." (Mt.7:21–23)**

> **But my righteous one shall live by faith, and if he shrinks back, my soul has no pleasure in him. But we are not of those who shrink back and are destroyed, but of those who have faith and preserve their souls. (He.10:38–39)**

> **They went out from us, but they were not of us; for if they had been of us, they would have continued with us. But they went out, that it might become plain that they all are not of us. (1 Jn.2:19)**

> **Everyone who goes on ahead and does not abide in the teaching of Christ, does not have God. Whoever abides in the teaching has both the Father and the Son. (2 Jn.9)**

Like Peter, the believer may have a failure of faith. But the true believer will be genuinely broken by their failure, as Peter was (Mt.26:75; Mk.14:72; Lu.22:62). Surely, the Lord Jesus intercedes before the throne of the Father for all His dear followers who will face the possibility of laying down their lives for His sake, just as He prayed for Peter (Lu.22:32). How encouraging and comforting to know, that, if we must make that choice, He will be praying for us, praying for our faith to not fail.

The believer whose faith does fail will face the loss of rewards they could have received had they stood faithful to Christ (1 Co.3:15). They will hang their heads in agonizing shame at the Judgment Seat of Christ (1 Jn.2:28). A rich reward is promised for believers who are faithful unto death (Jas.1:12; Re.2:10). Tragically, the believer whose faith fails will be denied that reward.

> **Blessed is the man who remains steadfast under trial, for when he has stood the test he will receive the crown of life, which God has promised to those who love him. (Jas.1:12)**

> **Do not fear what you are about to suffer. Behold, the devil is about to throw some of you into prison, that you may be tested, and for ten days you will have tribulation. Be faithful unto death, and I will give you the crown of life. (Re.2:10)**

The Son of Man Himself will execute the judgment of which Jesus speaks (Jn.5:22; Ac.10:42; 17:31). He alone is the one man who lived and experienced all the temptations and trials of life, yet He never sinned. He alone has been through it all and conquered all. He alone is worthy to judge. He alone knows . . .

- what a person truly is—the true condition of the heart
- what a person truly believes and does not believe—whether a person has genuinely believed unto salvation
- what a person can and cannot do
- what a person does and fails to do

> **Before him will be gathered all the nations, and he will separate people one from another as a shepherd separates the sheep from the goats. (Mt.25:32)**

> **For the Father judges no one, but has given all judgment to the Son. (Jn.5:22)**

---

3   John F. Walvoord and Roy B. Zuck, *The Bible Knowledge Commentary: An Exposition of the Scriptures by Dallas Seminary Faculty*, (Wheaton, IL: Chariot-Victor Books, 1983). Via Wordsearch digital edition.

And he commanded us to preach to the people and to testify that he is the one appointed by God to be judge of the living and the dead. (Ac.10:42)

Because he has fixed a day on which he will judge the world in righteousness by a man whom he has appointed; and of this he has given assurance to all by raising him from the dead. (Ac.17:31)

On that day when, according to my gospel, God judges the secrets of men by Christ Jesus. (Ro.2:16)

Why do you pass judgment on your brother? Or you, why do you despise your brother? For we will all stand before the judgment seat of God. (Ro.14:10)

I charge you in the presence of God and of Christ Jesus, who is to judge the living and the dead, and by his appearing and his kingdom. (2 Ti.4:1)

c. Fear the unpardonable sin: Blasphemy against the Holy Spirit (vv.9–10).

Jesus went on to say that those who speak against Him can be forgiven. If a person denies Christ or even curses Christ and truly wants forgiveness, God will forgive them if they repent.

However, blasphemy against the Holy Spirit is not forgiven; it is the unpardonable sin. This sin is not referring to just *speaking* words against the Spirit. It means setting one's mind and heart and life against the Spirit. It means that the words spoken against the Spirit come from a heart set against the Spirit and the work of the Spirit. It is the hardening of one's heart against the work of the Spirit, rejecting the Spirit's work in one's life (see note—Mt.12:31-32 for a thorough discussion of the unpardonable sin).

d. Do not fear persecution or trials: The Holy Spirit will empower you (vv.11–12).

Having spoken to His disciples about all these matters, Jesus concluded by encouraging them to not fear persecution and trials. He did not want them to worry about being dragged before the authorities for their faith. They did not need to prepare defenses or plan what they would say. Why? Because, at that moment, the Holy Spirit would give them the words to say.

The Holy Spirit dwells within and empowers the believer. Whenever a believer faces persecution, whether mild ridicule or physical abuse and martyrdom, the Holy Spirit will give them power, the strength to bear and the words to speak. He will give the boldness needed to stand faithful to Christ, to not deny Him. He will give the words to say. The believer who triumphs in persecution, who is faithful even unto death, is the one who recognizes his or her own inability and leans fully on the ability of the Holy Spirit.

Very simply, we are to trust God in the hour of trial, trust Him for the strength to bear whatever people may do to us. This does not mean we should not be praying and thinking, but it means that we are to trust God for our defense. There is a reason for this. Only God knows the heart of the persecutors and any others who are present. Thus, He alone knows what needs to be said to touch their hearts or else to serve as a witness against them in the future.

When they deliver you over, do not be anxious how you are to speak or what you are to say, for what you are to say will be given to you in that hour. (Mt.10:19)

For I will give you a mouth and wisdom, which none of your adversaries will be able to withstand or contradict. (Lu.21:15)

And we impart this in words not taught by human wisdom but taught by the Spirit, interpreting spiritual truths to those who are spiritual. (1 Co.2:13)

Now therefore go, and I will be with your mouth and teach you what you shall speak. (Ex.4:12)

And I have put my words in your mouth and covered you in the shadow of my hand, establishing the heavens and laying the foundations of the earth, and saying to Zion, "You are my people." (Is.51:16)

(12:4) **Fear—Persecution:** fear of man is a terrible thing. It is a subject that needs to be looked at closely.

1. The fear of man causes several things.
   - ➤ It causes a person to become disturbed within the heart and mind: the loss of peace.
   - ➤ It causes a person to lose fervor: the loss of commitment.
   - ➤ It causes a person to be either sidetracked from or to give up what they know to be God's will: the loss of mission and meaning and purpose.

   For God gave us a spirit not of fear but of power and love and self-control. (2 Ti.1:7)

   There is no fear in love, but perfect love casts out fear. For fear has to do with punishment, and whoever fears has not been perfected in love. (1 Jn.4:18)

   Fear not, for I am with you; be not dismayed, for I am your God; I will strengthen you, I will help you, I will uphold you with my righteous right hand. (Is.41:10)

   But now thus says the LORD, he who created you, O Jacob, he who formed you, O Israel: "Fear not, for I have redeemed you; I have called you by name, you are mine. When you pass through the waters, I will be with you; and through the rivers, they shall not overwhelm you; when you walk through fire you shall not be burned, and the flame shall not consume you. For I am the LORD your God, the Holy One of Israel, your Savior. I give Egypt as your ransom, Cush and Seba in exchange for you." (Is.43:1–3)

2. There are several reasons why man is not to be feared.
   a. Man can only kill the body, not the soul. Human power is limited; people can go no further. They cannot touch a person's soul or life.
   b. Man can only send us out of this world, not out of heaven. "To be with Christ . . . is far better" anyway (Ph.1:23; 3:20–21).
   c. Man can only separate us from this world, not from life. We have eternal life. Death is not a part of the experience of the believer, for the believer will not "taste" death. Christ "tasted," that is, experienced, death for the believer (He.2:9). The believer has already passed from death to life and lives forever (Jn.5:24). When we face death, we are merely transferred from this world, from the physical dimension of being, into the next world, the heavenly or spiritual dimension of being (see DEEPER STUDY # 1—2 Ti.4:18).

   Truly, truly, I say to you, whoever hears my word and believes him who sent me has eternal life. He does not come into judgment, but has passed from death to life. (Jn.5:24)

   The Lord will rescue me from every evil deed and bring me safely into his heavenly kingdom. To him be the glory forever and ever. Amen. (2 Ti.4:18)

   But we see him who for a little while was made lower than the angels, namely Jesus, crowned with glory and honor because of the suffering of death, so that by the grace of God he might taste death for everyone. For it was fitting that he, for whom and by whom all things exist, in bringing many sons to glory, should make the founder of their salvation perfect through suffering. For he who sanctifies and those who are sanctified all have one source. That is why he is not ashamed to call them brothers. (He.2:9–11; see vv.12–18)

   d. Man can only cut us off from the unbelievers and believers of this earth, not from the love of God and the saints in glory.

   Who shall separate us from the love of Christ? Shall tribulation, or distress, or persecution, or famine, or nakedness, or danger, or sword? As it is written, "For your sake we are being killed all the day long; we are regarded as sheep to be slaughtered." No, in all these things we are more than conquerors through him who loved us. For I am sure that neither death nor life, nor angels nor rulers, nor things present nor things to come, nor powers, nor height nor depth, nor anything else in all creation, will be able to separate us from the love of God in Christ Jesus our Lord. (Ro.8:35–39)

3. There are two *primary* reasons why we should not fear man and persecution.
   a. God has given us a great and glorious cause: to reach people for Christ. Very practically some do not want to be reached; therefore, they rail and react and become our persecutors. But some do want to be saved, and the fact that they can receive eternal life is so glorious that it is worth whatever price we have to pay in order to see them saved. Remember that Paul was saved after witnessing faithful Stephen lay down his life for Christ (Ac.7:54–8:3).

   > For God so loved the world, that he gave his only Son, that whoever believes in him should not perish but have eternal life. For God did not send his Son into the world to condemn the world, but in order that the world might be saved through him. (Jn.3:16–17)

   > For the wages of sin is death, but the free gift of God is eternal life in Christ Jesus our Lord. (Ro.6:23)

   > Consequently, he is able to save to the uttermost those who draw near to God through him, since he always lives to make intercession for them. (He.7:25)

   > Let him know that whoever brings back a sinner from his wandering will save his soul from death and will cover a multitude of sins. (Jas.5:20)

   > There is no fear in love, but perfect love casts out fear. For fear has to do with punishment, and whoever fears has not been perfected in love. (1 Jn.4:18)

   b. God has given us a great hope (see Thought—Mt.10:26–27).

   > Having a hope in God, which these men themselves accept, that there will be a resurrection of both the just and the unjust. So I always take pains to have a clear conscience toward both God and man. (Ac.24:15–16)

   > For we know that if the tent that is our earthly home is destroyed, we have a building from God, a house not made with hands, eternal in the heavens. (2 Co.5:1)

   > But our citizenship is in heaven, and from it we await a Savior, the Lord Jesus Christ, who will transform our lowly body to be like his glorious body, by the power that enables him even to subject all things to himself. (Ph.3:20–21)

   > Because of the hope laid up for you in heaven. Of this you have heard before in the word of the truth, the gospel. (Col.1:5)

   > So when God desired to show more convincingly to the heirs of the promise the unchangeable character of his purpose, he guaranteed it with an oath, so that by two unchangeable things, in which it is impossible for God to lie, we who have fled for refuge might have strong encouragement to hold fast to the hope set before us. We have this as a sure and steadfast anchor of the soul, a hope that enters into the inner place behind the curtain, where Jesus has gone as a forerunner on our behalf, having become a high priest forever after the order of Melchizedek. (He.6:17–20)

   > Blessed be the God and Father of our Lord Jesus Christ! According to his great mercy, he has caused us to be born again to a living hope through the resurrection of Jesus Christ from the dead, to an inheritance that is imperishable, undefiled, and unfading, kept in heaven for you. (1 Pe.1:3–4)

4. There is a remedy to keep us from fearing man: God. God is to be feared (see note—Mt.10:28). Note several things.
   a. God can destroy us, both body and soul, and put both "in hell" (see DEEPER STUDY # 2—Mt.5:22). By "destroy" Jesus did not mean that a person's body and soul would cease to exist, but they would live a worthless existence, be ruined and suffer in ruin forever (see DEEPER STUDY # 1—Mt.10:28).
   b. Jesus was speaking to believers in this passage. God is to be feared much more and much sooner than man. The terror of humans pales into absolute insignificance in comparison to the terror of God. Imagine this one fact alone. The terror of mankind is but for a short while at most, but the terror of God is *forever*. The Bible says it never ends. The point is clear: before caving in to man's persecution, we need to remember the *fear of God*.
   c. The destruction of the soul comes from God, not from man. The power to destroy the soul is God's power alone. How fearful we must be of God—even we who are believers (see note—Mt.10:28)!

And do not fear those who kill the body but cannot kill the soul. Rather fear him who can destroy both soul and body in hell. (Mt.10:28)

And if you call on him as Father who judges impartially according to each one's deeds, conduct yourselves with fear throughout the time of your exile. (1 Pe.1:17)

Honor everyone. Love the brotherhood. Fear God. Honor the emperor. (1 Pe.2:17)

And "If the righteous is scarcely saved, what will become of the ungodly and the sinner?" (1 Pe.4:18)

And he said with a loud voice, "Fear God and give him glory, because the hour of his judgment has come, and worship him who made heaven and earth, the sea and the springs of water." (Re.14:7)

Now then, let the fear of the LORD be upon you. Be careful what you do, for there is no injustice with the LORD our God, or partiality or taking bribes. (2 Chr.19:7)

**M. The Parable of the Rich Fool:
Guard Against Greed or Covetousness, 12:13–21**

1. **A request for Jesus to render a judicial decision**
   a. A brother's desire for his part of an inheritance
   b. Jesus' firm refusal to get involved in worldly affairs
2. **Beware: Life does not consist merely of things**
   a. The serious warning: Watch out— Beware!
   b. The big sin: Greed or covetousness[DS1]

   c. The big "I" (6 times, 17–19a): Aggressively self-centered

   d. The big mistake: Self-indulgence and extravagant living
3. **Beware: Your life may be required and demanded tonight**

4. **Beware: Wealth is not a permanent possession—someone else gets it**

¹³ Someone in the crowd said to him, "Teacher, tell my brother to divide the inheritance with me."

¹⁴ But he said to him, "Man, who made me a judge or arbitrator over you?" ¹⁵ And he said to them, "Take care, and be on your guard against all covetousness, for one's life does not consist in the abundance of his possessions."

¹⁶ And he told them a parable, saying, "The land of a rich man produced plentifully, ¹⁷ and he thought to himself, 'What shall I do, for I have nowhere to store my crops?' ¹⁸ And he said, 'I will do this: I will tear down my barns and build larger ones, and there I will store all my grain and my goods. ¹⁹ And I will say to my soul, 'Soul, you have ample goods laid up for many years; relax, eat, drink, be merry.' ²⁰ But God said to him, 'Fool! This night your soul is required of you, and the things you have prepared, whose will they be?' ²¹ So is the one who lays up treasure for himself and is not rich toward God."

Division V

The Son of Man's Great Journey to Jerusalem (Stage I): His Mission and Public Challenge, 9:51–13:21

M. The Parable of the Rich Fool: Guard Against Greed or Covetousness, 12:13–21.

12:13–21
Introduction

God's Word commands us not to love "the things in the world" including the material things our eyes desire—money and possessions (1 Jn.2:15-17). Unquestionably, some of these things are essential for living in this world, and Scripture teaches us to be content with these necessities (1 Ti.6:8). When we crave more and more, we open ourselves up to a world of temptations and fall into one of Satan's destructive traps (1 Ti.6:9-10). Therefore, we have to constantly battle the love of money and possessions, and we need to continually remind ourselves that life is about much more than accumulating the things in this world. This truth is exactly what Jesus is trying to instill in our hearts and minds in this passage. This is, *The Parable of the Rich Fool: Guard Against Greed or Covetousness,* 12:13-21.

1. A request for Jesus to render a judicial decision (vv.13-14).
2. Beware: Life does not consist merely of things (vv.15-19).
3. Beware: Your life may be required and demanded tonight (v.20).
4. Beware: Wealth is not a permanent possession—someone else gets it (vv.20-21).

1 A request for Jesus to render a judicial decision.

While Jesus was teaching on intense spiritual matters, one man in the audience was focused on money. He did not ask Jesus for forgiveness or healing, but for a judicial ruling on a financial dispute between him and his brother.

> [13] Someone in the crowd said to him, "Teacher, tell my brother to divide the inheritance with me."
> [14] But he said to him, "Man, who made me a judge or arbitrator over you?"

a. A brother's desire for his part of an inheritance (vv.13-14).

The money-minded man was having a dispute with his brother over the inheritance of his father's estate. The law gave two-thirds to the older son and one third to the younger son. The man felt he was not getting his legal share, so he appealed to Jesus for help. It was a common practice for rabbis to settle legal disputes.

What the man wanted was significant. His request concerned money and property. He appealed to Jesus for help in getting what had probably been *stolen from him*. More than likely the property was rightfully his anyway. It would have been an act of justice to straighten out the inheritance.

b. Jesus' firm refusal to get involved in worldly affairs (v.14).

Jesus refused the man's request rather sternly, saying that it was not His place to judge the matter. The Lord refused to become involved in worldly affairs, in settling property and money disputes.

The man had exposed a serious flaw in his spiritual life. Jesus had just preached on critical spiritual truths. Apparently, the man *had not heard the message*. He was there, but he was too preoccupied with the thoughts of property and money to really hear the Word and receive the message.

The contrast between the man's priorities and Jesus' priorities is significant. The man's mind was set on the things of the earth and the world, on property and money, wealth and selfishness. The Lord's mind was set on higher and nobler affairs, on salvation and life, on heaven and eternity. Jesus' mission was not to give people property and possessions, but to give life, both abundant and eternal. Material possessions are nothing without life.

THOUGHT 1. Listening to the Word being preached does not mean that we "hear the Word," nor that we learn from it. The Word, salvation, and spiritual maturity are not received by a wandering mind or a worldly life.

> He who has ears to hear let him hear. (Mt.11:15)

> Set your minds on things that are above, not on things that are on earth. (Col.3:2)

> Therefore put away all filthiness and rampant wickedness and receive with meekness the implanted word, which is able to save your souls. (Jas.1:21)

> Son of man, you dwell in the midst of a rebellious house, who have eyes to see, but see not, who have ears to hear, but hear not, for they are a rebellious house. (Ezk.12:2)

2 Beware: Life does not consist merely of things.

Jesus turned the man's request into an opportunity to impart spiritual truth to the crowd. He issued three warnings in regard to possessions and life. The first: life does not consist merely of things.

12:15–19

¹⁵ And he said to them, "Take care, and be on your guard against all covetousness, for one's life does not consist in the abundance of his possessions."

¹⁶ And he told them a parable, saying, "The land of a rich man produced plentifully,

¹⁷ and he thought to himself, 'What shall I do, for I have nowhere to store my crops?'

¹⁸ And he said, 'I will do this: I will tear down my barns and build larger ones, and there I will store all my grain and my goods.

¹⁹ And I will say to my soul, "Soul, you have ample goods laid up for many years; relax, eat, drink, be merry."'"

a. **The serious warning: Watch out—beware (v.15a)!**
By giving a double warning, Jesus issued a strong charge:
➤ *"Take care"* or *"take heed"* or *"watch out"* (Gk. horate, *hor-ah'-teh*)—the warning was to be given close attention.
➤ *"Be on your guard"* or *"beware"* (phulassesthe, *foo-las'-sehs-thay*) means to protect or guard yourself from some enemy.

b. **The big sin: Greed or covetousness (v.15b).**
The enemy which Jesus cautioned us to beware of is the sin of *covetousness* (see Deeper Study # 1; Deeper Study # 1—Jas.4:1–3 for more discussion). Covetousness or greed is the big sin of the world—the sin of craving more and more. However, Jesus taught that life is about far more than accumulating money and possessions. Our happiness and comfort, soul and body do not depend on what we have; many who have little are happy and comfortable with healthy souls and bodies. Life does not consist merely of possessions—a beautiful home, the latest clothes, a new car, property, money, or wealth.

c. **The big "I": Aggressively self-centered (vv.16–19).**
To explain and enforce this truth, Jesus told a parable about a wealthy man who was *aggressively self-centered*. He was obsessed with the big "I." In just three short verses describing his thoughts, the rich man in Jesus' parable said, "I" six times and "my" five times. The man's attention was solely upon himself. Now note what the parable reveals about him:
➤ The man was blessed materially, tremendously blessed, but he did not thank God for his blessings.
➤ The man called the harvest his ground produced and the possessions he had, *"my grain"* or *"crops"* and *"my goods"* (vv.17–18).
➤ The man called his soul, *"my soul"* (v.19). There is no indication he had given his soul to God.
➤ He became *puffed up*, prideful of what he had done. He began to think of *bigger* and *better*, to focus on *I* and *me*, and *my* and *mine*.

d. **The big mistake: Self-indulgence and extravagant living (v.19b).**
This man's sole purpose was to live in ease, to have plenty to eat and drink, and to enjoy life as he wished. His mistake was the big mistake of all who are consumed with money and possessions: *selfishness*, self-indulgence, and extravagant living (see Deeper Study # 1—Lu.16:19–21). He thought only of self, of living at ease and in comfort, of indulging self and being as extravagant as he wished. He gave no thought to helping others. He forgot that he lived in a needy world that was lost and dying.

In addition, he put off living and enjoying life until he got his barns built. The idea is that he was a *workaholic* who was consumed with the passion to get what he wanted. (How many are just like him when they want something!)

But grasp the sobering point of the parable: he only *thought* these things. He never accomplished them; they were only thoughts of his heart. Something unexpected happened that prevented him from building his wealth as quickly as possible and retiring young.

But the cares of the world and the deceitfulness of riches and the desires for other things enter in and choke the word, and it proves unfruitful. (Mk.4:19)

But those who desire to be rich fall into temptation, into a snare, into many senseless and harmful desires that plunge people into ruin and destruction. (1 Ti.6:9)

Take care lest you forget the LORD your God by not keeping his commandments and his rules and his statutes, which I command you today, lest, when you have eaten and are full and have built good houses and live in them, and when your herds and flocks multiply and your silver and gold is multiplied and all that you have is multiplied, then your heart be lifted up, and you forget the LORD your God, who brought you out of the land of Egypt, out of the house of slavery. (De.8:11–14)

There is a grievous evil that I have seen under the sun: riches were kept by their owner to his hurt. (Ec.5:13)

Woe to those who join house to house, who add field to field, until there is no more room, and you are made to dwell alone in the midst of the land. (Is.5:8)

DEEPER STUDY # 1

(12:15) **Covetousness or Greed** (pleonexias. *pleh-on-ex-ee'-ahce*): a craving, a desire for more. It is dissatisfaction with what is enough. It includes the cravings for both material things and fleshly indulgences. It is desiring what belongs to others; snatching at something that belongs to others; a love of having, a cry of *give me, give me* (see 2 Pe.2:14).

➢ It is a desire so deep within a person that they find their happiness in things instead of in God.

➢ It is a covetousness so deep that it desires the power that things bring more than the things themselves.

➢ It is an intense appetite for gain; a passion for the pleasure that things can bring. It goes beyond the pleasure of possessing things for their own sakes.

No one can serve two masters, for either he will hate the one and love the other, or he will be devoted to the one and despise the other. You cannot serve God and money. (Mt.6:24)

For what will it profit a man if he gains the whole world and forfeits his soul? Or what shall a man give in return for his soul? (Mt.16:26)

But sexual immorality and all impurity or covetousness must not even be named among you, as is proper among saints. . . . For you may be sure of this, that everyone who is sexually immoral or impure, or who is covetous (that is, an idolater), has no inheritance in the kingdom of Christ and God. (Ep.5:3, 5)

For many, of whom I have often told you and now tell you even with tears, walk as enemies of the cross of Christ. Their end is destruction, their god is their belly, and they glory in their shame, with minds set on earthly things. (Ph.3:18–19)

Put to death therefore what is earthly in you: sexual immorality, impurity, passion, evil desire, and covetousness, which is idolatry. On account of these the wrath of God is coming. (Col.3:5–6)

For we brought nothing into the world, and we cannot take anything out of the world. But if we have food and clothing, with these we will be content. But those who desire to be rich fall into temptation, into a snare, into many senseless and harmful desires that plunge people into ruin and destruction. For the love of money is a root of all kinds of evils. It is through this craving that some have wandered away from the faith and pierced themselves with many pangs. (1 Ti.6:7–10)

Keep your life free from love of money, and be content with what you have, for he has said, "I will never leave you nor forsake you." (He.13:5)

You shall not covet your neighbor's house; you shall not covet your neighbor's wife, or his male servant, or his female servant, or his ox, or his donkey, or anything that is your neighbor's. (Ex.20:17)

If I have made gold my trust or called fine gold my confidence, if I have rejoiced because my wealth was abundant or because my hand had found much, this also would be an iniquity to be punished by the judges, for I would have been false to God above. (Jb.31:24–25, 28)

Put no trust in extortion; set no vain hopes on robbery; if riches increase, set not your heart on them. (Ps.62:10)

Incline my heart to your testimonies, and not to selfish gain! (Ps.119:36)

> Do not toil to acquire wealth; be discerning enough to desist. When your eyes light on it, it is gone, for suddenly it sprouts wings, flying like an eagle toward heaven. (Pr.23:4–5)
>
> Remove far from me falsehood and lying; give me neither poverty nor riches; feed me with the food that is needful for me. (Pr.30:8)
>
> He who loves money will not be satisfied with money, nor he who loves wealth with his income; this also is vanity. (Ec.5:10)
>
> For from the least to the greatest of them, everyone is greedy for unjust gain; and from prophet to priest, everyone deals falsely. (Je.6:13; see Je.8:10)
>
> You have sown much, and harvested little. You eat, but you never have enough; you drink, but you never have your fill. You clothe yourselves, but no one is warm. And he who earns wages does so to put them into a bag with holes. (Hag.1:6)

12:20a

3 Beware: Your life may be required and demanded tonight.

[20] "But God said to him, 'Fool! This night your soul is required of you, and the things you have prepared, whose will they be?'"

As the covetousness man made His plans to accumulate more and more, God spoke. The man would die that night, and all of his wealth would be left behind. It was God who knew the man's thoughts. It was God who knew the man was to die that very night. The man did not know it, nor did anyone else.

The man's "soul" was required. God required and demanded it. His *soul* was not going to cease existing. It was to exist in another world. Existence was not over for the man. The man's soul was simply to be in another world, in the spiritual dimension of existence.

The man was called a "fool" by God. He had lived as a fool, lived entirely for himself. He had refused to think about the truth, about the uncertainty of life, and about what would become of him after he died.

THOUGHT 1. We need to beware, for our life might be required and demanded *tonight*. Just like the man in Jesus' parable, we all have our *night*—appointed time—to die. Each of us has an appointment with death (He.9:27), and, like this man, we do not know the day or time of that appointment. How critical it is that we live each day with an awareness of death and eternity, that we make preparations for our soul and eternity. If we do not, like this man, we too are fools.

> The wicked shall return to Sheol, all the nations that forget God. (Ps.9:17)
>
> Therefore, just as sin came into the world through one man, and death through sin, and so death spread to all men because all sinned. (Ro.5:12)
>
> And just as it is appointed for man to die once, and after that comes judgment. (He.9:27)
>
> For I know that you will bring me to death and to the house appointed for all living. (Jb.30:23)
>
> For they will soon fade like the grass and wither like the green herb. (Ps.37:2)
>
> For he sees that even the wise die; the fool and the stupid alike must perish and leave their wealth to others. (Ps.49:10)
>
> A time to be born, and a time to die; a time to plant, and a time to pluck up what is planted. (Ec.3:2)
>
> It is better to go to the house of mourning than to go to the house of feasting, for this is the end of all mankind, and the living will lay it to heart. (Ec.7:2)

12:20b–21

4 Beware: Wealth is not a permanent possession—someone else gets it.

[20] "But God said to him, 'Fool! This night your soul is required of you, and the things you have prepared, whose will they be?'
[21] So is the one who lays up treasure for himself and is not rich toward God.'"

The greedy man in Jesus' parable had devoted his life to accumulating more and more. But when he died, he left every penny behind (v.20b). He took nothing with him. Jesus is exhorting us to beware, for wealth is not a permanent possession. When we die, someone else gets it.

Why is this true? This is a point seldom thought about. We can take nothing with us because the strength, the energy, the power, the life of our body leaves when we die. The Bible reveals . . .

- that the life of a person's body is their spirit
- that the spirit lives forever

When the spirit leaves the body, the strength and energy and power of the body are gone. Our bodies have to lie down. Note something else: *our spirits are spiritual*, of another dimension of being. They belong to another world, another life. Therefore, all *material* possessions have to be left behind. They are of this life, of this world, of this dimension. They cannot be transported into the spiritual dimension.

Jesus concluded this man's sad story by driving home the point of the parable: instead of storing up wealth in this life, we need to be "rich toward God" (v.21). Instead of laying up treasure in this world, we need to lay up treasure in heaven, invest in that which endures beyond this life (Mt.6:19-21). We need to live for the spiritual and eternal, not the material and temporal.

> Do not lay up for yourselves treasures on earth, where moth and rust destroy and where thieves break in and steal, but lay up for yourselves treasures in heaven, where neither moth nor rust destroys and where thieves do not break in and steal. For where your treasure is, there your heart will be also. (Mt.6:19-21)

> For we brought nothing into the world, and we cannot take anything out of the world. (1 Ti.6:7)

> Your gold and silver have corroded, and their corrosion will be evidence against you and will eat your flesh like fire. You have laid up treasure in the last days. (Jas.5:3)

> Surely a man goes about as a shadow! Surely for nothing they are in turmoil; man heaps up wealth and does not know who will gather! (Ps.39:6)

> For he sees that even the wise die; the fool and the stupid alike must perish and leave their wealth to others. (Ps.49:10)

> I hated all my toil in which I toil under the sun, seeing that I must leave it to the man who will come after me. (Ec.2:18)

N. The Genuine Believer: Do Not Worry About Necessities, 12:22–34

(Mt.6:25–34)

1. Do not worry about food or clothing

   a. The reason: Your life and body mean more than things
   b. Illustration 1: The ravens are fed by God

   c. Illustration 2: Your lifespan is not altered an hour by worry

   d. Illustration 3: The lilies and grass are clothed by God

   e. A tragic truth: Worry shows you have little faith[DS1]

2. Do not be wrapped up in seeking food or drink, or doubt God's care

   a. Such behavior is worldly
   b. God knows your needs

3. Seek the kingdom of God
   a. God provides necessities
   b. God gives you the kingdom

   c. God gives treasures that do not age, fail, or corrupt; nor can they be stolen

   d. God warns: Your heart will be where your treasure is

22 And he said to his disciples, "Therefore I tell you, do not be anxious about your life, what you will eat, nor about your body, what you will put on. 23 For life is more than food, and the body more than clothing. 24 Consider the ravens: they neither sow nor reap, they have neither storehouse nor barn, and yet God feeds them. Of how much more value are you than the birds! 25 And which of you by being anxious can add a single hour to his span of life? 26 If then you are not able to do as small a thing as that, why are you anxious about the rest? 27 Consider the lilies, how they grow: they neither toil nor spin, yet I tell you, even Solomon in all his glory was not arrayed like one of these. 28 But if God so clothes the grass, which is alive in the field today, and tomorrow is thrown into the oven, how much more will he clothe you, O you of little faith! 29 And do not seek what you are to eat and what you are to drink, nor be worried. 30 For all the nations of the world seek after these things, and your Father knows that you need them." 31 Instead, seek his kingdom, and these things will be added to you. 32 Fear not, little flock, for it is your Father's good pleasure to give you the kingdom. 33 Sell your possessions, and give to the needy. Provide yourselves with moneybags that do not grow old, with a treasure in the heavens that does not fail, where no thief approaches and no moth destroys. 34 For where your treasure is, there will your heart be also."

Division V

The Son of Man's Great Journey to Jerusalem (Stage I): His Mission and Public Challenge, 9:51–13:21

N. The Genuine Believer: Do Not Worry About Necessities, 12:22–34

(Mt.6:25–34)

12:22–34
Introduction

Jesus is continuing to teach *His disciples* (v.22). After exhorting them to not fear persecution (vv.1-12) and to guard against covetousness (vv.13-21), He now instructs them to not worry but to trust God for *all* their needs. Again, this message is not for the world in general; it is for disciples, the followers of Jesus. *Being anxious* or *worrying* about having what we need is a common concern in this world. However, it is not to be so among God's people, for our heavenly Father has promised to provide for us (see outline and notes—Mt.6:25-34 for more discussion and application). This is, *The Genuine Believer: Do Not Worry About Necessities*, 12:22-34.

1. Do not worry about food or clothing (vv.22-28).
2. Do not be wrapped up in seeking food or drink, or doubt God's care (vv.29-30).
3. Seek the kingdom of God (vv.31-34).

1 Do not worry about food or clothing.

The uncertainties of life in this world make it easy to worry about having the necessities of life. At some point in our lives, most of us will find ourselves in circumstances that threaten our security in having our needs met. Many people face this insecurity every day, not having adequate food or shelter. In poverty-stricken countries, life is a constant quest for food, water, clothing, and shelter. Our Lord charges us, His dear followers, not to be anxious or worry over such things. Jesus gives the reason why and then drives the point home with three illustrations.

a. The reason: Your life and body mean more than things (v.23).

Jesus is continuing to stress the lesson of the parable He had just given: life is about more than just material things (v.15). The life and the body mean much more than the food we eat and the clothes we wear. We are to focus on spiritual things, eternal things. Even the most basic needs of life—food and clothing—are not the things that are to consume our minds. As Jesus is about to say, if we will seek the kingdom of God, He will provide our necessities (v.31).

²² And he said to his disciples, "Therefore I tell you, do not be anxious about your life, what you will eat, nor about your body, what you will put on.

²³ For life is more than food, and the body more than clothing.

²⁴ Consider the ravens: they neither sow nor reap, they have neither storehouse nor barn, and yet God feeds them. Of how much more value are you than the birds!

²⁵ And which of you by being anxious can add a single hour to his span of life?

²⁶ If then you are not able to do as small a thing as that, why are you anxious about the rest?

²⁷ Consider the lilies, how they grow: they neither toil nor spin, yet I tell you, even Solomon in all his glory was not arrayed like one of these.

²⁸ But if God so clothes the grass, which is alive in the field today, and tomorrow is thrown into the oven, how much more will he clothe you, O you of little faith!"

At the same time, it is important to note what Jesus is *not* saying. Jesus is not saying that we should neglect caring for our bodies and lives. A *healthy body* will enhance our time on earth, and a *well-kept life* will assure a person of living *forever* in the presence of God. We are stewards of everything God has given us, including our bodies and our lives.

Nor is Jesus saying that we are not to think and plan for the necessities of life. He says we are not to *worry* and be anxious over the necessities of life. Everything in life takes some thought and some planning, but nothing should be so coveted that it causes anxiety and worry for us.

b. Illustration 1: The ravens are fed by God (v.24).

To illustrate the truth that we should not worry, Jesus points us to the ravens (crows). They are fed by God. Jesus said, "Consider"—think about the birds. They do not sow or reap their food. They do not store up their food. Yet, God provides food for them. They are able to find the food that they need.

Jesus then reminds us that we—God's dear children—are of much more value than the birds.

➤ We are higher beings, on a much higher level of creation. We are more noble and excellent, spiritual beings capable of a personal relationship with God (Jb.35:11; Jn.3:16).

➤ We are the children of God. God is the creator of birds, but He is the Father of believers (Ro.8:15-16; Ga.4:4-6).

➤ We are heirs of God. We are chosen to receive all that God possesses on that glorious day of redemption (Ro.8:16-17; Tit.3:7; 1 Pe.1:3-4).

Again, however, Jesus is not pampering His followers. He is absolutely not saying that we should avoid working to provide our needs. He is talking about *worrying* and *being anxious* over life's necessities. God does not put up with laziness and slothfulness, nor with lack of planning and initiative and effort. Jesus planned ahead (Jn.12:6) and preached industriousness (Lu.16:8; see 1-10). The Bible is clear that we should remain faithful while working at our place of employment, even working in order to have extra to give and to help meet the needs of others and of a desperate world (Ep.4:28; see note—Mt.6:25-34).

> For what does it profit a man if he gains the whole world and loses or forfeits himself? (Lu.9:25)

> Do not be anxious about anything, but in everything by prayer and supplication with thanksgiving let your requests be made known to God. And the peace of God, which surpasses all understanding, will guard your hearts and your minds in Christ Jesus. (Ph.4:6-7)

> Oh, how abundant is your goodness, which you have stored up for those who fear you and worked for those who take refuge in you, in the sight of the children of mankind! (Ps.31:19)

> You keep him in perfect peace whose mind is stayed on you, because he trusts in you. . . . Trust in the Lord forever, for the Lord God is an everlasting rock. (Is.26:3-4)

THOUGHT 1. The believer who truly trusts Jesus Christ will never be forsaken by God. This does not mean the believer will never suffer nor that the believer will never have to face difficulties. Suffering is sometimes necessary for the growth of the believer's faith and as a testimony to the world (see notes—Mt.5:10-12; 10:24-25). However, God never forsakes the believer. He takes care of the believer no matter what circumstances confront us. God cares for the believer and feeds us far more quickly than He feeds the ravens of the air.

> Then he ordered the crowds to sit down on the grass, and taking the five loaves and the two fish, he looked up to heaven and said a blessing. Then he broke the loaves and gave them to the disciples, and the disciples gave them to the crowds. And they all ate and were satisfied. And they took up twelve baskets full of the broken pieces left over. (Mt.14:19-20)

> Not that I am speaking of being in need, for I have learned in whatever situation I am to be content. I know how to be brought low, and I know how to abound. In any and every circumstance, I have learned the secret of facing plenty and hunger, abundance and need. I can do all things through him who strengthens me. . . . And my God will supply every need of yours according to his riches in glory in Christ Jesus. (Ph.4:11-13, 19)

> Trust in the Lord, and do good; dwell in the land and befriend faithfulness. (Ps.37:3)

> You visit the earth and water it; you greatly enrich it; the river of God is full of water; you provide their grain, for so you have prepared it. (Ps.65:9)

> Even to your old age I am he, and to gray hairs I will carry you. I have made, and I will bear; I will carry and will save. (Is.46:4)

c. Illustration 2: Your lifespan is not altered an hour by worry (vv.25-26).

English Bible versions vary on the translation of this verse. Some, including the ESV, speak of adding an hour to one's lifespan. Others, including the KJV and NKJV, speak of adding a cubit to one's stature. This is because the Greek word translated as *span of life* or *stature* (hēlikian, *hay-lick'-ih-ahn*) means height, quality, or status gained by growth; but sometimes it also means age. Likewise, the Greek word translated as *hour* or *cubit* (pēchun, *pay'-koon*) usually means a measure of distance (approximately 18 inches); but it can also mean a measure of time or age (Jn.9:21). So the verse can read either "who can add one cubit to his stature" or "one hour to his life span."

Regardless, the point is the same, and it is effective: worry is senseless—just as senseless as trying to add inches to our height or hours to our life. Both are beyond our control. We cannot make ourselves taller, and, ultimately, the exact time of our death is in God's hands. It is senseless to worry about things that are under God's control.

THOUGHT 1. Note the rich fool could not add one minute to his life. There was a time appointed for his death, and he could not change that time (see Lu.12:16–21).

Most short people, especially men, wish they were taller, and many tall people, especially ladies, wish they were shorter. But they cannot do anything to alter their God-ordained height. How do we keep from worrying about things that are beyond our control?

1) Realize there is a glorious hope for all (see note—Mt.6:27 for discussion).

2) Trust God's assuring promise to work all things out for good to those who truly love Him.

> And we know that for those who love God all things work together for good, for those who are called according to his purpose. (Ro.8:28)

3) Embrace the strong challenge to be content with one's state or lot in life.

> Only let each person lead the life that the Lord has assigned to him, and to which God has called him. This is my rule in all the churches. . . . Each one should remain in the condition in which he was called. . . . So, brothers, in whatever condition each was called, there let him remain with God. (1 Co.7:17, 20, 24; see vv.7–24)

> Not that I am speaking of being in need, for I have learned in whatever situation I am to be content. I know how to be brought low, and I know how to abound. In any and every circumstance, I have learned the secret of facing plenty and hunger, abundance and need. I can do all things through him who strengthens me. (Ph.4:11–13)

> Let the lowly brother boast in his exaltation, and the rich in his humiliation, because like a flower of the grass he will pass away. For the sun rises with its scorching heat and withers the grass; its flower falls, and its beauty perishes. So also will the rich man fade away in the midst of his pursuits. (Jas.1:9–11)

4) Obey God's command to trust His care.

> Casting all your anxieties on him, because he cares for you. (1 Pe.5:7)

> It is in vain that you rise up early and go late to rest, eating the bread of anxious toil; for he gives to his beloved sleep. (Ps.127:2)

d. Illustration 3: The lilies and grass are clothed by God (vv.27–28a).

In these verses Jesus proceeds to point His followers to the lilies and the grass. They are clothed by God. Again, Jesus says, "Consider"—look at and think about the lilies and grass of the field. Learn from what happens to them:

➢ Lilies do not toil for money to buy their clothing.

➢ Lilies do not spin to make their clothing.

➢ Yet, lilies are more arrayed than Solomon in all his glory.

➢ Grass is cut down and burned, yet God cares enough for it to provide for it.

We are of much more value than lilies and grass. With that being true, it is senseless to worry; God will clothe us.

THOUGHT 1. We need to seriously consider how concerned we often are with clothing. (Sometimes the concern becomes so strong it turns into a literal fear.) Note three concerns many people have about their clothing.

1) The concern of popularity. Some people fear not having the right clothing necessary to make them popular. Sometimes the concern is so great that they refuse to go to a particular function without the proper clothing.

2) The concern of style and fashion. Some are concerned with the very latest in style and fashion. They cannot accept their clothing's being the least bit outdated.

3) The concern of acceptability. Most adults would fall into this category. Clothing is a matter that actually involves inward feelings. The concern is really there. Time and thought and effort are expended to stay in style, at least enough to be acceptable.

> Do not let your adorning be external—the braiding of hair and the putting on of gold jewelry, or the clothing you wear—but let your adorning be the hidden person of the heart with the imperishable beauty of a gentle and quiet spirit, which in God's sight is very precious. (1 Pe.3:3-4)

e. A tragic truth: Worry shows you have little faith (v.28b).

Jesus emphasized that worrying about life's necessities reveals our lack of faith (see DEEPER STUDY # 1). We should not be anxious over life's necessities. Instead, we should trust God to provide the food and clothing we need. When we worry about these things, we are saying, essentially, that we do not believe God will take care of us.

DEEPER STUDY # 1

(12:28) **"O You of Little Faith":** see DEEPER STUDY # 1—Mt.6:30 for discussion.

12:29-30

29 "And do not seek what you are to eat and what you are to drink, nor be worried.
30 For all the nations of the world seek after these things, and your Father knows that you need them."

2 Do not be wrapped up in seeking food or drink, or doubt God's care.

Jesus said that we should not be wrapped up in seeking food and drink, nor should we worry about these things. When we are anxious about life's necessities, we doubt God's care for us. Note a significant fact: this is not a challenge; *it is a command*. Our primary focus is not to be on material things, even the most basic things we need. Jesus gives two reasons for this command.

a. Such behavior is worldly (v.30a).

Focusing primarily on material things is what worldly people do. It is what *the nations of the world*, the Gentiles, the heathen, the lost, do. Their lives revolve around getting things that pertain to this life and this world. Christ's followers are not to be seeking after these things. We are to be different, have different priorities and a different focus.

> For the Gentiles seek after all these things, and your heavenly Father knows that you need them all. (Mt.6:32)

> But watch yourselves lest your hearts be weighed down with dissipation and drunkenness and cares of this life, and that day come upon you suddenly like a trap. (Lu.21:34)

> Set your minds on things that are above, not on things that are on earth. (Col.3:2)

b. God knows your needs (v.30b).

Jesus assured us that our heavenly Father knows our needs. We are to rest in that assurance and not have a *doubtful* and *anxious mind* about them. We are to trust God and His ability to provide the things we need to live in this world.

> And Jesus said to him, ". . . All things are possible for one who believes." (Mk.9:23)

> For everyone who has been born of God overcomes the world. And this is the victory that has overcome the world—our faith. (1 Jn.5:4)

> Commit your way to the LORD; trust in him, and he will act. (Ps.37:5)

> The LORD has remembered us; he will bless us; he will bless the house of Israel; he will bless the house of Aaron. (Ps.115:12)

> Trust in the LORD with all your heart, and do not lean on your own understanding. (Pr.3:5)

3 Seek the kingdom of God.

Instead of seeking material things, even life's most basic necessities, Jesus commands us to seek the kingdom of God (see DEEPER STUDY # 3—Mt.19:23–24). Our lives are not to revolve around seeking the things of this world. We are to focus our lives on the kingdom of God and the work God has given us to do. We are to leave our welfare in the hands of God. In relation to this, Jesus makes three great promises and delivers one significant warning.

> [31] "Instead, seek his kingdom, and these things will be added to you.
> [32] Fear not, little flock, for it is your Father's good pleasure to give you the kingdom.
> [33] Sell your possessions, and give to the needy. Provide yourselves with moneybags that do not grow old, with a treasure in the heavens that does not fail, where no thief approaches and no moth destroys.
> [34] For where your treasure is, there will your heart be also."

a. God provides necessities (v.31).

Jesus promises that God will provide the necessities of life for the person who seeks God first. If we will focus on seeking His kingdom, He will see to it that our needs are met. When we seek the spiritual and eternal, God will give us the material things life requires.

> And I tell you, ask, and it will be given to you; seek, and you will find; knock, and it will be opened to you. For everyone who asks receives, and the one who seeks finds, and to the one who knocks it will be opened. What father among you, if his son asks for a fish, will instead of a fish give him a serpent; or if he asks for an egg, will give him a scorpion? If you then, who are evil, know how to give good gifts to your children, how much more will the heavenly Father give the Holy Spirit to those who ask him! (Lu.11:9–13)
>
> And will not God give justice to his elect, who cry to him day and night? Will he delay long over them? (Lu.18:7)
>
> If you ask me anything in my name, I will do it. (Jn.14:14)

b. God gives you the kingdom (v.32).

God wants to give us something far greater than food and drink and clothing. He wants to give us His kingdom. God will give the kingdom to His "little flock," those who truly seek God's kingdom first and trust Him to care for them. Note the term "little flock." It tells us two things.

First, the number is small. Only a few really seek God's kingdom first.

> For the gate is narrow and the way is hard that leads to life, and those who find it are few. (Mt.7:14)
>
> For many are called, but few are chosen. (Mt.22:14)
>
> Then the King will say to those on his right, "Come, you who are blessed by my Father, inherit the kingdom prepared for you from the foundation of the world. For I was hungry and you gave me food, I was thirsty and you gave me drink, I was a stranger and you welcomed me." (Mt.25:34–35)
>
> For the kingdom of God is not a matter of eating and drinking but of righteousness and peace and joy in the Holy Spirit. (Ro.14:17)
>
> Listen, my beloved brothers, has not God chosen those who are poor in the world to be rich in faith and heirs of the kingdom, which he has promised to those who love him? (Jas.2:5)

Second, God's care is sure. He is the Shepherd and His true followers are *His* flock, the sheep of *His* pasture (Ps.100:3). The Lord will take care of His sheep.

> To him the gatekeeper opens. The sheep hear his voice, and he calls his own sheep by name and leads them out. When he has brought out all his own, he goes before them, and the sheep follow him, for they know his voice. (Jn.10:3–4)
>
> I am the good shepherd. I know my own and my own know me, . . . And I have other sheep that are not of this fold. I must bring them also, and they will listen to my voice. So there will be one flock, one shepherd. (Jn.10:14, 16)
>
> The LORD is my shepherd; I shall not want. (Ps.23:1; see vv.2–6)

c. God gives treasures that do not age, fail, or corrupt; nor can they be stolen (v.33).

Instead of focusing on receiving what we need and accumulating possessions beyond what we need, Jesus calls us to focus on giving to those who have needs. In return, Jesus promises that God will give us treasure in heaven, treasure that endures throughout eternity.

This concept is revolutionary. Again and again, Jesus preached strongly against accumulating possessions. The parable He has just given emphasizes the foolishness of doing so (vv.15-21). We live in a world so full of needs, a world that is lost and dying. Once our own needs have been met, we are to give of our abundance to meet the needs of others. Our position or profession or how much income we have does not matter. Once our needs are met, we are to begin meeting the needs of the world. In fact, believers are commanded to work so that we can have *more* to give to the needy (Ep.4:28). Our purpose for working is not to achieve a reputable position nor to gain wealth. It is for the purpose of seeking God's kingdom, of spreading the love of God by meeting the needs of others.

> Give to the one who begs from you, and do not refuse the one who would borrow from you. (Mt.5:42)

> And he answered them, "Whoever has two tunics is to share with him who has none, and whoever has food is to do likewise." (Lu.3:11)

> In all things I have shown you that by working hard in this way we must help the weak and remember the words of the Lord Jesus, how he himself said, "It is more blessed to give than to receive." (Ac.20:35)

> Contribute to the needs of the saints and seek to show hospitality. (Ro.12:13)

> So then, as we have opportunity, let us do good to everyone, and especially to those who are of the household of faith. (Ga.6:10)

> Let the thief no longer steal, but rather let him labor, doing honest work with his own hands, so that he may have something to share with anyone in need. (Ep.4:28)

> They are to do good, to be rich in good works, to be generous and ready to share. (1 Ti.6:18)

> Do not neglect to do good and to share what you have, for such sacrifices are pleasing to God. (He.13:16)

Nothing of this earth lasts throughout eternity. Just like the foolish rich man in Jesus' parable, we leave all our earthly possessions behind when we die. But when we give what we have to meet the desperate needs of others—both physical and spiritual needs—we fill our bag with *real treasure*, eternal treasure that will . . .

- never age
- never fail
- never be stolen
- never be destroyed

> Indeed, I count everything as loss because of the surpassing worth of knowing Christ Jesus my Lord. For his sake I have suffered the loss of all things and count them as rubbish, in order that I may gain Christ (Ph.3:8)

> Thus storing up treasure for themselves as a good foundation for the future, so that they may take hold of that which is truly life. (1 Ti.6:19)

> Blessed be the God and Father of our Lord Jesus Christ! According to his great mercy, he has caused us to be born again to a living hope through the resurrection of Jesus Christ from the dead, to an inheritance that is imperishable, undefiled, and unfading, kept in heaven for you. (1 Pe.1:3-4)

> I counsel you to buy from me gold refined by fire, so that you may be rich, and white garments so that you may clothe yourself and the shame of your nakedness may not be seen, and salve to anoint your eyes, so that you may see. (Re.3:18)

Jesus calls us to secure the treasures of God's approval and of souls won in heaven. These treasures will never fail nor corrupt nor be stolen.

> For what is our hope or joy or crown of boasting before our Lord Jesus at his coming? Is it not you? (1 Th.2:19)

d. **God warns: Your heart will be where your treasure is (v.34).**

In verse 34, Jesus warns His followers: our hearts will be where our treasure is. If our treasure is in this world, if we live indulgent and extravagant lives, our hearts will be in the world. But if our treasure is in heaven, if we invest our money and possessions in the Lord's work of helping others and reaching souls, our hearts will be in heaven.

> But lay up for yourselves treasures in heaven, where neither moth nor rust destroys and where thieves do not break in and steal. (Mt.6:20)

The kingdom of heaven is like treasure hidden in a field, which a man found and covered up. Then in his joy he goes and sells all that he has and buys that field. (Mt.13:44)

Jesus said to him, "If you would be perfect, go, sell what you possess and give to the poor, and you will have treasure in heaven; and come, follow me." (Mt.19:21)

And all who believed were together and had all things in common. And they were selling their possessions and belongings and distributing the proceeds to all, as any had need. (Ac.2:44–45)

There was not a needy person among them, for as many as were owners of lands or houses sold them and brought the proceeds of what was sold and laid it at the apostles' feet, and it was distributed to each as any had need. (Ac.4:34–35)

Do not love the world or the things in the world. If anyone loves the world, the love of the Father is not in him. For all that is in the world—the desires of the flesh and the desires of the eyes and pride of life—is not from the Father but is from the world. And the world is passing away along with its desires, but whoever does the will of God abides forever. (1 Jn.2:15–17)

O. The Parable of the Faithful and Unfaithful Managers: A Strong Warning—Be Prepared, 12:35–48

(Mt.24:37–25:30)

1. The charge: Be watching—be ready for the Lord's return
   a. Because your master—the Lord—is returning

   b. Because you will be served by your master—Christ Himself

   c. Because you will be blessed (it will be good for you)

   d. Because you must not be caught unprepared

   e. Because Christ will come when least expected

2. The parable of the managers
   a. Peter's question
   b. Jesus' answer regarding a faithful and wise manager
      1) He is a manager who oversees others

      2) He is also a servant
      3) He is found doing—serving faithfully
      4) He will be rewarded, put in charge

   c. An unfaithful and unwise manager
      1) He presumes there is plenty of time
      2) He does what he wants, abusing others and living a worldly life
      3) He will be judged with the unbelievers

35 "Stay dressed for action and keep your lamps burning,

36 and be like men who are waiting for their master to come home from the wedding feast, so that they may open the door to him at once when he comes and knocks.

37 Blessed are those servants whom the master finds awake when he comes. Truly, I say to you, he will dress himself for service and have them recline at table, and he will come and serve them.

38 If he comes in the second watch, or in the third, and finds them awake, blessed are those servants!

39 But know this, that if the master of the house had known at what hour the thief was coming, he would not have left his house to be broken into.

40 You also must be ready, for the Son of Man is coming at an hour you do not expect."

41 Peter said, "Lord, are you telling this parable for us or for all?"

42 And the Lord said, "Who then is the faithful and wise manager, whom his master will set over his household, to give them their portion of food at the proper time?

43 Blessed is that servant whom his master will find so doing when he comes.

44 Truly, I say to you, he will set him over all his possessions.

45 But if that servant says to himself, 'My master is delayed in coming,' and begins to beat the male and female servants, and to eat and drink and get drunk,

46 the master of that servant will come on a day when he does not expect him and at an hour he does not know, and will cut him in pieces and put him with the unfaithful.

47 And that servant who knew his master's will but did not get ready or act according to his will, will receive a severe beating. **48** But the one who did not know, and did what deserved a beating, will receive a light beating. Everyone to whom much was given, of him much will be required, and from him to whom they entrusted much, they will demand the more."

d. The unfaithful managers' fate
   1) Those who sinned deliberately— knew the Lord's will—will be judged harshly
   2) Those who sinned in ignorance— did not know the Lord's will—will be judged less harshly
   3) The principle of judgment is perfect justice: Receiving much requires giving much

Division V

The Son of Man's Great Journey to Jerusalem (Stage I): His Mission and Public Challenge, 9:51–13:21

O. The Parable of the Faithful and Unfaithful Managers: A Strong Warning—Be Prepared, 12:35–48

(Mt.24:37–25:30)

12:35–48
Introduction

As Jesus continues speaking to His disciples, He is still dealing with the subject of covetousness, of being focused on and consumed with accumulating money and possessions (vv.13-21; vv.22-34). The believer's mind is to be focused on holiness and service, not on possessions and cares of this world. Our Lord has committed His work to us. He has left us responsible for taking the gospel to the world and making disciples (Mt.28:18-20). But He is coming again, and He will hold us accountable for our faithfulness or unfaithfulness to Him and His work. We need to be prepared for His return, always watching and ever busy about His work. This is, *The Parable of the Faithful and Unfaithful Managers: A Strong Warning—Be Prepared*, 12:35-48.

1. The charge: Be watching—be ready for the Lord's return (vv.35-40).
2. The parable of the managers (vv.41-48).

1 The charge: Be watching—be ready for the Lord's return.

In these verses, Jesus shares a gripping illustration. The picture is that of a master who has gone off to attend a great marriage celebration. His servants have been left behind to look after the household and to wait for his return. The servants should be diligently looking after everything until he returns, and they should be waiting to greet him upon his return.

The point of the illustration is, believers are to live in a constant state of readiness (v.35). We are always to be prepared, always watching and waiting for our Lord's return.

➢ We are to be fully dressed, ready for action. Most literally translated, this phrase is *your loins* (Gk. osphues,

35 "Stay dressed for action and keep your lamps burning,
36 and be like men who are waiting for their master to come home from the wedding feast, so that they may open the door to him at once when he comes and knocks.
37 Blessed are those servants whom the master finds awake when he comes. Truly, I say to you, he will dress himself for service and have them recline at table, and he will come and serve them.
38 If he comes in the second watch, or in the third, and finds them awake, blessed are those servants!
39 But know this, that if the master of the house had known at what hour the thief was coming, he would not have left his house to be broken into.
40 You also must be ready, for the Son of Man is coming at an hour you do not expect."

401

os-foo'-es) *having been girded* (periezōsmenai, *peh-rih-eh-zōs-men'-eye*). In the East, men wore robes that came down over their knees. These loose robes hampered movement and work. When working or battling, they raised their robes and tied them with a belt at the waist so they could move quickly and freely. Jesus is speaking of personal preparation: keeping your heart and life pure and staying ever ready to move and meet the Lord, as well as being constantly ready to serve the Lord.

➤ We are to keep our lamps burning, never allowing them to go out. This statement refers to serving and laboring for the Lord. We are to keep the lights of labor burning by faithfully serving and working for the Lord. It also speaks of watching expectantly for the Lord's return.

The idea behind both images is, of course, *readiness*: being prepared in body and labor, being pure and faithful. The believer must never lie down or slumber, never be caught off guard or unprepared. Jesus gives six reasons for living in a constant state of readiness, of purity and faithfulness.

a. Because your master—the Lord—is returning (v.36).

The believer is to stay ready because the Lord is returning. He is the *master* in the illustration, the head of the house; He owns the property. He did not desert the house or the property. He left to attend a great marriage feast. He will be returning to *His home and His property* (world).

Most literally translated, this verse begins, "and you yourselves be like men . . ." The words "your" (v.35) and "you yourselves" are emphatic. No matter what others may do, "your loins" and "your lamps" must be prepared. You must be like people who wait and stay awake and look and are prepared for their Lord. You must be *ready* to open the door *immediately* when He knocks, for He is going to return. His return is an absolute certainty (see Jn.14:2–3; Tit.2:12–13).

> But he remained silent and made no answer. Again the high priest asked him, "Are you the Christ, the Son of the Blessed?" And Jesus said, "I am, and you will see the Son of Man seated at the right hand of Power, and coming with the clouds of heaven." (Mk.14:61–62)

> And then they will see the Son of Man coming in a cloud with power and great glory. (Lu.21:27)

> And said, "Men of Galilee, why do you stand looking into heaven? This Jesus, who was taken up from you into heaven, will come in the same way as you saw him go into heaven." (Ac.1:11)

> For the Lord himself will descend from heaven with a cry of command, with the voice of an archangel, and with the sound of the trumpet of God. And the dead in Christ will rise first. (1 Th.4:16)

> So Christ, having been offered once to bear the sins of many, will appear a second time, not to deal with sin but to save those who are eagerly waiting for him. (He.9:28)

THOUGHT 1. An application to salvation may be made here as well. A person must be ready to open the door of his or her heart immediately when Jesus knocks.

> Behold, I stand at the door and knock. If anyone hears my voice and opens the door, I will come in to him and eat with him, and he with me. (Re.3:20)

b. Because you will be served by your master—Christ Himself (v.37).

Jesus gives a second reason why we are to be prepared and watching for His return: because we will be served by Christ Himself. This is a most precious and wonderful promise, a most unusual promise. Imagine the Lord of the universe *serving* us at a banquet! Yet it is the promise made by Jesus. Why would such a promise be made to the believer?

God has only one Son, and God loves His only Son *so much* that He promises to elevate to the highest position any person who serves His Son. Any person who serves God's Son will be highly honored by God.

> If anyone serves me, he must follow me; and where I am, there will my servant be also. If anyone serves me, the Father will honor him. (Jn.12:26)

The person who believes in God's Son is adopted as a child of God's, and that person becomes a brother or sister to Christ and an heir of God.

> For you did not receive the spirit of slavery to fall back into fear, but you have received the Spirit of adoption as sons, by whom we cry, "Abba! Father!" The Spirit himself bears witness with our spirit

that we are children of God, and if children, then heirs—heirs of God and fellow heirs with Christ, provided we suffer with him in order that we may also be glorified with him. For I consider that the sufferings of this present time are not worth comparing with the glory that is to be revealed to us. (Ro.8:15-18)

But when the fullness of time had come, God sent forth his Son, born of woman, born under the law, to redeem those who were under the law, so that we might receive adoption as sons. And because you are sons, God has sent the Spirit of his Son into our hearts, crying, "Abba! Father!" So you are no longer a slave, but a son, and if a son, then an heir through God. (Ga.4:4-7)

Believers are to stay ready because the very thing for which we have been working is Christ's return. When Christ gathers us all together, His heart will be so overflowing with love and joy (as will ours) that *He* will serve *us*. In this world, we have served Him. But when He comes for us and takes us to His home—heaven—He will serve us. What a humbling thought!

In my Father's house are many rooms. If it were not so, would I have told you that I go to prepare a place for you? And if I go and prepare a place for you, I will come again and will take you to myself, that where I am you may be also. (Jn.14:2-3)

But our citizenship is in heaven, and from it we await a Savior, the Lord Jesus Christ, who will transform our lowly body to be like his glorious body, by the power that enables him even to subject all things to himself. (Ph.3:20-21)

When Christ who is your life appears, then you also will appear with him in glory. (Col.3:4)

So that he may establish your hearts blameless in holiness before our God and Father, at the coming of our Lord Jesus with all his saints. (1 Th.3:13)

Note the statement, "He will dress Himself for service" or "gird Himself." This is the same image conveyed of Christ's first coming to earth as a man; He took off the outward glories of His deity and took on Himself "the form of a servant" (Ph.2:7-8). When Christ came the first time, He came to serve us by becoming one of us and laying down His life on the cross. Jesus did not come to be served, but to serve by giving His life as a ransom for our sins (Mk.10:45). Our Lord portrayed this precious truth when He washed His disciples' feet. He took off His outer garments and girded Himself in the servant's apron—the towel—and humbly washed their feet, symbolizing the spiritual cleansing He gives to all who believe (Jn.13:4-8).

Now we are told that He will once again put on the servant's apron when He comes for us. He who washed us in His own blood will serve us in glory! How can we not be moved by this thought? How can we not serve Him with all of our strength? How can we not give Him everything we are and have?

c. **Because you will be blessed (it will be good for you) (v.38).**
The third reason we are to stay ready is because we will be blessed. The word *blessed* (makarioi, *mah-kah'-rih-oy*) speaks of those who have been made happy or blessed. The idea is that Christ is going to make the faithful believers—those who are watching for His return—happy and blessed. Happiness and blessedness will become a state of being, the constant experience of the believer. But note two points.

First, this blessing is conditional. We must be watching and ready for the Lord's coming (pure and faithful) if we are to receive this blessing.

Second, it is for those whose faithfulness endures until Christ returns. The night was divided into four watches by the Romans and into three watches by the Jews. Christ may not return in the first watch; His return may be in the second or third watch. The point is the importance of being ready and staying ready, of continuing to be faithful until the Lord returns, no matter how long the wait is. The hour of His return is unknown, but He is returning. It may be immediately; it may be later. The idea is that no one knows the time, but we must stay ready—be prepared—if we wish to be blessed. We must not quit after the "first watch." We must keep serving, keep watching until the night is over—until the Lord comes.

Let your reasonableness be known to everyone. The Lord is at hand. (Ph.4:5)

You also, be patient. Establish your hearts, for the coming of the Lord is at hand. (Jas.5:8)

I am coming soon. Hold fast what you have, so that no one may seize your crown. (Re.3:11)

d. Because you must not be caught unprepared (v.39).

The fourth reason the believer is to stay ready is because Christ will come unexpectedly. The illustration is clear: the hour of the Lord's return is not known; His return is going to be unexpected. The believer . . .

- must not be careless: get tired of waiting up, get sleepy, be caught off guard, begin to disbelieve. (All of this can happen to a house owner waiting on a burglar.)
- must watch: secure, sit up, stay awake, listen, look, take notice of all noises and sights (signs). (The burglar always comes in an unexpected hour.)

The believer must watch and be prepared as much as a home owner would watch and prepare if he knew a burglar were coming.

> For as the lightning comes from the east and shines as far as the west, so will be the coming of the Son of Man. . . . But concerning that day and hour no one knows, not even the angels of heaven, nor the Son, but the Father only. (Mt.24:27, 36)

> Therefore stay awake—for you do not know when the master of the house will come, in the evening, or at midnight, or when the rooster crows, or in the morning. (Mk.13:35)

e. Because Christ will come when least expected (v.40).

The fifth reason the believer is to stay ready is because Christ will come when *least* expected. Jesus could not have stated it any clearer; He could not have spoken any plainer. When we do not expect Him, He will come. Therefore, we must always "be ready."

> Therefore you also must be ready, for the Son of Man is coming at an hour you do not expect. (Mt.24:44)

> And while they were going to buy, the bridegroom came, and those who were ready went in with him to the marriage feast, and the door was shut. Afterward the other virgins came also, saying, "Lord, lord, open to us." But he answered, "Truly, I say to you, I do not know you." Watch therefore, for you know neither the day nor the hour. (Mt.25:10–13, see vv.6–9)

> For you yourselves are fully aware that the day of the Lord will come like a thief in the night. (1 Th.5:2)

> Remember, then, what you received and heard. Keep it, and repent. If you will not wake up, I will come like a thief, and you will not know at what hour I will come against you. (Re.3:3)

12:41–48

> Behold, I am coming like a thief! Blessed is the one who stays awake, keeping his garments on, that he may not go about naked and be seen exposed! (Re.16:15)

⁴¹ Peter said, "Lord, are you telling this parable for us or for all?"

⁴² And the Lord said, "Who then is the faithful and wise manager, whom his master will set over his household, to give them their portion of food at the proper time?

⁴³ Blessed is that servant whom his master will find so doing when he comes.

⁴⁴ Truly, I say to you, he will set him over all his possessions.

⁴⁵ But if that servant says to himself, 'My master is delayed in coming,' and begins to beat the male and female servants, and to eat and drink and get drunk,

⁴⁶ the master of that servant will come on a day when he does not expect him and at an hour he does not know, and will cut him in pieces and put him with the unfaithful.

⁴⁷ And that servant who knew his master's will but did not get ready or act according to his will, will receive a severe beating.

⁴⁸ But the one who did not know, and did what deserved a beating, will receive a light beating. Everyone to whom much was given, of him much will be required, and from him to whom they entrusted much, they will demand the more."

2 The parable of the managers.

Jesus went on to explain this truth so clearly that nobody could misunderstand what He was saying. In the parable that follows, the *master* is the Lord Himself, and the *manager* or *steward* is the servant of Jesus Christ.

a. Peter's question (v.41).

Peter wanted to know if Jesus' message on watching and readiness was for the disciples only or did it apply to the world as well. Jesus answered by giving a parable known as the parable of the managers or stewards.

b. Jesus' answer regarding a faithful and wise manager (vv.42–44).

Jesus told first of a faithful and wise manager. The Lord said four things about this servant who fulfilled his responsibilities diligently and faithfully.

First, he was a *manager* or *steward* (oikonomos, *oy-kon-om'-os*; v.42). A manager was just what Jesus said he was: a man who was set over his master's household. He oversaw the master's estate and business and was responsible for all of it, including the master's servants.

> For it will be like a man going on a journey, who called his servants and entrusted to them his property. To one he gave five talents, to another two, to another one, to each according to his ability. Then he went away. (Mt.25:14-15)

> Calling ten of his servants, he gave them ten minas, and said to them, "Engage in business until I come." (Lu.19:13)

Second, he was a *servant* (doulos, *doo'-los*), a bond-slave, a man under his master's will entirely (v.43a). His very life depended on doing everything his master said (see note, *Slave*—Ro.1:1).

Third, he was found "so doing," that is, serving faithfully when his master returned (v.43b). His master found him *doing exactly* what he should have been doing (1 Co.4:2).

➤ He was overseeing the Master's household.

> For you were bought with a price. So glorify God in your body. (1 Co.6:20)

> Therefore, my beloved brothers, be steadfast, immovable, always abounding in the work of the Lord, knowing that in the Lord your labor is not in vain. (1 Co.15:58)

> Rendering service with a good will as to the Lord and not to man. (Ep.6:7)

> By the Holy Spirit who dwells within us, guard the good deposit entrusted to you. (2 Ti.1:14)

> Obey your leaders and submit to them, for they are keeping watch over your souls, as those who will have to give an account. Let them do this with joy and not with groaning, for that would be of no advantage to you. (He.13:17)

> Shepherd the flock of God that is among you, exercising oversight, not under compulsion, but willingly, as God would have you; not for shameful gain, but eagerly; not domineering over those in your charge, but being examples to the flock. (1 Pe.5:2-3)

➤ He was feeding the Master's family faithfully.

> When they had finished breakfast, Jesus said to Simon Peter, "Simon, son of John, do you love me more than these?" He said to him, "Yes, Lord; you know that I love you." He said to him, "Feed my lambs." (Jn.21:15; see vv.16-17)

> Moreover, it is required of stewards that they be found faithful. (1 Co.4:2)

> Keep a close watch on yourself and on the teaching. Persist in this, for by so doing you will save both yourself and your hearers. (1 Ti.4:16)

> As each has received a gift, use it to serve one another, as good stewards of God's varied grace. (1 Pe.4:10)

Fourth, he was to be rewarded, *promoted over all* that the Lord had (v.44). The idea is that the faithful and wise servants of the Lord will be placed as high as they can be placed. They will be given all that the Master and Lord has, that is, a complete estate to manage (see notes—Lu.16:10-12; 19:15-23; 22:28-30).

> His master said to him, "Well done, good and faithful servant. You have been faithful over a little; I will set you over much. Enter into the joy of your master." (Mt.25:23)

> And he said to him, "Well done, good servant! Because you have been faithful in a very little, you shall have authority over ten cities." (Lu.19:17)

> You are those who have stayed with me in my trials, and I assign to you, as my Father assigned to me, a kingdom. (Lu.22:28-29)

> Or do you not know that the saints will judge the world? And if the world is to be judged by you, are you incompetent to try trivial cases? (1 Co.6:2)

> If we endure, we will also reign with him; if we deny him, he also will deny us. (2 Ti.2:12)

> And from Jesus Christ the faithful witness, the firstborn of the dead, and the ruler of kings on earth. To him who loves us and has freed us from our sins by his blood and made us a kingdom, priests to his God and Father, to him be glory and dominion forever and ever. Amen. (Re.1:5-6)

c. **An unfaithful and unwise manager (vv.45-46).**

Jesus then told of an unfaithful, unwise manager. The Lord said three things about this servant who failed in his responsibilities.

First, the unfaithful manager presumed there was *plenty of time* (v.45a). Why? Because his master had delayed His coming; therefore, the manager thought his return was a long way off. Note that he did not doubt his master's return. He knew his master was returning, but he did not think it would be soon.

> And I will say to my soul, "Soul, you have ample goods laid up for many years; relax, eat, drink, be merry." (Lu.12:19)

> And as he reasoned about righteousness and self-control and the coming judgment, Felix was alarmed and said, "Go away for the present. When I get an opportunity I will summon you." (Ac.24:25)

> Come now, you who say, "Today or tomorrow we will go into such and such a town and spend a year there and trade and make a profit"—yet you do not know what tomorrow will bring. What is your life? For you are a mist that appears for a little time and then vanishes. (Jas.4:13–14)

> Do not boast about tomorrow, for you do not know what a day may bring. (Pr.27:1)

> "Come," they say, "let me get wine; let us fill ourselves with strong drink; and tomorrow will be like this day, great beyond measure." (Is.56:12)

Second, he did his own will, his own thing (v.45b). He mistreated and abused the servants under his authority, both male and female. And he was unfaithful to his duties. Instead of working, he indulged in the fleshly pleasures of partying and carousing, eating and drinking.

> And as for what fell among the thorns, they are those who hear, but as they go on their way they are choked by the cares and riches and pleasures of life, and their fruit does not mature. (Lu.8:14)

> One who is faithful in a very little is also faithful in much, and one who is dishonest in a very little is also dishonest in much. (Lu.16:10)

> But she who is self-indulgent is dead even while she lives. (1 Ti.5:6)

> For we ourselves were once foolish, disobedient, led astray, slaves to various passions and pleasures, passing our days in malice and envy, hated by others and hating one another. (Tit.3:3)

> You have lived on the earth in luxury and in self-indulgence. You have fattened your hearts in a day of slaughter. (Jas.5:5)

> You shall not oppress a hired worker who is poor and needy, whether he is one of your brothers or one of the sojourners who are in your land within your towns. (De.24:14)

Third, he was to be judged with the unfaithful or unbelievers (v.46). The Lord was very clear about this.

➤ The unfaithful manager will be caught by his master *unaware*; the master will return when the manager is not expecting him.

> For as in those days before the flood they were eating and drinking, marrying and giving in marriage, until the day when Noah entered the ark, and they were unaware until the flood came and swept them all away, so will be the coming of the Son of Man. (Mt.24:38–39)

> But watch yourselves lest your hearts be weighed down with dissipation and drunkenness and cares of this life, and that day come upon you suddenly like a trap. For it will come upon all who dwell on the face of the whole earth. (Lu.21:34–35)

> For man does not know his time. Like fish that are taken in an evil net, and like birds that are caught in a snare, so the children of man are snared at an evil time, when it suddenly falls upon them. (Ec.9:12)

➤ The Lord will "cut him in pieces" or "in two." This means he will be condemned to death, cut off from among the living, exiled from eternal life. Most tragic, he shall be *cut off* from God's presence.

➤ The Lord will appoint the unfaithful manager his portion with the unfaithful or unbelievers. Why? Because he was not genuine. He was a hypocrite.

These details reveal the answer to Peter's question (v.41). The Lord's message was to all, to unbelievers as well as His followers. The return of Christ will mean judgment on those who never believed in Him, never prepared for eternity by accepting the salvation He offers through repentance and faith.

> And will cut him in pieces and put him with the hypocrites. In that place there will be weeping and gnashing of teeth. (Mt.24:51)

When the Son of Man comes in his glory, and all the angels with him, then he will sit on his glorious throne. Before him will be gathered all the nations, and he will separate people one from another as a shepherd separates the sheep from the goats. And he will place the sheep on his right, but the goats on the left. Then the King will say to those on his right, "Come, you who are blessed by my Father, inherit the kingdom prepared for you from the foundation of the world. . . ." Then he will say to those on his left, "Depart from me, you cursed, into the eternal fire prepared for the devil and his angels. . . ." And these will go away into eternal punishment, but the righteous into eternal life. (Mt.25:31-34, 41, 46)

To fill his belly to the full, God will send his burning anger against him and rain it upon him into his body. . . . The heavens will reveal his iniquity, and the earth will rise up against him. The possessions of his house will be carried away, dragged off in the day of God's wrath. This is the wicked man's portion from God, the heritage decreed for him by God. (Jb.20:23, 27-29)

Let him rain coals on the wicked; fire and sulfur and a scorching wind shall be the portion of their cup. (Ps.11:6)

d. The unfaithful managers' fate (vv.47-48).

Jesus identified the unfaithful managers and their fate. Note that Jesus is answering Peter's question in these two verses as well. He was speaking to both believers and unbelievers. Who is to be watching and living in a state of readiness? Who is to be served by Christ and greatly blessed? The answer is clear: the faithful manager, not the unfaithful manager. Who then is the unfaithful manager? Two classes are named:

Class 1: the *servant* who knew his master's will and did not prepare himself (v.35), nor did he do the Lord's will (v.47). This servant's judgment is tragic, for he knew God's will, but deliberately rejected it. Therefore, he will receive severe judgment and punishment.

His winnowing fork is in his hand, to clear his threshing floor and to gather the wheat into his barn, but the chaff he will burn with unquenchable fire. (Lu.3:17)

But for those who are self-seeking and do not obey the truth, but obey unrighteousness, there will be wrath and fury. There will be tribulation and distress for every human being who does evil, the Jew first and also the Greek. (Ro.2:8-9)

And to grant relief to you who are afflicted as well as to us, when the Lord Jesus is revealed from heaven with his mighty angels in flaming fire, inflicting vengeance on those who do not know God and on those who do not obey the gospel of our Lord Jesus. They will suffer the punishment of eternal destruction, away from the presence of the Lord and from the glory of his might. (2 Th.1:7-9)

Then the Lord knows how to rescue the godly from trials, and to keep the unrighteous under punishment until the day of judgment. (2 Pe.2:9)

And if anyone's name was not found written in the book of life, he was thrown into the lake of fire. (Re.20:15)

Class 2: those who did not know the Lord's will; therefore, they were not able to prepare themselves as they should have, nor were they able to faithfully serve the Lord (v.48). However, note a critical point: these still committed acts worthy of punishment. Therefore, they will be judged and condemned as well, but not as severely as those who knew the Lord's will (see Ro.1:20f; 2:11-16).

The principle of God's judgment is perfect justice. Note that degrees of rewards and punishment are being taught. Those who knew the fullness of the Father's will, the full message of the gospel, and rejected it will be judged more severely than those who did not. Likewise, there are degrees of rewards for believers. Those who were given much—greater abilities and opportunities—will be judged more severely than those who were given less. We are to use all the Lord has committed to us, holding nothing back.

P. The Three Gross Misconceptions People Have about the Messiah, 12:49–59

1. **Misconception 1: The Messiah came to bring peace on earth**
   a. Truth 1: Christ came to bring judgment
   b. Truth 2: Christ came to suffer and die
   c. Truth 3: Christ came to bring division

2. **Misconception 2: The Messiah has not yet come**
   a. Truth 1: People discern the weather, that is, earthly events

   b. Truth 2: People do not discern the signs of the times, the Messianic Age

   c. Truth 3: People do not discern spiritual matters

3. **Misconception 3: People have no need to make peace with God**
   a. Truth 1: People have a bad case before God, the Judge
   b. Truth 2: The time is urgent—be reconciled to the Judge
   c. Truth 3: Payment, that is, judgment, is a sure thing

⁴⁹ "I came to cast fire on the earth, and would that it were already kindled!

⁵⁰ I have a baptism to be baptized with, and how great is my distress until it is accomplished!

⁵¹ Do you think that I have come to give peace on earth? No, I tell you, but rather division.

⁵² For from now on in one house there will be five divided, three against two and two against three.

⁵³ They will be divided, father against son and son against father, mother against daughter and daughter against mother, mother-in-law against her daughter-in-law and daughter-in-law against mother-in-law."

⁵⁴ He also said to the crowds, "When you see a cloud rising in the west, you say at once, 'A shower is coming.' And so it happens.

⁵⁵ And when you see the south wind blowing, you say, 'There will be scorching heat,' and it happens.

⁵⁶ You hypocrites! You know how to interpret the appearance of earth and sky, but why do you not know how to interpret the present time?

⁵⁷ And why do you not judge for yourselves what is right?

⁵⁸ As you go with your accuser before the magistrate, make an effort to settle with him on the way, lest he drag you to the judge, and the judge hand you over to the officer, and the officer put you in prison.

⁵⁹ I tell you, you will never get out until you have paid the very last penny."

Division V

The Son of Man's Great Journey to Jerusalem (Stage I):
His Mission and Public Challenge, 9:51–13:21

P. The Three Gross Misconceptions People Have about the Messiah, 12:49–59

Jesus' message in this chapter begins with the Lord preaching to His disciples (v.1). But as He proceeds, Jesus transitions to preaching to all who were present, unbelievers as well as believers (vv.41–48). Now, Jesus concludes the message by preaching to the unbelievers in the crowd. Clearly and straightforwardly, Jesus covers three serious misconceptions that unbelievers have, dangerous errors that condemn a person for eternity. This is, *The Three Gross Misconceptions People Have about the Messiah,* 12:49–59.

1. Misconception 1: The Messiah came to bring peace on earth (vv.49–53).
2. Misconception 2: The Messiah has not yet come (vv.54–57).
3. Misconception 3: People have no need to make peace with God (vv.58–59).

1 Misconception 1: The Messiah came to bring peace on earth.

The first misconception is that the Messiah came to bring peace. People usually think of Christ as having brought the message of peace to earth, and He did. He brought *peace with God* to people's hearts and the *peace of God* to people's lives (see note, *Peace*—Jn.14:27). But the Jewish people expected Him to bring peace to the world. They thought He was coming to establish a political kingdom, to overthrow the Roman Empire and set up a government that was perfectly just and fair. However, as Christ explained, He came for a totally different purpose.

⁴⁹ "I came to cast fire on the earth, and would that it were already kindled!
⁵⁰ I have a baptism to be baptized with, and how great is my distress until it is accomplished!
⁵¹ Do you think that I have come to give peace on earth? No, I tell you, but rather division.
⁵² For from now on in one house there will be five divided, three against two and two against three.
⁵³ They will be divided, father against son and son against father, mother against daughter and daughter against mother, mother-in-law against her daughter-in-law and daughter-in-law against mother-in-law."

a. **Truth 1: Christ came to bring judgment (v.49).**
Jesus said that He came to cast fire on the earth, that is, judgment. Fire is usually a symbol of judgment in the Bible. This is the clearest meaning here, for Christ was talking about His death (v.50), both the judgment for our sin that would be upon Him, and the judgment His death would bring to the world.

Jesus went on to say that He wished the fire "were already kindled." Christ was wishing that the cross was already over with. The judgment as the *sin-bearer* of the world was almost too much for Him to bear (see Lu.22:39–46, Gethsemane). It was Christ's death that brought the fire of judgment to the world.

➤ His death judged (condemned) sin in the flesh.

For God has done what the law, weakened by the flesh, could not do. By sending his own Son in the likeness of sinful flesh and for sin, he condemned sin in the flesh. (Ro.8:3)

For Christ also suffered once for sins, the righteous for the unrighteous, that he might bring us to God, being put to death in the flesh but made alive in the spirit. (1 Pe.3:18)

➤ His death judged (condemned) the prince of this world.

Now is the judgment of this world; now will the ruler of this world be cast out. And I, when I am lifted up from the earth, will draw all people to myself. (Jn.12:31–32)

Concerning judgment, because the ruler of this world is judged. (Jn.16:11)

➤ His death caused people to judge themselves to be sinners, sinners who were spiritually dead to God.

> **For the love of Christ controls us, because we have concluded this: that one has died for all, therefore all have died; and he died for all, that those who live might no longer live for themselves but for him who for their sake died and was raised. (2 Co.5:14–15)**

> **He himself bore our sins in his body on the tree, that we might die to sin and live to righteousness. By his wounds you have been healed. (1 Pe.2:24)**

➤ His death caused people to judge themselves in the flesh, that is, to judge their flesh as being weak and subject to sin. Mankind's sinful, carnal nature needs to be controlled and denied and brought into subjection to Christ.

> **And he said to all, "If anyone would come after me, let him deny himself and take up his cross daily and follow me." (Lu.9:23)**

> **We know that our old self was crucified with him in order that the body of sin might be brought to nothing, so that we would no longer be enslaved to sin. . . . For the death he died he died to sin, once for all, but the life he lives he lives to God. So you also must consider yourselves dead to sin and alive to God in Christ Jesus. Let not sin therefore reign in your mortal body, to make you obey its passions. Do not present your members to sin as instruments for unrighteousness, but present yourselves to God as those who have been brought from death to life, and your members to God as instruments for righteousness. (Ro.6:6, 10–13)**

> **For I know that nothing good dwells in me, that is, in my flesh. For I have the desire to do what is right, but not the ability to carry it out. For I do not do the good I want, but the evil I do not want is what I keep on doing. Now if I do what I do not want, it is no longer I who do it, but sin that dwells within me. (Ro.7:18–20)**

b. **Truth 2: Christ came to suffer and die (v.50).**
Christ came to suffer and die, that is, to be baptized with the judgment of death and to be separated from God. The term "a baptism to be baptized with" refers to Christ's death. He was to be immersed, placed into a state of death, of separation from God *for man*. His suffering in bearing the judgment of God was to be beyond imagination. Note that Jesus used the metaphors of both *fire* and *baptism* to describe His death. Note also that He was *distressed*, pressured to get the ordeal of the judgment over, to have the judgment accomplished and humanity's salvation completed.

> **And they were on the road, going up to Jerusalem, and Jesus was walking ahead of them. And they were amazed, and those who followed were afraid. And taking the twelve again, he began to tell them what was to happen to him, saying, "See, we are going up to Jerusalem, and the Son of Man will be delivered over to the chief priests and the scribes, and they will condemn him to death and deliver him over to the Gentiles. And they will mock him and spit on him, and flog him and kill him. And after three days he will rise." . . . Jesus said to them, "You do not know what you are asking. Are you able to drink the cup that I drink, or to be baptized with the baptism with which I am baptized?" (Mk.10:32–34, 38)**

c. **Truth 3: Christ came to bring division (vv.51–53).**
Jesus corrected the people's concept of the Messiah, telling them that He had come to bring division—not peace—to the earth (v.51; see outline and notes—Mt.10:34–37 for more discussion and application). The world would be divided by the question, "What do you think about the Christ? Whose Son is He?" (Mt.22:42).

This division would even occur in families (v.52). Belief in Christ often sets a family member against his or her family. It is important to see this. Christ calls a person out of the world: to be separate from the world and to go about correcting the sin and evil of the world. If a family continues to live in sin and to walk ever onward toward the grave without turning to God and a life of righteousness, two things usually happen:

➤ The believer struggles to witness to his or her loved ones, no matter the cost and opposition he/she may face.

➤ The family members often rebel against the righteousness and efforts of the believer.

Believers are called to a life of righteousness and to a life of warfare against sin and evil. If a member of a believer's family is engaged on the side of evil, there is *a natural conflict* between them and the family member. The family member is still living primarily to satisfy their worldly desires. They repress and subdue the thought of God so that they can pursue their physical and material desires.

On the other hand, the believer is living primarily for God and His righteousness, to reach people with the glorious gospel of Christ. They no longer live to satisfy worldly desires, but to accomplish spiritual purposes.

The two natures—the sinful human nature and the divine nature—differ drastically. They are diametrically opposed to one another (Ga.5:17). Worldly people primarily talk about the world and live for the pursuit of the world. Spiritual people make God the primary force of their life: they talk about God and the things of righteousness, and they pursue God and His righteousness.

As believers, we are to love our families deeply, but we are to love God first and foremost. Our first loyalty is to God. Two terrible things happen when we put our families before God.

First, our families cannot be what they should be without God. No family can reach its full potential without God. There will be a lack of spiritual growth and strength, of conviction and commitment, of confidence and assurance, of purpose and meaning, of life and God—and it will be for eternity. There will be no sense, no assurance of anything beyond this life.

Second, God cannot look after our families unless He is given His rightful place in the family. If the family takes control, ignoring God and His control, then what happens to the family is in its hands. God is put off to the side, excluded, and shut out. He has no part in the welfare of the family. The family is left all to itself, and trouble usually follows. There is certainly a lack of spiritual strength to face the trials and crises that confront every family during life.

What these two facts teach is this: we need to love God supremely, putting Him before all—even before our families. When we do, our families can be everything they should be and have the hope of being looked after and cared for by God (Mt.6:33). Therefore, a person's decision to follow Christ, no matter the sacrifice to their family, is a wise decision; in fact, it is the only reasonable decision.

Do not think that I have come to bring peace to the earth. I have not come to bring peace, but a sword. For I have come to set a man against his father, and a daughter against her mother, and a daughter-in-law against her mother-in-law. And a person's enemies will be those of his own household. Whoever loves father or mother more than me is not worthy of me, and whoever loves son or daughter more than me is not worthy of me. (Mt.10:34-37)

I appeal to you therefore, brothers, by the mercies of God, to present your bodies as a living sacrifice, holy and acceptable to God, which is your spiritual worship. Do not be conformed to this world, but be transformed by the renewal of your mind, that by testing you may discern what is the will of God, what is good and acceptable and perfect. (Ro.12:1-2)

Keep yourselves in the love of God, waiting for the mercy of our Lord Jesus Christ that leads to eternal life. (Jude 21)

You shall love the Lord your God with all your heart and with all your soul and with all your might. (De.6:5)

And now, Israel, what does the Lord your God require of you, but to fear the Lord your God, to walk in all his ways, to love him, to serve the Lord your God with all your heart and with all your soul. (De.10:12)

2 Misconception 2: The Messiah has not yet come.

The second misconception is that the Messiah has not yet come. People in Jesus' day did not believe that He was the Messiah, and multitudes of people today do not believe that He is the Messiah.

a. Truth 1: People discern the weather, that is, earthly events (vv.54–55).

Jesus points out that people interpret or discern the weather, that is, physical matters of the world. People's natural senses can be very discerning and sharp. They are

54 He also said to the crowds, "When you see a cloud rising in the west, you say at once, 'A shower is coming.' And so it happens.
55 And when you see the south wind blowing, you say, 'There will be scorching heat,' and it happens.
56 You hypocrites! You know how to interpret the appearance of earth and sky, but why do you not know how to interpret the present time?
57 And why do you not judge for yourselves what is right?"

skillful in studying and experimenting and in drawing conclusions from the natural world. Weather is the example Christ used; but the subject could be finances, medicine, society, geography, or any other earthly subject. Jesus says people are very capable in discerning the material and physical matters of their world.

b. Truth 2: People do not discern the signs of the times, the Messianic Age (v.56).

However, people *fail to interpret* or *discern* the times, that is, the coming of the Messiah. Even in Jesus' day, the signs that pointed to Jesus' being the Messiah were visible. A thoughtful and genuinely spiritual person could see these signs, but most were neither thoughtful nor spiritual.

c. Truth 3: People do not discern spiritual matters (v.57).

People fail to *judge* or discern spiritual matters. When it comes to the spiritual senses, most are dead and undiscerning. They do not take time to observe the spiritual signs nor to experience the spiritual world, not really. Some people in Jesus' day had seen the signs that identified Him as the Messiah, for instance Simeon and Anna (Lu.3:25f). Some of these signs were as follows:

➤ The scepter, that is, the lawgiver, had actually come from Judah in the person of Jesus Christ (Mt.1:2).

➤ The weeks and ages predicted by Daniel were closing out (see note and DEEPER STUDY # 1—Mt.24:15).

➤ The prophet Elijah, the forerunner of the Messiah, had come and proclaimed the Messiah to be Jesus (Mt.3:1–12).

➤ The baby Jesus had been born in Bethlehem (Mt.2:1).

➤ Many throughout the world were expecting the coming of some great person, some Messiah (Mt.1:18).

➤ Many godly Jews were looking for the coming of the Messiah, God's great Deliverer of Israel (Lu.2:25f).

➤ The message and works of Jesus were great evidence, phenomenal miracles given by God to substantiate His claims (see note and DEEPER STUDY # 1—Jn.14:11).

In addition to these, what greater signs could God give than the signs that radically change lives? Unbelief is without excuse. The problem is that people want signs of their own choosing, not the signs which God has chosen to give. People are always wanting God to deal with them through some . . .

- spectacular sign
- brilliant sight
- astounding truth
- irrefutable argument
- miraculous experience
- unbelievable deliverance

God's great concern is not *signs from heaven*, not signs outside man. God's great concern is meeting people in their lives, within their hearts, where they really need help. People must discern the times if they are to live abundantly while on this earth and live eternally in the next world. God wants to meet people in their sickness and sorrow and lostness. Meeting people in the areas of their need is an irrefutable sign given to every generation.

Jesus' question is one of the most honest, thought-provoking, and revealing questions ever asked of human beings. And it takes a person who is honest and open—a person who is willing to have their heart exposed for what it really is—to answer the question. "Why do you not judge for yourselves what is right?"

THOUGHT 1. What is the answer to Jesus' question? Why do people not discern, not judge what is right?

1) Why do people not discern that God *is*, that He exists?

> **For what can be known about God is plain to them, because God has shown it to them. For his invisible attributes, namely, his eternal power and divine nature, have been clearly perceived, ever since the creation of the world, in the things that have been made. So they are without excuse. (Ro.1:19–20)**

Therefore, as to the eating of food offered to idols, we know that "an idol has no real existence," and that "there is no God but one." (1 Co.8:4)

For there is one God, and there is one mediator between God and men, the man Christ Jesus, who gave himself as a ransom for all, which is the testimony given at the proper time. (1 Ti.2:5–6)

In the beginning, God created the heavens and the earth. (Ge.1:1)

You are the LORD, you alone. You have made heaven, the heaven of heavens, with all their host, the earth and all that is on it, the seas and all that is in them; and you preserve all of them; and the host of heaven worships you. (Ne.9:6)

That they may know that you alone, whose name is the LORD, are the Most High over all the earth. (Ps.83:18)

For thus says the LORD, who created the heavens (he is God!), who formed the earth and made it (he established it; he did not create it empty, he formed it to be inhabited!): "I am the LORD, and there is no other." (Is.45:18)

2) Why do people not discern that Jesus Christ is truly the Son of God?

And those in the boat worshiped him, saying, "Truly you are the Son of God." (Mt.14:33)

The beginning of the gospel of Jesus Christ, the Son of God. (Mk.1:1)

And I have seen and have borne witness that this is the Son of God. (Jn.1:34)

Jesus heard that they had cast him out, and having found him he said, "Do you believe in the Son of Man?" He answered, "And who is he, sir, that I may believe in him?" Jesus said to him, "You have seen him, and it is he who is speaking to you." (Jn.9:35–37)

Jesus said to her, "I am the resurrection and the life. Whoever believes in me, though he die, yet shall he live, and everyone who lives and believes in me shall never die. Do you believe this?" She said to him, "Yes, Lord; I believe that you are the Christ, the Son of God, who is coming into the world." (Jn.11:25–27)

Whoever confesses that Jesus is the Son of God, God abides in him, and he in God. (1 Jn.4:15)

3) Why do people not discern that righteousness is the way for them to live and the way for communities and the world to conduct their affairs?

For I tell you, unless your righteousness exceeds that of the scribes and Pharisees, you will never enter the kingdom of heaven. (Mt.5:20)

For the kingdom of God is not a matter of eating and drinking but of righteousness and peace and joy in the Holy Spirit. (Ro.14:17)

Wake up from your drunken stupor, as is right, and do not go on sinning. For some have no knowledge of God. I say this to your shame. (1 Co.15:34)

For the love of money is a root of all kinds of evils. It is through this craving that some have wandered away from the faith and pierced themselves with many pangs. But as for you, O man of God, flee these things. Pursue righteousness, godliness, faith, love, steadfastness, gentleness. Fight the good fight of the faith. Take hold of the eternal life to which you were called and about which you made the good confession in the presence of many witnesses. (1 Ti.6:10–12)

Training us to renounce ungodliness and worldly passions, and to live self-controlled, upright, and godly lives in the present age, waiting for our blessed hope, the appearing of the glory of our great God and Savior Jesus Christ. (Tit.2:12–13)

Jesus was saying that the signs of the times—the signs of every generation—the signs of nature itself—are enough to point toward God in all His love and righteousness. Why, then, do people not judge for themselves what is right?

3 Misconception 3: People have no need to make peace with God.

The third misconception is that people have no need to make *peace with God*. Jesus used an earthly illustration—a guilty person being taken to court—to explain the truth of our condition before God.

[58] "As you go with your accuser before the magistrate, make an effort to settle with him on the way, lest he drag you to the judge, and the judge hand you over to the officer, and the officer put you in prison.

[59] I tell you, you will never get out until you have paid the very last penny."

a. Truth 1: People have a bad case before God, the Judge (v.58a).

Because we have sinned against God, we have made God our *accuser* or *adversary*. However, God is also the Judge before whom we must stand. And we have a bad case; in fact, we have *no* case at all, no defense. We are guilty as charged of sinning against God.

> For all have sinned and fall short of the glory of God. (Ro.3:23)

> Therefore, just as sin came into the world through one man, and death through sin, and so death spread to all men because all sinned. (Ro.5:12)

> If we say we have no sin, we deceive ourselves, and the truth is not in us. (1 Jn.1:8)

> They have all fallen away; together they have become corrupt; there is none who does good, not even one. (Ps.53:3)

> We have all become like one who is unclean, and all our righteous deeds are like a polluted garment. We all fade like a leaf, and our iniquities, like the wind, take us away. (Is.64:6)

b. Truth 2: The time is urgent—be reconciled to the Judge (v.58b).

When a person has a hopeless case with an adversary, the best thing to do is to try to *settle out of court*. This is what Jesus is saying we sinners need to do. We need to settle our sin debt with God, and we need to settle now, while there is time. The time will come for each of us when it is too late to be reconciled to Him.

> Therefore, we are ambassadors for Christ, God making his appeal through us. We implore you on behalf of Christ, be reconciled to God. For our sake he made him to be sin who knew no sin, so that in him we might become the righteousness of God. Working together with him, then, we appeal to you not to receive the grace of God in vain. For he says, "In a favorable time I listened to you, and in a day of salvation I have helped you." Behold, now is the favorable time; behold, now is the day of salvation. (2 Co.5:20–6:2)

c. Truth 3: Payment, that is, judgment, is a sure thing (v.59).

Otherwise, we are going to be judged by God and have to pay *every penny*—the full penalty of every sin we have committed. Again, the hour is urgent. People need to make peace with God, and they need to do so immediately. If they fail to make peace with God, then they will have to pay the most severe penalty, which is death—eternal separation from God in hell.

> You serpents, you brood of vipers, how are you to escape being sentenced to hell? (Mt.23:33)

> Do you suppose, O man—you who judge those who practice such things and yet do them yourself— that you will escape the judgment of God? (Ro.2:3)

> How shall we escape if we neglect such a great salvation? It was declared at first by the Lord, and it was attested to us by those who heard. (He.2:3)

> See that you do not refuse him who is speaking. For if they did not escape when they refused him who warned them on earth, much less will we escape if we reject him who warns from heaven. (He.12:25)

> Be assured, an evil person will not go unpunished, but the offspring of the righteous will be delivered. (Pr.11:21)

THOUGHT 1. Out of His great mercy and grace, God longs to settle our sin debt and has made a way to do so. Because our debt to Him is greater than we can pay, God gave His Son to pay it for us. All we have to do is accept the salvation God offers through repentance and faith in Christ.

> For God so loved the world, that he gave his only Son, that whoever believes in him should not perish but have eternal life. (Jn.3:16)

> But God shows his love for us in that while we were still sinners, Christ died for us. (Ro.5:8)

> For the wages of sin is death, but the free gift of God is eternal life in Christ Jesus our Lord. (Ro.6:23)

> For our sake he made him to be sin who knew no sin, so that in him we might become the righteousness of God. (2 Co.5:21)

> But he was pierced for our transgressions; he was crushed for our iniquities; upon him was the chastisement that brought us peace, and with his wounds we are healed. All we like sheep have gone astray; we have turned—every one—to his own way; and the Lord has laid on him the iniquity of us all. (Is.53:5–6)

Q. The Truth About Suffering and Sin: The Great Need for All to Repent, 13:1–9

(Mt.21:18-21; Mk.11:12-14, 20-26; Is.5:1-7)

There were some present at that very time who told him about the Galileans whose blood Pilate had mingled with their sacrifices.

² And he answered them, "Do you think that these Galileans were worse sinners than all the other Galileans, because they suffered in this way?

³ No, I tell you; but unless you repent, you will all likewise perish.

⁴ Or those eighteen on whom the tower in Siloam fell and killed them: do you think that they were worse offenders than all the others who lived in Jerusalem?

⁵ No, I tell you; but unless you repent, you will all likewise perish."

⁶ And he told this parable: "A man had a fig tree planted in his vineyard, and he came seeking fruit on it and found none.

⁷ And he said to the vinedresser, 'Look, for three years now I have come seeking fruit on this fig tree, and I find none. Cut it down. Why should it use up the ground?'

⁸ And he answered him, 'Sir, let it alone this year also, until I dig around it and put on manure.

⁹ Then if it should bear fruit next year, well and good; but if not, you can cut it down.'"

1. **People do not suffer because they are worse sinners than others**[DS1]
   a. Event 1: The latest news of a horrible, murderous event
      1) Did they suffer because they were worse sinners?

      2) No! *All* must repent or perish

   b. Event 2: The latest news of a terrible tragedy
      1) Did they suffer because they were worse sinners?

      2) No! *All* must repent or perish

2. **People must bear fruit or else they will perish**
   a. The fig tree's privilege: It was in the vineyard
   b. The fig tree's purpose: To bear fruit
   c. The day for reaping came
      1) Found no fruit
      2) Found that the tree was using up space on the ground and producing nothing
   d. The mercy of God
      1) Gave the tree another chance
      2) Fertilized and fed it
   e. The judgment was to be based on the fruit the tree bore

Division V

The Son of Man's Great Journey to Jerusalem (Stage I):
His Mission and Public Challenge, 9:51–13:21

Q. The Truth About Suffering and Sin: The Great Need for All to Repent, 13:1–9

(Mt.21:18–21; Mk.11:12–14, 20–26; Is.5:1–7)

13:1–9
Introduction

One of the world's most perplexing problems is, why do people suffer? Some people feel that suffering is a punishment for sin; therefore, those who suffer more are worse sinners than those who suffer less. The result, too often, is that many who suffer feel this is true; consequently, they end up with all sorts of guilt and emotional problems. They think their suffering is due to some serious sin they have committed and that God is punishing them because they have been such flagrant sinners. Is suffering God's punishment for sin? Jesus answers that question in this passage. This is, *The Truth About Suffering and Sin: The Great Need for All to Repent,* 13:1–9.

1. People do not suffer because they are worse sinners than others (vv.1–5).
2. People must bear fruit or else they will perish (vv.6–9).

13:1–5

There were some present at that very time who told him about the Galileans whose blood Pilate had mingled with their sacrifices.

² And he answered them, "Do you think that these Galileans were worse sinners than all the other Galileans, because they suffered in this way?

³ No, I tell you; but unless you repent, you will all likewise perish.

⁴ Or those eighteen on whom the tower in Siloam fell and killed them: do you think that they were worse offenders than all the others who lived in Jerusalem?

⁵ No, I tell you; but unless you repent, you will all likewise perish."

1 People do not suffer because they are worse sinners than others.

Two recent events had set the people to judging and talking about those affected by tragedy. The common thinking of the day was that such catastrophes happen to people because of their appalling sins. Jesus confronted this erroneous thinking, making it clear that people do *not* suffer because they are *worse sinners* than others.

a. **Event 1: The latest news of a horrible, murderous event (vv.1–3).**
Some shared with Jesus the latest news of a horrible massacre (v.1). Some Galileans were in the temple in the midst of worship, offering their sacrifices to God, when Herod had them attacked and slaughtered by his soldiers (see DEEPER STUDY # 1). The crowd was making a very harsh judgment. They were saying the Galileans were murdered because they were *worse sinners* (v.2). The crowd brought this subject up in response to what Jesus had taught, that people must make peace with God before it is too late (Lu.12:58–59). They were saying the Galileans were swept down upon, just like Jesus had described; therefore, their sins must have been great.

Jesus was pointed and clear in refuting their thoughts. Note that the people had not spoken their thoughts; they had *only related* the story. However, Jesus *knew* their thoughts, and they were thinking at that exact moment that the Galileans had suffered such a horrible death because they were worse sinners. Or to express it as it is so often stated: suffering is due to sin.

Jesus said, "No! But unless you repent, you will all likewise perish" (v.3). Such an argument has its basis in self-righteousness. The point is unmistakable: all people must repent of sin, for all people are sinners, not just those who suffer greatly.

b. **Event 2: The latest news of a terrible tragedy (vv.4–5).**
This subject is so important, and it is so critical that people understand it that Jesus referred to a recent event—the tragedy of a tower's falling on eighteen construction workers. It is

significant that Jesus used a tragedy as a second illustration instead of an event similar to the murderous act just discussed. His point is unquestionable; suffering is not necessarily due to sin or to degrees of sin (v.4). The people killed in the fall of the tower were no greater sinners than all the other people of Jerusalem. If suffering were due to sin, then there would be no life whatsoever. Why? Because *all people are so sinful* that we are worthy of only the most severe punishment that can be suffered—death itself. Thus, Jesus stressed His point: *all* people must repent or else perish (v.5; see DEEPER STUDY # 2—Lu.5:23; note—Jn.9:1–3).

Note exactly what Jesus says:

➤ Suffering is not always due to *sin*.

> Or how can you say to your brother, "Let me take the speck out of your eye," when there is the log in your own eye? (Mt.7:4)

> When the native people saw the creature hanging from his hand, they said to one another, "No doubt this man is a murderer. Though he has escaped from the sea, Justice has not allowed him to live." (Ac.28:4; see outline and notes—1 Co.1:3–11; 1:3–4 for more discussion and verses)

➤ All people are guilty of sinning exceedingly, sinning enough to cause us to perish.

> As it is written: "None is righteous, no, not one; no one understands; no one seeks for God. All have turned aside; together they have become worthless; no one does good, not even one." "Their throat is an open grave; they use their tongues to deceive." "The venom of asps is under their lips." "Their mouth is full of curses and bitterness." "Their feet are swift to shed blood; in their paths are ruin and misery, and the way of peace they have not known." "There is no fear of God before their eyes." (Ro.3:10–18)

> For all have sinned and fall short of the glory of God. (Ro.3:23)

> Now the works of the flesh are evident: sexual immorality, impurity, sensuality, idolatry, sorcery, enmity, strife, jealousy, fits of anger, rivalries, dissensions, divisions, envy, drunkenness, orgies, and things like these. I warn you, as I warned you before, that those who do such things will not inherit the kingdom of God. (Ga.5:19–21)

➤ All people are doomed to perish.

> For the wages of sin is death, but the free gift of God is eternal life in Christ Jesus our Lord. (Ro.6:23)

> But as for the cowardly, the faithless, the detestable, as for murderers, the sexually immoral, sorcerers, idolaters, and all liars, their portion will be in the lake that burns with fire and sulfur, which is the second death. (Re.21:8)

> The soul who sins shall die. The son shall not suffer for the iniquity of the father, nor the father suffer for the iniquity of the son. The righteousness of the righteous shall be upon himself, and the wickedness of the wicked shall be upon himself. (Ezk.18:20)

➤ There is only one way to keep from perishing: repent.

> And Peter said to them, "Repent and be baptized every one of you in the name of Jesus Christ for the forgiveness of your sins, and you will receive the gift of the Holy Spirit." (Ac.2:38)

> Repent therefore, and turn back, that your sins may be blotted out. (Ac.3:19)

> Repent, therefore, of this wickedness of yours, and pray to the Lord that, if possible, the intent of your heart may be forgiven you. (Ac.8:22)

> The times of ignorance God overlooked, but now he commands all people everywhere to repent. (Ac.17:30)

DEEPER STUDY # 1

(13:1–5) **Suffering—Galileans—Construction Workers:** Who were the Galileans slaughtered by Herod and the construction workers upon whom the tower fell? There is no sure record of either group other than what is given here. The best *theories* are as follows:

Two suggestions are made about the Galileans. First, they were followers of Judas of Galilee who opposed taxation imposed by the Romans (Ac.5:37). Herod either knew that some of Judas' followers were in the temple worshiping or mistook some group of Galileans as Judas' followers and had them slaughtered. This much is known: Pilate set out to build a new water system for Jerusalem. It was a huge construction project, and to finance the work, Pilate had to insist that the money be taken from the temple finances. This of course enraged the Jews, for the temple monies were gifts to God and belonged to God. The Galileans were an easily provoked people; therefore, they were usually in the forefront of trouble. Second, some commentators think that the slaughtered Galileans were revolutionaries who had moved into the city to carry out terrorist acts against the government. Herod knew about it and caught them off guard while they were worshiping. Note they were caught so much by surprise that their blood actually flowed and mingled with the blood of the animal sacrifices they were offering to God.

The construction workers are thought by most to have been repairing one of the towers which served as part of the fortifications on the walls of Jerusalem. It is thought to have been near the pool of Siloam.

13:6-9

⁶ And he told this parable: "A man had a fig tree planted in his vineyard, and he came seeking fruit on it and found none.

⁷ And he said to the vinedresser, 'Look, for three years now I have come seeking fruit on this fig tree, and I find none. Cut it down. Why should it use up the ground?'

⁸ And he answered him, 'Sir, let it alone this year also, until I dig around it and put on manure.

⁹ Then if it should bear fruit next year, well and good; but if not, you can cut it down.'"

2 People must bear fruit or else they will perish.

Jesus wanted to drive home the need for repentance by sharing a parable of a man's seeking fruit from a fig tree. The truth of the parable is, people must bear fruit or else they will perish. The man in the parable represents God; the vinedresser represents Christ; the vineyard represents either the world or Israel. Note the following facts about the fig tree:

a. The fig tree's privilege: It was in the vineyard (v.6a).

The fig tree was greatly privileged. It was *in the vineyard*. This detail signifies that it was planted (born) by the vineyard keeper (God or Christ) himself. God causes every person to be born into the world. He stands behind every person as that person's creator and Lord.

For "In him we live and move and have our being"; as even some of your own poets have said, "For we are indeed his offspring." (Ac.17:28)

The Spirit of God has made me, and the breath of the Almighty gives me life. (Jb.33:4)

Know that the Lᴏʀᴅ, he is God! It is he who made us, and we are his; we are his people, and the sheep of his pasture. (Ps.100:3)

Have we not all one Father? Has not one God created us? Why then are we faithless to one another, profaning the covenant of our fathers? (Mal.2:10)

In addition, it was planted right where other trees were bearing fruit. It had the same soil, nourishment, rain, and sun from heaven these fruitful trees had. This is true of all persons who are born in nations where the gospel is freely preached.

b. The fig tree's purpose: To bear fruit (v.6b).

The fig tree had been *planted* for the purpose of bearing fruit, and it *existed* to bear fruit. It was by nature a *fruit* tree; therefore, it was supposed to bear fruit. So it is with people (Lu.10:27; Ga.5:22-23; see Dᴇᴇᴘᴇʀ Sᴛᴜᴅʏ # 1—Jn.15:1-8).

c. The day for reaping came (v.7).

The day came when the vineyard owner, God Himself, came looking for fruit from the tree. Note that the reaper was not someone else; it was God Himself. He planted the tree to get fruit (God put human beings on earth to bear fruit). He expected fruit, for He was the one who had planted the tree.

So, every healthy tree bears good fruit, but the diseased tree bears bad fruit. (Mt.7:17)

I am the vine; you are the branches. Whoever abides in me and I in him, he it is that bears much fruit, for apart from me you can do nothing. (Jn.15:5)

> But the fruit of the Spirit is love, joy, peace, patience, kindness, goodness, faithfulness, gentleness, self-control; against such things there is no law. (Ga.5:22–23)

However, the vineyard owner found no fruit. The tree was bare. It failed in its purpose, and the owner's investment in the tree was wasted.

> As for what was sown among thorns, this is the one who hears the word, but the cares of the world and the deceitfulness of riches choke the word, and it proves unfruitful. (Mt.13:22)

> He dug it and cleared it of stones, and planted it with choice vines; he built a watchtower in the midst of it, and hewed out a wine vat in it; and he looked for it to yield grapes, but it yielded wild grapes. (Is.5:2)

Note the details revealed about the tree. First, the vineyard owner had been patient with the tree. For three years, he had come time after time, looking for fruit. The tree had plenty of time to bear fruit if it were ever going to bear fruit.

> The Lord is not slow to fulfill his promise as some count slowness, but is patient toward you, not wishing that any should perish, but that all should reach repentance. (2 Pe.3:9)

Second, the tree was wasting and misusing space. The purpose of the vineyard, the very reason for its existence, was to produce fruit for the owner.

➢ All space on the tree was needed for fruit.
➢ No space could be allowed to be wasted indefinitely.
➢ The tree was hurting the production of the vineyard.

THOUGHT 1. In the same way the fruitless tree was hindering the vineyard, the example of false believers affects the whole work of Christ. They cheapen the vineyard (world, church), causing others not to want its fruit.

> Because he has fixed a day on which he will judge the world in righteousness by a man whom he has appointed; and of this he has given assurance to all by raising him from the dead. (Ac.17:31)

> You who boast in the law dishonor God by breaking the law. For, as it is written, "The name of God is blasphemed among the Gentiles because of you." (Ro.2:23–24)

> And many will follow their sensuality, and because of them the way of truth will be blasphemed. (2 Pe.2:2)

Third, the tree was to be cut down. The owner pronounced judgment.

> Before him will be gathered all the nations, and he will separate people one from another as a shepherd separates the sheep from the goats. (Mt.25:32)

> For the wages of sin is death, but the free gift of God is eternal life in Christ Jesus our Lord. (Ro.6:23)

> Do not be deceived: God is not mocked, for whatever one sows, that will he also reap. For the one who sows to his own flesh will from the flesh reap corruption, but the one who sows to the Spirit will from the Spirit reap eternal life. (Ga.6:7–8)

d. The mercy of God (v.8).

The vineyard dresser interceded for the unfruitful tree. He asked for another year, one last chance for the tree. The owner granted one last chance, one last opportunity. This detail speaks of the longsuffering and mercy of God.

e. The judgment was to be based on the fruit the tree bore (v.9).

The next year was to be the last chance, the last opportunity for the tree. If the tree did not bear fruit then, it was to be cut down. The vineyard owner would have no more patience with it.

THOUGHT 1. It is critical—eternally critical—that every person grasp the lessons of this parable.
1) God has given every person the privilege of life and the opportunity to bear fruit—to live productively, to do works that have eternal significance.
2) God is patient, extremely longsuffering. He gives people opportunity after opportunity to repent.

And Jesus said, "Father, forgive them, for they know not what they do." And they cast lots to divide his garments. (Lu.23:34)

Who is to condemn? Christ Jesus is the one who died—more than that, who was raised—who is at the right hand of God, who indeed is interceding for us. (Ro.8:34)

Consequently, he is able to save to the uttermost those who draw near to God through him, since he always lives to make intercession for them. (He.7:25)

3) The tree's judgment was based on its fruit (see outline and notes—Jn.15:1–8; Ga.5:22–23). The proof of genuine repentance is fruit; all who have genuinely repented of their sins will bear fruit for the Lord.

Bear fruit in keeping with repentance. (Mt.3:8)

By this my Father is glorified, that you bear much fruit and so prove to be my disciples. . . . You did not choose me, but I chose you and appointed you that you should go and bear fruit and that your fruit should abide, so that whatever you ask the Father in my name, he may give it to you. (Jn.15:8, 16)

4) The Lord's patience is long, but it will run out. A final opportunity to repent will come to all. God will judge all who do not bear fruit—who do not genuinely repent.

Even now the axe is laid to the root of the trees. Every tree therefore that does not bear good fruit is cut down and thrown into the fire. (Mt.3:10)

If anyone does not abide in me he is thrown away like a branch and withers; and the branches are gathered, thrown into the fire, and burned. (Jn.15:6)

But if it bears thorns and thistles, it is worthless and near to being cursed, and its end is to be burned. (He.6:8)

For their vine comes from the vine of Sodom and from the fields of Gomorrah; their grapes are grapes of poison; their clusters are bitter; their wine is the poison of serpents and the cruel venom of asps. "Is not this laid up in store with me, sealed up in my treasuries? Vengeance is mine, and recompense, for the time when their foot shall slip; for the day of their calamity is at hand, and their doom comes swiftly." (De.32:32–35)

THOUGHT 2. Jesus' parable had a special application to the nation of Israel. In the Old Testament, one of the symbols of Israel is the fig tree (Je.24:1–10; Ho.9:10; Mi.7:1). God had planted the nation of Israel in the earth and had given it special privileges. When the Messiah came, He came first to Israel. The three years in the parable represent Christ's three years of public ministry before Israel (v.7). Yet, the nation never brought forth fruit, never repented and received Christ as its Savior and Lord.

O Jerusalem, Jerusalem, the city that kills the prophets and stones those who are sent to it! How often would I have gathered your children together as a hen gathers her brood under her wings, and you were not willing! (Mt.23:37)

He came to his own, and his own people did not receive him. (Jn.1:11)

But you denied the Holy and Righteous One, and asked for a murderer to be granted to you. (Ac.3:14)

Brothers, my heart's desire and prayer to God for them is that they may be saved. (Ro.10:1)

R. People vs. Religion: Which Is More Important? 13:10–17

13:10–17

¹⁰ Now he was teaching in one of the synagogues on the Sabbath.

¹¹ And behold, there was a woman who had had a disabling spirit for eighteen years. She was bent over and could not fully straighten herself.

¹² When Jesus saw her, he called her over and said to her, "Woman, you are freed from your disability."

¹³ And he laid his hands on her, and immediately she was made straight, and she glorified God.

¹⁴ But the ruler of the synagogue, indignant because Jesus had healed on the Sabbath, said to the people, "There are six days in which work ought to be done. Come on those days and be healed, and not on the Sabbath day."

¹⁵ Then the Lord answered him, "You hypocrites! Does not each of you on the Sabbath untie his ox or his donkey from the manger and lead it away to water it?

¹⁶ And ought not this woman, a daughter of Abraham whom Satan bound for eighteen years, be loosed from this bond on the Sabbath day?"

¹⁷ As he said these things, all his adversaries were put to shame, and all the people rejoiced at all the glorious things that were done by him.

1. **Jesus taught in the synagogue on the Sabbath**
2. **The woman was a worshiper of God**
   a. She was faithful to worship, v.10
   b. She was crippled by a curvature of the spine
   c. She was seen and called forward by Jesus

   d. She received Jesus' Word and touch
   e. She immediately glorified God

3. **The ruler (religionist) was a worshiper of God**[DS1]
   a. He became angry with the people
   b. He corrupted God's Word[DS2]
   c. He rejected Christ

   d. He was hypocritical
      1) He placed animals above people

      2) He placed religion above people

4. **The effect of Jesus' works and words: The opponents were humiliated, while crowds rejoiced**

Division V

The Son of Man's Great Journey to Jerusalem (Stage I): His Mission and Public Challenge, 9:51–13:21

R. People vs. Religion: Which Is More Important? 13:10–17

Introduction

So much of what is done in the name of religion is far from what God commands and from what pleases Him. Many adhere to the practicing of rituals and requirements while seemingly oblivious to a personal relationship with God and what He truly commands of people. Others, like the Jewish religious leaders of Jesus' day, elevate their traditions and strict rules above people and their needs. On a contentious Sabbath day, Jesus confronted this problem head-on. This is, *People vs. Religion: Which Is More Important?*, 13:10–17.

1. Jesus taught in the synagogue on the Sabbath (v.10).

2. The woman was a worshiper of God (vv.11–13).
3. The ruler (religionist) was a worshiper of God (vv.14–16).
4. The effect of Jesus' works and words: opponents were humiliated, while crowds rejoiced (v.17).

13:10

1 Jesus taught in the synagogue on the Sabbath.

[10] Now he was teaching in one of the synagogues on the Sabbath.

The event recorded in this passage took place as Jesus was teaching in the synagogue on the Sabbath. Three significant facts need to be seen:

➢ This was the last time Jesus was ever in a synagogue as far as we know. From this point on He was such a controversial figure that no synagogue would allow Him in the pulpit.

➢ This healing miracle took place on the Sabbath, and healing was not allowed on the Sabbath. It was considered work unless it was a matter of life and death. The fact that Jesus broke the Sabbath law was what caused the present dispute.

➢ Both the woman and the synagogue ruler were worshipers of God (vv.11–16).

THOUGHT 1. Jesus was worshiping on the Sabbath, doing exactly what He should have been doing.

THOUGHT 2. There is a difference between worshipers. This is seen in the afflicted woman and the religious leader (vv.11–16). She sought to draw near the Lord for deliverance, whereas the religionist only practiced his ceremony and ritual.

13:11–13

2 The woman was a worshiper of God.

[11] And behold, there was a woman who had had a disabling spirit for eighteen years. She was bent over and could not fully straighten herself.
[12] When Jesus saw her, he called her over and said to her, "Woman, you are freed from your disability."
[13] And he laid his hands on her, and immediately she was made straight, and she glorified God.

As Jesus was teaching in the synagogue, one of the attendees was a woman who stood out in the crowd due to a disabling physical affliction. Yet, in spite of her crippling infirmity, she was there, worshiping God in sincerity.

a. She was faithful to worship (v.11a).

This woman's habit was to worship, to seek the face of God in looking after her life. Therefore, she was where she was supposed to be on this particular Sabbath: in worship. And because she was there, she was to receive a very special touch from God. She did not know it yet, but she was. Why her? Because she was sincere, ever so sincere in seeking God and His care.

God is spirit, and those who worship him must worship in spirit and truth. (Jn.4:24)

Ascribe to the LORD the glory due his name; bring an offering and come before him! Worship the LORD in the splendor of holiness. (1 Chr.16:29)

O LORD, I love the habitation of your house and the place where your glory dwells. (Ps.26:8)

One thing have I asked of the LORD, that will I seek after: that I may dwell in the house of the LORD all the days of my life, to gaze upon the beauty of the LORD and to inquire in his temple. (Ps.27:4)

Blessed is the one you choose and bring near, to dwell in your courts! We shall be satisfied with the goodness of your house, the holiness of your temple! (Ps.65:4)

I was glad when they said to me, "Let us go to the house of the LORD!" (Ps.122:1)

b. She was crippled by a curvature of the spine (v.11b).

Apparently, the woman had a curvature of the spine, as she was bent over and could not straighten herself. For eighteen years, she had suffered from this deformity.

The woman's physical affliction had a spiritual source: she had a "disabling spirit" or "a spirit of infirmity." Jesus said plainly that she had been bound by Satan (v.16). Thus, the woman needed spiritual healing as well as physical healing.

Despite her deformity, the woman still worshiped God. Her deformity was severe: she was stooped over and unable to straighten up. No doubt, her pain was sometimes severe. Yet, her habit was to attend worship and to seek the favor and help of God in her life.

> But seek first the kingdom of God and his righteousness, and all these things will be added to you. (Mt.6:33)

> And I tell you, ask, and it will be given to you; seek, and you will find; knock, and it will be opened to you. For everyone who asks receives, and the one who seeks finds, and to the one who knocks it will be opened. (Lu.11:9–10)

> That they should seek God, and perhaps feel their way toward him and find him. Yet he is actually not far from each one of us. (Ac.17:27)

> Seek the LORD and his strength; seek his presence continually! (Ps.105:4)

> For thus says the LORD to the house of Israel: "Seek me and live." (Am.5:4)

c. She was seen and called forward by Jesus (v.12).

The woman's faithfulness in the worship of God, despite her deformity and pain, attracted Jesus' attention. He knew both her condition with all its pain and inconvenience as well as the great sacrifice she made to worship God. He was moved with compassion for her. Note that she did not have to call to Jesus for help; Jesus called her *to Him*.

> Who shall separate us from the love of Christ? Shall tribulation, or distress, or persecution, or famine, or nakedness, or danger, or sword? (Ro.8:35)

> Casting all your anxieties on him, because he cares for you. (1 Pe.5:7)

> But the steadfast love of the LORD is from everlasting to everlasting on those who fear him, and his righteousness to children's children. (Ps.103:17)

> The steadfast love of the LORD never ceases; his mercies never come to an end. (Lam.3:22)

d. She received Jesus' Word and touch (v.13a).

Jesus had called her to come over to Him. She had to respond to His call; she had to take the step of coming herself. When she obeyed, Jesus spoke the Word to her, the *good news* that she was set free from her infirmity (v.12; keep in mind that her problem had been both spiritual and physical). Jesus reached out and touched her, and she was "made straight." She stood upright. She experienced *both the power of Jesus' Word and touch*. But note: it was because she came when Jesus called, and Jesus called to her because she was there worshiping God, seeking His grace and care.

THOUGHT 1. The Lord alone can heal those who are bowed down. Souls as well as bodies that are bent or bowed down can be lifted up by Jesus, no matter what it is that has caused the bowing:

- humiliation and shame
- sin
- lack of education
- loss of everything
- accident
- disease
- appearance and looks
- personality

> That evening they brought to him many who were oppressed by demons, and he cast out the spirits with a word and healed all who were sick. This was to fulfill what was spoken by the prophet Isaiah: "He took our illnesses and bore our diseases." (Mt.8:16–17)

> How God anointed Jesus of Nazareth with the Holy Spirit and with power. He went about doing good and healing all who were oppressed by the devil, for God was with him. (Ac.10:38)

> I am utterly bowed down and prostrate; all the day I go about mourning. For my sides are filled with burning, and there is no soundness in my flesh. I am feeble and crushed; I groan because of the tumult of my heart. O Lord, all my longing is before you; my sighing is not hidden from you. My heart throbs; my strength fails me, and the light of my eyes—it also has gone from me. (Ps.38:6–10)

The LORD opens the eyes of the blind. The LORD lifts up those who are bowed down; the LORD loves the righteous. (Ps.146:8)

e. She immediately glorified God (v.13b).

The jubilant woman's first impulse was to glorify God for her deliverance. She recognized that the Lord was the source of her healing, that only the Lord could have set her free from her infirmity, an affliction that was both physical and spiritual.

But thanks be to God, who gives us the victory through our Lord Jesus Christ. (1 Co.15:57)

Giving thanks always and for everything to God the Father in the name of our Lord Jesus Christ. (Ep.5:20)

Through him then let us continually offer up a sacrifice of praise to God, that is, the fruit of lips that acknowledge his name. (He.13:15)

Oh give thanks to the LORD; call upon his name; make known his deeds among the peoples! (1 Chr.16:8)

Offer to God a sacrifice of thanksgiving, and perform your vows to the Most High. (Ps.50:14)

It is good to give thanks to the LORD, to sing praises to your name, O Most High. (Ps.92:1)

13:14–16

3 The ruler (religionist) was a worshiper of God.

¹⁴ But the ruler of the synagogue, indignant because Jesus had healed on the Sabbath, said to the people, "There are six days in which work ought to be done. Come on those days and be healed, and not on the Sabbath day."
¹⁵ Then the Lord answered him, "You hypocrites! Does not each of you on the Sabbath untie his ox or his donkey from the manger and lead it away to water it?
¹⁶ And ought not this woman, a daughter of Abraham whom Satan bound for eighteen years, be loosed from this bond on the Sabbath day?"

Luke shifts the spotlight from the woman to another worshiper there that day: the ruler of the synagogue (see DEEPER STUDY # 2—Mt.4:23; 9:18-19). However, he was a different kind of worshiper than the disabled woman. Whereas the woman sought God through her need of His help, the ruler sought God through *form and ritual, ceremony and rules.* There is a vast difference between the two approaches. The Lord taught that we have to approach Him as a child, dependent, and needy. The head of the synagogue's reaction to the woman's healing reveals the true condition of his heart: his religion was outward only (see outline and notes—Mt.12:1-8; 12:9-13 for more discussion and application).

a. He became angry with the people (v.14a).

The ruler was indignant over what had taken place. In fact, the very people with whom he became angry were his neighbors, the persons who sat in worship with him every week. He allowed his temper to get out of control. The people were merely seeking help, for they were in desperate need, especially the woman; and he knew it. However, because he differed with them, he flared up against them.

THOUGHT 1. How many have hot tempers! How many strike out when they differ! How few control themselves!

Let all bitterness and wrath and anger and clamor and slander be put away from you, along with all malice. (Ep.4:31)

Know this, my beloved brothers: let every person be quick to hear, slow to speak, slow to anger. (Jas.1:19)

Righteous lips are the delight of a king, and he loves him who speaks what is right. (Pr.16:13)

Be not quick in your spirit to become angry, for anger lodges in the heart of fools. (Ec.7:9)

THOUGHT 2. The man lost his temper in the presence of Jesus. Every flare-up is seen by God, and He knows the sin being committed.

b. He corrupted God's Word (v.14b).

The ruler misunderstood and corrupted God's law (Sabbath). In his mind, Jesus had committed a serious crime. He had healed on the Sabbath day (see Deeper Studies 1, 2). But note that the pious man attacked the people rather than Jesus, blaming them for coming to the synagogue on the Sabbath (see Deeper Study # 3)! He was afraid to take Jesus on, for he knew that Jesus was stronger and more capable than he. So, he struck out against the weaker persons. How like the angry person!

c. He rejected Christ (v.14c).

By rejecting Jesus' authority to heal on the Sabbath, the religionist was rejecting Christ. He was refusing to acknowledge the Messiah, God's Son, who was actually standing right before him (see outline and notes—Ro.11:28-29; 1 Th.2:15-16 for discussion).

> Not everyone who says to me, "Lord, Lord," will enter the kingdom of heaven, but the one who does the will of my Father who is in heaven. (Mt.7:21)

> So everyone who acknowledges me before men, I also will acknowledge before my Father who is in heaven, but whoever denies me before men, I also will deny before my Father who is in heaven. (Mt.10:32-33)

> Jesus said to him, "I am the way, and the truth, and the life. No one comes to the Father except through me." (Jn.14:6)

> For there is one God, and there is one mediator between God and men, the man Christ Jesus, who gave himself as a ransom for all, which is the testimony given at the proper time. (1 Ti.2:5-6)

> And this is his commandment, that we believe in the name of his Son Jesus Christ and love one another, just as he has commanded us. (1 Jn.3:23)

d. He was hypocritical (vv.15–16).

Jesus asserted His authority over the synagogue's ruler as well as all the Jewish religious leaders, calling them hypocrites (v.15). The Lord pointed out that they placed both animals and *their religion* above people. They met their livestock's needs on the Sabbath, but they objected to Jesus' meeting of people's greater needs on the Sabbath. Their manmade religious traditions and rituals, ceremonies and rules were more important than meeting the basic needs of human life: the need for God and the need for spiritual, physical, and mental help. These all were to take a back seat to their religious formalities.

The religionists' offense was serious. Jesus hammered at the depths and damaging results of their hypocrisy by pointing out facts about the afflicted woman whose deliverance the synagogue's ruler so piously protested. She was . . .

- a "daughter of Abraham," a Jew and a professed believer in God
- a woman who had been bound by Satan, who had a great spiritual need
- a woman who had suffered for eighteen years

> And if you had known what this means, "I desire mercy, and not sacrifice," you would not have condemned the guiltless. For the Son of Man is lord of the Sabbath. (Mt.12:7-8)

> "Teacher, which is the great commandment in the Law?" And he said to him, "You shall love the Lord your God with all your heart and with all your soul and with all your mind. This is the great and first commandment. And a second is like it: You shall love your neighbor as yourself." (Mt.22:36-39)

> Woe to you, scribes and Pharisees, hypocrites! For you clean the outside of the cup and the plate, but inside they are full of greed and self-indulgence. You blind Pharisee! First clean the inside of the cup and the plate, that the outside also may be clean. Woe to you, scribes and Pharisees, hypocrites! For you are like whitewashed tombs, which outwardly appear beautiful, but within are full of dead people's bones and all uncleanness. So you also outwardly appear righteous to others, but within you are full of hypocrisy and lawlessness. (Mt.23:25-28)

> And he said to them, "Well did Isaiah prophesy of you hypocrites, as it is written, 'This people honors me with their lips, but their heart is far from me; in vain do they worship me, teaching as doctrines the commandments of men.' You leave the commandment of God and hold to the tradition of men." And he said to them, "You have a fine way of rejecting the commandment of God in order to establish your tradition!" (Mk.7:6-9)

> This testimony is true. Therefore rebuke them sharply, that they may be sound in the faith, not devoting themselves to Jewish myths and the commands of people who turn away from the

truth. . . . They profess to know God, but they deny him by their works. They are detestable, disobedient, unfit for any good work. (Tit.1:13–14, 16)

Religion that is pure and undefiled before God the Father is this: to visit orphans and widows in their affliction, and to keep oneself unstained from the world. (Jas.1:27)

By this we know love, that he laid down his life for us, and we ought to lay down our lives for the brothers. But if anyone has the world's goods and sees his brother in need, yet closes his heart against him, how does God's love abide in him? Little children, let us not love in word or talk but in deed and in truth. By this we shall know that we are of the truth and reassure our heart before him. (1 Jn.3:16–19)

DEEPER STUDY # 1

(13:14) **Sabbath Law—Religionists:** the crime committed by Jesus was breaking the Sabbath law, that is, *working* on the Sabbath day. This was a serious matter to the orthodox Jew. Just how serious can be seen in the strict demands governing the Sabbath. Law after law was written to govern all activity on the Sabbath. A person could not travel, fast, cook, buy, sell, draw water, walk beyond a certain distance, lift anything, fight in a war, or heal on the Sabbath unless life was at stake. A person was not even to contemplate any kind of work or activity. A good example of the legal restriction and the people's loyalty to it is seen in the women who witnessed Jesus' crucifixion. Despite their enormous love for Him, they would not even walk to His tomb to prepare the body for burial until the Sabbath was over (Mk.16:1f, Mt.28:1f).

It was a serious matter to break the Sabbath law. A person who broke the law was condemned, and if the offence were serious enough, the person was sentenced to die.

This may seem harsh to some. But when dealing with the Jewish nation, one must remember that it was their religion that held them together as a nation through centuries and centuries of exile. Their religion—in particular their beliefs about God's call to their nation, the temple, and the Sabbath—became the *binding force* that kept Jews together and maintained their distinctiveness as a people. It protected them from alien beliefs and from being swallowed up by other people through intermarriage. No matter where they were, they met together and associated together and held on to their beliefs. A picture of this can be seen in the insistence of Nehemiah when he led some Jews back to Jerusalem (Ne.13:15–22; see Je.17:19–27; Ezk.46:1–7).

All the above explains to some degree why religionists opposed Jesus with such hostility. Their problem was that they had allowed religion and ritual, ceremony and liturgy, and probably position, security, and recognition to become more important than the basic essentials of human life: personal need and compassion, and the true worship and mercy of God. (See note and DEEPER STUDY # 1—Mt.12:10. This is an important note for more discussion on this point.)

DEEPER STUDY # 2

(13:14) **Religionists—Word of God:** religionists (Jewish teachers) corrupted God's Word in two ways (Re.22:18–19; Pr.30:6).

1. By taking away from the words of God's Scripture. A person takes away from God's Word by denying sections that he or she does not like or understand, by neglecting to live by the whole counsel of God, and by interpreting some commandments too loosely.

2. By adding to the words of God's Scripture. A person adds to God's Word by interpreting it too strictly. This exalts the flesh and is nothing more than extreme discipline and self-control. Of course, both discipline and self-control are commendable and are qualities demanded by God's Word, but they are not an end in themselves.

God's Word is practical and leads to an abundant life, to real living. It is not cold, harsh, restrictive, monastic, unrealistic, or impractical. God did not give His Word for a select group (clergy); He gave it for the common people. "His commandments are not burdensome" (1 Jn.5:3).

The Sadducees were especially guilty of taking away from God's Word, whereas the Pharisees and Scribes were especially guilty of adding to God's Word (see DEEPER STUDY # 2—Ac.23:8; DEEPER STUDY # 1—Lu.6:2).

> For truly, I say to you, until heaven and earth pass away, not an iota, not a dot, will pass from the Law until all is accomplished. (Mt.5:18)
>
> And if anyone takes away from the words of the book of this prophecy, God will take away his share in the tree of life and in the holy city, which are described in this book. (Re.22:19)
>
> You shall not add to the word that I command you, nor take from it, that you may keep the commandments of the LORD your God that I command you. (De.4:2)
>
> Everything that I command you, you shall be careful to do. You shall not add to it or take from it. (De.12:32)
>
> Every word of God proves true; he is a shield to those who take refuge in him. Do not add to his words, lest he rebuke you and you be found a liar. (Pr.30:5–6)

DEEPER STUDY # 3

(13:15-16) **Man, Deceived:** the ruler became angry with Jesus, but he camouflaged it by attacking the people over a religious tradition. His life had become so routine that he was warped: he showed more concern for animals than he did for human beings. Jesus' blunt rebuke indicates that the man had probably never even thought of his plight. If he had, Jesus would likely have tried to stir him to a proper decision.

4 The effect of Jesus' works and words: The opponents were humiliated, while crowds rejoiced.

13:17

[17] As he said these things, all his adversaries were put to shame, and all the people rejoiced at all the glorious things that were done by him.

Jesus' opponents were humiliated by His condemnation of their detestable attitude. Like a penetrating fire, what Jesus had said burned through the outer trappings of all their rigid religious pomp, baring the ungodly darkness of their self-righteous souls. The crowds, however, had a different reaction. They rejoiced at the healing of the woman who had been bowed so low by her disability and spiritual oppression, as well as at all the "glorious things" Jesus had done.

S. The Parables of the Mustard Seed and Yeast (Leaven): The Kingdom of God, 13:18–21

(Mt.13:31–33; Mk.4:30–32)

1. The kingdom of God illustrated

2. It is like a mustard seed[DS1]
    a. It is planted by God
      1) As a small seed
      2) In His garden
    b. It grows to be great[DS2]
    c. It provides lodging for all

3. It is like yeast (leaven) working in bread[DS3, 4]
    a. It is taken and mixed into flour
    b. It works through until the whole amount (world) is changed

18 He said therefore, "What is the kingdom of God like? And to what shall I compare it?

19 It is like a grain of mustard seed that a man took and sowed in his garden, and it grew and became a tree, and the birds of the air made nests in its branches."

20 And again he said, "To what shall I compare the kingdom of God?

21 It is like leaven that a woman took and hid in three measures of flour, until it was all leavened."

Division V

The Son of Man's Great Journey to Jerusalem (Stage I): His Mission and Public Challenge, 9:51–13:21

S. The Parables of the Mustard Seed and Yeast (Leaven): The Kingdom of God, 13:18–21

(Mt.13:31–33; Mk.4:30–32)

13:18–21
Introduction

Jesus was still in the synagogue teaching. Some had rejected Him; others had accepted Him (v.17). This stirred Him to teach them about the kingdom of God, a subject that people needed to understand fully. To help the people comprehend kingdom truth, the Lord shared two revealing parables. This is, *The Parables of the Mustard Seed and Yeast (Leaven): The Kingdom of God*, 13:18-21.
    1. The kingdom of God illustrated (v.18).
    2. It is like a mustard seed (v.19).
    3. It is like yeast (leaven) working in bread (vv.20-21).

13:18

18 He said therefore, "What is the kingdom of God like? And to what shall I compare it?"

1 The kingdom of God illustrated.

Jesus turned His teaching to the subject of God's kingdom. Before giving two illustrations of the kingdom, Jesus stirred thought about it by asking two synonymous questions:
    ➤ What is the kingdom of God like?
    ➤ To what can the kingdom of God be compared?

2 It is like a mustard seed.

Jesus first used a mustard seed to illustrate what God's kingdom is like (see DEEPER STUDY # 1). From this tiny seed with great potential, Jesus taught three truths about the kingdom.

a. It is planted by God.

The man in the parable is God; thus, the mustard seed (kingdom) was planted by God. Note the word *took* (Gk. labōn, *lah-bone'*). It means to take deliberately, to take with purpose and thought. The seed was not planted by chance; it did not just happen. With purpose and thought, God planted and nourished the seed (kingdom).

> [19] "It is like a grain of mustard seed that a man took and sowed in his garden, and it grew and became a tree, and the birds of the air made nests in its branches."

➤ He planted it as a small seed.
➤ He planted it in His garden—the world, the creation of His own hand.

In the beginning, God created the heavens and the earth. (Ge.1:1)

You are the LORD, you alone. You have made heaven, the heaven of heavens, with all their host, the earth and all that is on it, the seas and all that are in them; and you preserve all of them; and the host of heaven worships you. (Ne.9:6)

Of old you laid the foundation of the earth, and the heavens are the work of your hands. (Ps.102:25)

b. It grows to be great.

The tiny mustard seed grew to be great; it became a large tree. This is really the major point of Luke, both in his Gospel and in *Acts*, to show how the kingdom was to grow from a few persons into a great worldwide movement. Imagine the scene. There stood Jesus in the synagogue with only a few persons who truly believed that He was bringing the kingdom of God to earth. In fact, most of the ones sitting before Him did not believe in Him at all; they opposed Him. But He knew something. God was planting the kingdom on earth through Him; therefore the kingdom was destined to grow and succeed (see DEEPER STUDY # 2).

Therefore let it be known to you that this salvation of God has been sent to the Gentiles; they will listen. (Ac.28:28)

So that in Christ Jesus the blessing of Abraham might come to the Gentiles, so that we might receive the promised Spirit through faith. (Ga.3:14)

This mystery is that the Gentiles are fellow heirs, members of the same body, and partakers of the promise in Christ Jesus through the gospel. (Ep.3:6)

Of the increase of his government and of peace there will be no end, on the throne of David and over his kingdom, to establish it and to uphold it with justice and with righteousness from this time forth and forevermore. The zeal of the LORD of hosts will do this. (Is.9:7)

For you will spread abroad to the right and to the left, and your offspring will possess the nations and will people the desolate cities. (Is.54:3)

Behold, you shall call a nation that you do not know, and a nation that did not know you shall run to you, because of the LORD your God, and of the Holy One of Israel, for he has glorified you. (Is.55:5)

c. It provides lodging for all.

The mustard bush provided lodging for the birds of the air. The birds' flocking to the tree is a picture of the people and nations of the earth seeking refuge in the covering of Christianity.

Some say the birds are those in the world who find their lodging in the kingdom—the kingdom (the church, Christianity) that had so small a beginning but has now grown into a remarkable, unstoppable movement. Many in the world, believers and nonbelievers alike, have found help and safety under its branches. To a large extent, laws and institutions of mercy, justice, and honor have evolved from this magnificent movement. This interpretation relies heavily on a picture painted by the Old Testament. A great empire is said to be like a tree, and conquered nations are said to be like birds who lodge under its shadow (Ezk.17:22-24; 31:6; Dan.4:14).

Others say the birds are Satan and his forces who infiltrate the kingdom (the church) and seek to devour its fruit. In the Parable of the Sower, Jesus used birds to represent Satan, and they devoured some of the seed that was sown (Lu.8:5, 12).

The Law and the Prophets were until John; since then the good news of the kingdom of God is preached, and everyone forces his way into it. (Lu.16:16)

DEEPER STUDY # 1

(13:19) **Mustard Seed:** the mustard seed was not actually the smallest seed known in Jesus' day, but the seed was very small, resulting in it being used as a common symbol of small-ness. However, the mustard bush grew as large as some trees. It has been reported that a rider on horseback could find shade under its branches. The fact that such a small seed could produce such huge results caused people to also use the mustard seed as a proverbial saying to describe the growth potential of something so small.

DEEPER STUDY # 2

(13:19) **Christianity—Kingdom of God:** several facts show just how small the beginning of the kingdom or of Christianity really was.

1. It began in the soul of a single person. Jesus launched the movement all by Him-self. The idea, the dream, was in no one else's soul but His. He moved out alone—in God's strength.

2. It was born in the soul of a carpenter from an obscure village, Nazareth, and from an obscure and despised nation, Israel (see note—Mt.8:5-13; Lu.7:4-5).

3. It was carried forth by men with no position and no prestige. There were no mighty, no noble, no famous persons among its early followers. They were but common folk, some from honorable professions such as the fishing industry (Mt.4:18-21), and some from despised professions such as tax collecting (Mt.9:9; see 1 Co.1:26).

4. It grew from just a few persons who had very *little faith* (see Mt.14:31; Lu.12:32).

5. It was formed as a church and numbered only one hundred and twenty in the very beginning (Ac.1:15).

13:20-21

20 And again he said, "To what shall I compare the kingdom of God?

21 It is like leaven that a woman took and hid in three measures of flour, until it was all leavened."

3 It is like yeast (leaven) working in bread.

Giving a second illustration, Jesus said that the kingdom of God is like yeast (leaven) working in bread. As a small amount of yeast affects an entire batch of bread, the king-dom of God will affect the whole world. Note two major points.

a. It is taken and mixed into flour (v.21).

The leaven (expansion of God's kingdom or gospel outreach) is deliberately taken and placed into the meal (world). The growth of the kingdom of God and the gospel are not by chance (see DEEPER STUDY # 2, pt.1—v.19).

For God so loved the world, that he gave his only Son, that whoever believes in him should not perish but have eternal life. (Jn.3:16)

But God shows his love for us in that while we were still sinners, Christ died for us. (Ro.5:8)

For there is no distinction between Jew and Greek; for the same Lord is Lord of all, bestowing his riches on all who call on him. (Ro.10:12)

Who desires all people to be saved and to come to the knowledge of the truth. (1 Ti.2:4)

He is the propitiation for our sins, and not for ours only but also for the sins of the whole world. (1Jn.2:2)

Turn to me and be saved, all the ends of the earth! For I am God, and there is no other. (Is.45:22)

The purpose of the kingdom is to leaven, that is, to change the whole of an individual and of society itself. It seeks to leaven individuals: to penetrate them with the gospel until the *whole being* is transformed. In addition, it seeks to leaven society as a whole: to penetrate society with the gospel until the whole of society is transformed.

Therefore, if anyone is in Christ, he is a new creation. The old has passed away; behold, the new has come. (2 Co.5:17)

And to be renewed in the spirit of your minds, and to put on the new self, created after the likeness of God in true righteousness and holiness. (Ep.4:23-24)

And have put on the new self, which is being renewed in knowledge after the image of its creator. (Col.3:10)

b. It works through until the whole amount (world) is changed. (v.21)

Leaven has a changing, transforming, fulfilling, and satisfying power (see DEEPER STUDY # 1— Lu.12:1 for discussion). The leaven (kingdom) works until the whole batch of dough (world) is changed (see DEEPER STUDIES 3, 4). The gospel will spread throughout the entire world, changing lives and changing society.

Jesus then said to them, "Truly, truly, I say to you, it was not Moses who gave you the bread from heaven, but my Father gives you the true bread from heaven. For the bread of God is he who comes down from heaven and gives life to the world." (Jn.6:32-33)

Jesus said to them, "I am the bread of life; whoever comes to me shall not hunger, and whoever believes in me shall never thirst." . . . I am the bread of life. Your fathers ate the manna in the wilderness, and they died. This is the bread that comes down from heaven, so that one may eat of it and not die. I am the living bread that came down from heaven. If anyone eats of this bread, he will live forever. And the bread that I will give for the life of the world is my flesh. . . . This is the bread that came down from heaven, not like the bread the fathers ate, and died. Whoever feeds on this bread will live forever. (Jn.6:35, 48-51, 58)

For he satisfies the longing soul, and the hungry soul he fills with good things. (Ps.107:9)

As with the mustard seed, many see the leaven as evil: evil will seep into the kingdom (church, Christianity) and corrupt it. In the Old Testament, leaven was a symbol of evil (Ex.12:14-20). In other teachings, Jesus had described the teaching of the Pharisees and Sadducees as well as Herod as leaven (Mt.16:12; Mk.8:15). The fact that Jesus gave these parables immediately after condemning the religious leaders as hypocrites supports the interpretation regard.

DEEPER STUDY # 3

(13:21) **Leaven—Transformation—Gospel—Kingdom of God:** leaven changes and transforms bread. Bread made from water is hard, dry, and not very nourishing; but leaven, mixed in with dough, changes and transforms bread tremendously. It does at least four things for bread.

1. Leaven makes bread soft, no longer hard. The leaven of the gospel does the same; it penetrates people's hearts and softens the hardness of their lives. Thereby people become much softer toward the Lord and toward the needs of others. They become more caring and giving. Softness is definitely one of the trademarks of a transformed person.

2. Leaven makes bread porous and moist, no longer dry. The leaven of the gospel does the same; it penetrates the dryness of people's hearts and lives. Thereby the gospel penetrates, creates pores in their lives, and moistens their hearts so they can grow into a moist or fruitful person.

3. Leaven makes bread satisfying, no longer dissatisfying. Again, the gospel does the same for the person who lives a life with no purpose, meaning, or significance. The gospel

leavens, that is, transforms a person's heart and life, giving purpose and joy and hope—all the satisfaction a person could ever desire.

4. Leaven makes bread nourishing, no longer of little benefit. The leaven of the gospel does the same thing for the person who seems to accomplish so little in life. The gospel not only gives *purpose* but it *inspires, commissions,* and *causes* a person to *feed others.* A person transformed by the gospel is able to feed the truth to the world. The gospel is able to explain the reasons for the emptiness and loneliness of the human heart and God's provision for such.

DEEPER STUDY # 4

(13:21) **Leaven:** note several important facts about how leaven works.
1. Leaven works quietly and silently. It works without fanfare and the spectacular. There is a thoughtful lesson here on how the gospel should be presented (see outline and notes—Mt.4:5-7; 12:38-40).

> And the Lord's servant must not be quarrelsome but kind to everyone, able to teach, patiently enduring evil, correcting his opponents with gentleness. God may perhaps grant them repentance leading to a knowledge of the truth. (2 Ti.2:24–25)

> To speak evil of no one, to avoid quarreling, to be gentle, and to show perfect courtesy toward all people. (Tit.3:2)

> Who is wise and understanding among you? By his good conduct let him show his works in the meekness of wisdom. (Jas.3:13)

> But in your hearts honor Christ the Lord as holy, always being prepared to make a defense to anyone who asks you for a reason for the hope that is in you; yet do it with gentleness and respect. (1 Pe.3:15)

2. Leaven finishes its work. Once it is inserted into the dough, nothing can stop it or ever pluck it out. It will transform the dough. This is a great lesson on the security of those who genuinely allow the gospel to penetrate their hearts and lives.

> I give them eternal life, and they will never perish, and no one will snatch them out of my hand. (Jn.10:28)

> And I am sure of this, that he who began a good work in you will bring it to completion at the day of Jesus Christ. (Ph.1:6)

> But the Lord is faithful. He will establish you and guard you against the evil one. (2 Th.3:3)

> Which is why I suffer as I do. But I am not ashamed, for I know whom I have believed, and I am convinced that he is able to guard until that day what has been entrusted to me. (2 Ti.1:12)

> Who by God's power are being guarded through faith for a salvation ready to be revealed in the last time. (1 Pe.1:5)

> Now to him who is able to keep you from stumbling and to present you blameless before the presence of his glory with great joy, to the only God, our Savior, through Jesus Christ our Lord, be glory, majesty, dominion, and authority, before all time and now and forever. Amen. (Jude 24–25)

3. Leaven works slowly and gradually, yet consistently. It takes time for it to leaven the whole lump. The believer can learn at least two lessons from this fact.
   a. It will take time to personally grow in the gospel. Just as a child grows physically through proper nourishment, so believers will grow spiritually if they receive proper nourishment. Their spiritual growth will take time; but it will be consistent and sure.

> And now I commend you to God and to the word of his grace, which is able to build you up and to give you the inheritance among all those who are sanctified. (Ac.20:32)

> Do your best to present yourself to God as one approved, a worker who has no need to be ashamed, rightly handling the word of truth. (2 Ti.2:15)

> All Scripture is breathed out by God and profitable for teaching, for reproof, for correction, and for training in righteousness. (2 Ti.3:16)

Like newborn infants, long for the pure spiritual milk, that by it you may grow up into salvation—if indeed you have tasted that the Lord is good. (1 Pe.2:2-3)

    b. It will take time for their own witnessing and work to produce bread. Yet their leavening (service and ministry) will leaven the lump of meal (people) with whom they work.

4. Leaven changes the quality, not the substance, of the dough. It is still dough, yet it is changed. People who receive the gospel remain human beings; but they are changed people, people of quality, people of God.

5. Leaven changes the whole lump. It permeates every pore of the dough's being. So it is with a person. Once the gospel genuinely penetrates, it permeates and affects all of their life (see 2 Co.5:17; Ga.6:15; Ep.4:23-24; Col.3:10).

OUTLINE AND SUBJECT INDEX

When you look up a subject and turn to the Scripture reference, you not only have the Scripture, you have *an outline and a discussion* (commentary) of the Scripture and subject.

This valuable feature of the everyWORD™ series becomes even more valuable once you have the complete set of books. Once you have all volumes, you will have access to each book's index, including a list of all the subjects and their Scripture references, and you will also have . . .

- an outline of *every* Scripture and subject in the Bible.
- a discussion (commentary) on every Scripture and subject.
- every subject supported by other Scriptures or cross references.

See for yourself how the index works. Quickly glance in the sample below to the very first subject of the Index of Luke. It is:

ACCEPTANCE—ACCEPTABLE
Discussed. 9:49-50

Turn to the first reference. Glance at the Scripture and outline of the Scripture, then read the commentary. As you familiarize yourself with the OUTLINE AND SUBJECT INDEX, you will likely find it to be a useful tool in your use of the everyWORD™ series.

BAPTISM (*Continued*)
Obedience & approval. 3:21-22
Of repentance. Meaning. 3:3
Results. Secures God's approval & blessings. Threefold. 3:22

BEAM
Parable of. Watch hypocrisy & criticizing. 6:41-42

BEHAVIOR
Golden Rule. 6: 31
Principles governing. 6:27-31

BELIEVE—BELIEVING—BELIEF
Vs. fear. 8:25

BELIEVER—BELIEVERS (See **APOSTLES; DISCIPLES; LABORERS; MINISTERS**)
Described.
As babes. 10:21
As builder. True vs. false discipleship. 6:46-49
Duty—Behavior—Life—Walk.
Not above Master, but treated the same as the Master. 6:40
Not to worry about necessities. 12:22-34
One thing needed. 10:38-42
Rules for discipleship. 6:39-45
To accept others. 9:49-50
To be conformed to Christ. 6:40
To be prepared for Jesus' return. 12:35-48
To die to self. (See **SELF-DENIAL**)
To fear the Lord. 8:25
To help the needy. 10:29-37
To watch. Fear certain things. 6:39-45
Toward money. (See **STEWARDSHIP**)
False. (See **DISCIPLE**, False)
Hall of Fame. Many wrote on life of Christ. 1:1
Hope of. (See **HOPE**)
Position.
Not above Master, but treated same as the Master. 6:40
Privileges of.
Discussed. 10:21-24
Trusted by Christ. 8:23
Truth revealed to. 10:21

BENEDICTUS
Song of Zacharias. 1:67-80

BETHLEHEM
City of Jesus' birth. Prophesied. 2:3

BETROTHED
Engagement before marriage. 1:27

BIRDS
Fed by God. 12:24

BLASPHEMY
Against the Holy Spirit. 12:9-10

BLIND—BLINDNESS, SPIRITUAL
Caused by. Spiritual dullness. 9:44-45
Parable of. Blind leading the blind. 6:39
Results. Causes others to be blind (followers, children). 6:39

BODY
Deformed. How to keep from worrying about. 12:25

Duty. Not to be anxious about the **b.** even if deformed. 12:22-28; 12:25
Indulgence of. (See **INDULGENCE**)

BONDAGE
List of. Several things. 9:47

BOOK OF LIFE
Duty. To rejoice that one's name is written in heaven. 10:20

BORROW—BORROWING (See **LENDING**)

BOTTLES
New vs. old **b.** New life & joy. Purpose of Jesus. 5:36-39, esp. 37-38

BRIDEGROOM
Symbolizes. Jesus death. Mission of dying. 5:35

BROKEN-HEARTED (See **CONTRITION; SORROW, GODLY**)
Healed by Jesus. 4:17-19
Touches Christ. 7:12-13

BROTHERHOOD
Basis of.
God binds together. 8:21
Not of flesh or blood or will. 8:20
Principles governing. Fivefold. 6:27-31
Discussed. 8:19-21
Example. Demonstrating & showing **b.** vs. not demonstrating. 10:29-37
Failure in. Some things often put before **b.** 10:29-37
Meaning. What true **b.** is. 8:19-21
Results. Overcomes prejudice. 10:29-37
Source of. 8:19-21
Discussed. 10:29-37
True **b.** 8:19-21
What binds believers together. 8:21

BRUISED
Physically, mentally, spiritually. Jesus heals. 4:17-19

BUSYNESS
Caused by. Distraction. 10:40

CAESAR
Tiberius. Discussed. 3:1

CAIAPHAS
High Priest. Discussed. 3:1-6

CALL—CALLED
Commitment to. Reluctant obedience. 5:1-11; 9:57-62
Importance of. 6:12
Nature of **c.** Personal & dynamic. 3:2
Of disciples. Jesus chooses His men. 6:12-19
Purpose.
To catch men; to fish for souls. 5:10
To discipleship. Steps to. 6:1-11
To serve God, not religion. 3:2
Source. Of God & Christ, not of religion. 3:2

CAPERNAUM
Headquarters of Jesus. 4:31
Jesus' ministry in C. 4:31-44

CAPTIVE—CAPTIVATED
Delivered by. Christ. 4:17-19
Who is **c.** People. 4:18

CARE—CARING
Duty to **c.**
For children. 2:41-52
For the less fortunate & the weak. 7:2
Show **c.** for all men, even enemies. 10:25-37
Example of. Centurion soldier for servant. 7:2
Of God. Provides necessities of life for His people. 12:22-34
Of Jesus Christ. Identified with man. Every conceivable experience. 2:40

CARES OF WORLD
Duty. Not to be anxious over. 12:22-34
Results. Chokes life out of a person. 8:11-15

CARNAL—CARNALITY
Described as. Powerlessness. 9:37-45
Mind of. Vs. spiritual **m.** 12:13-21

CENTURION
Example of. Great faith of. 7:1-10

CEREMONY—CEREMONIAL LAW (See **SCRIBAL LAW; RELIGION; RITUAL**)
Facts about.
Superseded by need. 6:1-11
Laws of.
Cleanliness, purity. Washing hands. **C.** 11:37-38
Walking over graves. 11:44

CHEEK
Striking—slapping. Attitude toward being slapped. 6:27-31

CHILDISHNESS
Of generation. 7:32
Of unbelievers. 7:32

CHILDREN—CHILDLIKENESS
Duties of.
To be faithful to God. 2:49-50
To be faithful to parents. 2:51
To study—learn—share. 2:46-47
Jesus and **c.** Discussed. 9:46-48
Symbolize—Illustrate.
Greatness. 9:46-48
Treatment—Reactions toward.
By Jesus. 9:47
To be received. 9:46-48

CHRISTIAN (See **BELIEVER**)

CHRISTIANITY
Growth of. Great. 13:19
Source. New life & movement brought by Christ. 5:36-39

CHURCH
Attendance. Reasons. False vs. true. 8:4-15
Basis—Foundation.
God binds together by Word. 8:21
To be centered in homes, families. 9:4; 10:5-6

CIRCUMCISION
Physical **c.**
Performed on the eighth day. 1:59
The time when a child was named. 1:59-63

CITIZENSHIP (See **GOVERNMENT; NATIONS**)

CLOAK (See **OUTER GARMENT**)

CLOTHING (See **DRESS**)
Duty. To trust God & not to worry about fashion. 12:22-34

CLOUD
At Transfiguration of Christ. 9:34; 9:35
Meaning. 9:35

COMMANDMENT—COMMANDMENTS
Greatest c. Discussed. 10:25-37

COMMISSION
Discussed. 9:1-9; 10:1-16; 10:17-20
  How to go forth. 10:1-16
  The 70 symbolize five things. 10:1-16; 10:1
Given to. Disciples & preachers. 9:1-9
Great C.
  Fivefold mission. 5:27-39
  Threefold mission. 6:17-19

COMMIT—COMMITMENT (See **DEDICATION**)
Kind of c.
  Half-hearted. 9:57-62
  Reluctant c. 5:4-6; 9:57-62

COMPASSION
Duty. To show c.
  For all men, even for enemies. 10:25-37
  Upon the different. 10:25-37
  Upon the neglected and injured. 10:25-37
Example.
  Good Samaritan. 10:25-37
Failure to show c.
  Duty placed before c. 10:29-37
  Fear or unconcern prevents c. 10:29-37
Meaning. 7:13
Of God.
  For the sorrowful. 7:11-17
Of Jesus Christ.
  For a mother with a dead son. 7:12-13
  For the diseased, the crippled, & the needy. 13:11-16
  For the most unclean. 5:13
  For the needy who are faithful in worship. 13:11-16
  Verses. List of. 7:12-13
Results. Overcomes prejudice. 10:33-37
Stirred by. Four things. 7:12-13
Verses. List of. 10:33-37

COMPLACENT—COMPLACENCY
Example. Reluctance to obey. 5:4-5
Result. Secures little if anything. 8:18
Verses. List of. 8:18

COMPLAINING
Caused by. Anxiety, worry. 10:40

COMPROMISE
Judgment of. Warning. 6:24-26
Temptation to. Discussed. 4:5-8

CONDEMN—CONDEMNATION
Caused by. Are as vipers, biting & poisonous. 3:7

CONFESS—CONFESSION
Fear to c. Christ. 12:4-12
Essential.
  C. vs. being ashamed. 12:4-12
  Must c. for restoration. 15:20-21
  Must make a personal c. 1:43-44; 9:20; 12:4-12
  To confess sin, reluctance to obey. 5:8-9
Verses. List of. 5:8-9; 9:20

CONFORMED—CONFORMITY
To Christ. Goal of believers. 6:40

CONSERVATIVE
Vs. Indulgent. Unbelievers reject both approaches to the gospel. 7:33-34

CONSTRUCTION WORKERS
Tower fell on. Thought to be great sinners. 13:1-5

CONTRITION (See **HUMILITY; SORROW, GODLY**)
Essential.
  To confess sin, reluctance to obey. 5:8-9
  Verses. List of. 5:8-9; 5:12

CONVERSATION
Duty. To waste no time in needless c. 10:4

CONVERSION—CONVERTED (See **SALVATION**; Related Subjects)
Dramatic. Lacks depth. 8:11-15
How a person is c.
  Various types. 8:4-15
Warning. Snatched away by the devil. 8:5, 12

COVENANT, NEW
Established. By Christ. Brings salvation. 1:68-75

COVET—COVETOUSNESS
Discussed. 12:13-21
Illust. 12:13-21
Meaning. 12:15
Result.
  Failure to use wealth wisely. 12:13-21
  Judgment. 12:20-21
Sin of.
  Big sin of world. 12:15-19
Verses. List of. 12:15-19; 12:15

CREATION
Of man.
  Every man owes his existence to God. 13:6-9
Responsibility for c.
  Man. To bear fruit. 13:6-9

CRITICISM—CRITICIZING
Cause of. Anxiety & worry. 10:40
Nature. Blinds a person to his own faults. 6:41-42
Warning against. Watch hypocrisy & c. Four points. 6:41-42

CROSS—SELF-DENIAL (See **JESUS CHRIST, DEATH; CROSS**)
Duty.
  To bear one's c. 9:23
  To take up the c. 9:23-27
Meaning. Taking up the cross. 9:23

Reactions to.
  Man accepts or is repulsed by. 2:35

CROWDS
Thousands followed Christ. 8:4

CURSING—SWEARING
Attitude toward. Those who c. us. 6:27-31

DAILY CROSS (See **CROSS**)

DARKNESS
Nature. Men try to hide four things. 8:17

DAVID
Illustration. Putting need before religious rules. 6:1-5
Kingdom of. Given to Christ. 1:31-33; 1:32-33; 3:24-31

DEAR
Meaning. 7:2

DEATH—DYING
Dead raised. Widow's son. Great compassion & power. 7:11-17
Described. As sleep. 8:51-53
Fact.
  Comes to rich. Rich not exempt. 12:20
  Touches Christ. 7:12-13
To self. (See **CROSS; SELF-DENIAL**)

DECEIVE—DECEPTION
Error of. Hidden behind ritual. 13:14

DECISION (See **INDECISION**)
Duty—Essential.
  Must be made. Choice essential. 2:34
  Neutrality impossible. 9:57-62; 11:23
  To hear the Word of Christ. 9:35
Facts.
  Can wait too late. 13:25
  Man hedges in making a d. 9:57-62
  Spirit will not always strive after man. 4:28-30
Rejected.
  Discussed. 9:57-62
  Excuses given. 9:57-62
Results. Determines a person's destiny. 11:23
Verses. List of. 9:61-62

DEDICATION—DEDICATED (See **COMMITMENT; FAITHFULNESS; SURRENDER**)
Described as.
  Half-hearted. 9:57-58
Duty—Essential.
  To forsake all for Christ. 5:11
Results. God knows & richly blesses. 2:25-27

DEFORMITY
Healed by Jesus. Man more important than religion. 13:11-13

DELIVERANCE
From sin. List of things which enslave. 9:47

DEMONS (See **EVIL SPIRITS**)

DENY—DENIAL (See APOSTASY; BACKSLIDING)
Warning against.
Fear denying Christ. 12:4-12

DESERTION (See APOSTASY; DENIAL)

DESPERATION (See SEEKING)

DESTINY
Determined by. Decision for Christ. Neutrality impossible. 11:23

DEVOTION—DEVOTIONS
Duty.
Daily meditation essential. 10:41-42
To sit at Christ's feet. 10:38-42
To take time alone with God & to rest. 9:10
Verses. List of. 9:10; 10:41-42

DILIGENCE—DILIGENTLY (See ENDURANCE; PERSEVERANCE; STEDFASTNESS; ZEAL)
Duty.
To act & act now. 9:59-60
To labor even if tired. 9:11

DISCIPLE—DISCIPLES (See APOSTLES; BELIEVER; LABORER; MINISTERS)
Call.
Jesus chooses His men. Who & why. 6:12-19
Steps to c. 5:1-11; 6:12-19
Character—Traits. Genuine vs. counterfeit. 6:46-49
Commission. (See COMMISSION; MISSION)
Disbelief of.
Predictions of Jesus' death. 9:44-45
Duty.
To be conformed to Christ. 6:40
To fear hypocrisy. 12:1-3
Failure of. Power lost. 9:37-40
False. Lays no foundation. 6:49
Mission—Commission. (See COMMISSION; MISSION)
Of Jesus. Numbered many more than just twelve. 10:1
Position.
Not above Master. But treated same as M. 6:40
Power of. (See POWER)
Privileges of. Discussed. 10:21-24
Resources. (See RESOURCES)
Sent forth. (See COMMISSION; MISSION)

DISCIPLESHIP
Call of. Step to c. 5:1-11
Cost of.
Great c. 9:57-62
Discussed.
Reason people follow Christ. 7:11
Terms of. 9:23-27
Essential.
Sacrifice, self-denial. 9:57-62
Examples of. 9:57-62
Failure of.
Divided allegiance. 9:59-60
Lack of commitment. Three examples. 9:57-62
Looking back. 9:61-62
Putting family before Christ. 9:59-62; 12:51-53

Reluctant to respond to call. 5:1-11; 9:57-62
To count cost. 9:57-62
False (See PROFESSION, False)
Meaning. 9:23
Rules for. Fourfold. 6:39-45
True vs. false. Two foundations. 6:46-49
Verses. List of. 9:61-62

DISCIPLINE—CHASTISEMENT OF GOD
Caused by. Unbelief. Not believing the promise of God. 1:20-22
Response to. Obedience. 1: 63

DISCIPLINE, CHURCH (See CHURCH DISCIPLINE)

DISCRIMINATION
Overcome by.
Compassion. 10:33-37

DOUBLE-MINDED (See DECISION; NEUTRALITY)
Duty. To decide. Not to be d. 9:57-62; 11:23

DRESS (See CLOTHING)
Can cause problems.
Extravagant living. 7:25
Warning against.
Extravagant—exposed d. 7:25

DULL—DULLNESS
Caused by. Spiritual insensitivity. 9:44-45
Verses. List of. 9:44-45

DUTY
Placed before compassion. 10:29-37

ELECT—ELECTION (See CHOSEN; PREDESTINATION)

ELIJAH
Appeared at Jesus' transfiguration. Reason. 9:30-31

ELIZABETH, MOTHER OF JOHN THE BAPTIST
Picture of godly parents. 1:5-25
Supernatural proclamation. Unusual testimony. 1:39-45

EMBARRASSED
Things e. about. Discussed. 9:26

EMPATHY (See SYMPATHY)

EMPTY—EMPTINESS
Answer to. Seeking Jesus. 5:27-29; 5:30-32

ENCOURAGE—ENCOURAGEMENT
Duty. To e. the weaker. 1:43-44
Example. Two with similar circumstances. 1:39-42

END TIME (See JESUS CHRIST, Return)

ENDURANCE (See PERSEVERANCE; STEDFASTNESS)
Duty. To e. in prayer. 11:5-10

ENEMIES
Attitude toward. (See PERSECUTION)
Discussed. 6:20-23; 6:27-31

ESCAPISM
Of generation. Discussed. 7:33-34

Results.
Hard hearts. 7:33-34
Rejection of Jesus. 7:33-34
Shirking of duty. 7:33-34

ESPOUSED
Discussed. Engagement before marriage. 1:27

ETERNAL LIFE
How to secure. Giving everything. 10:25-37
Results of rejecting. Losing one's life. 9:24
Source. How to inherit. 10:25-37

EVALUATION
Needed. Time for e. is essential. 9:10

EVANGELISM—EVANGELIZE
And Jesus. Was the ministry of Jesus. 4:17-19; 19:10, see Mt.28:19-20
Dangers to. Sensationalism. Jesus tempted to use e. 4:9-12
How to e. Discussed. 10:1-16
Method.
House e. 9:4; 10:5-6
Meaning. 8:1
To be centered in homes. 9:4
Why e. Harvest is great. 10:2

EVIL SPIRITS
Acknowledged Jesus' deity. Rejected by Jesus. 4:33-37; 4:41
Delivered from.
An only child. Rebuke of present generation. 9:37-45
Most unclean. 4:33-37; 8:1
Discussed. 9:39
Character & work. 8:26-39
Power over.
By Jesus.
Proves deity of Christ. 11:14-28
Christian witness given power over. 10:17-18
To free men. 8:26-39
Work of. Wish to inhabit men. 11:24-26

EXCESS (See INDULGENCE)

EXCUSES
For not following Christ. Discussed. 9:57-62

EXORCIST
Jewish e. In Jesus' day. 11:19

EXPOSURE—EXPOSED
Of all things. Discussed. 8:17
Verses. List of. 8:17; 12:1-3

EYE
Described as. Healthy vs. diseased. Man has either h. or d. eye. 11:33-36

FAITH (See BELIEVE; TRUST)
Duty.
To believe "nothing is impossible." 1:36-37
To believe the miraculous. 1:34-35
To trust God to take care of needs & necessities. 10:4
Example of.
Centurion. Great f. in a soldier. 7:1-10
Friends. Brings about forgiveness. 5:18-20

Great **f.** Found in a soldier. 7:1-10
Lack of. (See **UNBELIEF**)
Meaning. 7:6-8
Reward. Of true **f.** 8:40-56
Source. Jesus' power. 7:6-8; 7:9-10
Stages - kinds of.
    Great **f.** 7:1-10
    Persisting **f.** 5:18-20; 8:41-42;
      8:49-56
    Reluctant **f.** 5:4-11
Vs. fear. 8:25

FAITHFUL—FAITHFULNESS (See
    DEDICATION)
Duty.
    Despite lack of blessing from God.
      1:8-9
    To be **f.** until Jesus returns.
      12:41-48
Results. Secures more & more. 8:18

FAITHLESSNESS
Meaning. 9:41
Of whom.
    Of a generation. 9:41
    Of men. 8:22-25
Sin of. Present generation. 9:41

FAMILY (See **PARENTS**)
Basis of a **f.** Discussed. 8:19-21
Danger.
    Often divided over Christ. 12:51-53
    Putting before Christ. 9:59-62;
      12:51-53
Duty.
    Not to be put before Christ. 12:51-53
    To be Godly **f.** Picture of. 1:5-25
    To witness to **f.** 8:38-39
Parents. Godly **p.** 1:5-25
Purpose. To be the center of the
    church's ministry. 9:4

FAMILY OF GOD
Basis. Not of heritage, flesh, or will.
    8:21

FASTING
Of Jesus. Criticized because He fasted
    so little. 5:33-34

FAVOR—FAVORED (See **BLESSINGS;**
    GRACE; PROMISES)
Example of. Mary, mother of Jesus.
    1:28

FEAR
Caused by. Jesus' power. 7:16
Causes one to.
    Glorify God. 7:16
Meaning. 7:16-17
Results. Stirs reverence for the Lord.
    8:25
Vs. faith. 8:25
What is **f.** List of twelve things feared.
    9:26
What to fear. 12:1-12; 12:13-21
    Covetousness & selfishness.
      12:13-21
    God. Results. 7:16-17
    Judgment—soul being required
      tonight. 12:20-21
    Not to **f.** men. Reasons. 12:4-12
    Things to **f.** & not to **f.** 12:1-12;
      12:13-21

FEED—FEEDING
Miracle of. By Christ. How to minister.
    9:10-17

FELLOWSHIP
Basis—Source. Discussed. 8:21

FICKLENESS
Characteristic of Jesus' age. 7:29-35

FIG TREE
Parable of. Must bear fruit or perish.
    13:6-9

FIRE
Described. As unquenchable. Meaning.
    3:17

FOLLOW—FOLLOWING
Of Jesus.
    Discussed. 9:23

FOOD (See **NEED—NECESSITIES**)
Duty. Not to worry about. God
    provides. 12:22-34

FORFEITED
Meaning. 9:25

FORGIVENESS, SPIRITUAL
Condition. Repentance. 3:3
How one receives.
    By forgiving others. 11:2-4
    Prayer for. 11:2-4
Results.
    Proves Christ's power. 5:17-26
Steps to. Discussed. 5:17-26

FORSAKING
F. all. (See **SELF-DENIAL**)

FOUNDATIONS
Of life. Two **f.** True vs. false
    discipleship. 6:46-49, see
    Mt.7:24-27

FREEDOM
Of Christ. Delivers. List of things. 9:47

FRUIT BEARING (See **BELIEVER;**
    DEDICATION)
Duty.
    To give **f.** to God. 13:6-9
    To repent & bear **f.** 3:8
Essential.
    Judgment based upon. 13:6-9
    Must bear **f.** or perish. 13:6-9
Results. Reveals one's nature. 6:43-45

FULL, THE (The Well-fed)
Judgment of. Are warned. 6:24-26,
    esp.v.25

GABRIEL
Angel. Discussed. 1:19
Work of. Sent to an unknown person
    with God's message. 1:26

GALILEANS
Slaughtered by Herod. Thought to be
    great sinners. 13:1-5

GARMENT
Parable of. New vs. old. To bring new
    life, joy. 5:33-34

GENERATION
Described.
    By Jesus. 7:32-35
    Evil. Reasons. 11:31

Rebuke of. 9:37-45
Welfare of. Determined by concern for
    righteousness. 10:2

GENTILES
Salvation of **G.** Predicted.
    At Jesus' birth. 2:28-32
Vs. Jews. Prejudice between. 7:4

GIVE—GIVING (See **STEWARDSHIP**)
Duty.
    To give to help meet needs.
      6:27-31
    To give when asked. 6:27-31
    To seek heavenly treasures by **g.**
      12:31-34
    To work so one is able to **g.** & meet
      the needs of others. 12:31-34
Facts—Principles.
    Judged by the amount kept back, not
      given. 21:3
    More one **g.**, more he receives.
      6:37-38
Verses. List of. 9:16-17

GLORIFY—GLORIFYING
Of God.
    After being blessed & healed. 5:26;
      13:13

GLORY
Shekinah. 2:8-12
Source. Prayer & Jesus' presence. 9:29

GOD
And the Holy Spirit. Gives the Spirit to
    those who ask. 11:11-13
Description of. Discussed. 1:46-56
Existence.
    Must believe God is—does exist.
      12:54-57
    Verses. List of. 12:54-57
Holy—Holiness. Declared by Mary.
    1:49-50
Knowledge of—Omniscience.
    Mutual **k.** between God & Christ &
      the believer. 10:22
Mercy. God's glorious **m.** & deliverance.
    1:46-56
Nature.
    Goodness of. Is good not evil.
      11:11-13
Power.
    All things are possible to God. 1:36-
      37; 1:57
    To send the Messiah, born of a
      virgin. 1:49-50
Providence—Sovereignty.
    Reversed the order of things on
      earth. 1:51-53
    Rules over events to fulfill Scripture.
      Christ's birth. 2:1-6
Will of. Submission to. 1:26-38
Works of.
    Movement in history. 1:46-56
    To reverse order of five things.
      1:51-53

GOLDEN RULE
Discussed. 6:31

GOOD—GOODNESS
Misconception of. (See
    SELF-RIGHTEOUSNESS)

GOOD SAMARITAN
Parable of. Supreme questions of life.
10:25-37

GOSPEL
Duty. To guard, protect. 10:5-6
Message of.
 Certainty of. The truth of the Word.
  1:1-4
 Concerns the Lord Jesus Christ. 1:1
Of Luke.
 Based upon many written accounts.
  1:1
 Historical, orderly, accurate account.
  1:1-4
Power of. Transforming **p**. 13:21
Response to. Some refuse to hear.
 6:27-31
Source.
 Eyewitnesses & ministers of the
  Word. 1:2
 God. 1:3

GOVERNMENT (See **CITIZENSHIP;
NATION**)

GRATITUDE (See
THANKFUL—THANKSGIVING)

GREAT—GREATNESS
Discussed. 9:46-50

GROWTH, SPIRITUAL
Essential. Must **g**. before serving. 5:14
Need for. To grow strong in spirit.
 1:80

GUESTS
Courtesies to. 7:44-46

HANDS
Washing. Part of Jewish ceremonial law.
 Purity, cleanliness. 11:37-38

HAPPINESS
Of world. Judgment of. Warning to.
 6:24-26

HARD—HARDNESS OF HEART
Results.
 Close minds to the truth. 8:9-10
 Reject Jesus. Hard heart. 4:28-30;
  7:33-34
 Reject the Word. 8:11-15

HATE—HATRED
Attitude—Duty toward. Do good to
 those who **h**. us. 6:27-31

HAUGHTY—HAUGHTINESS (See
**ARROGANCE; PRIDE; SELF-
SUFFICIENCY; BOASTING**)

HEALS—HEALING
By Jesus Christ. Example of.
 All diseases. Helpless who seek Him.
  4:40
 Centurion's servant. Great
  compassion & faith. 7:1-10
 Deformity. People more important
  than religion. 13:11-13
 Demon-possessed.
  Delivers most unclean. 4:33-37
  Many. 4:41
  Possessed son. 9:37-45
 Hemorrhaging woman. Faith of a
  hopeless women. 8:43-48

Leper.
 Most untouchable. 5:12-16
Man with withered hand. Saving life.
 6:6-11
Most needful. Peter's mother-in-law.
 4:38-39
Mute man. 11:14
Neglected. Reason. A greater need,
 faith. 9:11
Paralyzed man. Power to forgive sins.
 5:18-26
Raises the dead.
 Jairus' daughter. 8:40-42, 49-56
 Widow's son. 7:11-17

HEAR
Duty. To hear the Word of Christ. 9:35

HEART
Duty.
 Must be cleansed. 11:39-41
 To give **h**. to God. 11:39-41
Inside vs. outside. Purity, cleanliness.
 11:39-41
Source. Of evil, impurity. 11:39-41
State—Kinds of.
 Honest & good **h**. 8:15
 Indifferent. 8:11-15
 Wayward. 9:41
What the **h**. does. Believes. 8:15

HEAVEN
Characteristics—nature.
 Life in. Differs from this life.
  12:41-48
How to enter.
 By putting treasure in **h**. 12:33
 Must have name written in **h**., Book
  of life. 10:20

HELL
Described. Unquenchable fire. 3:17

HELPLESS
Needs met. By Jesus. 4:40

HEMORRHAGING WOMAN
Healed by Jesus. Reward of true faith.
 8:43-48

HERITAGE
Honor of. By religionists. Error of.
 11:47-51

HEROD ANTIPAS (4 B.C.–A.D. 39)
Discussed. 3:1-2
Disturbed by disciples' teaching. 9:7-9

HIDE
Men try to **h**. four things. 8:17

HIGH PRIESTHOOD
Of Jesus. Discussed. Verses of prophecy
 & fulfillment. 3:32-38

HISTORY
Christ & **h**. Invasion into **h**. by Jesus.
 Divides ages & time. 7:28
Pivotal points of.
 Christ. Coming of. 3:1-6; 7:28; 11:23
 Launched. By John the Baptist. 3:1-6

HOLY SPIRIT
And God. Given by God to all who ask.
 11:11-13
Facts. Will not always strive with man.
 4:28-30

Infilling.
 Due to obedience. 1:41
 Follows obedience & the discipline
  of God. 1:67
 Upon Simeon. 2:25
Sins against. Blasphemy. Unpardonable.
 12:9-10
Source of. Given in answer to prayer.
 11:11-13
Work of.
 Came upon. Mary. 1:35
 To give the believer inspiration when
  needed. 12:4-12
 To speak through the believer when
  needed. 12:4-12

HOME (See **FAMILY**)
Duty. To witness to own **h**. & family.
 8:38-39
To be center of church's ministry. 9:4

HONOR
Duty. To **h**. Jesus Christ. 11:19
Seeking worldly **h**. Discussed. 11:43

HOPE
In God. Greatly blessed. 2:36
Result. Eases fear when persecuted.
 12:4-12
Verses. List of. 12:14

HOSPITALITY
Duty. Discussed. 10:8-9

HOUR, THE
Urgency of. 10:4

HOUSE—HOUSES
Described as.
 Built upon rock & sand. True vs.
  false. 6:46-49
 Divided **h**. cannot stand. 11:17-18
 Of rich. 7:36
Discussed. 5:19
Duty. To trust God for shelter, & not to
 worry. 12:22-34

HUMANISM—HUMANIST
Described. 10:21
Discussed. 10:21
Judgment of. 10:21
View - Position.
 Reject demands of Christ. 2:34-35
Warning to. 9:23

HUMILITY
Duty.
 To seek forgiveness in **h**. 5:12
 To seek Jesus in **h**. 5:12
Essential.
 For God to use. 1:47-48
 Necessary for greatness. 9:46-50
 To sense "nothingness." 1:47-48;
  7:37-38
Example of.
 Centurion soldier. 7:3
 Mary, the mother of Jesus. 1:47-48
Source - Comes by.
 Abasing oneself. 1:47-48
 Sensing one's sinfulness &
  unworthiness. 7:37-38

HUNGER, SPIRITUAL (See
SATISFACTION, SPIRITUAL)
Answer to. God & His Word, not
 physical food. 4:3-4

Duty. To **h.** for the Word of God. 5:1;
  10:38-42, esp. 39
Meaning. 6:20-23
Verses. List of. 5:1

HYPOCRISY—HYPOCRITE
Answer to. The one essential. 10:40
Cause.
  Seeking God through form & ritual.
  13:14-16
Described. As leaven. 12:1-3
Duty. To fear being a **h.** 12:1-3
Traits of. Places form & ritual before
  people in need. 13:14-16
Verses. List of. 12:1-3

IDENTIFY—IDENTIFYING
Duty. To **i.** with people. 10:8-9
Of Christ with believers. 10:16

IMMORALITY—IMMORAL
Example of. Woman. Repents & is
  saved. 7:36-50

INCARNATION
Reveals. The power of God. 8:22-23

INDOLENT (See **COMPLACENT**)

INDULGE—INDULGENCE
Described.
  As extravagant living. 12:13-21
  As trying to save life in this world.
  9:24
Example.
  Rich fool. 12:13-21
Judgment of. 6:24-26
Verses. List of. 12:15-19
Vs. giving one' life to Christ. 9:24

INDWELLING PRESENCE
Of the Holy Spirit.
  Given by God to all who ask.
  11:11-13
  Purpose of. 11:11-13

INHERITANCE
Dispute over. Jesus asked for an answer.
  12:13-14
Law governing. 12:13-14

INTERCESSION
Result. To delay judgment. 13:6-9

INTOLERANCE
Reasons for. 9:49-50

IRRESPONSIBILITY
Behavior. 10:29-37

ISRAEL
Consolation of. 2:25
History. Discussed. 6:2

JAIRUS
Daughter raised from the dead. Reward
  of true faith. 8:40-56

JAMES
Men in the New Testament named
  James. 5:10

**JAMES THE APOSTLE, THE SON OF
  ZEBEDEE**
Misunderstood Jesus' mission. 9:52-54

JEALOUSY (See **ENVY**)
Caused by.
  Position. 9:49-50

JERUSALEM
Jesus' great journey to. 9:51-19:28

JESUS CHRIST
Accused—Accusations against. (See
  JESUS CHRIST, Charges Against)
  Of Beelzebub. 11:14-16
  Of breaking the Sabbath law. 6:1-5;
  13:10-17
  Of ceremonial uncleanness.
  11:37-38
Age when launched ministry. Thirty.
  Reasons. 3:23
And children. (See **CHILDREN**)
Authority. (See **POWER**)
  Over Sabbath—Sunday. 6:1-11
Baptism—Baptized.
  By fire & Holy Spirit. Meaning. 3:16
  Obedience & God's approval.
  3:21-22
  Of death. Discussed. 12:50
  Of judgment. Discussed. 12:50
Birth. (See **VIRGIN BIRTH**)
  In Bethlehem. Reasons. 2:1-6
  Praised by a prophetess. 2:36-38
  Proclaimed to be the Salvation of
  God. 2:36-38
  Prophesied. 2:1-6
  Shocking circumstances of. 2:7
  Unusual events. 2:1-24
Call—Calling of (See **CALL—CALLED**)
Challenged about. (See **JESUS CHRIST**,
  Accused—Accusation)
Charges against. (See **JESUS CHRIST**,
  Trials, Legal)
Childhood.
  Dedicated in the temple. 2:28-35
  First recognition of Messiahship. At
  twelve years old. 2:41-52
  Growth of. 2:39-40; 2:43-45
  Lost by parents. 2:41-52
  Why came to earth as a child & not
  as a man. 2:40
Claims.
  Foundation Rock. True vs. false
  discipleship. 6:46-49
  Light of the world. 11:33-36
  Son of God. 10:22
  Son of Man. Described. 9:57-58
  Sovereign. Supreme place in
  universe. 10:22
  To be central figure in history. 11:23
  To be the fulfillment of Scripture.
  4:20-21
  To be the Light which men must
  seek. 11:33-36
  To be the Messiah of prophecy.
  4:17-21
Compassion of. (See **COMPASSION**, Of
  Jesus Christ)
Concepts of.
  Christ of God. 9:20
  Elijah. 9:18-19
  John the Baptist risen from the dead.
  9:18-19
  People's **c.** vs. true **c.** 9:18-22
  Prophet. 9:18-19
Cross. (See **JESUS CHRIST**, Death)
  Is the only way to God. 4:9-12
  Must resist any other way to God.
  4:9-12

Reveals the inner thoughts of man's
  heart. 2:34-35
Weight of. Pressure. Caused by
  foreseeing. 9:28
Crowds follow. Thousands. 12:1
Ct. Adam. Why **C.** entered the world as
  a child and not as a man. 2:40
Death—Crucifixion.
  Baptism of. 12:49-53
  Destined—Determined.
  Set for death. 9:51
  Necessity. Driven toward
  Jerusalem. 9:51
  Foreseeing. Pressure, weight of.
  9:28-36
  Necessity.
  Set for Jerusalem. 9:51-56
  Predicted—Foretold. 9:22; 9:44-45;
  12:50
  By Simeon when **J.** was a child.
  2:34-35
  Discussed. 9:44-45
  Second **p.** 9:44-45
  Results—Effects.
  Brought the fire of judgment to
  the world. Four ways. 12:49
  Fourfold. 12:49-53
  How **d.** should affect disciples.
  5:35
  Judged, condemned Satan. 10:18
  Symbolized.
  By the Bridegroom. Mission of
  dying. 5:35
Deity. (See **MESSIAH—MESSIAHSHIP**)
  Claims. (See **JESUS CHRIST**, Claims)
  Demonstrated. **D.** and Sovereignty.
  8:22-25
  King. Verses & fulfillment of Davidic
  prophecies. 3:24-31
  Mediator.
  Verses. List of. 11:31-32
  Messianic heir: Prophet, Priest, &
  King. Verses & fulfillment. 3:23-38
  Priest. Verses & fulfillment. 3:32-38
  Proclaimed
  Before birth. 1:43-44; 1:68-75
  In dedication of—as a child in the
  temple. 2:28-33
  To be Messiah as a child. 2:28-33
  Proof.
  By changed lives. 20:6
  Fourfold. 5:22-26
  Great **p.** Resurrection. 11:29-36
  Is Son of God. Men fail to see.
  12:54-57
  Six **p.** 11:14-28
  Prophet. Verses & fulfillment. 3:38
  Sovereign. Supreme place in
  universe. 10:22
Denial. (See **DENY—DENIAL**)
Devotion. (See **COMMITMENT;
  DEDICATION; DEVOTION**)
Disciples of. (See **APOSTLES; DISCIPLES**)
Family.
  Embarrassed over Jesus & His claims.
  8:19
  Mother. Mary. Submission to God's
  will. 1:26-38
  Parents.
  Were faithful in worship. 2:41-42
  Were poor. 2:24

Stone. (See **JESUS CHRIST**,
  Names–Titles)
Sufferings of.(See **JESUS CHRIST**, Death)
  S. every trial of man. Listed. 2:40
Support of. Financial. By women. 8:2-3
Teaching.
  Taught with authority. 4:31
Temptation of. Conquering–victory
  over. 4:1-15
Transfiguration. Events of. 9:28-36
Virgin Birth. (See **VIRGIN BIRTH**)
Who **J.** is. 9:18-22
Word of. To be heard, listened to. 9:35
Work of.
  Discussed. 1:68-80; 2:25-35
  Mission. (See **JESUS CHRIST**,
    Mission)
  Proclaimed by John. Fourfold. 3:5
  Revealed. By **J.** Himself. 5:27-39
  Sent forerunners ahead to prepare.
    10:1
  To be the High Priest. Verses of
    prophecy & fulfillment. 3:32-38
  To be the Mediator, Messianic High
    Priest. Verses of prophecy &
    fulfillment. 3:32-38
  To be the Prophet of God. Verses of
    prophecy & fulfillment. 3:38
  To cast out evil spirits. Proves deity.
    11:14-28
  To destroy Satan. Six areas. 10:18;
    11:21-22
  To experience & suffer every trial of
    man. 2:40
  To give light. Three groups. 1:76-79
  To reverse the order of three things.
    1:51-53

JEWS
History of. 6:2
Teachers. Some **t.** in Jesus day. 2:46-47
Vs. Gentiles. Prejudice between. 7:4

JOANNA
Discussed. Supported, Jesus. 8:3

JOHN THE APOSTLE
Misunderstood Jesus' mission. 9:52-54

JOHN THE BAPTIST
Birth & naming. An event for all
  generations. 1:57-66
Discussed. 3:1-6
Forerunner. Pivotal point of history.
  3:1-6
Greatest among men. 7:28
Message of. Eight points. 3:7-20
Parents of. Picture of godly **p.** 1:5-25
Prophecy of. Person & ministry. Why
  he was sent into the world. 1:76-80
Proves deity of Christ. 7:21-23
Questions Jesus' Messiahship. Proof of
  M. 7:18-28
Response to. By sinners & people.
  7:29-31

JONAH
Symbolized the resurrection of Christ.
  11:30

JOY
Basis for. Salvation, not power. 10:20
Cause of. Name written in heaven, in
  Book of Life. 10:20

Meaning. 10:17
Of Jesus. 10:21
Source.
  Comes from two things. 6:20-23,
    esp. v.21
  Presence of Jesus Christ. 5:33-34

JUDGE–JUDGING OTHERS (See
  CRITICISM; DIVISION)
Duty. Watch **j.** 6:41-42
Principles of new life. 6:27-38

JUDGMENT (See **END TIME**)
Degrees of–Basis of.
  Based upon privilege. 12:47-48
  Rewards and punishment. 12:41-48
Described.
  All things to be revealed. 8:17-18
  Cut in pieces. 12:46
  Severe. Many blows. 12:47-48
  Unquenchable fire. 3:17
How God **j.** By Christ. 12:4-12;
  12:49-53
Proof of. Scripture. 10:10-15
Results. Sin exposed. 12:1-3
Sure.
  Inevitable. No escape. Is definitely
    coming. 12:58-59
Verses. List of. 10:10-15; 11:50-51;
  12:41-48
Who is to be **j.**
  All who make excuses. 9:61-62
  All who reject Jesus Christ. 10:10-15
  Covetous & selfish. 12:20-21
  Person who builds upon a false
    foundation. 6:49
  The rejecter. 10:10-15
  This generation. 11:30-32
  Unfaithful manager. 12:41-48
Why God **j.** Failing to bear fruit. 3:9

JUSTICE
Duty.
  To meet the needs of the poor &
    oppressed. 11:42
  To preach social justice. 3:10-14
Fact. More important than religion.
  11:42

KING
Christ is **K.** Verses & fulfillment of
  Davidic prophecies. 3:24-31

KINGDOM OF DAVID
Promised.
  To Christ. Eternal. 1:31-33; 1:32-33
  Verses & fulfillment. 3:24-31

KINGDOM OF GOD
Citizens of.
  Least in **k.** greater than the greatest
    of the prophets. 7:28
  Who is unfit for. 9:62
Duty.
  To preach. 9:60
  To seek. 12:31-34
Facts about.
  Several **f.** 13:19; 13:20-21
Message of.
  Preached by Jesus. 8:1
Nature of.
  Age of **k.** vs. age of promise. 7:28
Nature of.
  Universal. 13:20-21

Ushered in by Christ. 7:28
  What it is like. 13:18-21
  "Within" a person. 17:20-21
Power of. Transforming **p.** 13:21
Promised.
  To believers. As reward. 6:20; 9:27
  To Christ. Eternal. 1:31-33; 1:32-33
Time of.
  Is come to men. 11:20
  Is near. 10:11
  Ushered in.
    By Christ. 11:20

KINGDOM OF HEAVEN (See
  KINGDOM OF GOD)

KINSHIP (See **BROTHERHOOD;**
  FAMILY)
Basis. Discussed. 8:19-21

KNOW–KNOWING–KNOWLEDGE
Christ. Known only by revelation.
  10:22
Of Christ. (See **CHRIST**, Knowledge of)
Of God. (See **GOD**, Knowledge of)

LABOR–LABORERS (See **BELIEVERS;**
  DISCIPLES; MINISTERS)
Call of. (See **CALL–CALLED**)
Duty.
  To **l.** for money to meet need of
    others. 12:33-34
  To pray for laborers. 10:2
Mission of laborers. Discussed. 10:1-16
Power of laborers. Discussed. 10:17-20
Privileges of laborers. Discussed.
  10:21-24
Sins of. Different professions. 3:10-14

LAST DAYS (See **END TIME**)

LAST TIME (See **END TIME**)

LAUGH–LAUGHTER
Of world. Judgment of. 6:24-26

LAW
Importance.
  To Jewish nation. 6:2, 7
Relation to Christ.
  Fulfilled by Christ.
    As a child. 2:21-23
    Two reasons. 2:39
Scribal law. (See **SCRIBAL LAW**)

LEADERS
Call of. To be ambassadors &
  shepherds. 6:13

LEAVEN
Discussed. 12:1-3
Parable of. Kingdom of God. 13:18-19
Power of. What it does. Transforming
  p. of. 13:21

LEGALISM–LEGALIST
Discussed. 6:2, 7
Error–Problem with. Places form
  & ritual before people in need.
  13:14-16
In Jewish religion. Reason for. 6:2, 7

LEND–LENDING
Duty. To **l.** when asked. 6:29-31; 6:35

LEPER–LEPROSY
Discussed. 5:12

LETHARGY (See **COMPLACENT**)

LIBERAL
Vs. conservative. Unbelievers reject both approaches to the gospel. 7:33-34

LIBERTY (See **FREEDOM; DELIVERANCE**)
Vs. license. Unbelievers reject both approaches to the gospel. 7:33-34

LICENSE
Vs. liberty. Unbelievers reject both approaches to the gospel. 7:33-34

LIFE
Concepts of. Consists in things. 12:15-19
Dangers—Problems—Errors of.
  Can be choked by three things. 8:11-15
  Wasting in worldly, indulgent living. 12:15-19
Essential—Duty.
  Losing vs. gaining l. 9:24
  To make a decision for life. 11:23
  To make prayer the breath of life; major characteristic of l. 3:21
Foundation of—Privileges of.
  Christ and l. Christ brings a new l. 5:36-39
  Discussed. 6:46-49
  Principles of. Discussed. 6:27-38; 8:16-18
Kinds of.
  Genuine vs. counterfeit. 6:46-49
Parable of. House built upon rock & sand. 6:46-49
Purpose.
  Threefold. 9:24
  To gather, not to scatter sheep. 11:23
Questions of. Supreme q. 10:25-37
Source—Energy of l.
  Christ. New l. & joy brought by Christ. 5:33-34
  Sitting at Jesus' feet. 10:40
Storms of. (See **TRIALS**)
  Calmed by Christ. 8:24
  Deliverance. Only if life is built on sure foundation. 6:46-49
Vs. materialism. More important than things. 12:22

LIGHT
Described. As the resurrection of Christ. Is the great l. 11:33-36
Duty. To let the light shine in one's dark life. 11:33-36
Purpose of.
  Discussed. 8:16
  Misuse of. 8:16
Source.
  Jesus Christ gives l. to three groups. 1:76-79
  Verses. List of. 11:33-36

LILIES
Clothed by God. Will c. believer. 12:27

LONELY—LONELINESS
Answer to. Seeking Jesus. 5:27-29; 5:30-32

LOST
Judgment of. (See **JUDGMENT**)
Meaning. 9:25
Results.
  Receives forgiveness. 7:47-48

LOVE
Discussed. 10:25-37
Essential—Duty.
  Discussed. 6:27-38
  To l. enemies. Discussed. 6:27-31
  To l. God. 10:25-37
  To l. neighbor. 10:25-37
Verses. List of. 10:25-28

LOW—LOWLINESS (See **HUMILITY**)

LUKE
Luke based his gospel upon the writings of many. 1:1
Truth of Luke's gospel account. 1:1-4

LYSANIUS
Discussed. 3:1-6

MAGNIFICAT
Song of Mary. 1:46-56

MANAGER
Meaning. 12:41-48
Parable of. Faithful & unfaithful. Warning. Be prepared. 12:41-48

MANKIND
Creation of.
  By God. Every man owes his existence to God. 13:6-9
Duty—Behavior.
  Not to be anxious about the body. 12:22-34
  To live productively for God. 13:6-9
  To give fruit to God. 13:6-9
  To have a healthy eye, not a diseased e. 11:33-36
Errors of—Misconceptions of.
  Being deceived. By religion. 13:10-17
  Gross e. of. 12:49-59
  Placing tradition over people. 13:10-17
  Sensing no need for God. 10:21
  Thinking Christ came to bring peace only. 12:49-53
  Thinking the Messiah has not yet come. 12:54-54
  Thinking there is no need to "make peace with God." 12:58-59
  Threefold. 12:49-59
  Unbelief & not understanding. 11:29
Lost. (See **LOST**)
Love for. (See **LOVE**, Essential—Duty) 10:29-37
Nature.
  Sinful. 13:1-9
State of—Present.
  All are sinful. 13:1-9
  Deserves to be rebuked. 9:37-45
  Truth hid from. Reasons. 10:21
  Welfare of. Determined by concern for righteousness. 10:2
Trials of (See **TRIALS**)
Value—Worth.
  More important than religion. 13:10-17
  More valuable than birds. 12:24

MANIFEST—MANIFESTATION
To believer. Very special m. of God's approval. Threefold. 3:22

MARRIED—MARRIAGE
Duty. To be faithful before God. 1:5-25
Espoused. Engagement before m. Discussed. 1:27

MARTHA
Discussed. Character of. 10:38-39

MARY MAGDALENE
Discussed. 8:2
Supported Jesus. 8:2-3

MARY, MOTHER OF JESUS
Acknowledged that she needed a Savior. 1:47-48
An event for all generations. 1:47-48
Humility of. 1:47-48
Magnificent song describing God. 1:46-56
Proclaimed to be blessed. Reasons. 1:45
Submission to God's will. 1:26-38
Virgin. Proof. 1:27
Visited Elizabeth, John the Baptist's mother. 1:39-45

MATERIALISM (See **MONEY; RICHES; WEALTH**)
Caused by—Source. Distraction. 10:40
Discussed. 9:23-27; 12:13-21
  The man of wealth. 12:13-21
Duty.
  Not to be anxious about. 12:22-34
  Not to seek m., but to trust God. 12:29-30
Judgment of. Eight reasons listed. 9:26
Results.
  Causes one to lose self. 9:23-27
  Chokes the Word. 8:7, 14
  Distracts from the essential. 10:40
  Perils of. Discussed. 6:20-26
Vs. being spiritually minded.
  Discussed. 12:13-21
  Seeking m. 9:46
Vs. Christ.
  Preferred over salvation & Jesus. 8:36-37
Warning against.
  Discussed. 9:23-27

MATTHEW—LEVI, THE APOSTLE
Call of. 5:27-32

MATURITY (See **GROWTH, SPIRITUAL**)

MEDITATE—MEDITATION
Verses. List of. 9:36; 10:41-42

MESSAGE (See **PREACHING**)
Content.
  Peace. 10:5-6
  Social justice. 3:10-14
  The kingdom of God. 8:1; 9:59-60; 10:9

MESSIAH—MESSIAHSHIP
Claimed. 22:67-68
  By Jesus. When launching His ministry. 4:16-30
  Recognition of. First r. by Jesus. 2:49-50
Discussed. 9:20

Exaltation. (See **PROPHECY**, About Christ)

False concept—Misunderstood.
Came to bring peace. 12:49-53
Earthly kingdom. 7:18-28; 7:18-20
Man's c. vs. true c. 9:18-22
Messiah has not yet come. 12:54-57
Messianic ruler of judgment. 9:52-54
Kingdom of. (See **KINGDOM OF GOD**)
Messianic heir. 3:23-38
Names—Titles.
Messianic King. 7:18-20; 7:21-23
Proclaimed at birth.
By angel to shepherds. 2:11
By Anna, a prophetess. 2:36-39
By Simeon, a godly man. 2:25-35
Proclaimed. Before birth.
By the angel Gabriel. 1:26-33
By Elizabeth. 1:43
By Zechariah. 1:67-75
Proof.
Final **p.** of Messiah. Fourfold. 7:18-28
Great **p.** Resurrection. 11:29-36
Ministry & message of Jesus. 7:18-28
Six **p.** 11:14-28
Prophecies. (See **PROPHECY**, About Christ)

MINISTERS (See **BELIEVERS; DISCIPLES**)
Appearance. Attitude toward dress & **a.** 9:3-5
Attitude toward other **m.**
Jealousy—envy. 9:46-50
Call—Called.
Chosen by Christ. Who & why. 6:12-19
Reluctant to respond to **c.** Reasons. 5:1-11; 9:57-62
Steps to **c.** 5:1-11
To be ambassadors & shepherds. 6:13
Trusted by Christ. 8:23
Commission—Mission. 9:1-9
Eight things. 10:1-16
Great **m.** Fivefold. 5:27-39
To center ministry in homes. 9:4
To minister, to serve. 4:17-19
Dangers.
Leaving one's first love. 9:61-62
Looking back. 9:61-62
Described. As shepherd. 11:23
Duty—Work. (See
MINISTRY—MINISTERING)
Day of. Typical **d.** in life of Jesus. 4:31-44
Discussed. 10:1-16
Faithful and unfaithful. 12:35-48
How to minister. 9:10-17
Minister to whom. 10:29-37
Not to lose power. 9:37-40
To accept compensation. 10:7
To be ambassadors. 6:13
To be hospitable, adaptable. 10:7
To gather, not scatter the flock. 11:23
To guard the message. 10:5-6
To honor Jesus Christ. 11:19
To live free of materialism & concern for appearance. 9:3-5
To minister in the home. 9:4
To minister the Word. 1:2

To pray for laborers. 10:2
To preach. 4:43-44; 8:1; 9:59-60; 10:8-9
To receive other **m.** 9:49-50
To reject those who reject Christ. 9:49-50
To teach and preach with power. 4:31-32, 43-44
To trust God for money, care. 10:4
To walk away from rejecters. 10:10-15
To warn & leave rejecters alone. 9:4
To waste no time in empty conversation. 10:4
To work so will have to give & meet needs. 12:31-34
Equipped—Resources.
Given power over evil, over Satan. 9:1
Message. Kingdom of God. 8:1; 9:60
Problems.
Dangers. Attempts to sidetrack. 4:43-44
Support of. Financial. 10:7
Treatment. Rejected. How to respond when **r.** 8:40
Unity of. (See **UNITY**)
Vision of. (See **VISION**)

MINISTRY—MINISTERING
Attitude toward. Right vs. wrong **a.** 9:12
Burdened down with. 10:40
Duty—Work.
How to minister. 9:10-17
To accept others. 9:49-50
To identify with people. 10:8-9
To meet both physical & spiritual needs. 9:11; 10:8-9
To **m.** & not live on spiritual highs. 9:32-33
To **m.** even if tired. 9:11
To **m.** to the needy who are faithful in worship. 13:11-13
To **m.** to the poor. 11:42
To support the **m.** 8:1-3
Example. Of not helping the needy. 10:31
Meaning. Discussed. 9:48
Methods. To be centered in home. 9:4; 10:5-6
Of Jesus Christ. Identified with man in every conceivable experience. 2:40
Preparation. Launching a new **m.** 4:1-2
Problems.
Distracted from the **m.** 10:40
Stressing spiritual need as an excuse for no power in the physical. 9:11
Results. Fourfold. Parable of Seed. 8:4-15
Verses. List of. 9:11; 9:16-17; 10:29-37; 11:42

MISLEADING OTHERS (See **STUMBLING BLOCK**)

MISSION—MISSIONS (See **JESUS CHRIST**, Mission)
Dangers to. Attempts to sidetrack. 4:43-44
Discussed. 10:1-16
Great.
Fivefold. **m.** 5:27-39
Threefold **m.** 6:18-19

Sent forth.
Discussed. 9:1-9
To preach, heal, & share the power of Christ. 6:18-19

MISSIONARIES
Duty. To be adaptable. 10:8-9

MONEY (see **MATERIALISM; RICHES; STEWARDSHIP; WEALTH**)

MORALS—MORALITY
Duty.
To live a pure life. 1:27
Verses. List of. 1:27
Essential. For God to use. 1:27

MOTHERS
A Godly **m.** 1:26-38

MULTITUDES
Fed by Christ. 9:10-17
Followed Christ. By the thousands. 8:4

MURMUR—MURMURING
Cause. Anxiety, worry. 10:40

MUSTARD SEED
Discussed. 13:19
Parable of. 13:18-21

NAIN
City of. Discussed. 7:11

NATIONS (See **CITIZENSHIP; GOVERNMENT**)

NAZARETH
Discussed. 1:26
Rejected Christ. 4:16-30

NEEDS—NECESSITIES (See **CARES OF WORLD**)
Attitude toward. Right vs. wrong. 9:12
Concern for **n.** causes.
Anxiety. 10:40
Distraction. 10:40
Distracted by. 10:40
Duty.
Not to fear **n.** 12:4-12
To be met by believers. 11:42
To supersede religion, rituals, rules. 6:1-11
To trust God to take care of **n.** 10:4
Met—Provided.
By God. 12:22-34
By Jesus Christ. Proves the love & power of God. 11:29
By prayer. 9:28-36
How to get **n.** met.
Met by sitting at Jesus' feet. 10:40; 10:41
Seeking vs. trusting God. 12:29-30
Temptation to secure apart from God. 4:3-4
Temptation to secure **n.** illegally. 4:3-4
Verses. List of. 8:14

NEIGHBOR (See **LOVE**)
Love for. Ministering to. 10:29-37
Who is my **n.** 10:29-37

NEUTRALITY (See **DECISION**)
Fact.
Cannot be indecisive. 9:57-62; 11:23

Perseverance in.
    Discussed. 11:5-10
    Verses. List of. 9:28; 11:5-10;
      11:11-13
Prayer life of Christ. (See **JESUS**
  CHRIST, Prayer Life)
When to **p**. Three significant times.
  9:18-19

PREACHING
Call to. Primary **c**. 8:1
Discussed. 8:1
Duty.
    To **p**. peace. 10:5-6
    To **p**. social justice. 3:10-14
    To **p**. the kingdom of God. 9:59-60;
      10:8-9
Meaning. 8:1
Message of. Kingdom of God. 8:1; 9:59-
  60; 10:8-9
Mission.
    Of Christ. 4:17-19
    Of John the Baptist. Eight points.
      3:7-20
Response to.
    Fourfold. 8:4-15
    Refuse to hear. 6:27-31

PREJUDICE
Broken down—Abolished.
    By compassion. 10:29-37
Caused by. Listed. 9:49-50
Results. Prevents compassion.
  10:29-37

PREPARE—PREPARATION
Essential. To be tried & proven. 4:1-2
Spiritual **p**.
    Must **p**. for Jesus' coming. 3:4-6
    Needed after being disciplined by
      God. 1:23-25

PRESSURE (See STRESS)

PRIDE—PROUD
Caused by.
    Ambition. 9:46-50
    Discussed. 7:39
    Self-righteousness. 7:39
    Self-sufficiency. 10:21
Described. Believing one is good
  enough to be acceptable. 3:8; 7:39
Judgment of. 6:24-26
Verses. List of. 10:21
Warning to. To be scattered, lost.
  1:51-53

PRIEST—PRIESTS
Division of **p**. in Christ's day. 1:5
Names of some **p**. Zacharias, John the
  Baptist's father. 1:8-9
Privilege of. Burning incense
  considered highest privilege.
  1:8-10

PRIESTHOOD
Division of. In Christ's day. 1:5
Of Jesus. Verses of prophecy &
  fulfillment. 3:23-38

PROFESSION
Dramatic. Often lacks depth. 8:11-15
Misconception: **p**. is enough.
  Obedience is essential. 6:46
True. Kind of heart. 8:11-15

PROFESSION ONLY—PROFESSION, FALSE
Error—Misconception.
    Attends church, but sits off to the
      side. 8:11-15
    Reasons why people follow Christ.
      7:11
Example of. Three ex. of failing to count
  the cost. 9:57-62
Judgment of. Discussed. 10:10-15

PROMINENCE
Love of. Is wrong. 11:43

PROMISE
Age of **p**. vs. age of God's kingdom.
  7:28

PROPHECY
About Christ's first coming.
By Zechariah. Four. 1:68-75
    Discussed. Verses of prophecy &
      fulfillment. 3:23-38
    Events & fate of child's life. 2:25-35
    Fulfilled. Christ. Birth. 2:1-24
    Work of. To reverse order of five
      things. 1:51-53

PROPHET
Christ is **p**. of God. Verses of prophecy
  & fulfillment. 3:38

PROSTITUTE
Repents. Is saved. 7:37-38

PROVISION (See NEEDS—NECESSITIES)

PRUDENT
Of world. Truth hid from. 10:21

PURE—PURITY (See MORALS—MORALITY)

PURPOSE
Of man. To bear fruit. 13:6-9

QUEEN OF SHEBA
Example. Of seeking the truth. 11:31

QUESTIONS
About Christ. (See **JESUS CHRIST**;
  Related Subjects)
    His Deity. 7:18-28

QUIETNESS
Essential. To be still in the presence of
  God. 9:36
Verses. List of. 9:36

RAVENS
Fed by God. 12:24

READINESS (See JESUS CHRIST, Returns)
Duty. To watch for the Lord's return.
  12:35-48

RECEIVING OTHERS
Discussed. 9:49-50

RECKLESS—RECKLESSNESS
Example of. A foolish traveler. 10:29-37

RECOGNITION
Seeking. Discussed. 11:43

REDEMPTION
Message. Verses. List of. 2:38
Source. Jesus Christ. 2:38

REFORMATION
Inadequate. Corrupts even more.
  11:24-26
Vs. regeneration. 11:24-26

REGENERATION (See BORN AGAIN; NEW BIRTH)
Vs. reformation. 11:24-26

REJECTION
Duty. To warn & leave alone. 9: 5
Judgment of. 10:10-15
Of Jesus Christ.
    His claims to be Messiah. 4:24-27
    His cross. 2:34-35
    Will not always strive with man.
      4:28-30

REJOICING
Meaning. 10:21
Of Jesus. 10:21
Source. Name being written in heaven,
  in Book of Life. 10:20

RELATIONSHIPS (See BROTHERHOOD)

RELIGION—RITUAL
Described as.
    Rules and regulations. 5:30-35
Need.
    To know need has precedence over
      r. 6:1-11
    To know **r**. is less important than
      man. 6:1-11; 13:10-17
    To know **r**. is superseded by saving
      life. 6:6-11
Of feelings. Sensationalism. Temptation
  of. 4:9-12
Problem with.
    Placed before compassion. 10:29-37
    Tendency to become
      institutionalized. Put before men
      & needs. 6:1-11; 10:29-37
True **r**.
    Man is greater than **r**. 13:10-17
    Need supersedes **r**. 6:1-11

RELIGIONISTS
Accusations against. Seven charges.
  11:37-54
Described.
    As fools. 11:39-41
    As self-righteous. 11:39-41
Opposed Christ.
    Accused Christ. Of being demon-
      possessed. 11:14-16
    Broke tradition. Scribal law. 6:1-5
    Insane anger, wrath. 6:1-11
    Investigating committee. Observed
      Jesus. 5:17
    Questioned Christ, His source of
      power. 11:14-16
    Reasons. 13:14
    Sought to kill Jesus & prophets.
      11:47-51
Position—Hold to.
    Rules and regulations. 5:30-35
Problem with.
    Corrupted the Word of God. How
      they corrupted it. 11:52; 13:14
    Honored the past, its heritage;
      neglected the present. 11:47-51
    Hypocrisy. See leaven. 12:1-3

RELIGIONISTS (*Continued*)
Life warped. 13:14
Placed form & ritual before people in need. 6:1-11; 10:29-37
Plunder the way of God. 11:39-41
Self-righteous **r.**—self-justification.
Five faults. 7:36-50
Many faults. 11:37-54
Not acceptable to God. 11:39-41
Sins of.
"Sat by," critical, refused to participate. 5:17

RELUCTANCE
Illustration of **r.** to obey. 5:4-5

REMORSE (See **CONFESSION; CONTRITION; REPENTANCE**)

REPENT—REPENTANCE (See **SALVATION**; Related Subjects)
Baptism of **r.** Meaning. 3:3
Duty.
Called to **r.** 3:3
To call sinners to **r.** 5:30-32
Essential.
Attitude of **r.** vs. self-righteous. 7:36-50
Great need for all to **r.** 13:1-9
Without excuse if do not **r.** 11:30-32
Results.
Bears fruit. 3:8
Verses. List of. 11:31-32

REPORTING
Time for **r.** essential. 9:10

RESOURCES
Attitude toward. Right vs. wrong. 9:12
Described—Listed.
Power. 10:17-20
Privileges. 10:21-24
Provision of necessities. 12:22-34

REST, PHYSICAL
Time for **r.** essential. 9:10
Verses. List of. 9:10

REST, SPIRITUAL
Essential. Time for spiritual renewal & **r.** 9:10
Verses. List of. 9:10

RESURRECTION
How the dead are raised.
Because of the great compassion of Christ. 7:12-13
By the great power of Christ. 7:14-15
Stages. Past. By Jesus, **r.** a widow's son at Nain. 7:11-17

RETURN OF JESUS CHRIST (See **JESUS CHRIST**, Return)

REVEALED—REVELATION (See **MANIFESTATION**)
All things shall be **r.** Nothing hid. 8:17
Insight into. Given only to believers. 10:21
Of spiritual world. By Christ only. 10:22

REVIVAL
False vs. true. 8:4-15
Thousands followed Christ. 8:4
Widespread throughout Israel. 3:1-20; 7:17

REWARDS
Degrees. 12:44
Described.
God's kingdom. 9:27
Great in heaven. 6:20-23; 8:18
Reciprocal, equal. 6:35-36; 6:37-38
Three great **r.** 6:35-36
Verses. List of. 12:41-48
How to secure—Basis of.
Faithfulness and being responsible. 10:15-20
Ministering. 9:48
Obedience. 6:35-36
Receiving people. Threefold. 9:48

RICH—RICHES (See **MATERIALISM; MONEY; WEALTH**)
Duty.
To fear death. 12:20
Facts.
Die just as everyone else. 12:20
Not a permanent possession.
Someone else gets. 12:20-21
Judgment of.
Are warned. 6:24-26
To be stripped, emptied. 1:51-53
Saved—salvation of.
The man of wealth. 12:13-21
Results.
Chokes the life out of a person. 8:11-15
Verses. List of. 6:24-26; 8:11-15; 12:20-21

RICH FOOL
Parable of. Man of wealth. 12:13-21

RIGHTEOUS—RIGHTEOUSNESS
Duty.
To know that it is time to live a **r.** life. 12:54-57
To live a **r.** life. 1:68-75
Meaning. 6:20-23, esp.v.21
Vs. self-righteousness. Discussed. 11:39-41

RITUAL (See **RELIGION**)

RULES—REGULATIONS
Facts about.
Inward purity more important than ceremony. 11:37-39
Superseded by need. 6:1-11

RULING & REIGNING (See **REWARDS**)
Reward of believers. For faithfulness. 12:41-48

SABBATH—SUNDAY
Discussed. 6:1
Fact. Need supersedes the **s.** 6:1-11

SALVATION—SAVED
Deliverance.
List of things. 9:47
Duty.
To rejoice not in power but in **s.** 10:20
To strive to enter the narrow gate. 13:24
Error—misconception.
Can approach God in one's own way. 11:39-41
Will be **s.** later. 13:25

Fact.
Can act too late. 13:25
Few saved. 13:24
Rejection of. Judgment will be terrible. 10:10-16
Source—How one is **s.**
Faith. 7:50
Mission of the Lord. 9:51-56
Repentance. 7:50
Revelation of Christ necessary for **s.** 10:22
Work vs. self-denial. 6:32-34
Who is **s.**
Anyone—Christ turns no one away. 4:40
Helpless. 4:38-39; 4:40
Most unclean. 4:33-37
Outcasts. 5:27-29
Sinners. 5:30-32
Untouchable. 5:12-16

SAMARIA
Discussed. 10:33

SAMARITAN, GOOD
Parable of. Supreme questions of life. 10:25-37

SAMARITANS
Discussed. 10:33
Rejected Jesus. Reason. 9:52-54

SATAN
Defeated—destroyed.
By Christ.
Four ways. 11:21-22
Purpose of Jesus. 9:1; 9:42-43; 10:18
Six areas. 10:18
Existence—Nature of.
Not a mistaken notion. 11:17-18
Taught by Christ. 11:17-18
Power of. Is strong, but Jesus is stronger. 11:21-22
Victory over.
By believer. 10:17-18
By Christ. (See **SATAN**, Defeated)
Work—strategy of.
To destroy man & the work of God. 11:17-18
To hurt & cause pain to God. 11:17-18

SATISFACTION, SELF (See **COMPLACENT**)

SATISFACTION, SPIRITUAL (See **HUNGER, SPIRITUAL**)
Source.
God & His Word, not physical food. 4:3-4
Gospel. Works like leaven. 13:20-21

SCRIBAL LAW
Discussed. 6:2; 6:7
Importance of. Considered more important than God's law. 11:45

SCRIBES
Discussed. 6:2; 6:7
Problem with. Charges against. 11:37-54
Vs. Jesus.
Opposed Jesus. 5:17; 6:7

SCRIPTURE
Fulfilled—Fulfillment of.
By Christ. 7:22
Misuse of. Interpretation of. Some
twist S. 4:11; 11:52

SEA OF GALILEE
Discussed. 8:22

SECRET—SECRECY
Impossible. 8:17
Of men. Try to hide four things. 8:17

SECURITY
Of believer.
Is assured. 13:21
Power over all enemies. 10:19

SEEK—SEEKING
Christ s. men.
Will not always s. & strive after men.
4:28-30
Duty.
To s. Christ despite all difficulties.
11:31-32
To s. wisdom despite all difficulties.
11:31-32
Men s. Christ.
By a man needing help for a servant.
7:4
By most untouchable. 5:12-16
By soldier rejecting false gods. 7:4
To s. Christ despite all difficulties.
11:31-32
Results. Secures more & more. 8:18
Verses. List of. 11:31-32

SELF-CONFIDENCE (See
SELF-SUFFICIENCY)

SELF-DENIAL (See **CROSS**)
Cost of. Discipleship. Discussed.
9:57-58
Discussed. Terms of discipleship.
9:23-27
Duty.
To forsake all to serve Christ. 5:11;
5:27
Meaning. Discussed. 9:23

**SELF-RIGHTEOUS—SELF-
RIGHTEOUSNESS**
Attitude—Spirit of.
Pride. 7:39; 7:44-50
Self-righteous vs. repentant. 7:36-50
Thinking one is good enough to be
acceptable to God. 3:8; 7:39
Need of. Discussed. 7:44-50
Verses. List of. 10:21
Vs. righteousness. Discussed. 11:39-41

SELF-SEEKING (See **AMBITION;
SELFISHNESS**)
Sin of.
Seeking greatness. 9:46
Seeking position & titles. 11:43

SELF-SUFFICIENCY—SELF-SUFFICIENT
Described. As worldly wise & prudent.
10:21
Discussed. 10:21
Temptation of. Discussed. 4:9-12
Results.
Truth hid from. Reasons. 10:21
Verses. List of. 10:21

SELFISHNESS
Described.
Big "I." 12:16-19
Results. Judgment. 12:16-21
Sin of.
Discussed. 12:13-19
Seeking greatness. Wrong ambition.
9:46
Verses. List of. 12:15-19

SENSATIONALISM—SPECTACULAR
(See **SIGNS**)
Temptation of. 4:9-12
Why men seek. 11:14-16

SERVE—SERVICE (See **BELIEVERS;
MINISTERS—MINISTERING;
MINISTRY**)
Duty.
To be faithful till Christ returns.
12:41-48

SEVENTY DISCIPLES
Of Lord. Sent out. 10:1-16; 10:17-20

SHEBA, QUEEN OF
Illustrates how Christ should be sought
despite great difficulty. 11:30-32

SHEEP
Vs. wolf. Persecution. 10:3

SHEKINAH GLORY
Described. Seen in Christ. 9:32-33

SHELTER
Duty. Not to worry about s.; God
provides. 12:22-34

SHEPHERDS
At the birth of Christ. 2:8-12; 2:15-18;
2:20
Duty. To gather not scatter sheep. 11:23
Reputation of. Base, irreligious. 2:8-12

SHOWBREAD
Discussed. 6:3-4

SICKNESS
Caused by. Not because of sin. 13:1-9

SIGNS
Desire for.
Exciting, sensational s. 11:14-16
Problem with. Enough evidence
already. 11:29
Why men seek. 11:14-16
Greatest s. Resurrection of Jesus.
Threefold sign. 11:29-30

SIMEON
Discussed. 2:25-28; 2:25-35

SIMON THE PHARISEE
Invited Jesus to dinner. 7:36

SIN—SINS
Acts—Behavior of.
Attitudes of sinful and self-
righteous. 7:36-50
Being religious. (See **RELIGIONISTS**)
Burdening men with rules &
regulations. 11:45-46
Clean outside, unclean inside.
11:39-41
Disloyalty. 12:4-12
Distracted. 10:40
Divided attention. 9:59-60

Failure to count the cost. 9:57-58
Lack of faith. Faithless. 9:41
Acts—Behavior of.
Looking back. 9:61-62
Misleading others. 11:44
Omitting justice & love. 11:42
Perverse. 9:41
Powerlessness. 9:37-40
Putting heritage before present need.
11:47-51
Reluctant obedience. 9:57-62
Seeking position. 11:43
Seeking titles. 11:43
Taking away the key of knowledge
about God. 11:52
Wayward heart. 9:41
And suffering. Thought to be the cause
of suffering. 13:1-9
Deliverance from.
Forgiven because of friends'
perseverance. 5:18-20
Forgiveness of. Discussed. 5:21-26
Duty.
To confess sin. (See **CONFESSION**)
To preach against. 3:7-20
To rebuke sin in high places. 3:19-20
Exposed. (See **JUDGMENT**)
Known by Christ. 12:1-3
Verses. List of. 8:17; 12:1-3
Judgment of. (See **JUDGMENT**)
Meaning.
Big "I." 12:16-19
Selfishness. 12:16-19
Results.
Truth about. 13:1-9
Unpardonable s. 12:10
Secret (See **SIN**, Exposed)
Results. Misleads others. 11:44
To be exposed. 12:1-3
Symbol—Type of. Leprosy. 5:12-16
Unpardonable s. Blasphemy against the
Holy Spirit. 12:10

SIN AND SUFFERING
Not because of sin. 13:1-9

SINNER—SINNERS
And Christ.
Jesus associates with. 5:27-32
Jesus came to save. 5:27-32
Deliverance.
Must repent. 5:30-32
S. saved. 7:36-50
Fact. All men are s. 13:1-9

SLEEPINESS (See **SLOTHFUL**)

SLOTHFUL – SLOTHFULNESS (See
COMPLACENT)
God doesn't tolerate. 12:24

SLUGGARD (See **COMPLACENT;
SLOTHFULNESS**)

SOCIAL JUSTICE
Preached. By John the Baptist. 3:10-14

SOCIETY
Hope of. New principles of life. 6:27-38

SODOM
Judgment. Like that of rejecters. 10:12

SOLDIER
Great faith found in s. 7:1-10

SOLOMON
Illustrates. How a person must seek
Christ above all else. 11:30-32

SORROWFUL
Meaning. 6:20-23

SOVEREIGNTY
Of Christ. Over nature. 8:22-25

SPECK IN EYE
Parable of. Watch hypocrisy &
criticizing. 6:41-42

SPIRITUAL BLINDNESS (See
BLINDNESS, Spiritual)
Discussed. 11:45-46

SPIRITUAL GROWTH (See **GROWTH,
SPIRITUAL**)

SPIRITUAL HUNGER (See **HUNGER &
THIRST**)

SPIRITUAL INSENSITIVITY
(See **BLINDNESS, SPIRITUAL;
DULLNESS, SPIRITUAL**)

SPIRITUAL INSIGHT
Into truth. Given to believers only.
10:21

**SPIRITUAL
INVESTMENTS—TREASURES**
Duty.
To seek treasure in God's kingdom.
12:31-34

**SPIRITUAL MIND—SPIRITUALLY
MINDED**
Vs. worldly **m.** 12:13-21

SPIRITUAL STRUGGLE (See **DECISION;
NEUTRALITY**)
Caused by.
Indecision. Choosing other things
before God. 9:57-62; 11:23

**SPIRITUAL WORLD—SPIRITUAL
DIMENSION**
Reality—truth of. Unknown to man.
Must be revealed. 10:22
Vs. physical world, dimension.
Discussed. 10:22

STEDFASTNESS
Duty. To be **s.** To endure, hope for
salvation. 2:36

STEWARD (See **MANAGER**)

STEWARDSHIP (See **GIVE—GIVING**)
Duty.
Not to misuse money, but to meet
needs of people. 11:42
To accept compensation. 10:7
To give what we have. 9:16-17
To meet needs of poor & oppressed.
11:42
To support ministers. 10:7
To trust God & set an example. 9:16-
17; 10:4
To trust God, not money. 12:30
To work so we will have to give &
meet needs. 12:31-34
Purpose. To gain heavenly treasure.
12:31-34
Verses. List of. 9:16-17
Women who supported Jesus. 8:1-3

STILLNESS (See **QUIETNESS**)

STORMS OF LIFE (See **LIFE**, Storms of)

STRESS (See **ANXIETY**)

STUDY
Duty. To meditate & **s.** 10:41-42
Verses. List of. 10:41-42

STUMBLING BLOCK
Results. Misleading others. 11:44

SUBMIT—SUBMISSION
Duty. To **s.** to God's will. 1:26-38; 1:38

SUFFERING
Caused by.
Is not because of sin. 13:1-9
Discussed. 13:1-9
Purpose. Why men **s.** 13:1-9

SUNDAY (See **SABBATH**)

SUPPLY (See **NEEDS—NECESSITIES**)

SUSANNA
Discussed. Supported Jesus. 8:3

SYMPATHY—EMPATHY (See
CARE—CARING)
Duty. To show compassion for all men,
even enemies. 10:33-37
Of Jesus Christ. Identified with every
conceivable experience of men.
2:40

SYNAGOGUE
Last time Jesus was in the **s.** 13:10

TAX COLLECTOR
Discussed. 5:27
Rejected by the people. 7:29-31

TAXATION
Used by God to cause Jesus' birth in
Bethlehem. 2:1-6

TEACHERS
Some well-known **t.** in Jesus' day.
2:46-47

TEACHERS, FALSE
Nature. Blind. 6:39
Results. Cause followers to be blind.
6:39

TEMPTATION
Conquering—Deliverance.
Discussed. 4:2
Discussed. 4:2
Kinds of **t.** To by-pass God. 4:9-12
Of Jesus Christ. Discussed. 4:1-15
Purpose. To prepare for service. 4:1-2
Results. Blessed if conquered. 4:13-15

TESTIMONY (See
WITNESS—WITNESSING)

THANKSGIVING (See **GRATITUDE;
THANKFUL; WORSHIP**)
Duty.
To give **t.** after healing. Woman with
deformity. 13:11-13
To give **t.** publicly after blessing.
13:11-13

THEOPHILUS
Man to whom Luke writes gospel &
Acts. 1:3

TIME
Is short. 9:59-60; 12:58
Jesus—pivotal point of history. (See
HISTORY) 7:28; 11:23
Urgency of. 10:1-4

TITHE—TITHING (See **GIVE—GIVING;
STEWARDSHIP**)
Duty. Not to misuse money, but use to
meet needs. 11:42
Of religionists. Strict. 11:42
Warning. Against using **t.** for attention.
11:43

TITLE
Seeking. Discussed. 11:43

TOLERANCE
Discussed. 9:49-50

TRADITION (See **RELIGION—RITUAL**)
Error—Problem with. Placed before
man. 13:14-16

TRANSFIGURED—TRANSFIGURATION
Of Christ. 9:28-36

TRANSFORMS—TRANSFORMATION
How gospel **t.** 13:21

TREASURE, SPIRITUAL
Duty. To seek. 12:31-34
Vs. earthly **t.** 12:31-34

TREE
Parable of good and corrupt **t.** 6:43-45

TRIALS—TRIBULATION (See **LIFE**,
Storms of)
Deliverance through.
By the power of Christ. 8:24
By two in similar circumstances.
1:39-42
Only if life built on sure foundation.
6:46-49
Of man. Christ experienced & suffered
every trial of man. 2:40

TRIALS, POLITICAL (See **JESUS
CHRIST**, Trials of)

TRIBULATION, GREAT (See **END TIME**)

TRUST—TRUSTED
Believers **t.** by Christ. 8:23
Duty. To **t.** God to take care of needs,
necessities. 10:4; 12:22-34
Verses. List of. 10:4
Vs. fear. 8:25

TRUSTS, FALSE
Problem with. False basis. Building a
life upon. 6:49

TRUTH
Fact. Concealed. Reason. 8:9-10
Nature. Is very narrow. 8:18
Problem.
Counterfeit. The *seemingly true.* 8:18
Hid to natural man. Reason. 10:21
Revealed.
To believers only. 10:21
Vs. hidden. 10:21
Reward of. Seekers & achievers given
more. 8:18
Seek—seeking.
How one is to **s.** 11:31
To seek diligently. 11:31

UNBELIEF (See **REJECTION**)
In Christ. By hometown. Seek to kill.
4:24-27; 4:28-30
Warning—Danger of.
To rejecters. 10:10-15
Truth hid from. 10:21

UNCONCERN
Results. Prevents compassion.
10:29-37

UNDERSTAND—UNDERSTANDING
Lack of. Spiritual dullness. 9:44-45

UNFAITHFUL—UNFAITHFULNESS
Caused by.
Ignoring the Lord's return. 12:41-48
Manager or Steward. Parable of.
Warning. Be prepared. 12:35-48

UNITY (See **BROTHERHOOD;**
DIVISION)
Basis. Word of God. 8:21
Essential for ministry. Togetherness
essential. 9:1
Source.
God binds hearts together. 8:21
Not of flesh, heritage, or will.
8:20

UNLEAVENED BREAD, FEAST OF (See
FEASTS)

UNPARDONABLE SIN
Discussed. 12:10

UNREADINESS
Duty. To watch for Lord's return.
12:35-48

UNSAVED (See **LOST, THE;**
UNBELIEVERS)

UNTHANKFULNESS (See
THANKFULNESS)

UNTOUCHABLE
Cleansed. By Jesus. Must seek in
humility. 5:12-16

UNWORTHINESS
Sense of. Example of. Centurion
soldier. 7:3

URGENT—URGENCY
To go, minister. Hour is **u.** 9:59-60;
10:1-4

VICTORY
By believers. Over Satan. 9:1; 9:42-43;
10:18
By Christ. Over Satan. 9:1; 9:42-43;
10:18

VIRGIN BIRTH
Of Christ.
By Holy Spirit. Meaning. 1:27;
1:34-35
Necessary. Eight reasons. 1:27

VISION, WORLDWIDE
Need for.
To pray for laborers. 10:2
To see people, people who need
God's Word. 8:1
Verses. List of. 9:11

WARNING
Meaning of "woe." 10:13

WATCH—WATCHING
Duty.
To **w.** for Lord's return. Five reasons.
12:35-40
Need to. Rules for discipleship.
Fourfold. 6:39-45

WEALTH—WEALTHY (See **MONEY;**
RICHES; STEWARDSHIP;
MATERIALISM)
Dangers - Problems with.
Covetousness—Selfishness. 12:13-21
Leads one to trust in **w.** 12:15-19
Not a permanent possession.
Someone else gets. 12:20-21
Duty.
To fear death. 12:20
Judgment of.
Discussed. 6:24-26; 12:20-21
Parable of Rich Fool. The man of
wealth. 12:13-21
Verses. List of. 6:24-26; 8:11-15; 12:15;
12:20-21
Vs. true spiritual **w.** 12:31-34

WIDOW
Duty. To be faithful to God. 2:36
Touches Christ's heart. 7:12-13

WIDOW'S SON
Raised from dead. Great compassion &
power. 7:11-17

WISDOM
Duty. To seek **w.** despite all difficulties.
11:30-32
Result. Declares Jesus is Son of God.
7:35, see vv.33-34

WISE
Identified. As person who declares
Jesus is of God. 7:35
Of world.
Described. Reasons. 10:21
Truth hid from. 10:21

WITNESS—WITNESSING
Duty.
To evaluate efforts in **w.** 9:10
To go to hometown. 8:38-39
To **w.** in meekness & quietness.
13:21
To **w.** to all who look for redemption.
2:38
To **w.** to family. 8:38-39
To **w.** to friends. 5:27-29
Example of.
Anna. After seeing God's redemption.
2:38
Seventy sent forth. 10:1-16
How to go—Method.
Discussed. 10:1-16
Not being offended by Christ. 7:23;
9:26
Sharing one's testimony. 8:38-39
To be centered in homes. 9:4; 10:5-6
Joy of. 15:6
Verses. List of. 8:38-39

WOE
Meaning. 10:13

WOMAN WITH CURVATURE OF
SPINE
Healed by Jesus. 13:11-13

WOMEN
Example. Of a prophetess. Anna.
2:36-38
Ones who supported Jesus. 8:1-3
Young. Chosen by God. Reasons.
Submission. 1:26-38

WORD OF GOD
Adding to - Abuse of. 11:45
Corrupted by religionists. 13:14
Turning people to own ideas &
positions. 11:52
Twisting, corrupting. 11:52
Duty.
To believe. 1:45
To have a vision of peoples' need for
Word. 5:1
To hear & keep. 11:27-28
To hear the Word of Christ. 9:35
Nature of.
A record of eyewitnesses & ministers
of the Word. 1:2
God. 1:3
Truth. Historical, orderly, accurate
account. 1:1-4
Response to.
False vs. true. 8:4-15
Refuse to hear. 6:27-31
What the **W.** does.
Delivers from anxiety, pressure,
stress. 10:38-42

WORK (See **LABOR**)

WORKS
Vs. self-denial. 6:32-34

WORLD
Deliverance from.
An event for all the **w.** 1:57-66
Hope of. New principles of life.
6:27-38
Described.
As evil. Reasons. 11:31
As wolves. Persecution. 10:3
By Jesus. Threefold. 7:29-35
Judgment of—End of.
Signs of the end time. (See **END**
TIME)
Warning about. Fate of. Parable of
Seed. 8:4-15
State of—Problems with.
Refusing to face the reality of the **w.**
6:24-26
Verdict of. By Jesus. Threefold.
7:29-35
Warning about.
Rebuke of. Three reasons. 9:37-45
Welfare of. Determined by concern for
righteousness. 10:2

WORLDLY—WORLDLINESS (See
MATERIALISM; MONEY; WEALTH)
Caused by.
Covetousness, selfishness. 12:13-21;
12:31-34
List of **c.** Judgment of. 9:26
Discussed.
Saving life in this world vs. losing life
for Christ. 9:23-27
Duty.
To resist temptation of. 4:5-8
To seek heavenly treasure. 12:31-34
Judgment of. 6:24-26

WORLDLY—WORLDLINESS

(*Continued*)

Results—Effects of.
   Chokes life out of men. Three things.
      8:11-15
Sin of.
   Discussed. 12:13-19
   Seeking. 9:46
Verses. List of. 8:11-15
Vs. being spiritually minded.
   12:13-21
Vs. God.
   Vs. trusting God. 12:29-30
Warning against.
   Discussed. 9:24

WORLDLY MINDED

Vs. spiritually **m**. 12:13-21

WORSHIP

Duty.
   Not to neglect public **w**. despite
      affliction. 13:11-13
   To be faithful no matter
      circumstances. 13:11-13
Example of.
   By woman severely deformed.
      13:11-13
   Faithfulness. 2:37; 2:41-42
Reasons.
   False vs. true. 8:4-15

WRATH

Caused by—Reason. Are as vipers,
   biting, poisonous. 3:7

WRITING

As a ministry.
   By Luke. 1:3
   By many of the early believers. 1:1

YOUTH

Chosen by God. Submission to God's
   will. 1:26-38

ZEAL (See **DILIGENCE**)

Duty.
   To act and act now. 9:59-60
   To serve even if tired. 9:11

ZECHARIAH

Father of John the Baptist. Picture of
   godly parents. 1:5-25
Predicts. Person & ministry of God's
   Savior & His forerunner. 1:67-80

LEADERSHIP MINISTRIES WORLDWIDE

Leadership Ministries Worldwide (LMW) exists to equip ministers, teachers, and lay workers in their understanding, preaching, and teaching of God's Word by publishing and distributing worldwide *The Preacher's Outline & Sermon Bible®* and related Outline Bible Resources; to reach & disciple men, women, boys, and girls for Jesus Christ.

OUTLINE BIBLE RESOURCES

The **Outline Bible Resources** have been given to LMW for printing and distribution worldwide at/below cost, by those who remain anonymous. Our daily prayer is that each volume will lead thousands, millions, yes even billions, into a better understanding of the Holy Scriptures and a fuller knowledge of Jesus Christ the Incarnate Word, of whom the Scriptures so faithfully testify.

This material, like similar works, has come from imperfect man and is thus susceptible to human error. We are nevertheless grateful to God for both calling us and empowering us through His Holy Spirit to undertake this task. Because of His goodness and grace, *The Preacher's Outline & Sermon Bible®* New Testament and the Old Testament volumes are complete and are now being revised and expanded in the **everyWORD®** commentary series.

In addition, *The Minister's Personal Handbook, The Believer's Personal Handbook, The Business Leader's Personal Handbook* and other helpful **Outline Bible Resources** are available in printed form as well as on various digital platforms.

Our Mission is to make the Bible so understandable—its truth so clear and plain—that men and women everywhere, whether teacher or student, preacher or hearer, can grasp its message, receive Jesus Christ as Savior, and become fully-equipped disciples of Jesus Christ. It is our goal that every leader around the world, both clergy and lay, will be able to understand God's Holy Word and present God's message with more clarity, authority, and understanding—all beyond his or her own power.

God has given the strength and stamina to bring us this far. Our confidence is that as we keep our eyes on Him and remain grounded in the undeniable truths of the Word, we will continue to produce other helpful **Outline Bible Resources** for God's dear servants to use in their Bible study and discipleship.

We offer this material first to Him in whose name we labor and serve and for whose glory it has been produced and, second, to everyone everywhere who studies, preaches and teaches the Word.

LMW (Leadership Ministries Worldwide) publishes the world's leading outline commentary Bible series, *The Preacher's Outline & Sermon Bible®*. Our mission is to provide pastors in the global church with this and other gospel-centered resources:

The Preacher's Outline & Sermon Bible® - a Bible outline commentary series (44 volumes in KJV, 40 in NIV).

The LMW app - our Bible outline commentary digital app

everyWord - our Bible outline commentary series in ESV (call for availability)

Handbook Series
What the Bible Says to the Believer – The Believer's Personal Handbook
What the Bible Says to the Minister – The Minister's Personal Handbook
What the Bible Says to the Business Leader – The Business Leader's Personal Handbook
What the Bible Says about the Tabernacle
What the Bible Says about the Ten Commandments

The Teacher's Outline & Study Bible™ - various New Testament books

Practical Illustrations
Practical Word Studies in the New Testament
Old Testament Prophets Supplement

Study Booklets:
Faith
Prayer
The Passion of Jesus
Wisdom

All books are available at **lmw.org**, on **amazon.com**, and at your local bookstore. *The Preacher's Outline & Sermon Bible®* is also available for sale digitally from Wordsearch, Logos, Olive Tree, Accordance and others.

Proceeds from sales, along with donations from donor partners, go to underwrite our translation and distribution projects. These projects equip pastors and leaders in the global church who have limited access to the books, resources, and training they need to prepare them to preach the Word of God clearly, plainly, and confidently.

Visit LMW's website at **lmw.org** to learn more about our mission and how you can partner with us:

PRAY: Please pray for the spread of the gospel and our role in it. Go to **lmw.org/stories** to join our prayer network.

CONNECT: LMW partners with other like-minded ministries around the world. Do you know someone who might like to connect with us? Let us know at: **info@lmw.org**

GIVE: The work of LMW is sustained by faithful giving. Impact the world with God's Word at **lmw.org/give.**

LMW is a 501(c)(3) ministry founded in 1992 to share God's Word, clearly explained, with pastors, bible students and Christian leaders worldwide.

lmw.org   1928 Central Ave.   1-(800) 987-8790
info@lmw.org   Chattanooga, TN 37408   (423) 855-2181

www.ingramcontent.com/pod-product-compliance
Lightning Source LLC
Chambersburg PA
CBHW080921100426
42812CB00007B/2343